MAGILL INDEX
TO
CRITICAL SURVEYS

MAGILL INDEX
TO
CRITICAL SURVEYS

Cumulative Indexes

1981–1988

SALEM PRESS

Pasadena, California   Englewood Cliffs, New Jersey

Library of Congress Cataloging-in-Publication Data
Magill index to critical surveys.
　　p. cm.
　　ISBN 0-89356-591-1
　　1. Literature—History and criticism—Dictionaries.　2.
Literature—Bio-bibliography.　3. Authors—Biography.　I.
Magill, Frank Northen, 1907-　. II Title: Index to critical
surveys.
PN524.M34　1990　　　　　　　　　　　　　90-8340
016.809--dc20　　　　　　　　　　　　　　　　CIP

PUBLISHER'S NOTE

This index to Magill's *Critical Survey* series combines and collates the indexes from the seven multivolume reference sets in this comprehensive survey of both English-language and foreign-language writers: the Critical Surveys of Short Fiction (seven volumes), Long Fiction (thirteen volumes), Poetry (thirteen volumes), Drama (twelve volumes), their Supplements (one volume each for Long Fiction, Short Fiction, Poetry, and Drama), Mystery and Detective Fiction (four volumes), and Literary Theory (four volumes). Hence, the current index offers, in one location, a valuable guide to discussion of books, plays, stories, poems, and authors appearing in the fifty-seven volumes of the series, along with cross-references from foreign-language titles, alternative titles, and pseudonyms.

Entries are followed by a code indicating the Critical Survey in which the discussion appears, which in turn is followed by the page or pages locating the discussion:

DEng   Critical Survey of Drama: English Language Series
DFor   Critical Survey of Drama: Foreign Language Series
DSup   Critical Survey of Drama: Supplement
LFEng Critical Survey of Long Fiction: English Language Series
LFFor Critical Survey of Long Fiction: Foreign Language Series
LFSup Critical Survey of Long Fiction: Supplement
LTh   Critical Survey of Literary Theory
M&D   Critical Survey of Mystery and Detective Fiction
PEng   Critical Survey of Poetry: English Language Series
PFor   Critical Survey of Poetry: Foreign Language Series
PSup   Critical Survey of Poetry: Supplement
ShF   Critical Survey of Short Fiction
ShFSup Critical Survey of Short Fiction: Supplement

Boldface entries signal the existence of a complete article on the topic in question.

Alphabetization is by word rather than letter, and transposed elements are disregarded; hence, "Jacob, Max," precedes *"Jacob and the Angel."* Hyphenated compounds are treated as two separate words if the two elements could stand independently (as in "fifty-five") but are treated as one word if one of the elements could not stand alone (as in "non-being"). Numerals are alphabetized as though they were spelled out (*"1919"* under "nineteen-nineteen"), as are common abbreviations: "Mr." as "mister"; "Mrs." as "mistress"; "St." as "saint"; "Dr." as "doctor." The *Mc* particle in names such as McPherson is alphabetized as though it were spelled *Mac*.

There are two prominent exceptions to the alpha-by-word rule: First, surnames composed of more than one element are alphabetized as though one word; hence, "Le Carré, John" is preceded by *"Leatherstocking Tales."* Second, series of enumerated titles by the same author (such as the plays *Henry IV, Part I, Henry IV, Part II*, and *Henry V*, all by William Shakespeare) appear in numerical order rather than alphabetical order, for the sake of logical consistency.

Titles of books, plays, stories, essays, and poems are followed, in parentheses, by the author's surname; in an index of this size and scope, the editors found that further identification, by means of a first initial or a first name, was sometimes necessary to avoid confusion with another author.

Code System

ShF   *Critical Survey of Short Fiction.* 7 vols. Salem Press, Englewood Cliffs, N.J. 1981.

PEng   *Critical Survey of Poetry, English Language Series.* 8 vols. Salem Press, Englewood Cliffs, N.J. 1982.

LFEng   *Critical Survey of Long Fiction, English Language Series.* 8 vols. Salem Press, Englewood Cliffs, N.J. 1983.

PFor   *Critical Survey of Poetry, Foreign Language Series.* 5 vols. Salem Press, Englewood Cliffs, N.J. 1984.

LFFor   *Critical Survey of Long Fiction, Foreign Language Series.* 5 vols. Salem Press, Englewood Cliffs, N.J. 1984.

DEng   *Critical Survey of Drama, English Language Series.* 6 vols. Salem Press, Englewood Cliffs, N.J. 1985.

DFor   *Critical Survey of Drama, Foreign Language Series.* 6 vols. Salem Press, Englewood Cliffs, N.J. 1986.

LFSup   *Critical Survey of Long Fiction, Supplement.* 1 vol. Salem Press, Englewood Cliffs, N.J., and Pasadena, Calif. 1987.

ShFSup   *Critical Survey of Short Fiction, Supplement.* 1 vol. Salem Press, Englewood Cliffs, N.J., and Pasadena, Calif. 1987.

PSup   *Critical Survey of Poetry, Supplement.* 1 vol. Salem Press, Englewood Cliffs, N.J., and Pasadena, Calif. 1987.

DSup   *Critical Survey of Drama, Supplement.* 1 vol. Salem Press, Englewood Cliffs, N.J., and Pasadena, Calif. 1987.

LTh   *Critical Survey of Literary Theory.* 4 vols. Salem Press, Englewood Cliffs, N.J., and Pasadena, Calif. 1987.

M&D   *Critical Survey of Mystery and Detective Fiction.* 4 vols. Salem Press, Englewood Cliffs, N.J., and Pasadena, Calif. 1988.

MAGILL INDEX
TO
CRITICAL SURVEYS

A

"A" (Zukofsky). PEng 3225-3226.

"A & P" (Updike). ShF 98-99.

A ciascuno il suo. See *Man's Blessing, A.*

"A Cristo crucificado." *See* "To Christ Crucified."

"A halál lovai." *See* "Death's Horsemen."

"A Kolota partján." *See* "On the Banks of the Kalota."

A la pintura (Alberti). PFor 23.

À la recherche du temps perdu. See *Remembrance of Things Past.*

"A la vida religiosa" (León). PFor 843.

"À la voix de Kathleen Ferrier" (Bonnefoy). PSup 46.

"A Leopoldo II." *See* "To Leopold II."

À l'ombre des jeunes filles en fleurs. See *Within a Budding Grove.*

"A Luigia Pallavicini caduta da cavallo." *See* "To Louise Pallavicini Fallen from a Horse."

"A mi hermano Miguel in memoriam." *See* "To My Brother Miguel in Memoriam."

"A mia figlia." *See* "To My Daughter."

"A mia moglie." *See* "To My Wife."

A minden titkok verseiből. See *Of All Mysteries.*

"A Nuestra Señora." *See* "To Our Lady."

"A parteneide" (Manzoni). PFor 958.

À rebours. See *Against the Grain.*

"A Roosevelt." *See* "To Roosevelt."

"A Santiago." *See* "To Santiago."

A secretio agravio, secreta venganza. See *Secret Vengeance for Secret Insult.*

"A Silvia." *See* "To Sylvia."

"A Sion-hegy alatt." *See* "Under Mount Sion."

"A stesso." *See* "To Himself."

"A szétszóródás elött." *See* "Before the Diaspora."

À toi, pour toujours, ta Marie-Lòu. See *Forever Yours, Marie-Lou.*

À vau-l'eau. See *Down Stream.*

"A veces una hoja des prendida. . ." (González Martínez). PFor 611.

"A Víctor Hugo" (Darío). PFor 421-422.

"À Villequier" (Hugo). PFor 736. See also *Contemplations, Les.*

"À Zurbarán" (Gautier). PFor 537-538. See also *España.*

Aarestrup, Emil. PFor 2166.

Abad, Per. *See* Per Abad.

Abaddón, el exterminador (Sabato). LFFor 1467-1468.

Abbas, K. A. ShF 649.

"Abbé Aubain, The" (Mérimée). ShF 198.

Abbé Mouret's Transgression (Zola). LFFor 1990. See also *Rougon-Macquart, Les.*

Abbey, Kieran. *See* **Reilly, Helen.**

Abbot, Anthony. M&D 1-5.

"ABC to the Virgin, An" (Chaucer). ShF 1101.

"Abduction, The" (Kunitz). PSup 249.

Abe, Kōbō. DFor 2434; LFFor 1-9.

"Abe Lincoln" (Guest). PEng 1166.

Abe Lincoln in Illinois (Sherwood). DEng 1807-1808.

Abel, Robert H. ShF 2487.

Abel et Bela (Pinget). DSup 306-307.

Abel Sánchez (Unamuno). LFEng 3302-3303; LFFor 1792-1793, 2391.

Abelard, Peter. LTh 1653.

Abell, Kjeld. DFor 1-10, 2480.

Abén Humeya (Martínez de la Rosa). DFor 1274-1275.

"Abend, Der." *See* "Evening."

"Abenjacán the Bojarí, muerto en su laberinto." *See* "Ibn Hakkan al-Bokhari, Dead in His Labyrinth."

"Abenland." *See* "Occident I, The."

Abenteuerliche Simplicissimus, Der. See *Adventurous Simplicissimus, The.*

Aber die Nachtigall jubelt (Kunze). PFor 805.

Abhijñānaśakuntala. See *Śakuntalā.*

Abish, Walter. ShF 2488.

"Abominable" (Brown). ShF 564.

"Abominable History of the Man with the Copper Fingers, The" (Sayers). ShF 758.

Abominable Man, The (Sjöwall and Wahlöö). M&D 1499.

Abortion, The (Brautigan). LFEng 292-293.

"Abou Ben Adhem" (Hunt). PEng 1464-1465.

About Face (Fo). DSup 114.

About That (Mayakovsky). PFor 990-991.

Adams, Alice. ShFSup 1-6.

Adams, Andy. *See* Gibson, Walter B.

Adams, Cleve F. M&D 6-10.

Adams, Henry. LTh 160.

"Add nekem a szemeidet." *See* "Give Me Your Eyes."

"Adda, L'" (Manzoni). PFor 957.

Addicción del diálogo (Torres Naharro). DFor 1874-1875.

Adding Machine, The (Rice). DEng 1584-1586.

Addison, Joseph. DEng 1-10, 2177; LTh 7-12, 176, 240, 772, 775, 908-909, 1530, 1532, 1598, 1600-1601, 1684-1685, 1689; PEng 6-13, 3472; ShF 155-156, 824-829, 2264-2269. *See also* Steele, Sir Richard.

Address Delivered Before the Senior Class in Divinity College, Cambridge, An. See *Divinity School Address.*

Adefesio, El (Alberti). DFor 2506.

Adelchi (Manzoni). DFor 2408

Adelphoe. See *Brothers, The.*

Adler, Stella. DEng 2528.

"Adlestrop" (Thomas, E.). PEng 2893.

"Administrativnyi vostorg." *See* "Power-Drunk."

Admirable Crichton, The (Barrie). DEng 121-123.

"Admiral and the Nuns, The" (Tuohy). ShF 2346-2347.

"Admiral Fan, The" (Williams). PSup 389-390.

"Admiralteyskaya Igla." *See* "Admiralty Spire, The."

"Admiralty Spire, The" (Nabokov). ShFSup 220.

"Adolescence" (Wescott). ShF 2423.

Adolphe (Constant). LFFor 2123-2124; LTh 1181.

Adonais (Shelley). PEng 2559-2560.

"Adónde te escondiste." *See* "Spiritual Canticle, The."

Adone, L' (Marino). PFor 974-976, 2017-2018.

Adonis (La Fontaine). PFor 813-814.

"Adoración de los magos, La." *See* "Adoration of the Magi, The."

"Adoration of the Magi, The" (Cernuda). PFor 322. See also *Nubes, Las.*

"Adoration of the Magi, The" (Yeats). ShF 2473.

Adorjan, Carol Madden. ShF 2490.

Adorno, Theodor. LTh 13-18, 137-138, 142, 1767, 1808.

Adrastea (Herder). LTh 671.

Adriatische Rosemund, Die (Zesen). LFFor 2151.

Adrienne Mesurat. See *Closed Garden, The.*

Adult Bookstore (Shapiro). PEng 2542.

"Adulterous Woman, The" (Camus, A.). ShF 1047-1048.

Advance and Reformation of Poetry, The (Dennis). LTh 1688.

Advance of the American Short Story, The (O'Brien, Edward). ShF 84.

Advancement of Learning (Bacon). LTh 75, 77, 1675.

"Adventure of the Camberwell Beauty, The" (Derleth). ShF 1258.

"Adventure of the Egyptian Tomb, The" (Christie). ShF 1146-1147.

"Adventure of the Empty House, The" (Doyle). ShF 1304.

"Adventure of the Remarkable Worm, The" (Derleth). ShF 1257-1258.

"Adventure of the Rudberg Numbers, The" (Derleth). ShF 1256-1257.

"Adventure of the Speckled Band, The" (Doyle). ShF 1299.

Adventurer (Hawkesworth). ShF 1605, 1606, 1607, 1608.

Adventurer, The (Johnson, S.). ShF 1708.

"Adventures of a Monkey, The" (Zoshchenko). ShFSup 379.

Adventures of Augie March, The (Bellow). LFEng 227, 3106.

Adventures of Caleb Williams, The. See *Caleb Williams.*

Adventures of Ferdinand, Count Fathom, The. See *Ferdinand, Count Fathom.*

Adventures of Gil Blas of Santillane, The (Le Sage). LFEng 3103-3104.

Adventures of Huckleberry Finn, The (Twain). LFEng 2667-2668, 3105; ShF 615.

Adventures of Master F. J., The (Gascoigne). PEng 1064-1065.

Adventures of Peregrine Pickle, The. See *Peregrine Pickle.*

Adventures of Pinocchio, The (Collodi). ShF 684-685.

Adventures of Roderick Random, The. See *Roderick Random.*

"Adventures of Shamrock Jolnes, The" (Henry). ShF 1630.

Age of Wonders, The (Appelfeld). LFSup 35-38.

Agee, James. LFSup 1-7.

Agents and Patients (Powell). LFEng 2117.

"Aghwee the Sky Monster" (Ōe). ShFSup 234.

"Agitated Meditation" (Tranströmer). PFor 1527.

Aglaura (Suckling). PEng 2777.

Agnes Bernauer (Hebbel). DFor 889.

Agnes de Castro (Behn). LFEng 221-222.

Agnès de Méranie (Ponsard). DFor 1490.

Agnon, Shmuel Yosef. LFFor 10-23; ShF 422, 830-835.

"Agonia." *See* "Agony."

Agonía del cristianismo, La. See *Agony of Christianity, The.*

Agonie du Cristianisme, L'. See *Agony of Christianity, The.*

"Agony" (Ungaretti). PFor 1565. See also *Allegria, L'.*

"Agony. As New., An" (Baraka). PEng 86.

Agony of Christianity, The (Unamuno). PFor 1557.

Agua Viva (Lispector). LFSup 246.

¿Aguila o sol? See *Eagle or Sun?*

Aguilera Malta, Demetrio. LFFor 2295; LFSup 8-15.

Aguirre, Isidora. DFor 31-38, 2443.

"Aguri" (Tanizaki). ShFSup 315.

Ah Q cheng chi. See *True Story of Ah Q, The.*

Ah Q cheng-chuan. See *True Story of Ah Q, The.*

Ahl al-kahf (Hakim). DSup 174.

Ahl al-qamar. See *Poet on the Moon.*

Ahlin, Lars. LFFor 2359.

Ahnfrau, Die. See *Ancestress, The.*

Ahnung und Gegenwart (Eichendorff). LTh 435.

Aho, Juhani. LFFor 2342-2343.

"Ahogado más hermos del mundo, El." *See* "Handsomest Drowned Man, The."

"Ai Poeti Del Secolo XIX." *See* "Thoughts Addressed to the Poets of the Nineteenth Century."

Aias. See *Ajax.*

Aichinger, Ilse. ShF 2491.

Aickman, Robert. ShF 2492.

Aigle à deux têtes, L'. See *Eagle Has Two Heads, The.*

Aiken, Conrad. LFEng 15-24; PEng 20-26; ShF 258-259, **836-841.**

Ainsworth, William Harrison. LFEng 25-34.

"Air and Fire" (Berry). PEng 153.

Air Raid (MacLeish). DEng 1219.

"Airiños, airiños, aires." *See* "Breezes, Breezes, Little Breezes."

"Airship Boys in Africa, The" (Cassity). PSup 62-63.

Aissa Saved (Cary). LFEng 455.

Ajax (Sophocles), DFor 2103-2104.

Akalaitis, JoAnne. DSup 1-7.

Akhmatova, Anna. LTh 1607; PFor 9-16, 237, 2146.

Akhnaton, King of Egypt (Merezhkovsky). LFFor 1139.

Akiko, Yosano. *See* **Yosano Akiko.**

Akropolis (Wyspiański). DFor 2029-2031.

Aksakov, Sergey. LFFor 2315.

Aksyonov, Vassily. LFSup 16-21.

Akt des Lesens, Der. See *Act of Reading, The.*

Akt przerywany. See *Interrupted Act, The.*

"Akter." *See* "Actor, The."

Akutagawa, Ryūnosuke. ShFSup 7-12.

Al gözüm seyreyle Salih. See *Seagull.*

Aladdin (Oehlenschläger). DFor 1439-1440.

Alaham (Greville). PEng 1157-1158.

Alain-Fournier. LFFor 24-39.

Alan of Lille. LTh 19-23; PFor 2114.

Alanus de Insulis. *See* **Alan of Lille.**

Alarcón, Pedro Antonio de. LFFor 2383; ShF 842-848.

Alarcón y Mendoza, Juan Ruiz de. See **Ruiz de Alarcón, Juan.**

Alas, Leopoldo. *See* **Clarín.**

Alastor (Shelley). PEng 2551-2552.

Albany Cycle, The (Kennedy). LFSup 195-199.

"Albatross, The" (Lem). ShFSup 153.

Albee, Edward. DEng 11-23, 2408-2409; DSup 407.

Alberic. LTh 1651.

Albert von Stade. LTh 22.

Alberti, Leon Battista. LTh 1661.

Alberti, Rafael. DFor 2506; PFor 17-24.

Albertine disparue. See *Sweet Cheat Gone, The.*

Albertine in Five Times (Tremblay). DSup 356.

"Albertus: Soul and Sin" (Gautier). PFor 535.

Albigenses, The (Maturin). LFEng 1841.

Albine: Or, The Abbé's Temptation. See *Abbé Mouret's Transgression.*

Alcaeus. PFor 1759-1761.

Alcalde de Zalamea, El. See *Mayor of Zalamea, The.*

Alcayaga, Lucila Godoy. *See* **Mistral, Gabriela.**

Alceste (Quinault). DFor 1507-1508.

Alcestis (Euripides). DFor 573-574, 2110-2111.

"Alchemist, The" (Bogan). PEng 236-237.

Alchemist, The (Jonson). DEng 1021-1023, 2285; ShF 1715-1716.

Alcibiades (Otway). DEng 1442-1443.

Alcman. PFor 1762.

Alcools (Apollinaire). PFor 53-54.

Alcuin. PFor 2113.

Alcyone (D'Annunzio). PFor 387-388. See also *Laudi, Le.*

Aldan, Daisy. ShF 2493.

Alden, Michele. *See* **Avallone, Michael.**

Aldington, Richard. LFEng 35-47.

Aldiss, Brian. ShF 779-780, 2494.

Aldrich, Thomas Bailey. LFEng 48-58; M&D 11-15; PEng 27-36; ShF 587.

Aleck Maury, Sportsman (Gordon). LFEng 1176.

Alecsandri, Vasile. DFor 2296-2297.

Alegría, Ciro. LFFor 40-48.

Alehouse Sonnets (Dubie). PSup 105.

Aleichem, Sholom. ShF 849-854.

Aleixandre, Vicente. PFor 25-32; PSup 403.

Aleksandriya. LFFor 2302.

Aleksandrov, Josip Murn. PFor 2269.

Alemán, Mateo. LFEng 3102.

Alencar, José de. LFFor 2281.

Alepoudhélis, Odysseus. *See* **Elýtis, Odysseus.**

Aleramo, Sibilla. LFFor 2238; PFor 2032.

Alexander, Sidney. ShF 2495.

Alexander, Campaspe and Diogenes. See *Campaspe.*

Alexander Romance (Pseudo-Callisthenes). LFFor 2014.

Alexanderplatz, Berlin (Döblin). LFFor 477-478, 2194.

Alexander's Feast (Dryden). PEng 878.

Alexandria Quartet, The (Durrell). LFEng 844-847.

"Alexandrian Kings" (Cavafy). PFor 298-299, 1956.

Alfieri, Vittorio. DEng 2348; DFor 39-49, 2406-2407; PFor 2022-2024.

Alfonso, King of Castile (Lewis). DEng 1129, 1135-1136.

Algabal (George). LTh 574; PFor 547-548.

Algren, Nelson. LFSup 22-30; ShF 269, 855-858.

Alguma poesia (Drummond de Andrade). PSup 98.

Alguns contos (Lispector). ShFSup 166.

Al-Hakim, Tawfiq. *See* **Hakim, Tawfiq al-.**

Ali Pacha (Payne). DEng 2397.

Aliatar (Saavedra). DFor 1615.

Alibi for Murder. See *Dream Walker, The.*

"Alice Addertongue" (Franklin). ShF 1410-1411.

Alice's Adventures in Wonderland (Carroll). PEng 440-443.

"Alien Corn, The" (Maugham). ShF 1904.

Alighieri, Dante. *See* **Dante.**

Alison, Archibald. LTh 1745.

Alive and Dead (Ferrars). M&D 601.

Aliya. See Second *Aliya* and Fifth *Aliya.*

Alkēstis. See *Alcestis.*

All About H. Hatterr (Desani). LFFor 2220.

"All Bread" (Atwood). PEng 69.

"All Choice Is Error" (Cunningham). PSup 77.

All Citizens Are Soldiers. See *Sheep-Well, The.*

All Fools (Chapman). DEng 354-356.

All for Love (Dryden). DEng 521-522.

All God's Dangers (Rosengarten). ShF 627, 1430-1431.

All Green Shall Perish (Mallea). LFFor 1054-1056.

"All-Knowing Rabbit" (Kennedy). PEng 1570-1571.

"All Legendary Obstacles" (Montague). PEng 2035.

All Men Are Brothers. See *Water Margin.*

All Men Are Enemies (Aldington). LFEng 42-43.

All Men Are Mortal (de Beauvoir). LFFor 116-117.

All My Friends Are Going to Be Strangers (McMurtry). LFEng 1755-1756.

"All My Pretty Ones" (Sexton). PEng 2523.

All My Pretty Ones (Sexton). PEng 2523.

All My Sons (Miller). DEng 1338-1339, 2406.

All Our Yesterdays. See *Dead Yesterdays.*

All Quiet on the Western Front (Remarque). LFFor 1398-1401, 2191.

"All-Seeing, The" (Nin). ShF 1950.

"All soul, no earthly flesh" (Nashe). PEng 2073.

"All Souls' Day" (Pascoli). PFor 1141.

All That Fall (Beckett). DEng 153-154; DFor 161-162.
All the King's Men (Warren). LFEng 2775-2776.
"All the Soul Indrawn. . ." (Mallarmé). PFor 926-927.
"All You Zombies'" (Heinlein). ShF 1619.
"Allal" (Bowles). ShF 992.
"All'amica risanata." *See* "To the Healed Friend."
"Allant châtier la rebellion des Rochelois" (Malherbe). PFor 921-922.
Allegoria del Poema (Tasso). PFor 1501.
Allegories of Reading (de Man). LTh 349.
Allegory of Love, The (Lewis). LTh 896.
Allegria, L' (Ungaretti). PFor 1564-1566.
Allegria di naufragi. See *Allegria, L'*.
"Allegro, L'" (Milton). PEng 2007.
Allegro Barbaro (Bartók). PEng 3505-3508, 3511, 3512.
"Alleluia Meadow, The" (Holz). PFor 694-695.
Allen, Grant. M&D 16-22.
Alley, Henry. ShF 2496.
Alley Jaggers (West). LFSup 372.
Alleyn, Edward. DEng 2522-2523.
"Alligator Bride, The" (Hall). PEng 1202.
Alligator Bride, The (Hall). PEng 1197, 1201-1202.
Allingham, Margery. M&D 23-28.
Allingham, William. PEng 37-46.
"All'Italia." *See* "To Italy."
All's Well That Ends Well (Shakespeare). DEng 1709-1710, 2280.
Alma (Prior). PEng 2290-2291.
"Almanac, An" (Schuyler). PEng 2483.
"Almanac of Pain, An" (Dazai). ShFSup 93.
Almas perdidas (Hernández). DFor 2442.
Al-Mawākib. See *Procession, The*.
"Almond-Blossom" (Lawrence, D. H.). PEng 1684.
Almoran and Hamet (Hawkesworth). ShF 1608-1609.
Almqvist, Carl Jonas Love. DFor 2469; LFFor 2337; PFor 2167.
Alnæs, Finn. LFFor 2363.
Alonso, Dámaso. LTh 24-28.
Alouette, L'. See *Lark, The*.
Alpenkönig und der Menschenfeind. See *Mountain King and Misanthrope*.
"Alpha" (Brathwaite). PEng 272.

"Alpha" (Różewicz). PFor 1368-1369.
Alphabet of Elegies (Quarles). PEng 2299.
Alphabetical Order (Frayn). DSup 127-128.
Alphonsus of Arragon (Greene, R.). DEng 2270.
Altamirano, Ignacio Manuel. LFFor 2284.
"Altar, The" (Herbert). PEng 1298, 1299.
"Altarwise by Owl-Light" (Thomas, D.). PEng 2884-2885.
"Alternative, The" (Baraka). ShF 923.
"Altes Blatt, Ein." *See* "Old Manuscript, An."
"Although by Night" (John of the Cross). PFor 766.
Althusser, Louis. LTh 416-417, 503-504, 845, 1767.
"Altura y pelos." *See* "Height and Hair."
Álvarez Gardeazábal, Gustavo. LFFor 2300-2301.
Alvarez Journal, The (Burns). M&D 250.
Álvarez Quintero, Serafín, and Joaquín Álvarez Quintero. DFor 50-58, 2502-2503.
Alvaro, Corrado. DFor 2415; LFFor 2246.
"Always to Be Named" (Bobrowski). PFor 206.
Alyagrov. *See* **Jakobson, Roman.**
Alzire (Voltaire). DFor 1968-1969.
"Am I Insane?" (Maupassant). M&D 1209.
"Am Sonnabend Abend." *See* "On a Saturday Evening."
"Am/Trak" (Baraka). PEng 89-90.
Ama de la casa, El (Martínez Sierras). DFor 1284-1285.
Amade, László. PFor 1977.
Amadeus (Shaffer, P.). DEng 1685-1687.
Amadis de Gaula (de Montalvo). ShF 144.
Amadis of Gaul (Vicente). DFor 1959.
Amado, Jorge. LFFor 49-56.
"Amado dueño mio" (Cruz). PFor 378.
"Amai." *See* "I Loved."
"Amante di Gramigna, L'" *See* "Gramigna's Mistress."
"Amante dulce del alma" (Cruz). PFor 380.
"Amaranta" (Alberti). PFor 20.
Amateur Cracksman, The (Hornung). M&D 906.
Amateurs (Barthelme). ShFSup 24.
Amazing Stories. ShF 773-774.
Amazing Web, The (Keeler). M&D 956-957.
"Amazon, The" (Leskov). ShFSup 159.
Amazoulous, Les (Kâ). DFor 2270.
Ambarvalia (Clough). PEng 519.

Ambassadors, The (James, H.). LFEng 1436, 1448-1449.
"Amber Bead, The" (Herrick). PEng 1311.
Ambiguous Adventure (Kane). LFFor 2035.
Ambitious Step-Mother, The (Rowe). DEng 1633-1634.
Ambito (Aleixandre). PFor 29.
Ambler, Eric. M&D 29-34.
Ambra (Poliziano). PFor 1256. See also *Sylvae.*
Ambrogini, Angelo. *See* **Poliziano.**
"Ambrose His Mark" (Barth). ShF 928.
Ambrosio. See *Monk, The.*
Ambrosio (Lewis, M.). ShF 730-731.
Ambrosius Theodosius Macrobius. *See* **Macrobius.**
A.M.D.G. (Pérez de Ayala). LFFor 1256.
Âme enchantée, L'. See *Soul Enchanted, The.*
Âme romantique et la rêve, L' (Béguin). LTh 1151.
Amelia (Fielding). LFEng 3073.
Amelia (Patmore). PEng 2194.
Amen Corner, The (Baldwin). DEng 74-75.
America (Blake). PEng 213-214.
"America" (Wheatley). PEng 3053.
"America! America!" (Schwartz). ShF 2207-2208.
American, The (James, H.). DEng 994.
"American Authors of Today" (Boynton). ShF 72.
American Buffalo (Mamet). DEng 1240-1243, 2413.
American Democrat, The (Cooper). LFEng 607.
American Dream, The (Albee). DEng 2408.
American Dream, An (Mailer). LFEng 1779-1781.
"American Eagle, The" (Lawrence, D. H.). PEng 1683-1684.
"American Glamour" (Young). PEng 3216.
"American History" (Harper). PSup 162.
American Hunger (Wright, R.). ShF 579.
"American Letter" (MacLeish). PEng 1855.
"American Literature" (Fuller). LTh 524-525.
American Magazine. ShF 588.
"American Portrait: Old Style" (Warren). PEng 3028.
American Renaissance (Matthiessen). LTh 1009-1012.
American Scene, The (James, H.). LFEng 1435.

American Scholar, The (Emerson). LTh 455, 457-458; ShF 219.
American Short Stories, "Introduction" (Current-Garcia and Patrick). ShF 74.
"American Short Story, The" (Column). ShF 73.
"American Short Story, The" (Gerould). ShF 77.
"American Short Story, The" (Mirrielees). ShF 83.
American Short Story, The (Peden). ShF 86, 317.
American Short Story, The (Ross, D.). ShF 88.
"American Short Story, The" (Smertenko). ShF 89.
American Short Story, The (Voss). ShF 93.
"American Short Story, The" (West, R. B.). ShF 93.
"American Short Story During the Twenties, The" (Peden). ShF 86.
"American Short Story in the First Twenty-five Years of the Twentieth Century, The" (Newman). ShF 84.
American Short Story in the Twenties, The (Wright, A.). ShF 94.
"American Short Story Today, The" (Geismar). ShF 77.
"American Takes a Walk, An" (Whittemore). PEng 3079.
American Tragedy, An (Dreiser). LFEng 836-838, 3051, 3180-3183.
American Visitor, An (Cary). LFEng 456.
"American Way, The" (Corso). PEng 578.
Americana (DeLillo). LFSup 85-86.
America's Coming-of-Age (Brooks, V.). LTh 226.
Amerika (Kafka). LFFor 898-900.
Amers. See *Seamarks.*
Âmes du Purgatoire, Les (Mérimée). LFFor 1148.
Âmes fortes, Les (Giono). LFFor 657.
Amichai, Yehuda. PSup 1-7.
Aminta (Tasso). DFor 1816-1819, 2399-2400; PFor 2015.
"Amirauté, L' " (Follain). PSup 128-129.
Amis, Kingsley. LFEng 59-70; LFSup 401.
"Amitié, L' " (Follain). PSup 128.
Ammianus Marcellinus. *See* Marcellinus, Ammianus.
Ammons, A. R. PSup 8-14.

"Among School Children" (Yeats). PEng 3199-3203.

"Among Tenses" (Morgenstern). PFor 1058. See also *Gallows Songs, The.*

"Amor." *See* "Love."

"Amor dormido." *See* "Love Asleep."

Amor es más laberinto (Cruz). DFor 443-444.

Amore, Un. See *Love Affair, A.*

Amore della tre melarance, L'. See *Love of the Three Oranges, The.*

"Amore e morte." *See* "Love and Death."

Amores (Ovid). PFor 1122-1123, 1124.

"Amoret" (Congreve). PEng 555.

Amoretti (Spenser). PEng 2714-2715.

Amos, Alan. *See* **Knight, Kathleen Moore.**

"Amos Barton" (Eliot, G.). ShF 1334.

Amour fou, L' (Breton). LTh 215.

"Amoureuse, L'." *See* "Woman in Love, A."

Amours de Voyage (Clough). PEng 520-521.

Amphitryon (Hacks). DFor 853.

Amphitryon (Kleist). DFor 1076-1078.

Amphitryon (Plautus). DFor 1484.

Amphitryon 38 (Behrman). DEng 187.

Amphitryon 38 (Giraudoux). DFor 725-726.

Amrita (Jhabvala). LFSup 171-172.

Amtmandens døttre (Collett). LFFor 2338.

"Amuck in the Bush" (Callaghan). ShFSup 69.

"Amusing Adventure, An" (Zoshchenko). ShFSup 380.

"Amy Foster" (Conrad). LFEng 3282-3284.

Amy Robsart (Hugo). DFor 969.

"An die Dichter." *See* "To the Poets."

"An die Freude." *See* "Ode to Joy."

"An ein fallendes Blatt." *See* "To a Falling Leaf."

An Giall (Behan). DEng 166.

"An Klopstock." *See* "To Klopstock."

"An Nelly Sachs." *See* "To Nelly Sachs."

"An Tieck." *See* "To Tieck."

Anabase. See *Anabasis.*

Anabasis (Perse). PFor 1195.

Anacreon. PFor 33-39.

Anakomidhi (Pentzíkis). PFor 1190.

"Analyse structurale en linguistique et en anthropologie, L'." *See* "Structural Analysis in Linguistics and in Anthropology."

Anand, Mulk Raj. LFFor 2218-2220; ShF 645, 646.

"Anaphora" (Bishop). PEng 187.

"Anatomy Lesson, The" (Connell). ShF 1176-1177.

Anatomy of Criticism (Frye). LTh 508-509, 512, 1432, 1756-1757.

Anatomy of Nonsense, The (Winters). LTh 1568.

Anatomy of the World, An (Donne). PEng 834-835.

Anaya, Rudolfo A. ShF 2497.

Ancel, Paul. *See* **Celan, Paul.**

Anceschi, Luciano. LTh 29-35.

Ancestral Power (Awoonor). DEng 2421.

Ancestress, The (Grillparzer). DFor 821-822, 824.

Anciennes Odeurs, Les. See *Remember Me.*

"Ancient Hungarian Lament of Mary." PFor 1974.

"Ancient Lights" (Clarke). PSup 70-71.

"Ancient Torso of Apollo" (Rilke). PFor 1331. See also *New Poems.*

Ancius Manlius Severinus Boethius. *See* Boethius.

And Be a Villain (Stout). M&D 1543-1544.

"And Death Shall Have No Dominion" (Thomas, D.). PEng 2883-2884.

"And I Lounged and Lay on Their Beds" (Cavafy). PFor 300.

And Miss Reardon Drinks a Little (Zindel). DEng 2128-2131.

And on the Eighth Day (Queen). M&D 1380.

And Quiet Flows the Don. See *Silent Don, The.*

And So Ad Infinitum. See *Insect Play, The.*

And They Put Handcuffs on the Flowers (Arrabal). DFor 128-129.

And Things That Go Bump in the Night (McNally). DEng 1228, 1229-1230.

"And You?" (Foscolo). PFor 493-494. *See also* "Sonetti."

Andersch, Alfred. ShF 2498.

Andersen, Benny. PFor 2197.

Andersen, Hans Christian. DFor 2469; LTh 1723; ShF 859-866.

Andersen, Vita. PFor 2198.

Anderson, Maxwell. DEng 24-29.

Anderson, Robert. DEng 30-40.

Anderson, Sherwood. LFEng 71-80; ShF 247-248, 540-541, 723, 815, 867-874.

Andersson, Claes. PFor 2200.

Ando Tsuguo. PFor 2079.

Andorra (Frisch). DFor 648-649.

André (Dunlap). DEng 532-533.

André le Chapelain. PFor 1836.

"Andrea" (O'Hara). ShF 2016-2017.

Andrea, Marianne. ShF 2499.

"Andrea del Sarto" (Browning, R.). PEng 341-343.

Andreas. ShF 433.

Andreas-Salomé, Lou. LFFor 2183-2184.

Andress, Lesley. *See* **Sanders, Lawrence.**

"Andreuccio of Perugia" (Boccaccio). ShFSup 49.

Andreyev, Leonid. DFor 59-67; LFFor 2321.

Andria. See *The Woman from Andros, The.*

Andrian-Werburg, Leopold von. LFFor 2188.

Andrić, Ivo. LFFor **57-71,** 2075-2076.

Andromache (Euripides). DFor 2113.

Andromache (Racine). DFor 1514-1516; LTh 840, 1198-1199, 1687.

Andromaque. See *Andromache.*

"Anfang." *See* "Beginning."

"Ange heurtebise, L'" (Cocteau). PFor 372. See also *Opéra.*

Angel at the Gate, The (Harris). LFSup 149.

Ángel fieramente humano (Otero). PFor 1114-1115.

Angel Fire (Oates). PEng 2119.

Angel in the House, The (Patmore). PEng 2190-2192.

"Angel Levine" (Malamud). ShF 1863-1864.

"Angel of the Odd, The" (Poe). ShF 2108-2109.

Angel of the Revolution, The (Griffith). LFEng 3207-3208.

Angel Pavement (Priestley). LFEng 2142-2143.

Angèle (Dumas, père). DFor 490-491.

"Angelfish" (Dent). M&D 485.

"Angelic Guidance" (Newman). PEng 2104.

"Angelic Imagination, The" (Tate). LTh 1428.

"Angelina or l'Amie Inconnue" (Edgeworth). ShF 1324.

Angelo, Tyrant of Padua (Hugo). DFor 970.

Angels Fall (Wilson). DEng 2102.

"Angels of Detroit, The" (Levine). PEng 1716.

Angels' Prayer (Hakim). DSup 178.

"Angelus, The" (Harte). PEng 1241.

"Anger" (Creeley). PEng 683-684.

"Angle of Geese" (Momaday). PEng 2019.

Angle of Repose (Stegner). LFEng 2499, 2500-2502.

Anglo-Saxon Attitudes (Wilson, A.). LFEng 2901-2902.

Angst des Tormanns beim Elfmeter, Die. See *Goalie's Anxiety at the Penalty Kick, The.*

Anguriya Binimoy (Mukherjee). LFFor 2216.

Anhelli (Slowacki). PFor 1444-1445.

Aniara (Martinson). PSup 272-273.

Anika's Times (Andrić). LFFor 66-67.

Anikina vremena. See *Anika's Times.*

Anile, Antonio. PFor 2045.

Animal de fondo (Jiménez). PFor 754.

Animal Farm (Orwell). LFEng 2059-2061.

Animal Kingdom, The (Barry). DEng 134-135.

"Animal That Drank Up Sound, The" (Stafford). PEng 2723.

"Animal, Vegetable, Mineral" (Bogan). PEng 236.

"Animals Are Passing from Our Lives" (Levine). PEng 1715.

"Anitachi." *See* "My Older Brothers."

Ankerfeste (Hauge). LFFor 800. See also *Cleng Peerson.*

Anklagung des verderbten Geschmackes (Bodmer). LTh 176.

Anmerkungen über die "Geschichte der Kunst des Alterthums" (Winckelmann). LTh 1564.

Ann Veronica (Wells). LFEng 2810.

Anna Karenina (Tolstoy). LFFor 1725-1727, 2317.

Anna Kleiber (Sastre). DSup 323-324.

Anna Liisa (Canth). DFor 328-329.

Anna of the Five Towns (Bennett). LFEng 241-242.

Anna Snegina (Esenin). PFor 480.

Anna Sophie Hedveg (Abell). DFor 6-8.

Anna Svärd (Lagerlöf). LFFor 986, 988-989. See also *Ring of the Löwenskölds, The.*

Annaeus Lucanus, Marcus. *See* **Lucan.**

Annals of Newgate, The (Villette). ShF 748.

"Annamalai" (Narayan). ShFSup 228.

Annensky, Innokenty. PFor **40-46,** 2145-2146.

Anni Mirabiles, 1921-1925 (Blackmur). LTh 160.

Anniversaries (Johnson). LFFor 892-893.

Anno Domini MCMXXI (Akhmatova). PFor 12.

Annonce faite à Marie, L'. See *Tidings Brought to Mary, The.*

Annus Mirabilis (Dryden). PEng 873.

"Anonymiad" (Barth). ShF 931-932.

Anonymous Sins (Oates). PEng 2118.

"Anorexia" (Boland). PSup 38.

Another Country (Baldwin). LFEng 137-139.

"Another Night in the Ruins" (Kinnell). PEng 1596-1597.

"Another Spring" (Sassoon). PEng 2474.

"Another Texas Ghost Story" (Brautigan). ShFSup 57.

"Another upon her weeping" (Herrick). PEng 1311-1312.

"Another Voice" (Wilbur). PEng 3095.

Another's Nest (Benavente). DFor 176-177.

Anouilh, Jean. DFor **68-83**, 2355-2356.

Anpao (Highwater). LFEng 1361-1362.

"Anrufung des grossen Bären." *See* "Evocation of the Great Bear."

Ansichten eines Clowns. See *Clown, The.*

"Answer, The" (Cotton). PEng 581, 584.

"Answer, An" (Suckling). PEng 2781.

Answer from Limbo, An (Moore, B.). LFEng 1889-1890.

"Answer to some Verses made in his praise, An" (Suckling). PEng 2782.

Answered Prayers (Capote). LFEng 443, 449-450.

"Answers in Progress" (Baraka). ShF 924-926.

"Antéros" (Nerval). PFor 1088.

"Anthem for Doomed Youth" (Owen). PEng 2162.

Anthologie auf das Jahr 1782. See *Anthology for the Year 1782.*

Anthology for the Year 1782 (Schiller). PFor 1404, 1406.

Anthropological Principle in Philosophy, The (Chernyshevsky). LTh 288.

Antic Hay (Huxley). LFEng 1401-1402.

"Anti-Christ" (Chesterton). PEng 494-495.

Anticlaudian, The (Alan of Lille). LTh 20-23.

Anticristo, El (Ruiz de Alarcón). DFor 1607-1608.

Anti-Death League, The (Amis). LFEng 64, 67-68.

Antigone (Alfieri). DFor 46-47.

Antigone (Anouilh). DFor 78-79, 2355-2356.

Antigone (Cocteau). DFor 417-419.

Antigone (Sophocles). DFor 1729-1732, 2104-2105.

"Antigua, Penny, Puce." See *Antigua Stamp, The.*

Antigua Stamp, The (Graves, R.). LFEng 1195.

Anti-platon (Bonnefoy). PSup 44.

Anti-Story (Stevick, ed.). ShF 90.

Antoine, André. DEng 2195-2196, 2232-2233; DFor 2347.

Antoninus, Brother. *See* **Everson, William.**

Antonio Foscarini (Niccolini). DFor 1432.

Antonius Diogenes. LFFor 2000, 2014.

Antony (Dumas, *père*). DFor 488-489.

Antony and Cleopatra (Shakespeare). DEng 1721-1722, 2283.

Antropologicheskii printsip v filosofii. See *Anthropological Principle in Philosophy, The.*

Antschel, Paul. *See* **Celan, Paul.**

"Anyone lived in a pretty how town" (Cummings). PEng 707-708.

Anzai Hitoshi. PFor 2080.

Anzengruber, Ludwig. DFor **84-92**, 2373.

"Aoi Hano." *See* "Aguri."

Aoi no ue. See *Lady Aoi, The.*

Apartment in Athens (Wescott). LFEng 2838.

Ape and Essence (Huxley). LFEng 1408-1409.

"Apennine" (Pasolini). PFor 1149. See also "Gramsci's Ashes."

Apes of God, The (Lewis, W.). LFEng 1685-1686.

Aphrodite in Aulis (Moore, G.). LFEng 1902-1903.

"A-Playin' of Old Sledge at the Settlemint" (Murfree). ShF 226.

"Apogee of Celery" (Neruda). PFor 1076. See also *Residence on Earth.*

"Apoges del apio." *See* "Apogee of Celery."

Apollinaire, Guillaume. DEng 2203; LTh 213, 996; **PFor 47-56**, 1883-1884.

Apollodorus of Carystus. DFor 2134.

Apollonius of Rhodes. LTh 264.

"Apollonius of Tyana, A Dance, with Some Words, for Two Actors" (Olson). PSup 308.

Apollonius Rhodius. PFor **57-63**, 253.

"Apología pro vita sua" (Cernuda). PFor 323. See also *Como quien espera el alba.*

Apologie for Poetry. See *Defence of Poesie.*

Apologie of the Schoole of Abuse, An (Gosson). LTh 613.

Apology for Poetry, An (Sidney). LTh 609, 611, 1345-1346, 1349, 1442, 1665, 1669-1671, 1675.

Apology for the Life of Mrs. Shamela Andrews, An. See *Shamela.*

"Apparently with no surprise" (Dickinson). PEng 809-810.

"Apparition de la vieille" (Follain). PSup 131.

"Apparition of Splendor" (Moore). PEng 2047.

"Appel du chevalier, L'" (Follain). PSup 128.

Appelfeld, Aharon. LFSup 31-42.

"Appennino, L'." *See* "Apennine."

Arias tristes (Jiménez). PFor 750.
Aridoshi (Zeami). DFor 2042.
Ariel (Rodo). LFFor 2286.
Arion. DFor 2088-2089.
Ariosto, Ludovico. DFor 103-110, 2396; LTh 131, 366, 584, 1040, 1662; PFor 93-100, 163, 2012-2014.
Aristocracy (Howard, B.). DEng 971-972.
Aristophanes. DEng 2137; DFor 111-120, 2091-2092, 2095, 2123-2130.
Aristos (Fowles). LFEng 1008.
Aristotle. DEng 2138-2143; DFor 2094-2095; LTh 22, **36-44**, 77, 258, 272-274, 276-277, 280, 301-302, 305, 309-310, 323, 384, 405, 529, 584-587, 614, 779, 781-782, 840, 855, 862, 882, 906, 939, 952, 958, 1038-1041, 1111, 1143-1145, 1200, 1282-1283, 1285-1286, 1320, 1347, 1461, 1636-1637, 1648-1649, 1661, 1665, 1799, 1832.
"Aristotle and the Hired Thugs" (Gold). ShF 1503-1504.
Ariwara no Narihira. PFor 2059-2060.
Ark (Johnson). PSup 214-215.
Aškerc, Anton. PFor 2269.
Arlatan's Treasure (Daudet). ShF 1242.
"Arlésienne, L' " (Daudet). ShF 1240.
Armah, Ayi Kwei. LFEng 81-93.
Armance (Stendhal). LFFor 1653-1655.
Arme Heinrich, Die. See *Poor Henry.*
Arme Konrad, Der (Wolf). DFor 2019.
Arme Spielmann, Der. See *Poor Fiddler, The.*
Armed Descent (Kelly). PSup 219-220.
Ärmer Mörder. See *Poor Murderer.*
"Armidale" (Simpson). PEng 2609.
Armies of the Night, The (Mailer). LFEng 1772, 1783-1785.
"Arminius" (Praed). PEng 2279.
"Arms" (Beer). PEng 119.
"Arms and the Boy" (Owen). PEng 2162.
Arms and the Man (Shaw). DEng 1729-1731.
Armstrong, Charlotte. M&D 35-41.
Armstrong's Last Goodnight (Arden). DEng 47-48.
Arnaldo da Brescia. See *Arnold of Brescia.*
Arniches, Carlos. DFor 2502.
Arnim, Achim von. LTh 1706.
Arnold, Matthew. LTh **45-50**, 160, 459, 498, 752, 873, 1087, 1245, 1256, 1349, 1400, 1405-1406, 1456, 1732-1733; PEng **47-56.**
Arnold of Brescia (Niccolini). DFor 1432-1434.

Aronpuro, Kari. PFor 2199.
Arouet, François-Marie. See **Voltaire.**
Around the World in Eighty Days (Verne). LFFor 1874.
Arp, Hans. PFor 101-107.
Arp, Jean. See **Arp, Hans.**
Arpino, Giovanni. LFFor 2248, 2252.
Arrabal, Fernando. DFor 121-131, 2260-2261, 2359-2360, 2507.
Arrah-na-Pogue (Boucicault). DEng 269.
Arraignment of Paris, The (Peele). DEng 1490, 1491.
Arrival and Departure (Koestler). LFEng 1552-1553.
Arrivants, The (Brathwaite). PEng 268-271; PFor 212-216.
Arriví, Francisco. DFor 2446.
Arrow-Odd. See *Örvar-Odds saga.*
Arrow of God (Achebe). LFEng 6, 9-11.
Arrow of Gold, The (Conrad). LFEng 587.
Arrow Pointing Nowhere (Daly, E.). M&D 453.
Arrowsmith (Lewis, S.). LFEng 1677-1678.
Ars amatoria. See *Art of Love, The.*
Ars poetica. See *Art of Poetry, The.*
"Ars Poetica" (MacLeish). PEng 1854-1855.
"Ars Poetica?" (Milosz). PFor 1035.
"Ars Poetica" (Wright, C.). PEng 3149.
"Arsène in Prison" (Leblanc). M&D 1036-1037.
"Arsenio" (Montale). PFor 1048. See also *Bones of the Cuttlefish.*
"Art" (Gautier). PFor 539. See also *Enamels and Cameos.*
"Art" (Levertov). PEng 1706.
"Art and Formula in the Short Story" (Beck). ShF 71.
Art and Morality (Brunetière). LTh 235.
Art and Social Life (Plekhanov). LTh 1122.
"Art as Technique" (Shklovsky). ShF 89.
Art de Tragédie (La Taille). LTh 277.
"Art for Art's Sake" (Forster). LTh 499.
Art of Courtly Love, The (Capellanus). ShF 443.
Art of Fiction, The (James). LTh 753-754; LFEng 3047.
Art of Letters, The (Ts'ao P'i). LTh 1774.
"Art of Love, The" (Koch). PEng 1628-1629.
Art of Love, The (Koch). PEng 1627, 1629.
Art of Love, The (Ovid). PFor 1123-1125.

"Aspasia" (Leopardi). PFor 863. See also *Canti*.

Aspects of Eve (Pastan). PEng 2174.

Aspects of the Modern Short Story (Ward). ShF 93.

Aspects of the Novel (Forster). LTh 499-500, 925; ShF 1387.

Aspenström, Werner. PFor 2187.

Asphalt Jungle, The (Burnett). M&D 244-245.

"Asphodel, That Greeny Flower" (Williams, W. C.). PEng 3119-3120.

Aspidistra in Babylon, An (Bates). LFEng 185.

"Assassin" (Tomlinson). PEng 2910.

Assassin Who Gave Up His Gun, The (Cunningham). M&D 441.

Assassins, The (Prokosch). LFEng 2161.

Assassins Have Starry Eyes. See *Assignment: Murder.*

Assassins Road (Harvester). M&D 849.

"Assembling a Street" (Galvin). PEng 1055.

Assignment, The (Dürrenmatt). M&D 560.

Assignment: Murder (Hamilton). M&D 816.

Assistant, The (Malamud). LFEng 1790, 1795-1797, 3067; ShF 417.

Assommoir, L' (Zola). LFFor 1990-1992. See also *Rougon-Macquart, Les.*

"Assyrian king, in peas with fowle desyre, Th'" (Surrey). PEng 2789.

Asteropherus, Magnus Olai. DFor 2465.

Asthetische Erfahrung und literarische Hermeneutik. See *Aesthetic Experience and Literary Hermeneutics.*

Astillero, El. See *Shipyard, The.*

Astounding Science Fiction. ShF 775-776.

Astrate (Quinault). DFor 1506-1507.

Astrea (d'Urfé). LFFor 1809-1811, 2026, 2114; ShF 145.

Astrée, L'. See *Astrea.*

Astrologer, The (Della Porta). DFor 478.

Astronauci (Lem). LFFor 1009.

Astronomer and Other Stories, The (Betts). ShF 961-962.

Astrophel and Stella (Sidney, P.). PEng 2573-2574, 2575-2580.

Asturias, Miguel Ángel. LFFor 81-88, 2294; **ShF 882-888**; ShFSup 387.

Asylum Piece (Kavan). ShF 275-276, 1737-1739.

"At a Party" (Bogan). PEng 235, 237.

"At Ann Lee's" (Bowen). ShF 254-255.

At Fault (Chopin). LFEng 527-529.

At Heaven's Gate (Warren). LFEng 2772.

"At His Nativity" (Isvaran). ShF 644-645.

"At Jane's" (Stern). PSup 376-377.

At Lady Molly's (Powell). LFEng 2118-2119.

At My Heart's Core (Davies). DEng 470-471.

At Play in the Fields of the Lord (Matthiessen). LFEng 1822-1823, 1825, 1826-1830.

"At Provincetown" (Hoffman). PEng 1358.

"At Rhodes" (Durrell). PEng 919-920.

"At Sallygap" (Lavin). ShF 1782-1783.

At Swim-Two-Birds (O'Brien, F.). LFEng 2026, 2027-2028.

At Terror Street and Agony Way (Bukowski). PEng 360.

"At the Bay" (Mansfield). ShF 1884.

"At the Bomb Testing Site" (Stafford). PEng 2723.

At the Bottom. See *Lower Depths, The.*

"At the 'Cadian Ball" (Chopin). ShF 1135.

"At the Edge of the World" (Leskov). ShFSup 160.

"At the End of September" (Petőfi). PFor 1224-1225.

At the End of the Open Road (Simpson). PEng 2603-2604.

"At the Executed Murderer's Grave" (Wright, J.). PEng 3161-3163.

"At the Indian Killer's Grave" (Lowell, R.). PEng 1788-1789.

"At the Market" (Arany). PFor 83.

"At the Prophet's" (Mann). ShF 1877.

"At the Rendezvous of Victory" (Gordimer). ShFSup 110.

"At the Seminary" (Oates). ShF 709-710.

"At the Theatre" (Cavafy). PFor 300.

At the Top of My Voice (Mayakovsky). PFor 991, 992.

At the Villa Rose (Mason). M&D 1197.

"At Twilight" (Monroe). PEng 2028.

At være eller ikke være. See *To Be, or Not to Be?*

Atala (Chateaubriand). LFFor 338-339.

Atalanta in Calydon (Swinburne). DEng 1897-1898; PEng 2813.

Athawar House (Nagarajan). ShF 644.

Atheist, The (Otway). DEng 1449.

Atheist's Tragedy, The (Tourneur). DEng 1941-1943, 2292.

"Athénaïse" (Chopin). ShF 1134-1135.

Atlakviða. See *Lay of Atli.*

Atlantic Flyway (Galvin). PEng 1055-1057.

Auto da sibila Cassandra. See *Play of the Sibyl Cassandra, The.*

Auto de barca do inferno (Vicente). DFor 2173.

Auto de barca do purgatorio (Vicente). DFor 2177.

Auto de los Reyes Magos. DFor 2170.

"Autobiografia" (Saba). PSup 343, 345.

Autobiographies (Yeats). LTh 1589.

"Autobiography" (Barth). ShF 929.

Autobiography (Hunt). PEng 1462.

"Autobiography" (Seifert). PSup 355.

"Autobiography of a Comedian" (Ciardi). PEng 503.

Autobiography of Miss Jane Pittman, The (Gaines). LFEng 1047-1048; ShF 1430-1431.

"Automa, L'." *See* "Fetish, The."

"Automatons" (Hoffmann). ShF 1648.

Autonomia ed eteronomia dell'arte (Anceschi). LTh 31.

"Autor als Produzent, Der." *See* "Author as Producer, The."

Autre Monde, L'. See *Other Worlds.*

Autre Tartuffe, L'. See *Frailty and Hypocrisy.*

"Autumn Begins in Martin's Ferry, Ohio" (Wright, J.). PEng 3165.

"Autumn Day" (Gallant). ShF 1439-1440.

Autumn Journal (MacNeice). PEng 1872-1875.

"Autumn Maneuvers" (Bachmann). PFor 128. See also *Gestundete Zeit, Die.*

Autumn of the Patriarch, The (García Márquez). LFFor 619.

"Autumn Passed Through Paris" (Ady). PFor 6.

Autumn Sonata (Valle-Inclán). LFFor 1835. See also *Pleasant Memoirs of the Marquis de Bradomín, The.*

"Autumnal, The" (Donne). PEng 828-829.

"Autumnal" (Glück). PSup 137.

Avallone, Michael. M&D 42-47. *See also* **Carter, Nick.**

Avariés, Les. See *Damaged Goods.*

"Ave Atque Vale" (Swinburne). PEng 2821-2822.

Avenarius, Richard. LTh 944.

Avenging Angel, The (Burns). M&D 252-253.

Avenir de la science, L'. See *Future of Science, The.*

Aventure ambiguë, L'. See *Ambiguous Adventure.*

Aventures prodigieuses de Tartarin de Tarascon. See *Tartarin of Tarascon.*

Avenue Bearing the Initial of Christ into the New World (Kinnell). PEng 1594-1596.

Averroës. LTh 1038, 1648.

Aves sin nido (Turner). LFFor 2283.

Aveva due pistole con gli occhi bianchi è neri (Fo). DSup 110-111.

"Avtor i geroi v esteticheskoi deyatel'nosti." *See* "Author and Hero in Aesthetic Activity."

Awake and Sing (Odets). DEng 1398-1399, 2403-2404.

"Awake, my Eyes, at Night my Thoughts pursue" (Sedley). PEng 2506.

Awakening, The (Chopin). LFEng 526-527, 529-532; ShF 1131, 1132.

"Awakening" (Herbert). PFor 655.

"Awareness" (Madhubuti). PEng 1892.

Awooner, Kofi. PFor 108-116.

Awooner-Williams, George. *See* **Awoonor, Kofi.**

Axe, The (Undset). LFFor 1804. See also *Master of Hestviken, The.*

Axel and Anna (Bremer). LFFor 2337.

Axel's Castle (Wilson). LTh 1548.

Axion Esti, The (Elýtis). PFor 464-465, 1967-1968.

Axton, David. *See* **Koontz, Dean R.**

Aya no tsuzumu. See *Damask Drum, The.*

Ayckbourn, Alan. DEng 60-69; DSup 407.

Aydi ai-na'imah, al-. See *Tender Hands.*

"Aye, There It Is! It Wakes To-night" (Brontë). PEng 298-299.

Ayraud, Pierre. *See* **Narcejac, Thomas.**

Ayukawa Nobuo. PFor 2078.

"Az éden elvesztése." *See* "Loss of Paradise, The."

"Az elveszett alkótmany" (Arany). PFor 76.

Az ember tragédiája. See *Tragedy of Man, The.*

Azma iroikó ke penthimo yia ton haméno anthipolohaghó tis Alvanías. See *Heroic and Elegiac Song for the Lost Second Lieutenant of the Albanian Campaign.*

Azul (Darío). PFor 422-423.

B

"B Negative" (Kennedy). PEng 1570.
"Babas del diablo, Las." *See* "Blow-Up."
Babbitt (Lewis, S.). LFEng 1675-1677.
Babbitt, Irving. LTh **68-74,** 1011, 1256-1257, 1319, 1566, 1818.
Babel, Isaac. DFor 2462; ShF **899-904.**
Babel-17 (Delany). LFEng 715, 717-718.
Babelandia (Aguilera Malta). LFSup 13-14.
Babe's Bed, The (Wescott). ShF 2423.
Babička. See *Grandmother, The.*
Babits, Mihály. PFor **117-123,** 1984.
"Babiy Yar" (Yevtushenko). PFor 1710.
Babouc (Voltaire). ShFSup 329-330.
Babruis. ShF 379, 380.
Babson, Marian. M&D **48-52.**
"Baby Is Three" (Sturgeon). LFEng 2584.
"Baby Villon" (Levine). PEng 1715.
"Babylon Revisited" (Fitzgerald). ShF 1373-1374.
Babyloniaca (Iamblichus). LFFor 2001.
"Babysitter, The" (Coover). LFEng 3329; ShF 1191-1192.
Bacchae, The (Euripides). DFor 577, 2117-2119.
Bacchides. See *Two Bacchides, The.*
Bacchus (Cocteau). DFor 422.
"Bacchus" (Empson). PEng 970-971.
Bacchylides. PFor 1945.
Bachelard, Gaston. LTh 1149.
"Bachelor" (Meredith). PEng 1956-1957.
Bachelor of Arts, The (Narayan). LFEng 1968.
Bachman, Richard. *See* **King, Stephen.**
Bachmann, Ingeborg. LFFor 2199; PFor **124-130,** 1934; ShF 2502.
"Back" (Corman). PEng 571.
Back Country, The (Snyder). PEng 2672-2674.
Back to Methuselah (Shaw). DEng 2382.
Backtrack (Hansen). M&D 832-833.
Backward Place, A (Jhabvala). LFSup 174.
Bacon, Francis. LTh **75-81,** 1675, 1677; PEng 596.
"Bad Blood" (Rimbaud). PFor 1339-1340. See also *Season in Hell, A.*
"Bad Characters" (Stafford). ShF 2262-2263.
"Bad Dreams" (Pinsky). PEng 2218.

Bad Man, A (Elkin). LFEng 888-889.
Bad Man from Bodie. See *Welcome to Hard Times.*
Bad Seed (Anderson, M.). DEng 2202.
"Bad Time for Poetry" (Brecht). PFor 224-225.
Badenheim, 'ir nofesh. See *Badenheim 1939.*
Badenheim 1939 (Appelfeld). LFSup 33-35.
Badgers, The (Leonov). M&D 1059-1060.
Bad-tempered Man, The (Menander). DFor 1306-1308, 2133.
Baggesen, Jens. PFor 2163.
Bagley, Desmond. M&D **53-58.**
Bagrovy ostrov. See *Crimson Island, The.*
Bahía de silencio, La. See *Bay of Silence, The.*
Bahnwärter Thiel. See *Flagman Thiel.*
Bahr, Hermann. LFFor 2184.
Baikie Charivari, The (Bridie). DEng 278-279.
"Bailbondsman, The" (Elkin). LFEng 890; ShF 1341-1342.
"Bailes y las comedias, Los" (Feijóo). LTh 476.
Bailey, H. C. M&D **59-66;** ShF 755-756.
Baiser au lépreux, Le. See *Kiss for the Leper, A.*
Bajazet (Racine). DFor 1518.
Bajazet, preface to (Racine). LTh 1199.
Bajka (Ćosić). LFFor 388-389.
Bajza, Jozef Ignác. LFFor 2068; PFor 1808.
Bakchai. See *Bacchae, The.*
Baker, Asa. See **Halliday, Brett.**
Baker, George Pierce. DEng 2399.
Baker, Houston A., Jr. LTh 546, 550.
Baker, Will. ShF 2503.
Bakhtin, Mikhail. LTh **82-89,** 440, 832-833, 1437, 1799, 1821.
"Balaam and His Master" (Harris, J.). ShF 1590-1591.
"Balada de la placeta." *See* "Ballad of the Little Square."
"Balada del Andaluz perdido." *See* "Ballad of the Lost Andalusian."
Baladas de primavera (Jiménez). PFor 751.
Balaka. See *Flight of Swans, A.*
Balassi, Bálint. PFor 1976.
Balbín, Bohuslav. PFor 1798.

Balcony, The (Genet). DFor 683-685, 2260.

Balcony, The (Heiberg, G.). DFor 895.

Bald Soprano, The (Ionesco). DFor 995-997, 2248-2250, 2357.

Baldur hiin gode (Oehlenschläger). DFor 1441-1442.

Baldwin, James. DEng 70-78; LFEng 128-145, 3068; ShF 556, 581, 905-910, 1855.

Bale, John. DEng 79-91.

"Balek Scales, The" (Böll). ShF 974-975.

Balkonen. See *Balcony, The.*

Ball, Doris Collier. See **Bell, Josephine.**

Ball, John. M&D 67-73.

"Ball of Malt and Madame Butterfly, A" (Kiely). ShF 1742-1744.

"Ballad" (Khodasevich). PSup 228.

Ballad and the Source, The (Lehmann). LFSup 231-234.

"Ballad of a Streetwalker" (Manger). PFor 949-950.

"Ballad of a Sweet Dream of Peace" (Warren). PEng 3025.

"Ballad of Babie Bell, The" (Aldrich). PEng 30.

"Ballad of Birmingham" (Randall, D.). PEng 2316.

"Ballad of Bouillabaise, The" (Thackeray). PEng 2874-2875.

"Ballad of Dead Ladies" (Villon). PFor 1658.

"Ballad of East and West, The" (Kipling). PEng 1608, 1609.

"Ballad of Hanna'leh the Orphan, The" (Manger). PFor 950.

Ballad of Love, A (Prokosch). LFEng 2166.

Ballad of Reading Gaol, The (Wilde). PEng 3107-3108.

"Ballad of Sue Ellen Westerfield, The" (Hayden). PEng 1253.

"Ballad of the Bridal Veil" (Manger). PFor 950.

"Ballad of the Children of the Czar, The" (Schwartz). PEng 2489.

"Ballad of the Harp-Weaver, The" (Millay). PEng 2002.

"Ballad of the Little Square" (García Lorca). PFor 516.

"Ballad of the Lost Andalusian" (Alberti). PFor 23.

"Ballad of the Oedipus Complex" (Durrell). PEng 923.

Ballad of the Sad Café, The (McCullers). LFEng 1734-1736, 3309-3311; ShF 481, 1846-1847.

"Ballad of the White Horse, The" (Chesterton). PEng 493-494.

"Ballad of William Sycamore, The" (Benét). PEng 143.

"Ballad on the Gospel 'In the Beginning Was the Word'" (John of the Cross). PFor 766.

"Ballad on the Poet François Villon" (Biermann). PFor 190.

"Ballad on the Psalm 'By the Waters of Babylon'" (John of the Cross). PFor 766.

"Ballad upon a Wedding, A" (Suckling). PEng 2781-2782.

Ballade at the Reverence of Our Lady, Qwene of Mercy (Lydgate). PEng 1808.

"Ballade auf den Dichter François Villon." *See* "Ballad on the Poet François Villon."

"Ballade des Äusseren Lebens" (Hofmannsthal). PFor 674.

"Ballade des dames du temps jadis." *See* "Ballad of Dead Ladies."

"Ballade von einem Traum" (Zweig). PFor 1726.

Ballades en jargon. See *Poems in Slang.*

Ballads (Stevenson). PEng 2757.

Ballads and Other Poems (Longfellow). PEng 1749.

Ballads of a Bohemian (Service). PEng 2516.

Ballady i romanse (Mickiewicz). PFor 2124.

Balladyna (Słowacki). DFor 1715-1716, 2276.

Ballard, J. G. LFEng 146-154; LFSup 401; ShF 779-780, **911-916;** ShFSup 387.

Ballard, W. T. *See* **Carter, Nick.**

"Balloon, The" (Barthelme). ShFSup 23.

Balloon (Colum). DEng 386.

"Baltazar's Marvellous Afternoon" (García Márquez). ShF 1455.

"Balthasar" (France). ShF 1403-1404.

Balthazar (Balzac). See *Quest of the Absolute, The.*

Balthazar (Durrell). See *Alexandria Quartet, The.*

Baltics (Tranströmer). PFor 1528-1529.

Balzac, Honoré de. LFFor **89-102,** 2126-2127, 2130, 2131; LTh 253, 554, 937, 1173, 1395, 1420, 1711; M&D **74-81;** ShF 172, 464, **917-921.**

Balzac, Jean-Louis Guez de. LTh 1687.

"Balzac and Reality" (Butor). LTh 253.

"Bartleby the Scrivener" (Melville). LFEng
3278-3280; ShF 205, 207-208, 796-798,
1915-1918.
Bartlett, Paul Alexander. ShF 2506.
Bartolozzi, Lucia Elizabeth. *See* Vestris,
Madame.
"Base and Superstructure in Marxist Cultural
Theory" (Williams). LTh 1544.
"Basement Room, The" (Greene, G.). ShF
272-273, 786, 1543-1544.
Bashō, Matsuo. *See* **Matsuo Bashō.**
Basic Training of Pavlo Hummel, The (Rabe).
DEng 1547-1548.
Basil (Collins, W.). M&D 388.
Basket Case, The (McInerny). M&D 1162.
Bass, Rochelle. *See* **Owens, Rochelle.**
Bassani, Giorgio. LFFor 2253.
Bassetto, Corno di. *See* **Shaw, George
Bernard.**
"Bat, The" (Sitwell). PEng 2629.
Bataille, Henri. DFor 2349.
Bataille de Pharsale, La. See *Battle of
Pharsalus, The.*
Batailles dans la montagne (Giono). LFFor
656.
"Bateau ivre, Le." *See* "Drunken Boat, The."
**Bates, H. E. LFEng 178-186; ShF 270-271;
ShFSup 27-34.**
"Bath, The" (Carver). ShFSup 81.
Bathhouse, The (Mayakovsky). DFor 1296-
1297.
"Bathhouse, The" (Zoshchenko). ShFSup 379.
Batiushkov, Konstantin. PFor 2136.
Batrachoi. See *Frogs, The.*
"Batter my heart, three-personed God" (Donne).
PEng 836.
Battered Wife and Other Poems, The (Davie).
PSup 91.
Battle, The (Romains). LFFor 1444. See also
Men of Good Will.
Battle of Agincourt, The (Drayton). PEng 854.
Battle of Alcazar, The (Peele). DEng 1491-
1492.
"Battle of Finney's Ford, The" (West). ShFSup
362.
"Battle of Hastyngs" (Chatterton). PEng 471.
Battle of Maldon. ShF 431-432.
Battle of Pharsalus, The (Simon). LFFor 1609-
1611.
Battle of the Books, The (Swift). LTh 1690.

"Battle of the Lake Regillus, The" (Macaulay).
PEng 1827.
Battle Pieces and Aspects of the War (Melville).
PEng 1945, 1950.
"Battle Problem" (Meredith). PEng 1954-1955.
"Battle with the Dragon, The" (Schiller). PFor
1409.
Battles of Coxinga, The (Chikamatsu). DFor
395-397.
Baty, Gaston. DFor 2351.
"Bau, Der." *See* "Burrow, The."
Baudelaire, Charles. LTh 109-114, 551, 555,
1087-1088, 1273-1274, 1568, 1697, 1702,
1732-1733; **PFor 131-140,** 1875-1876.
Bauer mit dem Blerr, Der (Sachs). DFor 1625.
Baumbach, Jonathan. ShF 2507.
Baumgarten, Alexander Gottlieb. LTh 31.
"Bavarian Gentians" (Lawrence, D. H.). PEng
1685-1686.
Bax, Roger. *See* **Garve, Andrew.**
Bay Boy, The (Tyler). DEng 1945-1946.
Bay of Silence, The (Mallea). LFFor 1053-
1054.
Bay Psalm Book. LTh 1740.
Baza de espadas. See *Ruedo ibérico, El.*
Bazin, André. DEng 2518.
Be Careful How You Live (Lacy). M&D 1019.
Beach, The (Pavese). LFFor 1247-1248.
"Beach of Falesá, The" (Stevenson, R. L.).
ShF 2285.
"Beach Party, The" (Grau). ShF 1531, 1532-
1533.
Beach Red (Bowman). ShF 130-131.
"Beacons" (Baudelaire). PFor 134-135.
Bećković, Matija. PFor 2258.
Beal, M. F. ShF 2508.
"Beantwortung einer Anfrage." *See* "Response
to a Request."
"Bear, The" (Faulkner). LFEng 3272-3273,
3274-3276; ShF 11, 12, 13, 14, 1363-1365.
"Bear, The" (Kinnell). PEng 1597.
"Bear on a Plate" (Malgonkar). ShF 650.
Beard, Thomas. ShF 499.
Beardsley, Monroe C. LTh 1554, 1812.
"Beast, The" (Brecht). ShF 1005-1006.
"Beast in the Jungle, The" (James, H.). LFEng
3321-3323; ShF 232-233, 1683-1685.
Beast in View (Millar). M&D 1221.
Beastly Beatitudes of Balthazar B., The
(Donleavy). LFEng 785-786.
Beast's Story, A (Kennedy). DSup 216.

"Beato sillón." *See* "Blessed Armchair."
Béatrice du Congo (Dadié). DFor 2269, 2270.
Beattie, Ann. **LFEng 187-194;** LFSup 401;
ShF 552; **ShFSup 35-43.**
Beau Brummell (Fitch). DEng 620-621, 2399.
"Beau Monde of Mrs. Bridge, The" (Connell).
ShF 1178.
Beauchampe (Simms). LFEng 2413.
Beauchamp's Career (Meredith). LFEng 1867-
1869.
Beaumarchais, Pierre-Augustin Caron de.
DEng 2182, 2334; **DFor 144-153,** 2340.
Beaumont, Francis. DEng 139-145; **PEng 92-**
97.
Beaumont, Francis, and John Fletcher. DEng
2290, 2299-2301.
Beautiful and Damned, The (Fitzgerald, F. S.).
LFEng 959-962.
Beautiful Days (Innerhofer). LFFor 2206.
"Beautiful Girl" (Adams). ShFSup 6.
Beautiful Greed, The (Madden). LFEng 1761-
1763.
Beautiful People, The (Saroyan). DEng 1657-
1658.
"Beautiful Stranger, The" (Jackson). ShF 1670.
"Beautiful Young Nymph Going to Bed, A"
(Swift). PEng 2808.
"Beautiful Youth" (Benn). PFor 173.
Beautyful Ones Are Not Yet Born, The (Armah).
LFEng 84-86.
Beauvoir, Simone de. **LFFor 112-120;** LFSup
401.
Beaux' Stratagem, The (Farquhar). DEng 583-
584.
"Because I could not stop for Death"
(Dickinson). PEng 812, 3387.
Becher, Johannes R. PFor 1813, 1817, 1929.
Beck, Julian. DEng 2481, 2482.
Beck, Warren. **ShF 934-936.**
Becker, Stephen. **LFEng 195-204.**
Becket (Anouilh). DFor 81-82.
Becket (Tennyson). DEng 1918-1919.
Beckett, Samuel. **DEng 146-158,** 2207, 2384-
2385; **DFor 154-166,** 2241, 2245-2248,
2359; DSup 407; **LFEng 205-216; LFFor**
121-132, 2146; LFSup 401; LTh 1318;
PEng 98-107; PFor 141-150; PSup 403;
ShF 674, **937-941;** ShFSup 387.
Beclch (Owens). DEng 1458-1459.
Becque, Henry. DEng 2195; **DFor 167-173,**
2347.

Bécquer, Gustavo Adolfo. **PFor 151-159,**
2224.
"Bedbug, The" (Harrison). PSup 168.
Bedbug, The (Mayakovsky). DFor 1295-1296;
PFor 986.
Beddoes, Thomas Lovell. **PEng 108-114.**
Bede. PEng 416-418.
Bedford, Donald F. *See* **Fearing, Kenneth.**
"Bednaya Liza." *See* "Poor Liza."
Bednaya nevesta. See *Poor Bride, The.*
Bednost ne porok. See *Poverty Is No Crime.*
"Beds" (Barnard). PSup 25.
"Bee, The" (Lyly). PEng 1819-1821.
"Bee Meeting, The" (Plath). PEng 2229.
Beeding, Francis. **M&D 94-98.**
"Beep Beep Poem, The" (Giovanni). PEng
1100-1101.
Beer, Patricia. **PEng 115-122;** PSup 403.
Beer, Thomas. ShF 251.
Beerbohm, Max. **ShF 942-947.**
Beer-Hofmann, Richard. LFFor 2188.
Befehl, Der. See *Order, The.*
"Before an Old Painting of the Crucifixion"
(Momaday). PEng 2018-2019.
Before Cannae (Munk). DFor 1393.
Before Dawn (Hauptmann). DFor 869-871,
2375.
Before Dawn (Holz and Schlaf). LFFor 2181.
"Before Parting" (Pasternak). ShF 2062.
Before the Brave (Patchen). PEng 2187.
"Before the Diaspora" (Ady). PFor 7.
Before the Fact (Berkeley). M&D 121-122.
"Before the Law" (Kafka). ShF 1732-1733.
Befristeten, Die. See *Numbered, The.*
Beg. See *Flight.*
Beggar in Jerusalem, A (Wiesel). LFFor 1926-
1927.
Beggar on Horseback (Kaufman and Connelly).
DEng 419-420.
"Beggars, The" (O'Flaherty). ShF 2010-2011.
Beggar's Opera, The (Gay). DEng 732-734,
2179, 2458-2459, 2465; PEng 1067.
Beggarwoman of Locarno, The (Kleist). ShF
1762.
"Beginning" (Novalis). PFor 1095-1096.
"Beginning" (Orr). PEng 2150.
Beginning and the End, The (Jeffers). PEng
1496.
Beginning on the Short Story, A (Williams, W.
C.). ShF 94.
"Beginnings" (Hayden). PEng 1249-1250.

"Beginnings of and for the True Short Story in England" (Harris, W.). ShF 78.

Begović, Milan. DFor 2293; PFor 2263.

Béguin, Albert. LTh 1151, 1808.

Begum's Fortune, The (Verne). LFFor 1875.

Behan, Brendan. DEng 159-167.

"Behaving Like a Jew" (Stern). PSup 370-371.

"Behind the Automatic Door" (Robbe-Grillet). ShF 2156.

Behn, Aphra. DEng 168-178; LFEng 217-223, 3018-3019; PEng 123-131; ShF 502.

"Behold the Lilies of the Field" (Hecht). PEng 1279-1281.

Behrman, S. N. DEng 179-189.

Beiden Klingsberg, Die. See *Father and Son.*

"Beim Bau der Chinesischen Mauer." *See* "Great Wall of China, The."

Being and Nothingness (Sartre). LTh 1274.

Being There (Kosinski). LFEng 1563-1564.

"Bekenntnis zur Trümmerliteratur." *See* "Defense of Rubble Literature."

Bela e a fera, A (Lispector). ShFSup 168.

Bela Lugosi's White Christmas (West). LFSup 373.

Belaia staia (Akhmatova). PFor 12.

Belarmino and Apolonio (Pérez de Ayala). LFFor 1261-1263.

Belasco, David. DEng 190-199.

Belaya gvardiya. See *White Guard, The.*

Belfagor. See *Story of Belphagor the Arch Demon, The.*

Belfry of Bouges and Other Poems, The (Longfellow). PEng 1749.

"Believe It" (Logan). PEng 1743.

Belinda, Aunt. *See* **Braddon, M. E.**

Belinsky, Vissarion. LFFor 2314; LTh 115-123, 285, 288, 388, 394, 396-398, 946, 1104, 1108, 1122, 1179, 1446, 1502; PFor 2140-2141.

Bell, Josephine. M&D 99-106.

Bell for Adano, A (Hersey). LFEng 1352, 1355-1356.

Bellamy, Joe David. ShF 2509.

Belle Saison, La (Martin du Gard). LFFor 1114-1115. See also *World of the Thibaults, The.*

"Belle Zoraïde, La" (Chopin). ShF 1133.

Belleau, Rémy. PFor 2115.

Bellefleur (Oates). LFEng 2015.

Belles Images, Les (de Beauvoir). LFFor 119.

Belles-sœurs, Les (Tremblay). DSup 349-350.

Bellman, Carl Michael. LFFor 2335; PFor 2161.

Belloc, Hilaire. PEng 132-139.

Bellow, Saul. LFEng 224-236, 3067; ShF 549-550, **948-952,** 1855; ShFSup 387.

"Bells for John Whiteside's Daughter" (Ransom). PEng 2327-2329.

"Bells in Winter" (Milosz). PFor 1036.

"Bells of San Blas, The" (Longfellow). PEng 1748.

Bellum civile. See *Pharsalia.*

Beloved Hedgerose, The (Gryphius). DFor 839.

Bely, Andrey. LFFor 2320; LTh **124-130,** 975.

Bembo, Pietro. LTh **131-136,** 1459, 1462-1463; PFor **160-169.**

"Ben venga maggio." *See* "Oh, Welcome May."

Benavente y Martínez, Jacinto. DFor **174-182,** 2501-2502.

Bend in the River, A (Naipaul). LFEng 1962-1964.

Bend Sinister (Nabokov). LFEng 1951-1952.

Bendigo Shafter (L'Amour). LFSup 225.

Bending the Bow (Duncan). PEng 905.

"Benediction" (Kunitz). PSup 243.

Benediktsson, Einar. PFor 2175.

Benefactors (Frayn). DSup 130-131.

Benet, Juan. LFFor 133-143.

Benét, Stephen Vincent. PEng **140-145;** ShF 259, 543-544, **953-959.**

Beniak, Valentín. PFor 1811.

Beniowski (Słowacki). PFor 1445-1446, 2125.

"Benito Cereno" (Melville). LFEng 3311-3313; ShF 116.

Benjamin, Walter. LTh **137-143;** 416-417, 1366, 1808.

Benn, Gottfried. PFor **170-176,** 1929, 1933.

Bennett, Arnold. LFEng **237-248,** 3052, 3082; M&D **107-111.**

Bennett, John. ShF 2510.

Benson Murder Case, The (Van Dine). M&D 1638.

"Benson Watts Is Dead and in Virginia" (Betts). ShF 962-964.

"Bent Tree, The" (Manger). PFor 950.

Bentham, Jeremy. LTh 1030-1031, 1730.

Bentley, E. C. M&D 112-117.

Bentley, Eric. LTh **144-151,** 1101, 1328.

Bentley, Richard. LTh 1689-1690.

Between the Acts (Woolf). LFEng 1428, 2957-2959.

Beulah Land (Davis). LFEng 677-678.

Beulah Quintet, The (Settle). LFSup 345-349.

Bevis of Hampton. ShF 141.

Beware the Curves (Gardner, E.). M&D 691.

Bewitched, The (Barnes). DSup 12-13.

"Bewitched Jacket, The" (Buzzati). ShFSup 63-64.

Beyle, Marie-Henri. *See* **Stendhal.**

Beyond Culture (Trilling). LTh 1455.

Beyond Desire (Anderson). LFEng 79.

Beyond Human Power. See *Beyond Our Power.*

Beyond Our Power (Bjørnson). DFor 216.

"Beyond the Alps" (Lowell, R.). PEng 1790.

Beyond the Bedroom Wall (Woiwode). LFSup 395-396.

"Beyond the Desert" (Rhodes). ShF 604.

"Beyond the Glass Mountain" (Stegner). ShF 2271-2272.

Beyond Therapy (Durang). DSup 104.

Bezdenezhe. See *Poor Gentleman, A.*

"Bezhin Meadow" (Turgenev). ShF 201, 202-203, 2352-2354.

B. F.'s Daughter (Marquand). LFEng 1818.

Bhagavad Gītā. LFSup 172, 174.

Bhattacharya, Bhabani. ShF 651-652.

Białe małżeństwo. See *White Marriage.*

Bias of Communication, The (Innis). LTh 958.

Biedermann und die Brandstifter. See *Firebugs, The.*

"Biedny chrześcijanin patrzy na getto." See "Poor Christian Looks at the Ghetto, A."

Bierce, Ambrose. M&D 124-129; ShF 182, 231-232, 536.

Biermann, Wolf. PFor 186-192, 1813, 1818, 1820.

Biernat of Lublin. PFor 2119.

Big as Life (Doctorow). LFEng 773-775.

"Big Blonde" (Parker). ShF 2054-2055.

Big Bow Mystery, The (Zangwill). M&D 1731-1733.

"Big-City Lights" (Zoshchenko). ShFSup 382.

Big Clock, The (Fearing). M&D 596-597.

Big Heat, The (McGivern). M&D 1156-1157.

Big House, The (Robinson). DEng 1619-1621.

Big Knife, The (Odets). DEng 1402-1403.

"Big Mama's Funeral" (García Márquez). ShF 1454.

"Big Meeting" (Hughes). ShF 1660-1661.

Big Money, The (Dos Passos). LFEng 797-798.

Big Night, The. See *Dreadful Summit.*

Big Rock Candy Mountain, The (Stegner). LFEng 2498, 2499-2500.

Big Sin, The (Webb). M&D 1690-1691.

Big Sleep, The (Chandler). LFEng 492-494; M&D 304-305.

Big Toys (White). DSup 395-396.

"Big Two-Hearted River" (Hemingway). LFEng 1339-1340; ShF 1624-1625.

Biggers, Earl Derr. M&D 130-135.

"Biggest Band, The" (Cassill). ShF 1070-1071.

Biglow Papers, The (Lowell, J. R.). PEng 1780.

Bijou (Madden). LFEng 1765-1766.

Bijoux indiscrets, Les. See *Indiscreet Toys, The.*

Bila nemoc. See *Power and Glory.*

"Bildner, Der" (Zweig). PFor 1725-1726.

Bill, Max. PFor 592.

Bill of Rites, A Bill of Wrongs, A Bill of Goods, A (Morris). LFEng 1905.

Billard um halbzehn. See *Billiards at Half-Past Nine.*

Billiards at Half-Past Nine (Böll). LFFor 182-184.

"Billie" (Young). PEng 3218.

Billy Budd, Foretopman (Melville). LFEng 1859-1861, 3280-3282; PEng 1944.

Billy Liar (Hall and Waterhouse). DEng 869-871.

Billy Phelan's Greatest Game (Kennedy). LFSup 197-198. See also *Albany Cycle, The.*

Biloxi Blues (Simon). DEng 1831-1832.

Bilvav Yamin. See *In the Heart of the Seas.*

Bingham, Sallie. ShF 2516.

Biographia Literaria (Coleridge, S. T.). PEng 3478-3479; LTh 3, 303-304, 1696, 1701.

Biography (Behrman). DEng 186, 187.

Biography (Mi-la Ras-pa). PFor 2247-2248.

Biography of the Life of Manuel, The (Cabell). LFEng 406-407.

Bios kai politela tou Alexe Zormpa. See *Zorba the Greek.*

Birchwood (Banville). LFSup 45-46.

"Bird, The" (Paz). PFor 1172.

Bird, Robert Montgomery. DEng 207-218.

Bird in Hand (Drinkwater). DEng 512.

Birds, The (Aristophanes). DFor 117-118, 2126-2127.

"Birds, The" (du Maurier). M&D 554-555.

"Birds, The" (Galvin). PEng 1057.

Birds (Perse). PFor 1196-1197.

"Black-Smith, The" (D'Urfey). PEng 912.

Blackstone, Harry. *See* **Gibson, Walter B.**

"Blackstone Rangers, The" (Brooks, G.). PEng 315-317.

Blackwood, Caroline. PEng 1797, 1798, 1799.

Blaine, James. *See* **Avallone, Michael.**

Blair, Eric Arthur. *See* **Orwell, George.**

Blaisdell, Anne. *See* **Linington, Elizabeth.**

Blaise, Clark. ShF 2518.

Blake, Margaret. *See* **Gill, B. M.**

Blake, Nicholas. M&D 136-143.

Blake, Robert. *See* **Davies, L. P.**

Blake, William. LFEng 2862, 2870-2871; LTh 5, 448-449, 1696, 1700; **PEng 203-219,** 3335, 3342, 3428, 3429.

Blanche, August Theodore. DFor 2469-2470.

Blanchette (Brieux). DFor 249-250.

Blanco (Paz). PFor 1174.

Blancs, Les (Hansberry). DEng 878, 882-884.

"Blandings Novels, The" (Wodehouse). LFEng 2921-2922.

Blasco Ibáñez, Vicente. LFFor 164-177.

"Blasphemies" (MacNeice). PEng 1869.

Blätter für die Kunst (George). LTh 571-576.

Blaze of Roses, A (Trevor). M&D 1603.

"Blazon" (Darío). PFor 423. See also *Profane Hymns and Other Poems.*

Bleak House (Dickens, C.). LFEng 3077-3078; M&D 503-504.

Blechtrommel, Die. See *Tin Drum, The.*

Bleeck, Oliver. *See* **Thomas, Ross.**

"Bleeding Heart, The" (Stafford). ShF 2261-2262.

Bleich, David. LTh 686, 688, 736, 1764.

Blendung, Die. See *Auto-da-Fé.*

"Blessed Armchair" (Guillén). PFor 625. See also *Cántico.*

"Blessed Damozel, The" (Rossetti, D. G.). PEng 2427-2428.

"Blessed Is the Man" (Moore). PEng 2047.

"Blessed Longing" (Goethe). PFor 588. See also *West-Eastern Divan.*

"Blessing, The" (Kizer). PEng 1620-1621.

"Blessing, A" (Wright, J.). PEng 3168.

"Blessing of Women, A" (Kunitz). PSup 248.

Blessing Way, The (Hillerman). M&D 879-880.

"Blight, A" (Newman). PEng 2104.

Blind Beggar of Alexandria, The (Chapman). DEng 354.

Blind Cyclos (Ikiddeh). DEng 2422.

Blind Date (Kosinski). LFEng 1564-1566.

"Blind Man's Tale, A" (Tanizaki). ShFSup 316.

"Blind Singer, The" (Hölderlin). PFor 686. See also *Nachtgesänge.*

"Blinde Sänger, Der." *See* "Blind Singer, The."

Blindenschrift (Enzensberger). PFor 469.

"Blinder" (Gordimer). ShFSup 110.

Blindness (Green). LFEng 1208-1209.

Blindness and Insight (de Man). LTh 1153.

Bliss, James L. *See* **Henry, O.**

Blithedale Romance, The (Hawthorne). LFEng 1324-1325, 3089.

Blixen-Finecke, Karen. *See* **Dinesen, Isak.**

"Blizzard, The" (Pushkin). ShFSup 253.

Bloch, Robert. M&D 144-148.

Block, Lawrence. M&D 149-154.

Blok, Aleksandr. PFor 193-201, 2145.

"Blonde Eckbert, Der" (Tieck). LFEng 3242-3246.

Blood, Matthew. *See* **Halliday, Brett.**

"Blood-Burning Moon" (Toomer). ShF 2341-2342.

Blood Is a Beggar (Kyd). M&D 1013.

Blood Knot, The (Fugard). DEng 700-701.

Blood Meridian (McCarthy). LFSup 269-270.

Blood of Others, The (de Beauvoir). LFFor 115-116.

Blood of the Lamb, The (De Vries). LFEng 739-740.

"Blood of the Walsungs" (Mann). ShF 1877.

Blood on Baker Street. See *Case of the Baker Street Irregulars, The.*

Blood on the Bosom Devine (Kyd). M&D 1012-1014.

Blood Oranges, The (Hawkes). LFEng 1307-1309; ShF 1603-1604.

Blood Red, Sister Rose (Keneally). LFSup 186-187, 190.

Blood Relations (Örkény). DSup 300.

Blood Tie (Settle). LFSup 347-348.

Blood Wedding (García Lorca). DFor 662-663, 2505.

Bloodline (Gaines). ShF 1431, 1434-1435.

Bloodlines (Wright, C.). PEng 3149-3150.

Bloody Poetry (Brenton). DSup 35.

Bloom, Harold. LTh 162-167, 306, 646-647, 1033, 1245, 1413, 1776, 1797, 1816, 1833.

Bloomers, The (Sternheim). DFor 1736-1737.

Bloomfield, Leonard. LTh 1441; PFor 1736.

Blot in the 'Scutcheon, A (Browning). DEng 292-294.

"Blow, The" (Seifert). PSup 357.
"Blowing of the Seed, The" (Everson). PEng 989.
"Blow-Up" (Cortázar). ShF 786, 1203-1204.
Blue Boy (Giono). LFFor 655.
Blue Hammer, The (Macdonald). LFSup 278-279.
"Blue Hotel, The" (Crane, S.). ShF 598-599, 799-800, 1217, 1219-1220; LFEng 3305-3307.
"Blue Island" (Powers). ShF 2120-2121.
Blue Juniata (Cowley, M.). PEng 603-605, 607.
"Blue Kimono, The" (Callaghan). ShFSup 71.
"Blue Meridian" (Toomer). PEng 2918-2919.
Blue Movie (Southern). LFEng 2470-2472.
Blue Sash and Other Stories, The (Beck). ShF 935.
"Blue Swallows, The" (Nemerov). PEng 2087-2088.
"Blue Symphony" (Fletcher, J. G.). PEng 1027.
Blue Voyage (Aiken). LFEng 17-19.
"Bluebeard's Egg" (Atwood). ShFSup 17-18.
Bluebeard's Egg and Other Stories (Atwood). ShFSup 18.
"Bluebell Meadow" (Kiely). ShF 1745-1747.
"Bluebirds, The" (Thoreau). PEng 2903.
Blues for Mister Charlie (Baldwin). DEng 71, 75-78.
Bluest Eye, The (Morrison). LFEng 1916-1917.
Blumen-, Frucht- und Dornenstücke. See *Flower, Fruit, and Thorn Pieces.*
Blumenboot, Das (Sudermann). DFor 1765.
Blunck, Hans Friedrich. LFFor 2195.
"Bluspels and Flalansferes" (Lewis). LTh 895, 897.
Bly, Robert. PEng 220-228; PSup 403.
"Boarding House, The" (Joyce). ShF 1721.
Boas, Frederick S. PEng 1901, 1903.
"Boast no more, fond Love, thy Power" (D'Urfey). PEng 913.
Boat, The (Hartley). LFEng 1300-1301.
Bobette. *See* Simenon, Georges.
Bobrowski, Johannes. PFor 202-208, 1817, 1821.
Boccaccio, Giovanni. LFEng 3216-3218, 3219-3222; LTh 133-135, 168-173, 283, 967, 1433, 1655-1656, 1661; PEng 3243; PFor 2009, 2114-2115; ShFSup 44-50.
Bocksgesang. See *Goat Song.*

Bodas de sangre. See *Blood Wedding.*
Bodel, Jean. DFor 2163-2164, 2175.
Bödeln. See *Hangman, The.*
Bodelsen, Anders. LFFor 2367.
"Bodies" (Oates). ShF 1965-1966.
Bodily Harm (Atwood). LFEng 100-102.
Bodmer, Johann Jakob. DFor 2363; LTh 174-177.
"Body, The" (Simic). PEng 2592.
Body in the Boudoir (Vulliamy). M&D 1660, 1662.
Body in the Library, The (Christie). LFEng 540.
Body in the Silo, The (Knox). M&D 1000.
Body's Rapture, The (Romains). LFFor 1441.
Boesman and Lena (Fugard). DEng 700, 701-702.
Boethius. LTh 20; PFor 2112.
Bogan, Louise. PEng 229-239.
"Bogataia zhizn." *See* "Lucky Draw, The."
"Bogland" (Heaney). PEng 1269.
Bogmail (McGinley). M&D 1148-1149.
Bogus, S. Diane. ShF 2520.
"Bohemian, The" (O'Brien, F-J.). ShF 1979-1980.
Bohemian Lights (Valle-Inclán). DFor 1924-1925.
Boiardo, Matteo Maria. PFor 2012-2013.
Boileau, Pierre, and Thomas Narcejac. M&D 155-160.
Boileau-Despréaux, Nicolas. LFFor 2114; LTh 178-183, 371-372, 479, 481, 841, 853-854, 908, 969, 1180, 1195, 1515, 1684, 1693; PFor 1855.
Boisrobert, François de. LTh 1683.
Boitempo (Drummond de Andrade). PSup 101-102.
Bok, Edward W. ShF 589.
Boke of Cupide, The (Clanvowe). PEng 3272.
Boker, George H. DEng 219-226, 2398.
Bola de nieve, La (Tamayo y Baus). DFor 1806.
Boland, Eavan. PSup 33-41.
Bold Stroke for a Wife, A (Centlivre). DEng 349.
Boleslavsky, Richard. DEng 2528, 2529.
Böll, Heinrich. LFFor 178-189, 2198-2199; LFSup 401; ShF 971-976.
"Bolond Istók." *See* "Crazy Steve."
Bolt, Robert. DEng 227-242.
Bolton, Guy. DEng 2468.

28

Bolzano, Bernard. PFor 1799-1800.

"Bona and Paul" (Toomer). ShF 2342.

Bond, Edward. DEng 243-252.

Bond, Ruskin. ShF 652.

Bonds of Interest, The (Benavente). DFor 177-179, 2502.

Bonduca (Fletcher). DEng 635.

Bondy, Sebastián Salazar. DFor 2445.

Bone of My Bones (Wilkinson). LFEng 2894-2895.

Bones of the Cuttlefish (Montale). PFor 1046, 1048-1050.

Bonheur Fou, Le. See *Straw Man, The.*

Bonjour, là, bonjour (Tremblay). DSup 353.

Bonjour Tristesse (Sagan). LFFor 1472-1473.

Bonne Chanson, La (Verlaine). PFor 1628.

Bonnefoy, Yves. PSup 42-49.

Bønnelycke, Emil. LFFor 2354; PFor 2184.

Bonner, Robert. ShF 584.

Bonnes, Les. See *Maids, The.*

Bontempelli, Massimo. LFFor 2243.

Bontly, Thomas. ShF 2521.

"Bontsha the Silent" (Peretz). ShF 2087-2088.

Bony Buys a Woman (Upfield). M&D 1618-1620.

Boogie Woogie Landscapes (Shange). DSup 329-330.

Book Against the Barbarians, The (Erasmus). LTh 470-471.

"Book as Object, The" (Butor). LTh 252.

Book of Ahania, The (Blake). PEng 216.

"Book of Ancestors" (Atwood). PEng 68.

Book of Bebb, The (Buechner). LFEng 353-354.

Book of Changes. LTh 1775.

Book of Common Prayer, A (Didion). LFEng 763-766.

Book of Daniel, The (Doctorow). LFEng 775-777.

Book of Exercises (Seferis). PFor 1416-1417.

"Book of Four Ladies, The" (Chartier). PFor 347.

Book of Hours, The (Gomringer). PFor 595.

Book of Hours, The (Rilke). PFor 1328, 1330.

Book of Laughter and Forgetting, The (Kundera). LFFor 954-956.

Book of Life (Madhubuti). PEng 1896-1897.

Book of Lights, The (Potok). LFSup 318-319.

Book of Los, The (Blake). PEng 215.

Book of Martyrs, The (Foxe). ShF 497-498.

Book of Masks, The (Gourmont). LTh 622.

Book of Nightmares, The (Kinnell). PEng 1597-1598, 1599.

Book of Settlements (Thorgilsson). ShF 388.

Book of Songs (Confucius, editor). LTh 1773, 1785; PFor 1778-1779, 1781.

Book of Songs (Heine). PFor 644, 645, 647, 648-649.

Book of Stories. ShF 415.

Book of the Courtier, The. See *Courtier, The.*

Book of the Duchess, The (Chaucer). PEng 481; ShF 1102-1103.

Book of the Green Man, The (Johnson). PSup 212-213.

Book of the Hopi (Waters). LFEng 2781.

Book of the Icelanders (Thorgilsson). ShF 387.

Book of the Pious. ShF 415-416, 417.

Book of Thel, The (Blake). PEng 209.

Booke of Ayres, A (Campion). PEng 427-428.

Books Do Furnish a Room (Powell). LFEng 2121.

Boom Boom Room. See *In the Boom Boom Room.*

Boors, The (Goldoni). DFor 760-761.

"Boot, The" (Giusti). PFor 574.

Booth, Edwin. DEng 2525, 2526.

Booth, Irwin. *See* **Hoch, Edward D.**

Booth, Philip. PSup 403.

Booth, Wayne C. LTh 184-189, 560, 1817, 1825.

"Bopeep: A Pastoral" (Howells). PEng 1422.

Bopp, Franz. PFor 1732.

Boquitas pintadas. See *Heartbreak Tango.*

Bor, Matej. PFor 2270.

Borchert, Wolfgang. DFor 2380; ShF 2522.

"Bordal." *See* "Wine Song."

Bording, Anders. PFor 2158.

Borenstein, Audrey F. ShF 2523.

Borgen, Johan. LFFor 2352, 2353-2354.

Borges, Jorge Luis. LFEng 3225-3226; LFFor 2292, 2293; LTh 190-197; M&D 161-167; ShF 997-982; ShFSup 387.

"Borgo, Il" (Saba). PSup 347.

Boris Godunov (Pushkin). DFor 1496-1497, 2453; LTh 1178-1179; PFor 1292, 1293-1294.

Born in the Gardens (Nichols). DSup 283-284.

"Born Yesterday" (Larkin). PEng 1672.

Borough, The (Crabbe). PEng 641-643.

"Borrowed Time" (Bachmann). PFor 128. See also *Gestundete Zeit, Die.*

Boscán, Juan. PFor 2216-2217.

Bose, Buddhadeva. LFFor 2225, 2226.
Böse Geist Lumpazivagabundus, Der (Nestroy). DFor 1419-1422.
Böse Weib, Das (Sachs). DFor 1626.
Bösen Köche, Die. See *Wicked Cooks, The.*
Bosnian Chronicle (Andrić). LFFor 60-63.
Bosnian Story. See *Bosnian Chronicle.*
Bosoms and Neglect (Guare). DEng 862.
Boston (Sinclair, U.). LFEng 2424-2425.
Boston, Bruce. ShF 2524.
Bostonians, The (James, H.). LFEng 1446-1448.
Boswell (Elkin). LFEng 888.
Both Your Houses (Anderson, M.). DEng 28.
Bothie of Tober-na-Vuolich, The (Clough). PEng 518-519.
Bottega del caffe, La. See *Coffee-house, The.*
"Bottle" (Zoshchenko). ShFSup 379.
"Bottle of Milk for Mother, A" (Algren). ShF 857.
Botto, Ján. PFor 1809.
Bottomley, Gordon. DEng 253-261.
Bouc émissaire, Le. See *Scapegoat, The.*
Boucher, Anthony. M&D 168-172.
Bouchon de cristal, Le. See *Crystal Stopper, The.*
Boucicault, Dion. DEng 262-270, 2360, 2398, 2526.
Bouge of Court, The (Skelton). PEng 2635, 2636-2637.
"Bought and Sold" (Moravia). ShFSup 199.
Boughton, Rutland. DEng 2461.
Bound to Violence (Ouologuem). LFFor 2037, 2041.
Bourget, Paul. LTh 198-203, 1391, 1421.
Bourgmestre de Stilemonde, Le. See *Burgomaster of Stilemonde, The.*
Bourne, Peter. *See* **Graeme, Bruce.**
Boursiquot, Dionysius Lardner. *See* **Boucicault, Dion.**
"Bouteille à la mer, La" (Vigny). PFor 1642.
Bouts de bois de Dieu, Les. See *God's Bits of Wood.*
Bouvard and Pécuchet (Flaubert). LFFor 556-557.
Bovio, Giovanni. DFor 2410.
Bow Bells. LFEng 33.
Bowden, James. ShF 2525.
Bowen, Elizabeth. LFEng 262-269; ShF 133, 254-255, 523, **983-989.**
Bower, Bertha M. LFEng 3195.

Bowles, Paul. LFSup 52-59; ShF 548, 990-993; ShFSup 387.
Bowles, William Lisle. PEng 249-256.
Box, Edgar. M&D 173-178.
Box Man, The (Abe). LFFor 7.
"Box Seat" (Toomer). ShF 2342-2343.
Boy (Hanley). LFEng 1246-1247.
"Boy at the Window" (Wilbur). PEng 3097-3098.
"Boy of Pergamum, The" (Petronius). ShF 2093.
Boye, Karin. PFor 2179.
Boyle, Kay. LFEng 270-281; ShF 265, 553, **994-1003.**
Boys and Girls Together (Saroyan). LFEng 2339-2340.
Boys in the Back Room, The (Romains). LFFor 1440.
Boys in the Band, The (Crowley). DSup 71-72.
Boys Who Stole the Funeral, The (Murray). PSup 290-291.
Bracco, Roberto. DFor 222-229.
"Bracelet, The" (Stanley). PEng 2728.
Brackenridge, Hugh Henry. ShF 528.
Bradamante (Garnier). DFor 670-671.
Bradbury, Ray. ShF 778-779.
Braddon, M. E. M&D 179-185.
Bradstreet, Anne. PEng 163, 257-264, 1375, 3371, 3384.
Braggart Warrior, The (Plautus). DFor 2141.
"Brahma" (Emerson). PEng 957-958.
Braine, John. LFEng 282-289; LFSup 401.
"Brama, La" (Saba). PSup 347.
Bramah, Ernest. M&D 186-191; ShF 516-517.
Brancati, Vitaliano. DFor 2415; LFFor 2246-2247.
"Branch Road, A" (Garland). ShF 1468-1469.
Branches of Adam (Fletcher, J. G.). PEng 1027-1028.
Brand (Ibsen). DFor 980-981, 2471.
Brand, Christianna. M&D 192-197.
Brand, Max. LFEng 3194-3195.
Brandes, Georg. LFEng 3172; LFFor 2338; LTh 1421, 1719, 1724.
Brandi, John. ShF 2526.
Brandt, Jørgen Gustava. PFor 2197.
Branner, Hans Christian. DFor 2480; LFFor 2355.
Brashers, Charles. ShF 2527.
Brass Ankle (Heyward). DEng 938.

Brat Farrar (Tey). M&D 1580, 1582.

Brathwaite, Edward Kamau. PEng 265-273; PFor 209-217; PSup 403.

Bratsk Station (Yevtushenko). PFor 1710-1711.

Bratskaya GES. See *Bratsk Station.*

Bratya Karamazovy. See *Brothers Karamazov, The.*

Braun, Volker. DSup 16-27; PFor 1818, 1821, 1824.

Brautigan, Richard. LFEng 290-295; LFSup 401; ShFSup 51-58.

Brave New World (Huxley). LFEng 1405-1406, 3211.

Bravery of Earth, A (Eberhart). PEng 928.

"Bread and Wine" (Hölderlin). PFor 687.

Bread and Wine (Silone). LFFor 1587-1588.

Breadwinner, The (Maugham). DEng 1310.

"Break, The" (Sexton). PEng 2525.

Break of Noon (Claudel). DFor 408-409.

Breakers and Granite (Fletcher, J. G.). PEng 1027.

Breakfast at Tiffany's (Capote). LFEng 447-448.

"Breakfast at Twilight" (Dick). ShF 1261-1262.

Breakheart Pass (MacLean). M&D 1175.

Breaking of the Vessels, The (Bloom). LTh 166.

"Breaking the Chain" (Harrison). PSup 170.

Breast, The (Roth). LFEng 2305.

"Breasts" (Simic). PEng 2592.

Breasts of Tiresias, The (Apollinaire). DEng 2203.

"Breath of Lucifer" (Narayan). ShFSup 228.

Brébeuf and His Brethren (Pratt). PEng 2284-2285.

Brecht, Bertolt. LTh 140-141, 144, 147-148, 204-211, 937-938, 1815; DEng 2205-2206, 2239; DFor 230-245, 611-612, 615, 2240, 2378-2379; DSup 17, 25, 116, 118-119, 321; PFor 218-227, 1813, 1817, 1819, 1822, 1931-1932; ShF 1004-1010.

"Breefe balet touching the traytorous takynge of Scarborow Castell, A" (Heywood, J.). PEng 1335-1336.

Breen, Jon L. M&D 198-202.

"Breeze Anstey" (Bates). ShF 270; ShFSup 31.

Breeze from the Gulf, A (Crowley). DSup 71-72.

"Breezes, Breezes, Little Breezes" (Castro). PFor 278. See also *Cantares gallegos.*

Breitinger, Johann Jakob. DFor 2363; LTh 174-175.

Brekke, Paal. LFFor 2363; PFor 2190.

Brekkukotsannáll. See *Fish Can Sing, The.*

Bremer, Fredrika. LFFor 2337.

Bremond, Claude. LTh 1762.

Brennan, Joseph Payne. ShF 2528.

Brentano, Clemens. PFor 1917-1918.

Brenton, Howard. DEng 2491, 2492-2493; DSup 28-37.

"Breslauer Ausarbeitung" (Dilthey). LTh 378.

Breton, André. DEng 2203; LTh 212-216, 1492, 1710, 1830; PFor 228-234, 1547, 1885.

Breton, Nicholas. PEng 274-282.

Bretón de los Herreros, Manuel. DFor 2498.

Breton's Bowre of Delights (Breton, N.). PEng 278.

Brett, Simon. M&D 203-209.

"Bréviaire des nobles, Le." *See* "Breviary for Nobles, The."

"Breviary for Nobles, The" (Chartier). PFor 348.

Brewsie and Willie (Stein). LFEng 2516-2517.

Brewster, Harry. ShF 566.

Breytenbach, Breyten. PSup 50-58.

Březina, Otokar. PFor 1803.

"Brick Moon, The" (Hale). ShF 770.

"Brickdust Row" (Henry). ShF 230.

Bridal Canopy, The (Agnon). LFFor 14-17.

Bridal Dinner, The (Gurney). DSup 164-165.

"Bridal Measure, A" (Dunbar). PSup 111.

"Bridal Photo, 1906" (Ciardi). PEng 503.

Bridal Wreath, The (Undset). LFFor 1803.

"Bride Comes to Yellow Sky, The" (Crane, S.). ShF 599-600, 1220-1221.

"Bride Waits, The" (Venkataramani). ShF 644.

"Bride Without a Dowry, A" (Amichai). PSup 4.

Bridegroom's Body, The (Boyle). LFEng 277-278.

Bridel, Bedřich. PFor 1798.

"Brides, The" (Hope). PSup 189.

Brides of Reason (Davie). PSup 85.

"Bride's Prelude, The" (Rossetti, D. G.). PEng 2428-2429.

Bride's Tragedy, The (Beddoes). PEng 111.

Brideshead Revisited (Waugh). LFEng 2798-2799.

Bridge, The (Crane, H.). PEng 651-652, 3365-3366, 3391.

"Bridge Builders, The" (Kipling). ShF 1751.
"Bridge of Dreams, The" (Tanizaki). ShFSup 317-318.
Bridge of San Luis Rey, The (Wilder). LFEng 2883.
"Bridge of Sighs, The" (Hood). PEng 1388-1389.
Bridge of Years, The (Sarton). LFEng 2347-2348.
Bridge on the Drina, The (Andrić). LFFor 63-64.
Bridgeman, Richard. *See* **Davies, L. P.**
Bridges, Robert. PEng 283-291.
Bridges at Toko-Ri (Michener). LFSup 300-301.
Bridie, James. DEng 271-280, 2383.
Brief an den Vater. See Letter to His Father.
"Brief eines Dichters an einen Andern." *See* "Letter from One Poet to Another."
Brief Life, A (Onetti). LFFor 1211-1212.
"Briefcase History" (Middleton, C.). PEng 1990.
Briefe, die neueste Litteratur betreffend (Lessing). LTh 668, 880.
Briefe über die ästhetische Erziehung des Menschen in einer Reihe von Briefen. See On the Aesthetic Education of Man.
Briefe zu Beförderung der Humanität. See Letters for the Advancement of Humanity.
Briefing for a Descent into Hell (Lessing). LFEng 1640.
Brief-Wechsel von der Natur des poetischen Geschmackes (Bodmer). LTh 176.
Brieux, Eugène. DFor 246-255, 2348.
Brigadier, The (Fonvizin). DFor 633-635.
Briggflatts (Bunting). PEng 367, 371.
Briggs, Charles F. ShF 588.
"Bright and Morning Star" (Wright, R.). ShF 579.
Bright Day (Priestley). LFEng 2143-2144.
"Bright Field, The" (Walcott). PEng 3006.
Bright Orange for the Shroud (MacDonald, J.). M&D 1132.
Brighton Beach Memoirs (Simon). DEng 1831.
Brighton Rock (Greene, G.). LFEng 1217-1219; M&D 791.
"Brim Beauvais" (Stein). ShFSup 309.
"Brindisi di Girella, Il." *See* "Girella's Toast."
"Bringing Up" (Harrison). PSup 168-169.
Brissac, Malcolm de. *See* **Dickinson, Peter.**
Bristo (Ferreira). DFor 591.

"Bristowe Tragedie: Or, The Deth of Syr Charles Bawdin" (Chatterton). PEng 471.
Britannia's Pastorals (Browne). PEng 320.
Britannicus (Racine). DFor 1516-1518.
Britannicus, prefaces to (Racine). LTh 1197, 1199.
Britten, Benjamin. DEng 2462-2463.
Britting, Georg. PFor 1931.
"Britva." *See* "Razor, The."
Broad and Alien Is the World (Alegría). LFFor 46-47.
"Broadsheet Ballad, A" (Coppard). ShF 1197.
Broch, Hermann. LFFor 190-201, 2194.
Brock, Rose. *See* **Hansen, Joseph.**
"Brodeuse d'abeilles, La" (Follain). PSup 130.
Brodsky, Joseph. PFor 235-243.
"Broken Connections" (Oates). PEng 2119.
"Broken Dark, The" (Hayden). PEng 1248-1249.
Broken Face Murders, The (Teilhets). M&D 1577.
Broken Ground, The (Berry). PEng 149-150.
"Broken Ground, The" (Berry). PEng 150.
Broken Gun, The (L'Amour). LFSup 224.
Broken Heart, The (Ford). DEng 655-658, 2289.
"Broken Homes" (Trevor). ShFSup 324.
Broken Pieces. See Cinq and *Like Death Warmed Over.*
Broken Water (Hanley). LFEng 1245.
"Broken World, A" (O'Faoláin). ShF 2000-2001.
Brokenbrow. See Hinkemann.
Broker of Bogotá, The (Bird). DEng 217-218.
Brome, Richard. DEng 281-288, 2298-2299.
Brontë, Charlotte. LFEng 296-305.
Brontë, Emily. LFEng 306-311, 3145-3146; **PEng 292-300.**
Bronze Horseman, The (Pushkin). PFor 1300-1301.
Brook, Peter. DEng 2489-2490, 2531-2532.
Brook Kerith, The (Moore, G.). LFEng 1902.
Brooke, C. F. Tucker. PEng 1903.
Brooke, Fulke Greville, First Lord. *See* **Greville, Fulke.**
Brooke, Rupert. PEng 301-308.
Brookhouse, Christopher. ShF 2529.
Brooklyn Murders, The (Coles). M&D 371.
Brookner, Anita. LFSup 60-69.
Brooks, Ben. ShF 2530.

Brooks, Cleanth. LTh 158, **217-222**, 306, 1011, 1148, 1424-1425, 1521-1523, 1554-1556, 1753-1754, 1818.

Brooks, Gwendolyn. PEng **309-317.**

Brooks, Van Wyck. LTh **223-230**, 316-319, 1011, 1550.

"Broom, The" (Leopardi). PFor 864-865. See also *Canti.*

Brorson, Hans Adolph. PFor 2159-2160.

Brot und Wein. See *Bread and Wine.*

"Brother Jacob" (Eliot, G.). ShF 1336.

"Brother John" (Harper). PSup 162.

Brother to Dragons (Warren). PEng 3025-3027.

Brotherly Love (Fielding). LFSup 116.

Brotherly Love (Hoffman). PEng 1360-1361.

Brothers, The (Terence). DFor 1826, 2143.

Brothers and Sisters (Compton-Burnett). LFEng 566-567.

Brothers in Arms (Denison). DEng 500-501.

Brothers in Confidence (Madden). LFEng 1761, 1764-1765.

Brothers Karamazov, The (Dostoevski). LFFor 515-517; M&D 524.

Brouette du vinaigrier, La (Mercier). DFor 1316-1317, 2342.

Brown, Charles Brockden. LFEng **312-324;** LTh 524; ShF 528, 529.

Brown, Douglas. *See* **Gibson, Walter B.**

Brown, Fredric. M&D **210-214;** ShF 2531.

Brown, Morna Doris. *See* **Ferrars, E. X.**

Brown, Rosellen. ShF 2532.

Brown, William Hill. LFEng 3039.

Browne, Barum. *See* **Beeding, Francis.**

Browne, William. PEng **318-322.**

Browning, Elizabeth Barrett. PEng **323-333.**

Browning, Robert. DEng **289-297;** LTh 524; PEng 325, **334-347.**

Browning Version, The (Rattigan). DEng 1561. See also *Playbill.*

Bruce, The (Barbour). PEng 3255, 3278.

Bruce, Leo. M&D **215-222.**

Bruckner, Ferdinand. DFor **256-265.**

Bruder Eichmann (Kipphardt). DFor 1055-1057.

Brulls, Christian. *See* **Simenon, Georges.**

Brumby Innes (Prichard). DEng 2433.

Brunetière, Ferdinand. LTh **231-236**, 859, 1421.

"Brunettina mia, La." *See* "My Brunette."

Bruno, Giordano. DFor 2397.

"Brush Fire" (Cain). ShF 1025-1027.

"Brushwood Boy, The" (Kipling). ShF 1751.

Brut (Layamon). PEng 1689-1694.

"Bruto Minore." *See* "Younger Brutus, The."

Brutus (Cicero). LTh 294-295, 1638.

Brutus (Payne). DEng 1486-1487.

Bruyn, Günter de. LFFor 2203.

Bryant, William Cullen. LTh 1744, 1746; PEng **348-353.**

Bryosov, Valery. LFFor 2320; LTh 975; PFor 2143.

Buccaneers, The (Wharton, Edith). LFEng 2858.

Buch der Bilder, Das (Rilke). PFor 1328.

Buch der Lieder. See *Book of Songs.*

"Buch vom mönchischen Leben, Das." *See* "Of the Monastic Life."

"Buch von der Armut und vom Tod, Das." *See* "Of Poverty and Death."

Buch von der deutschen Poeterey, Das (Opitz). PFor 1908.

"Buch von der Pilgerschaft, Das." *See* "Of Pilgrimage."

Buchan, John. LFEng **325-337; M&D 223-230.**

Büchner, Georg. DFor **266-275**, 2371.

Büchse der Pandora, Die. See *Pandora's Box.*

Buck (Ribman). DSup 315.

Buck, Pearl S. LFEng **338-346;** ShF **1011-1016.**

"Buck in the Hills, The" (Clark). ShF 1151-1152.

"Buckdancer's Choice" (Dickey, J.). PEng 798.

Buckdancer's Choice (Dickey, J.). PEng 797, 798.

Buckingham, George Villiers, second Duke of. See **Villiers, George.**

Buckley, William F., Jr. M&D **231-237.**

Buckower Elegies (Brecht). PFor 226.

Buckstone, John Baldwin. DEng 2358.

Bucolics. See *Eclogues.*

Bucolicum carmen. See *Eclogues.*

Buda halála. See *Death of King Buda, The.*

Buddenbrooks (Mann). LFFor 1077-1079, 2186.

Budō denraiki (Saikaku). ShFSup 270.

Buechner, Frederick. LFEng **347-356.**

"Buenaventura, La." *See* "Prophecy, The."

Buenaventura, Enrique. DFor 2445.

Buenos Aires Affair, The (Puig). LFFor 1353-1357; M&D 1371-1374.

Buero Vallejo, Antonio. DFor 276-286. DFor 2507.

Bufera e altro, La. See *Storm and Other Poems, The.*

"Buffalo, 12.7.41" (Howe). PSup 196.

Buffeting, The (Wakefield Master). DEng 1995.

Bug-Jargal. See *Noble Rival, The.*

Bugayev, Boris. *See* Bely, Andrey.

Bugles in the Afternoon (Haycox). LFEng 3195.

"Builders, The" (Orr). PEng 2153.

"Building, The" (Larkin). PEng 1670-1671, 1675-1676.

Buke giri monogatari. See *Tales of Samurai Honor.*

Bukowski, Charles. PEng 354-365; PSup 403.

Bukowski Sampler, A (Bukowski). PEng 360-361.

"Buladelah-Taree Holiday Song Cycle, The" (Murray). PSup 290.

Bulgakov, Mikhail. DFor 287-296, 2462; **LFFor 202-210,** 2327.

Bulgarin, Fadey. LFFor 2310.

Bull, Olaf. PFor 2176.

Bull from the Sea, The (Renault). LFEng 2220-2221.

Bullet Park (Cheever). LFEng 508-510.

Bullins, Ed. DEng 298-308, 2411, 2424, 2428, 2429.

Bulwer-Lytton, Edward. DEng 309-317.

Bungei Kyōkai. DFor 2432.

"Bungeijō no shizen shugi" (Hōgetsu). LTh 681.

Bunin, Ivan. LFFor 2321.

Bunte Steine (Stifter). LFFor 1669, 1671.

Bunting, Basil. PEng 366-372; PSup 404.

Bunyan, John. LFEng 357-363, 3018.

"Buoy, The" (Zoshchenko). ShFSup 382.

Burbage, James. DEng 2267.

Burbage, Richard. DEng 2522-2523.

"Burden of Itys, The" (Wilde). PEng 3105-3106.

"Bureau d'Echange de Maux, The" (Dunsany). ShF 743-744.

Bürger, Gottfried. LTh 1304-1305.

Bürger Schippel. See *Paul Schippel Esq.*

Bürger von Calais, Die. See *Citizens of Calais, The.*

Burger's Daughter (Gordimer). LFEng 1168-1170.

Burgess, Anthony. LFEng 364-372; LFSup 401-402.

Burgess, Trevor. *See* **Trevor, Elleston.**

Burglar in the Closet, The (Block). M&D 151.

"Burglar of Babylon, The" (Bishop). PEng 187-188.

Burgomaster of Stilemonde, The (Maeterlinck). DFor 1241-1242.

Burgraves, The (Hugo). DFor 970-971.

"Burial of Orgaz, The" (Rítsos). PFor 1349.

Buried Child (Shepard). DEng 1762, 1765-1766.

Buried City (Moss). PEng 2066.

Buried for Pleasure (Crispin). M&D 414.

Buried Land, A (Jones, M.). LFEng 1490-1491.

"Buried Life, The" (Arnold). PEng 52-53.

Buried Treasure, A (Roberts). LFEng 2279-2280.

Burke, Edmund. LTh 237-241, 722-723, 1218, 1601, 1700.

Burke, Kenneth. LTh 188, 242-248, 306, 315, 349, 980, 1222.

Burlador de Sevilla, El. See *Trickster of Seville, The.*

Burley, W. J. M&D 238-241.

Burlyuk, David. PFor 987.

Burmese Days (Orwell). LFEng 2057-2058.

Burn, The (Aksyonov). LFSup 19-20.

Burn, David. DEng 2431.

Burnett, W. R. M&D 242-248.

Burney, Fanny. LFEng 373-382.

"Burning" (Snyder). PEng 2672.

"Burning Babe, The" (Southwell). PEng 2690-2691.

"Burning Bush" (Untermeyer). PEng 2949.

Burning Court, The (Carr). ShF 728.

Burning Fountain, The (Wheelwright). LTh 1756.

Burning Heart: Women Poets of Japan, The (Rexroth, trans.). PFor 1716.

Burning House, The (Beattie). ShFSup 39.

Burning in Water, Drowning in Flame (Bukowski). PEng 362.

"Burning Light, The" (Varnalis). PFor 1959.

Burning Mountain, The (Fletcher, J. G.). PEng 1028.

"Burning Poem, The" (MacBeth). PEng 1835.

"Burning the Letters" (Jarrell). PEng 1482.

Burning World, The. See *Drought, The.*

Burns, Rex. M&D 249-254.

Burns, Robert. PEng 373-383, 3322, 3334-3335, 3341-3342.

Burr (Vidal). LFEng 2719-2721, 3154.

Burroughs, Edgar Rice. LFEng 3209.

Burroughs, William. LFEng 383-391; LFSup 402.

"Burrow, The" (Kafka). ShF 1733-1734.

Burton, Miles. *See* **Rhode, John.**

"Bus Along St. Clair: December, A" (Atwood). PEng 67.

Bus Stop (Inge). DEng 985-986.

"Busca en todas las cosas" (González Martínez). PFor 611.

Busch, Frederick. ShF 2534.

"Bush Trembles, Because, The" (Petőfi). PFor 1223-1224.

Bushman Who Came Back, The. See *Bony Buys a Woman.*

Bushrangers, The (Burn). DEng 2431.

Bushwhacked Piano, The (McGuane). LFSup 292.

Busie Body, The (Centlivre). DEng 347-349.

Busman's Honeymoon (Sayers). LFEng 2362-2363.

Bussy d'Ambois (Chapman). DEng 358-359, 2287-2288.

Bustan. See *Orchard, The.*

"Bustle in a House, The" (Dickinson). PEng 3387.

"Busy-Body Papers, The" (Franklin). ShF 1409-1410.

"But at the Stroke of Midnight" (Warner). ShFSup 356-357.

But for Whom Charley (Behrman). DEng 187.

"But He Was Cool or: he even stopped for green lights" (Madhubuti). PEng 1894.

Butcher's Dozen (Kinsella). PSup 236.

Butler, Samuel. LFEng 392-400; PEng 384-390.

Butler's Ghost (D'Urfey). PEng 911.

Butley (Gray). DEng 807-809.

Butor, Michel. LFFor 211-220; LTh 249-255.

Butt, Der. See *Flounder, The.*

"Buttered Greens" (Schuyler). PEng 2478-2479.

Butterfly, The (Cain). M&D 259.

"Butterfly, The" (Ponge). PFor 1263.

"Butterfly" (Sachs). PFor 1375.

"Butterfly Piece" (Hayden). PEng 1249.

Butterfly's Evil Spell, The (García Lorca). DFor 656-657.

Butters, Dorothy Gilman. *See* **Gilman, Dorothy.**

"Butylka." *See* "Bottle."

Buyer's Market, A (Powell). LFEng 2118.

Buzo, Alexander. DEng 318-324, 2436.

Buzzati, Dino. DFor 2415; LFFor 221-229, 2253; ShFSup 59-65.

"By Al Lebowitz's Pool" (Nemerov). PEng 2082-2083.

"By Candlelight" (Plath). PEng 2227-2228.

"By Coming to New Jersey" (Stern). PSup 369.

"By Frazier Creek Falls" (Snyder). PEng 2675.

By Love Possessed (Cozzens). LFEng 635-636.

"By Morning" (Swenson). PEng 2796-2797.

"By Occasion of the young Prince his happy Birth. May 29-1630" (King). PEng 1581-1582.

"By the Margin of the Great Deep" (Æ). PEng 18.

By the Open Sea (Strindberg). LFFor 1693-1694, 2340.

By Way of Sainte-Beuve (Proust). LTh 1172-1174, 1261.

Bye-Bye, Blackbird (Desai). LFEng 729-730.

Bygmester Solness. See *Master Builder, The.*

Byrne, John Keyes. *See* **Leonard, Hugh.**

"Byrnies, The" (Gunn). PEng 1174.

Byrom, John. PEng 391-399.

Byrom, Thomas. PEng 1701.

Byron, George Gordon, Lord. DEng 325-342; LTh 256-261, 1018, 1181, 1703, 1709; PEng 400-415, 3342-3343; ShF 472.

"Byron and Goethe" (Mazzini). LTh 1018-1019.

"Byzantium" (Yeats). PEng 3362.

C

Cab at the Door, A (Pritchett). LFEng 2152.

Cabal and Love (Schiller). DFor 1658.

Cabala, The (Wilder). LFEng 2882-2883.

"Caballero, El." See "Gentleman, The."

Caballero de Olmedo, El. See Knight from Olmedo, The.

Caballo del rey don Sancho, El (Zorrilla y Moral). DFor 2064.

Cabbages and Kings (Henry). M&D 854-855.

Cabell, James Branch. LFEng 401-410.

Cabellos de Absolón, Los (Calderón). DFor 307-308.

Cabin, The (Blasco Ibáñez). LFFor 171-173.

Cable, George Washington. LFEng 411-419; ShF 225-226, 534, 586, 616, **1017-1023.**

Cables to the Ace (Merton). PEng 1976-1977.

Cabot Wright Begins (Purdy). LFEng 2172.

Cabrera Infante, Guillermo. LFFor 2298.

Cabrujas, José Ignacio. DFor 2445.

Caccia al lupo, La. See Wolf Hunt, The.

Caccia alla volpe, La (Verga). DFor 1947.

Cadenus and Vanessa (Swift). PEng 2806-2807.

Cadillac Jack (McMurtry). LFEng 1756-1757.

Cadle, Dean. ShF 2535.

Cady, Jack. ShF 2536.

Caecilius of Calacte. LTh 904-905.

Caecilius Statius. DFor 2144-2145.

Caedmon. PEng 416-420.

Caeiro, Alberto. See Pessoa, Fernando.

Caelica (Greville). PEng 1156-1157, 3291.

Caesar, Gaius Julius. PFor 2093-2094.

"Caesar and His Legionnaire" (Brecht). ShF 1006-1007.

Caesar's Apostasy. See Emperor and Galilean.

Caesar's Column (Donnelly). LFEng 3207.

Cæsars frafald. See Emperor and Galilean.

Cage aux Folles, La (Fierstein). DEng 2409.

Cahier d'un retour au pays natal. See Return to My Native Land.

Cahier gris, Le (Martin du Gard). LFFor 1114. See also World of the Thibaults, The.

Caída de los Limones, La. See Fall of the House of Limón, The.

Cain (Byron). DEng 330.

Cain, James M. M&D 255-261; ShF 1024-1027.

Caine, Hall. DEng 2372.

Caine Mutiny, The (Wouk). LFEng 2965-2967.

Caius Gracchus (Knowles). DEng 1060-1061.

"Cake, The" (Baudelaire). PFor 139.

Cakes and Ale (Maugham). LFEng 1848-1849, 1850.

Cakes for Your Birthday (Vulliamy). M&D 1660.

"Calamus" (Whitman). PEng 3069.

Calderón de la Barca, Pedro. DEng 2162; DFor 297-309, 2494-2495; LTh 637; PFor 244-250.

Caldwell, Erskine. LFEng 420-428; LFSup 402; ShF 261-262, **1028-1033;** ShFSup 387.

Cale (Wilkinson). LFEng 2892-2893.

Caleb Williams (Godwin). M&D 751-755.

"Caliban" (Brathwaite). PEng 266; PFor 210, 215.

Caliban's Filibuster (West). LFSup 373-374.

California Suite (Simon). DEng 1829-1830.

Caligula (Camus). DFor 315-317, 2356-2357.

Calisher, Hortense. ShF 548, 1034-1040; ShFSup 387.

Calisto and Meliboea (Rastell?). DEng 2259.

Call for the Dead (Le Carré). LFEng 1611-1612.

Call Girls, The (Koestler). LFEng 1554-1555.

"Call of Cthulhu, The" (Lovecraft). ShF 1823-1825.

Call of the Wild, The (London). LFEng 1693-1694, 3179-3180.

Callaghan, Morley. LFEng 429-439; LFSup 402; ShF 545, 638; **ShFSup 66-74.**

"Called Home" (Beer). PEng 119.

Calligrammes (Apollinaire). PFor 54.

Callimachus. LTh 262-265, 1637; PFor 57-58, **251-258.**

Callimachus (Hroswitha). DFor 2153.

"Calm After the Storm, The" (Leopardi). PFor 861. See also Canti.

Calpurnius Siculus. PFor 2105.

Calvino, Italo. LFFor 230-250, 2251, 2255; LFSup 402; LTh 266-271; ShF 1041-1045; ShFSup 387-388.

Camaraderie, La (Scribe). DFor 1680-1681.

Cambises (Preston). DEng 2261.

Camera Obscura. See *Laughter in the Dark.*

Camilla (Burney). LFEng 380.

Camille (Dumas, *fils*). DFor 500-504, 2346.

Camino, El. See *Path, The.*

"Camionista, Il." *See* "Lorry Driver, The."

Camões, Luís de. PFor 259-265.

"Camouflage" (Pastan). PEng 2172.

Camp, The (Gambaro). DFor 2444; DSup 147-148.

Camp of Wallenstein, The (Schiller). DFor 1659, 2368. See also *Death of Wallenstein, The.*

"Campaign, The" (Addison). PEng 11-12.

Campana, Dino. PFor 2038-2039.

Campaspe (Lyly). DEng 1179-1182; ShF 1831-1832.

Campbell, John W., Jr. ShF 774-775, 776, 877, 2537.

"Camping Out" (Empson). PEng 969.

Campion, Thomas. LTh 1663; PEng 421-429.

Campo, El. See *Camp, The.*

"Campo di Fiori" (Miłosz). PFor 1033.

Campos, Álvaro de. *See* **Pessoa, Fernando.**

Campos de Castilla (Machado). PFor 914-915.

"Campus on the Hill, The" (Snodgrass). PEng 2660-2661.

Camus, Albert. DFor 72, 310-320, 2356-2357; LFFor 251-265, 2143-2144, 2145; LTh 1273; ShF 1046-1051.

Can Such Things Be? (Bierce). ShF 231-232.

Can You Forgive Her? (Trollope). LFEng 2656-2657.

Canaans Calamitie (Deloney). PEng 789-790, 791.

"Canada of Myth and Reality, The" (Davies). ShF 633.

"Canadians" (Gurney). PEng 1182-1183.

Cañas y barro. See *Reeds and Mud.*

"Cancer: A Dream" (Sissman). PEng 2620-2621.

Cancer Ward (Solzhenitsyn). LFFor 1643-1644.

Cancerqueen (Landolfi). ShFSup 131-132, 134.

Canción de cuna. See *Cradle Song, The.*

"Canción de jinete." *See* "Song of the Horseman, The."

"Canción que oyó en sueños el viejo, La." *See* "Song Which the Old Man Heard in His Dreams, The."

Canción rota, La (Hernández). DFor 2442.

Cancionero (Unamuno). PFor 1558-1559.

Cancionero apócrifo (Machado). PFor 915-916.

Cancionero sin nombre (Parra). PFor 1132.

Canciones rusas (Parra). PFor 1133-1134.

Cancroregina. See *Cancerqueen.*

Candelaio, Il (Bruno). DFor 2397.

Candida (Shaw). DEng 35, 1731-1733.

Candidate, The (Flaubert). LFFor 547.

Candide (Hellman and Bernstein). DEng 2474.

Candide (Voltaire). LFFor 1895, 1899-1901, 2118; ShFSup 329.

Candido (Sciascia). LFFor 1522.

"Candle, The" (La Fontaine). LTh 856.

"Candle, A" (Suckling). PEng 2778-2779.

Candy (Southern). LFEng 2469.

"Candy-Man Beechum" (Caldwell). ShF 1032.

Cane (Toomer). PEng 2912, 2913, 2914-2915, 2918; ShF 251, 252, 554, 577, 2340.

Canetti, Elias. LFFor 266-272, 2207; LFSup 402.

Cankar, Ivan. DFor 2294; LFFor 2078; PFor 2269.

Canne al vento (Deledda). LFFor 443-444.

Cannibal, The (Hawkes). LFEng 1305-1307.

Cannibal Masque, The (Ribman). DSup 316.

Cannibals and Missionaries (McCarthy). LFEng 1725.

Cannon, Curt. *See* **McBain, Ed.**

"Canon Alberic's Scrapbook" (James, M. R.). ShF 1689.

"Canonization, The" (Donne). PEng 829-830.

Canossa (Ernst). DFor 558-559.

Canotte, La (Labiche). DFor 1135-1137.

Cant (Munk). DFor 1391-1392.

"Cantar de amigo." *See* "Friend's Song."

Cantar de mío Cid. See *Poem of the Cid.*

Cantares gallegos (Castro). PFor 278.

Cantatrice chauve, La. See *Bald Soprano, The.*

Canterbury Tales, The (Chaucer). LTh 281-282; PEng 485-489, 3238, 3260-3267, 3490; ShF 139-140, 142, 1100, 1108-1109, 1113, 1116.

Canth, Minna. DFor 321-329.

Canti (Leopardi). PFor 857-865.

Canti di Castelvecchio (Pascoli). PFor 1141-1142.

Cántico (Guillén). PFor 624-625.

Cántico espiritual. See *Spiritual Canticle of the Soul, A.*

Cantilena of St. Eulalia. ShF 434.

"Canto dell'amore." *See* "Song of Love."

Canto for a Gypsy (Smith). M&D 1505.

Canto general (Neruda). PFor 1077.

"Canto notturno di un pastore errante dell'Asia." *See* "Night Song of a Nomadic Shepherd in Asia."

Canto novo (D'Annunzio). PFor 385.

Cantor, Eli. ShF 2538.

Cantos (Pound). PEng 2270-2275, 3365, 3390-3391.

Cantos de vida y esperanza (Darío). PFor 424.

Cantù, Cesare. LTh 365.

Canzio (Kivi). DFor 1068.

Canzoneri, Robert. ShF 2539.

Canzoniere (Petrarch). LTh 1093, 1658-1660; PFor 1234-1236, 2008-2009.

Canzoniere, Il (Saba). PSup 343, 345-346.

Cap de Bonne-Espérance, Le (Cocteau). PFor 370-371.

"Cap for Steve, A" (Callaghan). ShFSup 73.

Cape Cod Mystery, The (Taylor). M&D 1570.

Čapek, Karel. DFor 330-343, 2283; LFFor 273-279, 2066.

Capella, Martianus. PFor 2111-2112.

Capote, Truman. LFEng 440-450; LFSup 402; ShF 481, 554, **1052-1056;** ShFSup 388.

"Capra, La." *See* "Goat, The."

Captain of Köpenick, The (Zuckmayer). DFor 2073-2074.

Captain of the Gray Horse Troop, The (Garland). LFEng 1087-1089.

Captain of the Vulture, The (Braddon). M&D 183.

Captain Pantoja and the Special Service (Vargas Llosa). LFFor 1850-1851.

Captains Courageous (Kipling). LFEng 1543.

Captain's Daughter, The (Pushkin). LFFor 1363-1364, 1368-1371.

Captain's Verses, The (Neruda). PFor 1077-1078.

Captive, The (Proust). LFFor 1337-1339. See also *Remembrance of Things Past.*

Captives, The (Gay). DEng 732.

Captives, The (Plautus). DFor 2141.

"Captivity, The" (Goldsmith). PEng 1111.

Capture of Miletus, The (Phrynichus). DFor 2090, 2095.

Capuana, Luigi. DFor 2410-2411; LFFor 2231-2232; ShF 685-686.

Car Cemetery, The (Arrabal). DFor 124-126.

Cara de Dios (Valle-Inclán). LFFor 1836.

Caractères, Les. See *Characters, The.*

Caragiale, Ion Luca. DFor 344-351, 2298.

Caravans (Michener). LFSup 301-302.

Carcase for Hounds (Mwangi). LFFor 2051.

"Carcass, A" (Baudelaire). PFor 135-136.

Carcere, Il. See *Political Prisoner, The.*

"Carcere" (Pavese). ShF 2065.

Card Index, The (Różewicz). DFor 1581-1582.

Cardarelli, Vincenzo. PFor 2047.

Cardenio und Celinde (Gryphius). DFor 837.

Cardinal, The (Shirley). DEng 1819-1822, 2292.

"Cardinal, A" (Snodgrass). PEng 2659.

Cardinal of Spain, The (Montherlant). DFor 1356.

"Cardinal's First Tale, The" (Dinesen). LFEng 3265-3266.

Carducci, Giosuè. PFor 266-272, 2027-2029.

"Care--Charming Sleep" (Fletcher, J.). PEng 1014.

Careless Husband, The (Cibber). DEng 366-367.

Carelessness (Turgenev). DFor 1901-1904.

"Carentan O Carentan" (Simpson). PEng 2603.

Caretaker, The (Pinter). DEng 1517-1520.

Carew, Thomas. LTh 1675; PEng 430-436, 2726-2727, 2779, 2780.

"Cargoes" (Masefield). PEng 1922-1923.

Caridorf (Bird). DEng 214.

Carioca Fletch (Mcdonald). M&D 1126-1127.

Carlet, Pierre. See **Marivaux.**

Carleton, William. ShF 1057-1063.

Carling, Finn. LFFor 2363.

Carlson, Ron. ShF 2540.

Carlyle, Thomas. LFEng 3033; LTh 4, 459, 1019-1020, 1248, 1406, 1418, 1703, 1730-1731.

Carmelita (Iniss). DEng 2451.

Carmen (Mérimée). LFFor 1150-1152; ShF 1922-1923.

Carmen Saeculare (Prior). PEng 2288.

Carmichael, Harry. M&D 262-266.

"Carmilla" (Le Fanu). ShF 477, 736-737, 1798-1800.

Carminalenia (Middleton, C.). PEng 1987, 1990-1991.

"Carnal Knowledge" (Gunn). PEng 1170.

Carne, la morte, e il diavolo nella letteratura romantica, La. See *Romantic Agony, The.*

Carner, Josep. PFor 1774.

Carnival (Harris). LFSup 149.

Carnival, The (Prokosch). LFEng 2161.

Carnival Scenes (Caragiale). DFor 350.

Caro Michele. See *No Way.*

"Carogne" (Pavese). ShF 2065.

Caron, Pierre-Augustin. *See* **Beaumarchais, Pierre-Augustin Caron de.**

Carossa, Hans. PFor 1932.

Carpelan, Bo. PFor 2191.

Carpentier, Alejo. LFFor 280-288, 2294, 2296, 2299; ShF 1064-1068.

Carr, John Dickson. M&D 267-274; ShF 763.

Carr, Pat. ShF 2541.

Carrasquilla, Tomás. LFFor 2286.

"Carrefour" (Reverdy). PSup 321-322.

Carreta, La (Marqués). DFor 2446.

"Carriage from Sweden, A" (Moore). PEng 2046.

Carrie (King). LFSup 204-205.

Carrier of Ladders, The (Merwin). PEng 1982.

"Carriola, La." *See* "Wheelbarrow, The."

"Carrion Comfort" (Hopkins). PEng 1402.

Carroll, David. LTh 507.

Carroll, John D. *See* **Daly, Carroll John.**

Carroll, Lewis. PEng 437-453.

"Carski soneti" (Dučić). PFor 429.

"Cart with Apples, A" (Middleton, C.). PEng 1989.

Cartas eruditas y curiosas (Feijóo). LTh 475-476.

Carte, Richard D'Oyly. DEng 759, 2359.

Carter, Angela. LFSup 70-76.

Carter, Nick. M&D 275-288. *See also* **Avallone, Michael; Collins, Michael; Hanshew, Thomas W.; and Smith, Martin Cruz.**

Carus, Titus Lucretius. *See* **Lucretius.**

Carver, Raymond. ShFSup 75-82.

Cary, Joyce. LFEng 451-463.

Casa con dos puertas, mala es de guardar. See *House with Two Doors Is Difficult to Guard, A.*

Casa de Bernarda Alba, La. See *House of Bernarda Alba, The.*

Casa de campo. See *House in the Country, A.*

Casa e la città, La. See *City and the House, The.*

Casa Guidi Windows (Browning, E. B.). PEng 330-331.

Casa in collina, La. See *House on the Hill, The.*

Casa verde, La. See *Green House, The.*

Casamiento, El. See *Marriage, The.*

Casanova's Chinese Restaurant (Powell). LFEng 2119.

Case, The (Sukhovo-Kobylin). DFor 1774-1776. See also *Trilogy of Alexander Sukhovo-Kobylin, The.*

Case for Three Detectives (Bruce). M&D 218.

Case Is Altered, The (Jonson). DEng 2285.

Case of Kitty Ogilvie, The (Stubbs). M&D 1549.

"Case of Laker, Absconded, The" (Morrison). M&D 1243-1244.

"Case of Mr. Foggatt, The" (Morrison). M&D 1242-1243.

"Case of Oscar Brodski, The" (Freeman). M&D 669.

Case of Rebellious Susan, The (Jones, H. A.). DEng 1004.

Case of the Baker Street Irregulars, The (Boucher). M&D 170.

Case of the Missing Brontë, The (Barnard). M&D 85.

"Case of the Missing Hand, The" (Morrison). M&D 1244.

Case of the Russian Diplomat, The (Cunningham). M&D 442.

Case of the Seven of Calvary, The (Boucher). M&D 170.

Case of the Solid Key, The (Boucher). M&D 170-171.

Case of the Velvet Claws, The (Gardner, E.). M&D 691.

Casey, John. *See* **O'Casey, Sean.**

Casibus Illustrium Virorum, De (Boccaccio). PEng 1809-1810.

Casina (Plautus). DFor 1485.

Cask, The (Crofts). M&D 419.

"Cask of Amontillado, The" (Poe). ShF 192-193.

Casona, Alejandro. DFor 352-360, 2506.

Caspary, Vera. M&D 289-294.

Cassandra Singing (Madden). LFEng 1763-1764.

Cassaria, La. See *Coffer, The.*

Cassill, R. V. LFEng 464-471; LFSup 402; ShF 1069-1074; ShFSup 388.

"Cassinus and Peter" (Swift). PEng 2808.

Cassiodorus. PFor 2113.

Cassirer, Ernst. LTh 790, 1756; ShF 184-185.

Cassity, Turner. PSup 59-65.

"Castaway, The" (Cowper). PEng 615-616.

Castaway (Cozzens). LFEng 632-633.

Caste (Robertson). DEng 1609-1610.

Castellano, Il (Trissino). LTh 1462.

Castello dei destini incrociati, Il. See *Castle of Crossed Destinies, The.*

Castelvetro, Lodovico. DEng 2156, 2158; DFor 2199-2200; **LTh 272-278,** 310, 1664-1665.

Castiglione, Baldassare. LTh 131-132, 1462.

Castigo sin venganza, El. See *Justice Without Revenge.*

Castigos y ejemplos de Catón. PFor 2210.

Casting of Bells, The (Seifert). PSup 356.

Castle, The (Kafka). LFFor 902-904.

Castle Corner (Cary). LFEng 456.

Castle Gay (Buchan). LFEng 334.

Castle Keep (Eastlake). LFEng 853-855.

Castle of Crossed Destinies, The (Calvino). LFFor 246-247.

Castle of Hearts, The (Flaubert). LFFor 547.

Castle of Otranto, The (Walpole). LFEng 3121, 3124-3125, 3257-3259; ShF 179, 474, 730.

Castle of Perseverance, The. DEng 2253.

Castle of the Carpathians, The (Verne). LFFor 1876.

Castle Rackrent (Edgeworth, M.). LFEng 863-865.

Castle Spectre, The (Lewis). DEng 1132-1135.

Castle to Castle (Céline). LFFor 306, 311-313.

Castles of Athlin and Dunbayne, The (Radcliffe). LFEng 2199-2200; M&D 1390.

Castro, A. See *Ignez de Castro.*

Castro, Rosalía de. PFor 273-281.

Castro y Bellvís, Guillén de. DFor 2488.

Casualties of Peace, (O'Brien, E.). LFEng 2020-2021.

Cat, The (Colette). LFFor 370.

Cat and Mouse (Grass). LFFor 736.

Cat and Shakespeare, The (Rao). LFEng 2212-2213.

"Cat-Goddesses" (Graves). PEng 1132.

Cat Man (Hoagland). LFSup 153.

Cat of Many Tails (Queen). M&D 1379-1380.

Cat on a Hot Tin Roof (Williams, T.). DEng 2076-2080.

Cat's Cradle (Flower). M&D 632.

Cat's Cradle (Vonnegut). LFEng 2727-2728.

"Cat's Meow, The" (Morris). ShFSup 204-205.

Cataline (Ibsen). DFor 2471.

"Catastrophe" (Buzzati). ShFSup 63.

"Catastrophe de l'Igitur, La" (Claudel). PFor 359.

"Catch, The" (Ōe). ShFSup 232-234.

Catch-22 (Heller). LFEng 1329-1330, 1331-1334.

Catcher in the Rye, The (Salinger). LFEng 2321, 2325-2329.

"Categories" (Kennedy). PEng 1575.

Catharina von Georgien (Gryphius). DFor 836.

Cathay (Pound). PEng 2268.

"Cathedral" (Carver). ShFSup 80-81.

Cathedral, The (Lowell, J. R.). PEng 1780-1781.

Cathedral Folk, The (Leskov). ShFSup 159.

Cather, Willa. LFEng **472-484,** 3054; ShF 10, 587, 605, **1075-1081,** 1569.

Catherine Carmier (Gaines). LFEng 1044-1045.

Catherine Howard (Dumas *père*). DFor 491.

Catherine the Great. LFFor 2308-2309; LTh 1694.

Cathleen ni Houlihan (Yeats and Gregory). DEng 2118-2119.

Catholic, The (Plante). LFSup 311.

Catholics (Moore, B.). LFEng 1891.

Cathy Come Home (Sanford). DEng 2506.

Cathy of Heilbronn (Kleist). DFor 1078-1080.

Catiline His Conspiracy (Jonson). DEng 2286.

Cato. PFor 2088.

Cato (Addison). DEng 4, 7-9, 2342.

Catsplay (Örkény). DSup 298-299.

Cattafi, Bartolo. PFor 2051.

Catullus. DFor 2147; **PFor 282-291,** 2094-2095.

Caucasian Chalk Circle, The (Brecht). DFor 241-244.

Caudwell, Christopher. LFEng 3161; LTh 1540.

"Caupolicán" (Darío). PFor 422-423. See also *Azul.*

Cavafy, Constantine P. PFor 292-301, 1954-1957.

"Cavalcanti" (Pound). LTh 1156.

Cavalcanti, Guido. LTh 341-342; PFor 302-307.

Cavaliere inesistente, Il. See *Nonexistent-Knight, The.*

"Cavalla storna, La." *See* "Dapple-grey Mare, The."

Cavalleria rusticana (Verga). DFor 1944-1945, 2411; ShF 2379-2380.

"Cave, The" (Zamyatin). LFFor 1978-1979; ShFSup 371-372.

Cave Dwellers, The (Saroyan). DEng 1658.

Cave of Salamanca, The (Cervantes). DFor 366.

Caveat for Common Cursetors, Vulgarly Called Vagabonds, A (Harman). ShF 453-454.

Cavendish, Margaret. *See* Newcastle, Margaret Cavendish, Duchess of.

Caversham Entertainment, The (Campion). PEng 427.

Caves du Vatican, Les. See *Lafcadio's Adventures.*

Caviare at the Funeral (Simpson). PEng 2608-2609.

Caxton, William. LTh 1185; PEng 3269; ShF 143, 382.

"Ce que dit la bouche d'ombre." *See* "What the Mouth of the Shadow Says."

"Cebu" (Creeley). PEng 688-689.

Čech, Svatopluk. PFor 1802.

"Ceci n'est pas un conte." *See* "This Is No Yarn."

Cecilia (Burney). LFEng 379-380.

Cefalu. See *Dark Labyrinth, The.*

Cela, Camilo José. LFFor 289-301, 2393.

Celan, Paul. PFor 308-315, 1372, 1934-1935.

"Celebrated Jumping Frog of Calaveras County, The" (Twain). ShF 211-212, 2361-2362.

"Celebration, The" (Dickey, J.). PEng 798.

Celebration (Settle). LFSup 349-350.

"Celebrations" (Clarke). PSup 70.

Celestial Navigation (Tyler). LFEng 2679-2680.

"Celestial Omnibus, The" (Forster). ShF 521, 1391.

Celestina, La (Rojas). See *Comedia de Calisto y Melibea, La.*

"Celibacy" (Clarke). PSup 69.

Céline, Louis-Ferdinand. LFFor 302-314.

Celle qui n'était plus. See *Woman Who Was No More, The.*

Celles qu'on prend dans ses bras (Montherlant). DFor 1354.

Celos infundados, Los (Martínez de la Rosa). DFor 1272-1273.

Celtic Twilight, The (Yeats). LTh 1587; ShF 656-657.

Cement (Müller). DSup 260.

"Cemetery, The" (Gill). ShF 1487.

"Cena miserable, La." *See* "Wretched Supper, The."

Cena Trimalchionis (Petronius). ShF 2092, 2095-2096.

Cenci, The (Shelley). DEng 1746, 1747, 1752-1753.

Cendrars, Blaise. LFFor 315-323; PFor 1880.

"Ceneri." *See* "Ashes."

"Ceneri di Gramsci, Le." *See* "Gramsci's Ashes."

Cent Ballades (Christine de Pisan). PFor 352-353.

Centaur, The (Updike). LFEng 2687, 2699-2703.

"Center" (Miles). PSup 279.

Center of Attention, The (Hoffman). PEng 1358.

Centlivre, Mrs. Susannah. DEng 343-350, 2177.

Centuries of Meditations (Traherne). PEng 2925-2926.

Century. ShF 585, 586, 588.

Century of Hero-Worship, A (Bentley). LTh 146.

Cerco de Numancia, El. See *Siege of Numantia, The.*

Ceremony (Parker). M&D 1301.

"Ceremony" (Stafford). PEng 2723-2724.

Ceremony of Innocence, The (Ribman). DSup 314.

Cernuda, Luis. PFor 316-324.

"Cero." *See* "Zero."

Certain Bokes of Virgiles Aenis (Surrey). PEng 2790-2791.

Certain Notes of Instruction Concerning the Making of Verse or Rime in English (Gascoigne). PEng 3285.

Certain Sleep (Reilly). M&D 1404.

Certain Smile, A (Sagan). LFFor 1473-1474.

Certain Sourire, Un. See *Certain Smile, A.*

Certain Tragicall Discourses (Fenton). ShF 487-489.

Certayn Eglogus (Barclay). PEng 3286.

"Certayne Notes of Instruction Concerning the Making of Verse or Rhyme in English" (Gascoigne). LTh 543.

Cervantes, Miguel de. DFor 361-368, 2486-2487; LFEng 3222-3223, 3225-3227, 3231; LFFor 324-332, 2024-2026, 2373; PEng 3313; ShF 1082-1092.

Ces plaisirs. See *Pure and the Impure, The.*

Césaire, Aimé. DSup 38-44; LTh 1056, 1058; PFor 325-330; PSup 404.

Cesta kolem světa za 80 dni (Kohout). DSup 223.

Cetro de José, El (Cruz). DFor 444.

Cette Voix. See *That Voice.*

Cézanne, Paul. LTh 1493.

Chabot, Admiral of France (Chapman and Shirley). DEng 2287, 2288.

Chaffin, Lillie D. ShF 2542.

Chaikin, Joseph. DEng 2483.

"Chain of Love, A" (Price). ShF 2123.

"Chain Saw at Dawn in Vermont in Time of Drouth" (Warren). PEng 3027.

"Chained Stream, The" (Hölderlin). PFor 686. See also *Nachtgesänge.*

"Chainsaw" (Everson). PEng 993.

Chairs, The (Ionesco). DFor 998-999, 2251, 2357.

Chaises, Les. See *Chairs, The.*

"Chaka" (Senghor). PFor 1426. *See also* Hosties noires.

Chalbaud, Román. DFor 2445.

Chaleur Network, The. See *In Any Case.*

Challenge (Sapper). M&D 1468-1469.

Chalúpka, Ján. DFor 2284.

Chalúpka, Samo. PFor 1809.

Chamber Music (Joyce). PEng 1522-1525.

"Chambered Nautilus, The" (Holmes). PEng 1374-1375.

Chambre d'hôtel. See *Chance Acquaintances.*

Chambres de bois, Les. See *Silent Rooms, The.*

"Champion" (Lardner). ShF 1771.

Champs magnétiques, Les (Breton and Soupault). LTh 214.

Chance, John Newton. M&D 295-302.

Chance Acquaintances (Colette). LFFor 369.

"Chance to Work" (Gurney). PEng 1184-1185.

Chancellor, Le. See *Survivors of the Chancellor.*

Chances, The (Villiers). DEng 1982.

Chandler, Raymond. LFEng 485-499, 3189; M&D 303-311; ShF 761-762, 1093-1099.

Chang Chao. DFor 2328.

Ch'ang ho (Shen Tsung-wen). LFFor 2107.

Chang K'o-chiu. PFor 1791.

"Change" (Kunitz). PSup 242.

Change for the Angel (Kops). DEng 1081.

Change of Heart, A (Butor). LFFor 217-218; ShF 127-128, 132.

Change of Skin, A (Fuentes). ShF 130.

"Changed Woman, The" (Bogan). PEng 232, 233.

Changeling, The (Middleton and Rowley). DEng 1330-1332.

Changing Light at Sandover, The (Merrill). PEng 1966-1968.

Changing Mind (Aiken). PEng 24-25.

Changing Room, The (Storey). DEng 1889-1891.

"Changing the Wheel" (Brecht). PFor 226. See also *Buckower Elegies.*

Chang-Shêng tien. See *Palace of Eternal Youth, The.*

"Channel Crossing" (Plath). PEng 2229.

Channel Crossing and Other Poems, A (Swinburne). PEng 2820.

"Channel Firing" (Hardy). PEng 1221.

Channing, Edward Tyrrell. LTh 1743.

Channing, William E. LTh 1743-1744.

"Chanson d'automne." *See* "Song of Autumn."

"Chanson de l'oiseleur" (Prévert). PFor 1279.

Chanson de Roland. See *Song of Roland.*

"Chanson un peu naïve" (Bogan). PEng 232.

"Chansons les plus courtes. . ., Les" (Prévert). PFor 1280-1281.

Chant des morts, Le (Reverdy). PSup 325-326.

Chant du monde, Le. See *Song of the World, The.*

Chant of Jimmie Blacksmith, The (Keneally). LFSup 186-187.

Chants d'ombre (Senghor). PFor 1424.

Chants for Socialists (Morris). PEng 2060.

Chants pour Naëtt. See "Songs for Signare."

"Chants pour Signare." *See* "Songs for Signare."

Chants terrestres (Follain). PSup 126-128.

Chao Chih-hsin. LTh 1780.

"Chao-ch'êng hu." *See* "Tiger of Chaoch'êng, The."

Chaos of Crime (Linington). M&D 1082-1084.

Chapayev (Furmanov). LFFor 2324.
Chapeau de paille d'Italie, Un. See *Italian Straw Hat, The.*
Chapelain, Jean. LTh 277, 309-310, 1687.
Chapman, George. DEng 351-361, 2287-2288; **PEng 454-463.**
Char, René. PFor 331-336, 1892-1893; PSup 404.
"Character of a Happy Life, The" (Wotton). PEng 3144.
Characteristicks of Men, Manners, Opinions, Times (Shaftesbury). LTh 1319-1321, 1323, 1531.
Characters, The (La Bruyère). LTh 836-837, 839.
Characters (Theophrastus). ShF 155.
Charakteristiken und Kritiken (Schlegel, F.). LTh 1311.
Charcot, Jean-Martin. PFor 229-230.
Chareas and Callirhoe (Chariton). LFFor 2002-2003.
Charing Cross Mystery, The (Fletcher). M&D 625.
Charioteer, The (Renault). LFEng 2218-2219.
Chariton. LFFor 2002-2003.
Charlatanisme, Le (Scribe). DFor 1681-1682.
"Charles" (Jackson). ShF 1670.
Charles, Franklin. *See* **Adams, Cleve F.**
"Charles Baudelaire's 'Les Chats'" (Jakobson). LTh 749.
Charles Demailly (Goncourts). LFFor 712.
Charles d'Orléans. PEng 3272; **PFor 337-343,** 1845, 1846.
Charles Men, The (Heidenstam). LFFor 821-822.
Charles of Orleans. *See* **Charles d'Orléans.**
"Charles Simic" (Simic). PEng 2594-2595.
Charles XII (Planché). DEng 1525-1526.
Charley Is My Darling (Cary). LFEng 457-458.
Charlie (Mrożek). DFor 1381.
Charlotte Corday (Ponsard). DFor 1490, 1492.
Charlotte Löwensköld (Lagerlöf). LFFor 986-989. See also *Ring of the Löwenskölds, The.*
"Charlotte Russe" (Hale, N.). ShF 1570.
Charlotte Temple (Rowson). LFEng 2314-2316.
Charmed Circle, A (Kavan). LFEng 1510.
Charmed Life, A (McCarthy). LFEng 1722-1723.
Charnel Rose, The (Aiken). PEng 23.

"Charogne, Une." *See* "Carcass, A."
Charterhouse of Parma, The (Stendhal). LFFor 1660-1663.
Charteris, Leslie. M&D 312-318; ShF 764-765.
Chartēs, Ho (Sinópoulos). PFor 1972.
Chartier, Alain. PFor 344-349, 1844.
Chartreuse de Parme, La. See *Charterhouse of Parma, The.*
Chase, James Hadley. M&D 319-324.
Chase, Richard. LTh 1756.
Chase of the Golden Plate, The (Futrelle). M&D 676.
"Chaser, The" (Collier). ShF 121, 1169.
"Chassidische Schriften." *See* "Hasidic Scriptures."
Chast' rechi. See *Part of Speech, A.*
Chaste Maid in Cheapside, A (Middleton). DEng 1329-1330.
Chastelard (Swinburne). DEng 1898-1899.
Château des Carpathes, Le. See *Castle of the Carpathians, The.*
Château des cœurs, Le. See *Castle of Hearts, The.*
Chateaubriand, François René de. LFEng 3142; **LFFor 333-342;** LTh 1181, 1243, 1698.
Châtiments, Les (Hugo). PFor 735.
Chatte, La. See *Cat, The.*
Chatterton (Vigny). DFor 2344.
Chatterton, Thomas. PEng 464-474.
Chattopadhyaya, Harindranath. PFor 2000.
Chaucer, Geoffrey. DEng 2149; LTh 22-23, **279-284,** 967; **PEng 475-489,** 1288, 1802-1803, 1804, 3260-3267, 3490; PFor 1467; ShF 138-140, 142-143, 381, 447, **1100-1117.**
Chaulieu, Guillaume Amfryl. PFor 1859.
Chaussée, Pierre-Claude Nivelle de La. *See* **La Chaussée, Pierre-Claude Nivelle de.**
Chaves (Mallea). LFFor 1057-1058.
Chayka. See *Seagull, The.*
"Che Guevara" (Lowell, R.). PEng 1795.
Cheat, The (Čapek). LFFor 278-279.
"Cheating the Gallows" (Zangwill). M&D 1733.
"Cheat's Remorse, The" (Callaghan). ShFSup 72-73.
Checkmate (Le Fanu). M&D 1049.
Chee-Chee (Rodgers and Hart, L.). DEng 902-903.

Cheer, The (Meredith). PEng 1956.
Cheery Soul, A (White). DSup 394-395.
Cheever, John. LFEng 500-512; ShF 553-554, **1118-1123.**
Chef-d'œuvre inconnu, Le. See *Unknown Masterpiece, The.*
Chekhov, Anton. DFor 369-383, 782, 2457; LFEng 3172, 3300; ShF 462, **1124-1130.**
Chelsea Murders, The (Davidson). M&D 457-458.
Chemins de la liberté, Les. See *Roads to Freedom.*
Chemmeen (Pillai). LFFor 2226.
Ch'ên Tu-hsiu. LTh 704, 1781.
Chêng Hsüan. LTh 1774.
Chêng Kuang-chu. DFor 2316.
Chénier, André-Marie. PFor 1859, 1861, 1864.
Chéreau, Patrice. DFor 2355.
Chéri (Colette). LFFor 371-372.
Chérie (Goncourt, E.). LFFor 717.
Chernyshevsky, Nikolay. LFFor 2318; LTh 121, **285-291,** 386-388, 390, 396, 398, 946, 1104-1108, 1123, 1125, 1447, 1502.
Cherokee Night, The (Riggs). DEng 1592, 1596-1597.
Cheronis-Selz, Thalia. ShF 2543.
Cherry, Kelly. ShF 2544.
Cherry Orchard, The (Chekhov). DFor 380-383.
"Cherrylog Road" (Dickey, J.). PEng 797.
"Cherty dlia kharakteristiki russkogo prostonarod'ia." See "Features for Characterizing the Russian Common People."
Chesapeake (Michener). LFSup 302-303.
Chesnutt, Charles Waddell. LFEng 513-522; **ShFSup 83-90.**
Chester Cycle. DEng 2248-2249.
Chesterfield, Lord (Phillip Dormer Stanhope). LTh 1218.
Chesterton, G. K. M&D 325-332; PEng 490-**497;** ShF 754.
"Chestnut casts his flambeaux, The" (Housman). PEng 1415.
Chetki (Akhmatova). PFor 11-12.
Chetyrnadtsatoye dekabrya. See *December the Fourteenth.*
Cheuse, Alan. ShF 2545.
Chevengur (Platonov). LFFor 2323.
"Chèvre, La." See "Goat, The."

"Chèvre de M. Seguin, La." See "M. Seguin's Goat."
"Chèvrefeuille." See "Honeysuckle, The."
Cheyney, Peter. M&D 333-339.
Cheyney, Reginald Southhouse. See **Cheyney, Peter.**
Chez Nous (Nichols). DSup 282.
Chi, Juan. See **Juan Chi.**
Ch'i Ju-shan. DFor 2334.
Chia. See *Family, The.*
Chiabrera, Gabriello. PFor 2018.
Ch'iang K'uei. LTh 1777.
Chiang-chai shin-hua (Wang Fu-chih). LTh 1779-1780.
Chiao-jan. LTh 1776.
Chiarelli, Luigi. DFor 384-391.
Chiaroscuro (Deledda). LFFor 436-437.
Chiave a stella, La. See *Monkey's Wrench, The.*
Chicago Poems (Sandburg). PEng 2449, 2451.
"Chicago Train, The" (Glück). PSup 134.
"Chickamauga" (Bierce). ShF 793, 968-969.
Chicken Soup with Barley (Wesker). DEng 2016-2017.
Chickencoop Chinaman, The (Chin). DSup 46-48.
Chief Thing, The. See *Main Thing, The.*
Ch'ien, T'ao. See **T'ao Ch'ien.**
Chien couchant, Le (Sagan). LFFor 1477-1478.
"Chiens ont soif, Les" (Prévert). PFor 1280.
Chijin no ai (Tanizaki). LFFor 1712-1713.
Chikamatsu Monzaemon. DFor 392-400, 2426-2431; LTh 1790.
"Child, The" (Bates). ShF 270.
"Child by Fever" (Foote). LFEng 979.
"Child in the Hills" (Still). PEng 2764.
"Child in the House, The" (Pater). LFEng 2065.
"Child My Choice, A" (Southwell). PEng 2688.
"Child of Europe, A" (Miłosz). PFor 1033.
"Child of God, The" (O'Flaherty). ShF 2008-2009.
Child of Gold (McCarthy). LFSup 268.
Child of Pleasure, The (D'Annunzio). LFFor 409-411.
Child Story (Handke). LFFor 790.
"Child Who Favored Daughter, The" (Walker). ShFSup 337.
Childe Byron (Linney). DSup 238.

Childe Harold's Pilgrimage (Byron). LTh 1709; PEng 407-411.
"Childe Roland to the Dark Tower Came" (Browning, R.). PEng 343-344.
Childermass, The (Lewis, W.). LFEng 1685-1686.
Childers, Erskine. M&D 340-344.
"Childhood" (Justice). PEng 1533.
"Childhood of a Boss" (Sartre). LFFor 1514.
"Childhood of Liuvers, The" (Pasternak). PFor 1159. See also *My Sister, Life.*
"Childhood of Zhenya Luvers, The" (Pasternak). ShF 2060-2061.
"Childish Recollections" (Byron). PEng 405.
Children (Gurney). DSup 166-167.
"Children, The" (Oates). ShF 707.
Children at the Gate, The (Wallant). LFEng 2763-2764.
Children of a Lesser God (Medoff). DSup 244.
"Children of Adam" (Whitman). PEng 3068, 3069.
Children of Heracles, The (Euripides) 2113-2114.
Children of the Albatross (Nin). LFEng 1994.
Children of the Ash-Covered Loam (Gonzalez). LFEng 1139.
Children of the Black Sabbath (Hébert). LFFor 812-813, 814.
Children of the Game (Cocteau). LFFor 361-362.
Children's Hour, The (Hellmann). DEng 916-920.
Child's Garden of Verses, A (Stevenson). PEng 2755, 2756.
Chill, The (Macdonald). LFSup 275-276.
Chilly Scenes of Winter (Beattie). LFEng 190-192.
Chimera (Barth). LFEng 3327-3328.
Chimères, Les (Nerval). PFor 1087-1089.
"Chimes for Yahya" (Merrill). PEng 1964-1966.
Chimmoku. See *Silence.*
Chin, Frank. DSup 45-51.
Chin P'ing Mei (Wang Shih-chen). LFFor 2091, 2097-2099.
Chin Shêng-t'an. LTh 1779.
China Governess, The (Allingham). M&D 26-27.
China Trace (Wright, C.). PEng 3152-3153.
Chinese des Schmerzes, Der (Handke). LFFor 790.

Chinese Lake Murders, The (van Gulik). M&D 1643.
Chinese Nail Murders, The (van Gulik). M&D 1646.
"Chinese Nightingale, The" (Lindsay). PEng 1725-1726.
Chinese Wall, The (Frisch). DFor 643-645, 2261-2262.
Chinese Written Character as a Medium for Poetry, The (Pound). LTh 1159.
Ch'ing shan lei (Ma). DFor 2316.
Ch'ing-chao, Li. *See* **Li Ch'ing-chao.**
"Ch'ing-p'ing yüeh." *See* "Tune: Pure, Serene Music."
"Chiocciola, La." *See* "Snail, The."
"Chip of Glass Ruby, A" (Gordimer). ShFSup 107.
"Chiron" (Hölderlin). PFor 686. See also *Nachtgesänge.*
Chłopi. See *Peasants, The.*
Choephoroi. See *Libation Bearers.*
"Chœur des cèdres du Liban" (Lamartine). PFor 835-836.
Choice of a Tutor, The (Fonvizin). DFor 638.
Choise of Valentines (Nashe). PEng 2074.
"Chomei at Toyama" (Bunting). PEng 370.
Chomsky, Noam. LTh 1437, 1801, 1803, 1813, 1830; PFor 1736.
Chopin, Frédéric. LFFor 1489-1490.
Chopin, Kate. LFEng 523-532; ShF 1131-1136.
"Chor der Steine." *See* "Chorus of the Stones."
"Chorus of the Stones" (Sachs). PFor 1373-1374.
"Choruses Descriptive of Dido's State of Mind" (Ungaretti). PFor 1571. See also *Terra promessa, La.*
Chosen, The (Potok). LFSup 314-315.
Chosen Poems (Monroe). PEng 2029.
"Ch'ou Ch'ang shaofu." *See* "In Response to Vice-Magistrate Chang."
Chou-kung shê-chêng (Chêng). DFor 2316.
Chou Shou-jen. *See* Lu Hsün.
Chouans, The (Balzac). M&D 75.
Chrétien de Troyes. LFFor 2110; PFor 632, 1838; ShF 444, 1137-1142.
Christ and Antichrist (Merezhkovsky). LFFor 1138-1139.
Christ Legends (Lagerlöf). LFFor 979.
Christ Recrucified (Kazantzakis). LFFor 920.
Christ Stopped At Eboli (Levi). LFFor 2248.

Cien años de soledad. See *One Hundred Years of Solitude.*

Cíger-Hronský, Jozef. LFFor 2069.

Cimbrernes tog (Jensen). LFFor 883. See also *Long Journey, The.*

Cimbrians, The. See *Long Journey, The.*

Cimetière des voitures, La. See *Car Cemetery, The.*

"Cimetière marin, Le." See "Graveyard by the Sea, The."

Cinco horas con Mario (Delibes). LFFor 450-451.

"Cinderella" (Grimm). ShF 1561.

"Cinderella" (Jarrell). PEng 1483.

Cinderella (Walser, R.). ShFSup 347.

"Cinderella Waltz, The" (Beattie). ShFSup 39.

Cinna (Corneille). DFor 432-433.

Cinnamon Shops (Schulz). ShFSup 274-279.

Cino, Joseph. DEng 2480.

Cinq (Tremblay). DSup 353-354.

Cinq Cents Millions de la Bégum, Le. See *Begum's Fortune, The.*

Cinq Grandes Odes. See *Five Great Odes.*

"Cinque maggio, Il." *See* "Napoleonic Ode, The."

Cinthio, Giambattista Giraldi. *See* **Giraldi Cinthio, Giambattista.**

Cioso (Ferreira). DFor 591.

Cipreses creen en Dios, Los. See *Cypresses Believe in God, The.*

Circle, The (Maugham). DEng 1311-1312.

"Circle Game, The" (Atwood). PEng 64-65.

Circle Home, The (Hoagland). LFSup 153-154.

Circular Staircase, The (Rinehart). M&D 1430-1431.

Circular Study (Green). M&D 785.

Circus, Anthony. *See* **Hoch, Edward D.**

"Circus, The" (Koch). PEng 1628.

"Circus" (Porter). ShF 261.

"Circus in the Attic, The" (Warren). ShF 2406-2407.

"Circus Performers, The" (Tzara). PFor 1551.

Citadel, The (Cronin). LFEng 653, 656-658, 661.

Citadelle. See *Wisdom of the Sands, The.*

Cithara sanctorum (Tranovský, comp.). PFor 1807.

"Cities" (Hacker). PEng 1190-1191.

"Cities and Thrones and Powers" (Kipling). PEng 1608.

Cities of the Interior (Nin). LFEng 1992-1993.

Cities of the Plain (Proust). LFFor 1334-1337. See also *Remembrance of Things Past.*

"Cities, Plains and People" (Durrell). PEng 920-921.

Citizen Kane (Welles). DEng 2517.

Citizen of the World, The (Goldsmith). ShF 1512-1516.

Citizens of Calais, The (Kaiser). DFor 1019.

Città invisibili, Le. See *Invisible Cities.*

Città morta, La. See *Dead City, The.*

"Città vecchia." *See* "Old Town."

"City, The" (Æ). PEng 18.

City, The (Claudel). DFor 406-407.

City, The (Fitch). DEng 622-624.

City and the House, The (Ginzburg). LFSup 131.

City and the Mountains, The (Eça de Queiróz). LFFor 546.

City and the Pillar, The (Vidal). LFEng 2718-2719.

City Boy (Wouk). LFEng 2965.

"City in the Sea" (Poe). PEng 2246.

City Looking Glass, The (Bird). DEng 214.

City Madam, The (Massinger). DEng 2291.

City of God, The (Augustine). LTh 1646; ShF 892-894.

City of Illusions (Le Guin). LFEng 1633-1634.

City of Pleasure, The (Bennett). M&D 109.

"City of Satisfactions, The" (Hoffman). PEng 1359.

"City of the Dead, a City of the Living, A" (Gordimer). ShFSup 110.

"City of the Living, The" (Stegner). ShF 2272.

City of Trembling Leaves, The (Clark). LFEng 550.

City Politiques (Crowne). DEng 439-441.

City Primeval (Leonard). M&D 1056.

City Romance (Furetière). LFFor 2028.

City Solitary, A (Freeling). M&D 663-664.

Ciudad y los perros, La. See *Time of the Hero, The.*

Civil Poems (Miles). PSup 278.

Civil War, The (Foote). LFEng 969; ShF 288.

Civil War (Montherlant). DFor 1356-1357.

CIVIL warS, The (Wilson, Robert). DSup 402.

"Civilization" (Snyder). PEng 2674.

Clacson, trombette è pernacchi. See *About Face.*

Claiborne, Sybil. ShF 2548.

"Clair de lune." *See* "Moonlight."

Clam Shell, The (Settle). LFSup 347.

"Clamming" (Whittemore). PEng 3080.

Clamor (Guillén). PFor 625.

"Clara" (O'Brien, Edna). ShF 1974-1975.

Clare, John. PEng 506-515.

Clarel (Melville). PEng 1949.

Clarín. LFFor 343-355, 2385.

Clarissa (Richardson, S.). LFEng 2246-2247, 2250-2251; LTh 887; ShF 471.

Clark, Alfred Alexander Gordon. *See* **Hare, Cyril.**

Clark, Curt. *See* **Westlake, Donald E.**

Clark, Howard. *See* **Henry, O.**

Clark, Jean C. ShF 2549.

Clark, John Pepper. DSup 52-59.

Clark, LaVerne Harrell. ShF 2550.

Clark, Walter Van Tilburg. LFEng 544-552; ShF 547, 1150-1155.

Clarke, Anna. M&D 354-359.

Clarke, Arthur C. ShF 1156-1162; ShFSup 388.

Clarke, Austin. DEng 370-379; PSup 66-72.

Clarke, Martha. DSup 60-67.

Claro enigma (Drummond de Andrade). PSup 100.

Clash by Night (Odets). DEng 1402.

"Classic" (Herbert). PFor 656.

Classic Vision, The (Krieger). LTh 826.

"Classical Walpurgis Night" (Verlaine). PFor 1629.

Claudel, Paul. DFor 401-413, 2352; LFFor 1124; PFor 355-365, 1881, 1882-1883.

Claude's Confession (Zola). LFFor 1988-1989.

Claudianus, Claudius. PFor 2110.

Claudine à l'école. See *Claudine at School.*

Claudine à Paris. See *Claudine in Paris.*

Claudine and Annie (Colette). LFFor 371.

Claudine at School (Colette). LFFor 370-371.

Claudine en ménage. See *Claudine Married.*

Claudine in Paris (Colette). LFFor 371.

Claudine Married (Colette). LFFor 371.

Claudine s'en va. See *Claudine and Annie.*

Claudius Namatianus. *See* Namatianus, Claudius.

Claudius the God (Graves, R.). LFEng 1200-1201.

Claussen, Sophus. PFor 2172-2173.

Clavigo (Goethe). DFor 736.

"Clavo, El." *See* "Nail, The."

"Clay" (Joyce). ShF 115.

Clayhanger (Bennett). LFEng 244-245.

Clayton, Richard Henry Michael. *See* **Haggard, William.**

Clea. See *Alexandria Quartet, The.*

"Clean, Well-Lighted Place, A" (Hemingway). ShF 1625-1626; ShFSup 40.

Cleanness (Pearl-Poet). PEng 2197, 2200, 2202-2204, 3254; ShF 2068, 2069, 2070-2072.

Clear Light of Day (Desai). LFEng 731-732.

Clearing (Berry). PEng 154.

Clearing in the Woods, A (Laurents). DEng 1104-1105.

"Clearing the Title" (Merrill). PEng 1968.

Cleary, Jon. M&D 360-364.

Cleek, the Man of the Forty Faces. See *Man of the Forty Faces, The.*

Cleek, the Master Detective. See *Man of the Forty Faces, The.*

Clem Anderson (Cassill). LFEng 469.

Clemens, Samuel Langhorne. *See* **Twain, Mark.**

Cleng Peerson (Hauge). LFFor 799.

Cleopatra (Daniel). PEng 728.

Cléopâtre captive (Jodelle). DEng 2160.

"Clepsydra" (Ashbery). PEng 61.

Clerambault (Rolland). LFFor 1429-1430.

Clerihew, E. *See* **Bentley, E. C.**

"Clerk's Tale, The" (Chaucer). ShF 1113, 1114-1115.

Cleve, Anders. LFFor 2370.

Cleveland, Grover. LFEng 1025-1026.

"Cleveland Wrecking Yard, The" (Brautigan). ShFSup 54-55.

"Clickety-Clack" (Blackburn). PEng 199.

"Cliff, The" (Lermontov). PFor 874.

Cliges (Chrétien de Troyes). ShF 1141.

"Climbing Mount E-mei" (Li Po). PFor 888-889.

"Climbing the Peak of Mount T'ai-po" (Li Po). PFor 888-889.

Clitophon and Leucippe (Tatius). ShF 489.

Clizia (Machiavelli). DFor 1224-1225.

"CLM" (Masefield). PEng 1924.

"Clock, The" (Beer). PEng 117-118.

"Clock, The" (Dučić). PFor 429.

Clock Winder, The (Tyler). LFEng 2679.

Clock Without Hands (Kersh). M&D 980.

Clock Without Hands (McCullers). LFEng 1737.

Clockwork Orange, A (Burgess). LFEng 370-371.

Colette. LFFor 365-374, 2142; ShF 1163-1167.
Colin Clout (Skelton). PEng 2638-2639, 3286.
Coliphizacio. See *Buffeting, The.*
Collaborators (Mortimer). DEng 1358-1359.
Collages (Nin). LFEng 1996-1997.
"Collapsars" (McPherson). PEng 1882.
"Collar, The" (Herbert). PEng 1300, 1301.
Collected Longer Poems, The (Rexroth). PEng 2352.
Collected Poems (Barnard). PSup 24.
Collected Poems (Betjeman). PEng 167.
Collected Poems (Winters). PSup 399-400.
Collected Poems and Epigrams of J. V. Cunningham, The (Cunningham). PSup 74-75.
Collected Poems, 1950-1970 (Davie). PSup 88.
Collected Poems, 1930-1983 (Miles). PSup 279.
Collected Shorter Poems, The (Rexroth). PEng 2351.
Collected Stories (Stafford). ShF 2260.
Collected Stories (Taylor). ShF 550.
Collector, The (Fowles). LFEng 1014-1016.
Colleen Bawn, The (Boucicault). DEng 269.
Colliander, Tito. LFFor 2369.
Collier, Jeremy. DEng 2177.
Collier, John. ShF 258, 1168-1170.
Collier, Old Cap. See **Hanshew, Thomas W.**
Collier's. ShF 589.
Colline. See *Hill of Destiny.*
Collins, Hunt. See **McBain, Ed.**
Collins, Michael. M&D 379-386. *See also* **Carter, Nick.**
Collins, Wilkie. LFEng 553-562; M&D 387-393.
Collins, William. LFEng 553-555; PEng 546-552, 3331-3332.
Collinson, Peter. See **Hammett, Dashiell.**
"Colloque sentimentale." *See* "Sentimental Colloquium."
"Colloquy of the Dogs" (Cervantes). ShF 1086-1089.
Colmena, La. See *Hive, The.*
Cologne Epode (Archilochus). PFor 91-92.
Colomba (Mérimée). LFFor 1149-1150; ShF 1922.
"Colomber, The" (Buzzati). ShFSup 63.
Colombe's Birthday (Browning). DEng 295-296.
"Colombre, Il." *See* "Colomber, The."

Colonel Jack (Defoe). LFEng 690.
Colonel Julian and Other Stories (Bates). ShFSup 31.
Colonel Mint (West). LFSup 374-375.
Colonel's Daughter, The (Aldington). LFEng 41-42.
Colonel's Dream, The (Chesnutt). LFEng 521-522.
"Color of Darkness" (Purdy). ShF 2136-2137.
Color Purple, The (Walker). LFEng 2750, 2754-2756.
Colossus of Maroussi, The (Miller). LFEng 1873.
Colour of Murder, The (Symons). M&D 1563.
Colours in the Dark (Reaney). DEng 1576.
Colton, James. *See* **Hansen, Joseph.**
Colum, Padraic. DEng 380-394.
Columbian Ode, The (Monroe). PEng 2027.
Come and Kill Me. See *Brat Farrar.*
Come Back, Little Sheba (Inge). DEng 982-984.
"Come Back to the Raft Ag'in, Huck Honey!" (Fiedler). LTh 485.
Come le foglie. See *Like Falling Leaves.*
Come Morning (Gores). M&D 762.
"Come On, Ye Sons of Art" (Paley). ShF 2043.
Comedia de Calisto y Melibea, La (Rojas). DEng 2161; LFFor 2376-2377.
Comedia Himenea. See *Hymen.*
Comedia nueva, La (Moratín). DFor 1362-1363.
Comedia soldadesca (Torres Naharro). DFor 1872-1873.
Comédie de la mort, La. See *Drama of Death, The.*
Comédie humaine, La. See *Human Comedy, The* (Balzac).
Comédie sans comédie, La (Quinault). DFor 1504-1506.
Comedienne, The (Reymont). LFFor 1407-1408.
Comedy of Errors, The (Shakespeare). DEng 1703-1704, 2275.
Comedy of Human Life, The. See *Human Comedy, The.*
Comely Cook, The (Chulkov). LFFor 2305.
Comendador Mendoza, El. See *Commander Mendoza.*
"Comendadora, La." *See* "Nun, The."
Comenius. DFor 2282; PFor 1797.

Comfort Me with Apples (De Vries). LFEng 739.

Comforters, The (Spark). LFEng 2476, 2477-2479.

Comical History of the States and Empires of the World of the Moon and Sun. See *Other Worlds.*

Comical Revenge, The (Etherege). DEng 567-569, 2300-2301.

Comical Romance, The (Scarron). LFFor 2028.

Coming of Age in Soho (Innaurato). DSup 204-205.

"Coming of Light, The" (Strand). PEng 2772.

Coming to Terms (Miles). PSup 279.

Coming Up for Air (Orwell). LFEng 2058-2059.

Command and I Will Obey You (Moravia). ShFSup 198.

Commander Mendoza (Valera). LFFor 1822-1824.

Commedia. See *Divine Comedy, The.*

Comment c'est. See *How It Is.*

Commentaire sur Desportes (Malherbe). LTh 970-972.

Commentary on the "Dream of Scipio" (Macrobius). LTh 963-966, 1647.

"Commiato." See "Leavetaking."

Commodianus. PFor 2111.

Commodore's Daughters, The (Lie). LFFor 2342.

Common Chord, The (O'Connor, Frank). ShF 253-254.

"Common Dog, The" (Guest). PEng 1165.

"Common Meter" (Fisher). ShF 578.

Common Reader, The (Woolf). LTh 1575.

Common Story, A (Goncharov). LFFor 704-705.

"Commune présence" (Char). PFor 334.

"Communion" (Dunbar). PSup 115-116.

"Como chove mihudiño." *See* "How the Rain Is Falling Lightly."

"Como hermana y hermano." (González Martínez). PFor 612.

Como quien espera el alba (Cernuda). PFor 323.

Compagnon du tour de France, Le. See *Companion of the Tour of France, The.*

Companion of the Tour of France, The (Sand). LFFor 1491.

Companions of the Day and Night (Harris). LFSup 149.

Company (Beckett). LFEng 214-215; LFFor 130-131.

Company (Sondheim). DEng 2477.

Company of Poets, A (Simpson). PEng 2599.

Compass Flower, A (Merwin). PEng 1982.

Compassion (Pérez Galdós). LFFor 1282-1284.

"Complaint of Henry, Duke of Buckingham" (Sackville). PEng 2439, 2441-2442.

"Complaint of Mars, The" (Chaucer). ShF 1101.

Complaint of Nature, The (Alan of Lille). LTh 20, 22.

Complaint of Rosamond, The (Daniel). PEng 727-728.

Complaint of the Black Knight (Lydgate). PEng 1806-1807.

"Complainte de Lord Pierrot" (Laforgue). PFor 824-825. See also *Complaintes, Les.*

"Complainte des pianos qu'on entend dans les quartiers aisés" (Laforgue). PFor 824, 825. See also *Complaintes, Les.*

"Complainte du soir des comices agricoles" (Laforgue). PFor 823, 824. See also *Complaintes, Les.*

Complaintes, Les (Laforgue). PFor 824.

Complaints (Spenser). PEng 2716-2717.

Complaisant Lover, The (Greene, G.). DEng 831-833.

Complaynt of Phylomene, The (Gascoigne). LTh 543.

"Completed" (Williams, T.). ShF 2436-2437.

"Composed upon Westminster Bridge" (Wordsworth). PEng 3433.

Comptesse Coquette (Bracco). DFor 226.

Compton-Burnett, Ivy. LFEng 563-572; ShF 521.

"Computer's Karl Marx" (Middleton, C.). PEng 1988.

Comrade Kirillov (Rao). LFEng 2213-2214.

Comte, Auguste. LTh 1417, 1712, 1718, 1732.

Comte de Monte-Cristo, Le. See *Count of Monte-Cristo, The.*

Comus (Milton). PEng 2007.

Con il piedo straniero sopra il cuore (Quasimodo). PFor 1307.

Concept of Irony, The (Kierkegaard). ShFSup 24.

"Concept of Romanticism in Literary History, The" (Wellek). LTh 1538.

"Conception" (Miles). PSup 278.

"Conception and Technique" (Beck). ShF 71.
"Concepts of 'Tension,' 'Intensity,' and 'Suspense' in Short-Story Theory" (Dollerup). ShF 74.
"Concerning Short Stories" (Strong). ShF 90.
Concerning the Angels (Alberti). PFor 20.
"Concord Hymn" (Emerson). PEng 960.
Concrete (Bernhard). LFFor 161-162.
Concrete Island (Ballard). LFEng 151.
"Condemned Librarian, The" (West). ShFSup 364.
Condemned of Altona, The (Sartre). DFor 1644-1645, 1650-1651.
Condendado por desconfiado, El (Tirso). DFor 1847-1848.
"Condition Botanique, La" (Hecht). PEng 1278-1279.
Condition humaine, La. See *Man's Fate.*
"Condition of Art, The" (Conrad). ShF 814.
"Condominium, The" (Elkin). LFEng 890-891.
"Condor and the Guests, The" (Connell). ShF 1177.
Condor Passes, The (Grau). LFEng 1187-1188.
Confess, Fletch (Mcdonald). M&D 1128.
Confessio Amantis (Gower). PEng 1114, 1115, 1121-1123, 3259-3260.
"Confession, A" (MacBeth). PEng 1835.
Confession (Simms). LFEng 2414.
Confession de Claude, La. See *Claude's Confession.*
Confession of a Child of the Century, The (Musset). LTh 1709.
Confessions (Augustine). LTh 62-66, 1645-1646; ShF 890-892.
Confessions of a English Opium Eater (De Quincey). LTh 1709.
Confessions of a Fool, The (Strindberg). LFFor 1691-1693.
Confessions of a Mask (Mishima). LFFor 1156-1157.
"Confessions of Fitz-Boodle" (Thackeray). ShF 2315-2316.
Confessions of J.-J. Rousseau (Rousseau). LTh 1709.
Confessions of Nat Turner, The (Styron). LFEng 2589-2590, 2599-2601, 3154-3155.
Confessions of Zeno (Svevo). LFFor 1700-1702, 1705-1707.
Confianza (Salinas). PFor 1389.
Confidential Clerk, The (Eliot). DEng 554-555.

Conformist, The (Moravia). LFFor 1170-1171.
Confucius. LTh 1773; PFor 1779-1780.
Congiura dei Pazzi, La. See *Conspiracy of the Pazzi, The.*
"Congo" (Senghor). PFor 1427. See also *Hosties noires.*
Congreve, William. DEng 395-412, 2310; PEng 553-558; ShF 503, 504, **1171-1174.**
Conjectures on Original Composition (Young). LTh 1596-1599, 1601.
Conjuración de Venecia año de 1310, La. (Martínez de la Rosa). DFor 1269, 1275-1276.
Conjure Woman, The (Chesnutt). LFEng 513; ShF 575-576; ShFSup 85.
"Conjurer's Revenge, The" (Chesnutt). ShFSup 86-87.
Connaissance de l'est. See *East I Know, The.*
Connecticut General from Big Sur, A (Brautigan). LFEng 291-292.
Connecticut Yankee in King Arthur's Court, A (Twain). LFEng 2668-2669.
Connection, The (Gelber). DEng 739-742, 2481-2482.
Connell, Evan S., Jr. LFEng 573-583; ShF **1175-1181;** ShFSup 388.
Connelly, Marc. DEng 413-422.
Connoisseur, The (Connell). LFEng 580-581; ShF 1181.
Conquérants, Les. See *Conquerors, The.*
Conquerors, The (Malraux). LFFor 1063-1064.
Conquest of Plassans, The (Zola). LFFor 1990. See also *Rougon-Macquart, Les.*
Conquête de Plassans, La. See *Conquest of Plassans, The.*
"Conquistador" (Hope). PSup 189.
Conquistador (MacLeish). PEng 1856-1857.
Conrad, Joseph. LFEng 584-601, 983, 984, 994, 2772, 3048-3049, 3284, 3313; LTh 1524-1525; ShF 519, 520, 814, **1182-1188.**
Conrad, Michael Georg. LFFor 2180, 2182.
Consagración de la primavera, La (Carpentier). LFFor 287.
Conscious Lovers, The (Steele). DEng 1862-1865, 2329.
Conservationist, The (Gordimer). LFEng 1166-1168.
"Consider" (Auden). PEng 75-76.
Consider Her Ways (Grove). LFEng 1223.
"Considerando en frío. . . ." *See* "Considering Coldly. . . ."

Coover, Robert. LFEng 617-625, 3227, 3328-3329; LFSup 402; **ShF 1189-1193.**
"Cop and the Anthem, The" (Henry). ShF 230.
Cop Killer (Sjöwall and Wahlöö). M&D 1498.
Copains, Les. See Boys in the Back Room, The.
Copeau, Jacques. DEng 2237; DFor 2351.
Copeland, Ann. ShF 2556.
Cophetua (Drinkwater). DEng 508-509.
"Copley-Plaza, The" (Hale, N.). ShF 1570.
Coppard, A. E. ShF 257-258, **1194-1201.**
"Copper Ferule, The" (Otero). PFor 1114.
Coppia aperta, quasi spalancata. See Open Couple--Very Open, An.
Coquelin, Benoît-Constant. DEng 2525-2526.
Coral, The (Kaiser). DFor 1021-1023, 2378. See also *Gas* and *Gas II.*
Corbeaux, Les. See Vultures, The.
Corey, Paul. ShF 2557.
"Cori descrittivi di stati d'animo di Didone." *See* "Choruses Descriptive of Dido's State of Mind."
"Corinna's Going A-Maying" (Herrick, R.). PEng 1315-1317.
Coriolanus (Shakespeare). DEng 1722-1723, 2283.
Corman, Cid. PEng **567-573**; PSup 404.
"Corn" (Lanier). PEng 1661-1662.
Corn Is Green, The (Williams, E.). DEng 2063-2065.
"Corn Planting, The" (Anderson). ShF 873.
Corneille, Pierre. DEng 2171-2173; **DFor 424-437,** 1246; **LTh 308-313,** 403-404, 669, 708, 775, 838, 840, 880, 882, 1196-1197, 1393.
Cornelia (Garnier). DFor 669-670.
Cornelia (Kyd). DEng 1094-1095.
Cornelius Nepos. *See* Nepos, Cornelius.
Corner of Paradise, A (Holton). M&D 900.
Cornhuskers (Sandburg). PEng 2451.
Corning, Kyle. *See* **Gardner, Erle Stanley.**
"Cornwall" (Davie). PSup 89.
Cornwell, David John Moore. *See* **Le Carré, John.**
"Corona" (Celan). PFor 312. See also *Mohn und Gedächtnis.*
"Corona, La" (Donne). PEng 836.
Corona de fuego (Usigli). DFor 2442-2443.
Corona de luz (Usigli). DFor 2442-2443.
Corona de sombra. See Crown of Shadows.
Corona trágica, La (Vega). PFor 1603.
Coronation (Donoso). LFFor 492-495.

"Coronation, The" (Giusti). PFor 574-575.
Coronel no tiene quien le escriba, El. See No One Writes to the Colonel.
"Coronet for his Mistress Philosophy, A" (Chapman). PEng 459.
"Corpo, O" (Lispector). ShFSup 168.
"Corporal" (Brautigan). ShFSup 55-56.
"Corpse on the Wheat-Field" (Ady). PFor 6.
Correction (Bernhard). LFFor 160-161.
Correspondance, 1830-1880 (Flaubert). LFFor 547-548.
"Corridor, The" (Gunn). PEng 1170.
"Corridor, A" (Robbe-Grillet). ShF 2156.
Corridors of Power (Snow). LFEng 2463.
Corrington, John Williams. ShF 2559.
Corruption in the Palace of Justice (Betti). DFor 209-210.
Corso, Gregory. PEng 574-579.
"Corsons Inlet" (Ammons). PSup 10.
Cortázar, Julio. LFFor 375-384, 2292, 2298; LFSup 402; **ShF 1202-1205**; ShFSup 388.
Corte de los milagros, La. See Ruedo ibérico, El.
Cortegiano, Il. See Courtier, The.
Cortigiana, La. See Courtesan, The.
Corvo, Il (Gozzi). DFor 795-796.
Coryell, John Russell. *See* **Carter, Nick.**
Cosa e altri racconti, La. See Erotic Tales.
Coscienza di Zeno, La. See Confessions of Zeno.
Così è (se vi pare). See Right You Are (If You Think So.)
Ćosić, Dobrica. LFFor 385-392.
Cosmic Rape, The (Sturgeon). LFEng 2585-2586.
Cosmicomiche, Le. See Cosmicomics.
Cosmicomics (Calvino). LFFor 244-245.
Cosmopolitan. ShF 589, 771, 773.
Cosmos (Gombrowicz). LFFor 699.
Cosroès (Rotrou). DFor 1575.
"Cost, The" (Hecht). PEng 1281-1282.
"Côte Basque: 1965, La" (Capote). LFEng 450.
Côté de Guermantes, Le. See Guermantes Way, The.
"Cotter's Saturday Night, The" (Burns). PEng 377.
Cotton, Charles. PEng 580-587.
Coulter, John. DEng 2441.
Coulton, James. *See* **Hansen, Joseph.**

"Councillor Krespel" (Hoffmann). ShF 1647-1648.

Counselman, Mary Elizabeth. ShF 2560.

Counselor Ayres' Memorial (Machado de Assis). LFFor 1046-1047.

"Counsels" (Miłosz). PFor 1035.

Count Belisarius (Graves, R.). LFEng 1198-1199.

Count Julian (Landor). PEng 1642.

"Count Magnus" (James, M. R.). ShF 743.

Count of Monte-Cristo, The (Dumas, *père*). LFFor 526-528; M&D 544-547.

"Count the Almonds" (Celan). PFor 312. See also *Mohn und Gedächtnis*.

"Counter-Attack" (Sassoon). PEng 2471.

Counter Spy Murders, The. See *Dark Duet*.

Counterfeiters, The (Gide). LFFor 641-642, 646-649, 2139.

Countess Julie. See *Miss Julie*.

Countess of Pembroke's Passion, The (Breton, N.). PEng 280.

Country, The (Plante). LFSup 309-310. See also *Francoeur Novels, The*.

Country and the City, The (Williams, R.). PEng 3412-3413.

Country Comets (Day Lewis). PEng 757-758.

Country Doctor, A (Jewett). LFEng 1456-1459.

"Country Doctor, A" (Kafka). ShF 1734.

"Country Doctor, The" (Turgenev). ShF 201-202.

Country Girl, The (Odets). DEng 1403-1404.

Country Girls, The (O'Brien, E.). LFEng 2018-2019.

"Country Husband, The" (Cheever). ShF 1121-1122.

"Country Love Story, A" (Stafford). ShF 2262.

Country of Marriage, The (Berry). PEng 153-154.

Country of the Pointed Firs, The (Jewett). LFEng 1459-1461; ShF 1694.

"Country Passion, A" (Callaghan). ShFSup 68-69.

"Country Sunday, A" (Darley). PEng 733.

"Country Walk, A" (Kinsella). PSup 234.

Country Wife, The (Wycherley). DEng 2109-2111.

"Count's Wife, The" (Buzzati). ShFSup 64.

"County Ball, The" (Praed). PEng 2278.

County Kill (Gault). M&D 714-715.

Coup d'aile, Le (Curel). DFor 452-453.

Coup de dés jamais n'abolira le hasard, Un. See *Dice Thrown Never Will Annul Chance*.

Coup de Grâce (Yourcenar). LFFor 1962-1965.

Coup de lune, Le. See *Tropic Moon*.

Couples (Updike). LFEng 2689, 2690, 2691.

Courage (Grimmelshausen). LFFor 762.

Courrier sud. See *Southern Mail*.

Cours de linguistique générale. See *Course in General Linguistics*.

Cours de littérature dramatique. See *Vorlesungen über dramatische Kunst und Literatur*.

Cours de philosophie positive (Comte). LTh 1712.

Course in General Linguistics (Saussure). LTh 1761-1762.

"Course of a Particular, The" (Stevens). PEng 2749-2750.

Course of Lectures on Dramatic Art and Literature, A (Schlegel, A. W.). LTh 710, 1360-1361, 1707.

"Course of True Love Never Did Run Smooth, The" (Aldrich). PEng 34.

"Court Day" (Still). PEng 2763.

Courteline, Georges. DFor 2350.

Courtesan, The (Aretino). DFor 97-98.

Courtier, The (Castiglione). LTh 131-132, 1462; PFor 162-163; ShF 681-682.

Courtois d'Arras. DFor 2175.

Courts of the Morning, The (Buchan). LFEng 332.

Courtship of Miles Standish, The (Longfellow). PEng 1752.

"Courtship of the Family, The" (Stevenson). LTh 887.

"Courtship of the Yonghy-Bonghy-Bò, The" (Lear). PEng 1700.

Cousin Bazilio (Eça de Queiróz). LFFor 543-544.

Cousin Bette (Balzac). LFFor 100-101.

Cousin Phillis (Gaskell). LFEng 1101.

"Cousin Theresa" (Saki). ShF 2171-2172.

Covenant with Death, A (Becker). LFEng 199-200.

"Cover for Trout Fishing in America, The" (Brautigan). ShFSup 53-54.

Cover Her Face (James). M&D 933.

Covetous Knight, The (Pushkin). DFor 1497-1498. See also *Little Tragedies*.

"Cow in the House, A" (Kiely). ShF 1742.

"Cow of the Barricades, The" (Rao). ShF 648-649.

Coward, Noël. DEng 423-431, 2380-2381, 2382-2383; ShF 1206-1209.

Cowled Lover, The (Bird). DEng 214.

Cowley, Abraham. LTh 1349; PEng 588-597.

Cowley, Hannah. DEng 2335.

Cowley, Malcolm. LTh 314-320; PEng 598-609; ShF 296.

Cowper, William. PEng 610-619, 3331, 3333-3334, 3335.

"Cowslip Field, The" (Bates). ShFSup 32-33.

Cox, Anthony. *See* Berkeley, Anthony.

Cox, William. LTh 1744.

Cox, William Trevor. *See* Trevor, William.

Coxcomb, The (Beaumont and Fletcher). DEng 634.

Coxe, George Harmon. M&D 394-399.

Coxe, Louis Osborne. PEng 620-632; PSup 404.

Cozzens, James Gould. LFEng 626-637; ShF 1210-1215.

Crabbe, George. PEng 633-647, 3333.

Crackanthorpe, Hubert. ShF 515-516.

"Cracked Mother, The" (Brathwaite). PEng 270; PFor 214. *See also* "Limbo" and *Islands*.

Cradle Song, The (Martínez Sierras). DFor 1285-1286.

Craft of Fiction, The (Lubbock). LTh 756, 924-928.

"Craftsmen of Wine Bowls" (Cavafy). PFor 300-301.

Craig, Alisa. *See* MacLeod, Charlotte.

Craig, Gordon. DEng 2235-2236; DFor 2240.

"Crainquebille" (France). ShF 1405-1406.

Crane, Hart. PEng 648-658, 3365-3366, 3391.

Crane, R. S. LTh 187-188, 321-325, 782, 1755, 1817.

Crane, Stephen. LFEng 638-647; PEng 659-665; ShF 235-236, 536, 598, 1216-1221.

"Cranes of Ibycus, The" (Schiller). PFor 1406, 1409.

Cranford (Gaskell). LFEng 1098, 1100.

Crash (Ballard). LFEng 150-151.

Crashaw, Richard. PEng 666-674, 3309.

Crates. DFor 2122.

Cratinus. DFor 2121-2122.

Cratylus (Plato). LTh 1113.

Crawford, Marion F. ShF 536.

Crayencour, Marguerite de. *See* Yourcenar, Marguerite.

Crazy Hunter (Boyle). LFEng 277.

Crazy in Berlin (Berger). LFEng 253.

Crazy Kill, The (Himes). M&D 887-889.

"Crazy Steve" (Petőfi). PFor 1225.

Creasey, John. M&D 400-411.

Creation of the World and Other Business, The (Miller). DEng 1349-1350.

Creative Intuition in Art and Poetry (Maritain). LTh 1002.

"Creature, The" (O'Brien, Edna). ShF 1973-1974.

Crébillon, Claude. LFFor 2119.

Crébillon, Prosper Jolyot de. DFor 2338.

"Credo on a Good Morning" (Kunze). PFor 808.

Creeley, Robert. LTh 1076; PEng 60, 675-691; PSup 404.

Creepers, The (Creasey). M&D 404-405.

Crepusculario (Neruda). PFor 1072-1073.

Crescimbeni, Giovan Mario. LTh 1691.

Cress Delahanty (West). ShFSup 363.

Creutz, Gustaf Philip. PFor 2160-2161.

"Crewel Needle, The" (Kersh). M&D 982.

Crews, Frederick. PEng 3425-3426.

"Cricket, The" (Tuckerman). PEng 2940-2941.

Crime and Punishment (Dostoevski). LFFor 509-511, 2317; M&D 525-527.

Crime at Diana's Pool, The (Whitechurch). M&D 1714.

"Crime at the Tennis Club" (Moravia). ShFSup 195.

Crime de Sylvestre Bonnard, Le. See *Crime of Sylvestre Bonnard, The*.

Crime do Padre Amaro, O. See *Sin of Father Amaro, The*.

"Crime do professor de matemática." *See* "Crime of the Mathematics Professor, The."

Crime Doctor, The (Hornung). M&D 909.

"Crime of Mary Lynn Yager, The" (Cassill). ShF 1070, 1073.

Crime of Sylvestre Bonnard, The (France). LFFor 574-575; ShF 1403.

"Crime of the Mathematics Professor, The" (Lispector). ShFSup 167.

Crimes and Crimes (Strindberg). DFor 2476.

Crimes of the Heart (Henley). DSup 195-196.

Criminals, The (Bruckner). DFor 262-263.

Crimson Alibi, The (Cohen). M&D 366-367.

Crimson Island, The (Bulgakov). DFor 293-294.

"Crisalide." *See* "Chrysalis."

Crisi dell'eroe nel romazo vittoriano, La. See *Hero in Eclipse in Victorian Fiction, The*.

"Crisis, The" (Zoshchenko). ShFSup 381.

Crisis Achaiōn (Dionysius). LTh 1643.

"Crisis in Comparative Literature, The" (Wellek). LTh 1535, 1537.

"Crisis in London" (Gallico). ShF 1443-1444.

"Crisis of Culture, The" (Bely). LTh 128.

Crispin, Edmund. M&D 412-417.

Crispin, Rival of His Master (Lesage). DFor 1186-1187.

Cristo de Velázquez, El (Unamuno). PFor 1558.

Cristo si è fermato a Eboli. See *Christ Stopped at Eboli*.

Critic, The (Sheridan). DEng 1780-1781.

"Critic and Society: Barthes, Leftocracy, and Other Mythologies, The" (Soyinka). LTh 1372.

Critical and Historical Principles of Literary History (Crane, R. S.). ShF 173-174.

"Critical Approach to the Short Story, A" (Stroud). ShF 91.

Critical Understanding (Booth). LTh 188.

"Criticism: A Many-Windowed House" (Cowley). LTh 316.

"Criticism and Crises" (de Man). LTh 350.

Criticism and Ideology (Eagleton). LTh 415.

"Criticism and Symbolism" (Bely). LTh 126.

Criticism and Truth (Barthes). LTh 103, 106.

Criticism in the Wilderness (Hartman). LTh 645.

Critics and Criticism (Crane). LTh 322, 1755.

Critique de la critique. See *Literature and Its Theorists*.

Critique et vérité. See *Criticism and Truth*.

Critique of Judgment, The (Kant). LTh 791, 1296.

Critique of the School for Wives, The (Molière). DFor 1334-1335.

Critische Abhandlung von dem Wunderbaren in der Poesie und dessen Verbindung mit dem Wahrscheinlichen (Bodmer). LTh 176.

Critische Briefe (Bodmer). LTh 176.

Crnjanski, Miloš. PFor 2256.

Croce, Benedetto. LTh 31, **326-333**; 362-363, 627, 630, 982, 1100, 1129, 1168-1169, 1512.

Crochet Castle (Peacock). LFEng 2084-2085.

Crocodile on the Sandbank (Peters, Elizabeth). M&D 1314.

Croft-Cooke, Rupert. *See* **Bruce, Leo.**

Crofts, Freeman Wills. M&D 418-424.

Crome Yellow (Huxley). LFEng 1400-1401.

Cromedeyre-le-vieil (Romains). DFor 1551-1552.

Cromwell (Hugo). DFor 967-968.

Crónica de una muerte anunciada. See *Chronicle of a Death Foretold*.

Crónica del alba (Sender). LFFor 1551-1552.

Cronica Tripertita (Gower). PEng 1114.

Cronin, A. J. LFEng 648-662.

Crooked Lines of God, The (Everson). PEng 990.

Cross, The (Undset). LFFor 1804.

Cross, Amanda. M&D 425-430.

Cross Purpose. See *Misunderstanding, The*.

"Cross Ties" (Kennedy). PEng 1572.

"Crossed Apple, The" (Bogan). PEng 233.

"Crossing Brooklyn Ferry" (Jewett). ShF 1698.

"Crossing Brooklyn Ferry" (Whitman). PEng 3070.

"Crossing into Poland" (Babel). ShF 900-901.

Crotchet Castle (Peacock). LTh 1710.

Crow (Hughes, T.). PEng 1445, 3368-3369.

"Crow, The" (Meckel). ShFSup 188-189.

"Crow Jane" (Baraka). PEng 86.

Crowds and Power (Canetti). LFFor 266.

Crowe, C. B. *See* **Gibson, Walter B.**

Crowe, John. *See* **Collins, Michael.**

Crowley, Mart. DSup 68-73.

"Crown Is Older Than King Philip, The" (Walther). PFor 1678.

Crown of Shadows (Usigli). DFor 2442-2443; DSup 363-364.

Crowne, John. DEng 432-441.

Croxton *Play of the Sacrament*. DEng 2248, 2252.

"Cruche, La." *See* "Pitcher, The."

Crucible, The (Miller). DEng 1342-1343, 2407.

Crucifix in a Deathhand (Bukowski). PEng 359.

"Cruel and Barbarous Treatment" (McCarthy). ShF 1835-1836.

Cruikshank, George. LFEng 31.

Cruise of a Deathtime, The (Babson). M&D 50.

Cruise of the Breadwinner, The (Bates). LFEng 185.

"Cruise of the 'Idlewild,' The" (Dreiser). ShF 1308.

Crumbling Idols (Garland). ShF 234.

Crumley, James. M&D 431-436.

"Crusoe in England" (Bishop). PEng 189.

Cruz, Sor Juana Inés de la. DFor 438-446; PFor 375-381, 2220.

Cry Killer! See *Dagger of the Mind.*

Cry of Absence, A (Jones, M.). LFEng 1492-1493.

Cry, The Peacock (Desai). LFEng 725, 728.

Crying Game, The (Braine). LFEng 283.

Crying of Lot 49, The (Pynchon). LFEng 2191-2192.

Crystal, David. PEng 3456-3457.

Crystal Age, A (Hudson). LFEng 1384-1385, 1387.

Crystal and Fox (Friel). DEng 674-675.

"Crystal Palace, The" (Thackeray). PEng 2875-2876.

Crystal Stopper, The (Leblanc). M&D 1038.

Crystal World, The (Ballard). LFEng 149-150.

"Családi kör." *See* "Family Circle."

"Csárda romjai, A." *See* "Ruins of the *Csárda.*"

"Csatában." *See* "In Battle."

Csíky, Gergely. DFor 2287.

Csokonai Vitéz, Mihály. PFor 1978.

Csongor és Tünde (Vörösmarty). PFor 1667.

Csurka, István. DFor 2289.

Ctisis (Apollonius Rhodius). PFor 57.

"Cuartilla." *See* "Sheet of Paper."

Cuatro jinetes del Apocalipsis, Los. See *Four Horsemen of the Apocalypse, The.*

Cuban Thing, The (Gelber). DEng 744.

Čubranović, Andrija. PFor 2260.

Cueca larga, La (Parra). PFor 1133.

Cuentos andinos (López Albújar). ShF 699.

Cuentos de amor. See *Tales of Love.*

Cuernos de don Friolera, Los (Valle-Inclán). DFor 1925-1926.

Cuestión palpitante, La (Pardo Bazán). LFFor 1217-1218.

Cueva, Juan de la. DFor 2486.

Cueva de Salamanca, La. See *Cave of Salamanca, The.*

Cujo (King). LFSup 206.

Cullen, Countée. PEng 692-700.

Culler, Jonathan. LTh 425, 1801-1802, 1829.

Cultivation of Ideas, The (Gourmont). LTh 623.

Culture and Anarchy (Arnold). PEng 3482.

Culture des idées, La. See *Cultivation of Ideas, The.*

"Cultured Nation" (Kunze). PFor 806.

Culver, Kathryn. *See* **Halliday, Brett.**

Culver, Timothy J. *See* **Westlake, Donald E.**

Cumandá (Mera). LFFor 2283.

Cumberland, Richard. DEng 442-452.

Cummings, E. E. PEng 701-710.

Cunningham, E. V. M&D 437-444.

Cunningham, J. V. PSup 73-82.

Cuomo, George. ShF 2561.

Cuore. See *Heart.*

Cup, The (Tennyson). DEng 1919-1920.

"Cupid and my Campaspe played" (Lyly). PEng 1818.

"Cupid and Psyche" (Apuleius). LFFor 2016.

Cupido Conquered (Googe). PEng 3289.

Cupid's Revenge (Beaumont and Fletcher). DEng 631.

Curandero de su honra, El. See *Tiger Juan.*

Curé de Tours, Le. See *Vicar of Tours, The.*

Cure for Love (Ovid). PFor 1123-1125.

Curée, La. See *Kill, The.*

Curel, François de. DFor 447-454, 2347-2348.

Curious Savage, The (Patrick, J.). DEng 1466-1467.

Curry, Peggy Simson. ShF 2562.

Curse of Kehama, The (Southey). PEng 2682.

Curse of the Pharaohs, The (Peters, Elizabeth). M&D 1314-1315.

Curse of the Starving Class, The (Shepard). DEng 1762-1764.

Cursor Mundi. PEng 3490.

Curtin, Philip. *See* **Lowndes, Marie Belloc.**

Curtis, George William. ShF 588.

Curtis, Louisa Knapp. ShF 589.

Curtius, Ernst Robert. LTh 334-338.

Curve, The (Dorst). DSup 93.

Curzon, Daniel. ShF 2563.

"Custom House, The" (Hawthorne). LFEng 1320-1321; ShF 813.

Custom of the Country, The (Wharton, Edith). LFEng 2857-2858.

Cutting of an Agate, The (Yeats). LTh 1588.

"Cutting the Firebreak" (Everson). PEng 993.

Cuttlefish, The (Kantor). DSup 210.

Cyankali, Paragraph 218 (Wolf). DFor 2020.

Cyberiad, The (Lem). LFFor 1014.

D

Da (Leonard). DSup 230-233.
"Da-Da-Dee" (Himes). ShF 1643.
Da Silva da Silva's Cultivated Wilderness and
    Genesis of the Clowns (Harris). LFSup 149.
Da Ungaretti a D'Annunzio (Anceschi). LTh
    34.
Da Vinci's Bicycle (Davenport). ShF 1247.
Dachniki. See Summer Folk.
"Daddy" (Plath). PEng 2229, 3374.
Daddy Goriot. See Father Goriot.
"Daddy Long-Legs and the Fly, The" (Lear).
    PEng 1699.
Dadié, Bernard. DFor 2269, 2270.
"Dados eternos, Los." See "Eternal Dice, The."
Daffodil Sky, The (Bates). ShFSup 32.
Dage på en sky. See Days on a Cloud.
Dagerman, Stig. LFFor 2359.
Dagger of the Goth. (Zorrilla y Moral). DFor
    2064.
Dagger of the Mind (Fearing). M&D 595-596.
Dahl, Roald. ShF 1222-1228; ShFSup 388.
Dahl, Tor Edvin. LFFor 2364.
Dahlstierna, Gunno. PFor 2158.
Dahn, Felix. LFFor 2174.
Dahomean, The (Yerby). LFEng 2990-2992.
Dain Curse, The (Hammett). LFEng 1237.
Dainty Shapes and Hairy Apes (Kantor). DSup
    210.
Daisy Miller (James, H.). LFEng 1442-1443;
    ShF 215-216.
Daisy's Necklace and What Came of It
    (Aldrich). LFEng 50.
Daiyon kampyōki. See Inter Ice Age 4.
Dakghar. See Post Office, The.
Dal tuo al mio (Verga). DFor 1947-1948.
"Dalaim." See "My Songs."
D'ale carnavalului. See Carnival Scenes.
Daleko je sunce. See Far Away Is the Sun.
"Daleko u nama." See "Far Within Us."
D'Alembert, Jean. LTh 78.
Dalin, Olof von. DFor 2467.
Dalkey Archive, The (O'Brien, F.). LFEng
    2031.
Dalton, Priscilla. See Avallone, Michael.
Daly, Carroll John. M&D 445-449.

Daly, Elizabeth. M&D 450-454.
Daly, Maureen Patricia. ShF 551-552.
Dama boba, La. See Lady Nit-Wit, The.
Dama del alba, La. See Lady of Dawn, The
Dama duende, La. See Phantom Lady, The.
Damaged Goods (Brieux). DFor 253-254.
Damask Drum, The (Mishima). DFor 1323.
Damask Drum, The (Zeami). DFor 2040-2041.
Dame aux camélias, La. See Camille.
Dame Sirith. DEng 2256.
"Damnation of Byron, The" (Hope). PSup 191.
Damnation of Theron Ware, The (Frederic).
    LFEng 1029-1033.
"Damned Thing, The" (Bierce). ShF 969-970.
Damnée Manon, Sacée Sandra (Tremblay).
    DSup 355.
Damon and Pithias (Edward). DEng 2260-
    2261.
Dämonen, Die. See Demons, The.
Damy i huzary. See Ladies and Hussars.
Dana, Freeman. See Taylor, Phoebe Atwood.
Dana, R. H., Sr. LTh 1744.
Dana, Richard Henry, Jr. ShF 530.
Dance, Charles. See Planché, James Robinson.
"Dance for Militant Dilettantes, A" (Young).
    PEng 3212.
Dance of the Forests, A (Soyinka). DEng 1848-
    1851.
"Dance of the Happy Shades" (Munro).
    ShFSup 209.
Dance of the Machines, The (O'Brien, Edward).
    ShF 84.
Dance of the Seasons, The (Monroe). PEng
    2028.
"Dance of the Seven Deadly Sins, The"
    (Dunbar, W.). PEng 895.
Dance to the Music of Time, A (Powell).
    LFEng 2110-2112, 2114-2116, 2117-2122.
"Dancer" (Sachs). PFor 1375.
Dancer, Russell. See Pronzini, Bill.
"Dancer's Life, A" (Justice). PEng 1532.
"Dancing" (Young). PEng 3214-3215.
Dancing Bear (Crumley). M&D 433-435.
"Dancing Day to Day" (Young). PEng 3212.
Dancing Floor, The (Buchan). LFEng 334-335.

Darwin, Erasmus. PEng 3495.
Das, Manoj. ShF 651.
Das bist du (Wolf). DFor 2018-2019.
Dashiell, Samuel. *See* **Hammett, Dashiell.**
Dashing Charley. *See* **Hanshew, Thomas W.**
Dass, Petter. PFor 2159.
"Dasu Gemeine." *See* "Gemeine, Das."
D'Aubignac, Abbé. LTh 309-310.
Daudet, Alphonse. LFFor 416-427; ShF 459, 1236-1243.
Daughter of Jorio, The (D'Annunzio). DFor 460-461, 2412.
Daughter of the Legend (Stuart). LFEng 2576-2577.
Daughter of Time, The (Tey). M&D 1581.
Daughter's a Daughter, A (Christie). LFEng 536.
"Daughters of the Late Colonel, The" (Mansfield). ShF 114-115.
"Daumier-Smith's Blue Period" (Salinger). ShF 2179.
Davenant, Sir William. DEng 453-461; PEng 736-742.
Davenport, Guy. ShF 1244-1249; ShFSup 388.
DaviČo, Oskar. PFor 2256.
"David" (Birney). PEng 176-177.
David (Michelangelo). PFor 1006.
David, Jakob Julius. LFFor 2189.
David and Bethsabe (Peele). DEng 1494-1495.
David Garrick (Robertson). DEng 1606-1607.
David, It Is Getting Dark (Kops). DEng 1082-1083.
David Show, The (Gurney). DSup 165.
Davideis (Cowley, A.). PEng 595.
Davidson, Avram. *See* **Queen, Ellery.**
Davidson, Donald. LTh 1424-1425, 1753.
Davidson, Lionel. M&D 455-460.
Davie, Donald. PSup 83-92.
Davies, John. PEng 743-754.
Davies, L. P. M&D 461-465.
Davies, Rhys. ShF 255-256.
Davies, Robertson. DEng 462-474, 2441; LFEng 663-672; LFSup 402.
Daviot, Gordon. *See* **Tey, Josephine.**
Davis, Don. *See* **Halliday, Brett.**
Davis, H. L. LFEng 673-680.
Davis, Owen. DEng 475-480.
Davis, Robert Hart. *See* **Pronzini, Bill.**
Davita's Harp (Potok). LFSup 319-320.
Davor. See *Max.*

Dawkins, Cecil. ShF 2564.
"Dawn of Remembered Spring" (Stuart). ShF 2292-2293.
Dawn's Left Hand (Richardson, D.). LFEng 2241-2242.
"Day, The" (Kraus). PFor 797.
Day Book, A (Creeley). PEng 688.
Day by Day (Lowell, R.). PEng 1798-1800.
"Day Cools. . ., The" (Södergran). PSup 363-365.
Day for Anne Frank, A (Williams). PSup 389.
"Day He Himself Shall Wipe My Tears Away, The" (Ōe). ShFSup 234-236.
"Day in Late October, A" (Van Duyn). PEng 2964.
Day in the Death of Joe Egg, A (Nichols). DSup 278-289.
"Day Lady Died, The" (O'Hara). PEng 2127-2128.
Day Lewis, Cecil. PEng 755-762. *See also* **Blake, Nicholas.**
"Day of Judgment, The" (Watts). PEng 3047.
Day of the Leopards (Wimsatt). LTh 1555-1558.
Day of the Locust, The (West). LFEng 2841, 2845-2847.
"Day with the Foreign Legion, A" (Whittemore). PEng 3078.
Daybreakers, The (L'Amour). LFSup 222-223.
"Days" (Emerson). PEng 956-957.
Day's End and Other Stories (Bates). ShFSup 30.
"Days of Foreboding" (Kunitz). PSup 249-250.
Days of Hope. See *Man's Hope.*
"Days of Perky Pat, The" (Dick). ShF 1262-1263.
Days of the Turbins (Bulgakov). DFor 291-293.
Days on a Cloud (Abell). DFor 8.
Days Run Away Like Wild Horses over the Hills, The (Bukowski). PEng 361.
Dazai, Osamu. LFFor 428-435, 2278; ShFSup 91-96.
D'Azeglio, Massimo. LFFor 2231.
De amore (André le Chapelain). PFor 1836.
De arte poetica explicationes (Robortello). LTh 1664.
De Baudelaire au surréalisme. See *From Baudelaire to Surrealism.*
De civitate dei. See *City of God, The.*

De Constantia Jurisprudentis Liber Alter (Vico). LTh 1510.

De Copia. See *De Duplici Copia Verborum ac Rerum.*

De differentiis verborum (Isidore of Seville). LTh 741.

De Duplici Copia Verborum ac Rerum (Erasmus). LTh 411, 469, 471.

De imitations (Bembo). LTh 133

De inventione (Cicero). LTh 1651.

De la grammatologie. See *Of Grammatology.*

De la littérature considérée dans ses rapports avec les institutions sociales. See *Influence of Literature upon Society, The.*

De l'Allemagne. See *Germany.*

De l'idéal dans l'art. See *Ideal in Art, The.*

De l'influence des passions sur le bonheur des individus et des nations. See *Treatise on the Influence of the Passions upon the Happiness of Individuals and Nations, A.*

"De los álamos y los sauces" (Alberti). PFor 22.

De monarchia. See *On World Government.*

"De Mortuis" (Collier). ShF 1170.

De mundi universitate (Bernard Silvestris). LTh 20.

De nos oiseaux (Tzara). PFor 1550.

De Nuptiis Mercurii et Philologiae. See *On the Marriage of Mercury and Philology.*

De optimo genere dicendi. See *Orator ad M. Brutum.*

De oratore. See *On Oratory.*

De otio religioso (Petrarch). LTh 1660.

De poeta (Minturno). LTh 1669.

De poeta libri sex (Minturno). LTh 1039.

De poetica. See *Poetics.*

De rerum natura (Lucretius). PEng 3489; PFor 903-908.

De viris illustribus (Petrarch). LTh 1659.

De vulgari eloquentia (Dante). LTh 339-340, 344-345, 1459, 1462.

"Deacon's Masterpiece, The" (Holmes). PEng 1373-1374.

"Dead, The" (Brooke). PEng 306.

"Dead, The" (Joyce). LFEng 3320-3321; ShF 662-663, 1722-1723.

Dead at the Take-Off (Dent). M&D 485-486.

Dead City, The (D'Annunzio). DFor 460.

"Dead City, The" (Rossetti, C.). PEng 2417.

Dead Class, The (Kantor). DSup 210.

Dead End. See *Be Careful How You Live.*

Dead End (Kingsley). DEng 1040-1042.

Dead End Kids (Akalaitis). DSup 4-5.

"Dead End of Formalist Criticism, The" (de Man). LTh 349.

Dead Father, The (Barthelme). LFEng 172, 175-176.

"Dead Gallop" (Neruda). PFor 1075. See also *Residence on Earth.*

Dead Hand series (Sinclair, U.). LFEng 2416-2417.

Dead Letter (Pinget). DSup 304-306.

Dead Letter (Valin). M&D 1623.

"Dead Man" (Cain). ShF 1025.

"Dead Man, The" (Quiroga). ShF 695-696, 699.

Dead Man Leading (Pritchett). LFEng 2153-2156.

Dead of Spring, The. See *Empire City, The.*

Dead on Cue (Morice). M&D 1239.

"Dead Pan, The" (Browning, E. B.). PEng 329.

"Dead Past, The" (Asimov). ShF 880.

Dead Romantic (Brett). M&D 207-208.

Dead Souls (Gogol). LFFor 684-690, 2313.

Dead Stay Young, The (Seghers). LFFor 1529-1530.

"Dead World Relived, The" (Wolfe). ShF 2450-2451.

Dead Yesterdays (Ginzburg). LFSup 130.

Dead Zone, The (King). M&D 987-988.

Deadeye Dick (Vonnegut). LFEng 2731-2732.

Deadlock (Richardson, D.). LFEng 2240-2241.

Deadly Sex, The (Webb). M&D 1692.

Deagon, Ann. ShF 2565.

"Deal in Wheat, A" (Norris). ShF 234-235, 1958-1959.

Dealings with the Firm of Dombey and Son, Wholesale, Retail, and for Exportation. See *Dombey and Son.*

De Amicis, Edmondo. LFFor 2235-2236.

DeAndrea, William L. M&D 466-470.

Deane, Norman. *See* **Creasey, John.**

Dean's December, The (Bellow). LFEng 235-236.

Dear Brutus (Barrie). DEng 125-126.

Dear Michael. See *No Way.*

Dearest Enemy (Rodgers and Hart, L.). DEng 901-902.

Death and Devil (Wedekind). DFor 1980-1981.

"Death and the Compass" (Borges). M&D 164-165.

Death, Sleep & the Traveler (Hawkes). ShF 1600.

Death Stalks the Cobbled Square. See *Eye in the Darkness, The.*

Death Swap (Babson). M&D 51.

"Death the Proud Brother" (Wolfe). ShF 2452-2453.

Death Under Sail (Snow). LFEng 2458.

"Deathfeast" (Sinópoulos). PFor 1971-1972.

Death's Duell (Donne). PEng 821-822.

"Death's Horsemen" (Ady). PFor 6.

Death's Jest-Book (Beddoes). PEng 112-113.

Deathwatch (Genet). DFor 679-681, 2259-2260.

Deathwatch (Trevor). M&D 1605.

"Débat du cuer et du corps de Villon, Le." *See* "Dialogue of Villon's Heart and Body, The."

"Débat patriotique, Le." *See* "Patriotic Debate, The."

De Beauvoir, Simone. *See* **Beauvoir, Simone de.**

Debit and Credit. See *To Give and to Have.*

Debrett, Hal. *See* **Halliday, Brett.**

Debridement (Harper). PSup 163.

Debut, The (Brookner). LFSup 62-63.

Decadence. See *Artomonov Business, The.*

"Decadent Movement in Literature, The" (Symons). LTh 1412, 1736.

Decameron, The (Boccaccio). LFEng 3217-3218, 3219-3222, 3227-3228; LTh 171, 1433-1434, 1662; PEng 3243; ShF 139, 460, 679-680; ShFSup 46-49.

"Decapitated Chicken, The" (Quiroga). ShF 694, 697-699.

"Decay" (Clare). PEng 513.

"Decay of the Short Story, The" (Pugh). ShF 88.

Deceit, Desire, and the Novel (Girard). LTh 590-592.

"December Journal: 1968" (Blackburn). PEng 201.

December the Fourteenth (Merezhkovsky). LFFor 1139.

"December 27, 1966" (Sissman). PEng 2619.

"Decima" (Calderón). PFor 248-249.

"Décimas a la muerte." *See* "Decima."

Decimus Junius Juvenalis. *See* Juvenal.

Decimus Magnus Ausonius. *See* Ausonius, Decimus Magnus.

Decision (Boyle). LFEng 278-279.

Decline and Fall (Waugh). LFEng 2795-2796.

"Decline & Fall in Dingdong-Daddyland" (Algren). ShF 857.

"De Coverly Papers, The" (Addison). ShF 828.

Dedikation (Ekelöf). PFor 448-449.

Dedinac, Milan. PFor 2256.

Deep Blue Sea, The (Rattigan). DEng 1562.

Deep Sleep, The (Morris). LFEng 1910-1911.

Deephaven (Jewett). LFEng 1454-1456, 1459-1460.

Deer Park, The (Mailer). LFEng 1778-1779.

"Deer Park" (Wang Wei). PFor 1686-1687.

Defence and Illustration of the French Language, The (du Bellay). PFor 1850; LTh 409-413, 481, 1661.

Defence of Guenevere and Other Poems, The (Morris). PEng 2053-2054, 2061.

Defence of Poesie (Sidney, P.). PEng 2574-2575, 3284, 3468-3470. See also *Apology for Peotry, An.*

Defence of Poetry, A (Shelley). LTh 1332-1334, 1336-1337, 1349, 1703, 1709; PEng 2544-2545, 3479-3480.

Defence of Ryme, A (Daniel). LTh 1663-1664.

"Defending the Provinces" (Galvin). PEng 1056-1057.

"Defensa de la introducción de algunas voces peregrinas o nuevas en el idioma castellano" (Feijóo). LTh 476.

"Defensa de las mujeres" (Feijóo). LTh 476.

"Defense of Fiction" (Elliott, G. P.). ShF 75.

"Defense of Rubble Literature" (Böll). ShF 972.

Defense of the Sugar Islands, The (Cassity). PSup 64.

Deffence et illustration de la langue françoyse, La. See *Defence and Illustration of the French Language, The.*

De Filippo, Eduardo. DFor **463-470,** 2414-2415.

"Definitions" (Wright, C.). PEng 3148.

Defoe, Daniel. LFEng **681-696,** 3019-3021, 3023-3024, 3072; LFFor 1581-1582; ShF 151, 508-509.

De Forest, John William. LFEng **697-705.**

"Deformed Mistress, The" (Suckling). PEng 2779.

Deformed Transformed, The (Byron). DEng 330.

DeGrave, Philips. *See* **DeAndrea, William L.**

De Grazia, Emilio. ShF 2566.

Degré Zero de l'écriture, Le. See *Writing Degree Zero.*
Degrees (Butor). LFFor 218-219.
"Degrees of Gray in Philipsburg" (Hugo, R.). PEng 1450-1452.
Dei sepolcri. See *On Sepulchers.*
Deighton, Len. M&D 471-476.
"Déjame." See "Leave Me."
Dejection: An Ode (Coleridge, S. T.). PEng 542-543.
Dejemos hablar al viento (Onetti). LFFor 1214-1215.
Dekker, Carl. See **Collins, Michael.**
Dekker, Thomas. DEng 481-492, 2288; LFEng 3017; PEng 763-772.
Dekker His Dream (Dekker). PEng 771.
"Del dramma storio." See "On the Historical Drama."
De la Mare, Walter. LFEng 706-712; PEng 773-781; ShF 256-257, **1250-1254.**
Delaney, Shelagh. DSup 74-80.
Delany, Samuel R. LFEng 713-724; LFSup 402.
De la Roche, Mazo. ShF 637.
De La Torre, Lillian. M&D 477-482.
Delavrancea, Barbu Ştefanescu. DFor 2298-2299.
Delbanco, Nicholas. ShF 2567.
Delblanc, Sven. LFFor 2361.
"Delectable History of Sundry Adventures Passed by Dan Bartholomew of Bathe, The" (Gascoigne). PEng 1064.
Deledda, Grazia. LFFor **436-445,** 2236-2237; ShF 688.
Deleitoso, El (Rueda). DFor 1595-1597.
De León, Nephtalí. ShF 2568.
Deleuse, Gilles. LTh 850.
"Delfica" (Nerval). PFor 1088.
Delia (Daniel). PEng 727.
Delibes, Miguel. LFFor 446-454.
Delicate Balance, A (Albee). DEng 19-21.
Delicate Diet for Daintiemouthde Droonkardes, A (Gascoigne). LTh 542.
"Delicate Prey, The" (Bowles). ShF 991, 992.
"Delight in Disorder" (Herrick). PEng 1314-1315.
"Delight Song of Tsoai-talec, The" (Momaday). PEng 2019.
Delights of the Muses (Crashaw). PEng 668-669.
Delille, Jacques. PFor 1861-1862.

DeLillo, Don. LFSup 84-91.
"Délires I." *See* "Deliria I."
"Délires II: L'Alchimie du verbe." *See* "Deliria II: Verbal Alchemy."
"Deliria I" (Rimbaud). PFor 1340. See also *Season in Hell, A.*
"Deliria II: Verbal Alchemy" (Rimbaud). PFor 1339, 1340. See also *Season in Hell, A.*
"Delitto al circolo di tennis." *See* "Crime at the Tennis Club."
"Della Byron e Goethe." *See* "Byron and Goethe."
Della Porta, Giambattista. DFor 471-479, 2397.
Della Valle, Federico. PFor 2018-2019.
Delo. See *Case, The.*
Delo Artomonovykh. See *Artomonov Business, The.*
Deloney, Thomas. LFEng 3015-3016; PEng 782-791; ShF 496.
Deloria, Ella. ShF 568.
Delorme, Edmund. *See* **George, Stefan.**
Delta of Venus (Nin). ShF 1948-1949.
Delta Wedding (Welty). LFEng 2823-2824.
Deluge, The (Sienkiewicz). LFFor 1565, 1572, 1574.
"Deluge at Norderney" (Dinesen). ShF 1284-1285.
Del Valle-Inclán, Ramón Maria. *See* **Valle-Inclán, Ramón María del.**
De Man, Paul. LTh 165, **348-352,** 645-647, 828, 1033, 1035, 1152-1153, 1436, 1766, 1833.
De Marchi, Emilio. LFFor 2236.
Demesne of the Swans, The (Tsvetayeva). PFor 1535, 1536-1537.
Demetrios (Ernst). DFor 556-558.
Demian (Hesse). LFFor 828-829.
De Mille, Richard. ShF 2569.
Deming, Richard. *See* **Queen, Ellery.**
Demitrius (Metastasio). DSup 251-252.
Democracy and Esther (Linney). DSup 238.
Democracy and Poetry (Warren). LTh 1525.
Démocrite (Regnard). DFor 1541-1542.
Demoiselle à marier, La (Scribe). DFor 1678-1679.
Demolirte Literatur, Die (Kraus). PFor 793.
Demon, The (Lermontov). PFor 871-873.
"Demon Lover, The" (Bowen). ShF 987-989.
Demons, The (Doderer). LFFor 484-488; M&D 518-520.

Demosthenes. LTh 1643.

Denied a Country (Bang). LFFor 2339.

Denier du rêve. See *Coin in Nine Hands, A.*

Denison, Merrill. DEng 493-505, 2439.

Dennis, John. LTh 908, 1688.

"Dennis O'Shaughnessy Going to Maynooth" (Carleton). ShF 1060-1061.

"Dennitsa." *See* "Morning Star."

Dent, Lester. M&D 483-488.

Dentinger, Stephen. See **Hoch, Edward D.**

'dentity Crisis (Durang). DSup 102.

D'entre les morts. See *Living and the Dead, The.*

Denuestos del agua y del vino. See *Razón de amor.*

Deobe (Ćosić). LFFor 387-388.

"Deodand, The" (Hecht). PEng 1281.

"Departmental" (Frost). ShF 106.

"Departure" (Benn). PFor 174-176.

Departures (Justice). PEng 1532.

Dépeupleur, Le. See *Lost Ones, The.*

De Pre, Jean-Anne. *See* **Avallone, Michael.**

"Depressed by a Book of Bad Poetry, I Walk Toward an Unused Pasture and Invite the Insects to Join Me" (Wright, J.). PEng 3159.

"Depression" (Annensky). PFor 42.

Deptford trilogy. See *Fifth Business, Manticore, The,* and *World of Wonders.*

Deputy, The (Hochhuth). DFor 917-921, 2380.

De Quincey, Thomas. LTh 1705, 1709.

Derleth, August. M&D 489-496; ShF 746, **1255-1259,** 1827.

Dernier de l'empire, Le. See *Last of the Empire, The.*

Dernière Aimée, La (Njoya). DFor 2271.

"Dernière Classe, La." *See* "Last Class, The."

Derniers vers (Laforgue). PFor 827-828.

De Robertis, Giuseppe. PFor 2038.

De Roberto, Federico. LFFor 2223.

Derozio, Henry Louis Vivian. PFor 1994.

Derrida, Jacques. LTh 348, 353-361, 417, 503, 506, 527, 529, 645-647, 824-825, 828, 850, 890, 1033, 1035, 1070, 1152, 1436, 1628-1629, 1764-1766, 1802, 1820-1821, 1832.

Dersonne, Jacques. *See* **Simenon, Georges.**

Déry, Tibor. LFFor 2073.

Derzhavin, Gavrila. LTh 1694; PFor 2135.

Des bleus à l'âme. See *Scars on the Soul.*

Des Choses cachées depuis la fondation du monde. See *Things Hidden Since the Foundation of the World.*

Des fleurs de bonne volonté (Laforgue). PFor 826-827.

Desa aquests llibres al calaix de baix (Foix). PFor 489.

Desai, Anita. LFEng 725-732; LFFor 2223; LFSup 402.

De Sanctis, Francesco. LTh 362-368, 630-631.

Desatino, El (Gambaro). DSup 151.

"Descendant of El Cid, A" (Pardo Bazán). ShF 2048.

Descending Figure (Glück). PSup 136-137.

"Descent Through the Carpet, A" (Atwood). PEng 65.

Deschamps brothers. LTh 1707.

"Describing Poetic Structures" (Riffaterre). LTh 889.

"Description of a City Shower, A" (Swift). PEng 2086.

"Description of a Salamander, The" (Swift). PEng 2805-2806.

"Description of the Morning, A" (Swift). PEng 2806.

Desdén con el desdén, El. See *Love's Victory.*

"Desdichado, El" (Nerval). PFor 1087.

Desengaño en un sueño, El (Saavedra). DFor 1618-1619.

Désert de l'amour, Le. See *Desert of Love, The.*

Desert of Love, The (Mauriac). LFFor 1127.

"Deserted Church, The" (Coleridge, H.). PEng 530.

Deserted Village, The (Goldsmith). PEng 1109-1110, 3332.

Déserteur, Le. See *Point of Honor, The.*

Deserto dei Tartari, Il. See *Tartar Steppe, The.*

Desheredada, La. See *Disinherited Lady, The.*

"Design" (Frost). PEng 1045-1046.

"Design for Departure" (Algren). ShF 856.

Design for Living (Coward). DEng 429-430.

"Desire and the Black Masseur" (Williams, T.). 2437, 2438.

Desire in Language (Kristeva). LTh 833.

Desire to Kill (Clarke). M&D 355-356.

Desire Under the Elms (O'Neill). DEng 1410-1414, 2401.

"Désirée's Baby" (Chopin). ShF 1133-1134.

Desnos, Robert. PFor 1886.

"Desnudo." *See* "Nude."

Dexter, Colin. M&D 497-501.
Dey, Frederic M. Van Rensselaer. ShF 759. *See also* Carter, Nick.
Dhalgren (Delany). LFEng 720-722.
Dharma Bums, The (Kerouac). LFEng 1523-1524.
"Dhidhahi" (Pentzíkis). PFor 1188. See also *Ikones.*
"Dhoya" (Yeats). ShF 2470-2471.
Di Giacomo, Salvatore. PFor 2034; ShF 687, 688.
Diable boiteux, Le. See *Devil upon Two Sticks, The.*
Diable et le bon Dieu, Le. See *Devil and the Good Lord, The.*
Diaghilev, Sergei. DFor 415-416.
Dial. ShF 587.
Dialectic of Enlightenment (Adorno). LTh 17.
Dialogi (Lem). LFFor 1014.
Dialogic Imagination, The (Bakhtin). LTh 84-85, 87-88.
Diálogo del nascimiento (Torres Naharro). DFor 1873-1874.
Dialogo della lingue (Speroni). LTh 1661.
"Dialogue Between Mirth and Melancholy, A" (Newcastle). PEng 2095.
"Dialogue of Birds, A" (Newcastle). PEng 2094-2095.
Dialogue of Proverbs (Heywood, J.). PEng 1331-1334.
"Dialogue of Villon's Heart and Body, The" (Villon). PFor 1660.
"Dialogue on Poetry" (Schlegel, F.). LTh 1310, 1708.
Dialogues (Gregory the Great). ShF 427-428.
Dialogues of the Gods (Lucian). LTh 1644.
Dialogus, Cui Titulus Ciceronianus, Sive, de Optimo Dicendi Genere. See *Ciceronian, The.*
Diamant des Geisterkönigs, Der (Raimund). DFor 1529-1530.
"Diamond Cut Diamond" (Thackeray). ShF 2314-2315.
"Diamond Lens, The" (O'Brien, F-J.). ShF 770, 1978-1979.
Diana (Constable). PEng 562-564.
Diana of the Crossways (Meredith). LFEng 1870-1871.
Diario (Pavese). ShF 2065.
Diario de un poeta recién casado (Jiménez). PFor 749, 752.

Diary, A (Allingham). PEng 42.
Diary (Taylor). PEng 2843.
Diary of a Country Priest (Bernanos). LFFor 149-150.
Diary of a Mad Old Man (Tanizaki). LFFor 1715; ShFSup 318.
"Diary of a Madman" (Gogol). ShF 1496-1497.
"Diary of a Madman, The" (Lu Hsün). LFFor 2106; ShFSup 171-172.
Diary of a Rapist, The (Connell). LFEng 578-579.
Diary of a Scoundrel, The. See *Scoundrel, The.*
Diary of a Writer, The (Dostoevski). LTh 397.
Diary of Anaïs Nin, The (Nin). LFEng 1986, 1988.
"Diary Page 1980" (Kunze). PFor 808.
(Diblos) Notebook, The (Merrill). PEng 1958.
Dice Thrown Never Will Annul Chance (Mallarmé). LTh 979; PFor 928-929, 930-931.
"Dicen que no hablan las plantas." *See* "They Say That Plants Do Not Speak."
Dicenta y Benedicto, Joaquín. DFor 2501.
Dicerie sacre (Marino). PFor 975.
"Dichter, Der." *See* "Poet, The."
"Dichter und diese Zeit, Der." *See* "Poet and This Time, The."
Dichter und ihre Gesellen (Eichendorff). LTh 435.
Dichtoefeningen (Gezelle). PFor 554-555.
Dick, Philip K. LFSup 92-99; ShF 1260-1266; ShFSup 388.
Dick Gibson, Show, The (Elkin). LFEng 889-890.
Dickens, Charles. DEng 311; LFEng 555-556, 743-756, 1099-1100, 3032-3033, 3077-3078, 3153; M&D 502-507; ShF 464-465, 585, 734, 751, 1267-1273.
Dickens, John. LFEng 744.
Dickey, James. PEng 792-801; PSup 404.
Dickinson, Emily. PEng 802-813, 3371-3372, 3387-3388.
Dickinson, Peter. M&D 508-514.
Dickson, Carr. *See* Carr, John Dickson.
Dickson, Carter. *See* Carr, John Dickson.
"Dictatorship of the Proletariat" (Baraka). PEng 90-91.
"Diction" (Creeley). PEng 686-687.
Dictionary of the English Language, A (Johnson, S.). LTh 777; PEng 1498.

Dictys of Crete. LFFor 2014.

"Did You See the Coronation?" (Gallico). ShF 1443.

Diderot, Denis. DEng 2181-2182, 2333-2334; DFor 147-148, 2341-2342; **DSup 81-89;** LFFor **455-467,** 2120; LTh 78, **369-375,** 624, 708, 1688; PFor 1859; **ShF 1274-1280.**

Didion, Joan. LFEng **757-767;** LFSup 403.

Dido and Aeneas (Purcell). DEng 2457.

Dido Forsaken (Metastasio). DSup 250-251.

Dido, Queen of Carthage (Marlowe and Nashe). DEng 1249, 1364.

Didone abbandonata. See *Dido Forsaken.*

Diefendorf, David. ShF 2570.

Diehard, The (Potts). M&D 1350-1351.

Dieu (Hugo). PFor 738.

Dieu des corps, Le. See *Body's Rapture, The.*

Dieux ont soif, Les. See *Gods Are Athirst, The.*

Dieux s'en vont, D'Annunzio reste, Les (Marinetti). LTh 995.

Diez, Friedrich. LTh 335.

"Difference, The" (Glasgow). ShF 1490-1491, 1492.

Difference and Other Poems, The (Monroe). PEng 2028.

"Differences" (Kunert). PFor 1820.

Difficult Hour, I-III, The (Lagerkvist). DFor 1153.

Difficult Man, The (Hofmannsthal). DFor 938-941.

"Difficulties of a Revisionist" (Middleton, C.). PEng 1987.

Diggelmann, Walter Matthias. LFFor 2209.

"Digging" (Hall). PEng 1201.

"Digging for China" (Wilbur). PEng 3097.

"Digression" (Mickiewicz). PFor 1021-1022. See also *Forefathers' Eve.*

Dikē phōnēentōn. See *Consonants at Law, The.*

Diktonius, Elmer. PFor 2181.

"Dilemma" (Beer). PEng 117.

Dilemma of Human Identity, The (Lichtenstein). LTh 687.

Dillon, Millicent. ShF 2571.

Dilthey, Wilhelm. LTh **376-381,** 528, 530, 640, 642, 1809.

Dimanche. See *Sunday.*

Dimanche de la vie, Le. See *Sunday of Life, The.*

"Dimanches" (XXX) (Laforgue). PFor 826.

Dimitri Roudine. See *Rudin.*

Dimitri the Impostor (Sumarokov). DFor 1786-1787.

Dinner with the Family (Anouilh). DFor 77-78.

Dinesen, Isak. LFFor 2365; **ShF 1281-1286.**

"Ding-dong" (Beckett). ShF 939.

Dining Room, The (Gurney). DSup 167-168.

Dinner at Eight (Kaufman and Ferber). DEng 592-593.

Dinner at the Homesick Restaurant (Tyler). LFEng 2684-2685.

Dinner for Promotion (Henshaw). DEng 930-931.

Dio li fa e poi li accoppa (Fo). DSup 114.

Dione (Gay). DEng 732.

Dionysius of Halicarnassus. LTh **382-385,** 904-905, 1143, 1192, 1642-1643.

Dionysus in '69. DEng 2484.

"Dios bendiga todo, nena." *See* "God Blesses Everything, Child."

Dios deseado y deseante (Jiménez). PFor 754.

"Diotima" (Hölderlin). PFor 683.

Diphilus. DFor 2133.

Dipsychus (Clough). PEng 520.

"Dirge, A" (D'Urfey). PEng 913.

"Dirge, The" (King). PEng 1585-1586.

Dirty Hands (Sartre). DFor 1642-1643, 1649-1650.

Disappearance of God, The (Miller). LTh 1034-1035.

"Disappearance of Pratima Jena, The" (Mahaptra). ShF 654.

"Disappointment, The" (Behn). PEng 128.

Discarded Image, The (Lewis). LTh 893, 896.

Disch, Thomas M. ShF 780, **1287-1290;** ShFSup 388.

"Discipline" (Herbert). PEng 1301-1302.

"Discord in Childhood" (Lawrence, D. H.). PEng 1682.

Discorsi dell'arte poetica (Tasso). PFor 2015.

Discorso intorno al comporre dei romanzi. See *On Romances.*

Discorso intorno al comporre delle commedie e delle tragedie (Giraldi Cinthio). LTh 586.

Discorso o dialogo intorno a la nostra lingua (Machiavelli). LTh 1459, 1463.

Discos visuales (Paz). PFor 1174.

Discours (Corneille). LTh 309, 312, 1687.

Discours du grand sommeil (Cocteau). PFor 371.

Discours sur les sciences et les arts. See *Discourse on the Arts and Sciences, A.*

Discours sur Shakespeare et sur Monsieur de Voltaire (Baretti). LTh 90-91.

Discourse der Mahlern, Die (Bodmer). LTh 175.

Discourse of the Adventures Passed by Master F. J., The (Gascoigne). LTh 543.

"Discourse on Lyric Poetry, A" (Young). LTh 1597.

Discourse on the Arts and Sciences, A (Rousseau). LTh 1240-1241.

Discourse Which Carried the Praemium at the Academy of Dijon, The. See *Discourse on the Arts and Sciences, A.*

Discourses (Reynolds). LTh 1214, 1216-1217, 1219.

Discoveries (Jonson). LTh 779-782.

"Discovery" (Södergran). PSup 363-364.

"Discovery of the Pacific" (Gunn). PEng 1176.

Discrete Series (Oppen). PEng 2138.

Discussions of the Short Story (Summers). ShF 91.

"Disdaine returned" (Carew). PEng 434.

"Disent les imbéciles." See "Fools Say."

"Disillusionment of Ten O'Clock" (Stevens). PEng 2746.

Disinherited Lady, The (Pérez Galdós). LFFor 1276-1280.

D'Isly, Georges. See **Simenon, Georges.**

"Displaced Orpheus, A" (Untermeyer). PEng 2952-2953.

"Displaced Person, The" (O'Connor, Flannery). LFEng 3270-3272; ShF 798.

Dispossessed, The (Le Guin). LFEng 1636.

Disputation Between a Hee-Connycatcher and a Shee-Connycatcher, A (Greene, R.). ShF 1553.

Disraeli, Benjamin. LFEng 3078-3079.

"Dissentient Voice" (Davie). PSup 88.

Dissertations Moral and Critical (Beattie, J.). ShF 470.

"Distance" (Creeley). PEng 684.

"Distance" (Paley). ShF 2042-2043.

"Distant Episode, A" (Bowles). ShF 992.

Distant Horns of Summer, The (Bates). LFEng 184-185.

Distant Music, The (Davis). LFEng 679-680.

"Distant Orgasm, The" (Tate, J.). PEng 2837-2838.

Distant Relations (Fuentes). LFFor 596.

"Distant Steps, The" (Vallejo). PFor 1588, 1589.

Distant Trumpet, A (Horgan). LFSup 160-161.

Distortions (Beattie). ShFSup 36.

"Distracted Preacher, The" (Hardy). ShF 1582-1583.

Distrait, Le (Regnard). DFor 1540-1541.

Distressed Family, The (Mercier). DFor 1315-1316.

"District Doctor, The" (Turgenev). ShF 2354-2355.

"District in the Rear, A" (Pasternak). ShF 2062.

"Dithyramb to Women" (Illyés). PFor 744.

"Ditirambus a nőkhöz." See "Dithyramb to Women."

Ditte Menneskenbaren (Nexø).

"Dittié de Jeanne d'Arc, Le" (Christine de Pisan). PFor 353-354.

Divan (Hafiz). PSup 149, 152-157.

Divan-e Shams-e Tabriz (Rumi). PSup 340-341.

"Diver, The" (Hayden). PEng 1252-1253.

"Diver, The" (Schiller). PFor 1409.

"Diverting History of John Gilpin, The" (Cowper). PEng 616-617, 3330.

"Divided Heart, The" (Etherege). PEng 978-979.

Divided Heaven (Wolf). LFFor 1934-1935.

Dividend on Death (Halliday). M&D 811-813.

Divina commedia, La. See *Divine Comedy, The.*

Divinas palabras. See *Divine Words.*

Divine Comedy, The (Dante). LTh 66, 340-342, 345-346; PEng 498, 3243; PFor 397-416, 1467, 2006-2007; ShF 1230-1235.

Divine Fancies (Quarles). PEng 2298.

"Divine Mistress, A" (Carew). PEng 2779.

Divine Narcissus, The (Cruz). DFor 444; PFor 376, 381.

Divine Tragedy, The (Longfellow). PEng 1752-1753.

Divine Words (Valle-Inclán). DFor 1922-1924, 2503.

Diviners, The (Laurence). LFEng 1570-1571, 1574-1576.

"Diving into the Wreck" (Rich). PEng 2368-2369.

"Divining Rod" (Eichendorff). PFor 439.

Divinity School Address (Emerson). LTh 455; PEng 954.

Divino Narciso, El. See *Divine Narcissus, The.*

"Division of Parts, The" (Sexton). PEng 2522.

"Divorce" (Lu Hsün). ShFSup 181-183.

"Divorce of Lovers, A" (Sarton). PEng 2461.
Dīwān över fursten av Emgión (Ekelöf). PFor
452-453.
Dixon, Richard Watson. PEng 814-820.
Djinn (Robbe-Grillet). LFFor 1421.
"Djinns, The" (Hugo). PFor 733. See also
Orientales, Les.
Djulabije (Vraz). PFor 2262.
Djurdjević, Ignjat. PFor 2261.
Dnevnik pisatelya. See *Diary of a Writer, The.*
Dni Turbinykh. See *Days of the Turbins.*
Do Androids Dream of Electric Sheep? (Dick).
LFSup 97.
"Do ksiedza Ch." (Miłosz). PFor 1032.
Do, Lord, Remember Me (Garrett). LFEng
1093-1094.
"Do Robinsona Jeffersa." *See* "To Robinson
Jeffers."
Dobell Folio (Traherne). PEng 2927-2928.
Döblin, Alfred. LFFor 468-480, 2194, 2201.
Dobrolyubov, Nikolay. LTh 286-287, 289,
386-391, 395, 1104, 1106, 1108-1109,
1447, 1502.
Dobrovský, Josef. PFor 1799.
"Dobrozhelatel" (Zoshchenko). ShFSup 380.
Docherty, James L. *See* **Chase, James Hadley.**
Dock Brief, The (Mortimer). DEng 1354-1355.
Docker noir, Le (Sembène). LFFor 1536-
1538.
"Dockery and Son" (Larkin). PEng 1674.
Doctor Cobb's Game (Cassill). LFEng 470.
Doctor Copernicus (Banville). LFSup 46-47.
Doctor Faustus (Mann). LFFor 1083-1084.
Doctor Faustus (Marlowe). DEng 1260-1263,
2273.
Dr. Jekyll and Mr. Hyde (Stevenson). ShF
478, 479, 480.
Dr. Knock (Romains). DFor 1552-1553.
Doctor Zhivago (Pasternak). LFFor 1234-1238,
2327; PFor 1160-1161.
"Doctor's Son, The" (O'Hara). ShF 2018-
2019.
Doctorow, E. L. LFEng 768-780; LFSup 403.
Dodekalogos tou gypthou, Ho. See *Twelve
Words of the Gypsy, The.*
Dödens arlekin (Bergman). DFor 186.
**Doderer, Heimito von. LFFor 481-488; M&D
515-521.**
Dødes rige, Die (Pontoppidan). LFFor 2340.
Dodgson, Charles Lutwidge. *See* **Carroll,
Lewis.**

Dodsworth (Lewis, S.). LFEng 1680.
"Dodu" (Narayan). ShFSup 227.
Dodu and Other Stories (Narayan). ShFSup
227.
"Dodwells Road" (Wilbur). PEng 3095.
"Dog" (Ferlinghetti). PEng 1008-1009.
Dog Beneath the Skin, The (Auden and
Isherwood). DEng 53-56.
Dog in the Manger, The. See *Gardener's Dog,
The.*
"Dog Named Ego, the Snowflakes as Kisses,
A" (Schwartz). PEng 2492.
"Dog Sleeping on My Feet, A" (Dickey, J.).
PEng 796.
Dog Years (Grass). LFFor 736.
"Doge and Dogaressa" (Hoffmann). ShF 1648.
"Dogood Papers, The" (Franklin). ShF 1409.
"Doklad o zhurnalakh *Zvezda* i *Leningrad.*" *See*
"On the Journals *Zvezda* and *Leningrad.*"
Doktor Faustus. See *Doctor Faustus.*
"Doktor Murkes gesammeltes Schweiger." *See*
"Murke's Collected Silences."
Doktor Zhivago. See *Doctor Zhivago.*
Doll, The. See *Summer of the Seventeenth Doll,
The.*
Doll Trilogy, The (Lawler). DEng 1116.
Doll's House, A (Ibsen). DFor 981-982.
Dolore, Il (Ungaretti). PFor 1569-1570.
"Dolores" (Swinburne). PEng 2818-2819.
"Dolphin, The" (Lowell, R.). PEng 1797-1798.
Dolphin, The (Lowell, R.). PEng 1797-1798.
"Dolt, The" (Barthelme). ShFSup 23.
Dőlt vitorla (Illyés). PFor 743-744.
Dom Casmurro (Machado de Assis). LFFor
1045-1046.
Dom Juan. See *Don Juan.*
Dombey and Son (Dickens, C.). LFEng 751-
752, 3078.
Domecq, H. Bustos. *See* **Borges, Jorge Luis.**
"Domesday Book" (Lowell, R.). PEng 1799.
Domesday Book (Masters). PEng 1933-1934.
"Domestic Dilemma, A" (McCullers). ShF
1842-1843.
Dominic, R. B. *See* **Lathen, Emma.**
Don Alvaro (Saavedra). DFor 1612, 1617-
1618, 2498.
Don Braulio (Valera). LFFor 1824.
Don Carlos, Infante of Spain (Schiller). DFor
1658-1659.
Don Carlos, Prince of Spain (Otway). DEng
1443-1445, 1450.

Don Flows Home to the Sea, The. See *Silent Don, The.*

Don Gil de las calzas verdes (Tirso). DFor 1846.

Don Goyo (Aguilera Malta). LFSup 10-11.

Don Juan (Byron). PEng 411-414.

Don Juan (Molière). DFor 1336-1337.

Don Juan de Marana (Dumas, *père*). DFor 491.

Don Juan Tenorio (Zorrilla y Moral). DFor 2064-2065.

Don Juan und Faustus (Grabbe). DFor 803-804.

"Don Juan's Last Illusion" (Pardo Bazán). ShF 2049.

Don Quixote de la Mancha (Cervantes). DFor 361-362; LFEng 3223-3224, 3225-3226, 3327; LFFor 327-332, 420-421, 2024-2026, 2373, 2378-2380; PEng 388, 3313; ShF 144-145.

Don Sebastian, King of Portugal (Dryden). DEng 522-525.

Doña Luz (Valera). LFFor 1824-1826.

Doña Perfecta (Pérez Galdós). LFFor 1274-1276.

Doña Rosita the Spinster (García Lorca). DFor 664-665.

Donadieu (Hochwälder). DFor 929-930.

Donatus. LTh 1649-1650.

Donde habite el olvido (Cernuda). PFor 321.

"Dong with a Luminous Nose, The" (Lear). PEng 1700.

Donleavy, J. P. LFEng 781-788; LFSup 403.

"Donna me prega." *See* "My Lady Asks Me."

Donnadieu, Marguerite. *See* **Duras, Marguerite.**

Donne, John. LTh 783; **PEng 821-838,** 3298-3299, 3300, 3491-3492.

Donne di Messina, Le. See *Women of Messina.*

Donnelly trilogy (Reaney). DEng 1576, 1577.

Donnerstag (Hochwälder). DFor 931.

Donogoo (Romains). DFor 1553-1555.

Donoso, José. LFFor 489-502, 2297-2298.

Don's Party (Williamson). DEng 2093.

Don't Cry, Scream (Madhubuti). PEng 1894-1895.

Don't Lie to Me (Westlake). M&D 1703.

"Don't Look Now" (du Maurier). M&D 555.

Don't Monkey with Murder (Ferrars). M&D 600.

Don't Stop the Carnival (Wouk). LFEng 2970-2971.

Doolittle, Hilda. *See* **H. D.**

Doomsters, The (Macdonald). LFSup 273-274.

"Door, The" (Coover). ShF 1192-1193.

"Door, The" (Creeley). PEng 679.

"Door, A" (Merwin). PEng 1982.

Door into the Dark (Heaney). PEng 1264, 1268-1269.

"Doorbell, The" (Nabokov). ShFSup 218-219.

Doors of Stone, The (Prince). PSup 316.

"Doppioni." *See* "Doubles."

Dorfman, Ariel. ShF 693.

"Doris" (Congreve). PEng 555.

Dorn, Ed. PEng 839-846.

Dorothée (Camus, J. P.). ShF 498.

"Dorothy Q." (Holmes). PEng 1372-1373.

Dorsage, Jean. *See* **Simenon, Georges.**

Dorsan, Luc. *See* **Simenon, Georges.**

"Dorset" (Davie). PSup 90.

Dorst, Tankred. DSup 90-97.

Dorval (Diderot). DSup 84-85.

Dos caras del patroncito, Las (Valdez). DSup 370.

Doskonała próżnia. See *Perfect Vacuum, A.*

Dos Passos, John. LFEng 789-799; LTh 1273.

Dostoevski, Fyodor. LFEng 3147-3148; LFFor 503-517, 2314-2315, 2316-2317; LTh 120, 288, 290, 389, **392-400,** 947, 985, 1478; **M&D 522-528;** ShF 204, **1291-1296.**

Dostoevskii i Gogol (k teorii parodii) (Tynyanov). LTh 1477.

Dosutoefusukii no seikatsu (Kobayashi). LTh 821.

"Double, The" (Annensky). PFor 43.

"Double, The" (de la Mare). PEng 776.

Double, The (Dostoevski). LFEng 3296-3298; ShF 477.

"Double Axe, The" (Jeffers). PEng 1493-1494.

Double-Barrel (Freeling). M&D 663.

Double Barrelled Detective Story, A (Twain). M&D 1611-1612.

Double Dealer, The (Congreve). DEng 404-406.

Double Double (Yglesias). LFEng 3000-3001.

Double Honeymoon (Connell). LFEng 581-582; ShF 1181.

Double Image, The (MacInnes). M&D 1169.

"Double Image, The" (Sexton). PEng 2522.

Double Inconstance, La. See *Double Infidelity.*

Double Indemnity (Cain). M&D 258.

Double Infidelity (Marivaux). DFor 1264-1265.

Double Méprise, La. See *Slight Misunderstanding, A*.

Double PP, The (Dekker). PEng 771.

"Doubles" (Moravia). ShFSup 198.

Douglas, Gavin. PEng 3280.

Douglas, John. *See* **Collins, Michael.**

"Doux pays" (González Martínez). PFor 611-612.

"Dove in the Head, A" (Popa). PFor 1273.

"Dove of the East, A" (Helprin). ShFSup 116-117.

Dove of the East and Other Stories, A (Helprin). ShFSup 114-116.

"Dover Beach" (Arnold). PEng 54-55, 3229-3230.

Dover One (Porter). M&D 1340.

Dover Three (Porter). M&D 1340.

Dowd, T. B. *See* **Henry, O.**

Down and Out. See *Lower Depths, The*.

"Down at the Dinghy" (Salinger). ShF 2180.

Down Stream (Huysmans). LFFor 862-863.

Down the Long Hills (L'Amour). LFSup 225.

"Down Then By Derry" (Kiely). ShF 1747.

Down There. See *Là-Bas*.

"Downlook, The" (Lowell, R.). PEng 1800.

Downstream (Kinsella). PSup 233-234.

Dowson, Ernest. ShF 517.

Doyle, Arthur Conan. LFEng 800-813, 3079-3080; **M&D 529-537;** ShF 728, 751-752.

D'Oyly Carte, Richard. *See* Carte, Richard D'Oyly.

Dożywocie. See *Life Annuity, The*.

Dra-Dra, Der (Biermann). PFor 186.

Drabble, Margaret. LFEng 814-827.

Drachmann, Holger. LFFor 2338, 2339; PFor 2169.

Dracula (Stoker). LFEng 3129-3130, 3204; ShF 477, 736.

Drafts and Fragments of Cantos CX-CXVII (Pound). PEng 2274.

Dragon, The (Shvarts). DFor 1700-1702.

Dragon and the Unicorn, The (Rexroth). PEng 2353.

Dragon Can't Dance, The (Lovelace). LFEng 1702-1703.

Dragon Seed (Buck). LFEng 344-345.

Dragontea, La (Vega). PFor 1601.

Dragún, Osvaldo. DFor 2443-2444.

Drahtharfe, Die. See *Wire Harp, The*.

Drake, Albert Dee. ShF 2572.

Drake, Lisa. *See* **Hoch, Edward D.**

Drakon. See *Dragon, The*.

Dram of Poison, A (Armstrong). M&D 37.

Dram-Shop, The. See *Assommoir, L'*.

"Drama and the Revolutionary Ideal" (Soyinka). LTh 1375.

Drama in Muslin, A (Moore, G.). LFEng 1899-1900.

Drama nuevo, Un. See *New Drama, A*.

Drama of Death, The (Gautier). PFor 535-536.

"Drama of Exile, A" (Browning, E. B.). PEng 328, 332.

Drame des constructeurs, Le (Michaux). PFor 995.

Draper, Eliza. LFEng 2533.

Draussen vor der Tür. See *Man Outside, The*.

Drawers of Nets, The (Aeschylus). DFor 2119-2120.

"Drawing Lesson, The" (Orr). PEng 2154.

Drayton, Michael. PEng 847-856.

Dreadful Summit (Ellin). M&D 575.

"Dream, The" (Creeley). PEng 683.

"Dream at Daybreak" (Li Ch'ing-chao). PFor 883.

"Dream Boogie" (Hughes, L.). PEng 3400.

"Dream (1863), The" (Hayden). PEng 1250.

Dream Is Life, A (Grillparzer). DFor 2372.

Dream Journey, A (Hanley). LFEng 1251.

Dream Life of Balso Snell, The (West). LFEng 2843.

"Dream of a Ridiculous Man, The" (Dostoevski). ShF 1294-1295.

"Dream of Armageddon, A" (Wells). ShF 727.

Dream of Gerontius, The (Newman). PEng 2104-2105.

Dream of Governors, A (Simpson). PEng 2603.

Dream of Peter Mann, The (Kops). DEng 1081-1082.

Dream of Red Mansions, A. See *Dream of the Red Chamber*.

Dream of the Golden Mountains, The (Cowley). LTh 318.

Dream of the Red Chamber (Ts'ao Hsüeh-ch'in). LFFor 1749-1752, 1756-1767, 2091, 2099-2102.

Dream of the Rood, The (Unknown). PEng 711-712.

Dream on Monkey Mountain (Walcott, D. A.). DEng 2000-2002.

"Dream on the Eve of Success" (Hugo, R.). PEng 1457.

"Dream Pedlary" (Beddoes). PEng 112.

Dream Physician, The (Martyn). DEng 1281-1282.

Dream Play, A (Strindberg). DFor 1752-1754, 2476.

Dream Songs, The (Berryman). PEng 164, 3368, 3373-3374.

Dream Walker, The (Armstrong). M&D 39.

Dreambook for Our Time, A (Konwicki). LFFor 946-947.

Dreaming Jewels, The (Sturgeon). LFEng 2581-2584.

Dreaming of the Bones, The (Yeats). DEng 2120.

"Dreams" (Chekhov). ShF 1128-1129.

Dreams (Robertson). DEng 1607.

"Dreams Old and Nascent" (Lawrence, D. H.). PEng 1682.

"Dreamscape" (Booth). PEng 244-245.

"Dreamy" (Sonnett). ShF 709.

Dred (Stowe). LFEng 2560-2561.

Drei gerechten kammacher, Die. See *Three Righteous Combmakers, The.*

Drei Sprünge des Wang-lun, Die (Döblin). LFFor 474-476.

Dreigroschenoper. See *Threepenny Opera, The.*

Dreiser, Theodore. LFEng 828-839, 3049, 3050-3051; LTh 1454; ShF 539-540, 1306-1312.

Dressed Like an Egg (Akalaitis). DSup 2-3.

Dresser, Davis. *See* **Halliday, Brett.**

Dressing of Diamond, A (Freeling). M&D 663.

"Dressmaker's Dummy, The" (Robbe-Grillet). ShF 2154-2155.

Driemaal XXXIII kleengedichtjes (Gezelle). PFor 557-558.

"Drifting" (Quiroga). ShF 696, 697-698, 699.

"Drifting Down Lost Creek (Murfree). ShF 226-227.

"Drinking Alone in the Moonlight" (Li Po). PFor 891.

"Drinking from a Helmet" (Dickey, J.). PEng 797.

Drinkwater, John. DEng 506-513.

Dritte Buch über Achim, Das. See *Third Book About Achim, The.*

Dritte Walpurgisnacht, Die (Kraus). PFor 794-795.

Driver's Seat, The (Spark). LFEng 2482-2484.

"Driving Cross-country" (Kennedy). PEng 1573.

"Driving Through Sawmill Towns" (Murray). PSup 290.

"Driving West" (MacBeth). PEng 1835.

Droll Stories (Balzac). ShF 920.

Dronning går igen. See *Queen on Tour, The.*

Droome of Doomes Day, The (Gascoigne). LTh 542.

Droste-Hülshoff, Annette von. M&D 538-542; PFor 1919.

Drottningens juvelsmycke (Almqvist). LFFor 2337.

Drought, The (Ballard). LFEng 149.

Drought, James W. ShF 2573.

"Drought and Zazen" (Miyazawa). PSup 285.

"Drover's Wife, The" (Lawson). ShFSup 139.

Drowned World, The (Ballard). LFEng 148-149.

Drugie danie. See *Repeat Performance.*

"Drum, The" (Sitwell). PEng 2628-2629.

Drum-Taps (Whitman). PEng 3071-3072.

Drummer, The (Addison). DEng 6-7.

"Drummer of All the World, The" (Laurence). ShF 1776.

Drummond, John. *See* **Chance, John Newton.**

Drummond de Andrade, Carlos. PSup 93-102.

Drummond of Hawthornden, William. PEng 857-868.

Drums and Colours (Walcott, D. A.). DEng 2453.

Drums of Father Ned, The (O'Casey). DEng 1391-1392.

Drunk Man Looks at the Thistle, A (MacDiarmid). PSup 260-263.

"Drunkard, The" (O'Connor, Frank). ShF 672, 1992-1993.

"Drunkard's Dream, A" (Le Fanu). ShF 735.

"Drunken Boat, The" (Rimbaud). PFor 1337-1338.

Druyh sešit směšných lásek. See *Laughable Loves.*

Dry Heart, The (Ginzburg). LFSup 129-130.

Dry Season, The (Cowley, M.). PEng 605-607.

Dry Sun, Dry Wind (Wagoner). PEng 2989.

Dryden, John. DEng 514-525, 2175-2176; LTh 277, 312, 401-408, 772, 775, 779, 783, 908, 1140, 1530, 1688; PEng 127, 869-880, 2775-2776, 3298, 3299, 3315-3317, 3318, 3470-3472.

Drypoints of the Hasidim (Prince). PSup 317.
Držić, Džore. PFor 2260.
Držić, Marin. DFor 2292.
Du contrat social. See *Treatise on the Social Contract, A.*
Du côté de chez Swann. See *Swann's Way.*
Du mouvement et de l'immobilité de Douve. See *On the Motion and Immobility of Douve.*
Du sang pour un trône. DFor 2269, 2270.
Dubbi grammaticali (Trissino). LTh 1462.
Du Bellay, Joachim. LTh 409-413, 481; PFor 1850, 1851, 2115.
Dubie, Norman. PSup 103-108.
Dublin Magazine. ShF 675.
"Dublin Mystery, The" (Orczy). M&D 1283.
Dubliners (Joyce). LFEng 1496; ShF 242, 661-663, 1719, 1722-1723.
Dubois, Rochelle H. ShF 2574.
Du Bouchet, André. PFor 1893.
Dubrolyubov, Nikolay. LFFor 2318.
"Dubrovačke poeme" (Dučić). PFor 429.
Dubrovsky (Pushkin). LFFor 1363-1364, 1366-1368.
"Duchess and the Jeweller, The" (Woolf). ShF 2458-2459.
Duchess de la Vallière, The (Bulwer-Lytton). DEng 313.
Duchess of Malfi, The (Webster). DEng 2009-2010.
Duchesse de Langeais, La (Tremblay). DSup 354.
Dučić, Jovan. PFor 426-434, 2255.
Dudevant, Amandine-Aurore-Lucile Dupin, Baronne. See **Sand, George.**
Dudintzev, Vladimir. LFFor 2328.
Dudley-Smith, Trevor. See **Trevor, Elleston.**
Due zitelle, Le. See *Two Old Maids, The.*
"Duel, The" (Chekhov). LFEng 3300-3301.
Duenna, The (Sheridan). DEng 1776-1778.
Dueño de las estrellas, El (Ruiz de Alarcón). DFor 1609-1610.
Duffy, Marguerite. See **Terry, Megan.**
"Dug Out, The" (Sassoon). PEng 2472-2473.
Dugan, Alan. PEng 881-885; PSup 404.
Duineser Elegien. See *Duino Elegies.*
Duino Elegies (Rilke). PFor 1329, 1331-1332.
Duke, Will. See **Gault, William Campbell.**
Duke Humphrey's Dinner (O'Brien, F-J.). ShF 1980.
Duke of Gandia, The (Swinburne). DEng 1899.
Dukkehjem, Et. See *Doll's House, A.*

"Dulce et Decorum Est" (Owen). PEng 2160-2161.
"Dulcima" (Bates). LFEng 185.
Dulcy (Kaufman and Connelly). DEng 417-418.
Dullin, Charles. DFor 2351.
"Duma." See "Meditation."
Dumas, Alexandre, *fils.* DFor 494-506, **2346.**
Dumas, Alexandre, *père.* DFor 480-493, 2343-2345; LFEng 3152-3153; LFFor 518-530; M&D 543-550.
Du Maurier, Daphne. M&D 551-556.
Dumb Gods Speak, The (Oppenheim). M&D 1274.
Dumb Waiter, The (Pinter). DEng 1514-1517.
"Dun, The" (Edgeworth). ShF 1328-1329.
D'un château l'autre. See *Castle to Castle.*
"D'una letteratura europea." See "Of an European Literature."
Dunbar, Paul Laurence. PEng 3399-3400; PSup 109-118.
Dunbar, William. PEng 886-896, 3279-3280.
Duncan, Isadora. PFor 476.
Duncan, Robert. PEng 897-907; PSup 404.
Duncan, Robert L. See **Roberts, James Hall.**
Duncan, W. R. See **Roberts, James Hall.**
"Duncan spoke of a process" (Baraka). PEng 84-86.
Dunciad, The (Pope). PEng 2262.
Dunlap, William. DEng 526-534, 2397.
Dunne, Finley Peter. ShF 537.
Dunne, John Gregory. LFEng 758-759.
"Duns Scotus's Oxford" (Hopkins). PEng **1401.**
Dunsany, Lord. DEng 535-542; ShF 665, 743, 744, **1313-1318.**
"Dunwich Horror, The" (Lovecraft). ShF 1825-1827.
Du Perry, Jean. See **Simenon, Georges.**
Dupin, Amandine-Aurore-Lucile, Baronne Dudevant. See **Sand, George.**
Dupin, Jacques. PFor 1893.
Duplex, The (Bullins). DEng 308. See also Twentieth-Century Cycle.
Duplicate Death (Heyer). M&D 863.
Duque de Aquitania, El (Saavedra). DFor 1615-1616.
Durang, Christopher. DSup 98-105.
Duras, Marguerite. DFor 507-514; LFFor 531-539, 2146; LFSup 403.
D'Urfey, Thomas. PEng 908-915.

Durrant, Theo. *See* **Teilhet, Darwin L.**

Durrell, Lawrence. LFEng **840-848;** LFSup 403; **PEng 916-924;** PSup 404.

Dürrenmatt, Friedrich. DFor **515-525,** 2262-2263, 2380-2382; **M&D 557-561.**

Durych, Jaroslav. LFFor 2067.

Duse, Eleonora. DFor 457-458.

"Dusk" (Æ). PEng 18.

Dusklands (Coetzee). LFSup 78-79.

Dusty Answer (Lehmann). LFSup 228-229.

"Dusty Braces" (Snyder). PEng 2675.

Dutch Courtesan, The (Marston). DEng 1270-1271.

Dutch Lover, The (Behn). DEng 175.

Dutch Uncle (Gray). DEng 806-807.

Dutchman (Baraka). DEng 97-99.

Dutiful Daughter, A (Keneally). LFSup 190-191.

Dutt, Govin Chunder. PFor 1995.

Dutt, Michael Madhusan. PFor 1994-1995.

Dutt, Toro. PFor 1995-1996.

Dux Moraud. DEng 2252.

Dva brata. See *Two Brothers.*

"Dva chasa v rezervuare." *See* "Two Hours in a Reservoir."

Dvärgen. See *Dwarf, The.*

Dvenadtsat. See *Twelve, The.*

"Dvoinik." *See* "Double, The."

"Dvořákovo requiem." *See* "Requiem for Dvořák, A."

Dvoryanskoye gnezdo. See *House of Gentlefolk, A.*

Dwarf, The (Lagerkvist). LFFor 972-973; ShF 481.

"Dwarf House" (Beattie). ShFSup 36-37.

"Dwelling Place in Heaven" (León). PFor 843.

Dwight, Timothy. LTh 1739.

Dworzan, Hélène. ShF 2575.

Dwyer, Deanna. *See* **Koontz, Dean R.**

Dwyer, K. R. *See* **Koontz, Dean R.**

Dyadya Vanya. See *Uncle Vanya.*

Dybek, Stuart. ShF 2576.

"Dying: An Introduction" (Sissman). PEng 2615-2616.

Dying: An Introduction (Sissman). PEng 2615-2616.

Dying Inside (Silverberg). LFEng 3212.

"Dying Man's Confession, A" (Twain). M&D 1611.

"Dykes, The" (Kipling). PEng 1608.

Dym. See *Smoke.*

Dynamics of Literary Response, The (Holland). LTh 684-686, 1764.

Dynamite Voices (Madhubuti). PEng 1888.

Dynasts, The (Hardy). DEng 888-891; PEng 1222-1223.

Dyskolos. See *Bad-tempered Man, The.*

"Dyvers thy death do dyversely bemoan" (Surrey). PEng 2788.

Dziady. See *Forefathers' Eve.*

"Dziecie Europy." *See* "Child of Europe, A."

"Dzwony w zimie." *See* "Bells in Winter."

E

E. Kology (Koch). PEng 1623.

È stato così. See Dry Heart, The.

"E tu?" See "And You?"

"Each and All" (Emerson). PEng 958.

Each in His Own Way (Pirandello). DFor 1470-1471.

Each Man's Son (MacLennan). LFEng 1745-1746.

Eagle Has Two Heads, The (Cocteau). DFor 420-422.

"Eagle in New Mexico" (Lawrence, D. H.). PEng 1683.

Eagle on the Coin, The (Cassill). LFEng 468.

Eagle or Sun? (Paz). PFor 1172-1173.

Eagles' Nest (Kavan). LFEng 1511-1512.

Eagleton, Terry. LTh 137, 414-419, 758-759, 762, 912, 1541.

Early Americana (Richter). ShF 600, 602.

Early Autumn (Parker). M&D 1301.

Early Graves (Hansen). M&D 832.

Early Lessons (Edgeworth). ShF 1322-1323.

"Early Morning" (Bachmann). PFor 127-128.

Early Morning (Bond). DEng 247.

"Early Noon" (Bachmann). PFor 127. See also Gestundete Zeit, Die.

"Early Poems" (Justice). PEng 1531.

Early Sunday Morning (Hopper). PEng 3510, 3511, 3512.

Earmarked for Hell. See Pro Patria.

Earth Poetry (Everson). PEng 987.

Earth Spirit (Wedekind). DFor 1976-1977.

Earth Worms (Innaurato). DSup 201-202.

Earthbreakers, The (Haycox). LFEng 3196.

Earthly Paradise, The (Morris). PEng 2055, 2056, 2057-2058.

Earthly Possessions (Tyler). LFEng 2682.

Earthly Powers (Burgess). LFEng 369-370.

Earthquake in Chile, The (Kleist). LFEng 3248-3249; ShF 1759.

East, Charles. ShF 2577.

East I Know, The (Claudel). PFor 359-360.

"East of the Sun and West of the Moon" (Merwin). PEng 1981.

East River (Asch). LFFor 79.

"Eastbourne" (Montale). PFor 1051. See also Occasioni, Le.

"Easter Morning" (Ammons). PSup 13.

"Easter Procession, The" (Solzhenitsyn). ShF 2250.

"Easter-wings" (Herbert). PEng 1298, 1299.

Eastlake, William. LFEng 849-856; ShF 2578.

Eastman, Charles A. (Ohiyesa). ShF 567.

Eastward Ho! (Chapman, Jonson, and Marston). DEng 2286-2287.

"Eating the Pig" (Hall). PEng 1206.

Eaton, Charles Edward. ShF 2580.

Eaux et forêts, Les. See Rivers and Forests, The.

Eberhart, Mignon G. M&D 562-567.

Eberhart, Richard. PEng 925-935; PSup 404-405.

Ebert, Adolf. LTh 335.

Ebner-Eschenbach, Marie von. LFFor 2188.

Ebony Box, The (Fletcher). M&D 623-624.

"Ebony Tower, The" (Fowles). LFEng 1018-1020; ShF 1395, 1396.

Ebony Tower, The (Fowles). LFEng 1008, 1018-1020; ShF 1394.

Eça de Queiróz, José Maria de. LFFor 540-546.

"Ecce Puer" (Joyce). PEng 1526.

Ecclesiastes 1-5 (Surrey, paraphrase). PEng 2791.

Ecclesiastical History of the English People (Bede). PEng 416-418; ShF 428.

Ecclesiazusae (Aristophanes). DFor 118-119, 2123.

Echegaray y Eizaguirre, José. DFor 526-534, 2500.

"Echo and the Nemesis, The" (Stafford). ShF 2261.

"Echo's Bone" (Beckett). PEng 106; PFor 149.

Echo's Bones and Other Precipitates (Beckett). PEng 104; PFor 147.

"Eclogue" (Lear). PEng 1701.

"Eclogue for Christmas, An" (MacNeice). PEng 1871-1872.

Eclogues (Petrarch). PFor 1238.

Eclogues (Vergil). PFor 1607, 1608-1611; ShF 2384-2385.

Eclogues, Epitaphs, and Sonnets (Googe). PEng 3289.

Eco, Umberto. LFFor 2257; LTh 269, **420-426; M&D 568-573.**

École des femmes, L'. See *School for Wives, The.*

École des mères, L' (Marivaux). DFor 1263-1264.

"Ecologue" (Ginsberg). PEng 1094.

Écrits (Lacan). LTh 845-846, 849.

Écriture et la différence, L'. See *Writing and Difference.*

"Ecstasy, The" (Donne). PEng 830-831.

Ecstasy of Rita Joe, The (Ryga). DEng 1643-1646.

Ecuador (Michaux). PFor 999.

Ed è subito sera (Quasimodo). PFor 1307.

Edel, Leon. LTh **427-432.**

"Eden" (de la Mare). PEng 776.

Eden Cinema, The (Duras). DFor 511.

Eden End (Priestley). DEng 1536-1538.

Edgar Huntly (Brown, C. B.). LFEng 314, 320-324; ShF 528.

"Edge, The" (Glück). PSup 134-135.

Edge of Impossibility, The (Oates). LFEng 2010.

Edgeworth, Maria. LFEng **857-869,** 3031; ShF **1319-1322.**

Edgeworth, Richard Lovell. LFEng 859.

Edmonds, Helen (Woods). See **Kavan, Anna.**

Edmund Kean (Dumas, *père*). DFor 491-492.

Edna the Inebriate Woman (Sanford). DEng 2506.

Education of Henry Adams, The (Adams). ShF 219.

"Education of Millet, The" (Brecht). PFor 1819.

Éducation sentimentale, L'. See *Sentimental Education, A.*

"Edward Joseph O'Brien and the American Short Story" (Joselyn). ShF 80.

Edward I (Peele). DEng 1492.

Edward II (Marlowe). DEng 1257-1260, 2273; ShF 1896-1897.

Edwardes, George. DEng 2467-2468.

Edwards, Page. ShF 2581.

Edwards, R. T. See **Hoch, Edward D.**

Edwin (Mortimer). DEng 1359.

"Edwin and Angelina" (Goldsmith). PEng 1111.

Effect of Gamma Rays on Man-in-the-Moon Marigolds, The (Zindel). DEng 2126-2128.

Effets surprenants de la sympathie, Les (Marivaux). LFFor 1098-1099.

Effi Briest (Fontane). LFFor 564-566, 2178.

Egan, Lesley. See **Linington, Elizabeth.**

Egerton, Lucy. See **Gilbert, Anthony.**

"Egg, The" (Anderson). ShF 873, 112-113.

Egil's Saga. LFFor 2331; ShF 392-393.

Égloga de Cristino y Febea (Encina). DFor 542-543.

Égloga de los tres pastores (Encina). DFor 543.

Égloga de Plácido y Vitoriano (Encina). DFor 543-545.

Egloga, elegía, oda (Cernuda). PFor 320.

"Egloga primera." See "First Eclogue."

Égloga representada en reqüesta de unos amores (Encina). DFor 539-540.

Égloga representada por las mesmas personas (Encina). DFor 540-541.

"Egloga segunda." See "Second Eclogue."

Egmont (Goethe). DFor 739-740.

Egoist, The (Meredith). LFEng 1869-1870.

"Egri hangok." See "Sounds of Eger."

"Egy estém otthon." See "One Evening at Home."

Egy mondat a zsarnokságról. See *One Sentence on Tyranny.*

Eh? (Livings). DEng 1153-1154.

Ehe des Herrn Mississippi, Die. See *Marriage of Mr. Mississippi, The.*

Ehre, Die. See *Honor.*

Ehrenburg, Ilya. LFFor 2325, 2327.

Ehrengard (Dinesen). ShF 1284.

Eich, Günther. PFor 1930-1931.

Eiche and Angora. See *Rabbit Race, The.*

Eichendorff, Joseph von. LTh **433-439; PFor 435-444,** 1918.

Eigenart des Ästhetischen, Die (Lukács). LTh 939.

Eight Men (Wright, R.). LFEng 2974.

Eight Million Ways to Die (Block). M&D 152-153.

"Eight O'clock One Morning" (Grau). ShF 1533.

Eight Strokes of the Clock (Leblanc). M&D 1037-1038.

"Eight Views of Tokyo" (Dazai). ShFSup 94.

"Eighteen-Year-Old, The" (Morgenstern). PFor 1060.

170, **936-949,** 3356, 3358-3359, 3389, 3485-3488; ShF 177-178, 292.

Elisa (Goncourt, E.). LFFor 716-717.

Elixiere des Teufels, Die. See *Devil's Elixirs, The.*

"Elixir due Révérend Père Gaucher, L'." *See* "Reverend Father Gaucher's Elixir, The."

"Elizabeth" (Jackson). ShF 1669.

Elizabeth of England (Bruckner). DFor 263-264.

Elizabeth the Queen (Anderson, M.). DEng 27-28.

Elkin, Stanley. LFEng 884-893; LFSup 403; **ShF 1338-1343;** ShFSup 388.

Ellery Queen's Mystery Magazine. ShF 762.

Ellin, Stanley. M&D 574-578.

Elliott, George P. ShF 1344-1350.

Elliott, William D. ShF 2538.

Ellis, Henry Havelock. LTh 1737.

"Ellis Island" (Helprin). ShFSup 119-120.

Ellis Island and Other Stories (Helprin). ShFSup 117-118.

Ellison, Harlan. ShF 780, 781.

Ellison, Ralph. LFEng 894-905; LFSup 403; ShF 555-556.

Elmer Gantry (Lewis, S.). LFEng 1678-1680.

"Éloge de Richardson" (Diderot). LFFor 2120.

Éloges (Perse). PFor 1195.

Eloisa. See *New Héloïse, The.*

"Elpenor" (Sinópoulos). PFor 1971. See also *Metaichmio I.*

"Elsa's Eyes" (Aragon). PFor 70-71.

"Else Lasker-Schüler" (Bobrowski). PFor 205.

"Elsie in New York" (Henry). ShF 1630.

Elster, Kristian. LFFor 2340.

Éluard, Paul. PFor 455-460, 1886.

Elverhøj (Heiberg, J.). DFor 907.

"Elvis Presley" (Gunn). PEng 1172.

Ely, David. ShF 2584.

Elýtis, Odysseus. PFor 461-466, 1965-1968; PSup 405.

E. M. Forster (Trilling). LTh 500.

Emaux et camées. See *Enamels and Cameos.*

"Ember az embertelenségben." *See* "Man in Inhumanity."

Ember tragédiája, Az. See *Tragedy of Man, The.*

Embers (Beckett). DEng 154.

Embezzled Heaven (Werfel). LFFor 1911-1912.

Embezzler, The (Auchincloss). LFEng 111-112.

Embirikos, Andreas. PFor 1964-1965.

"Emblematics of Meaning, The" (Bely). LTh 127.

Emblemes (Quarles). PEng 2296-2297.

Emblems of a Season of Fury (Merton). PEng 1976.

"Embrace at Vergara, The" (Alarcón). ShF 845.

"Emergency Exit" (Silone). LFFor 1582.

Emergency Poems (Parra). PFor 1134.

Emerologio katastromatos I, II, and *III.* See *Logbooks.*

Emerson, Ralph Waldo. LTh 453-460, 524, 1012, 1567, 1746-1748; PEng 898, **950-962,** 3344, 3345, 3385-3386; ShF 219.

"Emerson, on Goethe" (Johnson). PSup 211-212.

Emigrès, The (Mrożek). DFor 1384-1385.

Emilia Galotti (Lessing). DFor 1205-1207.

Emily Dickinson in Southern California (Kennedy). PEng 1574-1575.

Emin, Fyodor. LFFor 2304-2305.

Emin, Nikolay. LFFor 2306.

Eminent Victorians (Strachey). LTh 431.

Emma (Austen). LFEng 122-124, 3132.

Emmanuel, Pierre. PFor 1890.

Emmett, R. T. *See* **Hanshew, Thomas W.**

Empedocles. PFor 1943-1944.

Empeños de una casa, Los. See *Household Plagued by Love.*

Emperor and Galilean (Ibsen). DFor 981.

Emperor Jones, The (O'Neill). DEng 1407-1410.

Emperor Julian, The. See *Emperor and Galilean*

"Emperor of Ice Cream, The" (Stevens). PEng 3392.

Emperor of the Moon, The (Behn). DEng 177.

"Emperor's New Clothes, The" (Andersen). ShF 864.

Empire and Communications (Innis). LTh 958.

Empire City, The (Goodman). LFEng 1148-1153.

Emploi de temps, L'. See *Passing Time.*

"Empress's Ring, The" (Hale, N.). ShF 1570.

Empson, William. LTh 350, **461-466,** 1222, 1797, 1818; **PEng 963-973.**

Empty Canvas, The (Moravia). LFFor 1171-1172.

En attendant Godot. See *Waiting for Godot.*

En Castellano (Otero). PFor 1115-1116.

"En el principio moraba." *See* "Ballad on the Gospel 'In the Beginning Was the Word.'"

"En Famille." *See* "Family Affair, A."

En la aradiente oscuriadad. See *In the Burning Darkness*

"En la fiesta de todos los santos." *See* "On the Holidays of All Saints' Day."

En las orillas del Sar. See *Beside the River Sar.*

En pièces détachées. See *Cinq* and *Like Death Warmed Over.*

En polsk familie (Hauch). LFFor 2336.

"En regardant vers le pays de France." *See* "While Looking Towards the Country of France."

"En sortant de l'école" (Prévert). PFor 1278.

"En una noche oscura." *See* "Dark Night, The."

"En voz baja" (González Martínez). PFor 611.

Enamels and Cameos (Gautier). PFor 538-540.

"Encampment at Morning, An" (Merwin). PEng 1982.

Enchanted, The (Giraudoux). DFor 726-727.

Enchanted Lake, The. See *Devil's Pool, The.*

Enchanted Night (Mrożek). DFor 1382.

"Enchanted Pilgrim, The" (Leskov). ShFSup 160.

"Encima de las corrientes." *See* "Ballad on the Psalm 'By the Waters of Babylon.'"

Encina, Juan del. DEng 2161-2162; DFor **535-545,** 2172, 2179, 2484.

Enckell, Rabbe. PFor 2181-2182.

"Encounter, An" (Joyce). ShF 1720.

Encounter (Sondhi). DEng 2418-2419.

"Encounter on the Parnassian Slope" (Beck). ShF 935.

Encyclopédie (Diderot). LFFor 457, 458, 459; LTh 370.

"End, The" (Beckett). ShF 938.

End and a Beginning, An. See *Fury Chronicle, The.*

"End of a Year" (Lowell, R.). PEng 1797.

End of an Ancient Mariner (Coles). M&D 373.

"End of Autumn, The" (Ponge). PFor 1265.

"End of Chronos, The" (Ungaretti). PFor 1568. See also *Sentimento del tempo.*

End of Summer (Behrman). DEng 185-186.

"End of Summer School, The" (Nemerov). PEng 2079.

End of the Affair, The (Greene, G.). DEng 827-828.

End of the Battle, The (Waugh). LFEng 2803.

End of the Game. See *Judge and His Hangman, The.*

End of the Road, The (Barth). LFEng 161-162.

"End of the Road, The" (Belloc). PEng 138.

"End of the Tether, The" (Conrad). ShF 1186.

"End of the World, The" (MacLeish). PEng 3501-3502, 3504, 3508-3509, 3511-3512.

End Zone (DeLillo). LFSup 86.

Endgame (Beckett). DEng 152-153, 2385; DFor 160-162, 2246-2247, 2359.

Endimion and Phoebe (Drayton). PEng 849.

Endō, Shusaku. LFSup 100-107.

Endymion (Heidenstam). LFFor 820.

Endymion (Lyly). DEng 1184-1185, 2269; PEng 1819; ShF 1832.

Enemies (Singer, Isaac). LFEng 2437-2439; LFFor 1623-1625.

Enemigos de alma, Los (Mallea). LFFor 1056-1057.

Enemy, The (Bagley). M&D 55-57.

"Enemy, The" (Buck). ShF 1012-1014.

Enemy of the People, An (Ibsen). DFor 2472.

Enemy of the People, An (Miller). DEng 1341-1342, 2406.

"Enfance d'un chef, L'." *See* "Childhood of a Boss."

"Enfant au tambour, L'" (Follain). PSup 128.

Enfant noir, L'. See *Dark Child, The.*

Enfant prodigue, L' (Becque). DFor 170.

"Enfantement" (Follain). PSup 130.

Enfants du sabbat, Les. See *Children of the Black Sabbath.*

Enfants terribles, Les. See *Children of the Game.*

"Enfermé, seul" (Éluard). PFor 459.

"Enfin" (Reverdy). PSup 325.

Engañados, Los (Rueda). DFor 1598-1600.

Engels, Friedrich. LTh 1712.

"Engführung." *See* "Stretto."

"England" (Davie). PSup 88.

England's Heroical Epistles (Drayton). PEng 850.

English Bards and Scotch Reviewers (Byron). LTh 256, 258, 261; PEng 406.

English Literature in the Sixteenth Century, Excluding Drama (Lewis). LTh 896-897.

English Murder, An (Hare). M&D 844-845.

English Poetry (Bateson). PEng 3408-3410.

"English Short Fiction in the Eighteenth Century" (Boyce). ShF 72.

"English Short Fiction in the 15th and 16th Centuries" (Schlauch). ShF 88.

"English Short Fiction in the Nineteenth Century" (Harris, W.). ShF 78.

"English Short Fiction in the Seventeenth Century" (Mish). ShF 83.

English Teacher, The (Narayan). LFEng 1968-1969.

English Traveler, The (Heywood, T.). DEng 2291.

"Englishman in Texas, An" (Middleton, C.). PEng 1988.

"Engraving" (Rítsos). PFor 1348-1349.

"Enigma, The" (Fowles). LFEng 1019; ShF 1397-1398.

Enneads (Plotinus). LTh 1129-1130, 1645.

Ennius, Quintus. DFor 546-551, 2139; LTh 1511; PFor 905, 2089-2090.

Ennodius. PFor 2111.

"Enoch Soames" (Beerbohm). ShF 943-944.

Enomoto Kikaku. *See* Takarai Kikaku.

"Enormous Radio, The" (Cheever). ShF 1122.

"Enough" (Creeley). PEng 684-685.

Enough Is Enough (Henshaw). DEng 931-933.

Enough Stupidity in Every Wiseman. See *Scoundrel, The.*

Enquist, Per Olov. LFFor 2361.

Enrico IV. See *Henry IV.*

"Enslaved Besieged, The" (Varnalis). PFor 1959.

Enter Solly Gold (Kops). DEng 1082.

"Entered as Second-class Matter" (Perelman). ShF 2082.

Entertainer, The (Osborne). DEng 1431-1432, 2386.

Entertaining Mr. Sloane (Orton). DEng 1420-1421.

Entertainment, The (Drummond). PEng 863, 866-867.

"Enthusiasm" (Byrom). PEng 397.

"Entrada a la madera." *See* "Entrance to Wood."

"Entrance into Life" (Hale, N.). ShF 1571.

Entrance to Porlock, The (Buechner). LFEng 352-353.

"Entrance to Wood" (Neruda). PFor 1076. See also *Residence on Earth.*

Entre Fantoine et Agapa. See *Between Fantoine and Agapa.*

Entre la vie et la mort. See *Between Life and Death.*

Entrekin, Charles. ShF 2585.

Entretiens sur "Le Fils naturel" (Diderot). LTh 372.

"Entropy" (Pynchon). ShF 2144-2145.

"Entzückung an Laura, Die." *See* "Rapture, to Laura."

"Enueg I" (Beckett). PEng 104-105; PFor 147-148.

Envers d'une sainte, L'. See *False Saint, A.*

"Envoy Extraordinary" (Golding). ShF 1507-1509.

"Envoy of Mr. Cogito, The" (Herbert). PFor 660.

Envy (Olesha). LFFor 2322-2323.

"Envy" (Ozick). ShF 2036-2038.

"Envy of Instinct, The" (Galvin). PEng 1053.

Enzensberger, Hans Magnus. PFor 467-472, 1935.

"Eolian Harp, The" (Coleridge, S. T.). PEng 533-535.

"Épars, l'indivisible, L'" (Bonnefoy). PSup 48.

Épaves. See *Strange River, The.*

"Ephelia to Bajazet" (Etherege). PEng 979.

Ephesiaca. See *Ephesian Tale.*

Ephesian History: Or, The Love Adventures of Abracoman and Anthia. See *Ephesian Tale.*

Ephesian Tale (Xenophon of Ephesus). LFFor 2003-2004.

Epic of Sheik Bedreddin, The (Hikmet). PSup 176, 178-179.

Epicharmus. DEng 2136; DFor 2097, 2137.

Epicœne (Jonson). DEng 1023-1024, 2285; LTh 781-782; ShF 1715.

Epigenes of Sicyon. DFor 2094.

Epigonen, Die (Immerman). LTh 1710.

Epigrames (Davies). PEng 748, 749.

Epigramme: Venedig. See *Venetian Epigrams.*

Epigrams (Callimachus). PFor 254, 256.

Epigrams (Jonson). PEng 1514-1515.

"Epilogue" (Lowell, R.). PEng 1800.

Épilogue (Martin du Gard). LFFor 1118. See also *World of the Thibaults, The.*

"Epilogue to *Semiramis*" (Sheridan). PEng 2565.

"Epilogue to *The Fatal Falsehood*" (Sheridan). PEng 2567.

"Epilogue to *The Rivals*" (Sheridan). PEng 2564, 2565.

Epipsychidion (Shelley). PEng 2556.

Episcopo and Company (D'Annunzio). LFFor 411.

"Erosion" (Pratt). PEng 2282-2283.

Erotic Tales (Moravia). ShFSup 199.

Erotica pathemata (Parthenius). LFFor 2000.

Erotika (Cankar). PFor 2269.

"Erotikos Logos" (Seferis). PFor 1415.

Erpingham Camp, The (Orton). DEng 1424-1425.

"Errata" (Simic). PEng 2597.

"Errigal Road, The" (Montague). PEng 2038-2039.

Ertel, Aleksandr. LFFor 2319.

Ervine, John Greer. *See* **Ervine, St. John.**

Ervine, St. John. DEng 559-565.

Erwin (Solger). LTh 1360.

"Erziehung der Hirse, Die." *See* "Education of Millet, The."

"Es färbte sich die Wiese grün." *See* "Meadow Turned Green, The."

Es lebe das Leben! See *Joy of Living, The.*

"Escalator, The" (Robbe-Grillet). ShF 2156.

"Escapade, An" (Callaghan). ShFSup 69.

Escape (Galsworthy). DEng 716.

"Escargots." *See* "Snails."

Esclusa, L'. See *Outcast, The.*

Escurial (Ghelderode). DFor 694-695.

Esenin, Sergei. PFor 473-481, 2148-2149.

Esfera, La. See *Sphere, The.*

Esmond in India (Jhabvala). LFFor 2222-2223; LFSup 172-173.

Espadas como labios (Aleixandre). PFor 29.

España (Gautier). PFor 536-538.

España, aparta de mí este cáliz. See *Spain, Take This Cup from Me.*

"Español habla de su tierra, Un." *See* "Spaniard Speaks of His Homeland, A."

"Esperanto" (Shalamov). ShFSup 290.

Espoir, L'. See *Man's Hope.*

Espriu, Salvador. PFor 1775.

Essai sur les fables de La Fontaine. See *La Fontaine et ses fables.*

Essai sur les fictions. See *Essay on Fiction.*

Essais (Montaigne). ShF 155.

Essais de critique et d'histoire (Taine). LTh 1417-1418, 1420.

Essais de psychologie contemporaine (Bourget). LTh 200, 1391.

Essais sur la littérature contemporaine (Brunetière). LTh 233.

"Essay at War, An" (Duncan). PEng 902.

Essay Concerning Human Understanding, An (Locke). LTh 1700.

Essay on Criticism, An (Pope). LTh 909, 1142-1143, 1145, 1689; PEng 2253-2255, 3323, 3472.

"Essay on Criticism, An" (Van Duyn). PEng 2963.

Essay on Fiction (Staël). LTh 1380, 1382.

Essay on Literature (Lu Chi). LTh 920, 922-923, 1774.

Essay on Man, An (Pope). LTh 1349; PEng 2258-2261, 3325.

"Essay upon Epitaphs" (Wordsworth). LTh 1581.

Essayes in Divinity (Donne). PEng 822.

Essays, The (Montaigne). LTh 1042, 1044, 1046-1047.

Essays and Studies (Swinburne). LTh 1401.

Essays in Criticism (Arnold). LTh 47-48, 1733; PEng 3484-3485.

Essays on European Literature (Curtius). LTh 336.

Essays on Shakespeare (Empson). LTh 464.

Essays on the Gogol Period of Russian Literature (Chernyshevsky). LTh 121, 287.

Essays Speculative and Suggestive (Symonds). LTh 1408.

"Essex" (Davie). PSup 89.

"Essex and Bacon" (Landor). PEng 1643.

Esson, Louis. DEng 2432.

Est-il bon? Est-il méchant? (Diderot). DSup 86-88.

"Est' tselomudrennye chary." *See* "There Are Chaste Charms."

Esta noche juntos, amándonos tanto. See *Together Tonight, Loving Each Other So Much.*

"Esta tarde, mi bien" (Cruz). PFor 378.

Estación total, La (Jiménez). PFor 753-754.

"Estatuto del vino." *See* "Ordinance of Wine."

Este domingo. See *This Sunday.*

Estetica come scienza dell'espressione e linguistica generale. See *Aesthetic as Science of Expression and General Linguistic.*

Esteticheskie otnosheniya iskusstva k deistvitel'nosti. See "Aesthetic Relationship of Art to Reality."

Esther. ShF 356-358.

"Esther" (Toomer). ShF 2341.

Esther Waters (Moore, G.). LFEng 1900-1901.

Esthétique de la langue française. See *What Is Pure French?*

Estío (Jiménez). PFor 752.

"Evening Land, The" (Lawrence, D. H.).
PEng 1683.

"Evening with Dr. Faust, An" (Hesse). ShF
1638.

"Evening with John Joe Dempsey, An"
(Trevor). ShFSup 321.

Evenings on a Farm near Dikanka (Gogol).
ShF 1496.

Evensmo, Sigurd. LFFor 2362.

"Eventide" (Purdy). ShF 2139.

Events and Wisdoms (Davie). PSup 87.

Everett, Edward. LTh 1743.

Everlasting Mercy, The (Masefield). PEng
1923-1924.

Everson, William. PEng 981-994; PSup 405.

Every Man a Murderer (Doderer). LFFor 484;
M&D 518.

Every Man in His Humour (Jonson). DEng
1018-1019, 2285.

Every Man out of His Humor (Jonson). DEng
2285.

Everyman. DEng 2253-2254.

"Everyone Sant" (Sassoon). PEng 2473.

"Everything and Nothing" (Borges). LTh 194.

"Everything Must Go!" (Elkin). ShF 1339-
1340.

Eve's Diary (Twain). ShF 374.

Evgeny Onegin. See *Eugene Onegin.*

Evidence of Love (Grau). LFEng 1188-1190.

"Evil May-Day" (Allingham). PEng 43-44.

Evil Wish, The (Potts). M&D 1351.

"Evocation of the Great Bear" (Bachmann).
PFor 128-129.

"Evolution" (Morgenstern). PFor 1060-1061.

*Évolution des genres dans l'histoire de la
littérature, L'* (Brunetière). LTh 233.

Evreinov, Nikolai. DFor 579-587.

Evropeiskaya noch' (Khodasevich). PSup 228-
229.

Evvie (Caspary). M&D 290, 292.

Ewald, Johannes. DFor 2467; PFor 2162-
2163.

"Ewigen Melodien" (Heyen). PEng 1325-1326.

"Ex Parte" (Lardner). ShF 1773.

Examens (Corneille). LTh 309, 312, 1687.

"Examination, The" (Snodgrass). PEng 2661.

"Excelente Balade of Charitie, as wroten by the
gode Prieste Thomas Rowley, 1464, An"
(Chatterton). PEng 470.

Excellent Women (Pym). LFEng 2181, 2182-
2183, 2185.

Except the Lord (Cary). LFEng 461-462.

"Excusation, L'." *See* "Excuse, The" (Chartier).

"Excuse, The" (Chartier). PFor 348.

"Excuse, The" (Oppenheimer). PEng 2144.

Executioner, The. See *Hangman, The.*

Executioner's Song, The (Mailer). LFEng
1785-1787; ShF 312.

Exemplary Novels (Cervantes). LFEng 3223,
3227; ShF 1083-1084, 1086.

"Exequy To his Matchlesse never to be
forgotten Freind, An" (King). PEng 1582-
1585.

Exercises in Style (Queneau). LFSup 326.

"Exhortation" (Bogan). PEng 237-238.

Éxi ke miá típsis yia ton ouranó. See *Six and
One Remorses for the Sky.*

Exile, An (Jones, M.). LFEng 1491-1492.

Exile and the Kingdom (Camus, A.). ShF
1047.

Exile of the Sons of Uisliu. ShF 434-435.

"Exiles" (Cavafy). PFor 298.

Exiles and Marriages (Hall). PEng 1198-1199.

Exile's Return (Cowley). LTh 314, 317-319.

Exister (Follain). PSup 126, 128.

Exit Lines (Hill). M&D 875.

Exit the King (Ionesco). DFor 1002-1003,
2255-2256, 2357.

Exodus. ShF 342-344.

Expedition of Humphry Clinker, The. See
Humphry Clinker.

"Expelled, The" (Beckett). ShF 939.

Expensive People (Oates). LFEng 2011-2012.

"Experience, An" (Hofmannsthal). PFor 675.

Experiment in Criticism, An (Lewis). LTh 895.

Experimental Novel, The (Zola). LTh 1618,
1711.

"Expiation, L'" (Hugo). PFor 735. See also
Châtiments, Les.

Explanation of America, An (Pinsky). PEng
2211-2212.

Explorations (Yeats). LTh 1588.

"Exploring the Province of the Short Story"
(Elliott, G. P.). ShF 75-76.

"Explosion of Seven Babies, An" (Crane, S.).
ShF 1217.

*Expositio Virgilianae continentiae secundum
philosophos moralis.* See *Content of Virgil.*

*Exposition of the Content of Virgil According to
Moral Philosophy, The.* See *Content of
Virgil.*

"Expostulation" (Byrom). PEng 396.

F

Fabbri, Diego. DFor 2414.
Fabeln (Lessing, G.). ShF 382.
"Faber Book of Modern Short Stories, The" (Bowen). ShF 71-72.
"Fable, The" (Winters). PSup 398.
"Fable from the Cayoosh Country" (Barnard). PSup 29-30.
"Fable of Pyramus and Thisbe, The" (Góngora). PFor 601.
Fable of the Bees, The (Mandeville). PEng 3406-3407.
"Fable of the Goat" (Agnon). ShF 831-833.
Fables (Gay). PEng 1075.
Fables (Henryson). PEng 1288-1290, 3279.
Fables (La Fontaine). PFor 810, 812-813, 816-818.
Fables (Marie de France). PFor 971; ShF 1891.
Fables, The, preface to (Dryden). LTh 406-407.
Fables and Fantasies for Adults (Das). ShF 643.
Fables of La Fontaine, The (Moore, trans.). PEng 2046-2047.
"Fábula de Píramo y Tisbe." *See* "Fable of Pyramus and Thisbe, The."
Fábula de Polifemo y Galatea. See *Polyphemus and Galathea*.
Fabulous Beasts, The (Oates). PEng 2119.
Fabulous Miss Marie, The (Bullins). DEng 308. *See also* Twentieth-Century Cycle.
Façade (Sitwell). PEng 2627-2629.
Faccio, Rina. *See* Aleramo, Sibilla.
Face of Another, The (Abe). LFFor 7.
Face of Fear, The (Koontz). M&D 1007.
"Face of Helen, The" (Christie). ShF 1144-1145.
"Face of Stone, A" (Williams, W. C.). ShF 2443-2444.
"Face on the Barroom Floor, The" (Algren). ShF 856.
"Faces" (Koch). PEng 1627.
Facing the Tree (Ignatow). PEng 1475.
"Facino Cane" (Balzac). ShF 920-921.
Fackel, Die. PFor 791-792, 792-793.

"Facts Concerning the Recent Carnival of Crime in Connecticut, The" (Twain). ShF 2362-2363.
"Facts in the Case of M. Valdemar, The" (Poe). ShF 739-740.
Fadeout (Hansen). M&D 830-831.
Fadeyev, Aleksandr. LFFor 2324.
Fadren. See *Father, The*.
Faerie Queene, The (Spenser). PEng 387-388, 2706, 2707-2708, 2710-2714; ShF 146.
"Fahrgast, Der." *See* "On the Tram."
Fair, A. A. *See* **Gardner, Erle Stanley.**
Fair Blows the Wind (L'Amour). LFSup 223-224.
"Fair Chloris in a pigsty lay" (Rochester). PEng 2400.
Fair Grit, The (Darin). DEng 2438.
Fair Haven, The (Butler). LFEng 393, 397.
Fair Jilt, The (Behn). LFEng 222; ShF 502.
Fair Maid of the West, The (Heywood, T.). DEng 952-953.
Fair Penitent, The (Rowe). DEng 1635-1636.
Fairbairn, Roger. *See* **Carr, John Dickson.**
"Faire roome, the presence of sweet beauty's pride" (Nashe). PEng 2072.
"Fairies, The" (Allingham). PEng 42.
Fairly Dangerous Thing, A (Hill). M&D 875-876.
Fairly Good Time, A (Gallant). LFEng 1054-1055.
Fairly Honourable Defeat, A (Murdoch). LFEng 1933-1937.
"Fairmount Cemetery" (Untermeyer). PEng 2949.
"Fairy Dream" (Petőfi). PFor 1221-1222.
"Fairy Goose, The" (O'Flaherty). ShF 2007-2008.
"Fairy Queen, The" (Newcastle). PEng 2095.
"Fairy Tale, The" (Goethe). LFEng 3238-3239; ShFSup 101.
Fairy Tale of New York, A (Donleavy). LFEng 786.
"Faith" (Guest). PEng 1166.
"Faith and Doubt" (Suckling). PEng 2778.
"Faith of Our Fathers" (Dick). ShF 1264-1265.

Faithful, The (Masefield). DEng 1289-1290.

Faithful Shepherd, The (Fanshawe). PEng 1000-1002.

Faithful Shepherd, The (Guarini). DEng 2158; DFor 844-847, 2400; PFor 2016.

Faithful Shepherdess, The (Fletcher, J.). DEng 630-631; PEng 1014-1017.

"Faithless Sally Brown" (Hood). PEng 1385-1386.

"Faithless Wife, The" (O'Faoláin). ShF 1999-2000.

Falcon, The (Tennyson). DEng 1919.

Falconer (Cheever). LFEng 510-512.

Falkberget, Johan. LFFor 2351.

Falkner (Shelley, M.). LFEng 2394-2395.

Fall, The (Camus). LFFor 262-264.

"Fall of a City" (Spender). PEng 2698.

Fall of America, The (Ginsberg) 1093-1094.

Fall of Hyperion, The (Keats). PEng 1550-1551.

Fall of the City, The (MacLeish). DEng 1218-1219.

Fall of the House of Limón, The (Pérez de Ayala). LFFor 1258-1259.

"Fall of the House of Usher, The" (Poe). LFEng 3128-3129; ShF 116, 162, 195-196, 473-474, 2105-2106.

Fall of the King, The (Jensen). LFFor 882, 2348.

Fallen Asleep While Young. See *Maid Silja, The*.

Fallen Idol, The (Film). ShF 786.

"Falling" (Dickey, J.). PEng 789-799.

"Falling" (Różewicz). PFor 1366.

Falling in Place (Beattie). LFEng 192-194.

"Falling Rocks, Narrowing Road, Cul-de-sac, Stop" (O'Faoláin). ShF 674, 2003.

Fallit, En. See *Bankrupt, The*.

Falls of Princes (Lydgate). PEng 1805, 1810-1811.

"False Burton Combs, The" (Daly, C.). M&D 447-448.

False Confessions, The (Marivaux). DFor 1266-1267.

False Delicacy (Kelly). DEng 2330.

False Messiah, The. See *Wunderbarliche Vogelsnest, Das*.

False One, The (Fletcher and Massinger). DEng 635-636.

False Saint, A (Curel). DFor 450-451.

"Falstaff's Lament over Prince Hal Become Henry V" (Melville). PEng 1950.

Faludi, Ferenc. PFor 1977.

"Fame" (Walker). ShFSup 340-341.

"Familia, La." See "Family, The."

Familia de Pascual Duarte, La. See *Family of Pascual Duarte, The*.

Familia lejana, Una. See *Distant Relations*.

"Familiale" (Prévert). PFor 1280.

"Familiar, The" (Le Fanu). ShF 735.

Familiar Epistle to the Author of the Heroic Epistle to Sir William Chambers, A (Sheridan). PEng 2566.

"Familiar Epistles to a Friend" (Byrom). PEng 396.

Familie Schroffenstein, Die. See *Schroffenstein Family, The*.

Familie Selicke, Die (Holz). LTh 692.

Familjen paa Gilje. See *Family at Gilje, The*.

"Family, The" (Cernuda). PFor 317-318. See also *Como quien espera el alba*.

Family, The (Pa Chin). LFFor 2107.

Family, The (Plante). LFSup 307-308. See also *Francoeur Novels, The*.

"Family Affair, A" (Maupassant). ShF 1909-1910.

Family and a Fortune, A (Compton-Burnett). LFEng 569-570.

Family and Friends (Brookner). LFSup 67-68.

Family Arsenal, The (Theroux). LFEng 2630, 2632-2633.

Family at Gilje, The (Lie). LFFor 2342.

"Family Circle" (Arany). PFor 79.

Family Idiot, The (Sartre). LTh 1274.

Family in Renaissance Florence, The (Alberti). LTh 1661.

Family Madness, A (Keneally). LFSup 191.

Family of Pascual Duarte, The (Cela). LFFor 292-295.

Family Reunion, The (Eliot). DEng 550-552.

Family Sayings (Ginzburg). LFSup 129-130.

Family Ties (Lispector). ShFSup 166-167.

Family Vault, The (MacLeod). M&D 1180-1181.

Famous Tragedy of the Queen of Cornwall, The (Hardy). DEng 891-893.

Famous Victories of Henry V, The. DEng 2265.

Fan Kuai p'ai chün nan (Chao Tsung). DFor 2305.

"Fanciullino, Il" (Pascoli). PFor 1136-1137.

"Fancy Woman, The" (Taylor). ShF 2310.
Fanny's Consent. See *When a Girl Says Yes.*
Fanon, Frantz. LTh 1062.
Fanshawe (Hawthorne). LFEng 1319-1320.
Fanshawe, Sir Richard. PEng 995-1003.
Fanshen (Hare). DSup 184.
Fantasia of the Unconscious (Lawrence, D. H.).
    LFEng 1583-1584.
Fantasio (Musset). DFor 1402-1403.
Fantastic, The (Todorov). LTh 1432, 1435;
    ShF 92.
Fantasticks, The. See Romantics, The.
"Fantasy, to Laura" (Schiller). PFor 1406.
Fantazy (Słowacki). DFor 1719-1721, 2276.
Fantesca, La (Della Porta). DFor 477-478.
Far Away Is the Sun (Ćosić). LFFor 386-387.
"Far East" (Snyder). PEng 2673.
Far from Cibola (Horgan). LFSup 159-160.
Far from the Madding Crowd (Hardy). LFEng
    1264-1266.
Far Journey of Ouidin, The (Harris). LFSup
    147. See also *Guiana Quartet, The.*
Far-off Hills, The (Robinson). DEng 1617-
    1618.
Far Princess, The (Rostand). DFor 1561-1562.
"Far Rockaway" (Schwartz). PEng 2490.
Far Tortuga (Matthiessen). LFEng 1822-1823,
    1826, 1827, 1830-1832.
"Far West, The" (Snyder). PEng 2672.
"Far Whistle, The" (Beck). ShF 936.
"Far Within Us" (Popa). PFor 1271.
Farce de Maître Pierre Panthelin. DFor 2177.
Farewell and Return, The (Crabbe). PEng 646.
"Farewell, Go with God!" (Unamuno). PFor
    1558.
Farewell, My Lovely (Chandler). LFEng 490;
    M&D 306-307, 309.
Farewell Party, The (Kundera). LFFor 954.
Farewell to Arms, A (Hemingway). LFEng
    1338, 1343-1346.
"Farewell to Cuba" (Cozzens). ShF 1212-1213.
"Farewell to Tobacco, A" (Lamb). PEng 1636.
"Farewell Without a Guitar, A" (Stevens).
    PEng 2750-2751.
Farigoule, Louis-Henri-Jean. *See* **Romains,
    Jules.**
"Faris" (Mickiewicz). PFor 1020-1021.
Färjesång (Ekelöf). PFor 449, 453.
Farmacia di turno (De Filippo). DFor 467-
    468.
Farmer (Harrison). LFEng 1290-1291.

Farmer Forsworn, The (Anzengruber). DFor
    89-90.
Farmer in His World, The. See *King and the
    Farmer, The.*
"Farmer's Daughter, The" (D'Urfey). PEng
    913.
"Farmers' Daughters, The" (Williams, W. C.).
    ShF 2444-2445.
Farming (Berry). PEng 152-153.
Farmyard (Kroetz). DFor 1123-1124.
Farquhar, George. DEng 579-585, 2177.
Farr, John. *See* **Webb, Jack.**
Farrell, James T. LFEng 906-913, 3062; ShF
    265-266, 545, **1351-1357.**
Farrell, J. G. LFSup **108-113.**
Farsa de Santa Susaña (Sánchez de Badajoz).
    DFor 2172.
Farther Off from Heaven. See *Dark at the Top
    of the Stairs, The.*
"Farys." *See* "Faris."
Fashionable Lover, The (Cumberland). DEng
    448-450.
Fashionable Prejudice (La Chaussée). DFor
    1141-1142.
Fassbinder, Rainer Werner. DFor 2383.
Fast, Howard Melvin. *See* **Cunningham, E. V.**
"Fast Train" (Kraus). PFor 797-798.
Fastes d'enfe. See *Chronicles of Hell.*
"Fastest Runner on Sixty-First Street, The"
    (Farrell). ShF 1355-1356.
Fata Morgana (Breton). PFor 234.
Fatal Curiosity (Lillo). DEng 1142-1143,
    1147-1150, 2178.
Fatal Interview (Millay). PEng 2001.
Fatal Inversion, A (Rendell). M&D 1408-1409.
Fatal Revenge (Maturin). LFEng 1838-1839.
Fatal Skin, The. See *Wild Ass's Skin, The.*
Fate at the Wedding. See *Blood Wedding.*
Fate of a Cockroach (Hakim). DSup 177.
Fate of the Jury, The (Masters). PEng 1933.
Fates of the Apostles, The (Cynewulf). PEng
    715-717.
Father, The (Dunlap). DEng 529-530, 2397.
Father, The (Strindberg). DFor 1750.
Father and Son (Kotzebue). DFor 1088.
"Father and Son" (Kunitz). PSup 243-244.
Father Goriot (Balzac). LFEng 3164; LFFor
    98-100; M&D 77.
Father Guzman (Stern). PSup 374-376.
Father Hubburd's Tale (Middleton, T.). PEng
    1995-1996.

Father of an Only Child, The (Dunlap). DEng 530-531.

Father of the Family, The (Diderot). DSup 85-87.

Father of the Plague-Stricken, The (Slowacki). PFor 1443-1444.

Fathers and Sons (Turgenev). LFFor 1775-1777, 2316.

Father's Words, A (Stern). LFSup 366-367.

Fauchono. See *Bristo.*

Faulkner, William. LFEng 914-937, 3058, 3063-3064, 3130-3131, 3155-3156; LTh 316, 1273; **M&D 585-591;** ShF 250-251, 544-545.

Fausses Confidences, Les. See *False Confessions, The.*

Faust (Goethe). DFor 741-743, 2366-2367.

Faust (Reynolds). ShF 732.

Faust, Frederick Schiller. *See* Brand, Max.

Faust, Irvin. ShF 2586.

Faustin, La (Goncourt, E.). LFFor 717.

"Faustina" (Bishop). PEng 187.

"Faustus" (Hope). PSup 191.

Faustus and the Censor (Empson). LTh 465.

Faute de l'abbé Mouret. See *Abbé Mouret's Transgression.*

Faux-monnayeurs, Les. See *Counterfeiters, The.*

Favores del mundo, Los (Ruiz de Alarcón). DFor 1608-1609.

Fawn, The (Marston). DEng 1271-1273.

Fazendeiro do ar (Drummond de Andrade). PSup 100.

Fear of Heaven, The (Mortimer). DEng 1359.

Fearful Joy, A (Cary). LFEng 458.

Fearing, Kenneth. M&D 592-598.

"Fears in Solitude" (Coleridge, S. T.). PEng 541.

Feast in Time of the Plague, The (Pushkin). DFor 1500. See also *Little Tragedies.*

Feast of Lupercal, The (Moore, B.). LFEng 1887-1888.

"Feast of Stephen, The" (Hecht). PEng 1282.

Feather Cloak Murders, The (Teilhet). M&D 1576-1577.

"Features for Characterizing the Russian Common People" (Dobrolyubov). LTh 389.

"February 1st, 1842" (Coleridge, H.). PEng 529-530.

Fecamps, Elise. *See* **Creasey, John.**

Federman, Raymond. ShF 2587.

Fedin, Konstantin. LFFor 2323.

Fédor, La (Daudet). ShF 1241.

Fedra. See *Phaedra.*

"Feed My Lambs" (O'Faoláin). ShF 2002.

Féerie pour une autre fois (Céline). LFFor 310-311.

Fegefeuer in Ingolstadt (Fleisser). DFor 610, 615-620.

"Fei-tsao." *See* "Bar of Soap, A."

Feijóo y Montenegro, Benito Jerónimo. LTh 473-477.

Felderman, Eric. ShF 2589.

"Feleségem és kardom." *See* "My Wife and My Sword."

Felhok. See *Clouds.*

Felicidada clandestina (Lispector). ShFSup 167-168.

"Félig csókolt csók." *See* "Half-Kissed Kiss."

"Felix Krull" (Mann). ShF 1877.

"Felix Randal" (Hopkins). PEng 1401.

"Feliz anniversário." *See* "Happy Birthday."

Fellow-Culprits, The (Goethe). DFor 735.

Fellowship of the Ring, The. See *Lord of the Rings, The.*

Female Consistory of Brockville, The (Caroli Candidus). DEng 2438.

"Female, Extinct" (Beer). PEng 121-122.

Female Imagination, The (Spacks). LTh 1769.

Female Imagination and the Modernist Aesthetic, The (Gilbert and Gubar). LTh 581.

Femme fardée, La. See *Painted Lady, The.*

"Femme noire." *See* "Black Woman."

"Fenchurch Street Mystery, The" (Orczy). M&D 1281-1282.

Fénelon, François de Salignac de La Mothe-. LTh 478-482.

Fenoglio, Beppe. LFFor 2252.

Ferber, Edna. DEng 586-595.

Ferdinand, Count Fathom (Smollett). LFEng 2449.

Ferdowsi. *See* **Firdusi.**

Ferdydurke (Gombrowicz). LFFor 698-699.

Ferguson, Helen. *See* **Kavan, Anna.**

Fergusson, Francis. LTh 242, 1756.

Ferlin, Nils. PFor 2178-2179.

Ferlinghetti, Lawrence. PEng 1004-1010, 3381; PSup 405.

Fermenty (Reymont). LFFor 1407-1408.

Fermo e Lucia. See *Betrothed, The.*

Fernández, Lucas. DFor 2172.

Fernández de Moratín, Leandro. *See* **Moratín, Leandro Fernández de.**

Feron, Jacques. ShF 640.

Ferrars, Elizabeth. *See* **Ferrars, E. X.**

Ferrars, E. X. M&D 599-604.

Ferreira, António. DFor 588-595.

Ferrements. See *Shackles.*

"Festival, The" (Duncan). PEng 901.

Fêtes galantes. See *Gallant Parties.*

"Fetish, The" (Moravia). ShFSup 197-198.

"Fetish for Love, A" (Laurence). ShF 1778.

Fetterley, Judith. LTh 1807.

Feuilles d'automne, Les (Hugo). PFor 733-734.

"Few Crusted Characters, A" (Hardy). ShF 1583-1584.

Feydeau, Georges. DFor 596-607, 2349.

ffinest ffamily in the Land, The (Livings). DEng 1154.

Fichte, Johann Gottlieb. LFFor 2164; LTh 1019, 1358, 1360, 1709.

Ficino, Marsilio. LTh 1127-1128, 1348, 1668.

Fiction and Repetition (Miller). LTh 1033, 1036.

Fiction and the Figures of Life (Gass). ShF 77.

"Fiction Writing in a Time of Troubles" (Wescott). ShF 2422-2423.

"Fictive Wish, The" (Everson). PEng 989.

"Fiddler, The" (Melville). ShF 1918-1919.

"Fiddler of the Reels, The" (Hardy). ShF 1581-1582.

Fiddler's House, The (Colum). DEng 388, 389-390.

"Fido: An Epistle to Fidelia" (Browne). PEng 321.

Fiedler, Leslie. LTh 483-488.

Field, Edward. ShF 316.

Field, Peter. *See* **Halliday, Brett.**

"Field Guide to the Western Birds" (Stegner). ShF 2272-2273.

"Field of Mustard, The" (Coppard). ShF 1196-1197.

Field Work (Heaney). PEng 1265, 1267, 1272-1273.

Fielding, Gabriel. LFSup 114-119.

Fielding, Henry. DEng 596-613, 2337-2338; LTH 1685; LFEng 938-952, 2247.

Fielding, William H. *See* **Teilhet, Darwin L.**

Fields, The (Richter). LFEng 2271.

Fields of Learning (Miles). PSup 278.

Fiend, The (Millar). M&D 1221.

Fiesco (Schiller). DFor 1657-1658.

"Fiesta" (Prévert). PFor 1280.

Fiesta in November (Mallea). LFFor 1052-1053.

"Fifteen: Spring" (West). ShFSup 363.

Fifth Business (Davies). LFEng 664-666, 668-669.

Fifth *Aliya.* LFFor 17-18.

5th of July (Wilson). DEng 2099.

"Fifty Males Sitting Together" (Bly). PEng 227.

Fifty Roads to Town (Nebel). M&D 1268.

Fig for Momus, A (Lodge). PEng 1733.

"Fig Tree" (Merwin). PEng 1982-1983.

"Fig Tree, The" (Porter). ShF 2114-2115.

"Fight, The" (Thomas). ShF 2323.

Fighting for Life (Ong). LTh 1084.

Fighting Terms (Gunn). PEng 1169, 1170.

Figlia di Jorio, La. See *Daughter of Jorio, The.*

"Figlio della Peppa, Il" (Saba). PSup 344.

Figure on the Boundary Line, The (Meckel). ShFSup 189.

"Figures" (Genette). LTh 560.

Figures for an Apocalypse (Merton). PEng 1975.

Figures in Modern Literature (Priestley). LTh 1264.

Figures of Earth (Cabell). LFEng 407-408.

Figures of Literary Discourse (Genette). LTh 559-560.

Figures of the Human (Ignatow). PEng 1473-1474.

"Figures of Thought" (Nemerov). PEng 2089.

Figures of Transition (Hicks). PEng 3410.

Fil à la patte, Un. See *Not By Bed Alone.*

Filippo. See *Phillip II.*

Fille des dieux, La (Kâ). DFor 2268-2269.

Fille Élisa, La. See *Elisa.*

"Filling Station" (Bishop). PEng 189.

Film (Beckett). DEng 156-157.

Filosofo, Il (Aretino). DFor 100.

Fils de Giboyer, Le. See *Giboyer's Son.*

Fils naturel, Le (Diderot). See *Dorval.*

Fils naturel, Le (Dumas, *fils*). See *Natural Son, The.*

Filumena Marturano (De Filippo). DFor 469-470.

Fin de Chéri, La. See *Last of Chéri, The.*

"Fin de l'automne, La." *See* "End of Autumn, The."

Fin de partie. See *Endgame.*

Fin de Satan, La (Hugo). PFor 737-738.

"For Fran" (Levine). PEng 1714.

"For George Lamming" (Birney). PEng 179-180.

"For Homer" (Corso). PEng 579.

"For Jan, in Bar Maria" (Kizer). PEng 1618.

"For John, Who Begs Me Not to Enquire Further" (Sexton). PEng 2523.

"For Koras and Balafong" (Senghor). PFor 1424-1425. See also *Chants d'ombre.*

"For Love" (Creeley). PEng 680-681.

For Love (Creeley). PEng 678, 679.

For Love Alone (Stead). LFEng 2492-2493.

"For My Daughter" (Kees). PEng 1563.

"For My Mother" (Glück). PSup 135.

"For My Son's Birthday" (Coxe). PEng 629.

"For Saundra" (Giovanni). PEng 1101.

For Services Rendered (Maugham). DEng 1310-1311.

"For the Fallen" (Levine). PEng 1717.

"For the Good of the Cause" (Solzhenitsyn). ShF 2250.

"For the Marriage of Faustus and Helen" (Crane, H.). PEng 650-651.

For the Unfallen (Hill, G.). PEng 1351.

"For the Union Dead" (Lowell, R.). PEng 1792-1793.

For the Union Dead (Lowell, R.). PEng 1792.

"For the Word Is Flesh" (Kunitz). PSup 242-243.

"For the Year of the Insane" (Sexton). PEng 2524.

"For Wei Pa, in Retirement" (Tu Fu). PFor 1542-1543.

For Whom the Bell Tolls (Hemingway). LFEng 1338-1339, 1346-1347.

"Forced March" (Radnóti). PFor 1315-1316.

Ford, Ford Madox. LFEng 982-990, 2227, 2230-2231, 3053.

Ford, Jesse Hill. ShF 1383-1386.

Ford, John. DEng 650-670, 2289-2290.

Forefathers' Eve (Mickiewicz). DFor 2276; PFor 1017-1019, 1021-1023.

Foreign Affairs (Lurie). LFSup 251-253.

Foreign Affairs, and Other Stories (O'Faoláin). ShF 666-667, 674.

Foreign Legion, The (Lispector). ShFSup 167.

Foreigner, The (Plante). LFSup 310-311.

Foreman, Richard. DSup 116-124.

Forerunner, The (Gibran). PEng 1084; PFor 567.

Forerunner, The (Merezhkovsky). See *Romance of Leonardo da Vinci, The.*

Forest, The (Ostrovsky). DFor 1451-1452.

Forest, Dial. *See* **Gault, William Campbell.**

"Forest Lake" (Södergran). PSup 364.

Forest of the Night (Jones, M.). LFEng 1489-1490.

Forester, C. S. M&D 640-645.

"Forests of Lithuania, The" (Davie). PSup 88-89.

"Forêt de longue actente, La" (Charles d'Orléans). PFor 342.

Foretaste of Glory (Stuart). LFEng 2575-2576.

Forever Yours, Marie-Lou (Tremblay). DSup 351-352.

Forges, A. de. *See* **Sue, Eugène.**

Forget-Me-Not Lane (Nichols). DSup 281.

"Foring Parts" (Thackeray). ShF 2315.

Forjættde land, Det. See *Promised Land, The.*

"Forks, The" (Powers). ShF 2119.

Forlorn Demon, The (Tate). LTh 1428.

Form of Victorian Fiction, The (Miller). LTh 1035.

"Form of Women, A" (Creeley). PEng 678-679.

"Formal Short Story in France and Its Development Before 1850, The" (Engstrom). ShF 76.

"Formation of a Separatist, I" (Howe). PSup 196.

"Forms of Art" (Bely). LTh 126.

Forms of Discovery (Winters). LTh 1569.

Forms of Fiction, The (Gardner and Dunlap, eds.). ShF 77.

Forner y Segarra, Juan Pablo. LTh 1693.

Fornés, María Irene. DEng 2487.

Forrest, Edwin. DEng 2525.

"Forsaken Garden, A" (Swinburne). PEng 2821.

"Forschungen eines Hundes." *See* "Investigations of a Dog."

Forse che si forse che no (D'Annunzio). LFFor 413-414.

"Forse perché della fatal quiete." *See* "Perhaps Because of the Fateful Quiet."

Forskrevet (Drachmann). LFFor 2339.

Forssell, Lars. PFor 2187.

Forster, E. M. LFEng 991-1007, 3053; LTh 496-501, 925, 927, 1404; ShF 121, 258, 521, 1387-1392.

Forsyth, Frederick. M&D 646-650.

"Forsythia" (Solt). PEng 3230, 3231.
Fort, Paul. *See* **Stockton, Frank R.**
Forth Feasting (Drummond). PEng 859.
Fortini, Franco. PFor 2050.
"Fortress, The" (Sexton). PEng 2523-2524.
Fortunata and Jacinta (Pérez Galdós). LFFor 1280-1282.
Fortunate Peasant, The (Marivaux). LFFor 1104-1106.
Fortunatus. LFFor 2150.
Fortunatus, Venantius. PFor 2113.
Fortune, My Foe (Davies). DEng 467, 472-473.
Fortunes and Misfortunes of the Famous Moll Flanders, The. See *Moll Flanders.*
Fortunes of Colonel Torlogh O'Brien, The (Le Fanu). LFEng 1623-1624.
Fortunes of Perkin Warbeck, The (Shelley, M.). LFEng 2392.
Forty Days of Musa Dagh, The (Werfel). LFFor 1910-1911.
"Forty-five a Month" (Narayan). ShFSup 227.
42nd Parallel, The (Dos Passos). LFEng 794-796.
"Forvandling" (Hauge). LFFor 802-803.
Foscolo, Ugo. DFor 2407; **PFor 491-498.**
Fossil, The (Sternheim). DFor 1739-1740.
Fossils, The (Curel). DFor 451-452.
Fotódhendro ke i dhékati tétarti omorfiá, To (Elýtis). PFor 466.
"Fou, Le" (Creeley). PEng 678.
"Fou, Un" (Maupassant). *See* "Madman, The."
"Fou?" *See* "Am I Insane?"
Fou d'Elsa, Le (Aragon). PFor 68, 71.
Foucault, Michel. LTh 195, **502-507,** 1070, 1152, 1476, 1804, 1821-1822, 1826.
"Foul Shots" (Matthews). PEng 1940.
"Found Drowned" (Phillpotts). M&D 1327-1328.
Foundation, The (Buero Vallejo). DFor 283-285.
"Foundations of American Industry, The" (Hall). PEng 1199.
"Founding and Manifesto of Futurism, The" (Marinetti). LTh 994.
Fountainville Abbey (Dunlap). DEng 532.
Four-Chambered Heart, The (Nin). LFEng 1994-1995.
Four Dissertations (Hume). LTh 724.
Four-Gated City, The (Lessing). LFEng 1645-1647, 3131.

Four Horsemen of the Apocalypse, The (Blasco Ibáñez). LFFor 175.
"Four Letters Confuted, The" (Nashe). PEng 2072
"Four Meetings" (James, H.). ShF 1677-1680.
"Four Poems" (Bishop). PEng 189.
Four P.P., The (Heywood, J.). DEng 945.
Four Quartets (Eliot). PEng 948.
"IV Rescue in Florida: The Friend" (Logan). PEng 1742.
Four Wise Men, The (Tournier). LFFor 1746-1747.
Four Zoas, The (Blake). PEng 217.
Fourchambault, Les. See *House of Fourchambault, The.*
Fourmi dans le corps, La (Audiberti). DFor 2359.
Fournier, Henri-Alban. *See* **Alain-Fournier.**
Fourteen Sonnets (Bowles). PEng 251.
Fourth Commandment, The (Anzengruber). DFor 91-92, 2373.
Fourth Deadly Sin, The (Sanders). M&D 1464.
Fourth Postman, The (Rice). M&D 1423-1424.
Fourth Protocol, The (Forsyth). M&D 648.
Fous des Bassan, Les. See *In the Shadow of the Wind.*
Fowler, Roger. PEng 3458-3459.
Fowles, John. LFEng 1008-1022; LFSup 403; **ShF 1393-1399.**
Fowre Hymnes (Spenser). PEng 2707.
"Fox, The" (Lawrence, D. H.). LFEng 3315-3317.
Fox, Robert. ShF 2593.
Fox Fables (Berechiah). ShF 380-381.
"Fox Hunt" (Still). PEng 2763.
Foxe, John. ShF 498.
Foxes of Harrow, The (Yerby). LFEng 2987-2988.
Foxprints (McGinley). M&D 1150-1152.
Fox's Paw, The (Pérez de Ayala). LFFor 1256-1257.
Foxx, Jack. *See* **Pronzini, Bill.**
Foxybaby (Jolley). LFSup 180-181.
Fra det moderne Amerikas aandsliv. See *Spiritual Life of Modern America, The.*
Fracastoro, Girolamo. PFor 499-510.
"Fragment of the Lives of Three Friends, A" (Hoffmann). ShF 1648.
"Fragment on Death" (Swinburne). PEng 2822.
Fragments (Anacreon). PFor 35-38.
Fragments (Archilochus). PFor 88-91.

98

Fragments (Armah). LFEng 86-88.

Fragments (Sappho). PFor 1396-1400.

"Fragments of a Liquidation" (Howe). PSup 195-196.

Frailty and Hypocrisy (Beaumarchais). DFor 153.

Frana allo scalo nord. See *Landslide.*

France, Anatole. LFFor 570-580; ShF 1400-1407.

Francesca da Rimini (Boker). DEng 222-224, 2398.

Francesca da Rimini (D'Annunzio). DFor 2412.

Francesco's Fortunes (Greene). PEng 1149-1150, 1151.

Franchiser, The (Elkin). LFEng 891-892.

Francis, Dick. M&D 651-655.

Francis, H. E. ShF 2594.

Franco, Marjorie. ShF 2596.

Francoeur Novels, The (Plante). LFSup 307-310.

Frank (Edgeworth). ShF 1323.

Frank, Leonhard. ShF 2597.

"Frank Courtship, The" (Crabbe). PEng 644.

Frankenstein (Shelley, M.). LFEng 2386, 2388-2389, 3129, 3139-3140, 3141; ShF 179, 475, 735.

Frankie and Johnnie (Kirkland). DEng 1048-1049.

Franklin, Benjamin. LTh 1741; ShF 1408-1414.

"Franklin's Tale, The" (Chaucer). PEng 3265-3266; ShF 1113, 1115-1116.

Franzén, Frans Mikael. PFor 2162.

Fraser, Lady Antonia. M&D 656-660.

Fraternity (Galsworthy). LFEng 1061-1062.

Frau Jenny Treibel. See *Jenny Treibel.*

Frau Jutta (Schernberg). DFor 2169-2170.

Frayn, Michael. DSup 125-132.

Frazer, Fred. *See* **Avallone, Michael.**

Frazer, Robert Caine. *See* **Creasey, John.**

Freddy's Book (Gardner, J.). LFEng 1079-1080.

Frederic, Harold. LFEng 1023-1033.

Frederic and Elfrida (Austen). ShF 896-897.

"Fredericksbury" (Aldrich). PEng 34.

Fredro, Aleksander. DFor 2277; DSup 133-141.

Free Fall (Golding). LFEng 1133-1134.

Free Fall in Crimson (MacDonald, J.). M&D 1132.

"Free Fiction" (Canby). ShF 72.

"Free Joe and the Rest of the World" (Harris, J.). ShF 1589-1590.

Free-Lance Pallbearers, The (Reed). LFSup 337.

Free Union (Breton). PFor 233-234.

Freedom for Clemens (Dorst). DSup 93.

"Freedom Kick, The" (Foote). LFEng 979.

Freedom of the City, The (Friel). DEng 675-676.

Freedom or Death (Kazantzakis). LFFor 920.

"Freedom's a Hard-Bought Thing" (Benét). ShF 956-957.

Freeing of the Dust, The (Levertov). PEng 1709.

Freeling, Nicholas. M&D 661-666.

Freeman, Mary E. Wilkins. ShF 228-229, 1415-1422.

Freeman, R. Austin. M&D 667-673; ShF 753.

Freeman, Susannah. *See* **Centlivre, Mrs. Susannah.**

Freeway, The (Nichols). DSup 282.

"Freezing" (Meredith). PEng 1957.

Freiheit für Clemens. See *Freedom for Clemens.*

Fremsynte, Den. See *Visionary, The.*

French Lieutenant's Woman, The (Fowles). LFEng 1016-1018.

French Revolution, The (Blake). PEng 213.

French Vulgate Cycle. LFEng 1802.

French Without Tears (Rattigan). DEng 1559-1561.

Freneau, Philip. PEng 1030-1038.

Frenssen, Gustav. LFFor 2182.

Frères Zemganno, Les. See *Zemganno Brothers, The.*

Frescoes for Mr. Rockefeller's City (MacLeish). PEng 1857.

Freud, Sigmund. LTh 214, 359, 685, 760, 833-834, 844-851, 890-891, 988, 1273, 1318, 1712, 1737, 1763-1764, 1767, 1822-1823; PEng 3419-3420; PFor 229-230.

Freund, Edith. ShF 2598.

Freyre, Isabel. PFor 523-524.

Freytag, Gustav. LFFor 2174.

Friar Bacon and Friar Bungay (Greene, R.). DEng 840-841, 2270-2271; PEng 1150.

"Friar Jerome's Beautiful Book" (Aldrich). PEng 31.

Fribytaren på Östersjön (Rydberg). LFFor 2337.

Fugitive, The (Fish). M&D 607.

Fühmann, Franz. PFor 1817, 1821, 1822, 1825.

Führer Bunker, The (Snodgrass). PEng 2664.

Fulgens and Lucres (Medwall). DEng 1315-1319, 2258; ShF 147.

Fulgentius. LTh **514-519**, 1647, 1654.

Full Moon (Wodehouse). LFEng 2921-2922.

Fuller, Margaret. LFEng 3041; LTh **520-526.**

Fumento, Rocco. ShF 2601.

Function of Criticism, The (Eagleton). LTh 418.

"Function of Criticism at the Present Time, The" (Arnold). LTh 48; PEng 3483.

Fundación, La. See *Foundation, The.*

Fundamentals of Language (Jakobson and Hale). LTh 1762.

Funeral Games (Renault). LFEng 2224.

Funeral in Berlin (Deighton). M&D 473-474.

"Funeral Ode on the Death of the Princess Charlotte" (Southey). PEng 2683.

Funeral Rites (Genet). LFFor 627.

"Funeral Wake, The" (D'Annunzio). ShF 687.

5 mal 1 Konstellation (Gomringer). PFor 595.

"Funland" (Abse). PEng 3, 4.

"Funnels, The" (Morgenstern). PFor 1059. See also *Gallows Songs, The.*

Funny Old Man, The (Różewicz). DFor 1585.

Funnyhouse of a Negro (Kennedy). DSup 213-215.

Fuoco, Il. See *Flame of Life, The.*

Für meine Genossen (Biermann). PFor 191-192.

Furetière, Antoine. LFFor 2028.

Furey, Michael. *See* **Rohmer, Sax.**

Furie des Verschwindens, Die (Enzensberger). PFor 469-470.

Furmanov, Dmitri. LFFor 2324.

Fürsorgliche Belagerung. See *Safety Net, The.*

Furtado, Joseph. PFor 2001.

Further Adventures of Nils, The (Lagerlöf). LFFor 978, 2344.

"Further Question" (Salinas). PFor 1387.

"Further Reminiscences of Ijon Tichy" (Lem). ShFSup 152.

Fury Chronicle, The (Hanley). LFEng 1245, 1247-1249.

"Fury of Aerial Bombardment, The" (Eberhart). PEng 931-932.

Furys, The. See *Fury Chronicle, The.*

Fusane's Trial (Hutchinson). DEng 2419-2420.

Fussy Man, The (Holberg). DFor 950-951.

Füst, Milán. PFor 1985.

Fūten rōjin nikki. See *Diary of a Mad Old Man.*

Futrelle, Jacques. M&D **674-679;** ShF 752.

Future Is Ours, Comrade, The (Kosinski). LFEng 1558-1559.

Future of Science, The (Renan). LTh 1417.

Futurisme, Le (Marinetti). LTh 995.

Futurological Congress, The (Lem). LFFor 1012.

Futz (Owens). DEng 1456-1457.

G

Gaboriau, Émile. M&D 680-686.

Gabriel (Pushkin). PFor 1296.

Gabriela, Clove and Cinnamon (Amado). LFFor 53-54.

Gabriela, cravo e canela. See *Gabriela, Clove and Cinnamon.*

Gadamer, Hans-Georg. LTh 527-532, 766, 1770.

Gadda, Carlo Emilio. LFFor 602-611, 2253.

Gaddis, William. LFEng 1034-1041; LFSup 403.

Gaines, Ernest J. LFEng 1042-1049; LFSup 403; ShF 582, 1429-1436.

Gaius Cornelius Gallus. *See* Gallus.

Gaius Julius Caesar. *See* Caesar, Gaius Julius.

Gaius Plinius Caecilius Secundus. *See* Pliny the Younger.

Gaius Sallustius Crispus. *See* Sallust.

Gaius Valerius Catullus. *See* **Catullus.**

Gaius Vetteius Aquilinus Juvencus. *See* Juvencus.

Gaj, Ljudevit. PFor 2262.

Gala (West). LFSup 375.

Galanskov, Yuri. PFor 2151.

Galanteries du duc d'Ossonne, Les (Mairet). DFor 1248-1249.

Galathea (Lyly). DEng 1182-1184.

Galaxy. ShF 585, 587-588, 767, 776.

Galdós, Benito Pérez. LFEng 3171.

"Galeso et Maximo, De" (Bembo). PFor 168.

Galgenlieder. See *Gallows Songs, The.*

Galich, Manuel. DFor 2445.

Galileo. See *Life of Galileo.*

Gallant, Mavis. LFEng 1050-1056; ShF 551, 640, 1437-1440; ShFSup 388.

Gallant Parties (Verlaine). PFor 1629-1631.

Gallery, The (Burns). ShF 274.

Gallicanus (Hroswitha). DFor 2153.

Gallico, Paul. ShF 1441-1445.

Gallina, Giacinto. DFor 2410.

Gallows of Chance, The (Oppenheim). M&D 1275.

Gallows Songs, The (Morgenstern). PFor 1057.

Gallus. PFor 2097.

"Galope muerto." *See* "Dead Gallop."

Galsworthy, John. DEng 709-717; LFEng 1057-1066, 3052, 3082; ShF 1446-1451.

Galton Case, The (Macdonald). LFSup 274-275.

Gálvez, Manuel. LFFor 2287.

Galvin, Brendan. PEng 1050-1057; PSup 405.

Gambaro, Griselda. DFor 2444; DSup 142-152.

Gambler, The (Betti). DFor 210.

Gamboa, Federico. DFor 2442; LFFor 2285.

Game, The (Euba). DEng 2422.

Game at Chess, A (Middleton). DEng 1326.

Game of Love and Chance, The (Marivaux). DFor 1265-1266, 2339.

"Games" (Popa). PFor 1270.

Gamester, The (Centlivre). DEng 346-347.

Gamlet (Sumarokov). DFor 1785-1786.

Gammer Gurton's Needle (Stevenson?). DEng 2257, 2264.

Ganar amigos (Ruiz de Alarcón). DFor 1606-1607.

"Gander-pulling, The" (Longstreet). ShF 1816-1817.

Gandhi (Trivadi). DFor 2391.

Gandhi, Mahatma. ShF 643.

"Gangrene" (Levine). PEng 1714.

"Gangu." *See* "Toys."

"Ganymed" (Goethe). PFor 585-586.

"Ganymed" (Hölderlin). PFor 686. See also *Nachtgesänge.*

Gao Ming. *See* Kao Ming.

Gao Tsê-ch'êng. *See* Kao Ming.

Gaol Gate, The (Gregory). DEng 853-854.

Går an, Det. See *Sara Videbeck.*

Garber, Eugene K. ShF 2602.

Garborg, Arne. DFor 2470-2471; LFFor 2341; PFor 2170.

García Guitiérrez, Antonio. DFor 2498.

García Lorca, Federico. DEng 2204; DFor 651-666; PFor 22, 511-520.

García Márquez, Gabriel. LFFor 612-620, 2292-2293, 2299; LFSup 403-404; ShF 694, 702, 704, 705, 1452-1457; ShFSup 388.

Garcilaso de la Vega. PFor 521-528, 2216-2217.

Garçon et l'aveugle, Le. DFor 2175.
"Garden, The" (Glück). PSup 136.
"Garden, The" (Marvell). PEng 1913-1915.
Garden, Ashes (Kiš). LFSup 214.
"Garden at St. Johns, The" (Swenson). PEng 2796.
Garden of Adonis, The (Gordon). LFEng 1178.
Garden of Earthly Delights, The (Clarke). DSup 64.
Garden of Earthly Delights, A (Oates). LFEng 2011.
"Garden of Love, The" (Blake). PEng 3428.
"Garden of Proserpine, The" (Swinburne). PEng 2819.
"Garden of the Forking Paths, The" (Borges). M&D 163-164; ShF 980-981.
Garden of Weapons, The (Gardner, J.). M&D 697.
Garden Party, The (Havel). DFor 878-879.
"Garden Party, The" (Mansfield). ShF 790.
"Gardener, The" (Kipling). ShF 1749, 1753-1755.
Gardener's Dog, The (Vega). DFor 1937.
Gardenia (Guare). DEng 863.
Gardeniny ikh dvornya priverzhentsy i vragi (Ertel). LFFor 2319.
"Gardens of the Villa d'Este, The" (Hecht). PEng 1279.
Gardner, Erle Stanley. LFEng 3189-3190; **M&D 687-693.**
Gardner, Helen. LTh 810-811.
Gardner, John. LFEng 1067-1082; LTh 260, **533-539; M&D 694-699; ShF 1458-1464;** ShFSup 388-389.
Gardner, Richard. ShF 2603.
Gargantua and Pantagruel (Rabelais). LFFor 1388, 1390-1394, 2112.
Gargoyles (Bernhard). LFFor 157-158.
Garibaldina, La (Vittorini). LFFor 1888-1889.
Garin, N. LFFor 2319.
Garland, Hamlin. LFEng 1083-1089; LTh 1749-1750; ShF 230-231, 586, 589.
Garland of Laurel, The (Skelton). PEng 2639-2640.
Garner, Hugh. ShF 640.
Garnier, Robert. DFor 667-673.
Garrett, George. LFEng 1090-1096; LFSup 404; **ShF 1472-1477;** ShFSup 389.
Garrick, David. DEng 2322, 2324, 2326, 2327, 2524.
Garve, Andrew. M&D 700-704.

Gas (Kaiser). DFor 1021-1023, 2378. See also *Coral* and *Gas II.*
Gas II (Kaiser). DFor 1021-1023, 2378. See also *Coral* and *Gas.*
Gascoigne, George. DEng 718-728; LTh 540-545, 1663; PEng 1058-1068, 3289-3290; ShF 484, 490.
"Gascoignes Lullabie" (Gascoigne). PEng 1066-1067.
"Gascoignes Memories" (Gascoigne). PEng 1062-1063.
"Gascoignes Wodmanship" (Gascoigne). PEng 1066.
"Gash, The" (Everson). PEng 992.
Gash, Jonathan. M&D 705-710.
Gaskell, Mrs. Elizabeth. LFEng 1097-1107, 3078.
Gaspard, Melchior et Balthazar. See *Four Wise Men, The.*
Gass, William H. LFEng 3329, 3330; **LFSup 120-126; ShF 1478-1483.**
Gastfreund, Der. See *Golden Fleece, The.*
Gaston, Wilber. See **Gibson, Walter B.**
Gaston de Blondeville (Radcliffe). LFEng 2200.
Gaston de Latour (Pater). LFEng 2075-2076.
"Gâteau, Le." *See* "Cake, The."
"Gates, The" (Rukeyser). PSup 334-335.
Gates, Henry Louis, Jr. LTh 546-550.
Gates of the Forest, The (Wiesel). LFFor 1924-1926.
Gathering of Fugitives, A (Trilling). LTh 1455.
Gathering Place, The (Breen). M&D 199-200.
Gathering Storm, The (Empson). PEng 965, 971.
"Gathering the Bones Together" (Orr). PEng 2151-2152.
Gatomachia (Vega). PFor 1603-1604.
Gatti, Armand. DFor 2360.
Gatto, Alfonso. PFor 2045, 2048.
Gattopardo, Il. See *Leopard, The.*
Gaudette (Hughes, T.). PEng 1445.
Gaudy Night (Sayers). LFEng 2361-2362; M&D 1477-1478.
Gault, William Campbell. M&D 711-716.
Gaunt, Graham. *See* **Gash, Jonathan.**
Gauntlet, A (Bjørnson). DFor 218.
Gauthier-Villars, Henri. LFFor 367-368.
Gautier, Théophile. LTh 113, 551-557, 1732; **PFor 529-541,** 1872-1873; ShF 172.
Gavriiliada. See *Gabriel.*

Gawain-Poet. *See* **Pearl-Poet, The.**
Gay, John. DEng **729-736,** 2179; PEng **1069-1078;** ShF 143, 455.
"Gazebo" (Carver). ShFSup 78.
"Gazing at Yellow Crane Mountain" (Li Po). PFor 891.
Gde tonko, tam i rvyotsya. See *Where It Is Thin, There It Breaks.*
Gdzie wschodzi słońce i kedy zapada (Miłosz). PFor 1035-1036.
"Gebet, Das." *See* "Prayer, The."
"Gebet des Zoraster." *See* "Prayer of Zarathustra."
"Gebildete Nation." *See* "Cultured Nation."
Gebir (Landor). PEng 1643.
Geburt der Tragödie aus dem Geiste der Musik, Die. See *Birth of Tragedy Out of the Spirit of Music, The.*
Gedanken über die Nachahmung der griechischen Werke in der Malerei und Bildhauerkunst. See *Reflections on the Paintings and Sculpture of the Greeks.*
"Gedicht, Das." *See* "Poem, The."
Gedichten, gezangen en gebeden (Gezelle). PFor 555-557.
"Gefesselte Strom, Der." *See* "Chained Stream, The."
Geijer, Erik Gustaf. PFor 2165-2166.
Geijerstam, Gustaf af. LFFor 2340.
Geistliche Lieder (Luther). See *Spiritual Songs.*
Geistliche Lieder (Novalis). See *Devotional Songs.*
Gelber, Jack. DEng **737-746,** 2481.
"Gelding of the Devil, The" (D'Urfey). PEng 912.
Geller, Ruth. ShF 2604.
Gellius, Aulus. LTh 1681.
Gelzer, Johann Heinrich. LTh 436.
"Gemeine, Das" (Dazai). ShFSup 95-96.
Gemini (Giovanni). PEng 1097, 1099, 1100, 1101-1102.
Gemini (Innaurato). DSup 202-203.
Gemini (Tournier). LFFor 1745-1746.
Gemini Contenders, The (Ludlum). M&D 1109-1110.
Genealogia deorum gentilium (Boccaccio). LTh 172, 1655, 1668-1669.
General Confession (Davies). DEng 469, 470.
"General Prologue, The" to *The Canterbury Tales* (Chaucer). PEng 486, 3262-3263.

"General William Booth Enters into Heaven" (Lindsay). PEng 1721, 1723-1724.
"General's Day, The" (Trevor). ShFSup 320-321.
General's Ring, The. See *Ring of the Löwenskölds, The.*
Generation Without Farewell (Boyle). LFEng 279-280.
"Generations" (Gurney). PEng 1180.
Generous Man, A (Price). LFEng 2131-2132.
Genesis. ShF 330-335, 337-342.
"Genesis" (Elýtis). PFor 465, 1967. See also *Axion Esti, The.*
"Genesis" (Hill, G.). PEng 1349-1352.
Genet, Jean. DFor **674-690,** 2258-2260, 2358; LFFor **621-634;** LFSup 404; LTh 1274.
Genette, Gérard. LTh 195, **558-564,** 1437.
Genezis z Ducha (Słowacki). PFor 1446.
Gengandere. See *Ghosts.*
"Genial Host, The" (McCarthy). ShF 124-125.
Génie du Christianisme, Le. See *Genius of Christianity, The.*
"Genio e tendenze di Tommasco Carlyle." *See* "On the Genius and Tendency of the Writing of Thomas Carlyle."
Genitrix (Mauriac). LFFor 1126-1127.
Genius, The (Brenton). DSup 34-35.
Genius and the Goddess, The (Huxley). LFEng 1409-1410.
Genius of Christianity, The (Chateaubriand). LFFor 333-334, 2124.
Genius of the Crowd, The (Bukowski). PEng 359.
Genji monogatari. See *Tale of Genji, The.*
"Genoveva" (Trench). PEng 2934-2935.
Gente conocida (Benavente). DFor 177.
Gentile, Giovanni. LTh 328.
"Gentilesse" (Chaucer). ShF 1101-1102.
Gentle Grafter, The (Henry). M&D 855-856; ShF 1632-1633.
Gentle Weight Lifter, The (Ignatow). PEng 1471.
"Gentleman, The" (Guillén). PFor 626-627.
Gentleman Dancing-Master, The (Wycherley). DEng 2107-2109.
"Gentleman of Shalott, The" (Bishop). PEng 185.
Gentleman Usher, The (Chapman). DEng 356-357.

"Gentlemen and Players" (Hornung). M&D 907.

Gentlemen, I Address You Privately (Boyle). LFEng 276-277.

Gentlemen in England (Wilson). LFSup 390-391.

Gentlemen in Their Season (Fielding). LFSup 117-118.

Geoffrey of Vinsauf. LTh 22, **565-570**, 1652.

"Geographer" (Hacker). PEng 1189-1190.

Geography of Lagaire, The (Merton). PEng 1977.

Geography of Poets, A (Field, ed.). ShF 316.

"Geography of the Near Past" (Young). PEng 3216-3217.

Geography of the Near Past (Young). PEng 3215.

"George" (Randall, D.). PEng 2314-2315.

George, Stefan. LTh **571-577**, 639-641; PFor **542-550**, 670-671, 1924.

George Silverman's Experiment (Dickens). ShF 1270-1271.

George Washington Poems, The (Wakoski). PEng 2997.

Georges, Georges-Martin. *See* **Simenon, Georges.**

George's Mother (Crane). LFEng 641.

Georgia Scenes (Longstreet). ShF 613, 1814.

"Georgia Theatrics" (Longstreet). ShF 1815-1816.

Georgics (Vergil). LTh 1043; PFor 1606, 1609-1611; ShF 2385.

Gerammelten Gedichte (Zweig). PFor 1725-1726.

Gerber, Merrill Joan. ShF 2605.

German Mythology (Grimm, J.). ShF 1556.

Germania Tod in Berlin (Müller). DSup 260-261.

"Germanic Materials and Motifs in the Short Story" (Pochman). ShF 87.

Germanicus. DFor 2147.

Germany: A Winter's Tale (Heine). LTh 663-664; PFor 648, 650.

Germany (Staël). LTh 1380, 1382-1383, 1696, 1704.

Germinal (Zola). LFFor 1994. See also *Rougon-Macquart, Les.*

Germinie Lacerteux (Goncourts). LFFor 714-715.

Gernsback, Hugo. LFEng 3209.

"Gerontion" (Eliot). PEng 943.

Gerould, Katherine Fullerton. ShF 177.

Geroy nashego vremeni. See Hero of Our Time, A.

Gerpla. See Happy Warriors, The.

Gerusalemme conquistata. See Jerusalem Conquered.

Gerusalemme liberata. See Jerusalem Delivered.

Gervinus, Georg Gottfried. LTh 436.

Gesammelte Werke in sieben Bänden (Ausländer). PSup 18.

"Gesang für meine Genossen." *See* "Song for My Comrades."

Ge-sar epic, The. PFor 2245-2246.

Geschichte der alten und neuen Literatur. See Lectures on the History of Literature Ancient and Modern.

Geschichte der Kunst des Alterthums. See History of Ancient Art.

Geschichte der Poesie der Griechen und Römer (Schlegel, F.). LTh 1310.

Geschichte der poetischen Literatur Deutschlands (Eichendorff). LTh 436-438.

Geschichte der poetischen National-Literatur der Deutschen (Gervinus). LTh 436.

Geschichte des Fräuleins von Sternheim. See History of Lady Sophia Sternheim.

Geschichte und Klassenbewusstsein. See History and Class Consciousness.

Geschichten aus dem Wiener Wald. See Tales from the Vienna Woods.

Geschichten Jakobs, Die. See Tales of Jacob, The.

Gesellschaft im Herbst (Dorst). DSup 93-94.

Gespräch im Hause Stein über den abwesenden Herrn von Goethe, Ein (Hacks). DFor 854.

Gespräch über die Poesie. See "Dialogue on Poetry."

"Gest Historiale of the Destruction of Troy, The." ShF 447.

Gesta Danorum (Saxo Grammaticus). LFFor 2333.

Gesta Regum Anglorum. See Acts of the Kings.

Gestalt am Ende des Grundstücks, Die. See Figure on the Boundary Line, The.

Gesticulador, El (Usigli). DFor 2443; DSup 362-363.

Gestiefelte Kater, Der. See Puss-in-Boots.

Gestohlene Bachern, Der (Sachs). DFor 1625-1626.

Gestundete Zeit, Die (Bachmann). PFor 126-127.

"Get on with the Sleeping" (Zoshchenko). ShFSup 377-378.

Get Ready for Battle (Jhabvala). LFSup 174.

Geteilte Himmel, Der. See *Divided Heaven*

Getting a Way with Murder (McInerny). M&D 1162-1163.

Getting Away with Murder? See *Murder Post-Dated*.

"Getting into Death" (Disch). ShF 1288.

Getting into Death (Disch). ShF 1289-1290.

Getting Out (Norman). DSup 290.

Gewicht der Welt, Das. See *Weight of the World, The*.

"Gezeiten." *See* "Tides."

Gezelle, Guido. PFor 551-561.

Ghare baire. See *Home and the World*.

"Ghaselen II." *See* "Ghazel II."

"Ghazel II" (Hofmannsthal). PFor 673-674.

Ghelderode, Michel de. DFor 691-699.

Ghetto (Heijermans). DFor 813.

Ghose, Aurobindo. *See* Aurobindo, Sri.

Ghose, Kasiprasad. PFor 1994.

Ghose, Manmohan. PFor 1999.

Ghost in the Machine, The (Koestler). LFEng 1550.

Ghost It Was, The (Hull). M&D 917.

Ghost of Lucrece, The (Middleton, T.). PEng 1995.

Ghost Sonata, The (Strindberg). DFor 1754-1755.

Ghost Stories and Tales of Mystery (Le Fanu). ShF 1796.

Ghost Way, The (Hillerman). M&D 881-882.

Ghost Writer, The (Roth). LFEng 2308-2309.

"Ghostly Father, I Confess" (McCarthy). ShF 1837-1838.

Ghostly Lover, The (Hardwick). LFEng 1256-1257.

Ghosts (Ibsen). DFor 982-983, 2472.

Ghosts of the Heart (Logan). PEng 1740.

"Giacca stregata, La." *See* "Bewitched Jacket, The."

Giacosa, Giuseppe. DFor 700-710, 2410.

Giambi ed epodi (Carducci). PFor 270-271.

"Giardino incantato, Il" (Calvino). ShF 1043-1044.

Gibbs, Henry. *See* **Harvester, Simon.**

Giboyer's Son (Augier). DFor 138-140.

Gibran, Kahlil. PEng 1079-1087; PFor 562-570.

Gibson, Morgan. ShF 2606.

Gibson, Walter B. M&D 717-724.

Gibson, William. DEng 747-755; DSup 407.

Gide, André. LFFor 635-650, 2138-2140; LTh 1171.

Gierow, Karl Ragner. DFor 2479.

Gift, The (Nabokov). LFEng 1950-1951.

"Gift of the Magi, The" (Henry). LFEng 3218; ShF 230, 1630, 1631, 1632.

Gift Shop, The (Armstrong). M&D 39.

Giganti della montagna, I. See *Mountain Giants, The*.

Gigi (Colette). LFFor 372-373; ShF 1164-1165.

Gil Blas (Lesage). LFFor 1030-1035, 2029-2030, 2118.

Gilbert, Anthony. M&D 725-730.

Gilbert, Michael. M&D 731-738.

Gilbert, Nicolas-Joseph-Laurent. PFor 1862-1863.

Gilbert, Sandra. ShF 2607.

Gilbert, Sandra M., and Susan Gubar. LTh 578-582, 1769.

Gilbert, W. S. DEng 756-768, and Sir Arthur Sullivan. DEng 2460-2461, 2467.

Gilchrist, Ellen. ShF 2608.

Gilder, Richard Watson. ShF 586, 588.

Giles Goat-Boy (Barth). LFEng 165-167.

Gilgun, John. ShF 2609.

Gill, B. M. M&D 739-744.

Gill, Brendan. ShF 1484-1487.

Gill, Claes. PFor 2189.

Gill, Patrick. *See* **Creasey, John.**

Gilles et Jeanne (Tournier). LFFor 1747.

Gilman, Dorothy. M&D 745-749.

Gilman, George. LFEng 3198.

Gilroy, Frank D. DEng 769-782.

"Gimiendo." *See* "Groaning."

"Gimpel the Fool" (Singer). ShF 2242-2243.

"Ginestra, La." *See* "Broom, The."

Ginger Man, The (Donleavy). LFEng 783-784.

"Gingillino." *See* "Trifler, The."

Ginsberg, Allen. PEng 1088-1096; PSup 405.

Ginzburg, Natalia. DFor 2415-2416; LFFor 2255-2256; LFSup 127-132.

Giocatore, Il. See *Gambler, The*.

Gioconda (D'Annunzio). DFor 460.

Giono, Jean. LFFor 651-659.

Giorno, Il (Parini). LTh 1691; PFor 2021-2022.

Giorno della civetta, Il. See *Mafia Vendetta.*

Giovanni, Nikki. PEng 1097-1104; PSup 405.

Giovanni da Procida (Niccolini). DFor 1431-1432.

Giovanni Episcopo. See *Episcopo and Company.*

Giraffe (Plumly). PEng 2233, 2234, 2235-2237.

Giraldi Cinthio, Giambattista. DEng 2157; **DFor 711-719,** 2395; LTh **583-588,** 1667.

Giraldus Cambrensis. LTh 22.

Girard, James P. ShF 2610.

Girard, René. LTh 589-594.

Giraudoux, Jean. DFor **721-730,** 2353.

"Girella's Toast" (Giusti). PFor 575.

Girl from Samos, The (Menander). DFor 1304-1306, 2133.

"Girl in a Library, A" (Jarrell). PEng 1483.

"Girl in the Storm, The" (Cain). ShF 1025.

"Girl Named Peter, A" (Bates). ShFSup 31.

Girl of the Golden West, The (Belasco). DEng 197-199.

Girl Who Was Shorn, The (Menander). DFor 2133.

"Girls at War" (Achebe). ShF 822-823.

Girls in Their Married Bliss (O'Brien, E.). LFEng 2019-2020.

"Girls in Their Summer Dresses, The" (Shaw). ShF 2224-2225.

"Girl's Song" (Bogan). PEng 233.

Gironella, José María. LFFor 660-666.

Gísla saga. LFFor 2332.

Gisli's Saga. ShF 393.

Gissing, George. LFEng 1108-1116; ShF 516.

Gitanjali (Tagore). PFor 1482-1483, 1485.

"Giulia Lazzari" (Maugham). M&D 1203-1204.

Giusti, Giuseppe. PFor 571-577.

"Give All to Love" (Emerson). PEng 958-959.

"Give Me Your Eyes" (Ady). PFor 5.

"Giving Birth" (Atwood). ShFSup 16-17.

"Giving Blood" (Updike). ShF 2371-2373.

Gjedsted, Rolf. PFor 2198.

Gjuzel, Bogomil. PFor 2273.

"Glad Day (After a Color Print by Blake)" (Untermeyer). PEng 2951.

Gladiator, The (Bird). DEng 215-216.

Gladiators, The (Koestler). LFEng 1550-1551.

"Gladius Dei" (Mann). ShF 1877.

Glance Away, A (Wideman). LFSup 380-381.

Glas (Derrida). LTh 645.

Glaser, Isabel Joshlin. ShF 2611.

Glasgow, Ellen. LFEng 1117-1125, 3054; **ShF 1488-1494.**

Glaspell, Susan. ShF 541.

Glasperlenspiel, Das. See *Glass Bead Game, The.*

Glass Bead Game, The (Hesse). LFFor 833-834.

Glass Key, The (Hammett). LFEng 1239-1240; M&D 827.

Glass Menagerie, The (Williams, T.). DEng 36-37, 2068-2071, 2405; ShF 2436.

Glass of Blessings, A (Pym). LFEng 2181-2182, 2183-2184, 2185.

Glass of Water, The (Scribe). DFor 1679-1680, 2345.

Glass People, The (Godwin). LFSup 135-136.

"Glass Pigeon, The" (Johnson, J.). ShF 1703-1705.

"Glass Scholar, The" (Cervantes). ShF 1089-1090.

Glass-Sided Ants' Nest, The (Dickinson). M&D 510-511.

Glasse of Governement, The (Gascoigne). DEng 726-727; LTh 542.

Glaube Liebe Hoffnung (Horvath). DFor 960-961.

Glengarry Glen Ross (Mamet). DEng 1243-1244, 2394, 2413.

Glidden, Frederick Dilley. *See* Short, Luke.

Glimm, Adele. ShF 2612.

"Glimpse into Another Country" (Morris). ShFSup 205-206.

Glitter Dome, The (Wambaugh). M&D 1680-1681.

Glittering Gate, The (Dunsany). DEng 539-540.

"Gloria" (Elytis). PFor 465, 1967. See also *Axion Esti, The.*

Gloria Mundi (Frederic). LFEng 1027.

Gloria Star. See *Cinq.*

"Glorias de España, Las" (Feijóo). LTh 476.

"Glory at Twilight" (Bhattacharya). ShF 651.

Glory of Columbia--Her Yeomanry!, The (Dunlap). DEng 533.

Glory of Hera, The (Gordon). LFEng 1180.

Glory of the Hummingbird, The (De Vries). LFEng 741.

"Glove, The" (Schiller). PFor 1409.

"Gloworm, The" (Stanley). PEng 2729.
Glück, Louise. PSup 133-139.
Glynn, Thomas. ShF 2613.
Gnaeus Naevius. *See* Naevius, Gnaeus.
Gnomology. See *Theognidea.*
Gnomon (Kenner). LTh 801.
Go-Away Bird, The (Spark). ShF 2256-2257.
"Go Back to Your Precious Wife and Son" (Vonnegut). ShF 2396-2397.
Go-Between, The (Hartley). LFEng 1301-1302.
Go Down, Moses (Faulkner). LFEng 932-935.
Go in Beauty (Eastlake). LFEng 850-851.
Go, Lovely Rose (Potts). M&D 1349-1350.
"Go, lovely rose" (Waller). PEng 3015.
Go Tell It on the Mountain (Baldwin). LFEng 134-137.
Goalie's Anxiety at the Penalty Kick, The (Handke). LFFor 784-785.
"Goat, The" (Ponge). PFor 1265.
"Goat, The" (Saba). PSup 346.
Goat Song (Werfel). DFor 1997-1998.
"Goblin Market" (Rossetti, C.). PEng 2418, 2419.
Goblin Market and Other Poems (Rossetti, C.). PEng 2416.
Goblins and Pagodas (Fletcher, J. G.). PEng 1027.
"God" (Lawrence, D. H.). PEng 1685.
"God Abandons Antony, The" (Cavafy). PFor 299.
"God and the Bayadere, The" (Goethe). PFor 587-588.
God Bless You, Mr. Rosewater (Vonnegut). LFEng 2728-2729; ShF 2392-2393.
"God Blesses Everything, Child" (Castro). PFor 278. See also *Cantares gallegos.*
God of Quiet, The (Drinkwater). DEng 509.
"God Sees the Truth, but Waits" (Tolstoy). ShF 2333-2334.
God Without Thunder (Ransom). PEng 2324.
Godey's Lady's Book. ShF 585.
"Godfather Death" (Grimm). ShF 1557-1558.
"Godhead as Lynx, The" (Sarton). PEng 2461-2462.
"Godliness" (Anderson). ShF 871.
Godric (Buechner). LFEng 354-355.
Gods Are Athirst, The (France). LFFor 577-578.
Gods Are Not to Blame, The (Rotimi). DEng 1625, 1627-1629.

God's Bits of Wood (Sembène). LFFor 1540-1542, 2052, 2056.
Gods, Demons and Others (Narayan). ShF 643.
God's Deputy (Dosunmu). DEng 2421.
"Gods Determinations" (Taylor). PEng 2852.
God's Gentry (MacDonagh). DEng 1211.
God's Grace (Malamud). LFEng 1799-1800.
"God's Grandeur" (Hopkins). PEng 1400.
God's Little Acre (Caldwell). LFEng 425-427.
"Gods of Greece, The" (Schiller). PFor 1408.
Gods of the Mountain, The (Dunsany). DEng 540.

God's Promises (Bale). DEng 84-86.
"God's Spies" (Howe). PSup 196.
"God's Visit" (Cernuda). PFor 322. See also *Nubes, Las.*
"God's Youth" (Untermeyer). PEng 2948-2949.
Godwin, Gail. LFSup 133-141.
Godwin, William. M&D 750-757.
Godzinna myśli (Slowacki). PFor 1442.
Goethe, Johann Wolfgang von. DEng 2185, 2229; DFor **731-744,** 1838-1839, 2366-2367; LFEng 3234-3235, 3238-3239, 3240-3241; LFFor **667-682,** 2159, 2162, 2163; LTh 60, 118, 337, 437, **595-602,** 641-642, 663-664, 667-668, 790, 984-986, 1018, 1298, 1302, 1304-1306, 1382, 1698, 1710; PFor **578-589,** 1403, 1913-1914; **ShFSup 97-103.**
"Gog" (Praed). PEng 2277-2278.
Goggan, John Patrick. *See* **Patrick, John.**
Gogol, Nikolai. DFor **745-753,** 1771, 2453-2454; LFEng 3267, 3277-3278; LFFor **683-692,** 2312; LTh 119-120, 287, 442, 1108, 1180, 1448, 1478, 1614; ShF 187-188, 460, **1495-1500.**
"Gogol's Wife" (Landolfi). ShFSup 132-133.
Gogol's Wife and Other Stories (Landolfi). ShFSup 129.
Going Abroad (Macaulay). LFSup 262.
"Going, Going" (Larkin). PEng 1675.
"Going to Meet the Man" (Baldwin, James). ShF 907-908.
Going to Meet the Man (Baldwin, James). ShF 556, 907.
Going to Pot (Feydeau). DFor 606.
Gökçeli, Yaşar Kemal. *See* **Kemal, Yashar.**
"Gold" (Hall). PEng 1203.

Gold, Herbert. ShF **1501-1505;** ShFSup 389.

"Gold Bug, The" (Poe). M&D 1333.

Gold by Gemini (Gash). M&D 708.

"Gold Coast" (McPherson). ShF 1855-1856.

Gold Coast Customs (Sitwell). PEng 2630.

Goldberg, Lester. ShF 2614.

Golden Apples, The (Welty). ShF 2418.

Golden Ass, The. See *Metamorphoses.*

Golden Bowl, The (James, H.). LFEng 3047-3048.

Golden Boy (Odets). DEng 1400-1401.

"Golden Chain, The" (Peretz). ShF 2085.

Golden Crucible, The (Stubbs). M&D 1550-1551.

Golden Fleece, The (Graves, R.). See *Hercules, My Shipmate.*

Golden Fleece, The (Grillparzer). DFor 822-826.

Golden Flower Pot, The (Hoffmann). ShF 1646.

Golden Fruits, The (Sarraute). LFFor 1503-1504.

"Golden Honeymoon" (Lardner). ShF 1772-1773.

"Golden Hour, The" (Claudel). PFor 360. See also *East I Know, The.*

Golden Keel, The (Bagley). M&D 54.

Golden Legend, The (Longfellow). PEng 1753-1754.

Golden Lotus, The. See *Chin P'ing Mei.*

Golden Notebook, The (Lessing). LFEng 1640, 1643-1645.

Golden Serpent, The (Alegría). LFFor 41-43.

"Golden Verses" (Nerval). PFor 1089.

Goldene Vliess, Das. See *Golden Fleece, The.*

"Goldfish" (Chandler). ShF 1097.

Golding, William. LFEng **1126-1138;** LFSup 404; ShF **1506-1510;** ShFSup 389.

Goldmann, Lucien. LTh 1421.

Goldoni, Carlo. DEng 2333; DFor **754-763,** 790, 2403-2405.

Goldsmith, Jeanette Erlbaum. ShF 2615.

Goldsmith, Oliver. DEng **783-794,** 2334; LFEng 3073; PEng **1105-1111,** 3332; ShF **1511-1517.**

Goldsmith, Peter. *See* **Priestley, J. B.**

Goldstone, Lawrence A. *See* **Treat, Lawrence.**

"Goldyn Targe, The" (Dunbar, W.). PEng 890, 891-892.

"Golem Death!" (Sachs). PFor 1374.

"Golem Tod!" *See* "Golem Death!"

Golk (Stern). LFSup 361-362.

Golob, Zvonimir. PFor 2266.

Golos iz khora. See *Voice from the Chorus, A.*

Goluben' (Esenin). PFor 478-479.

Goly god. See *Naked Year, The.*

Goly koral. See *Naked King, The.*

Gombrowicz, Witold. DFor **764-776;** LFFor **693-700,** 2064; LTh **603-608.**

Gommes, Les. See *Erasers, The.*

Gomringer, Eugen. PFor **590-597,** 1935.

Goncharov, Ivan. LFFor **701-708,** 2315-2316; LTh 389.

Goncourt, Edmond de. LFFor 709-718; LTh 1711.

Goncourt, Edmond de and **Jules de.** LFFor **709-718.**

Goncourt, Jules de. LTh 1711.

Gondibert (Davenant). PEng 736, 740-741.

"Gondolatok a könyvtárban." *See* "Thoughts in the Library."

Gondoliers, The (Gilbert and Sullivan). DEng 767.

Gondreville Mystery, The. See *Historical Mystery, An.*

Gone, No Forwarding (Gores). M&D 760-761.

Gone Out (Różewicz). DFor 1586-1587.

Gone with the Wind (Mitchell). LFEng 3151-3152.

Góngora y Argote, Luis de. LTh 26-27; PFor **598-604,** 1384, 2218-2219.

"Gonzaga Manuscripts, The" (Bellow). ShF 950-951.

González Martínez, Enrique. PFor **605-613,** 2226.

Gonzalez, N. V. M. LFEng 1139-1144; ShF 2616.

Good and Faithful Servant, The (Orton). DEng 1421-1422.

Good as Gold (Heller). LFEng 1335-1336.

Good Companions, The (Priestley). LFEng 2142.

"Good Corn, The" (Bates). ShFSup 32.

"Good Country People" (O'Connor, Flannery). ShF 720-721, 1985.

Good Day to Die, A (Harrison). LFEng 1289-1290.

"Good Deed, The" (Buck). ShF 1014-1016.

Good Earth, The (Buck). LFEng 339, 342-343.

Good Fight, The (Kinsella). PSup 236-237.

Good Friday (Masefield). DEng 1287-1288.

"Good Friday, 1613" (Donne). PEng 837.

Gover, Robert. ShF 2617.

Government Inspector, The. See *Inspector General, The.*

Government of the World in the Moon, The. See *Other Worlds.*

Governo della famiglia. See *Family in Renaissance Florence, The.*

Govinda Samantha (Day). LFFor 2216-2217.

Govoni, Corrado. PFor 2037, 2048.

Gower, John. PEng 1112-1123.

Goy, The (Harris). LFEng 1280-1281.

Goyen, William. ShF 1525-1529; ShFSup 389.

Goytisolo, Juan. LFFor 2393.

Gozzano, Guido. PFor 2037.

Gozzi, Carlo. DFor 788-798; ShF 683.

Grabbe, Christian Dietrich. DFor 799-808.

Grace Abounding to the Chief of Sinners (Bunyan). LFEng 359-361.

Gradnik, Alojz. PFor 2270.

Grady, Tex. See **Webb, Jack.**

Graeme, Bruce. M&D 769-773.

Graeme, David. See **Graeme, Bruce.**

Graff, Gerald. LTh 810-811.

Graham, Winston. M&D 774-779.

Grain of Wheat, A (Ngugi). LFEng 1980-1983; LFFor 2052.

"Gramigna's Mistress" (Verga). ShF 2381.

Grammaire du Décaméron (Todorov). LTh 1432-1433.

Grammar of Motives, A (Burke, K.). LTh 244-245.

Grammar of Stories, A (Prince). ShF 87.

Grammatica Slavica (Bernolák). PFor 1807.

Gramsci, Antonio. LTh 363, 627-632, 1543.

"Gramsci's Ashes" (Pasolini). PFor 1144, 1148-1150.

"Gran aventura, La." See "Sublime Adventure, The."

Gran carpa de los rasquachis, La (Valdez). DSup 371.

Gran Galeoto, El. See *Great Galeoto, The.*

Gran teatro del mundo, El. See *Great Theater of the World, The.*

Granby (Lister). LFEng 3134-3137.

Grand Écart, The (Cocteau). LFFor 360.

"Grand Galop" (Ashbery). PEng 60.

Grand Meaulnes, Le. See *Wanderer, The.*

Grand Piano, The. See *Empire City, The.*

Grand Testament, Le. See *Great Testament, The.*

Grand Troupeau, Le. See *To the Slaughterhouse.*

"Grande Bretèche, The" (Balzac). ShF 920.

Grande ritratto, Il. See *Larger than Life.*

Grandfather, The (Pérez Galdós). DFor 1458-1461, 2501.

Grandissimes, The (Cable). LFEng 416-417.

Grandmother, The (Němcová). LFFor 2065.

Grandmothers, The (Wescott). LFEng 2832, 2834-2836.

Grandower, Elissa. See **Waugh, Hillary.**

Grangecolman (Martyn). DEng 1280-1281.

Grant, Ambrose. See **Chase, James Hadley.**

Grant, John. See **Gash, Jonathan.**

Grant, Maxwell. See **Collins, Michael,** and **Gibson, Walter B.**

Granville-Barker, Harley. DEng 795-803.

Grapes of Wrath, The (Steinbeck). LFEng 2525-2526, 3062; ShF 2275.

Grasemann, Ruth. See **Rendell, Ruth.**

Grass, Günter. DSup 153-161; LFFor 730-739, 2199, 2201.

Grass Harp, The (Capote). LFEng 446-447.

Grass Is Singing, The (Lessing). LFEng 1641-1643.

Grass-Widow's Tale, The (Peters, Ellis). M&D 1320-1321.

"Grasshopper" (Cummings). PEng 3230.

"Grasshopper, The" (Lovelace). PEng 1758-1759.

Grateful to Life and Death. See *English Teacher, The.*

"Gratiana dancing and singing" (Lovelace). PEng 1759, 1760.

"Gratulatory to Mr. Ben Johnson for His adopting of Him to be His Son" (Randolph). PEng 2322.

Grau, Shirley Ann. LFEng 1182-1190; ShF 552, 1530-1534; ShFSup 389.

Grau Delgado, Jacinto. DFor 2504.

"Grave, A" (Moore). PEng 2044.

Graves, Caroline Elizabeth. LFEng 556-557.

Graves, Robert. LFEng 1191-1204; LFSup 404; PEng 167, 1124-1134; PSup 405; ShF 2618.

"Graveyard by the Sea, The" (Valéry). LTh 1491-1493; PFor 1578-1582.

Gravina, G. W. PFor 2019.

"Gravities" (Heaney). PEng 1268.

Gravity's Rainbow (Pynchon). LFEng 2192-2194.

Gray, Simon. **DEng 804-813; DSup 407.**
Gray, Thomas. **PEng 1135-1143,** 3329, 3331, 3332.
"Grayling" (Simms). ShF 2236-2237.
Grayson, Richard. ShF 2619.
Grazie, Le (Foscolo). PFor 496-497.
Grażyna (Mickiewicz). PFor 1019.
"Great American Novel, The" (De Forest) 700-701.
Great American Novel, The (Roth). LFEng 2305-2306.
"Great Blue Heron, The" (Kizer). PEng 1620.
"Great Breath, The" (Æ). PEng 12.
Great Circle (Aiken). LFEng 17-18, 19-20.
"Great Cossack Epic, The" (Thackeray). PEng 2873-2874.
Great Days (Barthelme). ShFSup 24.
Great Exhibition, The (Hare). DSup 184.
Great Expectations (Dickens, C.). LFEng 3163-3165.
Great Galeoto, The (Echegaray). DFor 531-532, 2500.
Great Gatsby, The (Fitzgerald, F. S.). LFEng 956, 961-964, 3060-3061, 3087; ShF 1317, 1372.
Great Goodness of Life (Baraka). DEng 101.
Great Hunger, The (Kavanagh). PEng 1539-1540.
Great Instauration, The (Bacon). LTh 77.
Great Jones Street (DeLillo). LFSup 86-87.
Great Meadow, The (Roberts). LFEng 2278-2279.
"Great Pax Whitie, The" (Giovanni). PEng 1103.
Great Peace, The (Braun). DSup 25-26.
"Great Pegram Mystery, The" (Barr). M&D 89.
Great Testament, The (Villon). PFor 1654, 1655, 1657-1659.
Great Theater of the World, The (Calderón). DFor 303-304.
Great Tirade at the Town-Hall (Dorst). DSup 93-94.
Great Victorian Collection, The (Moore, B.). LFEng 1891-1892.
"Great Wall of China, The" (Kafka). ShF 1733-1734.
Great Wash, The (Kersh). M&D 981.
Great White Hope, The (Sackler). DEng 1651-1652.
Greban, Arnoul. DFor 2166.

"Greedy Milkwoman, The" (Zoshchenko). ShFSup 380.
Greek Passion, The. See *Christ Recrucified.*
Green, Anna Katharine. **M&D 780-788.**
Green, Charles M. *See* **Gardner, Erle Stanley.**
Green, Geoffrey. ShF 2620.
Green, Henry. **LFEng 1205-1212.**
Green, Julien. **LFFor 740-750.**
Green, Paul. **DEng 814-823.**
Green Card (Akalaitis). DSup 5.
Green Centuries (Gordon). LFEng 1178.
"Green Eye, The" (Merrill). PEng 1961.
Green Flash, The (Graham). M&D 778.
Green for Danger (Brand). M&D 194.
Green Grow the Lilacs (Riggs). DEng 1591, 1594-1595.
Green Henry (Keller). LFFor 928-930.
"Green Hills of Earth, The" (Heinlein). ShF 1617-1618.
Green House, The (Vargas Llosa). LFFor 1848-1849.
"Green Lampshade" (Simic). PEng 2596.
Green Man, The (Amis). LFEng 64, 68-69.
Green Mansions (Hudson). LFEng 1385-1386.
Green Pastures, The (Connelly). DEng 413-414, 420-422.
Green Pope, The (Asturias). LFFor 87.
"Green Shelf, The" (Hall). PEng 1204.
"Green Tea" (Le Fanu). ShF 728, 1798, 1800-1802.
Green Water, Green Sky (Gallant). LFEng 1053-1054.
Green Years, The (Cronin). LFEng 653, 659-660, 661.
Greenberg, Alvin. ShF 2621.
Greenberg, Barbara L. ShF 2622.
Greenberg, Joanne. **ShF 1535-1539.**
Greene, Graham. **DEng 824-835; LFEng 1213-1222; LFSup 403; M&D 789-794; ShF 523, 1540-1547.**
Greene, Robert. **DEng 836-846,** 1364, 2270-2271; LFEng 3014, 3016; **PEng 1144-1152;** ShF 454, 455, 491, 495, **1548-1554.**
Greene's Groatsworth of Wit (Greene, R.). DEng 839.
"Greenleaf" (O'Connor, Flannery). ShF 107.
Greenmantle (Buchan). LFEng 332-333.
Gregorčič, Simon. PFor 2268-2269.
Gregorius (Hartmann von Aue). PFor 633-635.
Gregory, Lady Augusta. **DEng 847-856,** 2445; ShF 658.

Greimas, A. J. LTh 1762.
Grendel (Gardner, J.). LFEng 1073-1074.
Grendon, Stephen. *See* **Derleth, August.**
Gressmann, Uwe. PFor 1817, 1822.
"Gretel in Darkness" (Glück). PSup 135.
Grettir's Saga. ShF 393.
Greve, Felix Paul. *See* Grove, Frederick Philip.
Grevenius, Herbert. DFor 2479.
Greville, Fulke. PEng 1153-1159.
Grey, Mostyn. *See* **Christie, Agatha.**
Grey, Romer Zane. *See* **Pronzini, Bill.**
Grey, Zane. LFEng 3193-3194.
"Grey Light, The" (Sinópoulos). PFor 1972.
"Greyhound People" (Adams). ShFSup 3.
Griboyedov, Alexander. DFor 807-817.
Gridr's Fostering, Illugi. ShF 399.
Grieg, Nordahl. DFor 2480; PFor 2183.
Grieve, Christopher Murray. *See* **MacDiarmid, Hugh.**
"Grifel' naia oda." *See* "Slate Ode."
Griffi, Giuseppe Patroni. DFor 2415.
Griffin's Way (Yerby). LFEng 2988-2989.
Griffith, Patricia Browning. ShF 2623.
Grigorovich, Dmitrí. LFFor 2314.
Grigoryev, Apollon. LTh 395.
Grile, Dod. *See* **Bierce, Ambrose.**
Grillparzer, Franz. DFor 818-828, 2371-2372; LTh 633-638.
Grimes, Martha. M&D 795-800.
Grimm, Jakob. LTh 1502, 1704.
Grimm, The Brothers. ShF 1555-1562.
Grimmelshausen, H. J. C. von. LFFor 751-764, 2152.
Grimms' Fairy Tales (Grimm). ShF 1556, 1558, 1559-1562.
Grindel, Eugène. *See* **Éluard, Paul.**
Gringa, La (Sánchez). DFor 2442.
Gripenberg, Bertil. PFor 2174.
"Groaning" (Alberti). PFor 20.
Grób Agamemnona. See *Agamemnon's Grave.*
Gröber, Gustav. LTh 335.
"Grobovshchik" *See* "Undertaker, The."
Grooks (Hein). PFor 640.
"Gross Fifi, La" (Rhys). ShFSup 259-260.
Grosse Fahrt, Die (Blunck). LFFor 2195.
Grosse Schmährede an der Stadtmauer. See *Great Tirade at the Town-Hall.*
Grosser Frieden. See *Great Peace, The.*
Grossmüttiger Rechts-Gelehrter (Gryphius). DFor 837-838.

Grotesque in Art and Literature, The (Kayser). ShF 712.
Grotowski, Jerzy. DEng 2241; DFor 2241-2242.
"Groundhog, The" (Eberhart). PEng 929-930.
"Groundhog Revisiting, The" (Eberhart). PEng 933.
Group, The (McCarthy). LFEng 1723-1724.
"Group Life: Letchworth" (Betjeman). PEng 171-172.
Group of Noble Dames, A (Hardy). ShF 1584.
Group Portrait with Lady (Böll). LFFor 186-188.
Grove, Frederick Philip. LFEng 1223-1231; ShF 637.
Groves of Academe, The (McCarthy). LFEng 1722.
"Growing Season, The" (Caldwell). ShF 1031.
"Growing Stone, The" (Camus, A.). ShF 1049-1050.
Growth of Love, The (Bridges). PEng 287.
Growth of the Soil (Hamsun). LFFor 774-775, 2346.
Groza. See *Storm, The.*
Gruber, Ludwig. *See* **Anzengruber, Ludwig.**
Gruk. See *Grooks.*
Grumbler. *See* **Twain, Mark.**
Grün, Max von der. LFFor 2199.
Grundtvig, N. F. S. PFor 2165.
Grüne Heinrich, Der. See *Green Henry.*
Grupa Laokoona (Różewica). DFor 1582-1583.
Gruppenbild mit Dame. See *Group Portrait with Lady.*
"Gruselett." *See* "Scariboo."
Gryll Grange (Peacock). LFEng 2085-2086.
Gryphius, Andreas. DFor 829-840; PFor 1909.
Guard of Honor (Cozzens). LFEng 634-635.
"Guardapelo, El." *See* "Locket, The."
Guardian, The (Steele, R.). ShF 2267-2268.
Guardsman, The (Molnár). DFor 1346.
Guare, John. DEng 857-864.
Guareschi, Giovanni. LFFor 2253.
Guarini, Giambattista. DEng 2157; DFor 841-848, 2400; PFor 2016.
Guattari, Félix. LTh 850.
Gubar, Susan. *See* **Gilbert, Sandra M.**
Gucio zaczarowany (Miłosz). PFor 1034.
Gudrun (Jensen). LFFor 882.
Guerillas (Hochhuth). DFor 922.

H

H As in Hangman (Treat). M&D 1598.

H As in Hunted (Treat). M&D 1600.

"H. Scriptures, The" (II) (Herbert). PEng 1297.

Ha estallado la paz. See *Peace After War.*

"Ha férfi vagy, légy férfi." *See* "If You Are a Man, Then Be One."

Haabløse Slægter (Bang). LFFor 2339.

Håakansson, Björn. PFor 2192.

Haavikko, Paavo. LFFor 2368; PFor 2191; **PSup 140-148.**

Haavio, Martti. *See* Mustapää, P.

Hachnasat Kala. See *Bridal Canopy, The.*

Hacker, Marilyn. LFEng 714-715; **PEng 1186-1193; PSup 405.**

Hacks, Peter. DFor 849-855.

Haddon, Christopher. *See* **Beeding, Francis.**

Hadrian's Memoirs. See *Memoirs of Hadrian.*

"Haecceity" (Cunningham). PSup 77.

Hafiz. PSup 149-157.

Hafstein, Hannes. PFor 2170.

"Häftlinge, Die." See *Irren-die Häftlinge, Die.*

"Hag of Beare, The" (Montague). PEng 2036.

Hager, Stan. ShF 2624.

Haggard, H. Rider. LFEng 3202.

Haggard, William. M&D 801-807.

Hagiwara Sakutarō. PFor 2075, 2076.

"Haguruma." *See* "Cogwheels."

Hail and Farewell (Moore, G.). LFEng 1895-1896.

Haindl, Marieluise. *See* **Fleisser, Marieluise.**

"Hair, Lips, Eyes" (Vörösmarty). PFor 1666-1667.

"Haircut" (Lardner). ShF 108, 1772.

"Hairless Mexican, The" (Maugham). M&D 1203.

"Haj, száj, szem." *See* "Hair, Lips, Eyes."

Hakim, Tawfiq al-. DSup 169-180.

Hakon Jarl (Oehlenschläger). DFor 1440-1441.

Hákonarmál. See *Lay of Hákon, The.*

Hakootoko. See *Box Man, The.*

Hale, Nancy. ShF 1568-1574.

Ha-Levy, Judah. *See* **Judah ha-Levi.**

"Half an Hour" (Cavafy). PFor 300.

"Half-Kissed Kiss" (Ady). PFor 5. See also *New Verses.*

Haliburton, Thomas Chandler. ShF 635.

Halidon Hill (Minot). PEng 3255.

Hall, Adam. *See* **Trevor, Elleston.**

Hall, Donald. PEng 1194-1206; PSup 405.

Hall, James Byron. ShF 2625.

Hall, John. LTh 908.

Hall, Willis. DEng 865-873.

Hallam, Arthur Henry. PEng 1207-1211, 2861, 2864-2865.

Halle, Morris. PEng 3456.

"Hallelujah" (Sachs). PFor 1374.

"Hallelujawiese, Die." *See* "Alleluia Meadow, The."

Hallgrímsson, Jónas. PFor 2167-2168.

Halliday, Brett. M&D 808-814.

Halliday, M. A. K. PEng 3454-3455.

Halliday, Michael. *See* **Creasey, John.**

Hallinan, Nancy. ShF 2627.

Hall-Stevenson, John. LFEng 2531.

"Halt in the Wilderness, A" (Brodsky). PFor 242.

Halvfärdiga himlen, Den (Tranströmer). PFor 1529.

Ham Funeral, The (White). DSup 394.

"Hamann" (Bobrowski). PFor 205.

Hamann, Johann Georg. LTh 437, 669.

"Hamatraya" (Emerson). PEng 957.

Hamblen, Abigail Ann. ShF 2628.

Hamburg Dramaturgy (Lessing). LTh 881-882.

Hamburgische Dramaturgie. See *Hamburg Dramaturgy.*

Hamðismal. ShF 429.

Hamilton, Donald. M&D 815-821.

Hamlet (Döblin). LFFor 479-480.

Hamlet (Shakespeare). DEng 1716, 2281-2282; ShF 2214-2216.

"Hamlet and His Problems" (Eliot). LTh 448, 450.

Hamlet of A. MacLeish, The (MacLeish). PEng 1853.

Hamlet of Stepney Green, The (Kops). DEng 1079-1080.

"Hamlet of the Shchigrov District, The" (Turgenev). ShF 2355-2356.

Hamlet, Revenge! (Innes). M&D 924.

Hamletmachine (Müller). DSup 261-262.

Hammer of the Village, The (Petőfi). PFor 1219.

Hammett (Gores). M&D 761.

Hammett, Daghull. *See* **Hammett, Dashiell.**

Hammett, Dashiell. LFEng 1232-1242; M&D 822-828; ShF 543, 761, **1575-1578.**

Hammett, Mary Jane. *See* **Hammett, Dashiell.**

Hāmojō no umi. See *Sea of Fertility, The.*

Hamri, Thorsteinn fra. PFor 2200.

Hamsun, Knut. DFor 2476; LFFor **765-777,** 2345-2346.

Han d'Islande. See *Hans of Iceland.*

Han kung ch'iu. See *Sorrows of Han, The.*

Han sidder ved smeltediglen. See *He Sits at the Melting Pot.*

Han som fick leva om sitt liv. See *Man Who Lived His Life Over, The.*

Han Yü. PFor 1787.

"Hana." *See* "Nose, The."

"Hand, The" (Maupassant). M&D 1208.

Hand and Glove (Machado de Assis). LFFor 1042.

Hand and Ring (Green). M&D 784.

"Hand at Callow Hill Farm, The" (Tomlinson). PEng 2909.

"Hand-Rolled Cigarettes" (Yevtushenko). PSup 247.

Handel, George Frederick. DEng 2457, 2458.

Handful of Blackberries, A (Silone). LFFor 1588-1589.

Handful of Dust, A (Waugh). LFEng 2796-2798.

Handful of Rice, A (Markandaya). LFFor 2222.

"Handing Down, The" (Berry). PEng 152.

Handke, Peter. DFor **856-864,** 2243, 2383; LFFor **778-791,** 2207; LFSup 404.

"Hands" (Anderson). ShF 870.

Hands of Its Enemy, The (Medoff). DSup 244.

"Handschuh, Der." *See* "Glove, The."

Handske, En. See *Gauntlet, A.*

"Handsomest Drowned Man, The" (García Márquez). ShF 1455-1456.

Handy, Lowney. LFEng 1477-1478.

Hanged Man's House (Ferrars). M&D 601.

Hanging Captain, The (Wade). M&D 1667.

Hangman, The (Lagerkvist). DFor 1156, 2477-2478.

Hanjo (Mishima). DFor 1324-1325.

Hanka, Václav. PFor 1798.

"Hank's Woman" (Wister). ShF 596.

Hanley, James. LFEng **1243-1252.**

Hannibal (Grabbe). DFor 806-807.

Hannon, Ezra. *See* **McBain, Ed.**

Hans Alienus (Heidenstam). LFFor 820-821.

"Hans Carvel" (Prior). PEng 2290.

Hans Faust. See *Hinze und Kunze.*

Hans of Iceland (Hugo). LFFor 851-853.

Hansberry, Lorraine. DEng **874-884,** 2427-2428.

Hansen, Joseph. M&D **829-834;** ShF 2629.

Hansen, Martin Alfred. LFFor 2356.

Hansen, Thorkild. LFFor 2366-2367.

Hanshew, Thomas W. M&D **835-840.** *See also* **Carter, Nick.**

Hansson, Ola. PFor 2170.

"Hap" (Hardy). PEng 1219.

"Happie obtaining the Great Galleazzo, The" (Deloney). PEng 785.

"Happiest Man on Earth, The" (Maltz). ShF 1872-1873.

"Happily Neighing, the Herds Graze" (Mandelstam). PFor 936.

"Happiness" (Glück). PSup 137.

"Happiness" (Lavin). ShF 1786.

"Happiness of Others, The" (Price). ShF 2124-2125.

Happy as Larry (MacDonagh). DEng 1204-1206.

"Happy Birthday" (Lispector). ShFSup 167.

Happy Days (Beckett). DEng 155-156; DFor 163-164.

Happy Death, A (Camus). LFFor 257.

"Happy Death, A" (Lavin). ShF 1783-1784.

Happy Haven, The (Arden). DEng 45.

Happy Journey to Trenton and Camden, The (Wilder). DEng 2046.

Happy Marriage, The (MacLeish). PEng 1852.

Happy Pair, The (Sedley). PEng 2510.

Happy Valley (White, P.). LFEng 2864.

Happy Warriors, The (Laxness). LFFor 997.

Harambašić, August. PFor 2263.

Harbage, Alfred B. *See* **Kyd, Thomas.**

Hard Blue Sky, The (Grau). LFEng 1185.

"Hard Candy" (Williams, T.). ShF 2435, 2436.

Hard Freight (Wright, C.). PEng 3148.

Hard Life, The (O'Brien, F.). LFEng 2030-2031.

Hard Times (Dickens, C.). LFEng 3078.

Hard Winter, A (Queneau). LFSup 324-326.

Hardenberg, Friedrich von. *See* **Novalis.**

Harding, Gunnar. PFor 2193.

Hardwick, Elizabeth. LFEng 1253-1258; ShF 550.

Hardy, Thomas. DEng 885-894; LFEng 1259-1276, 3049-3050, 3079; LTh 1318; PEng 1212-1224, 3357; ShF 1579-1585.

Hare, Cyril. M&D 841-846.

Hare, David. DEng 2491, 2493; DSup 181-191.

Harington, Donald. ShF 2630.

Harknett, Terry. *See* Gilman, George.

Harlequinade (Rattigan). DEng 1562. See also *Playbill.*

Harmattan, L' (Sembène). LFFor 2052.

Harmonies poétiques et religieuses (Lamartine). PFor 834.

Harmonium (Stevens). PEng 2742-2743, 3391.

Harnack, Curtis. ShF 2631.

Harness Room, The (Hartley). LFEng 1299.

Harold (Tennyson). DEng 1917-1918.

Harp of a Thousand Strings (Davis). LFEng 676-677.

Harper, Michael S. PSup 158-165.

Harper's Monthly. ShF 585, 588.

Harper's Weekly. ShF 588.

Harris, Christopher. *See* **Fry, Christopher.**

Harris, Joel Chandler. ShF 223-225, 616, 1586-1591.

Harris, Mark. LFEng 1277-1285; LFSup 404.

Harris, Wilson. LFSup 142-150.

Harrison, Chip. *See* **Block, Lawrence.**

Harrison, Frederic. LTh 1738.

Harrison, Jim. LFEng 1286-1295; LFSup 404; PEng 1225-1236; PSup 405.

Harrison, Tony. PSup 166-172.

Harrowing of Hell, The. DEng 2246.

Harry and Lucy Concluded (Edgeworth). ShF 1329.

Harry and Lucy Concluded (Ruskin). ShF 2164-2165.

Harry, Noon and Night (Ribman). DSup 313.

Hart, Heinrich. LFFor 2179 Lth 1719.

Hart, Julius. LFFor 2179 Lth 1719.

Hart, Lorenz. DEng 895-905.

Hart, Lorenz, and Richard Rodgers. DEng 896, 898-899, 900, 901.

Hart, Moss. DEng 906-913.

Hart, Moss, and George S. Kaufman. DEng 906-907.

Harte, Bret. LTh 1749; PEng 1237-1245; ShF 210, 222-223, 533, 594, 1592-1597.

Harter, Penny. ShF 2632.

Hartley, L. P. LFEng 1296-1302.

Hartman, Geoffrey H. LTh 165, 306, 351, 644-648, 909, 1033, 1492, 1766, 1833.

Hartmann von Aue. PFor 629-636, 1900.

Hartzenbusch y Martínez, Juan Eugenio de. DFor 2498.

Haru no yuki. See *Spring Snow.*

"Haru to shura." *See* "Spring and Asura."

Harvest (Giono). LFFor 654.

Harvest on the Don. See *Virgin Soil Upturned.*

"Harvest Song" (Toomer). PEng 2917-2918.

Harvester, Simon. M&D 847-851.

Harvesters, The (Pavese). LFFor 1246-1247.

"Harzreise, Die." *See* "Journey to the Harz, The."

Hasdeu, Bogdan Petriceicu. DFor 2297.

Hašek, Jaroslav. LFFor 792-796, 2066.

"Hasidic Scriptures" (Sachs). PFor 1374.

Haslam, Gerald. ShF 2633.

Haste to the Wedding. See *Italian Straw Hat, The.*

Hastings, Roderic. See **Graeme, Bruce.**

Hasty Heart, The (Patrick, J.). DEng 1467-1468.

Hate of Treason (Breton, N.). PEng 282.

Hateful Contraries (Wimsatt). LTh 1556.

Hatter's Castle (Cronin). LFEng 648, 650-651, 652-653, 654-655, 661.

Hattyú, A. See *Swan, The.*

Hauch, Johannes Carsten. DFor 2469.

Hauge, Alfred. LFFor 797-804.

Hauge, Olav H. PFor 2194.

Haugen, Paal-Helge. LFFor 2364.

"Haunted" (de la Mare). PEng 778.

"Haunted and the Haunters, The" (Bulwer-Lytton). ShF 199-200.

"Haunted House, The" (Hood). PEng 1388.

Haunted House, The (Plautus). DFor 1486-1487, 2141.

"Haunted House, A" (Woolf). ShF 2455.

Haunted House and Other Short Stories, A (Woolf). ShF 2455.

Haunted Man, The (Dickens). ShF 1272.

"Haunted Palace, The" (Poe). PEng 2247.

"Haunted Valley, The" (Bierce). M&D 125.

Haunting of Hill House, The (Jackson). LFEng 1430-1431.

Hauptmann, Gerhart. DFor 865-875, 2375-2376; LFFor 2180-2181, 2183; LTh 986-987, 1721-1722, 1726.

Hauptmann von Köpenick, Der. See *Captain of Köpenick, The.*

Hauschner, Auguste. LFFor 2189.

Hauser, Marianne. ShF 2634.

Hausierer, Der (Handke). LFFor 784.

Haute Surveillance. See *Deathwatch.*

Hávamál. See *Sayings of the High One, The.*

Have Come, Am Here (Villa). PEng 2979-2981; PFor 1647.

Have with You to Saffron Walden (Nash). ShF 494-495.

Havel, Václav. DFor 876-882, 2283.

Havelok the Dane. ShF 448.

Havlíček Borovský, Karel. PFor 1800-1801.

"Hawk Roosting" (Hughes, T.). PEng 1443-1445.

Hawkes, John. LFEng 1303-1313; LFSup 404; ShF 1598-1604; ShFSup 389.

Hawkesworth, John. ShF 1605-1609.

Hawkline Monster, The (Brautigan). LFEng 293-294.

Hawthorne, Nathaniel. LFEng 1314-1328, 1855, 3041; LTh 524, 1012, 1567; ShF 112, 114, 160-161, 163, 181, 182-183, 185-187, 188-191, 449, 530-531, 769, 812-814, 1610-1614.

Hawthorne and the Modern Short Story (Rohrberger). ShF 88, 182-183.

"Hay Fever" (Hope). PSup 191.

Haycox, Ernest. LFEng 3195-3196.

Hayden, Robert. PEng 1246-1254.

"Haystack in the Floods, The" (Morris). PEng 2054.

Hayward, Richard. *See* **Kendrick, Baynard H.**

Hazard of New Fortunes, A (Howells). LFEng 1376-1378.

Hazards of Holiness, The (Everson). PEng 990-991.

Hazlitt, William. LTh 649-654, 798, 1701, 1705-1706, 1710.

H. D. LFEng 37-38; PEng 1255-1263.

"H. D. Book, The" (Duncan). PEng 897, 901.

"He?" (Maupassant). M&D 1209; ShF 1910-1911.

"He" (Porter). ShF 2113-2114.

"He Came into Her Line of Vision Walking Backward" (Backus). ShF 69-70.

"He Don't Plant Cotton" (Powers). ShF 2120.

He Sent Forth a Raven (Roberts). LFEng 2282-2283.

He Sits at the Melting Pot (Munk). DFor 1392-1393.

"He Swung and He Missed" (Algren). ShF 856.

He Wants Shih! (Owens). DEng 1460.

He Who Gets Slapped (Andreyev). DFor 65-66.

Head of a Traveller (Blake). M&D 140-141.

Head of the Bed, The (Hollander). PEng 1364, 1365.

Headbirths (Grass). LFFor 738.

Headlong Hall (Peacock). LFEng 2079-2080.

"Headwaters" (Momaday). PEng 2020-2021.

Healers, The (Armah). LFEng 91-92.

Healing Art, The (Wilson). LFSup 388.

Healing Song for the Inner Ear (Harper). PSup 164.

"Health Card" (Yerby). ShF 2477-2478.

"Healthiest Girl in Town, The" (Stafford). ShF 2262.

Heaney, Seamus. PEng 1264-1273, 3369-3370; PSup 405.

"Hearing" (Koch). PEng 1627.

Hearing Secret Harmonies (Powell). LFEng 2121-2122.

Heart (De Amicis). ShF 684.

Heart for the Gods of Mexico, A (Aiken). LFEng 18, 21-22.

Heart Is a Lonely Hunter, The (McCullers). DEng 1190; LFEng 1732-1733.

Heart of a Dog, The (Bulgakov). LFFor 209.

Heart of Darkness (Conrad). LFEng 229-230, 585, 589-593, 3048, 3284-3286; ShF 1184-1186.

Heart of Maryland, The (Belasco). DEng 195-196.

Heart of Midlothian, The (Scott). LFEng 2377-2382.

"Heart of Stone, A" (Zoshchenko). ShFSup 379.

"Heart of the Artichoke, The" (Gold). ShF 1502-1503.

Heart of the Matter, The (Greene, G.). LFEng 1219-1220; M&D 792.

"Heart of Thomas Hardy, The" (Betjeman). PEng 169-170.

Heartbreak Tango (Puig). LFFor 1351-1353.

Heartland (Harris). LFSup 148-149.

"Hearts' and Flowers'" (MacLeish). PEng 1854.

"Hearts Come Home" (Buck). ShF 1014.

Heart's Garden, The Garden's Heart, The (Rexroth). PEng 2353.

"Heart's Needle" (Snodgrass). PEng 2659-2660, 3372-3373.

Heart's Needle (Snodgrass). PEng 2658.

Heat and Dust (Jhabvala). LFSup 175.

Heat of the Day, The (Bowen). LFEng 267-268.

"Heathen Chinee, The." *See* "Plain Language from Truthful James."

Heather Field, The (Martyn). DEng 1277-1280.

"Heautontimoroumenos" (Baudelaire). PFor 138.

Heautontimorumenos. See *Self-tormentor, The.*

Heaven and Earth (Byron). DEng 330.

Heaven and Hardpan Farm (Hale, N.). ShF 1571.

"Heaven of Animals, The" (Dickey, J.). PEng 796.

"Heavenly City, Earthly City" (Duncan). PEng 901.

Heaven's My Destination (Wilder). LFEng 2884-2885.

"Heavy Bear Who Goes with Me, The" (Schwartz). PEng 2491-2492.

Heavysege, Charles. DEng 2438-2439.

Heb Sed. DFor 2085-2086.

Hebbel, Friedrich. DEng 2194-2195; **DFor 883-891,** 2373-2374; PFor 1921, 1922.

Hébert, Anne. LFFor 805-816.

"Hebräische Melodien." *See* "Hebrew Melodies."

"Hebrew Melodies" (Heine). PFor 651.

"Hebrew Poet, The" (Watts). PEng 3045.

Hecale (Callimachus). PFor 256, 257-258.

Hecht, Anthony. PEng 1274-1286; PSup 405-406.

Hecuba (Euripides). DFor 2113.

Hecyra. See *Mother-in-Law, The.*

Hedda Gabler (Ibsen). DFor 985-986.

Hedge, The (Delibes). LFFor 451-452.

Hedley, Leslie Woolf. ShF 2635.

"*Hee-Haw!*" (Warner). ShFSup 353.

Hegel, Georg Wilhelm Friedrich. DEng 2186; DFor 899; DSup 358; LFFor 2167-2168;

LTh 117, 206, 288, 364-365, 529-530, **655-659,** 936, 978, 1019, 1210, 1358-1359, 1361, 1710.

Heiberg, Gunnar. DFor 892-897, 2476.

Heiberg, Johan Ludvig. DFor 898-908, 2468.

Heidegger, Martin. LTh 528, 530-532, 767, 849, 1271.

Heidenstam, Verner von. LFFor 817-824, 2343-2344; PFor 2171.

"Height and Hair" (Vallejo). PFor 1592. See also *Human Poems.*

Heijermans, Herman. DFor 904-915.

Heike monogatari. LFFor 2265-2266, 2267.

Heilbrun, Carolyn G. *See* **Cross, Amanda.**

Heilige Experiment, Das. See *Strong Are Lonely, The.*

"Heimat, Die." *See* "Homeland."

Heimat. See *Magda.*

Hein, Piet. PFor 637-642, 2188; PSup 406.

Heine, Heinrich. LTh 437, **660-665,** 1361, 1696, 1710; **PFor 643-652,** 778, 1918-1919, 1920-1921.

Heinesen, William. LFFor 2355.

Heinlein, Robert A. ShF 775, 778, **1615-1620;** ShFSup 389.

Heinrich (Dorst). DSup 96.

Heinrich von Ofterdingen. See *Henry of Ofterdingen.*

Heinsius, Daniel. LTh 780, 782.

Heir Presumptive (Wade). M&D 1669.

"Heiress and Architect" (Hardy). PEng 1219.

Hekabē. See *Hecuba.*

Hektorović, Petar. PFor 2260.

Helen in Egypt (H. D.). PEng 1259, 1261-1262.

Helena (Machado de Assis). LFFor 1042.

Helga's Web (Cleary). M&D 363.

Heliand, The (Hartmann von Aue). PFor 1896.

Heliga Birgittas pilgrimsfärd (Heidenstam). LFFor 822-823.

Helige Cäcilie oder Die Gewalt der Musilke, Die. See *St. Cecilia or The Power of Music.*

Heliodorus of Emesa. LFFor 2005-2008, 2017.

Hell Has No Limits (Donoso). LFFor 497-498.

"Hell Screen" (Akutagawa). ShFSup 10.

Hellaakoski, Aaro. PFor 2182.

Heller, Joseph. LFEng 1329-1336; LFSup 404.

Heller, Steve. ShF 2636.

Hellman, Lillian. DEng 914-924, 2404; LFEng 1233-1234.

Hello (Creeley). PEng 688.
Hello America (Ballard). LFEng 152-153.
Hello, Darkness (Sissman). PEng 2618-2622.
Hello, La Jolla (Dorn). PEng 843-844.
Hello Out There (Saroyan). DEng 1658.
"Helmsman, The" (Cunningham). PSup 77-78.
Héloïse (Hébert). LFFor 814.
Héloise and Abélard (Moore, G.). LFEng 1902.
"Helping Hand, A" (Sansom). ShF 2184.
Helprin, Mark. ShFSup 113-121.
Helység-kalapácsa, A. See *Hammer of the Village, The.*
Hemingway, Ernest. LFEng 490, **1337-1349,** 3061-3062; LFSup 404; ShF 249-250, 544, 815, **1621-1628.**
Hemligheter på vägen (Tranströmer). PFor 1529.
Hemlock and After (Wilson, A.). LFEng 2900-2901.
Hemmer, Jarl. LFFor 2346-2347.
Hemsöborna. See *Natives of Hemsö, The.*
"Hen-Pecked" (Zoshchenko). ShFSup 378.
"Henceforth, from the Mind" (Bogan). PEng 238-239.
Henderson, Philip. PEng 1904.
Henderson the Rain King (Bellow). LFEng 229-231.
Henley, Beth. DEng 2411-2412; DSup 192-**197.**
Hennissart, Martha. *See* **Lathen, Emma.**
Henri Christoph (Walcott, D. A.). DEng 2453.
Henrietta, The (Howard, B.). DEng 970-971.
Henry, O. LTh 443; M&D 852-858; ShF 223, 229-230, 537-539, **1629-1633.**
Henry, Olivier. *See* **Henry, O.**
Henry and Emma (Prior). PEng 2290.
Henry James: A Life (Edel). LTh 428.
Henry of Ofterdingen (Novalis). LFFor 2166; LTh 1701.
Henry Stillings Jugend (Jung). LFFor 2156.
Henry III and His Court (Dumas, père). DFor 486-487, 2343.
Henry IV (Pirandello). DFor 1469-1470; LTh 1101.
Henry IV, Part I (Shakespeare). DEng 1701, 2277.
Henry IV, Part II (Shakespeare). DEng 1701-1702, 2277.
Henry V (Olivier's adaptation of Shakespeare). DEng 2519-2520.

Henry V (Shakespeare). DEng 1702-1703.
Henry VI, Part I (Shakespeare). DEng 1697-1698.
Henry VI, Part II (Shakespeare). DEng 1698.
Henry VI, Part III (Shakespeare). DEng 1698-1699.
Henry VIII (Shakespeare and Fletcher). DEng 636, 1703, 2284.
Henryson, Robert. PEng **1287-1293,** 3278-3279.
Henshaw, James Ene. DEng **925-933.**
Hepta epi Thebas. See *Seven Against Thebes.*
Heptameron, The (Marguerite de Navarre). LFFor 2111; ShF 144.
Heptateuchon (Thierry of Chartres). LTh 20.
"Hêr Bâbest." *See* "Sir Pope."
"Hêr Keiser." *See* "Sir Emperor."
"Her Person" (Guillén). PFor 627.
"Her Pure Fingernails on High Offering Their Onyx" (Mallarmé). PFor 928.
"Her Table Spread" (Bowen). ShF 985-987.
Her Victory (Sillitoe). LFEng 2402.
"Hera, Hung from the Sky" (Kizer). PEng 1619.
Heracles (Euripides). DFor 2114-2115.
Hērakleidai. See *Children of Heracles, The.*
Hērakles. See *Heracles.*
Herakles (MacLeish). DEng 1224.
Heraldos negros, Los (Vallejo). PFor 1587-1589.
Herberge, Die (Hochwälder). DFor 930.
Herbert, George. PEng **1294-1305.**
Herbert, Victor. DEng 2467.
Herbert, Zbigniew. PFor **653-661;** PSup 406.
"Herbstmanöver." *See* "Autumn Maneuvers."
Herceg, hátha megjön a tél is! (Babits). PFor 119-120.
"Hercules and Antaeus" (Heaney). PEng 1271.
Hercules furens. See *Mad Hercules.*
Hercules, My Shipmate (Graves, R.). LFEng 1201.
Hercules on Oeta (Seneca). DFor 2149.
Herder, Johann Gottfried. LFFor 2158; LTh 437, 596-597, **666-671,** 1560, 1697, 1699; PFor 1912-1913.
"Here" (Salinas). PFor 1386-1387.
"Here Comes the Maples" (Updike). ShF 2373.
"Here with the Long Grass Rippling" (Cowley, M.). PEng 607-608.
Hérédia, José-Maria de. PFor 1874.

Hereditary Forester, The (Ludwig). DFor 1214-1215.

Heritage (Cullen). PEng 696-697.

"Heritage" (Still). PEng 2764.

Herlihy, James Leo. ShF 559.

Herman, William. *See* **Bierce, Ambrose.**

"Herman Melville" (Auden). PEng 76-77.

Hermannschlacht, Die (Grabbe). DFor 807.

Hermes, pies i gwiazda (Herbert). PFor 657.

Hermine, L'. See *Ermine, The.*

Hermippus. DFor 2122.

"Hermit" (Updike). ShF 2368.

Hermlin, Stephan. PFor 1817, 1818, 1822, 1823, 1824, 1826.

Hermosura de Angélica, La (Vega). PFor 1601-1602.

Hernández, Antonio Acevedo. DFor 2442.

Hernani (Hugo). DEng 2188, 2189; DFor 968; LFFor 847; LTh 1710.

Hero and Leander (Chapman). PEng 460-461.

Hero and Leander (Marlowe). PEng 1902-1905; ShF 1893.

Hero in Eclipse in Victorian Fiction, The (Praz). LTh 1167.

Hero of Our Time, A (Lermontov). LFEng 3142-3144; LFFor 1021-1024, 2314; PFor 866.

Herod and Mariamne (Hebbel). DFor 888-889.

Herod the Great (Wakefield Master). DEng 1994.

Herod the King (Munk). DFor 1390.

Herodas. DFor 2135.

"Hérodias" (Flaubert). ShF 1381.

Herodias (Mallarmé). PFor 928-930.

Heroes and Heroines (Whittemore). PEng 3077-3078.

Heroes and Villains (Carter). LFSup 74.

Heroic and Elegiac Song for the Lost Second Lieutenant of the Albanian Campaign (Elýtis). PFor 1966.

"Heroic Poem in Praise of Wine" (Belloc). PEng 134-136.

Heroica de Buenos Aires (Dragún). DFor 2444.

Herr Sleeman kommer. See *Mr. Sleeman Is Coming.*

"Herrick" (Aldrich). PEng 32-33.

Herrick, Robert. PEng 1306-1318.

Herrington, John. LTh 1184.

Herself Surprised (Cary). LFEng 458-459.

Hersey, John. LFEng 1350-1358; LFSup 404-405.

Hertha (Bremer). LFFor 2337.

"Hertha" (Swinburne). PEng 2819-2820.

Hertz, Henrick. DFor 2469.

Hervey, Evelyn. *See* **Keating, H. R. F.**

Hervieu, Paul. DFor 2348.

"Herzeliebez Frowelîn." *See* "Little Maid So Dear."

Herzen, Aleksandr. LFFor 2318.

Herzog (Bellow). LFEng 231-232.

Herzog Theodor von Gothland (Grabbe). DFor 800-801.

Hesiod. PFor 662-669, 1757; ShF 135.

"Hesitations Outside the Room" (Atwood). PEng 67.

Hesperus (Jean Paul). LFFor 873-874.

Hesse, Hermann. LFFor 825-835, 2185, 2191-2193; ShF 1634-1639.

"Hessian Prisoner, The" (Bates). ShFSup 30.

"Hester" (Lamb). PEng 1636.

Het Pantser (Heijermans). DFor 914-915.

Hetty Dorval (Wilson, E.). LFEng 2911.

"Heure jaune, L'." *See* "Golden Hour, The."

Hext, Harrington. *See* **Phillpotts, Eden.**

"Hey Sailor, What Ship?" (Olsen). ShF 2021-2022.

Heyduk, Adolf. PFor 1802.

Heyen, William. PEng 1319-1328; PSup 406.

Heyer, Georgette. M&D 859-864.

Heym, Georg. PFor 1927-1928.

Heym, Stefan. LFFor 2204.

Heynen, Jim. ShF 2637.

Heyse, Paul. LFEng 3236-3237; LFFor 2172-2173.

Heyward, DuBose. DEng 934-939.

Heywood, John. DEng 940-947, 2154, 2256-2257; PEng 1329-1336.

Heywood, Thomas. DEng 948-956, 2291; PEng 1337-1343.

"Hi!" (de la Mare). PEng 776.

"Hi, Kuh" (Zukofsky). PEng 3223.

Hidden God, The (Brooks, C.). LTh 221.

"Hidden Things" (Cavafy). PFor 299.

"Hiding of Black Chief, The" (Henry). ShF 1630.

"Hiding Our Love" (Kizer). PEng 1618-1619.

Hiding Place (Wideman). LFSup 383-384. See also *Homewood Trilogy, The.*

Hier régnant désert (Bonnefoy). PSup 46.

Histoire de la littérature française classique
(Brunetière). LTh 233.
*Histoire de Vidocq, chef de la police de Sûreté:
Écrite d'après lui-même.* See *Memoirs of
Vidocq, Principal Agent of the French Police
Until 1827.*
*Histoire du chevalier des Grieux et de Manon
Lescaut.* See *Manon Lescaut.*
Histoires d'amour. See *Tales of Love.*
Historia (Gombrowicz). DFor 773-774.
Historia Apollonii regis Tyri. See *Old English
Apollonius of Tyre, The.*
Historia Britonum (Nennius). ShF 440.
Historia de El. See *Story of Him, The.*
Historia de las ideas estéticas en España
(Menéndez y Pelayo). LTh 1023-1024.
Historia de una pasión argentina (Mallea).
LFFor 1049, 1050.
Historia del corazón (Aleixandre). PFor 31.
Historia Regum Britanniae. See *History of the
Kings of Britain.*
Historias fingidas y verdaderas (Otero). PFor
1109, 1112.
Historias para ser contadas (Dragún). DFor
2444.
Historical Mystery, An (Balzac). M&D 76.
Historical Novel, The (Lukács). LTh 936.
Historical Odes and Other Poems (Dixon).
PEng 818, 819.
Historical Register for the Year 1736, The
(Fielding). DEng 610-612.
Historie of Samson, The (Quarles). PEng 2297-
2298.
"Historien." *See* "Stories."
Historische Roman, Der. See *Historical Novel,
The.*
History (Lowell, R.). PEng 1797.
History and Class Consciousness (Lukács).
LTh 759, 935-936.
History and Fall of Caius Marius, The (Otway).
DEng 1445-1447.
*History and Remarkable Life of the Truly
Honourable Col Jacque, Commonly Call'd
Col Jack, The.* See *Colonel Jack.*
"History as Appletree" (Harper). PSup 163.
"History as Personality" (Harper). PSup 163.
History Is Your Own Heartbeat (Harper). PSup
162.
"History of an Illness" (Zoshchenko). ShFSup
381.

History of Ancient Art (Winckelmann). LTh
669, 1563.
*History of Criticism and Literary Taste in
Europe from the Earliest Texts to the Present
Day, A* (Saintsbury). LTh 1265-1268, 1735.
*History of Eighteenth Century Literature 1660-
1780* (Gosse). ShF 508.
History of English Literature (Taine). LTh
1260, 1417-1418; PEng 3407-3408.
History of English Poetry, The (Warton, J.).
LTh 1532; PEng 3031-3032.
History of Gil Blas of Santillane, The. See *Gil
Blas.*
History of Henry Esmond, Esquire, The
(Thackeray). LFEng 2621-2623.
History of Italian Literature (De Sanctis). LTh
362-363, 366.
History of Lady Sophia Sternheim, The (La
Roche). LFFor 2155-2156.
History of Mr. Polly, The (Wells). LFEng
2811-2812.
History of Pendennis, The (Thackeray). LFEng
2620-2621.
History of Rasselas, The (Johnson, S.). PEng
3473; ShF 1709-1711.
*History of the Adventures of Joseph Andrews,
and of His Friend Mr. Abraham Adams.* See
Joseph Andrews.
History of the American Film, A (Durang).
DSup 101-102.
History of the Franks (Gregory of Tours). ShF
427.
History of the French Novel, A (Saintsbury).
LTh 1265-1266.
History of the Kings of Britain (Geoffrey of
Monmouth). PEng 1688-1689; ShF 441.
*History of the Life of the Late Mr. Jonathan
Wild the Great, The.* See *Jonathan Wild.*
History of the Lombards (Paul the Deacon).
ShF 428.
History of the Nun, The (Behn). LFEng 221;
ShF 502.
History of the Royal Society (Sprat). PEng
3493.
*History of the Valorous and Wittie Knight-
Errant, Don Quixote of the Mancha.* See
Don Quixote de la Mancha.
History of the World (Raleigh). PEng 2301.
History of Tom Jones, A Foundling, The. See
Tom Jones.

Hombres de maíz. See *Men of Maize*.

"Hombres necios" (Cruz). PFor 379.

"Home" (Beer). PEng 122.

"Home" (Guest). PEng 1165-1166.

Home (Storey). DEng 1887-1889.

Home and Beauty (Maugham). DEng 1310.

Home and the World (Tagore). LFFor 2218.

Home as Found (Cooper). LFEng 606-607.

Home at Seven (Sherriff). DEng 1791.

"Home Front, The" (Helprin). ShFSup 115-116.

"Home Is Where" (Adams). ShFSup 2.

Home of the Brave (Laurents). DEng 1101-1102.

"Home on the Range" (Dorn). PEng 842.

Home Place, The (Morris). LFEng 1904.

"Home Sickness" (Moore). ShF 660-661.

Home Truths (Gallant). LFEng 1053.

"Home/World" (Niedecker). PSup 299.

Homecoming (Ngugi). LTh 1062-1063.

"Homecoming, The" (Yerby). ShF 2478-2479.

"Homeland" (Hölderlin). PFor 681-682.

Homeless (Goldschmidt). LFFor 2337.

Homenaje (Guillén). PFor 625-626.

Homer. DFor 2087-2088; LFFor 1999; LTh 1143-1144, 1511; PFor 62, 85-86, **698-708,** 1750-1754; ShF 135, **1651-1655.**

Homero en Cuernavaca (Reyes). PFor 1322.

Homer's Daughter (Graves, R.). LFEng 1202.

Homestead Called Damascus, The (Rexroth). PEng 2352-2353.

"Hometown" (Galvin). PEng 1056.

Homeward: Songs by the Way (Æ). PEng 17-18.

Homeward to America (Ciardi). PEng 502.

Homewood Trilogy, The (Wideman). LFSup 383-385.

Homme approximatif, L'. See *Approximate Man*.

Homme aux quarante écus, L'. See *Man of Forty Crowns, The*.

Homme aux valises, L'. See *Man with Bags*.

"Homme paisible, Un." *See* "Tractable Man, A."

Homme qui rit, L'. See *Man Who Laughs, The*.

Hommes de bonne volunté, Les. See *Men of Good Will*.

Homo (Owens). DEng 1458.

Homo Faber (Frisch). LFFor 585-587.

Hondo (L'Amour). LFSup 221.

Honest John Vane (De Forest). LFEng 704.

"Honest Lover whosoever" (Suckling). PEng 2780.

Honest Whore, Part II, The (Dekker). DEng 488-492.

Honey and Salt (Sandburg). PEng 2452.

Honey in the Horn (Davis). LFEng 675-676.

Honeymoon, Bittermoon (Pérez de Ayala). LFFor 1259-1260.

"Honeysuckle, The" (Marie de France). ShF 1889.

Honneur et l'argent, L' (Ponsard). DFor 1491.

Honor (Sudermann). DFor 1762-1763.

Honorary Consul, The (Greene). M&D 792.

Honour and Offer (Livings). DEng 1153, 1156.

Honour of Valour (Breton, N.). PEng 282.

Honourable Schoolboy, The (le Carré). LFEng 1616-1617; M&D 1044.

Honshō nijū fukō (Saikaku). ShFSup 270.

Hood, Hugh. ShF 176, 640.

Hood, Thomas. **PEng 1377-1389.**

"Hook" (Clark). ShF 1155.

"Hook" (Wright, J.). PEng 3168.

Hooke, Sylvia Denys. *See* **Gilbert, Anthony.**

Hoop van zegen, Op. See *Good Hope, The*.

"Hop-Frog" (Poe). ShF 476.

"Hope" (Coleridge, H.). PEng 528.

"Hope" (Newman). PEng 2104.

Hope, A. D. PSup 184-192.

Hope, Brian. See **Creasey, John.**

"Hope Chest, The" (Stafford). ShF 2262.

Hopkins, Gerard Manley. PEng 815, **1390-1404.**

Hopley, George. *See* **Woolrich, Cornell.**

Hopley-Woolrich, Cornell George. *See* **Woolrich, Cornell.**

Hoppla! Such Is Life! (Toller). DFor 1863-1864.

Hopscotch (Cortázar). LFFor 379-380, 2292, 2298.

Hora da estrela, A. See *Hour of the Star, The*.

Horace. LTh 41-42, 63, 182, 260, 404, 584-585, 741, **695-700,** 799, 781-782, 854, 857, 952, 1039-1041, 1141, 1143, 1286, 1296, 1639-1641, 1652, 1665-1666, 1689; PFor 97, **709-719,** 1285, 1607, 2097, 2098; ShF 379-380.

Horace (Corneille). DFor 430-432.

Horacker (Raabe). LFFor 1383-1384.

Horae Lyricae (Watts). PEng 3046.

Horatian Ode upon Cromwell's Return from Ireland, An (Marvell). PEng 1909-1911.
"Horatius" (Macaulay). PEng 1826-1827.
Hordubal (Čapek). LFFor 276-277.
Horgan, Paul. LFSup 157-163.
Horizontal Man, The (Eustis). M&D 580-583.
Horkheimer, Max. LTh 13-14, 17, 137.
"Horla, The" (Maupassant). M&D 1210-1211.
Horniman, Anne. DEng 2375, 2446.
Hornissen, Die (Handke). LFFor 783.
Hornung, E. W. M&D 905-910.
"Horos kimitiriou" (Pentzíkis). PFor 1190. See also *Anakomidhi.*
Horovitz, Israel. DEng 957-964.
Horozsco, Sebastián de. DFor 2172.
Horribilicribrifax (Gryphius). DFor 838-839.
Horror Stories. ShF 741.
Horse and His Boy, The (Lewis, C. S.). LFEng 1657.
Horse and Two Goats and Other Stories, A (Narayan). ShFSup 228.
"Horse Chestnut Tree, The" (Eberhart). PEng 933.
"Horse Dealer's Daughter, The" (Lawrence, D. H.). ShF 1791-1792.
Horse Eats Hat. See *Italian Straw Hat, The.*
"Horse That Could Whistle 'Dixie', The" (Weidman). ShF 2411-2412.
"Horseback in the Rain" (Still). PEng 2764.
Horseman on the Roof, The (Giono). LFFor 658.
Horseman, Pass By (McMurtry). LFEng 1751-1752.
"Horses in Central Park" (Swenson). PEng 2795.
Horse's Mouth, The (Cary). LFEng 458, 460.
"Horses of Achilles, The" (Sikelianos). PFor 1957-1958.
"Horseshoe Finder, The" (Mandelstam). PFor 939-940.
Horsky hotel (Havel). DFor 881.
"Horus" (Nerval). PFor 1087.
Horvath, Odon von. DFor 953-962.
Horvatić, Dubravko. PFor 2266.
Horwitz, Julius. ShF 2645.
Hosanna (Quarles). PEng 2298.
Hosanna (Tremblay). DSup 354-355.
Hose, Die. See *Bloomers, The.*
Hospital, The (Fearing). M&D 594.
"Hospital Window, The" (Dickey, J.). PEng 796.

Hostage, The (Behan). DEng 165-167.
Hosties noires (Senghor). PFor 1426.
Hostrup, Jens Christian. DFor 2469.
Hot l Baltimore, The (Wilson). DEng 2100-2101.
Hotel, The (Bowen). LFEng 264.
Hotel du Lac (Brookner). LFSup 66-67.
Hotel New Hampshire, The (Irving). LFEng 1413, 1423-1425.
Hotel Play, The (Shawn). DSup 336-337.
Hotel Universe (Barry). DEng 136-137.
Hottentot Ossuary (Tate, J.). PEng 2838-2839.
Hound of the Baskervilles, The (Doyle). LFEng 807; M&D 532-535.
"Hounds of Tinaldos, The" (Long). ShF 565.
Hounds on the Mountain (Still). PEng 2762-2765.
"Hour, The" (Blackburn). PEng 195.
"Hour of Feeling, The" (Simpson). PEng 2608.
Hour of the Star, The (Lispector). LFSup 247.
Hours of Idleness (Byron). LTh 258; PEng 405.
"House, The" (Berry). PEng 151-152.
"House, The" (Creeley). PEng 690.
House Behind the Cedars, The (Chesnutt). LFEng 518-520.
House by the Churchyard, The (Le Fanu). LFEng 1624-1625; M&D 1050.
House by the Medlar Tree, The (Verga). DFor 2411; LFFor 1861-1864, 2232-2233; LTh 1497-1498.
House for Mr. Biswas, A (Naipaul). LFEng 1960.
House in Clewe Street, The (Lavin). ShF 1780.
House in Paris, The (Bowen). LFEng 265-266.
House in the Country, A (Donoso). LFFor 500-501.
"House in the Trees, The" (Booth). PEng 246.
"House in Turk Street, The" (Hammett). ShF 1577-1578.
House of Bernarda Alba, The (García Lorca). DFor 665, 2506.
House of Blue Leaves, The (Guare). DEng 861.
House of Cards (Ellin). M&D 577-578.
House of Children, A (Cary). LFEng 458.
House of Dust, The (Aiken). PEng 24.
"House of Ecstacy, The" (Farley). ShF 129-130.
House of Fame, The (Chaucer). LTh 282; PEng 481-482; ShF 1103.

House of Five Talents, The (Auchincloss).
LFEng 106-107.
House of Fourchambault, The (Augier). DFor
140-142.
House of Gentlefolk, A (Turgenev). LFFor
1774.
House of Incest (Nin). LFEng 1990-1991.
House of Life, The (Rossetti, D. G.). PEng
2431-2432, 2433.
House of Mirth, The (Wharton, Edith). LFEng
2852-2854.
"House of Night" (Freneau). PEng 1035.
House of the Arrow, The (Mason). M&D 1197-
1198.
House of the Dead, The (Dostoevski). LFFor
2317.
House of the Four Winds, The (Buchan).
LFEng 334.
House of the Prophet, The (Auchincloss).
LFEng 112-113.
House of the Seven Gables, The (Hawthorne).
LFEng 1322-1324.
House of the Sleeping Beauties, The
(Kawabata). LFFor 911-912.
House of the Solitary Maggot, The (Purdy).
LFEng 2174-2175.
House on Coliseum Street, The (Grau). LFEng
1185.
House on Marshland, The (Glück). PSup 135-
136.
House on the Hill, The (Pavese). LFFor 1248-
1250.
"House on the Hill, The" (Robinson). PEng
2388-2389.
House with Two Doors Is Difficult to Guard, A
(Calderón). DFor 301-302.
"Houseboat" (Nin). ShF 1949.
Household, Geoffrey. M&D 911-915.
Household Plagued by Love, A (Cruz). DFor
443.
Householder, The (Jhabvala). LFSup 173-174.
Housman, A. E. PEng 1405-1416.
"How Annandale Went Out" (Robinson). PEng
2391, 2392-2393.
"How Come?" (Ignatow). PEng 1472.
"How Dunbar Was Desired to Be a Friar"
(Dunbar, W.). PEng 888.
"How I Contemplated the World from the
Detroit House of Correction and Began My
Life Over Again" (Oates). ShF 1962-1963.

"How I Finally Lost My Heart" (Lessing, D.).
ShF 1806-1807.
How It Is (Beckett). LFEng 213; LFFor 129.
How Like a God (Stout). ShF 128.
How Like an Angel (Millar). M&D 1221-1222.
*How Mister Mockingpott Was Cured of His
Suffering* (Weiss). DFor 1990.
"How Mr. Rabbit Saved His Meat" (Harris, J.).
ShF 1587-1588.
"How Much Land Does a Man Need?"
(Tolstoy). ShF 2334-2335.
"How Pearl Button Was Kidnapped"
(Mansfield). ShF 1881.
"How Sharp Snaffles Got His Capital and His
Wife" (Simms). ShF 2233-2236.
How the Ancients Represented Death (Lessing).
LTh 882.
"How the Devil Came Down Division Street"
(Algren). ShF 857.
How the Plains Indians Got Horses (Plumly).
PEng 2235.
"How the Rain Is Falling Lightly" (Castro).
PFor 279. See also *Cantares gallegos.*
How to Do Things with Words (Austin). LTh
1827.
"How to Eat an Orange" (MacBeth). PEng
1834.
"How to Get on in Society" (Betjeman). PEng
171.
"How to Get Through Reality" (Blackburn).
PEng 196.
"How to Get Up Off It" (Blackburn). PEng
198.
"How to Read" (Pound). LTh 1156, 1158.
"How We Heard the Name" (Dugan). PEng
882-883.
Howard, Bronson. DEng 965-972.
Howard, Hartley. See **Carmichael, Harry.**
Howard, Henry. See **Surrey, Henry Howard,
Earl of.**
Howard, Sidney. DEng 973-978.
Howards End (Forster). LFEng 1001-1003.
Howe, Irving. LFEng 3252-3253.
Howe, Susan. PSup 193-199.
Howells, William Dean. LFEng 1368-1379,
3042-3043, 3049, 3173; LTh 1750; **PEng
1417-1427;** ShF 221, 233-234, 575, 586,
587, 589.
Howl (Ginsberg). PEng 1091-1092, 3380,
3393.

Howling at the Moon (Sakutarō). PFor 2075, 2076-2077.

Hrabal, Bohumil. LFFor 2067.

Hrafnkel's Saga. ShF 395-396.

Hreidar the Fool. ShF 396-397.

Hristić, Jovan. PFor 2257.

Hroswitha of Gandersheim. DEng 2244; DFor 2153-2154; PFor 2114.

"Hsaio-ch'ung-shan." *See* "Tune: Manifold Little Hills."

"Hsi furen." *See* "Lady Hsi."

Hsi-hsiang chi. See *Romance of the Western Chamber, The.*

Hsi-hsiang chi chu kung-tiao (Tung). DFor 2309.

Hsi-yu chi. See *Journey to the West, The.*

Hsi-Chou-shêng. *See* **P'u Sung-ling.**

Hsieh Ling-yün. PFor 720-726.

Hsing-shih yin-yüan chuan (P'u). ShFSup 238.

Hsü Wei. DFor 2323.

Hu Shih. LTh **701-706,** 1781.

Hu Ying-lin. LTh 1779.

"Hua ma." *See* "Picture Horse, The."

"Hua p'i." *See* "Painted Skin, The."

Huang Fang-yü. DFor 2324.

Huch, Friedrich. LFFor 2185.

Huch, Ricarda. LFFor 2184.

Huchel, Peter. PFor 1815, 1817, 1821, 1930.

Huddle, David. ShF 2646.

Hudibras (Butler). PEng 384-385, 386-390.

Hudson, W. H. LFEng 1380-1397.

"Hue and Cry" (McPherson). ShF 1856-1857.

Hue and Cry (McPherson). ShF 1855.

Huellas (Reyes). PFor 1321.

Huge Season, The (Morris). LFEng 1911-1912.

Hugh Selwyn Mauberley (Pound). PEng 2269, 3365, 3390.

Hughes, Colin. *See* **Creasey, John.**

Hughes, Langston. PEng **1428-1436,** 3393, 3400, 3401, 3402; ShF 266-267, 555, 578, **1656-1661.**

Hughes, Matilda. *See* **MacLeod, Charlotte.**

Hughes, Ted. PEng **1437-1446;** PSup 406.

Hugo (Bennett). M&D 108.

Hugo, Richard. PEng **1447-1459;** PSup 406.

Hugo, Victor. DEng 2188, 2189; DFor 963-972, 2344; LFFor 845-857; LTh **707-713,** 1383, 1395, 1696-1697, 1705-1707, 1709-1710, 1733; PFor **727-739,** 1870-1871; ShF 464.

Huguenots, Les (Scribe). DFor 1682-1684.

Huidobro, Vicente. LFFor 2291.

Huis-clos. See *No Exit.*

Huis van die dowe, Die (Breytenbach). PSup 53-54.

Huit Coups de l'horloge, Les. See *Eight Strokes of the Clock.*

"Huître, L'." *See* "Oyster, The."

Huldén, Lars. PFor 2200.

Hull, Richard. M&D 916-921.

"Hulla a búza-földön." *See* "Corpse on the Wheat-Field."

Hulme, T. E. LTh 306, **714-720,** 1554, 1810.

Human Age, The (Lewis, W.). LFEng 1688-1689.

Human, All Too Human (Nietzsche). LTh 1069.

Human Comedy, The (Balzac). LFFor 90-91, 92-94, 2126-2127; ShF 921.

Human Comedy, The (Saroyan). LFEng 2336-2337.

"Human Condition" (Gunn). PEng 1173.

"Human Element, The" (Maugham). ShF 1905.

Human Factor, The (Greene, G.). LFEng 1220-1221.

Human Landscapes (Hikmet). PSup 180-181.

Human Poems (Vallejo). PFor 1561, 1592-1593.

Human Season, The (Wallant). LFEng 2761-2762.

"Human Universe" (Olson). PSup 307.

Human Universe and Other Essays (Olson). LTh 1074.

Human Vibration (Richter). LFEng 2266-2267.

"Humanism and the Religious Attitude" (Hulme). LTh 716, 718.

"Humanitad" (Wilde). PEng 3106-3107.

"Humanitarians, The" (Giusti). PFor 575.

"Humble Bee, The" (Emerson). PEng 959-960.

Humble Romance and Other Stories (Freeman, M.). ShF 228.

Humboldt's Gift (Bellow). LFEng 234-235.

Hume, David. LTh 240, **721-725.**

"Hummingbirds" (Dubie). PSup 107.

Humor (Pirandello). LTh 148, 1097-1101.

Humourous Day's Mirth, An (Chapman). DEng 354.

Humphreys, David. LTh 1742.

Humphry Clinker (Smollett). LFEng 2450-251.

Hunchback of Notre Dame, The (Hugo). LFFor 853-854, 2125.

Hund des Generals, Der (Kipphardt). DFor 1055.

Hundejahre. See *Dog Years*.

Hundevakt (Hauge). LFFor 799-800. See also *Cleng Peerson*.

Hundred Sundrie Flowers Bound Up in One Small Poesie (Gascoigne). ShF 489-490.

Hundred-Thousand Songs (Mi-la Ras-pa). PFor 2247-2248.

Hundreth Sundrie Flowres, A (Gascoigne). LTh 541.

Hung-lou meng. See *Dream of the Red Chamber*.

Hung Shêng. DFor 2326.

Hung Wu. DFor 2319-2320.

Hunger (Hamsun). LFFor 769-771, 2345-2346.

Hunger and Thirst (Ionesco). DFor 2357.

Hunger Artist, The (Clarke). DSup 66-67.

"Hunger Artist, A" (Kafka). ShF 1733.

Hunger-Pastor, The (Raabe). LFFor 1380, 1381-1382.

"Hungry Man's Wheel, The" (Vallejo). PFor 1593. See also *Human Poems*.

Hunt, Kyle. *See* **Creasey, John.**

Hunt, Leigh. PEng 1460-1465.

Hunt, William Holman. LTh 1245.

Hunter, Evan. *See* **McBain, Ed.**

"Hunter Trials" (Betjeman). PEng 171.

"Hunting" (Snyder). PEng 2672.

"Hunting of the Hare, A" (Newcastle). PEng 2095.

Hunting of the Snark, The (Carroll). PEng 447-452.

"Hunting Season" (Greenberg). ShF 1538-1539.

Huntingtower (Buchan). LFEng 333-334.

Hurlyburly (Rabe). DEng 1553-1554.

"Hurrahing in Harvest" (Hopkins). PEng 1399-1400.

"Hurricane, The" (Freneau). PEng 1035.

Hurricane Lamp (Cassity). PSup 64-65.

Hurry Home (Wideman). LFSup 381-382.

Hurry on Down (Wain). LFEng 2738, 2739-2740.

"Hurry Up Please It's Time" (Sexton). PEng 2526.

Hurskas kurjuus. See *Meek Heritage*.

Hurston, Zora Neale. LFEng 1389-1397; ShF 577-578.

Husband and Wife (Fredro). DFor 2277; DSup 138.

Husfrue. See *Mistress of Husaby, The* and *Kristin Lavransdatter*.

Hussard sur le toit, Le. See *Horseman on the Roof, The*.

Husserl, Edmund. LTh 356-358, 379-380, 530-531, 685, 726-727, 767, 1149, 1227-1228, 1271, 1763, 1765, 1820.

"Huswifery" (Taylor). PEng 2844.

Hutcheson, Francis. LTh 723.

Huxley, Aldous. LFEng 1398-1412, 3059; ShF 245-246, 521.

Huxley, T. H. LTh 1738.

Huyendo del perejil (Tamayo y Baus). DFor 1805.

Huysmans, Joris-Karl. LFFor 858-867, 2135, 2136.

Hviezdoslav, Pavol Országh-. PFor 1809.

Hyde Park (Shirley). DEng 1815-1817, 2292.

"Hygeia at the Solito" (Henry). ShF 1630.

Hyman, Stanley Edgar. LTh 242.

Hymen (Torres Naharro). DFor 1869-1872.

"Hymn" (Caedmon). PEng 416-420.

"Hymn of Man" (Swinburne). PEng 2820.

"Hymn to a Woman Being Interrogated" (Kunze). PFor 806.

"Hymn to Adversity" (Gray). PEng 1139.

Hymn to Apollo (Callimachus). PFor 254, 257.

"Hymn to Christ, A" (Donne). PEng 837.

"Hymn to Death" (Ronsard). PFor 1358.

"Hymn to Freedom" (Hölderlin). PFor 685.

"Hymn to God the Father, A" (Donne). PEng 837.

"Hymn to Harmony, in Honour of St. Cecilia's Day, 1701, A" (Congreve). PEng 557.

"Hymn to Immortality" (Hölderlin). PFor 685.

"Hymn to Intellectual Beauty" (Shelley). PEng 2557-2558.

Hymn to Liberty, The (Solomòs). PFor 1452, 1454, 1455.

"Hymn to Life" (Schuyler). PEng 2479-2480.

"Hymn to Light" (Cowley, A.). PEng 595-596.

"Hymn to Satan" (Carducci). PFor 270.

"Hymn to the Morning, An" (Wheatley). PEng 3057-3058.

"Hymn to the Name and Honor of the Admirable Saint Teresa, A" (Crashaw). PEng 672-673.

I

I: six nonlectures (Cummings). PEng 702.

I, The (Holland). LTh 686.

"I Am" (Clare). PEng 514-515.

"I Am a Fool" (Anderson). ShF 106, 873.

"I Am a Horse" (Arp). PFor 105.

"I Am a Parcel of Vain Strivings Tied" (Thoreau). PEng 2903.

"I Am a Realist" (Różewicz). PFor 1367.

I Am Elijah Thrush (Purdy). LFEng 2173-2174.

I Am Mary Dunne (Moore, B.). LFEng 1890-1891.

I Am the Bitter Name (Williams). PSup 389.

"I Am 25" (Corso). PEng 577.

I Am Writing to You from a Far-Off Country (Michaux). PFor 999.

I asalefti zoi. See *Life Immovable.*

"I Believe, Unbelieving, in God" (Ady). PFor 6.

"I Cannot Know. . ." (Radnóti). PFor 1313.

I Ching. See *Book of Changes.*

I, Claudius (Graves, R.). LFEng 1200.

"I Don't Need You Any More" (Miller). ShF 1928.

"I dreaded that first Robin, so" (Dickinson). PEng 809.

"I Felt a Funeral, in my Brain" (Dickinson). PEng 811.

"I find no peace, and all my war is done" (Wyatt). PEng 3173-3174.

"I Gather the Limbs of Osiris" (Pound). LTh 1158.

"I Go into Darkened Temples" (Blok). PFor 198-199. See also *Stikhi o prekrasnoy dame.*

I Hardly Knew You (O'Brien, E.). LFEng 2022-2023.

"I Have a Premonition of You" (Blok). PFor 199. See also *Stikhi o prekrasnoy dame.*

"I Have Forgotten the Word I Wanted to Say" (Mandelstam). PFor 938. See also *Tristia.*

"I Have Fought a Good Fight" (Rossetti, C.). PEng 2420.

"I Have Not Heard the Tales of Ossian" (Mandelstam). PFor 937. See also *Stone.*

I havsbandet. See *By the Open Sea.*

"I heard a Fly buzz--when I died" (Dickinson). PEng 3372.

"I Keep to Myself Such Measures. . ." (Creeley). PEng 682.

"I Knew a Man by Sight" (Thoreau). PEng 2901.

"I Knew What I Was Doing" (Weidman). ShF 2411.

"I Know It as the Sorrow" (Everson). PEng 986.

"I know that He exists" (Dickinson). PEng 807-808.

"I like to see it lap the Miles" (Dickinson). PEng 805-806.

"I Love You, My Dear" (Petőfi). PFor 1225.

"I Loved" (Saba). PSup 346.

I Marry You (Ciardi). PEng 503.

"I' mi trovai fanciulle un bel mattino." See "I Went A-Roaming, Maidens, One Bright Day."

I Must Love Somebody (Kirkland). DEng 1051-1052.

I Never Sang for My Father (Anderson, R.). DEng 36-38.

"I Open" (Brathwaite). PFor 215-216.

I Ought to Be in Pictures (Simon). DEng 1830-1831.

"I Remember Galileo" (Stern). PSup 372.

"I Remember, I Remember" (Larkin). PEng 1672.

"I Screamed in the Night" (Różewicz). PFor 1364.

"I See the Mad" (Różewicz). PFor 1362, 1363-1364.

"I sing of Olaf glad and big" (Cummings). PEng 708-709.

"I skuchno i grustno. . ." See "It's Boring and Sad. . ."

"I Stand Here Ironing" (Olsen). ShF 113, 2021.

"I started Early--Took my Dog" (Dickinson). PEng 809.

"I, the Mournful God." See *Laughable Loves.*

"I Used to Have a Nail" (Castro). PFor 277.

"I Used to Live Here Once" (Rhys). ShFSup 262-263.

"I Wake and Feel the Fell of Dark, Not Day" (Hopkins). PEng 1402.

"I Walk Out Alone onto the Road" (Lermontov). PFor 875.

"I Was in Love" (Oates). ShF 1964.

"I Was Reading a Scientific Article" (Atwood). PEng 66.

"I Was Riding at Full Gallop Around the City Walls, Pursued by a Throng of Superstitious Coalmongers" (Foix). PFor 489-490.

"I Was Sitting upon a Rock" (Walther). PFor 1678-1679.

"I Went A-Roaming, Maidens, One Bright Day" (Poliziano). PFor 1254.

"I went into the Maverick Bar" (Snyder). PEng 2675.

I Will Marry When I Want (Ngugi and Ngugiwa). DEng 2419; DSup 267-268, 272-274.

I Would and Would Not (Breton, N.). PEng 281.

"Ia ne slyxal rasskazov Ossiana." *See* "I Have Not Heard the Tales of Ossian."

"Ia slova pozabyl, chto ia khotel skazat." *See* "I Have Forgotten the Word I Wanted to Say."

Iaia Garcia (Machado de Assis). LFFor 1042.

Iambi (Callimachus). PFor 256-257.

Iamblichus. LFFor 2001.

Iamvi kai anapaisti (Palamàs). PFor 1953.

"Iazvital'nyi." *See* "Stinger, The."

Ibn Ezra, Moses. PFor 777.

Ibn Gabirol, Solomon. PFor 777.

"Ibn Hakkan al-Bokhari, Dead in His Labyrinth" (Borges). M&D 163.

Ibn Nagrillah, Samuel. PFor 776-777.

Ibsen, Henrik. DEng 2191-2192; DFor 973-988, 2237, 2471-2472; LTh 1327-1329, 1724.

Ice (Kavan). LFEng 1512-1513.

Ice Age, The (Drabble). LFEng 825-826.

"Ice-Floes, The" (Pratt). PEng 2284.

"Ice House, The" (Gordon). ShF 1522-1524.

Icebound (Davis). DEng 478-479.

Iceman Cometh, The (O'Neill). DEng 1414-1417.

"Ich bin ein Pferd." *See* "I Am a Horse."

"Ich saz ûf eine Steine." *See* "I Was Sitting upon a Rock."

"Ichabod" (Whittier). PEng 3087.

Ichikawa Sadanji II. DFor 2432-2433.

"Ichinaka wa." *See* "In the City."

Ici ou ailleurs. See *Clope*.

"Icicles" (Gass). ShF 1480.

Iconographs (Swenson). PEng 2795-2796.

"¡Id con Dios!" *See* "Farewell, Go with God!"

Ida, A Novel (Stein). LFEng 2516.

Ida Brandt (Bang). LFFor 2339.

"Idea, The" (Carver). ShFSup 77.

Idea (Drayton). PEng 853.

"Idea of Order at Key West, The" (Stevens). PEng 3392.

Idea of the Humanities and Other Essays Critical and Historical, The (Crane). LTh 322.

Idea, the Shepherd's Garland (Drayton). PEng 849.

"Ideal Craftsman, An" (de la Mare). ShF 1253-1254.

Ideal Husband, An (Wilde). DEng 2037, 2038.

Ideal in Art, The (Taine). LTh 1420.

Idealist, En. See *Herod the King*.

Idea's Mirror (Drayton). PEng 849.

Ideas of Good and Evil (Yeats). LTh 1587.

Ideen über eine beschreibende und zergliedende Psychologie (Dilthey). LTh 378.

Idées de Madame Aubray, Les. See *Madame Aubray's Ideas*.

Identité (Pinget). DSup 305-306.

"Ides of March, The" (Hornung). M&D 908.

Ides of March, The (Wilder). LFEng 2885-2886.

Idiot, The (Dostoevski). LFFor 511-513.

Idiot de la famille, L'. See *Family Idiot, The*.

Idiot Lady, The. See *Lady Nit-Wit, The*.

Idiot's Delight (Sherwood). DEng 1806-1807.

Idiots Karamazov, The (Durang and Innaurato). DSup 101, 203.

"Idle Days on the Yann" (Dunsany). ShF 1317.

Idler, The (Johnson, S.). LTh 774, 1685; ShF 771, 1708-1709.

Idō. See *Move, The*.

"Idolaters, The" (D'Annunzio). ShF 687.

"Idyll" (Roethke). PEng 2409-2410.

Idylls (Theocritus). PFor 1508-1509.

Idylls of the King (Tennyson). PEng 2868.

"If from my lips some angry accents fell" (Lamb). PEng 1634-1635.

"If I have made, my lady, intricate" (Cummings). PEng 706.

"If I must die" (Nashe). PEng 2072.

If Morning Ever Comes (Tyler). LFEng 2676.

"If Not Higher" (Peretz). ShF 2089.

If Not Now, When? (Levi). LFSup 237-239.

If on a Winter's Night a Traveler (Calvino). LFFor 247-249.

"If poisonous minerals" (Donne). PEng 836.

"If There Were Not Death, but Oblivion" (Annensky). PFor 43.

"If We Must Die" (McKay). PEng 1845, 3392-3393, 3400.

"If You Are a Man, Then Be One" (Petőfi). PFor 1226.

"If You Don't Want to Live I Can't Help You" (Calisher). ShF 1037-1038.

"If you would seek a friend among men" (Crane, S.). PEng 663.

Ifigenia cruel (Reyes). PFor 1322.

"I. G." LTh 1668.

Igitur (Mallarmé). PFor 926-930.

Ignatow, David. PEng 1466-1477; PSup 406.

Ignez de Castro (Ferreira). DFor 592-594.

Ignjatović, Jakov. LFFor 2075.

"Igre." *See* "Games."

Ihara Saikaku. *See* **Saikaku, Ihara.**

Ihmiselon ihanuus ja kurjuus (Sillanpää). LFFor 1580.

Ihmiset suviyössä. See *People in the Summer Night.*

"Ihr Worte" (Bachmann). PFor 129.

Ikones (Pentzíkis). PFor 1187-1189.

"Ilama de amor viva." *See* "Living Flame of Love, The."

Île des esclaves, L' (Marivaux). DFor 1262-1263.

Île des pingouins, L'. See *Penguin Island.*

Île mystérieuse, L'. See *Mysterious Island, The.*

Iles, Francis. *See* **Berkeley, Anthony.**

Ilf, Ilya. LFFor 2325.

Ilić, Jovan. PFor 2254.

Ilić, Vojislav. PFor 2255.

Iliad (Homer). PFor 698-702, 704-708, 1747, 1750-1751, 1756-1757; ShF 1652-1653.

Ílios o protos, mazi me tis parallayiés páno se mián ahtídha (Elýtis). PFor 464, 1966.

I'll Be Home for Christmas (Anderson, R.). DEng 39-40. See also *You Know I Can't Hear You When the Water's Running.*

Ill Seen Ill Said (Beckett). LFEng 215; LFFor 131.

"Illinois Village, The" (Lindsay). PEng 1725.

Illness as Metaphor (Sontag). LTh 1366-1367.

Illuminations (Rimbaud). PFor 1341, 1342-1343.

"Illusion, The" (Everson). PEng 987.

Illusion and Reality (Caudwell). PEng 3411-3412.

Illusion comique, L' (Corneille). DFor 427-428.

Illustrations, The (Dubie). PSup 106.

Illustrious House of Ramires, The (Eça de Queiróz). LFFor 545-546.

Illyés, Gyula. DFor 2288; **PFor 740-746,** 1987.

Ilusiones del doctor Faustino, Las (Valera). LFFor 1821-1822.

Ilustre casa de Ramires, A. See *Illustrious House of Ramires, The.*

I'm Expecting to Live Quite Soon (West). LFSup 372-373.

I'm Herbert (Anderson, R.). DEng 38-39. See also *You Know I Can't Hear You When the Water's Running.*

Im Land der Umbramauten (Meckel). ShFSup 188.

I'm Not Stiller (Frisch). LFFor 583-585.

I'm Talking About Jerusalem (Wesker). DEng 2018.

"Im Unterreich." *See* "In the Subterranean Kingdom."

Im Westen nichts Neues. See *All Quiet on the Western Front.*

"Im Winter." *See* "In Winter."

"Images, The" (Rich). PEng 2371.

Images of Truth (Westcott). ShF 2423.

Imaginary Friends (Lurie). LFSup 254-255.

"Imaginary Iceberg, The" (Bishop). PEng 184, 188.

Imaginary Magnitude (Lem). ShFSup 150.

Imán. See *Pro Patria.*

Imitation de Notre-Dame la lune, L' (Laforgue). PFor 825-826.

Immanuel Kant (Bernhard). DFor 200-201.

"Immanuel Kant and the Hopi" (Stern). PSup 369.

Immensee (Storm). LFFor 1680-1681.

"Immer zu benennen." *See* "Always to Be Named."

Immermann, Karl Leberecht. LTh 1710.

Immobile Wind, The (Winters). PSup 396.

Immoralist, The (Gide). LFFor 640, 642-643, 2139-2140.

"Immortal Strangeness" (Everson). PEng 991.

Imnos is tin eleftheria. See *Hymn to Liberty, The.*

"Imperfect Conflagration, An" (Bierce). M&D 127.

"Imperial Adam" (Hope). PSup 189.

"Imperial Message, An" (Kafka). ShF 1733.

Imperium Pelagi (Young). LTh 1597.

Implied Reader, The (Iser). LTh 732-733.

Implizite Leser, Der. See *Implied Reader, The.*

Importance of Being Earnest, The (Wilde). DEng 2036, 2038-2040, 2366.

Imposteur, L'. See *Tartuffe.*

"Impostor" (Dick). ShF 1263.

Impromptu of Outrement, The (Tremblay). DSup 355-356.

Improvisatore, The (Andersen). LFFor 2336.

Improvisatore, The (Beddoes). PEng 110-111.

"In a Dark Time" (Roethke). PEng 2413-2414.

In a Free State (Naipaul). LFEng 1961-1962.

"In a Garden" (McPherson). PEng 1883.

In a Glass Darkly (Le Fanu). ShF 1798.

"In a Grove" (Akutagawa). ShFSup 10.

"In a Hard Intellectual Light" (Eberhart). PEng 929.

In a Shallow Grave (Purdy). LFEng 2175.

"In a Townsip of Asia Minor" (Cavafy). PFor 298.

In a Yellow Wood (Vidal). LFEng 2717-2718.

In Abraham's Bosom (Green). DEng 819-820.

"In Alexandria, 31 B.C." (Cavafy). PFor 298-299.

In Any Case (Stern). LFSup 362-363.

"In Battle" (Petőfi). PFor 1228.

"In Beirut" (Durrell). PEng 920-921.

"In Bertram's Garden" (Justice). PEng 1530.

In Broken Country (Wagoner). PEng 2988, 2989.

"In California" (Simpson). PEng 2604-2605.

In Celebration (Storey). DEng 1883-1885.

In Chancery (Galsworthy). LFEng 1064.

In Cold Blood (Capote). LFEng 448-449.

"In Dark Times" (Brecht). PFor 224.

In Defence of Shelley and Other Essays (Read). LTh 1212.

In Defense of Materialism (Plekhanov). LTh 1121.

"In Defense of the Short Story" (Hartley). ShF 79.

"In der blauen Ferne." *See* "In the Blue Distance."

"In der Flucht." *See* "Fleeing."

In der Sache J. Robert Oppenheimer. See *In the Matter of J. Robert Oppenheimer.*

"In der Strafkolonie." *See* "In the Penal Colony."

"In deserto" (Gautier). PFor 536-537. See also *España.*

"In Distrust of Merits" (Moore). PEng 2046.

"In Dreams Begin Responsibilities" (Schwartz, D.). ShF 549.

In Dreams Begin Responsibilities (Schwartz, D.). ShF 549, 2204.

In Dubious Battle (Steinbeck). LFEng 2522-2523.

In Evil Hour (García Márquez). LFFor 616-617.

"In Excelsis" (Lowell, A.). PEng 1771.

"In Faith of Rising" (Kennedy). PEng 1571.

"In finsteren Zeiten." *See* "In Dark Times."

"In Gallarus Oratory" (Heaney). PEng 1269.

In Goethes Hand (Walser, M.). DSup 388-390.

"In Greenwich There Are Many Gravelled Walks" (Calisher). ShF 1035-1037.

"In Her Own Image" (Boland). PSup 36-38.

In Her Own Image (Boland). PSup 34, 36-40.

In His Own Country (Callaghan). ShFSup 70.

"In His Own Image" (Boland). PSup 37.

"In Honour of Du Bartas" (Bradstreet). PEng 259-260.

"In Honour of St. Alphonsus Rodriguez: Laybrother of the Society of Jesus" (Hopkins). PEng 1401.

In hora mortis (Bernhard). PFor 182-183.

In Love and Trouble (Walker). ShFSup 335-336.

"In memoriam" (Senghor). PFor 1428. See also *Chants d'ombre.*

In Memoriam (Tennyson). PEng 2868-2870.

In Memoriam James Joyce (MacDiarmid). PSup 266.

"In Memory of Barry Cornwall" (Swinburne). PEng 2821.

"In memory of my dear grand-child Elizabeth Bradstreet" (Bradstreet). PEng 262-263.

"In Memory of W. H. Auden" (Stern). PSup 376.

"In morte di Carlo Imbonati" (Manzoni). PFor 958.

In My Father's House (Gaines). LFEng 1048-1049.

"In My Own Album" (Lamb). PEng 1637.

In New England Winter (Bullins). DEng 308.
See also Twentieth-Century Cycle.
"In Old Russia" (Zamyatin). ShFSup 371.
In Ole Virginia (Page). ShF 616.
"In Petersburg We Shall Meet Again"
(Mandelstam). PFor 938-939. See also
Tristia.
In Praise of Love (Rattigan). DEng 1563-1564.
"In railway halls, on pavement near the traffic"
(Spender). PEng 2700.
"In Response to Vice-Magistrate Chang" (Wang
Wei). PFor 1689-1690.
"In Sant' Ambrogio's" (Giusti). PFor 576-577.
"In Santa Maria del Popolo" (Gunn). PEng
1174-1175.
"In Savage Wastes" (Everson). PEng 991.
In Search of Love and Beauty (Jhabvala).
LFSup 175-176.
In Search of Theatre (Bentley). LTh 149.
In Sicily (Vittorini). LFFor 1885-1886, 2244.
"In Snow, a Possible Life" (Smith, D.). PEng
2644.
In somnium Scipionis. See *Commentary on the
"Dream of Scipio."*
"In Space" (Arp). PFor 106.
"In Summer" (Dunbar). PSup 116-117.
In Switzerland (Slowacki). PFor 1443.
"In the Alley" (Elkin). ShF 1341.
In the Beginning (Potok). LFSup 317-318.
"In the Beginning Was the Word" (Fiedler).
LTh 483-484.
In the Best Families (Stout). M&D 1544-1545.
"In the Blue Distance" (Sachs). PFor 1376.
In the Boom Boom Room (Rabe). DEng 1550-
1551.
In the Burning Darkness (Buero Vallejo). DFor
276-279.
"In the Cathedral" (Castro). PFor 281. See also
Follas novas.
"In the Central Blue" (Cassill). ShF 1070,
1071-1072.
"In the City" (Matsuo Bashō). PFor 983. See
also *Monkey's Raincoat*.
"In the Clay" (Moore). ShF 660.
"In the Corridors of the Metro" (Robbe-Grillet).
ShF 2156.
"In the Dream's Recess" (Everson). PEng 990.
"In the Eyes of the Gods" (Breton). PFor 232-
233.
"In the Fleeting Hand of Time" (Corso). PEng
576.

"In the Forest" (de la Mare). ShF 1252-1253.
In the Frame of Don Cristóbal (García Lorca).
DFor 658.
"In the Garden" (Paley). ShF 2043-2044.
"In the Grave No Flower" (Millay). PEng
2002.
In the Heart of the Country (Coetzee). LFSup
79.
"In the Heart of the Heart of the Country"
(Gass). LFSup 121; ShF 1482-1483.
*In the Heart of the Heart of the Country and
Other Stories* (Gass). LFSup 121.
In the Heart of the Seas (Agnon). LFFor 19-
22.
In the Heat of the Night (Ball). M&D 68-70.
"In the Holy Nativity of Our Lord" (Crashaw).
PEng 669-670.
In the Labyrinth (Robbe-Grillet). LFFor 1416-
1417.
In the Last Analysis (Cross). M&D 428.
"In the Lovely Half-light" (Breton). PFor 233.
In the Matter of J. Robert Oppenheimer
(Kipphardt). DFor 1053-1055, 2382.
In the Mecca (Brooks). PEng 3393.
"In the Miro District" (Taylor). ShF 624-635,
2309-2310.
"In the Mountain Tent" (Dickey). PEng 3566.
"In the Mountains: Question and Answer" (Li
Po). PFor 890.
"In the Naked Bed, in Plato's Cave"
(Schwartz). PEng 2489-2490.
"In the Night" (Schorer). ShF 2198-2199.
In the Outer Dark (Plumly). PEng 2234-2235.
"In the Penal Colony" (Kafka). ShF 1734.
"In the Region of Ice" (Oates). ShF 1965.
In the Shadow of the Glen (Synge). DEng
1906-1907.
In the Shadow of the Wind (Hébert). LFFor
811, 813-814.
"In the Stopping Train" (Davie). PSup 90-91.
"In the Subterranean Kingdom" (George). PFor
547. See also *Algabal*.
In the Tennessee Mountains (Murfree). ShF
226.
"In the Terror of the Night" (Pessoa). PFor
1208.
"In the Thicket" (Wescott). ShF 2423.
In the Time of Greenbloom (Fielding). LFSup
115-116.
"In the Train" (O'Connor, Frank). ShF 672,
1991.

Innerhofer, Franz. LFFor 2206.

Innes, Michael. M&D 922-927.

"Inni." *See* "Hymns."

Inni Sacri. See *Sacred Hymns, The.*

Innis, Harold. LTh 958-959.

"Inno a Satana." *See* "Hymn to Satan."

"Innocence" (Gunn). PEng 1173-1174.

Innocent, The (Jones, M.). LFEng 1487-1489.

Innocent and the Guilty, The (Warner). ShFSup 356.

Innocent Blood (James, P. D.). LFSup 167-168; M&D 937.

Innocent Traveller, The (Wilson, E.). LFEng 2912.

Innocent Wife, The. See *Claudine and Annie.*

Innocente, L'. See *Intruder, The.*

Innommable, L'. See *Unnamable, The.*

"Inonia" (Esenin). PFor 479.

Inquietudes de Shanti Andía, Las. See *Restlessness of Shanti Andia, The.*

Inquiry Concerning Virtue in Two Discourses, An (Shaftesbury). LTh 1321.

Inquiry Concerning Virtue or Merit, An (Shaftesbury). PEng 3126.

Inquiry into the Original of Our Ideas of Beauty and Virtue, An (Hutcheson). LTh 723.

Inquisiciones (Borges). LTh 194.

Inquisitory, The (Pinget). LFFor 1289-1290.

"Inscripción para la tumba de El Greco." *See* "Epitaph for the Tomb of El Greco."

Insect Play, The (Čapek and Čapek). DFor 337-338.

"Inside the Story" (Strand). PEng 2771-2772.

"Insistence of the Letter in the Unconscious, The" (Lacan). LTh 846, 849-850.

Insolación. See *Midsummer Madness.*

Inspector Calls, An (Priestley). DEng 1541-1543.

Inspector French's Greatest Case (Crofts). M&D 419-420.

Inspector General, The (Gogol). DFor 748-752, 2453-2454.

Inspector West Cries Wolf. See *Creepers, The.*

"Inspiration" (Thoreau). PEng 2903.

"Instance de la lettre dans l'inconscient ou la raison depuis Freud, L'." *See* "Insistence of the Letter in the Unconscious, The."

Instantanés. See *Snapshots.*

Institutio oratoria (Quintilian). LTh 1188-1193, 1641-1642.

Intellectual Things (Kunitz). PSup 242-243.

"Intensidad y altura." *See* "Intensity and Height."

"Intensity and Height" (Vallejo). PFor 1593. See also *Human Poems.*

"Intentional Fallacy, The" (Wimsatt and Beardsley). LTh 1554.

Inter Ice Age 4 (Abe). LFFor 5-6.

Intercom Conspiracy, The (Ambler). M&D 32-33.

Intereses creados, Los. See *Bonds of Interest, The.*

Interface (Gores). M&D 762.

Interfaces of the Word (Ong). LTh 1083.

Interior (Maeterlinck). DFor 1239.

Interludium de Clerico et Puella. DEng 2256.

Intermezzo (D'Annunzio). PFor 386.

Intermezzo (Giraudoux). See *Enchanted, The.*

"Interpretations of Dreams, The" (Koch). PEng 1627.

Interpreters, The (Soyinka). LFFor 2037, 2054-2055; LFSup 353-356.

Interrupted Act, The (Różewicz). DFor 1584.

"Interrupted Cadence, An" (Hoffmann). ShF 1648.

"Interrupted Elegy" (Paz). PFor 1172.

"Interruption, The" (Jacobs). M&D 929-930.

Intimate Relations (Cocteau). DFor 419-420.

"Into the Cone of Cold" (Elliott, G.). ShF 1347-1348.

"Into the Dusk-Charged Air" (Ashbery). PEng 60.

Into the Stone and Other Poems (Dickey, J.). PEng 795.

Into the Valley (Hersey). LFEng 1352.

Into Thin Air (Beck). ShF 934.

Intrigue and Love. See *Cabal and Love.*

Introduction à la littérature fantastique. See *Fantastic, The.*

Introduction à l'architexte (Genette). LTh 563.

Introduction à l'étude de la médecine expérimentale. See *Introduction to the Study of Experimental Medicine.*

Introduction to Poetics, An (Todorov). LTh 1435, 1437.

Introduction to the Study of Experimental Medicine (Bernard). LTh 1713.

Intruder, The (D'Annunzio). LFFor 411.

"Intruder, The" (Gordimer). ShFSup 107-108.

"Intruder, The" (Kizer). PEng 1620.

Intruder, The (Maeterlinck). DFor 1238-1239.

Island of Jewels, The (Planché). DEng 1527-1528.

"Island of Monkeys, The" (Dazai). ShFSup 94-95.

Island of Sheep, The. See *Man from the Norlands, The*.

Island Princess, The (Fletcher). DEng 637-638.

Islanders, The (Zamyatin). ShFSup 369-370.

Íslandingasögur (Þorðarsson). LFFor 994, 2332.

"Islands" (Brathwaite). PEng 271; PFor 215.

Islands (Brathwaite). PFor 214-215.

Islands of Unwisdom, The (Graves, R.). LFEng 1196-1197.

Íslandsklukkan (Laxness). LFFor 996.

Isle of Dogs, The (Jonson and Nashe). DEng 1364, 2271, 2286.

Islendingabók. See *Book of the Icelanders*.

Ismene (Rítsos). PFor 1970.

Issa. PSup 200-209.

"Ist die Geschichte gerecht?" (Zweig). PFor 1722.

Ist River. See *East River*.

Istanboul (Owens). DEng 1458.

Istituzioni della poesia, Le (Anceschi). LTh 32.

Istoria della volgar poesia (Crescimbeni). LTh 1691.

Istoricheskaya poetika (Veselovsky). LTh 1506.

"Istoriia bolezni." *See* "History of an Illness."

"István Öcsémhez." *See* "To My Younger Brother, István."

Isvaran, Manjeri. ShF 644.

It (King). LFSup 210.

It Catches My Heart in Its Hand (Bukowski). PEng 359.

"It Had to Be Murder" (Woolrich). M&D 1726.

"It Is Not Beauty I Demand" (Darley). PEng 733-734.

It Is So (If You Think So). See *Right You Are (If You Think So)*.

"It may be good, like it who list" (Wyatt). PEng 3176-3177.

"It May Never Happen" (Pritchett). ShF 2130-2131.

"It sifts from Leaden Sieves" (Dickinson). PEng 806.

It Walks by Night (Carr). M&D 268-269.

"It was not Death, for I stood up" (Dickinson). PEng 806-807.

Italian, The (Radcliffe). LFEng 2202-2203; M&D 1393.

"Italian Morning" (Bogan). PEng 236.

Italian Straw Hat, The (Labiche). DFor 1131-1133.

Italian Visit, An (Day Lewis). PEng 760-761.

Italienische Nacht (Horvath). DFor 955-958.

Itching Parrot, The (Lizardi). LFFor 2281-2282, 2286, 2296.

It's a Family Affair (Ostrovsky). DFor 1448.

"It's a Woman's World" (Boland). PSup 36-37.

"It's Boring and Sad. . ." (Lermontov). PFor 874-875.

"It's easy to invent a Life" (Dickinson). PEng 808.

Its Image on the Mirror (Gallant). LFEng 1054.

"It's Nation Time" (Baraka). PEng 88-89.

"Iudol." *See* "Vale of Tears."

Ivaanov, Vyacheslav. PFor 2145.

Ivan Vejeeghen (Bulgarin). LFFor 2310.

Ivan Vyzhigin. See *Ivan Vejeeghen*.

Ivanovskiye sitsi (Yevtushenko). PFor 1711-1712.

Ivar's Story. ShF 397.

"I've Brought to Art" (Cavafy). PFor 299.

Ivona (Gombrowicz). DFor 770-771.

"Ivy Gripped the Steps" (Bowen). ShF 255.

Iwein (Hartmann von Aue). PFor 633.

Iwona, ksiezniezka Burgunda. See *Ivona*.

"Iz Andreya Shenie." *See* "From André Chénier."

J

"Jabberwocky" (Carroll). PEng 445-448.
"Jack and the Other Jack" (Hall). PEng 1200.
Jack Gelber's New Play: Rehearsal (Gelber). DEng 745.
Jack Juggler (Udall?). DEng 2264.
Jack of Newbury (Deloney). LFEng 3016.
Jack Straw's Castle and Other Poems (Gunn). PEng 1169-1170, 1171.
Jackson, Shirley. LFEng 1426-1433; ShF 552, **1668-1674.**
Jacob, Max. PFor 1887-1888.
"Jacob and the Angel" (Everson). PEng 991.
"Jacob o la idea de la poesía" (Reyes). PFor 1322.
Jacobowsky, Ludwig. LFFor 2182.
Jacobowsky and the Colonel (Behrman). DEng 186-187.
Jacobs, W. W. M&D 928-931.
Jacob's Room (Woolf). LFEng 2947-2949.
Jacobsen, Jens Peter. LFFor 2338-2339; PFor 2169.
Jacobsen, Josephine. ShF 2650.
Jacobsen, Rolf. PFor 2189.
Jacobwsky and the Colonel (Werfel). DFor 1999-2000.
Jacques le fataliste et son maître. See *Jacques the Fatalist and His Master*.
Jacques the Fatalist and His Master (Diderot). LFFor 465-466.
Jagdgesellschaft, Die (Bernhard). DFor 198-200.
Jagua Nana (Ekwensi). LFFor 2047-2048.
Jahier, Piero. PFor 2038, 2045.
Jahr der Seele, Das. See *Year of the Soul, The*.
Jahrestage. See *Anniversaries*.
Jailbird (Vonnegut). LFEng 2730-2731.
"Jailer, The" (Plath). PEng 2224.
Jakobson, Roman. LFEng 3214-3215, 3331; LTh **744-749,** 828, 849, 889-890, 913, 1477, 1758, 1761-1762, 1800, 1815, 1822; PEng 3448-3450.
Jakšić, Djura. PFor 2254.
Jalousie, La. See *Jealousy*.
Jama (Kovačić). PFor 2265.
Jamaica Inn (du Maurier). M&D 553.

James, Henry. DEng **989-998;** LFEng 994, **1434-1451,** 2848-2849, 2851-2852, 3035, 3042, 3043, 3047-3049, 3055, 3082-3083, 3251-3252, 3262-3265, 3298; LTh 556, **750-757,** 926-927, 1012, 1454, 1549, 1568, 1750-1751; ShF 182, 213-214, 232, 518-519, 740-741, **1675-1687,** 2427-2428.
James, M. R. ShF 743, **1688-1693.**
James, P. D. LFSup **164-169;** M&D **932-938.**
James I. PEng 3272, 3278.
James IV (Greene, R.). DEng 842-844; PEng 1150-1151.
James, William. LFEng 3223-3224; LTh 146; PEng 900.
Jameson, Fredric. LTh 414, **758-763,** 1770, 1814.
Jammersminde. See *Memoirs of Leonora Christina*.
Jammes, Francis. PFor 1880.
Jandl, Ernst. PFor 1936.
"Jane" (Maugham). ShF 1904.
"Jane at Pigall's" (Hall). PEng 1204.
Jane Clegg (Ervine). DEng 561, 562, 563.
Jane Eyre (Brontë, C.). LFEng 301-302, 2228-2229, 2230, 2231-2232, 3162, 3163.
Jane Shore. See *Tragedy of Jane Shore, The*.
Janet, Pierre. PFor 229-230.
"Janet Waking" (Ransom). PEng 2329-2330.
"Janet's Repentance" (Eliot, G.). ShF 1335-1336.
Janevski, Slavko. PFor 2272-2273.
Janos the Hero (Petőfi). PFor 1219-1220.
János Vitéz. See *Janos the Hero*.
"January 1919" (Middleton, C.). PEng 1988.
"Janus" (Beattie). ShFSup 41-42.
"Jap, The" (Beck). ShF 935.
Japanese Family Storehouse, The (Saikaku). ShFSup 270-271.
"Japanese Way, The" (Pastan). PEng 2175.
Jardiel Poncela, Enrique. DFor 2506.
"Jardín de senderos que se bifurcan, El." *See* "Garden of the Forking Paths, The."
Jardines lejanos (Jiménez). PFor 750-751.
Jarnés, Benjamín. LFFor 2392.
Jarrell, Randall. PEng **1478-1486.**

Jarry, Alfred. DFor 1006-1015, 2349-2350; LTh 622, 996.

Jarvis, E. K. *See* Bloch, Robert.

Jason, Stuart. *See* Avallone, Michael.

Jason, Veronica. *See* Johnston, Velda.

Jatadharan (Venkataramani). ShF 644.

Játék a kastélyban. See *Play's the Thing, The.*

Jauss, David. ShF 2651.

Jauss, Hans Robert. LTh 685, 731, 733, 764-768, 1763, 1770, 1801.

"Javni" (Rao). ShF 648.

"Jaws of the Dog, The" (Greenberg). ShF 1539.

Jay, Martin. LTh 138.

J.B. (MacLeish). DEng 1220-1224.

"Je Suis le Plus Malade des Surrealistes" (Nin). ShF 1950.

"Je suis un cheval." See "I Am a Horse."

Je vous écris d'un pays lointain. See *I Am Writing to You from a Far-Off Country.*

Jealous God, The (Braine). LFEng 283, 286, 287-288.

"Jealous Hidalgo, The" (Cervantes). LFEng 3227, 3228-3230.

Jealous Old Husband, The (Cervantes). DFor 366.

Jealousy (Robbe-Grillet). LFFor 1415-1416, 2146.

Jean Barois (Martin du Gard). LFFor 1111-1112.

"Jean Beicke" (Williams, W. C.). ShF 2443.

Jean-Christophe (Rolland). LFFor 1427-1429, 2141-2142.

Jean de Meung and Guillaume de Lorris. PFor 614-621.

Jean de Meung. PFor 1839.

Jean le bleu. See *Blue Boy.*

Jean Paul. LFFor 868-878, 2162.

"Jean-ah Poquelin" (Cable). ShF 1021-1023.

Jeannot and Colin (Voltaire). ShFSup 330.

"Jeeves and Wooster Novels" (Wodehouse). LFEng 2922-2925.

Jeffers, Robinson. PEng 1487-1497.

Jefferson, Ian. *See* Davies, L. P.

Jefferson and/or Mussolini (Pound). LTh 1156.

Jeffrey, Lord. LTh 1708.

Jeffrey, William. *See* Pronzini, Bill.

Jeffries, Graham Montague. *See* Graeme, Bruce.

"Jen jednou." *See* "Once Only."

Jenko, Simon. PFor 2268.

Jenneval (Mercier). DEng 2183.

Jennie Gerhardt (Dreiser). LFEng 833-835.

"Jenny" (Rossetti, D. G.). PEng 2430.

Jenny (Undset). LFFor 1799.

Jenny Treibel (Fontane). LFFor 563-564, 2177-2178.

Jensen, Johannes V. LFFor 879-884, 2347-2348; PFor 2176-2177.

Jeppe of the Hill (Holberg). DFor 948-949, 2466.

"Jerboa, The" (Moore). PEng 2044-2045.

"Jeremiah Desborough: Or, The Kentuckian" (Richardson, J.). ShF 635.

Jeremy's Version (Purdy). LFEng 2173.

Jerome, Saint. LTh 1193; PFor 2110.

Jersild, Per Christian. LFFor 2361.

Jerusalem (Blake). PEng 218-219.

Jerusalem (Lagerlöf). LFFor 984, 2344.

Jerusalem Conquered (Tasso). PFor 1501.

Jerusalem Delivered (Tasso). PFor 1494-1495, 1496, 1498-1501, 2015.

Jerusalem the Golden (Drabble). LFEng 817-820.

Jerusalén conquistada (Vega). PFor 1602.

Jest of God, A (Laurence). LFEng 1573-1574.

Jest, Satire, Irony, and Deeper Significance (Grabbe). DFor 801-803.

"Jesu" (Herbert). PEng 1301.

Jeu d'Adam, Le. DFor 2162-2163.

Jeu de la feuillée (La Halle). DFor 2175.

Jeu de l'amour et du hasard, Le. See *Game of Love and Chance, The.*

Jeu de Robin et Marion, Le (La Halle). DFor 2175-2176.

Jeu de Saint-Nicolas, Le (Bodel). DFor 2163-2164, 2175.

Jew of Denmark, The (Goldschmidt). LFFor 2336.

Jew of Malta, The (Marlowe). DEng 1253-1256, 2272-2273; ShF 1896.

"Jew of Persia, A" (Helprin). ShFSup 116.

Jews, The (Lessing). DFor 1200-1201.

Jew's Beech Tree, The (Droste-Hülshoff). M&D 539-541.

Jewett, Sarah Orne. LFEng 1452-1463; ShF 227-228, 547, 1694-1699.

Jews in Babylonia (Reznikoff). PEng 2361.

Jhabvala, Ruth Prawer. LFFor 2222; LFSup 170-176; ShF 650.

Jidaimono. DFor 2427, 2430.

Jig of Forslin, The (Aiken). PEng 23-24.

Jig-Saw. See *Marylebone Miser, The.*
"Jigokuhen." *See* "Hell Screen."
"Jilting of Granny Weatherall, The" (Porter). ShF 801, 2114.
Jiménez, Juan Ramón. PFor 747-755, 2227.
Jimmy Shine (Schisgal). DEng 1664.
Jingling in the Wind (Roberts). LFEng 2282.
"Jinny the Just" (Prior). PEng 2291.
Jirásek, Alois. LFFor 2066.
Jiyugeki Kyōkai. DFor 2432-2433.
"Joal" (Senghor). PFor 1424. See also *Chants d'ombre.*
Job. ShF 346-348, 373.
Job (Roth). LFFor 1450-1452.
Job, the Victim of His People (Girard). LTh 592.
Jocasta (Gascoigne and Kinwelmershe). DEng 725-726, 2265.
Jocelyn (Lamartine). PFor 835.
Jochumsson, Matthiás. DFor 2474.
"Jockey, The" (McCullers). ShF 1841.
Jøde, En. See *Jew of Denmark, The.*
"Joe Eliot" (Farrell). ShF 1353-1355.
Joel Brand (Kipphardt). DFor 1055.
Johan Johan (Heywood, J.). DEng 945-946, 2256.
Johannessen, Georg. PFor 2194-2195.
Johannisfeuer. See *Fires of St. John.*
Johannsson, Ulrika Wilhelmina. *See* **Canth, Minna.**
John (Barry). DEng 136.
John Brown (Warren). LFEng 2770, 2773.
John Brown's Body (Benét). PEng 143-144.
"John Coltrane Dance, The" (Young). PEng 3212-3213.
"John Deth: A Metaphysical Legend" (Aiken). PEng 25.
"John Dryden" (Eliot). LTh 896.
John Ferguson (Ervine). DEng 561, 562, 563.
John Macnab (Buchan). LFEng 334-335.
John of Bordeaux (Greene, R.). DEng 844-845.
John of Salisbury. LTh 966, 1650.
John of the Cross, Saint. PFor 756-768.
"John Sherman" (Yeats). ShF 2471.
Johnny Johnson (Green). DEng 820-821.
Johnny Mangano and His Astonishing Dogs. See *Cinq.*
"Johnny Pye and the Fool-Killer" (Benét). ShF 957-959.
Johnson, Bengt Emil. PFor 2193.

Johnson, Eyvind. LFFor 2349-2350.
Johnson, Joe. ShF 2652.
Johnson, Josephine. ShF 1700-1705.
Johnson, Ronald. PSup 210-216.
Johnson, Samuel. LFEng 1464-1474, 3026, 3027; LTh 91-92, 260, 403, **769-778,** 1140, 1216, 1259, 1528-1529, 1533, 1684-1686, 1690; PEng 588, **1498-1507,** 3332; ShF **1706-1712.**
Johnson, Uwe. LFFor **885-893.**
Johnson Over Jordan (Priestley). DEng 1540-1541.
Johnston, Velda. M&D **939-942.**
Jókai, Mór. LFFor 2071-2072.
Joke, The (Kundera). LFFor 952-953.
Joker of Seville, The (Walcott, D. A.). DEng 2002.
Joking Apart (Ayckbourn). DEng 67-68.
Jokond ile Si-Ya-U (Hikmet). PSup 177.
Jolley, Elizabeth. LFSup **177-183.**
"Jolly Corner, The" (James, H.). LFEng 3298-3299; ShF 477, 741, 800, 1685-1686.
Jonah. ShF 358-360.
Jonah's Gourd Vine (Hurston). LFEng 1393, 1394-1395.
"Jonas" (Camus). LFFor 264.
Jónás könyve (Babits). PFor 122.
Jónasson, Jóhannes B. PFor 2186.
Jonathan Wild (Fielding). LFEng 949-950.
Jones, Annabel. *See* **Brand, Christianna.**
Jones, Everett Le Roi. *See* **Baraka, Amiri.**
Jones, Henry Arthur. DEng **999-1006.**
Jones, Inigo. DEng 2223.
Jones, James. LFEng **1475-1484.**
Jones, LeRoi. *See* **Baraka, Amiri.**
Jones, Madison. LFEng **1485-1495.**
Jones, Preston. DEng **1107-1013.**
Jones, William. PFor 1732, 1989-1990.
Jonson, Ben. DEng 283, **1014-1025,** 2167, 2285-2287, 2297, 2298; DFor 2227; LTh 450, **779-784,** 1184, 1665, 1676; PEng 93, **1508-1519,** 3305-3308, 3317-3318; ShF **1713-1717.**
Jordan County (Foote). LFEng 978-979.
"Jordan's End" (Glasgow). ShF 1493-1494.
Jordi de Sant Jordi. PFor 1771.
Jørgensen, Johannes. LFFor 2347; PFor 2172.
Jörn Uhl (Frenssen). LFFor 2182.
Jōruri. DFor 392-394.
"Joscelyn" (Simms). LFEng 2410-2411.
Josef Švejk (Kohout). DSup 222-223.

142

Joseph, Edward Lanza. DEng 2451.

Joseph and His Brothers (Mann). LFFor 1082.

Joseph Andrews (Fielding). LFEng 947-949.

Joseph, der Ernährer. See *Joseph the Provider.*

Joseph in Ägypten. See *Joseph in Egypt.*

Joseph in Egypt (Mann). LFFor 1082. See also *Joseph and His Brothers.*

Joseph the Provider (Mann). LFFor 1082-1083. See also *Joseph and His Brothers.*

Joseph und seine Brüder. See *Joseph and His Brothers.*

"Josephine the Singer, or the Mouse Folk" (Kafka). ShF 1733.

Josephson, Ragnar. DFor 2479.

Josh. *See* **Twain, Mark.**

Joshi, Arun. ShF 653.

"Joshua" (Grau). ShF 1531-1532.

Joshua Then and Now (Richer). LFEng 2260-2262.

Joueur, Le (Regnard). DFor 1539-1540.

"Joujou du pauvre, Le." *See* "Poor Child's Plaything, The."

Journal (Goncourts). LFFor 709.

Journal d'un curé de campagne. See *Diary of a Country Priest.*

"Journal for My Daughter" (Kunitz). PSup 246-247.

Journal in time (Queneau). LFSup 327-329.

Journal of the Plague Year, A (Defoe). LFEng 686-688.

"Journey" (Oates). ShF 131.

"Journey, The" (Winters). PSup 398-399.

Journey from St. Petersburg to Moscow, A (Radishchev). LFFor 2308.

Journey into Fear (Ambler). M&D 31.

Journey of Mr. Perrichon, The (Labiche). DFor 1133-1134.

Journey of Niels Klim to the World of the Underground (Holberg). LFFor 2334.

Journey of the Fifth Horse, The (Ribman). DSup 313-314.

Journey to London, A. See *Provok'd Husband, The.*

"Journey to Petrópolis" (Lispector). ShFSup 167.

Journey to the East, The (Hesse). LFFor 833.

Journey to the End of the Night (Céline). LFFor 306-308.

"Journey to the Harz, The" (Heine). PFor 649.

Journey to the Orient (Nerval). PFor 1085.

"Journey to the Seven Streams, A" (Kiely). ShF 1742.

Journey to the Sky (Highwater). LFEng 1362-1364.

Journey to the West, The (Wu Ch'eng-en). LFFor 1944-1949, 2091, 2095-2097.

Journey to the World Underground. See *Journey of Niels Klim to the World of the Underground.*

"Journey Toward Poetry" (Sarton). PEng 2460.

Journey's End (Sherriff). DEng 1785-1787, 1789-1790.

Jouve, Pierre-Jean. PFor 1890.

"Jou'vert." *See* "I Open."

Jouvet, Louis. DFor 2351.

Jovial Crew, A (Brome). DEng 287-288.

Jovine, Francesco. LFFor 2248.

"Joy of a Dog, The" (Guest). PEng 1164-1165.

Joy of Living, The (Sudermann). DFor 1765-1766.

Joy of Man's Desiring (Giono). LFFor 656.

"Joy to Great Caesar" (D'Urfey). PEng 915.

Joyce, James. LFEng 1496-1507, 3057-3058; LTh 424, 1413, 1573-1574; PEng 100, **1520-1527**; ShF 176, **1718-1723.**

"Joycelin Shrager Story, The" (Disch). ShF 1289.

József, Atlila. PFor 1985-1986.

JR (Gaddis). LFEng 1035, 1036, 1039-1040.

Ju-lin wai-shih. See *Scholars, The.*

"Ju meng ling." *See* "Tune: As in a Dream a Song."

Juan Chi. PFor **769-775,** 1784.

Juana Inés de la Cruz, Sor. *See* **Cruz, Sor Juana Inés de la.**

Juanita la larga (Valera). LFFor 1826-1828.

Juárez and Maximilian (Werfel). DFor 1998-1999.

Judah (Jones, H. A.). DEng 1004.

Judah ha-Levi. PFor **776-782.**

"Judas" (O'Connor, Frank). ShF 113-114, 368.

Judas (Patrick, R.). DEng 1479-1480.

Jude the Obscure (Hardy). LFEng 1274-1276, 3050, 3079.

Juden, Die. See *Jews, The.*

Judenauto, Das (Fühmann). PFor 1817.

Judenbuche, Die. See *Jew's Beech Tree, The.*

Judge, The (Gorky). See *Old Man.*

Judge, The (Mortimer). DEng 1356.

Judge and His Hangman, The (Dürrenmatt). M&D 558-559.

K

K voprosu o razvitii monisticheskogo vzgliada na istoriiu. See *In Defense of Materialism.*

K zvezdam. See *To the Stars.*

Kâ, Abdou Anta. DFor 2268-2269, 2270.

Kaalø, Steen. PFor 2198.

Kabale und Liebe. See *Cabal and Love.*

Kabaphēs, Kōnstantionos Petrou. *See* **Cavafy, Constantine P.**

"Kabnis" (Toomer). ShF 2343-2344.

"Kaddish" (Ginsberg). PEng 1092-1093.

Kafka, Franz. LFFor 199, **894-905,** 2189-2190; LTh 938, 1316; ShF **1729-1735.**

Kagi. See *Key, The.*

Kaicho-on (Ueda Bin). PFor 2074.

Kailas, Uuno. PFor 2182.

Kains, Josephine. *See* **Goulart, Ron.**

Kaiser, Georg. DFor **1016-1027,** 2239-2240, 2377-2378.

Kaiser Friedrich Barbarossa (Grabbe). DFor 804.

Kaiser Heinrich VI (Grabbe). DFor 804.

"Kaiserliche Botschaft, Eine." *See* "Imperial Message, A."

"Kak sdelana 'Shinel' Gogolia" (Eikhenbaum). LTh 442.

Kakinomoto no Hitomaro. PFor 2055-2057.

Kaksikymmentä ja yksi (Haavikko). PSup 146.

Kälberbrüten, Das (Sachs). DFor 1624-1625.

Kalechofsky, Roberta. ShF 2654.

Kalendergeschichten. See *Tales from the Calendar.*

Kalevala, The (epic). ShF 137.

Kalevala (Lönnrot). DFor 1063; PFor 2157.

Kaliber, Der (Müllner). M&D 1259-1262.

Kālidāsa. DFor **1028-1037,** 2387-2388.

Kalinčiak, Ján. LFFor 2068.

Kalkwerk, Das. See *Lime Works, The.*

Kallimachos. *See* **Callimachus.**

Kallman, Chester. DEng 53.

Kallocain (Boye). LFFor 2351.

Kálvos, Andreas. PFor 1950-1952.

"Kamakapala" (Rao). ShF 643.

Kamban, Guðmundur. DFor 2480; LFFor 2347.

Kamen no kokuhaku. See *Confessions of a Mask.*

"Kamennoe serdtse." *See* "Heart of Stone, A."

Kamera Obskura. See *Laughter in the Dark.*

Kamin. See *Stone.*

Kamin, Franz. ShF 2655.

Kaminsky, Stuart M. M&D 943-947.

Kammersänger, Der. See *Tenor, The.*

Kamo no Mabuchi. LTh 785-789, 1050-1052.

Kamouraska (Hébert). LFFor 812.

"Kampf mit dem Drachen, Der." *See* "Battle with the Dragon, The."

Kampmann, Christian. LFFor 2367.

Kamyenny gost. See *Stone Guest, The.*

Kan'ami Kiyotsugu. DFor 2422-2423.

"Kanbatsu to zazen." *See* "Drought and Zazen."

Kane, Cheikh Hamidou. LFFor 2035.

Kane, Wilson. *See* **Bloch, Robert.**

Kangaeru hinto (Kobayashi). LTh 821.

Kanjō-no maki. LFFor 2266. See also *Tale of Genji, The.*

Kant, Immanuel. LFFor 2160; LTh 378, 455, 531, **790-794,** 1019, 1296-1297, 1315, 1321-1322, 1697, 1756, 1810.

Kantan (Mishima). DFor 1324.

Kanteletar (Lönnrot). PFor 2157.

Kantemir, Antioch. PFor 2134.

Kanthapura (Rao). LFEng 2208-2210; LFFor 2220; ShF 648.

Kantor, Tadeusz. DSup 206-211.

Kao Ming. DFor 1038-1049, 2319-2321.

Kao Tsê-ch'êng. *See* Kao Ming.

Kapetan Michales, Ho. See *Freedom or Death.*

Kapitanskaya dochka. See *Captain's Daughter, The.*

Kaplan, Bernard. ShF 2656.

Kappa (Akutagawa). ShFSup 11.

Karamzin, Nikolay. LFFor 2307-2308; LTh 1694.

"Karintha" (Toomer). PEng 2915-2917.

Karkurit (Kivi). DFor 1067.

Karl Marx Play, The (Owens). DEng 1459-1460.

Karl Stuart (Fleisser). DFor 624.

Karlfeldt, Erik Axel. PFor 2171-2172.

"Karma" (Singh). ShF 650.
Karol. See *Charlie.*
Karolinerna. See *Charles Men, The.*
Karrig Niding (Ranch). DFor 2464.
Kartoteka. See *Card Index, The.*
"Karusel." *See* "Merry-Go-Round, The."
Karvaš, Peter. DFor 2285.
Karyotákis, Kostas. PFor 1959-1961.
Kaspar (Handke). DFor 859-860.
"Kaspar Is Dead" (Arp). PFor 104-105.
"Kaspar ist Tot." *See* "Kaspar Is Dead."
Kasprowicz, Jan. PFor 2127.
Kassák, Lajos. PFor 1985.
Kassette, Die. See *Strongbox, The.*
Kaštelan, Jure. PFor 2265.
Kästner, Erich. PFor 1931.
Katà Leukippēn kaì Kleitophōnta, Ta. See
   Leucippe and Cleitophon.
Kate Beaumont (De Forest). LFEng 703-704.
Käthchen von Heilbronn, Das. See *Cathy of
   Heilbronn.*
"Katherine Comes to Yellow Sky" (Helprin).
   ShFSup 115.
Kathleen ni Houlihan. See *Cathleen ni
   Houlihan.*
Kato Michio. DFor 2434.
Katona, József. DFor 2286.
"Katrina, Katrin" (Helprin). ShFSup 115.
Katz und Maus. See *Cat and Mouse.*
Kaufman, Bel. ShF 2657.
Kaufman, George S. DEng 1026-1034.
Kaufman, George S., and Moss Hart. DEng
   906-907.
Kaukasische Kreidekreis, Der. See *Caucasian
   Chalk Circle, The.*
**Kavan, Anna. LFEng 1508-1513; ShF 1736-
   1740.**
Kavanagh, Patrick. PEng 1535-1541.
Kavanagh, Paul. See **Block, Lawrence.**
Kavkazsky plennik. See *Prisoner of the
   Caucasus, The.*
Kawabata, Yasunari. DFor 1320; LFFor 906-
   914, 2277-2278.
Kayser, Wolfgang. ShF 712.
Kazan. See *Volcano.*
Kazan, Elia. DEng 2405, 2406, 2528-2529.
Kazantzakis, Nikos. LFFor 915-924; PFor
   783-790.
Kazinczy, Ferenc. PFor 1978.
Keach, William. PEng 1904.
Kean. See *Edmund Kean.*

Kean, Charles. DEng 2357-2358.
Kean, Edmund. DEng 2525.
Kearny, Jullian. See **Goulart, Ron.**
Keating, H. R. F. M&D 948-953.
Keats, John. LTh 259, **795-799,** 1583, 1701,
   1705; PEng **1542-1558,** 2408, 2744, 2745,
   2746, 2747, 3343, 3480-3481.
Keble, John. LTh 1703, 1709.
"Keela, the Outcast Indian Maiden" (Welty).
   ShF 2416-2418.
Keeler, Harry Stephen. M&D 954-959.
Keep Tightly Closed in a Cool Dry Place
   (Terry). DSup 343-344.
"Keeper of the Commandments, A" (Heywood,
   J.). PEng 1334.
Keepers of the House, The (Grau). LFEng
   1186-1187.
"Keeping It" (Oppenheimer). PEng 2145,
   2146.
Kees, Weldon. PEng 1559-1566.
Kein Ort. See *No Place on Earth.*
Keith, J. Kilmeny. *See* **Gilbert, Anthony.**
Kejser Julian, The. See *Emperor and Galilean.*
Kejser og Galilæer. See *Emperor and Galilean.*
Keller, Gottfried. LFFor **925-936,** 2171; ShF
   465.
Kellgren, Johan Henrik. DFor 2467; PFor
   2161-2162.
Kelly, Mary. M&D 960-964.
Kelly, Robert. PSup 217-222.
Kelly's Eye (Livings). DEng 1156.
Kemal, Yashar. LFFor **937-943;** LFSup 405.
Kemble, Charles. DEng 2525.
Kemelman, Harry. M&D 965-972.
Kendrake, Carleton. *See* **Gardner, Erle
   Stanley.**
Kendrick, Baynard H. M&D 973-978.
Keneally, Thomas. LFSup 184-192.
"Kenji Myazawa" (Ginsberg). PEng 1095.
Kennedy, Adrienne. DSup 212-217.
Kennedy, William. LFSup 193-200.
Kennedy, X. J. PEng **1567-1576;** PSup 406.
Kennedy's Children (Patrick, R.). DEng 1476-
   1478.
Kennelly, Tamara. ShF 2658.
Kenner, Hugh. LTh 800-805.
Kenny, Charles J. *See* **Gardner, Erle Stanley.**
Kenzaburo Ōe. *See* **Ōe, Kenzaburo.**
Kepler (Banville). LFSup 47-48.
"Kept" (Bogan). PEng 238.
"Kerchief, The" (Agnon). ShF 833-834.

Kermode, Frank. LTh 806-811.

Kern, Jerome. DEng 2469-2470.

Kerouac, Jack. LFEng 1514-1525; PEng 3380.

Kersh, Gerald. M&D 979-984.

Kesey, Ken. LFEng 1526-1536.

Kessler, Jascha. ShF 2659.

Kette, Dragotin. PFor 2269.

"Kew Gardens" (Woolf). ShF 2455.

Key, The (Tanizaki). LFFor 1714-1715; ShFSup 317.

Key to the Door (Sillitoe). LFEng 2401.

Key to Uncle Tom's Cabin, A (Stowe). LFEng 2557-2558.

Key-Aberg, Sandro. PFor 2188.

Keyes, Daniel. ShF 2661.

Keys of the Kingdom, The (Cronin). LFEng 653, 658-659, 661.

Keyser, Samuel Jay. PEng 3456.

Keyserling, Eduard, Graf von. LFFor 2185.

Kezermaister mit wort, würz und stain, Der (Sachs). DFor 1625.

Kézfogások (Illyés). PFor 743.

"Khat" (Dreiser). ShF 1308.

Khayyám, Omar. *See* Omar Khayyám.

Khodasevich, Vladislav. PSup 223-229.

Khorev (Sumarokov). DFor 1785, 2451.

Khorosho! See *Fine!*

"Khozhdeniye za tri morya Afanasiya Nikitina 1466-1472 gg." LFFor 2302-2303.

Khristos i Antikhrist. See *Christ and Antichrist.*

Khrouikhō, To (Sinópoulos). PFor 1972.

Khumish Lider (Manger). PFor 951-952.

Ki no Tsurayuki. *See* Tsurayuki, Ki no.

"Kicking the Leaves" (Hall). PEng 1206.

Kicking the Leaves (Hall). PEng 1198, 1205-1206.

Kid Stakes (Lawler). DEng 1116-1117.

Kiddush Hashem (Asch). LFFor 75-76.

Kidnapped (Stevenson, R. L.). LFEng 2550.

Kielland, Alexander. DFor 2470; LFFor 2341.

Kiely, Benedict. ShF 666, 1741-1747.

Kierkegaard, Søren. LTh 1361.

"Kierkegaard Unfair to Schlegel" (Barthelme). ShFSup 24.

Kihlaus (Kivi). DFor 1067.

Kihlman, Christer. LFFor 2370.

Kikaku, Takarai. *See* Takarai Kikaku.

Kiljan, Halldór. *See* Laxness, Halldór.

Kill, The (Zola). LFFor 1989. See also *Rougon-Macquart, Les.*

Kill Price, The (Yglesias). LFEng 3001-3002.

Killdeer, The (Reaney). DEng 1572-1575.

Killer, The (Ionesco). DFor 999-1001, 2255-2256.

Killer Inside Me, The (Thompson). M&D 1591-1592.

"Killers, The" (Hemingway). ShF 115, 785-786, 1626.

Killigrew, Thomas. DEng 2294, 2295.

Killing Frost, A (Wilkinson). LFEng 2891-2892.

Killing Ground, The (Settle). LFSup 348-349. See also *Beulah Quintet, The.*

"Killing of a State Cop, The" (Ortiz). ShF 570-571.

Killing of Abel, The (Wakefield Master). DEng 1991-1992.

Killing of Katie Steelstock, The. See *Death of a Favourite Girl.*

Killing Orders (Paretsky). M&D 1297.

Killing Time (Berger). LFEng 254-255.

Kilpi, Eeva. LFFor 2369.

Kilpi, Volter. LFFor 2357.

Kim. *See* Simenon, Georges.

Kim (Kipling). LFEng 1543-1545.

"Kimi shinitamō koto nakare." *See* "Never Let Them Kill You, Brother!"

Kimitake Hiraoka. *See* Mishima, Yukio.

Kinck, Hans Ernst. DFor 2476; LFFor 2345.

Kind of Testament, A (Gombrowicz). LTh 606.

"Kind pity chokes my spleen" (Donne). PEng 828.

"Kind Sir: These Woods" (Sexton). PEng 2523.

Kinder- und Hausmärchen. See *Grimms' Fairy Tales.*

Kindergeschichte. See *Child Story.*

Kinderspiel, Ein (Walser, M.). DSup 388.

Kindheitsmuster. See *Patterns of Childhood, A.*

Kindly Ones, The (Powell). LFEng 2119-2120.

Kinds of Affection (Miles). PSup 278.

Kineji, Maborushi. *See* Gibson, Walter B.

"King, The" (Babel). ShF 900.

King, The (Lagerkvist). DFor 1155.

King, Henry. PEng 1577-1588.

King, Stephen. LFSup 201-211; M&D 985-989; ShF 2662; ShFSup 122-126.

King and His Campaigners, A. See *Charles Men, The.*

King and No King, A (Beaumont and Fletcher). DEng 632.

King and the Farmer, The (Vega). DFor 1935.
King Coal (Sinclair, U.). LFEng 2423-2424.
King Coffin (Aiken). LFEng 17-18, 20-21.
"King Constantine Gave So Much" (Walther).
PFor 1679-1680.
King Horn. ShF 141.
King Hunger (Andreyev). DFor 64.
King Jesus (Graves, R.). LFEng 1201-1202.
King Johan (Bale). DEng 80-81, 88-90, 2260.
King John (Shakespeare). DEng 1700, 2276.
King Lear (Shakespeare). DEng 1719-1720,
2281, 2282.
King Lear's Wife (Bottomley). DEng 258-261.
King Leir and His Three Daughters. DEng
2266.
King Log (Hill, G.). PEng 1352, 1353.
King Must Die, The (Renault). LFEng 2220-
2221.
King Oedipus (Hakim). DSup 176.
"King of Asine, The" (Seferis). PFor 1416.
"King of the Bingo Game" (Ellison, R.). ShF
580-581.
King of the Dark Chamber, The (Tagore).
DFor 1796-1797.
King of the Golden River, The (Ruskin). ShF
2164, 2167-2168.
"King of the River" (Kunitz). PSup 245.
King Otakar's Rise and Fall (Grillparzer).
DFor 826-827.
King, Queen, Knave (Nabokov). LFEng 1949.
King Stag, The (Gozzi). DFor 796.
King, the Greatest Alcalde, The (Vega). DFor
1935.
"King Travicello" (Giusti). PFor 575.
"King's Indian, The" (Gardner). ShF 1461-
1462.
"Kingdom, The" (MacNeice). PEng 1868-
1869.
Kingdom Come, The (George). LTh 576.
"Kingdom of Darkness, The" (Dobrolyubov).
LTh 388.
Kingdom of God in Bohemia, The (Werfel).
DFor 1999.
Kingdom of This World, The (Carpentier).
LFFor 281-282.
Kingdoms of Elfin (Warner). ShFSup 358.
Kingery, Margaret. ShF 2663.
"Kingfisher Flat" (Everson). PEng 992-993.
"Kingfishers, The" (Olson). PSup 309-310.
Kingo, Thomas. PFor 2158-2159.
Kingsley, Charles. LFEng 3078.

Kingsley, Charlotte May. *See* **Hanshew,
Thomas W.**
Kingsley, Sidney. DEng 1035-1044.
Kinkakuji. See *Temple of the Golden Pavilion,
The.*
Kinnell, Galway. PEng 1589-1601; PSup 406.
Kinoshita Junji. DFor 2434.
Kinsella, Thomas. PSup 230-238.
Kinsella, W. P. ShF 2664.
"Kinsman of His Blood, A" (Wolfe). ShF
2451.
**Kipling, Rudyard. LFEng 1537-1546; PEng
1602-1611; ShF 518, 1748-1755, 1901.**
"Kipling's World" (Lewis). LTh 896.
Kipper, Die (Braun). DSup 20-22.
Kipphardt, Heinar. DFor 1050-1057, 2382.
Kireyevsky, Ivan Vasilyevich. LTh 1179.
Kirk, Hans. LFFor 2355.
Kirk, John Foster. ShF 588.
Kirkland, Jack. DEng 1045-1054.
Kirshner, Sidney. *See* **Kingsley, Sidney.**
Kirstinä, Väinö. PFor 2199.
Kiš, Danilo. LFSup 212-217.
Kisfaludy, Károly. DFor 2286.
Kisfaludy, Sándor. PFor 1979-1980.
"Kiss, The" (Chekhov). ShF 110.
Kiss, The (Nims). PEng 2113-2114.
Kiss, József. PFor 1983.
Kiss for the Leper, A (Mauriac). LFFor 1124-
1126.
"Kiss me, sweet: the wary lover" (Jonson).
PEng 1510.
Kiss of Kin, The (Settle). LFSup 345.
"Kiss of the Cross, The" (Everson). PEng 991.
Kiss of the Spider Woman (Puig). LFFor 1357.
Kit Brandon (Anderson). LFEng 79.
"Kith of the Elf-folk, The" (Dunsany). ShF
1316-1317.
Kittredge, G. L. LFEng 1803-1804.
Kivi, Aleksis. DFor 1058-1070, 2474.
Kizer, Carolyn. PEng 1612-1622; PSup 406.
Kjær, Nils. DFor 2477.
Kjærlighedens tragedie. See *Tragedy of Love,
The.*
Klage, Die (Hartmann von Aue). PFor 631.
Kleider machen Leute. See *Clothes Make the
Man.*
**Kleist, Heinrich, von. DFor 1071-1078, 2369;
LFEng 3247-3248, 3249; LTh 437-438, 812-
817, 986, 1704; ShF 1756-1763.**
Kline, Nancy. ShF 2665.

Klop. See *Bedbug, The.*

Klopstock, Friedrich Gottlieb. DEng 2349; LTh 175, 670, 1699; PFor 1911-1912.

Knack to Know a Knave, A (Greene, R.). DEng 844.

Knapp, Samuel. LTh 1746, 1770.

"Knee-Deep in June" (Riley). PEng 2379.

Knee Plays (Wilson). DSup 402.

"Kneel to the Rising Sun" (Caldwell). ShF 1030-1031.

"Knife, The" (Gill). ShF 1485-1486.

Knife of the Times and Other Stories, The (Williams, W. C.). ShF 2442.

"Knife That Killed Po Hancy, The" (Stockton). M&D 1537-1538.

Knight, Kathleen Moore. M&D 990-995.

Knight from Olmedo, The (Vega). DFor 1937-1938.

Knight of the Burning Pestle, The (Beaumont). DEng 143-145.

Knights, The (Aristophanes). DFor 117, 2124.

Knights of the Cross, The (Sienkiewicz). LFFor 1570-1572.

"Knights of the Open Palm" (Daly, C.). M&D 449; ShF 760.

"Knight's Tale, The" (Chaucer). PEng 3263-3264; ShF 1109-1110, 1111.

Kniha smichu a zapomnění. See *Book of Laughter and Forgetting, The.*

Knister, Raymond. ShF 638.

Knjiga boccadoro (Begović). PFor 2263.

Knock. See *Dr. Knock.*

"Knot, The" (Kunitz). PSup 247-248.

Know Nothing (Settle). LFSup 346-347. *See also* Beulah Quintet, The.

Knowledge of the Evening (Nims). PEng 2112.

Knowles, James Sheridan. DEng 1055-1063.

Knowles, John. ShF 1764-1769.

Knox, Ronald A. M&D 996-1004.

Kōshoku gonin onna. See *Five Women Who Loved Love.*

Kōshoku ichidai otoko. See *Life of an Amorous Man, The.*

Knuckle (Hare). DSup 185-186.

Knudsen, Erik. PFor 2189.

Knudsen, Jakob. LFFor 2347.

Knyaginya Ligovskaya. See *Princess Ligovskaya.*

Kobayashi Hideo. LTh 818-822, 1053.

Kobayashi Issa. PFor 2073.

Kobayashi Yatarō. *See* Issa.

"Kobutori." *See* "Taking the Wen Away."

Kocbek, Edvard. PFor 2270.

Koch, Claude. ShF 2666.

Koch, Kenneth. PEng 1623-1629; PSup 407.

Kochanowski, Jan. PFor 2119-2120.

Koestler, Arthur. LFEng 1547-1555.

"Kogda b ne smert', a zabyt'e." *See* "If There Were Not Death, but Oblivion."

"Kogda Psikheia-zhizn' spuskaetsia k teniam." *See* "When Psyche-Life Descends to the Shades."

Kogdá razguliayetsa. See *When the Skies Clear.*

"Kogda zhe pridet nostoiashchii den'?" *See* "When Will the Real Day Come?"

Kohout, Pavel. DSup 218-225.

Kojiki. See *Records of Ancient Matters.*

Kojinteki na taiken. See *Personal Matter, A.*

Kokinshū (Tsurayuki). LTh 1470.

Kokusenya kassen. See *Battles of Coxinga, The.*

Kolbenheyer, Erwin Guido. PFor 1932.

Kölcsey, Ferenc. PFor 1980.

Kollár, Ján. PFor 1799, 1808.

Kolonne Hund (Wolf). DFor 2019-2020.

"Kolybel'naia Treskovogo Mysa." *See* "Lullaby of Cape Cod."

Komachi, Ono no. *See* Ono no Komachi.

Komedia rybaltowska. DFor 2274.

Komediantka. See *Comedienne, The.*

Komenský, Jan Ámos. *See* Comenius.

Komet, Der (Jean Paul). LFFor 877.

Kommandørans døttre. See *Commodore's Daughters, The.*

Komornicka, Maria. PFor 2128.

Kompleks polski. See *Polish Complex, The.*

Konecky, Edith. ShF 2667.

Koneski, Blaže. PFor 2272-2273.

Kongens fald. See *Fall of the King, The.*

König Ottokars Glück und Ende. See *King Otakar's Rise and Fall.*

Konrad Wallenrod (Mickiewicz). PFor 1020.

Konstantinov-Džinov, Jordan Hadži. DFor 2294.

"Konstnär i norr, En." *See* "Artist in the North, An."

Kontraption (Owens). DEng 1460-1461.

Konungen. See *King, The.*

Konwicki, Tadeusz. LFFor 944-949.

"Kool-Aid Wino, The" (Brautigan). ShFSup 54.

Koontz, Dean R. M&D 1005-1009.

Köp den blindes säng (Ekelöf). PFor 449.

MAGILL INDEX TO CRITICAL SURVEYS

Kopfgeburten. See *Headbirths.*
Kopit, Arthur. DEng 1064-1076; DSup 407.
Kops, Bernard. DEng 1077-1085.
Kora. See *Bark.*
Koralle, Die. See *Coral, The.*
Korbal pravednykho. See *Ship of the Righteous, The.*
Kordian (Słowacki). DFor 1714-1715.
Koreni (Ćosić). LFFor 387.
"Korf's Clock" (Morgenstern). PFor 1058-1059. See also *Gallows Songs, The.*
"Korfsche Uhr, Die." *See* "Korf's Clock."
Korn, Henry. ShF 2668.
Korol', dama, valet. See *King, Queen, Knave.*
Korolenko, Vladimir. LFFor 2319.
Korpela, Jorma. LFFor 2368.
Korrektur. See *Correction.*
Korset. See *Cross, The,* and *Kristin Lavransdatter.*
"Koshka i liudi." *See* "Stove, The."
Kosinski, Jerzy. LFEng 1556-1566.
Kosmos. See *Cosmos.*
Kosoelv, Srečko. PFor 2270.
"Kost kosti." *See* "One Bone to Another."
Kosta, Victor. *See* **Simenon, Georges.**
Kostić, Laza. PFor 2254.
Kostrowitzky, Wilhelm Apollinaris de. *See* **Apollinaire, Guillaume.**
Kosztolányi, Dezső. PFor 1984.
Kötlum, Jóhannes úr. PFor 2186.
Kotzebue, August von. DEng 2178, 2332; DFor 1083-1093, 2370; LTh 1306.
Kouevuur (Breytenbach). PSup 54-55.
Kovačić, Ivan Goran. PFor 2265.
Kovan onnen lapsia (Canth). DFor 326-327.
Kozačinski, Emanuil. DFor 2291.
Kōzui wa waga tamashii ni oyobi (Ōe). LFFor 1200-1202.
"Krähe, Die." *See* "Crow, The."
Kralická Bible. PFor 1797.
Králik, Štefan. DFor 2285.
Králv, Janko. PFor 1809.
"Kraniche des Ibykus, Die." *See* "Cranes of Ibycus, The."
Kranjčević, Silvije Strahimir. PFor 2263.
Krankheit der Jugend (Bruckner). DFor 260-261.
Kransen. See *Bridal Wreath, The* and *Kristin Lavransdatter.*
Krapp's Last Tape (Beckett). DEng 154-155; DFor 162-163, 2247.

Krasicki, Ignacy. LFFor 2061; PFor 2122-2123.
Krasiński, Zygmunt. DFor 1094-1106, 1705, 1709-1710, 2276; PFor 2126.
"Krasnoe koleso" (Solzhenitsyn). LFFor 1646.
Kraszewski, Józef Ignacy. LFFor 2062.
Kraus, Karl. DFor 1107-1118; PFor 791-800.
Krechinsky's Wedding (Sukhovo-Kobylin). DFor 1773-1774. See also *Triology of Alexander Sukhovo-Kobylin, The.*
Křest svatého Vladimíra (Havlíček). PFor 1801.
Kretzer, Max. LFFor 2181.
Kreuzelschreiber, Die. (Anzengruber). DFor 90-91.
Krieger, Murray. LTh 823-830.
Kristensen, Tom. LFFor 2354; PFor 2184.
Kristeva, Julia. LTh 423, 831-835, 850, 1812, 1832.
Kristin Lavransdatter (Undset). LFFor 1803-1804, 2352.
Kristnihald undir Jökli. See *Christianity at Glacier.*
Kristuslegender. See *Christ Legends.*
Kritik der Urteilskraft. See *Critique of Judgment, The.*
Kritische Waffengänge (Harts). LTh 1719.
Kritische Wälder (Herder). LTh 669.
"Krizis." *See* "Crisis, The."
Krleža, Miroslav. DFor 2293; LFFor 2077; PFor 2264.
Krntikos, To (Solomòs). PFor 1456.
Kroetz, Franz Xaver. DFor 1119-1128, 2382-2383; DSup 407.
Krog, Helge. DFor 2480.
Król-Duch (Słowacki). PFor 1446-1447.
Krol Popiel i inne wiersze (Miłosz). PFor 1034.
Krolow, Karl. PFor 1934.
"Krône ist elter danne der künec Philippes sî, Diu." *See* "Crown Is Older Than King Philip, The."
Krst pri Savici (Prešeren). PFor 2268.
Krysl, Marilyn. ShF 2670
Krzyżacy. See *Knights of the Cross, The.*
"Który skrzywdziłeś." *See* "You Who Have Wronged."
Kuan Han-ch'ing. DFor 2314-2315.
"K'uang-jên jih-chi." *See* "Diary of a Madman, The."

150

"Kubla Khan" (Coleridge, S. T.). PEng 539-540.

"Kubla Khan" (Wheatley). PEng 3060.

Kubly, Herbert. ShF 2671.

Kuća nasred druma (Popa). PFor 1272.

Kuchibue o fuku toki. See *When I Whistle.*

"Kudzu" (Dickey, J.). PEng 797.

Kuhn, Thomas. LTh 765, 1819.

Kuhner, Herbert. ShF 2672.

Kukučín, Martin. LFFor 2068-2069.

Kulcskeresok (Örkény). DSup 300.

Kulisakh dushi. See *Theatre of the Soul, The.*

Kullervo (Kivi). DFor 1063-1064.

Kumbell, Kumbel. *See* **Hein, Piet.**

"Kumo no ito." *See* "Spider's Thread, The."

Kun en spillemand. See *Only a Fiddler.*

"Künc Constantin der gap sô vil." *See* "King Constantine Gave So Much."

Kundan the Patriot (Venkataramani). ShF 643.

Kundera, Milan. LFFor 950-957, 2067.

Kunert, Günter. PFor 1813, 1817, 1820, 1823, 1824.

"K'ung I-chi" (Lu Hsün). ShFSup 175-176.

K'ung Shang-jên. DFor 2327.

Kungaskald (Dahlstierna). PFor 2158.

Kunitz, Stanley. PSup 239-251.

"Kuno no nenkan." *See* "Almanac of Pain, An."

Kunst, Die (Holz). LTh 692-693, 1719-1720.

"Kunstwerk im Zeitalter seiner Reproduzierbarkeit, Das." *See* "Work of Art in the Age of Mechanical Reproduction, The."

Kuntsnmakher fun Lubin, Der. See *Magician of Lublin, The.*

Kunze, Reiner. PFor 801-809.

"Kuo Hsiangchi ssu." *See* "Visiting the Temple of Gathered Fragrance."

Kuo Mo-jo. LTh 1782.

Kuprin, Aleksandr. LFFor 2320-2321.

Kurka wodna. See *Water Hen, The.*

Kuruo paideía. See *Cyropaedia.*

Kurve, Die. See *Curve, The.*

Kurze Brief zum langen Abschied, Der. See *Short Letter, Long Farewell.*

Kusika's Short Stories (Madhaviah). ShF 643.

"Kusok mysa." *See* "Piece of Meat, A."

Kutonet veha-pasim. See *Tzili.*

Kuzari (Judah). PFor 779, 780.

Kvaran, Einar Hjörleifsson. LFFor 2343.

Kyd, Thomas. DEng 1086-1097, 2270; M&D 1010-1016.

Kyng Alisaunder. ShF 446.

"Kyōfu." *See* "Terror."

Kyūshū mondō (Yoshimoto). LTh 1594.

L

L. *Tolstoy i Dostoyevsky.* See *Tolstoy as Man and Artist, with an Essay on Dostoievski.*

Là-Bas (Huysmans). LFFor 865-866, 2136-2137.

Laberius, Decimus. DFor 2147.

Labiche, Eugène. **DFor 1129-1138,** 2349.

Labirynt (Ważyk). PFor 1695.

"Labor Day Dinner" (Munro). ShFSup 213-214.

Labrunie, Gérard. See **Nerval, Gérard de.**

La Bruyère, Jean de. LTh **836-842,** 1259.

Labyrinten (Baggesen). LFFor 2335.

"Labyrinth, The" (King). PEng 1586-1587.

"Labyrinth, The" (Nin). ShF 1950.

Labyrinthine Ways, The. See *Power and the Glory, The.*

"Lac, Le." *See* "Lake, The."

Lacan, Jacques. LTh 503, 833-834, **843-852,** 1767-1768, 1826; PEng 3424-3425.

Lacayos ladrones, Los. See *Registro de representantes.*

La Chaussée, Pierre-Claude Nivelle de. DEng 2181; **DFor 1139-1145,** 2340.

Laclos, Pierre Choderlos de. LFEng 3117-3120; LFFor 2121.

Laços de família. See *Family Ties.*

La Cour, Paul. PFor 2184.

Lacy, Ed. M&D 1017-1020.

Ladders to Fire (Nin). LFEng 1993-1994.

Ladies and Hussars (Fredro). DSup 138-139.

Ladies' Home Journal. ShF 589.

Lady, The (Richter). LFEng 2270.

"Lady and the Lion, The" (Grimm). ShF 1557.

Lady Aoi, The (Mishima). DFor 1324.

Lady Audley's Secret (Braddon). M&D 181-182.

Lady Chatterley's Lover (Lawrence, D. H.). LFEng 1601-1604.

Lady, Drop Dead (Treat). M&D 1600.

Lady Frederick (Maugham). DEng 1308-1309.

"Lady Geraldine's Courtship" (Browning, E. B.). PEng 329.

"Lady Hsi" (Wang Wei). PFor 1685-1686.

Lady in Peril (Dent). M&D 486.

Lady in the Dark (Hart, M.). DEng 911-913.

"Lady in the Looking Glass, The" (Woolf). ShF 2456.

Lady Jane Gray. See *Tragedy of Lady Jane Gray, The.*

Lady Julie. See *Miss Julie.*

"Lady Lazarus" (Plath). PEng 2229, 3374.

"Lady Lucifer" (O'Faoláin). ShF 2002.

"Lady Macbeth of the Mtsensk District" (Leskov). ShFSup 159.

Lady Nit-Wit, The (Vega). DFor 1936.

Lady of Dawn, The (Casona). DFor 355-357.

Lady of Lyons, The (Bulwer-Lytton). DEng 313-314.

Lady of Pleasure, The (Shirley). DEng 1817-1819, 2292-2293.

Lady of the Camillias, The. See *Camille.*

Lady of the Lake, The (Scott). PEng 2500, 2501-2502.

"Lady, or the Tiger?, The" (Stockton). M&D 1535-1536; ShF 588.

Lady Spider (MacDonagh). DEng 1208-1211.

Lady Susan (Austen). ShF 897-898.

Lady Windermere's Fan (Wilde). DEng 2036, 2037.

"Lady's Dressing Room, The" (Swift). PEng 2808.

Lady's Not for Burning, The (Fry). DEng 686-687.

Lady's Trial, The (Ford). DEng 666-669.

La Fayette, Madame de. LFFor **958-965,** 2028-2029, 2117.

Lafcadio's Adventures (Gide). LFFor 644-645, 2139.

La Fontaine, Jean de. LTh 481, **853-858,** 1419; **PFor 810-818,** 1856-1857; ShF 382.

La Fontaine et ses fables (Taine). LTh 1419.

Laforgue, Jules. **PFor 819-828,** 1879.

Lagar (Mistral). PFor 1040, 1043-1044.

Lagerkvist, Pär. **DFor 1146-1159,** 2477-2478; **LFFor 966-977,** 2350-2351; PFor 2177-2178.

Lagerlöf, Selma. **LFFor 978-990,** 2344; PFor 1371.

"Lágrimas que vierte un alma arrepentida" (Calderón). PFor 249.

La Halle, Adam de. DFor 2175-2176.
La Harpe, Jean-François de. LTh 859-864, 1180.
"Lai de plaisance, Le." *See* "Lay on Pleasure, The."
"Laid in my quyett bedd" (Surrey). PEng 2789.
Laine, Jarkko. PFor 2200.
Lais, Le. See *Legacy, The*.
Lais (Marie de France). PFor 964-971; ShF 1886, 1887.
"Lajwanti" (Anand). ShF 645.
"Lake, The" (Lamartine). PFor 832-833.
"Lake Isle of Innisfree, The" (Yeats). PEng 3190-3191.
Lalić, Ivan V. PFor 2257.
"Lamarck" (Mandelstam). PFor 940.
"Lamarck Elaborated" (Wilbur). PEng 3094-3095.
Lamartine, Alphonse de. LTh 1704; PFor 829-836, 1867-1868.
"Lamb, The" (Blake). PEng 209-210.
Lamb, Charles. LTh 1399, 1698, 1705, 1707, 1710; PEng 1630-1638.
"Lamb to the Slaughter" (Dahl). ShF 1223-1224.
Lambro, powstańca grecki (Slowacki). PFor 1442.
Lambros (Solomòs). PFor 1456.
"Lament, The" (Chekhov). ShF 1127-1128.
"Lament for Ignacio Sánchez Mejías" (García Lorca). PFor 21-22, 518-519.
Lament for the Bride (Reilly). M&D 1404.
"Lament for the Makaris" (Dunbar, W.). PEng 895-896.
"Lament on the Death of a Master of Arts" (Anand). ShF 646.
Lamentable Tragedy of Locrine, The (Stevenson?). DEng 2266.
"Lamentación de Navidad" (Reyes). PFor 1322.
"Lamentation of Mr. Pages Wife, The" (Deloney). PEng 785-786.
"Lamentationen." *See* "Lamentations."
"Lamentations" (Heine). PFor 651.
Laments (Kochanowski). PFor 2119.
La Mesnardière, Jules de. LTh 310.
Lamia (Keats). PEng 1552-1553.
Lamiel (Stendhal). LFFor 1663-1664.
LaMoore, Louis Dearborn. *See* **L'Amour, Louis.**

L'Amour, Louis. LFEng 3197; LFSup 218-226.
"Lamp, A" (Schorer). ShF 2200-2201.
"Lamp at Noon, The" (Ross, S.). ShF 638.
Lámpara maravillosa, La (Valle-Inclán). LFFor 1833-1834.
Lampe d'Aladin, La (Cocteau). PFor 370.
Lampedusa, Giuseppe Tomasi di. *See* **Tomasi di Lampedusa, Giuseppe.**
Lan-ling Wang ju chên ch'ü. DFor 2304.
Lancashire Witches, and Tegue o Divelly the Irish Priest, The (Shadwell). DEng 1673-1674.
Lancelot (Chrétien de Troyes). PFor 1838; ShF 444-445, 1140-1141.
Lancelot (Percy). LFEng 2096-2098.
Lancelot (Robinson). PEng 2393.
Lances de honor (Tamayo y Baus). DFor 1806-1807.
Land, The (Colum). DEng 388, 389.
"Land of the Dead, The" (Giusti). PFor 575.
"Land of Work" (Pasolini). PFor 1149-1150. See also "Gramsci's Ashes."
"Landarzt, Ein." *See* "Country Doctor, A."
Landessprache (Enzensberger). PFor 469.
"Landfall" (Wagoner). PEng 2992.
Landfall (Wagoner). PEng 2992-2993.
Landkjenning (Hauge). LFFor 800. See also *Cleng Peerson.*
Landnámabók. See *Book of Settlements.*
Landolfi, Tommaso. ShFSup 127-135.
Landor, Walter Savage. PEng 1639-1645.
Landsbybørnene (Ingemann). LFFor 2336.
"Landscape Near an Aerodrome, The" (Spender). PEng 2701-2702.
Landscape of the Body (Guare). DEng 861-862.
Landslide (Bagley). M&D 55.
Landslide (Betti). DFor 208-209.
Landstrykere. See *Vagabonds.*
Lang, Jack. DFor 2354-2355.
Langbaum, Robert. LFEng 3334.
Lange rejse, Den. See *Long Journey, The.*
Langgässer, Elisabeth. PFor 1931.
Langguth, A. J. ShF 2673.
Langland, William. PEng 1646-1655.
Langsame Heimkehr. See *Long Way Around, The.*
"Language" (Bobrowski). PFor 206.
Language as Gesture (Blackmur). LTh 159.
Language of the Self, The (Lacan). LTh 847.

Lanier, Sidney. PEng 1656-1666.
Lannigan, Harold. *See* Fugard, Athol.
Lanny Budd series (Sinclair, U.). LFEng 2425-2426.
Lanson, Gustave. LTh 235-236.
"Lantern Out of Doors, The" (Hopkins). PEng 1401.
Lantern to See By, A (Riggs). DEng 1593-1594.
Lanthorn and Candlelight (Dekker). PEng 770.
Lanuza (Saavedra). DFor 1615.
"Lanval" (Marie de France). ShF 444, 1887-1888.
Lao Shê. LFFor 2107.
Lao-ts'an Yu-chi. See *Travels of Lao Ts'an, The.*
Laocoön (Lessing). LTh 669, 880-881, 883, 1323.
Lap of Honour, A (MacDiarmid). PSup 267.
Lapot. *See* Leonov, Leonid Maksimovich.
"Lappin and Lapinova" (Woolf). ShF 2459-2460.
Laptev, Maksim. *See* Leonov, Leonid Maksimovich.
Lardner, Ring. ShF 251, 541, 1770-1774.
"Large Bad Picture" (Bishop). PEng 186.
"Large Red Man Reading" (Stevens). PEng 2746-2747.
"Larger Latitude, A" (Stanford). ShF 90.
Larger than Life (Buzzati). LFFor 227.
Largo lamento (Salinas). PFor 1387.
Lark, The (Anouilh). DFor 81.
Larkin, Philip. PEng 1667-1676, 3376, 3377-3378, 3455; PSup 407.
"Larks, The" (Hoffman). PEng 1358.
Larra, Mariano José de. DFor 2498.
Larsen, Marianne. PFor 2198.
Larson, Charles R. ShF 2674.
Lascelles, Lady Caroline. *See* Braddon, M. E.
Lasker-Schüler, Else. PFor 1928.
Lásky hra osudná (Čapek and Čapek). DFor 336.
Last Adam, The (Cozzens). LFEng 632.
Last Athenian, The (Rydberg). LFFor 2337-2338.
"Last Attachment, A" (Prince). PSup 317.
Last Battle, The (Lewis, C. S.). LFEng 1658.
"Last Chrysanthemum, The" (Hardy). PEng 1219-1220.
"Last Class, The" (Daudet). ShF 1241.

"Last Confession, A" (Rossetti, D. G.). PEng 2429-2430.
"Last Day, The" (Verga). ShF 2382.
Last Day in Dreamland (Hall). DEng 871-872.
"Last Day in the Field, The" (Gordon). ShF 1520-1521.
Last Days of Louisiana Red (Reed). LFSup 339-340.
Last Days of Mankind, The (Kraus). DFor 1112-1115; PFor 793-794.
"Last Escapade, The" (Alarcón). ShF 846.
"Last Gas Station, The" (Grau). ShF 1531.
Last Gentlemen, The (Percy). LFEng 2094-2095.
Last Good Kiss, The (Crumley). M&D 435.
Last Hero and Other Poems, The (Coxe). PEng 630-632.
Last Judgement (Clarke). M&D 355-357.
"Last Kiss" (Fitzgerald). ShF 1375-1376.
"Last Laugh" (Warren). PEng 3028.
Last Laugh, Mr. Moto (Marquand). M&D 1186.
"Last Leaf, The" (Henry). ShF 230.
"Last Leaf, The" (Holmes). PEng 1372.
Last Letters of Jacopo Ortis (Foscolo). PFor 491, 493.
"Last Love" (Novalis). PFor 1097.
Last Man, The (Shelley, M.). LFEng 2390-2392.
Last Mandarin, The (Becker). LFEng 203-204.
Last Meeting of the Knights of the White Magnolia, The (Jones, P.). DEng 1010. See also *Texas Trilogy, A.*
"Last Night That She Lived, The" (Dickinson). PEng 811-812.
Last of Chéri, The (Colette). LFFor 372.
Last of Mr. Moto, The. See *Stopover: Tokyo.*
Last of Mrs. Cheyney, The (Lonsdale). DEng 1171-1173.
Last of the Breed (L'Amour). LFSup 225.
Last of the Empire, The (Sembène). LFFor 2038.
"Last of the Light Brigade, The" (Kipling). PEng 1605.
Last of the Mohicans, The (Cooper). LFEng 606, 611-613.
Last of the Wine, The (Renault). LFEng 2219-2220.
Last Picture Show, The (McMurtry). LFEng 1752-1753.

Last Poems (Lawrence, D. H.). PEng 1685-1686.
"Last River, The" (Kinnell). PEng 1593.
Last Seen Wearing. . . (Waugh). M&D 1685.
Last September, The (Bowen). LFEng 264-265.
Last Stand at Papago Wells (L'Amour). LFSup 222.
"Last Stop" (Seferis). PFor 1417. See also *Logbooks*.
Last Temptation of Christ, The (Kazantzakis). LFFor 920-923.
Last Tycoon, The (Fitzgerald). ShF 1374, 1375, 1376.
"Last Word, The" (Hornung). M&D 908-909.
"Lastness" (Kinnell). PEng 1598-1599.
Låt människan leva. See *Let Man Live.*
La Taille, Jean de. LTh 277.
Late Bourgeois World, The (Gordimer). LFEng 1164.
"Late Flowering Lust" (Betjeman). PEng 172.
Late George Apley, The (Marquand). LFEng 1817.
Late Hour, The (Strand). PEng 2772-2773.
Late Mattia Pascal, The (Pirandello). LFFor 1302-1304, 2239.
Late Mrs. Null, The (Stockton). M&D 1537.
"Lately, Alas, I Knew a Gentle Boy" (Thoreau). PEng 2902.
Later (Creeley). PEng 688-690.
"Latest Literary Controversies, The" (Dostoevski). LTh 396.
Lathen, Emma. M&D 1021-1026.
Latimer, Jonathan. M&D 1027-1032.
Latin mystique, Le (Gourmont). LTh 624.
Latsis, Mary Jane. See Lathen, Emma.
Laudi, Le (D'Annunzio). PFor 387-388.
Laudi del cielo del mare della terra e degli eroi. See *Laudi, Le.*
Laughable Loves (Kundera). LFFor 950, 951, 952.
Laughing Matter, The (Saroyan). LFEng 2338-2339.
Laughing Policeman, The (Sjöwall and Wahlöö). M&D 1498.
Laughing Stock (Linney). DSup 238.
Laughter! (Barnes). DSup 13-14.
Laughter in the Dark (Nabokov). LFEng 1949-1950.
Laundromat, The. See *Third and Oak.*
Laune des Verliebten, Die. See *Wayward Lover, The.*

Laura (Caspary). M&D 290-292.
"Laura" (Saki). M&D 1458; ShF 2172.
"Laura am Klavier." *See* "Laura at the Piano."
"Laura at the Piano" (Schiller). PFor 1407.
Laurel de Apolo (Vega). PFor 1603.
Laurels Are Poison (Mitchell). M&D 1233.
Laurence, Margaret. LFEng 1567-1577; LFSup 405; ShF 1775-1779; ShFSup 389.
Laurence Bloomfield in Ireland (Allingham). PEng 44-45.
Laurents, Arthur. DEng 1098-1108.
"Laus Deo" (Whittier). PEng 3087-3088.
"Laüstic" (Marie de France). ShF 1888-1889.
Lautaro (Aguirre). DFor 37-38.
Lavers, Norman. ShF 2675.
Lavin, Mary. ShF 522, 675, 1780-1787; ShFSup 389.
"Law" (Radnóti). PFor 1312.
Law, William. PEng 397-398.
"Law of Life" (London). ShF 1811-1812.
Lawd Today (Wright, R.). LFEng 2978-2979.
Lawler, Ray. DEng 1109-1117, 2434-2435.
"Lawley Road" (Narayan). ShFSup 228.
Lawley Road and Other Stories (Narayan). ShFSup 227-228.
"Lawn in the Park" (Kraus). PFor 799.
Lawrence, D. H. LFEng 1578-1605, 3058-3059, 3316; LTh 865-870, 876, 1318, 1492; PEng 1677-1687; ShF 242-243-244, 520.
Lawrence, Frieda von Richthofen. LFEng 1581-1582.
Lawrence, Lydia Beardsall. PEng 1678.
Lawrence L'Imposteur (Aldington). LFEng 39.
Laws (Plato). LTh 1117-1118.
Lawson, Henry. ShFSup 136-141.
Lawson, Todd S. J. ShF 2676.
Lawton Girl, The (Frederic). LFEng 1027.
Laxdaela Saga. ShF 392.
Laxness, Halldór. LFFor 991-1003, 2357, 2358.
Lay By (Hare and others). DSup 184.
Lay of Atli. ShF 431.
Lay of Hákon, The (Skáldaspillir). PFor 2154.
Lay of Igor's Host, The. LTh 748; PFor 2132-2133.
Lay of the Last Minstrel, The (Scott). PEng 2500, 2501-2502.
Lay of the Sun, The. PFor 2155.
Lay of the White Steed. PFor 1974.
"Lay on Pleasure, The" (Chartier). PFor 347.
Layamon. PEng 1688-1694.

Legend of the Centuries, The (Hugo). PFor 736-737.

Legend of the Miraculous Stag. PFor 1974.

"Legend of the Origin of the Book Tao-Tê-Ching on Lao-tsû's Road into Exile" (Brecht). PFor 225.

Legenda o svaté Kateřině. See *Legend of St. Catherine, The.*

"Legende de Saint-Julien l'Hospitalier, La." See "Legend of Saint Julian the Hospitaller, The."

Légende des siècles, La. See *Legend of the Centuries, The.*

"Legende von der Entstehung des Buches Taoteking." See "Legend of the Origin of the Book Tao-Tê-Ching on Lao-tsû's Road into Exile."

Legends of Guatemala (Asturias). LFFor 84; ShF 883-884.

Léger, Alexis Saint-Léger. See **Perse, St.-John.**

Leggett, John. ShF 2679.

Legião estrangeira, A. See *Foreign Legion, The.*

Légitime Défense (Breton). LTh 214.

"Legs, The" (Graves). PEng 1130-1131.

Legs (Kennedy). LFSup 195-197. See also *Albany Cycle, The.*

Le Guin, Ursula K. LFEng 1629-1637; LFSup 405; ShF 552-553; **ShFSup 142-147.**

Lehmann, Rosamond. LFSup 227-234.

Lehmann, Wilhelm. PFor 1931.

Lehre der Sainte-Victoire, Der. See *Lesson of Mont-Sainte-Victoire, The.*

Lehtonen, Joel. LFFor 2356.

Lei-yü. See *Thunderstorm.*

Leiber, Fritz, Jr. ShF 2680.

Leibniz, Gottfried Wilhelm. LFFor 2153, 2154; LTh 78.

Leibowitz, Judith. LFEng 3251-3252.

Leiden des jungen Werthers, Die. See *Sorrows of Young Werther, The.*

Leila (Fogazzaro). LFFor 2235.

Leino, Eino. PFor 2173.

Lélia (Sand). LFFor 1492-1494.

Lem, Stanisław. LFFor 1004-1015; ShFSup 148-155.

Lemaître, Frédéric. DFor 2343.

"Lemon Trees, The" (Montale). PFor 1049. See also *Bones of the Cuttlefish.*

Lena (Ariosto). DFor 108-109.

Lenau, Nikolaus. PFor 1920.

"Lend Lease" (Shalamov). ShFSup 290.

Lengua poética de Góngora, La (Alonso). LTh 26.

"Leningrad" (Mandelstam). PFor 940.

Lenngren, Anna Maria. PFor 2162.

Lentricchia, Frank. LTh 506.

Lenz, Jakob Michael Reinhold. DFor 1160-1169.

Leo Armenius (Gryphius). DFor 836.

León, Luis de. PFor 837-844.

"Leonainie" (Riley). PEng 2375.

Leonard, Elmore. M&D 1053-1057.

Leonard, Hugh. DEng 2449; DSup 226-234.

Leonard, Lionel Frederick. See **Lonsdale, Frederick.**

Léonard, Nicolas-Germain. PFor 1863.

"Leonard and Susan" (Coleridge, H.). PEng 526.

Leonardo's Last Supper (Barnes). DSup 12.

Leonce and Lena (Büchner). DFor 273-274.

Leoni (Ruskin). ShF 2166-2167.

Leonidas of Tarentum. PFor 845-851.

Léonie est en avance (Feydeau). DFor 606-607.

Leonor de Guzman (Boker). DEng 224-225.

Leonov, Leonid Maksimovich. M&D 1058-1064.

Leopard, The (Tomasi di Lampedusa). LFFor 1730-1731, 1732-1737.

"Leopardi" (Strand). PEng 2773.

Leopardi, Giacomo. LTh 367, 1019, 1702, 1704, 1706, 1710; **PFor 852-865.**

Leopold, Karl Gustaf af. PFor 2162.

"Lepanto" (Chesterton). PEng 494.

Leper of Saint Giles, The (Peters, Ellis). M&D 1323.

Le Queux, William. M&D 1065-1070.

Lermontov, Mikhail. DFor 1170-1180; LFEng 3142-3144; LFFor 1016-1024, 2313-2314; LTh 119; **PFor 866-876, 2139-2140.**

Leroux, Gaston. M&D 1071-1077.

"Leroy" (Baraka). PEng 86.

Les. See *Forest, The.*

Les Blancs. See *Blancs, Les.*

Lesage, Alain-René. DFor 1181-1192, 2338; LFEng 3103; LFFor 1025-1036, 2029-2030, 2305.

"Lesbia" (Congreve). PEng 555.

Leskov, Nikolai. LFFor 2319; LTh 1356; **ShFSup 156-163.**

Leslie, Frank. ShF 588-589.

Lettres de mon moulin. See *Letters from My Windmill.*
Lettres persanes, Les. See *Persian Letters.*
Lettres portugaises. See *Five Love-Letters from a Nun to a Cavalier.*
Lettres portugaises (Guilleragues). See *Portuguese Letters.*
Letty Fox (Stead). LFEng 2492-2493.
"Letzte Liebe." *See* "Last Love."
Letzten Tage der Menschheit, Die. See *Last Days of Mankind, The.*
Leucippe and Cleitophon (Achilles Tatius). LFFor 2004-2005.
Leute von Seldwyla, Die. See *People of Seldwyla, The.*
"Levél Várady Antalhoz." *See* "Letter to Antal Várady."
Levelek Irisz koszorújából (Babits). PFor 119-120.
Levertov, Denise. PEng 1703-1711; PSup 407.
Levi, Carlo. LFFor 2247.
Levi, Primo. LFSup 235-240.
Levia gravia (Carducci). PFor 270.
Léviathan. See *Dark Journey, The.*
Leviathan (Hauge). LFFor 803-804.
Leviathan (Hobbes). ShF 505.
Levin, Meyer. ShF 2682.
Levin, Samuel. PEng 3452-3453.
Levine (Hanley). LFEng 1250-1251.
Levine, David M. ShF 2683.
Levine, Philip. PEng 1712-1718; PSup 407.
Lévi-Strauss, Claude. LTh 269, 503, 749, 845, **885-892**, 1280, 1761-1762, 1826.
Levnet og meninger (Ewald). LFFor 2335.
"Levsha." *See* "Lefty."
Levstik, Fran. PFor 2268.
Lewees, John. See **Stockton, Frank R.**
Lewes, George Henry. LFEng 872.
Lewis, Clayton W. ShF 2685.
Lewis, C. S. LFEng 1651-1660; LTh 95-96, **893-898**; PEng 164.
Lewis, Janet. PSup 252-257; ShF 2687.
Lewis, Mary. See **Brand, Christianna.**
Lewis, Matthew Gregory. DEng 1124-1140; LFEng 1661-1667, 3122-3123.
Lewis, Sinclair. LFEng 1668-1681, 3053-3054.
Lewis, Wyndham. LFEng 1682-1690.
Lexiphanes (Lucian). LTh 1644.

"Leyenda el sombrerón." *See* "Legend of the Big Hat."
Leyendas de Guatemala. See *Legends of Guatemala.*
L'Hermite, François. See **Tristan L'Hermite.**
Li Chih. LTh 1779.
Li Ch'ing-chao. PFor 877-884, 1789.
Li K'ai-hsiang. DFor 2323.
Li Mêng-yang. LTh 1777.
Li Po. PFor 885-893, 1540, 1542, 1785-1786.
Li Shang-yin. PFor 1787.
Li Ssŭ. PFor 1782.
Li Tung-yang. LTh 1777.
Liaisons dangereuses, Les. See *Dangerous Liaisons.*
Liang Ch'ên-yü. DFor 2323.
Liao-chai chih-i. See *Strange Stories from a Chinese Studio.*
"Liar!" (Asimov). ShF 877.
Liars, The (Jones, H. A.). DEng 1005.
Libation Bearers (Aeschylus). DFor 2101. See also *Oresteia.*
Libedinsky, Yuri. LFFor 2325.
Liber XXIV philosophorum. LTh 21.
Liberal Imagination, The (Trilling). LTh 1453-1454.
"Liberation, The" (Stafford). ShF 2262.
Liberties, The (Howe). PSup 195-196.
Libertine, The (Shadwell). DEng 1672.
"Liberty" (O'Faoláin). ShF 2002.
"Liberty and Peace" (Wheatley). PEng 3056.
Liberty Asserted (Dennis). DEng 2437-2438.
"Library of Babel, The" (Borges). ShF 981-982.
Libro de Alexandre. PFor 2207, 2008-2009.
Libro de Apolonio. PFor 2210.
Libro de buen amor (Ruiz). PFor 2210-2212.
Libro de Manuel. See *Manual for Manuel, A.*
Libro del cortegiano, Il. See *Courtier, The.*
"Libro Talonario, El." *See* "Stub-Book, The."
Licão de coisas (Drummond de Andrade). PSup 101.
"Licenciado Vidriera, El." *See* "Glass Scholar, The."
Licht (Meckel). ShFSup 189.
Lichtenstein, Alfred. PFor 1929-1930.
Lichtenstein, Heinz. LTh 687.
Lidman, Sara. LFFor 2360.
Lie, Árvid Torgeir. PFor 2196.
"Lie, The" (Raleigh). PEng 2307-2308.
Lie, Jonas. LFFor 2341-2342.

"Like Argus of Ancient Times" (London). ShF 1812.

Like Birds, Like Fishes (Jhabvala). ShF 650.

Like Death Warmed Over (Tremblay). DSup 351.

"Like Dolmens Round My Childhood the Old People" (Montague). PEng 2037.

Like Falling Leaves (Giacosa). DFor 705-708.

"Like the Night" (Carpentier). ShF 1065-1067.

"Lilac on the Gravestone" (Annensky). PFor 42.

"Lilacs" (Lowell, A.). PEng 1770.

Liliencron, Detlev von. LTh 1720; PFor 1923.

Liliom (Molnár). DFor 1345-1346.

Lilja. See *Lily, The.*

Lilla Weneda (Słowacki). DFor 1716-1717.

Lille, Per Räff. PFor 2155.

Lillo, George. DEng 1141-1150, 2178.

Lilly's Story (Wilson, E.). LFEng 2913-2914.

Lily, The. PFor 2155.

"Lily, The" (Bates). ShFSup 30.

"Limbo" (Brathwaite). PFor 214, 215. See also *Islands.*

"Limbo" (Coleridge, S. T.). PEng 544.

Lime Works, The (Bernhard). LFFor 158-159.

"Limerick Gloves, The" (Edgeworth). ShF 1326.

"Limoni, I." *See* "Lemon Trees, The."

Linares Rivas y Astray, Manuel. DFor 2503.

Lincoln, Geoffrey. *See* **Mortimer, John.**

"Lincoln Relics, The" (Kunitz). PSup 248-249.

"Lincolnshire Tale, A" (Betjeman). PEng 171.

Lindberg, Per. DFor 2477.

Lindegren, Erik. PFor 2186-2187.

Lindo don Diego, El (Moreto y Cabaña). DFor 1371-1372.

Lindsay, Vachel. PEng 1719-1728.

"Line" (Merwin). PEng 1982.

Line, David. *See* **Davidson, Lionel.**

Line in Water, A (Pritam). LFFor 2226.

Line of Fire (Hamilton). M&D 816.

"Lines" (Whittemore). PEng 3078.

"Lines About 'Lines'" (Sinclair). PEng 3455-3456.

Lines at Intersection (Miles). PSup 276-277.

"Lines by a Lady of Fashion" (Sheridan). PEng 2566-2567.

"Lines Composed a Few Miles Above Tintern Abbey" (Wordsworth). PEng 3128-3130, 3456.

"Lines for a Book" (Gunn). PEng 1172.

"Lines, Trees, and Words" (Blackburn). PEng 197.

"Lines Written in Anticipation of a London Paper Attaining a Guaranteed Circulation of Ten Million Daily" (Sassoon). PEng 2473.

"Lines Written on a Seat on the Grand Canal" (Kavanagh). PEng 1540.

Linguistic Moment, The (Miller). LTh 1036.

Ling-yün, Hsieh. *See* **Hsieh Ling-yün.**

Linhart, Antun Tomaž. DFor 2294.

Linington, Elizabeth. M&D 1078-1085.

Links (Heijermans). DFor 915.

Linna, Väinö. LFFor 2368.

Linnaeus. LFFor 2334.

Linnankoski, Johannes. LFFor 2346.

Linney, Romulus. DSup 235-239.

Lion Country. See *Book of Bebb, The.*

Lion in Love, The (Delaney). DSup 77-79.

Lion, the Witch, and the Wardrobe, The (Lewis, C. S.). LFEng 1656-1657.

"Lions, Harts, Leaping Does" (Powers). ShF 2121.

Lion's Meal, The (Curel). DFor 454.

Lippard, Lucy R. ShF 2688.

Lippincott's Magazine. ShF 587-588.

Lirismos (González Martínez). PFor 610.

Lisle, Leconte de. PFor 1874.

Lispector, Clarice. LFFor 2300; LFSup 241-248; ShFSup 164-169.

"List" (Popa). PFor 1269.

Listen to the Wind (Reaney). DEng 1575-1576.

"Listeners, The" (de la Mare). PEng 777-778.

"Listening to Foxhounds" (Dickey, J.). PEng 796.

"Listening to Lester Young" (Matthews). PEng 1938-1939.

"Listening to President Kennedy Lie About the Cuban Invasion" (Bly). PEng 224.

Lit défait, Le. See *Unmade Bed, The.*

Literarische Kunstwerk, Das. See *Literary Work of Art, The.*

Literary Criticism (Wimsatt and Brooks, C.). LTh 1556-1557.

"Literary Drug Traffic, The" (Hull). ShF 79.

"Literary Environment" (Eikhenbaum). LTh 443.

"Literary History as a Challenge to Literary Theory" (Jauss). LTh 766.

Literary Language and Its Public in Late Latin Antiquity and in the Middle Ages (Auerbach). LTh 60.

Live Bait and Other Stories (Tuohy). ShF 2348.

"Live Life Deeply" (West). ShFSup 364-365.

Live Like Pigs (Arden). DEng 45.

Live or Die (Sexton). PEng 2524.

"Lives" (Booth). PEng 247.

"Lives" (Rukeyser). PSup 331.

Lives of St. Edmund and St. Fremund, The (Lydgate). PEng 1808-1809.

Lives of the Artists (Vasari). ShF 681.

Lives of the English Poets (Johnson). LTh 1259.

Lives of the Poets (Johnson). PEng 3473-3475.

Lives of X (Ciardi). PEng 504.

"Living Alone" (Levertov). PEng 1709.

Living and the Dead, The (Boileau and Narcejac). M&D 158-159.

Living and the Dead, The (White, P.). LFEng 2864-2866.

Living End, The (Elkin). LFEng 892-893.

Living Flame of Love (John of the Cross). PFor 763, 766-767.

"Living Glass" (McPherson). PEng 1884.

"Living Relic, A" (Turgenev). ShF 2356-2357.

Living Room, The (Greene, G.). DEng 828-829.

Living Shadow, The (Gibson). M&D 720-721.

Living Temple, The (Fish). LTh 490.

"Living Temple, The" (Holmes). PEng 1375-1376.

Living Together (Ayckbourn). DEng 64-65. See also *Norman Conquests, The.*

Livings, Henry. DEng 1151-1157.

Livius Andronicus. DFor 2138; PFor 2088-2089.

"Livre de Créatures, Le" (Philippe de Thaon). PEng 3489.

Livre des masques, Le. See *Book of Masks, The.*

"Livre des quarte dames, Le." *See* "Book of Four Ladies, The."

Livsslaven. See *One of Life's Slaves.*

Livy. PFor 2098.

Liza. See *House of Gentlefolk, A.*

Liza of Lambeth (Maugham). LFEng 1845.

Lizard in the Cup, The (Dickinson). M&D 512-513.

Lizardi, José Joaquín Fernández de. LFFor 2281.

Lizárraga, Andrés. DFor 2444.

Lizzie Borden (Lowndes). M&D 1101.

Llama de amor viva. See *Living Flame of Love.*

Llanto por Ignacio Sánchez Mejías. See *Lament for Ignacio Sánchez Mejías.*

Llosa, Mario Vargas. *See* **Vargas Llosa, Mario.**

Llull, Ramon. PFor 1769-1771.

"L. N. Tolstoy's *Childhood* and *Boyhood* and *Military Tales*" (Chernyshevsky). LTh 289.

Lo Kuan-chung. LFFor 2081-2082, 2090, 2092-2094; ShF 135.

Lo que puede un empleo (Martínez de la Rosa). DFor 1272.

Lo-t'o Hsiang-tzu. See *Rickshaw Boy.*

"Loaf of Bread, The" (Ponge). PFor 1264-1265.

"Lobsters" (Nemerov). PEng 2080-2081.

Local Measures (Miles). PSup 277.

Locandiera, La. See *Mistress of the Inn, The.*

Locataire, Le. See *Lodger, The.*

Lock of Berenice (Callimachus). PFor 253.

Locke, John. LTh 238, 1700.

Locke-Elliott, Sumner. DEng 2434.

"Locket, The" (Pardo Bazán). ShF 2050.

Locklin, Gerald. ShF 2689.

Lockridge, Richard, and Frances Lockridge. M&D 1086-1092.

Lockwood Concern, The (O'Hara). LFEng 2052-2054.

Locrine (Swinburne). DEng 1899.

Locura de amor, La (Tamayo y Baus). DFor 1809.

"Locus" (Hayden). PEng 1252.

Lodge, Thomas. DEng 1158-1164, 2271; LTh 609, 613, 1186; PEng 1729-1736; ShF 491, 495.

Lodger, The (Lowndes). M&D 1102-1103.

Lodger, The (Simenon). M&D 1486.

"Lodging for the Night, A" (Stevenson, R. L.). ShF 2282-2283.

Lodore (Shelley, M.). LFEng 2392-2394.

Lodovico Sforza (Niccolini). DFor 1432.

Loerke, Oskar. PFor 1931.

Logan, Jake. *See* **Smith, Martin Cruz.**

Logan, John. PEng 1737-1743; PSup 407; ShF 2691.

Logbooks (Seferis). PFor 1417, 1962-1963.

"Logging" (Snyder). PEng 2671-2672.

Logic as the Science of the Pure Concept (Croce). LTh 330.

Logica come scienza del concetto puro. See *Logic as the Science of the Pure Concept.*

Logical Investigations (Husserl). LTh 379.

"Loon's Cry, The" (Nemerov). PEng 2083-2084.
"Loot" (Kipling). PEng 1606.
Loot (Orton). DEng 1422-1424.
Loot of Cities, Being the Adventures of a Millionaire in Search of Joy, The (Bennett). M&D 108.
López Albújar, Enrique. ShF 702, 705.
López de Ayala, Pero. PFor 2213.
López de Ayala y Herrera, Adelardo. DFor 2499-2500.
Lorca, Federico García. *See* **García Lorca, Federico.**
Lord, Albert B. PFor 1752-1754.
Lord Hay's Masque, The (Campion). PEng 426-427.
"Lord, I've seen too much" (Shapiro). PEng 2542.
Lord Jim (Conrad). LFEng 585, 593-597, 1762.
Lord Malquist and Mr. Moon (Stoppard). DEng 1866-1867.
Lord Mayor of Death, The (Babson). M&D 49.
Lord of the Flies (Golding). LFEng 1129, 1130-1131.
Lord of the Isles, The (Scott). PEng 2502.
Lord of the Rings, The (Tolkien). LFEng 2644-2646.
Lord Weary's Castle (Lowell, R.). PEng 1787-1789.
Lord's Masque, The (Campion). PEng 427.
Lorenc, Kito. PFor 1818, 1823-1824.
Lorenzaccio (Musset). DFor 1406-1408.
Lorenzaccio (Vigny). DFor 2344.
Lorris, Guillaume de. *See* **Guillaume de Lorris.**
"Lorry Driver, The" (Moravia). ShFSup 197.
"Lorsque l'enfant paraît." *See* "Infantile Influence."
Los de abajo. See *Underdogs, The.*
Los que se van (Aguilera Malta). LFSup 9.
Losing Battles (Welty). LFEng 2826-2827.
"Loss of Paradise, The" (Illyés). PFor 744-745.
"Loss of Sammy Crockett, The" (Morrison). M&D 1244.
"Losses" (Jarrell). PEng 1480-1481.
Lost and Found Stories of Morley Callaghan, The (Callaghan). ShFSup 73.
"Lost Children, The" (Jarrell). PEng 1484.
Lost Domain, The. See *Wanderer, The.*

Lost Empires (Priestley). LFEng 2144-2145.
"Lost Hearts" (James, M. R.). ShF 1689-1691.
Lost Honor of Katharina Blum, The (Böll). LFFor 188.
"Lost in the Funhouse" (Barth). ShF 928, 930-931.
Lost in the Funhouse (Barth). ShF 928.
Lost Lady, A (Cather). LFEng 480-481.
Lost Letter, The (Caragiale). DFor 348-350, 2298.
"Lost Luggage" (Adams). ShFSup 2.
Lost Ones, The (Beckett). LFEng 213-214; LFFor 129-130.
"Lost Phoebe, The" (Dreiser). ShF 1310-1311.
Lost Pilot, The (Tate, J.). PEng 2835-2836.
"Lost Princess, The" (Nahman). ShF 1942-1943.
Lost Profile (Sagan). LFFor 1476.
"Lost Sanjak" (Saki). M&D 1457.
"Lost Self" (Benn). PFor 173-174.
Lost Steps, The (Carpentier). LFFor 284-286.
"Lost Titian, The" (Rossetti, C.). PEng 2416.
Lost World, The (Doyle). LFEng 810-811.
"Lost World, The" (Jarrell). PEng 1484-1485.
Lost World, The (Jarrell). PEng 1484.
Lotman, Yuri. LTh 440, 745, **911-917.**
"Lotos-Eaters, The" (Tennyson). PEng 2862-2863.
"Lottery, The" (Edgeworth). ShF 1327.
Lottery, The (Fielding). DEng 604.
"Lottery, The" (Jackson). ShF 795-796, 1672-1674.
Lotus (Breytenbach). PSup 56.
"Lotus, The" (Rhys). ShFSup 260.
"Lough Derg Pilgrim, The" (Carleton). ShF 1060.
"Lough Neagh Sequence, A" (Heaney). PEng 1269.
Louis Lambert (Balzac). LFFor 96-97.
"Louis Lebeau's Conversion" (Howells). PEng 1421.
"Louisa, Please" (Jackson). ShF 1670.
Loupeznik. See *Robber, The.*
Loutherbourg, Philip James de. DEng 2227, 2325.
Louÿs, Pierre. PFor 1573.
"Love" (III) (Herbert). PEng 1304.
"Love" (Lispector). ShFSup 166.
"Love" (Zoshchenko). ShFSup 381.
Love Affair, A (Buzzati). LFFor 227-228.

Love Among the Cannibals (Morris). LFEng 1912.

"Love and Death" (Leopardi). PFor 863. See also *Canti.*

Love and Death in the American Novel (Fiedler). LTh 486.

Love and Friendship (Austen). ShF 897.

Love and Friendship (Lurie). LFSup 250-253.

"Love and Grief" (Dunbar). PSup 111-112.

Love and Its Derangements (Oates). PEng 2118.

Love and Like (Gold). ShF 1501-1502.

Love and Napalm (Ballard). ShF 914-915.

Love and Work (Price). LFEng 2132-2134.

"Love Asleep" (Guillén). PFor 626.

"Love Decoy, The" (Perelman). ShF 2083.

Love Eaters, The (Settle). LFSup 344-345.

Love Feast. See Book of Bebb, The.

Love for Love (Congreve). DEng 406-408.

Love for Lydia (Bates). LFEng 183-184.

Love Has No Alibi (Cohen). M&D 367.

Love in a Dry Season (Foote). LFEng 975-977.

Love in a Tub. See Comical Revenge, The.

Love in a Wood (Wycherley). DEng 2106-2107.

"Love in fantastic triumph sate" (Behn). PEng 128.

Love in Several Masques (Fielding). DEng 602.

Love in the Ruins (Percy). LFEng 2095-2096.

Love Is a Dog from Hell (Bukowski). PEng 362-363.

"Love Is a Piece of Paper Torn to Bits" (Bukowski). PEng 358.

Love Is Enough (Morris). PEng 2058-2059.

"Love Lies Sleeping" (Bishop). PEng 185.

"Love Match, A" (Warner). ShFSup 354-355.

Love Nest, The (Sherwood). DEng 1801.

"Love of Death, A" (Pinsky). PEng 2215-2218.

Love of Fame, the Universal Passion (Young). LTh 1597.

Love of the Three Oranges, The (Gozzi). DFor 794-795.

Love Poems (Sexton). PEng 2525.

"Love Song: I and Thou" (Dugan). PEng 883-884.

"Love Song of J. Alfred Prufrock, The" (Eliot). PEng 942-943.

"Love Sonnet" (Updike). PSup 382-383.

Love Suicide at Schofield Barracks, The (Linney). DSup 238.

Love Suicides at Amijima, The (Chikamatsu). DFor 398-399.

Love Suicides at Sonezaki, The (Chikamatsu). DFor 397-398, 2426.

"Love that doth raine and live within my thought" (Surrey). PEng 2786-2787.

Love You (Randall, D.). PEng 2317.

Lovecraft, H. P. ShF 744-746, **1820-1828.**

Loved and the Lost, The (Callaghan). LFEng 432, 435-437.

Loved One, The (Waugh). LFEng 2799-2800.

Lovejoy, Arthur O. LTh 1538.

Lovelace, Earl. LFEng **1700-1704.**

Lovelace, Richard. PEng **1755-1762.**

"Lover's Anger, A" (Prior). PEng 2289.

Lovers Are Never Losers (Giono). LFFor 654-655.

Lover's Melancholy, The (Ford). DEng 653-655.

Lover's Revolt, A (De Forest). LFEng 701.

Lover's Whim, The. See Wayward Lover, The.

"Lovers of Their Time" (Trevor). ShFSup 322-323.

"Lovers Relentlessly" (Kunitz). PSup 243.

"Love's Consolation" (Dixon). PEng 817-818.

"Love's Humility" (Dunbar). PSup 112.

Love's Labour's Lost (Shakespeare). DEng 1705-1706, 2276.

Love's Last Shift (Cibber). DEng 365-366, 2310.

Love's Metamorphosis (Lyly). DEng 1186-1188.

"Loves Offence" (Suckling). PEng 2781.

Love's Old Sweet Song (Saroyan). DEng 1657.

Love's Pilgrimage (Sinclair, U.). LFEng 2423.

Love's Questing (Romains). LFFor 1441. See also *Body's Rapture, The.*

Love's Sacrifice (Ford). DEng 658-661.

Love's Victory (Moreto y Cabaña). DFor 1370-1371.

Lovesey, Peter. M&D **1093-1098.**

Loving (Green). LFEng 1209-1211.

Lovo o polku Igoreve, S. See Lay of Igor's Host, The.

"Low Barometer" (Bridges). PEng 286-287.

"Low Lands" (Davie). PSup 87.

"Low-Lands" (Pynchon). ShF 2143-2144.

Löwe Leopold, Der (Kunze). PFor 801.

Lowell, Amy. PEng **1763-1772.**

Lowell, James Russell. LTh 525; PEng 1773-1782.

Lowell, Robert. DEng 2408; LFEng 1255-1256; PEng 1783-1800.

Löwensköldska ringen. See *Ring of the Löwenskölds, The.*

Lower Depths, The (Gorky). DFor 783-784.

"Lowest Room, The" (Rossetti, C.). PEng 2420.

Lowndes, Marie Belloc. M&D 1099-1105.

Lowry, Malcolm. LFEng 1705-1718; ShF 639.

Lowry, Margerie Bonner. LFEng 1708.

Loyal Subject, The (Fletcher). DEng 637.

Loyalties (Galsworthy). DEng 715-716.

Lu Ann Hampton Laverty Oberlander (Jones, P.). DEng 1010. See also *Texas Trilogy, A.*

"Lu chaih." *See* "Deer Park."

Lu Chi. LTh 901, 918-923, 1774; PFor 1784.

Lu Hsün. LFFor 2106-2107; ShFSup 170-184.

Lu Yu. PFor 1789-1790.

Lubbock, Percy. LTh 924-928.

Lucan. PFor 894-901, 2104-2105.

Luces de bohemia. See *Bohemian Lights.*

Lucian. LTh 929-933, 1643-1644.

Lucić, Hanibal. PFor 2260.

Lucidor, Lasse. PFor 2158.

Lucien Leuwen (Stendhal). LFFor 1657-1660.

Lucienne's Story (Romains). LFFor 1441. See also *Body's Rapture, The.*

Lucilius. LTh 697.

Lucius Annaeus Florus. *See* Florus.

Lucius Apuleius. *See* Apuleius.

Luck of Ginger Coffey, The (Moore, B.). LFEng 1888-1889.

"Luck of Roaring Camp, The" (Harte). ShF 222-223, 587.

"Lucky Draw, The" (Zoshchenko). ShFSup 378.

Lucky Jim (Amis). LFEng 63-65; PEng 3377.

"Lucky Life" (Stern). PSup 371-372.

Lucky Life (Stern). PSup 370.

Lucky Sam McCarver (Howard, S.). DEng 976-977.

Lucrèce (Ponsard). DFor 1489, 1492.

Lucretia Borgia (Hugo). DFor 969-970.

"Lucretia Burns" (Garland). ShF 1467-1468.

Lucretius. PFor 902-908, 2094-2095.

Lucretius Carus, Titus. *See* Lucretius.

Lucy Church Amiably (Stein). LFEng 2515.

Lucy Gayheart (Cather). LFEng 479.

"Lucy in Her Pink Jacket" (Coppard). ShF 1200.

Ludlum, Robert. M&D 1106-1111.

Ludus Coventriae. See *N-town Cycle.*

Ludvígsbakke. See *Ida Brandt.*

Ludwig, Jack. ShF 640.

Ludwig, Otto. DFor 1212-1217, 2374.

Lugar sin límites, El. See *Hell Has No Limits.*

Lugné-Poë, François. DFor 2349.

"Lui?" *See* "He?"

Luis de León. *See* León, Luis de.

Lukáč, Emil Boleslav. PFor 1811.

Lukács, Georg. LFEng 3158, 3160, 3234; LTh 416, 664, 759, 934-940, 1814.

"Luke Havergal" (Robinson, E. A.). PEng 3518-3529.

"Lullaby" (Auden). PEng 76.

"Lullaby" (Sexton). PEng 2521.

"Lullaby" (Silko). ShFSup 296-298.

"Lullaby of Cape Cod" (Brodsky). PFor 241, 242.

Lully, Jean-Baptiste. LTh 839.

Lun-wên. See *Art of Letters, The.*

"Luna." *See* "Moon."

Luna de miel, luna de hiel. See *Honeymoon, Bittermoon.*

Luna e i falò, La. See *Moon and the Bonfires, The.*

Lunacharsky, Anatoly. LTh 122, 941-950, 1125.

Lundbye, Vagn. LFFor 2367-2368.

Lundis (Sainte-Beuve). LTh 1259, 1263.

Lundkvist, Artur. PFor 2179.

Lung ch'êng lu (Liu Tsung-yüan). ShFSup 246.

"Lupa, La." *See* "She-Wolf, The."

Lupa, La (Verga). DFor 1946-1947.

Luria, Isaac. ShF 420-421.

Lurie, Alison. LFSup 249-257.

Lusíadas, Os. See *Lusiads, The* (Camões).

Lusiads, The (Camões). PFor 262-265.

Lusiads, The (Fanshawe). PEng 1002-1003.

Lustig comedia vid nampn Tisbe, En (Asteropherus). DFor 2465.

Lute, The (Kao Ming). DFor 1038-1039, 1042-1049, 2319.

Luther (Osborne). DEng 1432-1433.

Luther, Martin. PFor 1905-1907.

Lutherbibel (Luther). PFor 1906-1907.

Luv (Schisgal). DEng 1662-1663.

Luz de domingo. See *Sunday Sunlight.*

Luzán y Claramunt, Ignacio de. LTh 951-
955, 1692; PFor 2220-2221.
Luzi, Mario. PFor 2045.
Lvov, Pavel. LFFor 2306.
Lycée (La Harpe). LTh 863.
"Lycidas" (Milton). PEng 2007-2008.
Lycophron of Chalcis. DFor 2120, 2134.
Lycus, the Centaur (Hood). PEng 1384-1385.
"Lydford Journey" (Browne). PEng 322.
Lydgate, John. PEng 1801-1813, 3270-3271.
Lydie Breeze (Guare). DEng 863.
Lying Days, The (Gordimer). LFEng 1159-
1161.
"Lying in a Hammock at William Duffy's Farm
in Pine Island, Minnesota" (Wright, J.).
PEng 3158.
Lying Three (McInerny). M&D 1162, 1164.
Lykke-Per (Pontoppidan). LFFor 2339-2340.
Lyly, John. DEng 1178-1188, 2269-2270;
LFEng 3014; PEng 1814-1821; ShF 491,
492, 1829-1833.
Lymington, John. *See* Chance, John Newton.
Lynch, B. Suárez. *See* Borges, Jorge Luis.
Lynchers, The (Wideman). LFSup 382-383.
"Lynching, The" (McKay). PEng 1846.

"Lynching of Jube Benson, The" (Dunbar).
ShF 576-577.
Lynds, Dennis. *See* Collins, Michael.
Lyons, Grant. ShF 2693.
"Lyric Poetry and Experiment" (Bely). LTh
127.
"Lyric Short Story, The" (Baldeshwiler). ShF
70.
Lyrical Ballads (Wordsworth and Coleridge, S.
T.). LTh 1578-1579, 1581-1582, 1708;
PEng 3125-3128, 3342, 3475-3477; ShF
179-180.
Lyrical Poems (Dixon). PEng 819.
Lyrics and Rhythms, The (Carducci). PFor 272.
Lyrics from the Hearthside (Dunbar). PSup
111-112.
Lyrics of Love and Laughter (Dunbar). PSup
112.
Lyrics of Lowly Life (Dunbar). PSup 113-114.
Lys rouge, Le. See *Red Lily, The*.
Lysistrata (Aristophanes). DFor 2128.
Lytle, Andrew Nelson. ShF 2694.
Lyubimov. See *Makepeace Experiment, The*.
"Lyubka the Cossack" (Babel). ShF 900.
Lyutenant Shmidt. See *Lieutenant Schmidt*.

M

"M., Singing" (Bogan). PEng 235.

Ma Chih-yüan. DFor 2315.

"Ma Rainey" (Brown). PEng 3402-3403.

"Maaruf the Cobbler." ShF 411.

Mabou Mines. *See* Akalaitis, JoAnne.

Maça no escuro, A. See *Apple in the Dark, The.*

McAfee, Thomas. ShF 2695.

McAlmon, Robert. ShF 252-253.

MacAndrew, Elizabeth. ShF 724.

Macaulay, Rose. LFSup 258-264.

Macaulay, Thomas Babington. LFFor 2214; LTh 1730; **PEng 1822-1829.**

McBain, Ed. M&D 1112-1117.

Macbeth (Shakespeare). DEng 1720-1721, 2281, 2282-2283; PEng 1946.

MacBeth, George. PEng 1830-1837; PSup 407.

McCarthy, Cormac. LFSup 265-270.

McCarthy, Mary. LFEng 1719-1726; ShF 1834-1839; ShFSup 389.

McCartney, Dorothy. ShF 2696.

McCauley, Carole Spearin. ShF 2697.

McClure, James. M&D 1118-1123.

McClure's. ShF 589.

McCluskey, John A., Jr. ShF 2698.

McConkey, James. ShF 2699.

McCord, Howard. ShF 2700.

McCue, Lillian de la Torre Bueno. *See* **De la Torre, Lillian.**

McCullers, Carson. DEng 1190-1200; LFEng 1727-1737; ShF 550, 1840-1848.

MacDiarmid, Hugh. PSup 258-268.

MacDonagh, Donagh. DEng 1201-1212.

Mcdonald, Gregory. M&D 1124-1129.

Macdonald, John. *See* **Macdonald, Ross.**

MacDonald, John D. M&D 1130-1134.

Macdonald, John Ross. *See* **Macdonald, Ross.**

Macdonald, Ross. LFSup 271-280; **M&D 1135-1140;** ShF 763-764.

McDonald, Walter. ShF 2701.

McElroy, Colleen J. ShF 2702.

McElroy, Joseph. LFSup 281-289.

"McEwen of the Shining Slave Makers, (Dreiser). ShF 1308.

MacFlecknoe (Dryden). PEng 874-875.

McGerr, Patricia. M&D 1141-1147.

McGinley, Patrick. M&D 1148-1153.

McGivern, William P. M&D 1154-1159.

McGuane, Thomas. LFSup 290-297.

Mácha, Karel Hynek. PFor 1800.

Machado, Antonio. PFor 909-916, 2227.

Machado de Assis, Joaquim Maria. LFFor 1037-1048, 2285; ShF 1849-1853.

Machado, Manuel. PFor 910, 913.

Machar, Josef Svatopluk. PFor 1803.

Machiavelli, Niccolò. DFor 1218-1226, 2396-2397; LTh 366-367, 1459, 1463.

"Machine Stops, The" (Forster). ShF 1388.

Machine-wreckers, The (Toller). DFor 1860-1861.

"Machtmythus" (Holz). PFor 693.

Machwe, Prabhakar. LFFor 2225.

McInerny, Ralph. M&D 1160-1166.

MacInnes, Helen. M&D 1167-1171.

"McKabe" (Gallico). ShF 1442-1443.

McKay, Claude. PEng 1838-1846; ShF 578.

MacKay, John Henry. LFFor 2181.

McKeon, Richard. LTh 1817.

Mackerel Plaza, The (De Vries). LFEng 738-739.

Mackey, Ernan. *See* **McInerny, Ralph.**

Mackey, Mary. ShF 2703.

Mackintosh, Elizabeth. *See* **Tey, Josephine.**

Macklin, Charles. DEng 2523-2524.

MacLean, Alistair. M&D 1172-1176.

MacLeish, Archibald. DEng 1213-1225; **PEng 1847-1860.**

MacLennan, Hugh. LFEng 1738-1748.

MacLeod, Charlotte. M&D 1177-1183.

McLuhan, Marshall. LTh 956-962, 1079.

McMahon, Pat. *See* **Hoch, Edward D.**

McMillan, Florri. ShF 2704.

McMurtry, Larry. LFEng 1749-1757; LFSup 405.

McNally, Terrence. DEng 1226-1233; DSup 407.

McNamara, Eugene. ShF 2705.

MacNeice, Louis. PEng 1861-1877.

McNeile, Herman Cyril. *See* **Sapper.**
McPherson, James Alan. ShF 1854-1858.
McPherson, Sandra. PEng 1878-1885; PSup
407.
Macquarie (Buzo). DEng 321-322.
Macready, William Charles. DEng 2357, 2525.
Macrobius. LTh **963-968,** 1646-1647; PFor
2109.
Macropulos Secret, The (Čapek). DFor 340.
Macskajáték. See *Catsplay.*
Mactacio Abel. See *Killing of Abel, The.*
McTeague (Norris). LFEng 2002-2004.
Mad Hercules (Seneca). DFor 1692-1693,
2148.
Mad Lover, The (Fletcher). DEng 637.
Madach, Imre. DFor **1227-1234,** 2287.
"Madagascar" (Davenant). PEng 738-739.
Madagascar (Davenant). PEng 738.
Madame Aubray's Ideas (Dumas, *fils*). DFor
505.
Madame Bovary (Flaubert). LFEng 3162;
LFFor 550-553, 2332-2333.
"Madame de la Carlière" (Diderot). ShF
1279.
Madame de Sade (Mishima). DFor 1325-1326.
Madame Delphine (Cable). LFEng 417-419.
Madame d'Ora (Jensen). LFFor 881-882.
Madame Gervaisais (Goncourts). LFFor 716.
"Madame Tellier's Establishment"
(Maupassant). ShF 1909.
"Madame Zilenskey and the King of Finland"
(McCullers). ShF 1842.
Mädchen aus der Feenwelt, Das. See *Maid from
Fairyland, The.*
Madden, David. LFEng **1758-1768;** LFSup
405; ShF 2706.
Maddux, Rachel. ShF 2708.
Madeleine (Zola). DFor 2049.
Madeleine Férat (Zola). LFFor 1989.
Mademoiselle de Scudéry (Hoffmann). ShF
1647.
"Mademoiselle Panache" (Edgeworth). ShF
1325.
Madheart (Baraka). DEng 100-101.
Madhubuti, Haki R. PEng 1886-1897.
"Madman, The" (Maupassant). M&D 1210.
Madman and the Nun, The (Witkiewicz). DFor
2011.
Madness and Civilization (Foucault). LTh 504.
"Madonna Mia" (Swinburne). PEng 2819.
"Madonna Mia" (Wilde). PEng 3105.

"Madonna of the Evening Flowers" (Lowell,
A.). PEng 1771.
Madras House, The (Granville-Barker). DEng
800-801.
Madre, La. See *Mother, The.*
Madre naturaleza, La (Pardo Bazán). LFFor
1226-1227.
Madsen, Sven Åge. LFFor 2360, 2366.
Madwoman in the Attic, The (Gilbert and
Gubar). LTh 579, 1769.
Madwoman of Chaillot, The (Giraudoux). DFor
729-730.
Maecenas. PFor 1285.
Maeterlinck, Maurice. DEng 2198, 2199;
DFor 1235-1242, 2238, 2349.
Mafia Vendetta (Sciascia). LFFor 1519-1520.
Magazine of Fantasy & Science Fiction, The.
ShF 776.
Magda (Sudermann). DFor 1766-1767.
Maggie (Crane, S.). LFEng 640-641, 3177-
3179; ShF 536, 1309.
"Maggie Meriwether's Rich Experience"
(Stafford). ShF 2260-2261.
"Magic Barrel, The" (Malamud). ShF 1862-
1863.
Magic Christian, The (Southern). LFEng 2469-
2470.
"Magic Curtain, The" (Kunitz). PSup 246.
"Magic Egg, The" (Stockton). ShF 2287-2289.
Magic Mountain, The (Mann). LFFor 1080-
1082, 2193.
"Magic of Words, The" (Bely). LTh 126-127.
Magic Realists, The (Terry). DSup 342-343.
"Magic Striptease, The" (Garrett). ShF 1475-
1477.
Magic Striptease, The (Garrett). LFEng 1095.
Magic Toyshop, The (Carter). LFSup 72-73.
Magician of Lublin, The (Singer, Isaac).
LFEng 2435-2437; LFFor 1620-1622.
Magician's Nephew, The (Lewis, C. S.).
LFEng 1657.
"Magician's Song" (Fletcher, J.). PEng 1014.
Mágico prodigioso, El. See *Wonder-Working
Magician, The.*
Magie rouge. See *Red Magic.*
Magister Ludi. See *Glass Bead Game, The.*
Magistrate, The (Pinero). DEng 1501-1503.
Magnetic Mountain, The (Day Lewis). PEng
759.
Magnificence (Brenton). DSup 33-34.
Magnificence (Skelton). DEng 2259.

Malamud, Bernard. LFEng 1788-1800, 3067; LFSup 405; ShF 549, 1859-1864; ShFSup 389.

Malasangre, La (Gambaro). DSup 150-151.

Malatesta (Montherlant). DFor 1353.

Mālavikāgnimitra (Kālidāsa). DFor 1031-1033.

Malavoglia, I. See *House by the Medlar Tree, The.*

Malcolm (Purdy). LFEng 2170-2171.

Malcontent, The (Marston). DEng 1269-1270, 2291.

Malcontents, The (Snow). LFEng 2463-2464.

Malediction, The (Giono). LFFor 657.

"Malediction, The" (Williams, T.). ShF 2434.

Malefactors, The (Gordon). LFEng 1180.

Maleficio de la mariposa, El. See *Butterfly's Evil Spell, The.*

Malek-Adhél (Saavedra). DFor 1615.

Malentendu, Le. See *Misunderstanding, The.*

Malgonkar, Manohar. LFFor 2223; ShF 650.

Malgudi Days (Narayan). ShFSup 226.

Malherbe, François de. LTh 838, 969-974; PFor 917-923, 1855.

Malice Aforethought (Berkeley). M&D 121.

Malign Fiesta. See *Human Age, The.*

Malik Udib, al-. See *King Oedipus.*

Malina (Beck), Judith. DEng 2481, 2482.

Malinovski, Ivan. PFor 2196-2197.

Mallarmé, Stéphane. DEng 2198, 2199; LTh 213, 551, 555, 571-572, 623, 975-980, 1489-1491; PFor 924-931, 1878.

"Mallarmé et l'idée de décadence" (Gourmont). LTh 623.

Mallea, Eduardo. LFFor 1049-1058.

Malleson, Lucy Beatrice. *See* Gilbert, Anthony.

Mallowan, Agatha Christie. *See* Christie, Agatha.

Malone, Michael Patrick. ShF 2710.

Malone, Ruth. *See* Rice, Craig.

Malone Dies (Beckett). LFEng 211-212; LFFor 128.

Malone meurt. See *Malone Dies.*

Malory, Sir Thomas. LFEng 1801-1810; ShF 447, 1865-1869.

Malparte, Curzio. LFFor 2243.

Malquerida, La. See *Passion Flower, The.*

Malraux, André. LFFor 1059-1069, 2143.

Maltese Falcon, The (Hammett). LFEng 1237-1239, 3189; M&D 827.

Maltz, Albert. ShF 268, 1870-1874; ShFSup 389.

Malvaloca (Álvarez Quinteros). DFor 56-57.

Malzberg, Barry. ShF 781.

"Mama's Old Stucco House" (Williams, T.). ShF 2438.

"Mamay" (Zamyatin). ShFSup 372.

Mamba's Daughters (Heyward and Heyward). DEng 938.

"Mame" (Cummings). PEng 706.

Mamet, David. DEng 1234-1245, 2413; DSup 407-408.

"Man Alone" (Bogan). PEng 234.

Man and Boy (Morris). LFEng 1909-1910.

Man and His Picture, A (Sudermann). DFor 1763-1765.

Man and Superman (Shaw). DEng 1733-1736, 2382.

"Man and Two Women, A" (Lessing, D.). ShF 1807-1808.

Man and Wife (Collins, Wilkie). LFEng 557-558.

"Man and Wife" (Purdy). ShF 2137-2138.

"Man by the Name of Ziegler, A" (Hesse). ShF 1635-1636.

"Man Child, The" (Baldwin, James). ShF 906-907.

Man-Fate (Everson). PEng 992.

Man for All Seasons, A (Bolt). DEng 234-236.

"Man Friday" (Hope). PSup 191.

"Man from Mars, The" (Atwood). ShFSup 14-15.

Man from the Norlands, The (Buchan). M&D 226.

Man from the North, A (Bennett). LFEng 241.

"Man from the South" (Dahl). ShF 1225-1227.

"Man from the Top of the Mind, The" (Wagoner). PEng 2988.

Man Full of Nothing, A (Nestroy). DFor 1424-1426.

Man fun Notseres, Der. See *Nazarene, The.*

"Man I Parted from, Below, The" (Miyazawa). PSup 286.

"Man in Inhumanity" (Ady). PFor 7.

Man in the Black Coat Turns, The (Bly). PEng 226-227.

"Man in the Brooks Brothers Shirt, The" (McCarthy). ShF 1836-1837.

"Man in the Dead Machine, The" (Hall). PEng 1202.

Man in the Divided Sea, A (Merton). PEng 1974-1975.

Man in the High Castle, The (Dick). LFSup 95-96.

"Man in the Room, The" (Balmer and MacHarg). ShF 753.

"Man-Moth, The" (Bishop). PEng 184.

"Man of Adamant, The" (Hawthorne). ShF 477.

Man of Character, A (Henshaw). DEng 928-929.

Man of Forty Crowns, The (Voltaire). LFFor 1902-1903.

Man of Mode, The (Etherege). DEng 572-578.

Man of Property, The (Galsworthy). LFEng 1062-1064.

Man of the Forty Faces, The (Hanshew). M&D 838.

Man of the People, A (Achebe). LFEng 6, 11-13.

"Man on a Road" (Maltz). ShF 1873.

Man Outside, The (Borcherdt). DFor 2380.

"Man saw a ball of gold in the sky, A" (Crane, S.). PEng 664.

"Man That Corrupted Hadleyburg, The" (Twain). ShF 2363-2364.

"Man Who Became a Woman, The" (Anderson). LFEng 3288-3290; ShF 873.

Man Who Came to Dinner, The (Kaufman and Hart, M.). DEng 909-910.

Man Who Had All the Luck, The (Miller). DEng 1338.

"Man Who Had No Idee, The" (Disch). ShF 1290.

Man Who Invented Sin and Other Stories, The (O'Faoláin). ShF 1997.

Man Who Killed the Deer, The (Waters). LFEng 2785-2787.

Man Who Laughs, The (Hugo). LFFor 855-856.

Man Who Lived His Life Over, The (Lagerkvist). DFor 1154-1155.

"Man Who Lived Underground, The" (Wright). ShF 579, 2465-2467.

"Man Who Lost the Sea, The" (Sturgeon). ShF 2301.

Man Who Loved Children, The (Stead). LFEng 2490-2492.

Man Who Loved His Wife, The (Caspary). M&D 290-292.

"Man Who Was Almos' a Man, The" (Wright). ShF 580.

Man Who Was There, The (Morris). LFEng 1908-1909.

"Man Who Would Be King, The" (Kipling). ShF 112, 518, 1749-1751.

Man with Bags (Ionesco). DFor 1103-1104.

Man with the Blue Guitar, The (Stevens). PEng 3391.

Man with the Golden Arm, The (Algren). LFSup 26-28.

Man with the Golden Arm, The (Kirkland). DEng 1053.

Man with the Luggage, The. See *Man with Bags.*

"Man Without a Country, The" (Hale, E.). ShF 209.

Man Without a Soul, The (Lagerkvist). DFor 1155-1156.

"Man Without a Temperament, The" (Mansfield). ShF 114.

Man Without Qualities, The (Musil). LFFor 1186-1191, 2194.

Manassas (Sinclair, U.). LFEng 2420.

Manciata di more, Una. See *Handful of Blackberries, A.*

Mandarin, The (Eça de Queiróz). LFFor 544-545.

Mandarins, The (de Beauvoir). LFFor 117-119.

Mandate, The (Erdman). DFor 2460.

Mandel, Oscar. ShF 2711.

Mandell, Marvin. ShF 2712.

Mandelstam, Osip. PFor 932-942, 2147-2148.

Mandingo (Kirkland). DEng 1053.

Mandragola, La. See *Mandrake, The.*

Mandrake, The (Machiavelli). DFor 1222-1224, 2396-2397.

Man'en gan'nen no futtoboru. See *Silent Cry, The.*

"Manet" (Snodgrass). PEng 2662-2663.

Manette Salomon (Goncourts). LFFor 715-716.

Manfred (Byron). DEng 328.

Manfred, Frederick. ShF 2713.

Mangan Inheritance, The (Moore, B.). LFEng 1892-1893.

Manganilla de Melilla, La (Ruiz de Alarcón). DFor 1606.

Manger, Itzik. PFor 943-953.

"Mangler, The" (King). ShFSup 123.

Manhattan Transfer (Dos Passos). LFEng 793-794.

Manifest Detection of Dice-Play, A (Walker). ShF 453.

"Manifeste technique de la littérature futuriste." *See* "Technical Manifesto of Futurist Literature."

Manifesto of Surrealism (Breton). LTh 213-214.

Manivelle. See *Old Tune, The*.

Mann, Abel. *See* **Creasey, John.**

Mann, Heinrich. LFFor 2185-2186.

Mann ohne Eigenschaften, Der. See *Man Without Qualities, The*.

Mann, Thomas. LFEng 3333-3334; LFFor 195, **1070-1085**, 2186, 2193; LTh 937-938, **981-990**, 1316; ShF 713, **1875-1879**.

Mannen utan själ. See *Man Without a Soul, The*.

Manner, Eeva-Liisa. PFor 2190-2191.

Manninen, Otto. PFor 2174.

Mano (Dixon). PEng 816-817.

Manon Lescaut (Prévost). LFFor 1311, 1314-1316, 2119.

Manrique, Gómez. DFor 1252-1256, 2171, 2483.

Man's Blessing, A (Sciascia). LFFor 1520-1521.

Man's Fate (Malraux). LFFor 1065-1067.

Man's Hope (Malraux). LFFor 1067-1068.

Mansarda (Kiš). LFSup 213.

Manservant and Maidservant (Compton-Burnett). LFEng 570-571.

Mansfield, Katherine. ShF 242, 243-244, 520-521, **1880-1885.**

Mansfield Park (Austen). LFEng 120-122.

Manson, M. D. See *Citadel, The*.

Manticore, The (Davies). LFEng 666-667, 669-670.

"Mantis" (Zukofsky). PEng 3223-3224.

"Mantis" (Zukofsky). PEng 3223-3224.

"'Mantis,' An Interpretation" (Zukofsky). PEng 3223-3224.

Manto (Poliziano). PFor 1256. See also *Sylvae*.

Manton, Peter. *See* **Creasey, John.**

Manual for Manuel, A (Cortázar). LFFor 382-383.

"Manuelzinho" (Bishop). PEng 189.

"Ms. Found in a Bottle" (Poe). ShF 2107.

"Many Are Called" (Oates). PEng 2120.

Many Marriages (Anderson). LFEng 79.

Many Voices (Villa). PEng 2979; PFor 1647.

Man'yō kō (Mabuchi). LTh 786.

Manyōshū. LTh 785-789, 1784; PFor 2053, 2054-2055; PSup 284.

Manzoni, Alessandro. DFor 2407-2408; LFFor **1086-1094**, 2229-2231; LTh 367, 709, 1498; PFor 572, **954-961.**

Mao Ch'êng. LTh 1773.

Mão e a luva, A. See *Hand and Glove*.

Mao Tse-tung. LFFor 2084-2085; LTh 1782-1783.

Mao Tun. LFFor 2107; LTh 1782.

Mao-tan t'ing. See *Peony Pavilion*.

"Map, The" (Bishop). PEng 188.

Map of Misreading, A (Bloom). LTh 165.

"Map of Montana in Italy, A" (Hugo, R.). PEng 1453-1454.

"Map of Skye, A" (Hugo, R.). PEng 1453, 1454.

Map of the World, A (Hare). DSup 186.

"Map of Verona, A" (Reed, H.). PEng 2336-2337.

Map of Verona, A (Reed, H.). PEng 2335.

"Maple Syrup" (Hall). PEng 1205-1206.

Mappe meines Urgrossvaters, Die (Stifter). LFFor 1670-1671.

Mara, Sally. *See* **Queneau, Raymond.**

Maragall, Juan. PFor 1774.

Maraini, Dacia. DFor 2416.

Marat/Sade (Weiss). DFor 1986-1988, 2382.

"Marathon" (Glück). PSup 138.

Marble Faun, The (Hawthorne). LFEng 1325-1327.

Marcel, Gabriel. LFEng 2090.

Marcellinus, Ammianus. PFor 2110.

March, Ausiàs. PFor 1771-1772.

March, William. ShF 262.

"March Hare, A" (Leskov). ShFSup 161-162.

March Moonlight (Richardson, D.). LFEng 2242.

March to the Gallows (Kelly). M&D 962.

"Märchen, Das." *See* "Fairy Tail, The."

Marching Men (Anderson). LFEng 75-76.

Marco Polo Sings a Solo (Guare). DEng 860.

Marcovaldo ovvero le stagioni in città (Calvino). ShF 1044.

Marcus Annaeus Lucanus. *See* **Lucan.**

Marcus Aurelius Olympius Nemesianus. *See* Nemesianus.

Marcus Cornelius Fronto. *See* Fronto.

Marcus Fabius Quintilianus. *See* Quintilian.

Marcus Porcius Cato. *See* Cato.

Marcus Terentius Varro. *See* Varro.

Marcus Tullius Cicero. *See* Cicero.
Marcus Valerius Martialis. *See* Martial.
Marcuse, Herbert. LTh 1808.
Mare au diable, La. See *Devil's Pool, The.*
"Mareotis" (Durrell). PEng 920.
Marescalco, Il (Aretino). DFor 98-99.
Margarite of America, A (Lodge). ShF 492.
"Margens da alegria, As." *See* "Thin Edge of Happiness, The."
Mari Magno (Clough). PEng 521.
María (Isaacs). LFFor 2283.
Maria Magdalene (Hebbel). DFor 887-888.
Maria Nephele (Elýtis). PFor 1967.
Maria Stuart (Schiller). DFor 1660.
Mariana (Echegaray). DFor 533.
Mariana Pineda (García Lorca). DFor 657-658, 2505.
Mariane, La (Tristan). DFor 1890-1891.
Marie and Bruce (Shawn). DSup 336.
Marie de France. PFor 962-971; ShF 380, 444-445, **1886-1892.**
Marie Grubbe (Jacobsen). LFFor 2338.
Marilyn (Mailer). LFEng 1785.
Marina, Jeanne. ShF 2714.
"Marin-an" (Snyder). PEng 2673.
Marinetti, Filippo Tommaso. LTh 991-998; PFor 2037-2038.
Marino, Giambattista. PFor 972-977, 2017.
Marino Faliero, Doge of Venice (Byron). DEng 328-329, 339-340.
Mario and the Magician (Mann). ShF 1878.
Marion de Lorme (Hugo). DFor 968.
"Marionette Theater, The." *See* "About the Marionette Theater."
Mariquita y Antonio (Valera). LFFor 1818-1819.
Maritain, Jacques. LTh 154, 301, **999-1002.**
Marius the Epicurean (Pater). LFEng 2068-2075.
Marivaux. DEng 2332; DFor **1257-1268,** 2339-2340; LFFor **1095-1107,** 2030-2031, 2119.
"Marjorie Daw" (Aldrich). ShF 212.
Marjorie Morningstar (Wouk). LFEng 2967-2969.
"Mark of Apelles, The" (Pasternak). ShF 2059.
"Mark of Vishnu, The" (Singh). ShF 650.
"Mark on the Wall, The" (Woolf). ShF 2455-2456.
Markandaya, Kamala. LFFor 2222.
"Marked with D" (Harrison). PSup 171.

Markens grøde. See *Growth of the Soil.*
"Market at Turk" (Gunn). PEng 1172.
Markets of Paris, The. See *Savage Paris.*
Markham, Marion M. ShF 2715.
"Markheim" (Stevenson, R. L.). ShF 2283-2285.
Marksizm i filisofiya yazyka. See *Marxism and the Philosophy of Language.*
Markurells of Wadköping (Bergman). DFor 191-192.
Marlowe, Christopher. DEng 1246-1264, 2272-2273; PEng **1898-1907;** ShF **1893-1898.**
Marlowe, Stephen. *See* **Queen, Ellery.**
Marmion (Scott). PEng 2501-2502.
Marnie (Graham). M&D 776-777.
Maro, Publius Vergilius. *See* **Vergil.**
Marot, Clément. PFor 1848, 1850.
Marowitz, Charles. DEng 2489.
Marquand, John P. LFEng 1811-1821; M&D **1184-1188.**
Marqués, René. DFor 2446.
Marquina, Eduardo. DFor 2503.
Marquis of Keith, The (Wedekind). DFor 1979-1980.
Marquise of O . . . , The (Kleist). ShF 1757, 1760.
"Marriage" (Berry). PEng 151.
"Marriage" (Corso). PEng 577.
Marriage, The (Gombrowicz). DFor 771-773.
Marriage à la Mode (Dryden). DEng 517-519.
"Marriage Bond, The" (Zoshchenko). ShFSup 378.
"Marriage Ghazal" (Harrison). PEng 1234.
Marriage of Bette and Boo, The (Durang). DSup 104.
Marriage of Figaro, The (Beaumarchais). DFor 150-153, 2340.
Marriage of Heaven and Hell, The (Blake). PEng 211-213.
"Marriage of Helena and Menelaos, The" (Landor). PEng 1644.
Marriage of Mr. Mississippi, The (Dürrenmatt). DFor 519-521.
"Marriage Portion, A" (Foote). LFEng 978-979.
Marriages Between Zones Three, Four, and Five (Lessing). LFEng 1648-1650.
Marric, J. J. *See* **Creasey, John.**

Marrow of Tradition, The (Chesnutt). LFEng
520-521.
Marrying of Anne Leete, The (Granville-Barker).
DEng 798-799.
Mars (Zorn). LFFor 2209.
Marsden, James. *See* **Creasey, John.**
Marsh, Ngaio. M&D 1189-1194.
Marsh Hay (Denison). DEng 502-504, 2439.
Marshall, Raymond. *See* **Chase, James Hadley.**
"Marshes of Glynn, The" (Lanier). PEng 1664-
1666.
"Marsina stretta, La." *See* "Tight Frock Coat,
The."
Marsten, Richard. *See* **McBain, Ed.**
Marston, John. DEng **1265-1274,** 2290-2291.
Marta la piadosa (Tirso). DFor 1846.
"Marta Riquelme" (Hudson). LFEng 1383.
Martens, Adémar-Adolphe-Louis, *See*
Ghelderode, Michel de.
Martereau (Sarraute). LFFor 1502-1503.
"Martha Blake" (Clarke). PSup 70.
"Martha's Lady" (Jewett). ShF 1696.
Marthe (Huysmans). LFFor 861.
Martial. PFor 2104.
Martian Time-Slip (Dick). LFSup 96.
"Martian Way, The" (Asimov). ShF 879-880.
Martianus Capella. *See* Capella, Martianus.
Martin, Peter. *See* **Melville, James.**
Martin, Richard. *See* **Creasey, John.**
Martin, Stella. *See* **Heyer, Georgette.**
Martin Chuzzlewit (Dickens, C.). LFEng 749-
751.
Martin du Gard, Roger. LFFor 1108-1119.
Martin Eden (London). LFEng 1696-1697;
ShF 589-590.
Martin Faber (Simms). LFEng 2414.
Martin Salander (Keller). LFFor 934-935.
"Martin the Fisherman" (Knowles). ShF 1769.
Martínez, Enrique González. *See* **González
Martínez, Enrique.**
Martínez de la Rosa, Francisco. DFor **1269-
1277,** 2498.
Martínez Sierra, Gregorio, and **María
Martínez Sierra.** DFor **1278-1288,** 2503.
Martinsen, Martin. *See* **Follett, Ken.**
Martinson, Harry. PFor **2179-2180; PSup
269-274.**
Mártir del Sacramento, San Hermenegildo, El
(Cruz). DFor 444-445.
Marty (Chayefsky). DEng 2508.
Martyn, Edward. DEng **1275-1282.**

"Martyr, A" (Rossetti, C.). PEng 2420.
Martyrdom of Peter Ohey, The (Mrożek).
DFor 1380-1381.
"Martyr's Corner, The" (Narayan). ShFSup
228.
Martz, Louis L. PEng 1904.
Marulić, Marko. PFor 2259.
Marvell, Andrew. PEng **1908-1918.**
Marvellous Shoemaker's Wife, The. See
Shoemaker's Prodigious Wife, The.
"Marvels Beyond Thule, The" (Antonius
Diogenes). LFFor 2000, 2014.
Marx, Karl. LTh 936, 1295, 1712, 1718,
1721.
Marxism and African Literature (Ngugi). LTh
1065.
Marxism and Form (Jameson). LTh 760, 762.
Marxism and Literary Criticism (Eagleton).
LTh 415.
Marxism and Literature (Williams). LTh 1542.
Marxism and the Philosophy of Language
(Bakhtin). LTh 88.
Mary (Nabokov). LFEng 1949.
Mary Barton (Gaskell). LFEng 1099, 1103.
Mary O'Grady (Lavin). ShF 1780, 1785.
Mary Stuart (Słowacki). DFor 1712-1714.
Marylebone Miser, The (Phillpotts). M&D
1327.
"Mary's Song" (Plath). PEng 2225-2226.
"Marzo 1821" (Manzoni). PFor 960.
"Masa." *See* "Mass."
Masamune Hakuchō. LTh 1003-1008.
Masaoka Shiki. PFor 2075.
Maschera e il volto, La. See *Mask and the
Face, The.*
Maschinenstürmer, Die. See *Machine-wreckers,
The.*
Masculine Dead, The (Everson). PEng 987-
988.
Masefield, John. DEng **1283-1291; PEng
1919-1926.**
Mashen'ka. See *Mary.*
Masir Sursar. See *Fate of a Cockroach.*
Mask and the Face, The (Chiarelli). DFor 387-
390.
Mask for Dimitrios, A. See *Coffin for Dimitrios,
A.*
Mask of Apollo, The (Renault). LFEng 2221-
2222.
Masked Gods (Waters). LFEng 2781.
"Masked Woman's Song" (Bogan). PEng 234.

Mauriac, François. LFFor 1120-1132, 2142; LTh 1273.

Maurice (Forster). LFEng 1003-1004.

Mauser (Müller). DSup 260.

Mausoleum (Enzensberger). PFor 469-470.

Mauthner, Fritz. LFFor 2189.

"Mauvais sang." *See* "Bad Blood."

Mavor, Osborne Henry. *See* **Bridie, James.**

Mažuranić, Ivan. PFor 2262.

Max (Grass). DSup 159.

"Maximin" (George). PFor 550.

Maximus Poems, The (Olson). PEng 3366, 3367; PSup 310-311.

Maxwell, Mary Elizabeth Braddon. *See* **Braddon, M. E.**

May (Mácha). PFor 1800.

May, Karl. LFFor 2185.

May Day (Chapman). DEng 356.

"May Day Ode" (Thackeray). PEng 2875.

"May Day Sermon" (Dickey, J.). PEng 799.

"May Evening" (Eberhart). PEng 933.

"May Night" (Musset). PFor 1065-1066.

Mayakovsky, Vladimir. DFor 1289-1299; LTh 947; PFor 986-994, 2148-2149.

Mayflower, The (Blasco Ibáñez). LFFor 169-171.

Mayhall, Jane. ShF 2717.

Mayne, Ethel Colburn. ShF 517.

Mayor of Casterbridge, The (Hardy). LFEng 1270-1271, 3050.

Mayor of Zalamea, The (Calderón). DFor 306-307.

Mąż i żona. See *Husband and Wife.*

"Maze" (Eberhart). PEng 928-929.

Mazeppa (Słowacki). DFor 1717-1719.

Mazzini, Giuseppe. LTh 1015-1021, 1398.

"Me and Mrs. Mandible" (Barthelme). ShFSup 24-25.

"Me and the Girls" (Coward). ShF 1208.

"Meadow Turned Green, The" (Novalis). PFor 1100.

Mean Rufus Throw Down (Smith, D.). PEng 2644.

Measure for Measure (Shakespeare). DEng 1710, 2280-2281; ShF 2210.

"Meat" (Simic). PEng 2592.

"Mechón blanco, El." *See* "White Lock of Hair, The."

Meckel, Christoph. LFFor 2201; ShFSup 185-191.

Meczeństwo Piotra Oheya. See *Martyrdom of Peter Ohey, The.*

Medea (Euripides). DFor 574-575, 2111-2112.

Medea (Grillparzer). DFor 825. See also *Golden Fleece, The.*

Medea (Seneca). DFor 1689-1690, 2148-2149.

Medici, Lorenzo de'. PFor 2010-2011.

"Medicine" (Lu Hsün). ShFSup 176-177.

Medicine for Love (Henshaw). DEng 929-930.

Médico de su honra, El. See *Surgeon of His Honor, The.*

Medio tono (Usigli). DSup 361-362.

"Meditaciones rurales." *See* "Poem for a Day."

Meditation, A (Benet). LFFor 138-140.

"Meditation" (Lermontov). PFor 873.

"Meditation by the Stove" (Pastan). PEng 2174-2175.

"Meditation Eight" (Taylor). PEng 2846.

"Meditation Fifty-Six" (Taylor). PEng 2847-2849.

"Meditation Seventy-Nine" (Taylor). PEng 2850-2851.

"Meditation Thirty-Nine" (Taylor). PEng 2844-2846.

Méditations póetiques. See *Poetical Meditations, The.*

"Mediterranean, The" (Tate, A.). PEng 2827-2828.

Medium Is the Massage, The (McLuhan). LTh 958-959.

"Medium Is the Message, The" (Kennedy). PEng 1574.

Medjedović, Avdo. PFor 1753.

Medniy vsadnik. See *Bronze Horseman, The.*

Medoff, Mark. DSup 240-245.

Medora (Rueda). DFor 1596.

Medusa's Raft. See *Raft of the Medusa, The.*

Medwall, Henry. DEng 1314-1323.

Meek Heritage (Sillanpää). LFFor 1579.

Meet Me in the Green Glen (Warren). LFEng 2778-2779.

Meeting at Telgte, The (Grass). LFFor 737-738.

"Meeting-House Hill" (Lowell, A.). PEng 1770-1771.

"Meeting Place" (Ammons). PSup 13.

"Meeting Pool, The" (Bond). ShF 652-653.

"Meeting with Medusa, A" (Clarke, A.). ShF 1160-1161.

Mefisto (Banville). LFSup 49-50.

Megan Terry's Home (Terry). DSup 344-345.

Meglio gioventù, La (Pasolini). PFor 1148.

Mehren, Stein. PFor 2194.

Mei Lan-fang. DFor 2334.

Meier Helmbrecht (Hochwälder). DFor 929.

Mein Name sei Gantenbein. See *Wilderness of Mirrors, A.*

Meineidbauer, Die. See *Farmer Forsworn, The.*

Mejor alcalde, el rey, El. See *King, the Greatest Alcalde, The.*

"Melancholie an Laura." *See* "Melancholy, to Laura."

"Melancholy of Jason Kleander, Poet in Kommagini, a.d. 595" (Cavafy). PFor 299.

"Melancholy, to Laura" (Schiller). PFor 1407.

Mélanide (La Chaussée). DFor 1142-1144.

Melchoir, Ib. ShF 2718.

"Melicertus' Eclogue" (Greene). PEng 1148-1149.

Melincourt (Peacock). LFEng 2080-2082.

Melindres de Belisa, Los (Vega). DFor 1936.

"Melkii sluchai iz lichnoi zhizni." *See* "Personal Episode, A."

Mellichampe (Simms). LFEng 2411.

Melmoth the Wanderer (Maturin). LFEng 1835, 1840-1841, 3127, 3140-3141; ShF 513, 731.

Melodien, der blev vaek. See *Melody That Got Lost, The.*

Melodika russkogo liricheskogo stikha (Eikhenbaum). LTh 441.

Melody That Got Lost, The (Abell). DFor 4-6, 2480.

"Melusine, If Your Well Had Not" (Sachs). PFor 1373.

Melville, Herman. LFEng **1853-1862,** 3041-3042, 3148-3149; LTh 1012; PEng **1942-1951;** ShF 207, 367, **1913-1919.**

Melville, James. M&D 1213-1215.

Melville Goodwin, U.S.A. (Marquand). LFEng 1819.

Member of the Wedding, The (McCullers). DEng 1191, 1195-1198; LFEng 1736.

Memed, My Hawk (Kemal). LFFor 940-941.

Memleketimden insan manzaralari. See *Human Landscapes.*

Memnon: Histoire orientale. See *Zadig.*

Memnon: Or, Human Wisdom (Voltaire). ShFSup 330.

"Mémoire" (Reverdy). PSup 323-324.

Mémoires de Vidocq, chef de la police de Sûreté jusqu'en 1827. See *Memoirs of Vidocq,*

Principal Agent of the French Police Until 1827.

Mémoires d'Hadrien. See *Memoirs of Hadrian.*

Mémoires d'outre-tombe. See *Memoirs* (Chateaubriand).

Mémoires d'un honnête homme. See *Memoirs of a Man of Honor.*

Mémoires et avantures d'un homme de qualité. See *Memoirs of a Man of Quality.*

Memoirs (Chateaubriand). LFFor 334-335.

Memoirs and Adventures of a Man of Quality, The. See *Memoirs of a Man of Quality.*

Memoirs Found in a Bathtub (Lem). LFFor 1011.

Memoirs in Oxford (Prince). PSup 317.

Memoirs of a Man of Honor (Prévost). LFFor 1316-1318.

Memoirs of a Man of Quality (Prévost). LFFor 1310-1311, 1312-1314.

Memoirs of a Midget (de la Mare). LFEng 709, 710-711.

Memoirs of a Space Traveler (Lem). ShFSup 152.

Memoirs of a Survivor, The (Lessing). LFEng 1640-1641.

Memoirs of Hadrian (Yourcenar). LFFor 1965-1970.

Memoirs of Leonora Christina (Leonora Christina). LFFor 2334.

Memoirs of Vidocq, Principal Agent of the French Police Until 1827 (Vidocq). M&D 1651-1652.

Memorandum, The (Havel). DFor 879-880.

Memorandum on My Martinique. See *Return to My Native Land.*

Memorial de Ayres. See *Counselor Ayres' Memorial.*

Memórias póstumas de Braz Cubas. See *Posthumous Memoirs of Brás Cubas, The.*

"Memories" (Leopardi). PFor 861. See also *Canti.*

"Memories Sent to an Old Friend" (Akutagawa). ShFSup 11.

"Memory Clearing House, The" (Zangwill). M&D 1733.

Memory of Two Mondays, A (Miller). DEng 1343.

Me-mushiri ko-uchi (Ōe). LFFor 1196.

Men and Brethren (Cozzens). LFEng 633-634.

Men at Arms (Waugh). LFEng 2801.

Men in Her Death, The (Morice). M&D 1238.

Men in White (Kingsley). DEng 1039-1040.

Men livet lever. See *Road Leads On, The*.

"Men Loved Wholly Beyond Wisdom" (Bogan). PEng 233.

Men of Good Will (Romains). LFFor 1441-1444.

Men of Maize (Asturias). LFFor 84-85.

Men on Bataan (Hersey). LFEng 1352.

"Menace from Earth, The" (Heinlein). ShF 1618-1619.

Menaechmi. See *Twin Menaechmi, The*.

Menander. DEng 2144; DFor 1300-1308, 2131-2133.

Menaphon (Greene, R.). PEng 1149; ShF 1551-1552.

Menčetić, Šiško. PFor 2260.

Mencius. LTh 1467.

Mencken, H. L. LTh 71-72.

Mendiant de Jerusalem, Le. See *Beggar in Jerusalem, A*.

"Mending Wall" (Frost). PEng 1047.

Mendoza, Fray Iñigo de. DFor 2171.

Ménechmes, Les (Regnard). DFor 1543-1544.

Menéndez y Pelayo, Marcelino. LTh 1022-1026.

Mêng fêng chi (Wang). DFor 2324.

Menneskene og maktene. See *Floodtide of Fate*.

"Menons Klagen um Diotima." *See* "Menon's Laments for Diotima."

"Menon's Laments for Diotima" (Hölderlin). PFor 687.

Menorah Men, The (Davidson). M&D 456-457.

"Men's Room in the College Chapel, The" (Snodgrass). PEng 2661.

Men's Wives (Thackeray). ShF 2316-2317.

Mensagem (Pessoa). PFor 1206-1207.

Menschen und Leidenschaften (Lermontov). DFor 1177-1178.

Menschliches, Allzumenschliches. See *Human, All Too Human*.

"Menses" (Boland). PSup 39.

"Menses" (Millay). PEng 2002-2003.

Mensonge romantique et vérité romanesque. See *Deceit, Desire, and the Novel*.

Mentoria (Rowson). LFEng 2317-2318.

"Mentors" (Brooks, G.). PEng 3397.

"Menu/1965, The" (Brautigan). ShFSup 57-59.

Mercadé, Eustache. DFor 2166.

Mercer, David. DEng 2506.

"Merchant and the Jinni, The." ShF 410.

"Merchant of New Desires, The" (Elkin). ShF 1340.

Merchant of Venice, The (Shakespeare). DEng 1706-1707, 2278; ShF 2210.

"Merchant's Tale, The" (Chaucer). PEng 487; ShF 1113, 1115.

Mercian Hymns (Hill, G.). PEng 1346-1347, 1357, 3369.

Mercier, Louis-Sébastien. DEng 2182-2183; **DFor 1309-1318,** 2342.

Mercier and Camier (Beckett). LFEng 210-211; LFFor 126-127.

Mercière assassinée, La (Hébert). LFFor 806.

"Mère Sauvage, La" (Maupassant). ShF 114.

Meredith, Anne. See **Gilbert, Anthony.**

Meredith, George. LFEng 1863-1872, 3079.

Meredith, William. PEng 1952-1957.

Merely Murder. See *Death in the Stocks*.

Meres, Francis. LTh 1184.

Merezhkovsky, Dmitry. LFFor 1133-1141, 2319.

Meri, Veijo. LFFor 2368.

Meridian (Walker). LFEng 2749-2750, 2753-2754.

"Meriggiare pallido e assorto." *See* "Wall, The."

Mérimée, Prosper. LFFor 1142-1153, 2128; LTh 1395; ShF 459, **1920-1924.**

Merlin (Dorst). DSup 96.

"Merlin" (Emerson). PEng 956.

Merope (D'Annunzio). PFor 388. See also *Laudi, Le*.

Mérope (Voltaire). DFor 1969.

Meropius Pontius Paulinus. *See* Paulinus of Nola.

Merril, Judith. ShF 780.

Merrill, James. PEng 1958-1969; PSup 407.

Merry-Go-Round, The (Becque). DFor 171.

"Merry-Go-Round, The" (Zoshchenko). ShFSup 381.

Merry-Go-Round of Love, The (Pirandello). LFFor 1301-1302.

"Merry-Go-Round with White Swan" (Seifert). PSup 355.

Merry Death, A (Evreinov). DFor 583-584.

Merry Pranksters, The. LFEng 1527, 1528-1529.

Merry Wives of Windsor, The (Shakespeare). DEng 1709, 2279.

Merton, Thomas. PEng 1970-1978.

Merton of the Movies (Kaufman and Connelly). DEng 418-419.

Mertz, Barbara. *See* **Peters, Elizabeth.**

Merveilleux Nuages, Les. See *Wonderful Clouds, The.*

Merwin, W. S. PEng 1979-1983; PSup 407.

"Mes bouquins refermés sur le nom de Paphos." *See* "My Old Books Closed at the Name of Paphos."

Meshchane. See *Smug Citizen.*

"Message All Blackpeople Can Dig (& a few negroes too), A" (Madhubuti). PEng 1895.

Message from Hong Kong (Eberhart). M&D 565.

"Message from the Pig-Man, The" (Wain). ShF 2401.

Messe là-bas, La (Claudel). PFor 363.

Messenger, The (Kinsella). PSup 237.

Messenius, Johannes. DFor 2465.

Messiya. See *Akhnaton, King of Egypt.*

Mestiere di vivere, Il. See *This Business of Living.*

"Mestrović and the Trees" (Blackburn). PEng 196.

Mesyats v derevne. See *Month in the Country, A.*

Met ander woorde (Breytenbach). PSup 58-59.

"Metacommentary" (Jameson). LTh 762-763.

"Metafiction" (Scholes). ShF 88-89.

Metaichmio I (Sinópoulos). PFor 1971.

"Metamorphic Journal" (Levertov). PEng 1709-1710.

Metamorphoses (Apuleius). LFFor 2009-2010, 2012-2013.

Metamorphoses (Ovid). LTh 282; PFor 1125-1128; ShF 2025, 2026-2033.

"Metamorphosis" (Glück). PSup 137-138.

"Metamorphosis" (Kafka). LFEng 3317-3318; LFFor 897; ShF 108, 718-720, 1731-1732.

Metamorphosis (Sitwell). PEng 2629-2630.

Metaphor and Reality (Wheelwright). LTh 1756.

"Metaphysical Poets, The" (Eliot). LTh 447; PEng 3487.

Metaphysics (Aristotle). LTh 1636.

Metastasio, Pietro. DFor 2402-2403; **DSup 246-254;** PFor 2019-2020.

Metcalf, Paul. ShF 2719.

"Metel." *See* "Blizzard, The."

Meteor (Čapek). LFFor 277-278.

Météores, Les. See *Gemini.*

"Methodology of Narrative Structural Analysis" (Hendricks). ShF 79.

Metrical Letters (Petrarch). PFor 1238.

Metropolis, The (Sinclair, U.). LFEng 2422.

Metz, Roberta. ShF 2720.

"Metzengerstein" (Poe). ShF 2107.

Meung, Jean de. *See* **Jean de Meung.**

"Mexican Dust" (Adams). ShFSup 3.

Mexico Set (Deighton) 474-475.

Meyer, Conrad Ferdinand. LFFor 2173; PFor 1921, 1922-1923.

Meyerhold, Vsevolod. DEng 2238; DFor 2240, 2458-2461.

"Mezzogiorno d'inverno." *See* "Winter Noon."

"MHTIS. . .OU TIS" (Snodgrass). PEng 2658.

"Mi religión." *See* "My Religion."

Mi tío el empleado (Meza). LFFor 2285-2286.

Micah Clarke (Doyle). LFEng 808.

"Michael" (Wordsworth). PEng 3130-3132.

Michael Kohlhaas (Kleist). ShF 1760-1761.

Michael Robartes and the Dancer (Yeats). ShF 2472-2473.

Michael Scarlett (Cozzens). LFEng 630.

Michaels, Barbara. *See* **Peters, Elizabeth.**

Michaels, Leonard. ShF 2721.

Michaels, Steve. *See* **Avallone, Michael.**

Michaels, Walter Benn. LTh 1770.

Michaux, Henri. PFor 995-1002, 1891; PSup 407.

Michel, Jean. DFor 2166.

Michel Pauper (Becque). DFor 170-171.

Michelangelo. PFor 1003-1014.

Michener, James A. LFSup 298-305.

Michhil. See *Procession.*

Mickelsson's Ghosts (Gardner, J.). LFEng 1080-1082.

Mickiewicz, Adam. DFor 1705, 1708-1709, 2276; **PFor 1015-1024,** 1432, 1439, 1440-1441, 1448, 2124-2125.

"Microcosmic God" (Sturgeon). ShF 2299.

Micromegas (Voltaire). LFFor 1898-1899.

Midaregami. See *Tangled Hair.*

Midas (Lyly). DEng 1185-1186; PEng 1818.

"Mid-Country Blow" (Roethke). PEng 2409.

Middle Age of Mrs. Eliot, The (Wilson, A.). LFEng 2902-2903.

"Middle Drawer, The" (Calisher). ShF 1038-1040.

Middle Passage, The (Coxe). PEng 629-630.

"Middle Passage" (Hayden). PEng 1250.

Mimic Men, The (Naipaul). LFEng 1961.

Mimologiques (Genette). LTh 563.

"Mimosa, Le." *See* "Mimosa, The."

"Mimosa, The" (Ponge). PFor 1263.

"Mimsy Were the Borogoves" (Kuttner). ShF 565.

Min son på galejan (Wallenberg). LFFor 2335.

Mind Breaths (Ginsberg). PEng 1095.

"Mind, Intractable Thing, The" (Moore). PEng 2048.

"Mind Is an Enchanting Thing, The" (Moore). PEng 2046.

Mind of the Maker, The (Sayers). LFEng 2357-2358.

"Mind-Reader, The" (Wilbur). PEng 3098, 3099.

Mind to Murder, A (James). M&D 933-934.

Mine Boy (Abrahams). LFFor 2049.

"Mine own John Poyntz" (Wyatt). PEng 3178.

"Minek nevezzelek?" *See* "What Shall I Name You?"

Miner, Valerie. ShF 2728.

"Mines of Falun, The" (Hoffmann). ShF 1647.

Ming Huang. DFor 2305.

"Mingo: A Sketch of Life in Middle Georgia" (Harris, J.). ShF 1589.

"Minister's Black Veil, The" (Hawthorne). ShF 189-190.

Minister's Wooing, The (Stowe). LFEng 2561-2563.

Minkin, Stephen. ShF 2729.

Minna von Barnhelm (Lessing). DFor 1203-1205.

"Minneapolis Poem, The" (Wright, J.). PEng 3166-3168.

Minnesota Strip (Collins, M.). M&D 382, 384.

Minor, The (Fonvizin). DFor 635-638, 2452.

Minor Apocalypse, A (Konwicki). LFFor 947, 948-949.

Minor Poets of the Caroline Period (Saintsbury). LTh 1268.

Minot, Stephen. ShF 2730.

Minstrelsy of the Scottish Border, The (Scott). PEng 2500.

"Mint Quality, The" (Blackburn). PEng 200.

Minturno, Antonio. DEng 2156; **LTh 1038-1041,** 1669.

Minuta (Reyes). PFor 1322.

Miošić, Andrija Kačić. PFor 2261.

Mir zur Feier (Rilke). PFor 1328.

Mira de Amescua, Antonio. DFor 2493.

Miracle de la rose. See Miracle of the Rose.

Miracle de Théophile, Le (Rutebeuf). DFor 2164.

Miracle of the Rose (Genet). LFFor 629-631.

Miracle Worker, The (Gibson). DEng 752-754.

Mirour de l'Omme (Gower). PEng 1114, 1115, 1116-1118.

Mirra. See Murrha.

Mirror: Or, Book of Women (Roig). PFor 1772.

Mirror and the Lamp, The (Abrams). LTh 2-3, 850, 1370.

Mirror for Magistrates, A (Baldwin, W., comp.). PEng 2437-2439, 3294-3295.

Misal kneza Novaka. PFor 2259.

Misanthrope, The (Molière). DFor 1339; LTh 1687.

"Misanthrope, The" (Moravia). ShFSup 198.

"Misantropo, Il." *See* "Misanthrope, The."

Miscellaneous Observations on the Tragedy of Macbeth (Johnson). LTh 775.

Miscellaneous Pieces in Prose (Aiken and Barbauld). ShF 470.

"Miscellanies" (Cowley, A.). PEng 592-593.

Mischief (Armstrong). M&D 38.

Mischief of Being Clever, The (Griboyedov). DFor 812-816.

Misérables, Les (Hugo). LFFor 854.

Misericordia. See Compassion.

"Miserie" (Herbert). PEng 1303.

"Misfits, The" (Miller). ShF 1925, 1926-1927.

Misfortune of Being Clever, The. See Mischief of Being Clever, The.

Misfortunes of Arthur, The (Hughes). DEng 2265.

Misfortunes of Elphin, The (Peacock). LFEng 2083, 2084.

"Misgivings" (Melville). PEng 1945-1948.

Mishima, Yukio. DFor **1319-1327,** 2434; LFFor **1154-1160,** 2275, 2278; ShF **1931-1939.**

"Misoginia" (Pavese). ShF 2065-2066.

"Miss August" (Hale, N.). ShF 1570.

Miss Brown of X.Y.O. (Oppenheim). M&D 1274.

Miss Cayley's Adventures (Allen). M&D 18.

"Miss Coynte of Greene" (Williams, T.). ShF 2437-2438.

"Miss Cudahy of Stowe's Landing" (Elliott). ShF 1349-1350.

Moment in Eternity, A (MacDiarmid). PSup 260.

"Moment of Eternity, A" (Bhattacharya). ShF 651-652.

"Moments of Being" (Woolf). ShF 2456.

"Mōmoku monogatari." *See* "Blind Man's Tale, A."

Momos de doña Isabel para su hermano don Alfonso (Manrique). DFor 1255.

"Mon rêve familier." *See* "My Familiar Dream."

"Mon Roi." *See* "My King."

Monahan, John. *See* **Burnett, W. R.**

Monday After the Miracle (Gibson). DEng 754.

"Monday, Monday" (Blackburn). PEng 200.

Monday Night (Boyle). LFEng 278.

Monday Tales (Daudet). ShF 1241.

Monde comme il va, Le. See *Babouc.*

"Mondnacht." *See* "Moonlit Night."

"Monet's 'Waterlilies'" (Hayden). PEng 1249.

Money (Bulwer-Lytton). DEng 315-316, 2366.

Money Changers, The (Sinclair, U.). LFEng 2422-2423.

Money Order, The (Sembène). LFFor 1542, 1543.

Monk, The (Lewis, M.). LFEng 1661-1667, 2156-2160, 3126-3127.

Monk, Elizabeth Graham. ShF 2732.

Monk's-Hood (Peters, Ellis). M&D 1322.

Monkey. See *Journey to the West, The.*

"Monkey's Paw, The" (Jacobs). M&D 930.

Monkey's Raincoat (Matsuo Bashō). PFor 983.

Monkey's Wrench, The (Levi). LFSup 236-237.

Monody, Written at Matlock (Bowles). PEng 254-255.

"Monody Written Near Stratford Upon Avon" (Warton). PEng 3038.

Monroe, Harriet. PEng 2023-2030.

Monsieur (Durrell). LFEng 847, 3069.

Monsieur Beaucaire (Lonsdale). DEng 1169.

Monsieur d'Olive (Chapman). DEng 356, 357.

Monsieur Lecoq (Gaboriau). M&D 684.

Monsieur Ouine. See *Open Mind, The.*

"M. Pigeonneau" (France). ShF 1404.

"M. Seguin's Goat" (Daudet). ShF 1239.

"Monster, The" (Crane, S.). ShF 1221.

"Monster, The" (Gunn). PEng 1174.

Monster and Other Stories, The (Crane). LFEng 645-646.

Monstre Gai. See *Human Age, The.*

Mont Blanc (Shelley). PEng 2552-2554.

"Mont des Oliviers, Le" (Vigny). PFor 1640-1641.

Montague, John. PEng 2031-2039; PSup 408.

Montaigne, Michel Eyquem de. LTh 1042-1048.

Montale, Eugenio. PFor 1046-1053, 2040-2042, 2048-2049.

"Montana, Pastoral" (Cunningham). PSup 78.

"Monte Sant' Angelo" (Miller). ShF 1928-1929.

Montesquieu. LFEng 3110-3112; PFor 1858.

Montgomery, Marion. ShF 2733.

Montgomery, Max. *See* **Davenport, Guy.**

Montgomery, Robert Bruce. *See* **Crispin, Edmund.**

Month in the Country, A (Turgenev). DFor 1906-1908.

Month of Sundays, A (Updike). LFEng 2687, 2691.

Montherlant, Henry de. DFor 1350-1357, 2352-2353.

Monti, Vincenzo. DFor 2407; PFor 2024-2025.

Montiano y Luyando, Agustin. LTh 1692.

Montreal Smoked Meat. See *Cinq* and *Like Death Warmed Over.*

"Monument, The" (Bishop). PEng 186-187.

"Monument" (Brodsky). PFor 239.

Moodie, Susanna. ShF 635.

"Moon" (Unamuno). PFor 1558.

Moon and Sixpence, The (Maugham). LFEng 1847-1848, 1850.

Moon and the Bonfires, The (Pavese). LFFor 2250; ShF 2066.

"Moon-Bone Song, The" (Murray). PSup 290.

"Moongate" (Everson). PEng 993.

Moonlight, The (Cary). LFEng 458.

"Moonlight" (Verlaine). PFor 1627, 1630.

Moonlight Sonata, The (Rítsos). PFor 1350, 1970.

"Moonlit Night" (Eichendorff). PFor 441.

"Moonlit Night" (Tu Fu). PFor 1541, 1543.

"Moonshine War, The" (Stuart). ShF 2295.

Moonstone, The (Collins, W.). LFEng 560-561, 3186; M&D 389-390.

Moorcock, Michael. ShF 780.

Moore, Brian. LFEng 1883-1894; LFSup 405.

Moore, G. E. LTh 497, 1574.

Moore, George. LFEng 1895-1903, 3082; LTh 1089, 1735; ShF 655, 656, 659-661.

Moore, Marianne. PEng 2040-2049.

Moore, Raylyn. ShF 2734.

Moose, Ruth. ShF 2735.

"Morada del cielo." *See* "Dwelling Place in Heaven."

Moral Tales (Edgeworth). ShF 1323-1324, 1330.

Morall Fables of Esope (Henryson). ShF 143, 381.

Morall Philosophie of Doni, The. See *Pañcatantra.*

Moran of the Lady Letty (Norris). LFEng 2004-2005.

Morante, Elsa. LFFor 2255.

Moratín, Leandro Fernández de. DFor 1358-1366, 2497; LTh 1692.

Moravagine (Cendrars). LFFor 320-321.

Moravia, Alberto. DFor 2415; LFFor 1161-1173, 2254-2255; ShFSup 192-200.

Moravý sloup. See *Plague Column, The.*

Morayma (Martínez de la Rosa). DFor 1273-1274.

Morbid Taste for Bones, A (Peters, Ellis). M&D 1322-1323.

Mord den jeder begeht. See *Every Man a Murderer.*

More, Paul Elmer. LTh 68, 1011, 1257, 1566, 1818.

More, Thomas. LFFor 2022.

More de Venise, Le (Vigny). DFor 2344.

More Deaths Than One. See *And Be a Villain.*

"More Pansies" (Lawrence, D. H.). PEng 1685.

More Pricks Than Kicks (Beckett). ShF 938-939.

More Than Human (Sturgeon). LFEng 2582, 2584-2585.

More Women Than Men (Compton-Burnett). LFEng 567-569.

"Mores, The" (Clare). PEng 510-511.

Moreto y Cabaña, Agustín. DFor 1367-1372, 2495.

Moreton, Lee. *See* Boucicault, Dion.

Moretti, Marino. LFFor 2240.

Morgan, Claire. *See* Highsmith, Patricia.

Morgan, Lady. LTh 1392.

Morgan, Memo. *See* Avallone, Michael.

Morgan's Passing (Tyler). LFEng 2683-2684.

Morgante (Pulci). PFor 2012.

Morgante maggiore (Pulci). PFor 2012.

Morgante the Lesser (Martyn). DEng 1275.

Morgenlandfahrt, Die. See *Journey to the East, The.*

Morgenstern, Christian. PFor 1054-1062.

Mori Ōgai. LTh 1793-1795; PFor 2074.

Moriarty. See *Return of Moriarty, The.*

Morice, Anne. M&D 1236-1240.

Móricz, Zsigmond. LFFor 2073.

Mörike, Eduard. PFor 1919-1920.

"Morir en Bilbao." *See* "To Die in Bilbao."

Moritz Tassow (Hacks). DFor 852-853.

Morkinskinna. See *Rotten Skin.*

Morland, Dick. See Hill, Reginald.

Morley, John. LTh 1738.

Morley Callaghan's Stories (Callaghan). ShFSup 72.

Mörne, Arvid. PFor 2174.

"Morning" (Annensky). PFor 43.

"Morning Moon, The" (Walcott). PEng 3006.

Morning, Noon, and Night (Cozzens). LFEng 636-637.

"Morning of the Poem, The" (Schuyler). PEng 2479-2480, 2481-2482, 2483.

Morning Sacrifice (Cusack). DEng 2433.

Morning Song of Lord Zero, The (Aiken). PEng 25.

"Morning Star" (Pushkin). LTh 1179.

Morning Watch, The (Agee). LFSup 3-7.

Morphology of the Folktale (Propp). LTh 1762; ShF 87.

Morris, Wesley. LTh 507.

Morris, William. LTh 1245, 1739; PEng 2050-2062.

Morris, Wright. LFEng 1904-1914; ShF 548; ShFSup 201-207.

"Morris in Chains" (Coover). ShF 1193.

Morrison, Arthur. M&D 1241-1245; ShF 516.

Morrison, Toni. LFEng 1915-1924.

Morsztyn, Jan Andrzej. PFor 2121.

Mort à crédit. See *Death on the Installment Plan.*

Mort dans l'âme, La. See *Troubled Sleep.*

Mort d'Auguste, La. See *Old Man Dies, The.*

Mort de Chrispe, La (Tristan). DFor 1893.

"Mort de Guillaume Apollinaire, La." *See* "Death of Guillaume Apollinaire, The."

Mort de Pompée, La. See *Death of Pompey, The.*

Mort de quelqu'un. See *Death of a Nobody.*

Mort de Sénèque, La (Tristan). DFor 1892-1893.

"Mort d'Olivier Bécaille, La." *See* "Death of Olivier Bécaille, The."

"Mort du loup, La" (Vigny). PFor 1641-1642.

Mort du père, La (Martin du Gard). LFFor 1116. See also *World of the Thibaults, The.*

Mort heureuse, La. See *Happy Death, A.*

Mortal Acts, Mortal Words (Kinnell). PEng 1599-1600.

Mortal Stakes (Parker). M&D 1302.

"Mortality and Mercy in Vienna" (Pynchon). ShF 2142-2143.

Morte accidentale d'un anarchico. See *Accidental Death of an Anarchist.*

Morte d'Arthur, Le (Malory). LFEng 1801-1810.

Morte del re di Francia, La (Landolfi). ShFSup 129.

Morte d'Urban (Powers). LFEng 2125-2128.

Morte e a morte de Quincas Berro D'Agua, A. See *Two Deaths of Quincas Wateryell, The.*

"Morte e sole." *See* "Death and the Sun."

"Morte meditata, La." *See* "Death Meditated."

Mortimer, John. DEng 1352-1360; M&D **1246-1251.**

Mortimeriados (Drayton). PEng 850.

Morton, Anthony. *See* **Creasey, John.**

"Mosby's Memoirs" (Bellow). ShF 951-952.

"Moschus Moschiferus" (Hope). PSup 190.

Moscow Is Burning (Mayakovsky). DFor 1298.

Moscow on Fire. See *Moscow Is Burning.*

Moscow Road (Harvester). M&D 849.

Moseley, William. ShF 2736.

Mosén Millán. See *Requiem for a Spanish Peasant.*

Moses (Michelangelo). PFor 1008.

Moses, Man of the Mountain (Hurston). LFEng 1393.

Moskva gorit. See *Moscow Is Burning.*

Moskva kabatskaia (Esenin). PFor 477, 479-480.

Mosquito Coast (Theroux). LFEng 2631, 2633-2634.

Moss, Howard. PEng 2063-2067; PSup 408.

Moss, Rose. ShF 2737.

"Moss Gathering" (Roethke). PEng 2407.

Moss on the North Side (Wilkinson). LFEng 2891.

Mossén Cinto. *See* Verdaguer, Jacint.

"Most Elegant Drawing Room in Europe, The" (Hale, N.). ShF 1573.

Most Pleasant History of Ornatus and Artesia, The (Forde). ShF 496.

Most Pleasant History of Tom a Lincolne, The (Johnson, R.). ShF 495-496.

Mostellaria. See *Haunted House, The.*

"Mote in the Middle Distance, H*nry J*m*s, The" (Beerbohm). ShF 946.

"Moth and the Star, The" (Thurber). ShF 2329-2330.

"Mother, The" (Brooks, G.). PEng 313-314.

Mother, The (Buck). LFEng 343-344.

Mother, The (Čapek). DFor 341-342.

Mother, The (Deledda). LFFor 444-445.

Mother, The (Gorky). LFFor 725.

Mother and Two Daughters, A (Godwin). LFSup 139-140.

Mother Bombie (Lyly). DEng 1186.

Mother Courage and Her Children (Brecht). DFor 238-241.

Mother-in-Law, The (Terence). DFor 1828-1829, 2143.

Mother Night (Vonnegut). LFEng 2726-2727.

"Mother of God" (Sikelianos). PFor 1958.

Mother Poem (Brathwaite). PEng 272-273; PFor 216-217.

"Mother to Son" (Hughes, L.). PEng 1434.

Motion of History, The (Baraka). DEng 102-103.

Motke Ganev. See *Mottke the Thief.*

Motoori Norinaga. LTh 785, 789, 818, **1049-1053,** 1791-1792.

Motsart i Salyeri. See *Mozart and Salieri.*

Motte, Antoine Houdar de la. PFor 1859.

Mottke the Thief (Asch). LFFor 76.

Mouches, Les. See *Flies, The.*

"Mouchoir" (Cocteau). PFor 372. See also *Poésies, 1917-1920.*

"Moulin, Le." *See* "Mill, The."

Moulin de Pologne, Le. See *Malediction, The.*

"Mound of the Monkey's Grave, The" (Dazai). ShFSup 95.

Mountain Dialogues (Waters). LFEng 2781.

"Mountain Dulcimer" (Still). PEng 2764.

Mountain Giants, The (Pirandello). LFFor 1298.

Mountain King and Misanthrope (Raimund). DFor 1531-1532.

Mountain Meadow (Buchan). M&D 228. See also *Sick Heart River.*

"Mountain Tavern, The" (O'Flaherty). ShF 2011.

Murder Post-Dated (Morice). M&D 1238-1239.

"Murderer, The" (Ignatow). PEng 1470.

Murders in Praed Street, The (Rhode). M&D 1414.

"Murders in the Rue Morgue, The" (Poe). M&D 1334-1335; ShF 532, 749-750.

Murdoch, Iris. LFEng 1925-1944; LFSup 405.

Murfree, Mary Noailles. ShF 226-227.

"Murke's Collected Silences" (Böll). ShF 975-976.

Murphy (Beckett). LFEng 209; LFFor 125.

Murphy, Michael. ShF 2739.

Murray, Les A. PSup 288-293.

Murrha (Alfieri). DFor 46.

Murthy, U. R. Anantha. LFFor 2226.

Murtoleide, La (Marino). PFor 975.

Murugan the Tiller (Venkataramani). ShF 643.

Muschg, Adolf. LFFor 2210.

"Muse as Medusa, The" (Sarton). PEng 2462.

"Muse of Water, A" (Kizer). PEng 1621.

"Muse qui est la grâce, La." *See* "Muse Who Is Grace, The."

"Muse Who Is Grace, The" (Claudel). PFor 361. See also *Five Great Odes*.

"Muses, The" (Claudel). PFor 360-361. See also *Five Great Odes*.

Muses Are Heard, The (Capote). LFEng 444.

Muses' Elizium, The (Drayton). PEng 855-856.

Muses of One Mind (Trimpi). LTh 801.

Music, The (Duras). DFor 511.

"Music" (Thoreau). PEng 2901.

"Music Master, The" (Allingham). PEng 44.

"Music on the Muscatatuck" (West). ShFSup 362-363.

"Music School, The" (Updike). ShF 798-799, 2374-2375.

"Musician" (Bogan). PEng 237.

Musil, Robert. LFFor 1184-1191, 2188, 2194.

"Musk-ox, The" (Leskov). ShFSup 158.

Musophilus (Daniel). PEng 729.

Musset, Alfred de. DFor 1395-1409; LFFor 1489; LTh 1709; PFor 1063-1068, 1869-1870.

Mustapää, P. PFor 2182-2183.

Mustapha (Greville). PEng 1157.

"Mutability Cantos, The" (Spenser). PEng 2717.

"Mute Companions, The" (Narayan). ShFSup 226-227.

Mutmassungen über Jakob. See Speculations About Jacob.

Mutter Courage und ihre Kinder. See Mother Courage and Her Children.

Muzeeka (Guare). DEng 862.

My. See We.

My Ántonia (Cather). LFEng 476-477, 479-480; ShF 1569.

"My Brother Went to College" (Yerby). ShF 2479-2480.

"My Brother's Hand" (Zoshchenko). ShFSup 382.

"My Brunette" (Poliziano). PFor 1255.

My Childhood (Gorky). LFFor 727.

My Cousin Rachel (du Maurier). M&D 554.

"My Credo: Verbal Analysis" (Empson). LTh 462.

"My Death" (Strand). PEng 2770.

My Dinner with André (Shawn and Gregory). DSup 337.

My Fair Lady (Lerner and Loewe). DEng 2475.

"My Familiar Dream" (Verlaine). PFor 1628.

"My Father Is an Educated Man" (Stuart). ShF 2296.

"My father moved through dooms of love" (Cummings). PEng 707-708.

"My Father Sits in the Dark" (Weidman). ShF 2410.

"My Father's Garden" (Wagoner). PEng 2992.

"My Father's Ghost" (Wagoner). PEng 2992.

"My Favorite Murder" (Bierce). ShF 740.

"My First Acquaintance with Poets" (Hazlitt). LTh 652.

"My First Day as a Painter" (Harrison). PEng 1235.

"My First Tooth" (Shalamov). ShFSup 292.

My Friend Hitler (Mishima). DFor 1325-1327.

"My Great-Grandfather's Slaves" (Berry). PEng 150.

My Head! My Head! (Graves, R.). LFEng 1194.

My Heart and My Flesh (Roberts). LFEng 2282.

My Heart's in the Highlands (Saroyan). DEng 1655-1656.

"My Heat" (O'Hara). PEng 2125-2126.

"My King" (Michaux). PFor 1000-1001.

"My Kinsman, Major Molineux" (Hawthorne). ShF 160, 190.

"My Lady Asks Me" (Cavalcanti). PFor 306.

My Lady Clara. See *Dreams.*

"My Last Duchess" (Browning, R.). PEng 339.

"My Life" (Strand). PEng 2770.

My Life as a Man (Roth). LFEng 2306-2307.

"My Life by Somebody Else" (Strand). PEng 2770.

My Life in the Bush of Ghosts (Tutuola). LFFor 1787-1788.

"My Little Utopia" (Simic). PEng 2596.

"My lute awake" (Wyatt). PEng 3177-3178.

"My mother's maids, when they did sew and spin" (Wyatt). PEng 3178-3179.

My Name Is Aram (Saroyan). LFEng 2335-2336; ShF 2190.

My Name Is Asher Lev (Potok). LFSup 316-317.

My Next Bride (Boyle). LFEng 276.

"My Oedipus Complex" (O'Connor, Frank). ShF 672, 1992-1993.

"My Old Books Closed at the Name of Paphos" (Mallarmé). PFor 927-928.

"My Older Brothers" (Dazai). ShFSup 93-94.

"My Own Heart Let Me Have More Pity On" (Hopkins). PEng 1402.

My Own Murderer (Hull). M&D 919.

"My Poetry" (Dučić). PFor 432.

"My Religion" (Unamuno). PFor 1556-1557.

"My Sad Captains" (Gunn). PEng 1170, 1175.

My Sad Captains and Other Poems (Gunn). PEng 1169, 1170, 1171.

My Sister, Life (Pasternak). PFor 1157-1159.

"My Sisters, O My Sisters" (Sarton). PEng 2458-2459.

"My Songs" (Petőfi). PFor 1223.

"My sweet old etcetera" (Cummings). PEng 709.

My Uncle Dudley (Morris). LFEng 1908.

My Uncle Silas (Bates). ShF 270-271; ShFSup 31.

My Universities (Gorky). LFFor 727-728.

My Voice Because of You (Salinas). PFor 1387-1388.

My Wife and I. (Stowe). LFEng 2564.

"My Wife and My Sword" (Petőfi). PFor 1226.

"Mycerinus" (Arnold). PEng 50.

Myers, George, Jr. ShF 2740.

Myles, Simon. *See* **Follett, Ken.**

"Myopia: A Night" (Lowell, R.). PEng 1792.

Myortvye dushi. See *Dead Souls.*

Myrdal, Jan. LFFor 2362.

Myricae (Pascoli). PFor 1141.

"Myrtho" (Nerval). PFor 1087.

"Myself" (Creeley). PEng 690.

Mysli vrasplokh. See *Unguarded Thoughts.*

Mystère d'Adam. See *Jeu d'Adam, Le.*

Mystère de la chambre jaune, Le. See *Mystery of the Yellow Room, The.*

Mystère de la charité de Jeanne d'Arc, Le. See *Mystery of the Charity of Joan of Arc, The.*

Mystère de la parole. See *Mystery of the Word.*

Mystère de la passion, Le (Greban). DFor 2166.

Mystère des saints innocents, Le. See *Mystery of the Holy Innocents, The.*

Mystères de Paris, Les. See *Mysteries of Paris, The.*

Mysterier. See *Mysteries.*

Mysteries (Hamsun). LFFor 2346.

Mysteries of Paris, The (Sue). M&D 1554-1557.

Mysteries of Udolpho, The (Radcliffe). LFEng 2201-2202, 3125-3126; M&D 1392-1393.

Mysterious Affair at Styles, The (Christie). LFEng 536-537, 538-539; M&D 348-349.

Mysterious Island, The (Verne). LFFor 1874.

Mysterium (Hauge). LFFor 800-802.

Mystery and Manners (O'Connor, Flannery). LFEng 2040.

Mystery-bouffe (Mayakovsky). DFor 1294-1295; PFor 986, 990.

Mystery of Edwin Drood, The (Dickens). M&D 504-506.

Mystery of High Eldersham, The. See *Secret of High Eldersham, The.*

"Mystery of Marie Roget, The" (Poe). M&D 1335-1336; ShF 532, 750.

Mystery of the Cape Cod Players, The (Taylor). M&D 1568.

Mystery of the Charity of Joan of Arc, The (Péguy). PFor 1180-1181.

"Mystery of the Five Hundred Diamonds, The" (Barr). M&D 92.

Mystery of the Holy Innocents, The (Péguy). PFor 1181-1182.

Mystery of the Word (Hébert). LFFor 806, 809, 815.

Mystery of the Yellow Room, The (Leroux). M&D 1074-1075.

Mystery on Southampton Water (Crofts). M&D 422.

Mystic Masseur, The (Naipaul). LFEng 1959.

"Myth, Fiction, and Displacement" (Frye). ShF 77.

Myth, Literature, and the African World (Soyinka). LTh 1370.

Myth of Sisyphus, The (Camus). LFFor 251.

"Myth on Mediterranean Beach: Aphrodite as Logos" (Warren). PEng 3024.

Mythistorema (Seferis). PFor 1416, 1962.

Mythologia. See *Mythologies, The* (Fulgentius).

Mythologies (Barthes). LTh 105.

Mythologies, The (Fulgentius). LTh 514, 518-519.

Mythologiques (Lévi-Strauss). LTh 888.

Mythomystes (Reynolds). LTh 1675.

Myths and Texts (Snyder). PEng 2671-2672.

N

N or M? The New Mystery (Christie). LFEng 541.

"N (o)w/the" (Cummings). PEng 705.

N-town Cycle. DEng 2248, 2250-2251.

"N'a catedral." *See* "In the Cathedral."

Na dne. See *Lower Depths, The.*

Na Drini ćuprija. See *Bridge on the Drina, The.*

"Na kraiu sveta." *See* "At the Edge of the World."

"Na noite terrível." *See* "In the Terror of the Night."

Na pełnym mrozu. See *Out at Sea.*

Na vsyakogo mudretsa dovolno prostoty. See *Scoundrel, The.*

Nabokov, Vladimir. LFEng 1945-1954; LFFor 2328-2329; **ShFSup 215-223.**

Nabucco (Niccolini). DFor 1431.

"Nach der Lese." *See* "After the Harvest."

Nachdenken über Christa T. See *Quest for Christa T., The.*

Nachsommer, Der (Stifter). LFFor 1672-1673.

Nacht von Lissabon, Die. See *Night in Lisbon, The.*

Nachtgesänge (Hölderlin). PFor 685-686.

Nada como el piso 16. See *Nothing Like the Sixteenth Floor.*

Nada que ver (Gambaro). DSup 148-149.

"Nadgrobnoe slovo." *See* "Epitaph, An."

Nadja (Breton). LTh 214.

Nadobnisie i koczkodany. See *Dainty Shapes and Hairy Apes.*

Naevius, Gnaeus. DFor 1410-1414, 2139; PFor 2089.

Nagarajan, K. ShF 644.

Naharro, Bartolomé de Torres. *See* **Torres Naharro, Bartolomé de.**

Nahman of Bratslav, Rabbi. ShF 1940-1946.

Nahr al-junun. See *River of Madness, The.*

Naidu, Sarojini. PFor 1997-1998.

"Nail, The" (Alarcón). ShF 844-845.

Naipaul, V. S. LFEng 1955-1964.

Naissance de la clinique. See *Birth of the Clinic, The.*

Naissance de l'Odyssée (Giono). LFFor 654.

Nakanune. See *On the Eve.*

Naked and the Dead, The (Mailer). LFEng 1773-1776, 3064-3065.

"Naked and the Nude, The" (Graves). PEng 1128.

Naked King, The (Shvarts). DFor 1698-1700.

Naked Lunch, The (Burroughs). LFEng 384, 387-389.

Naked to the Grave (Carmichael). M&D 264.

Naked Year, The (Pilnyak). LFFor 2323.

Namatianus, Claudius. PFor 2109.

Name of the Rose, The (Eco). M&D 569-572.

Names, The (DeLillo). LFSup 88-89.

Names, The (Momaday). PEng 2019.

"Names" (Walcott). PEng 3005.

Names and Faces of Heroes, The (Price). ShF 2122-2123, 2126.

Names of Christ, The (León). PFor 841.

"Nametracks" (Brathwaite). PEng 272-273.

"Naming of Parts" (Reed, H.). PEng 2334, 2338.

Nana (Zola). LFFor 1992-1994. See also *Rougon-Macquart, Les.*

Nan-hsi. DFor 1039, 1042-1043, 1046, 2306, 2308, 2321-2322.

Nanshoku ōkagami (Saikaku). ShFSup 270.

Nansō Santomi hakkenden (Bakin). LFFor 2270-2273, 2275.

Năpasta (Caragiale). DFor 350.

Napis (Herbert). PFor 657, 659.

Napoleon (Grabbe). DFor 805-806.

Napoléon Bonaparte (Dumas, *père*). DFor 487-488.

"Napoleonic Ode, The" (Manzoni). PFor 960-961.

Napoli milionaria! (De Filippo). DFor 469.

Narayan, R. K. LFEng 1965-1972; LFFor 2220-2222; LFSup 405-406; ShF 646-647; **ShFSup 224-230.**

Narcejac, Thomas, and **Pierre Boileau. M&D 155-160.**

"Narchtliche Stunde." *See* "Nocturnal Hour."

Narcissus and Goldmund (Hesse). LFFor 832-833.

Narihira, Ariwara no. *See* Ariwara no Narihira.

Needle's Eye, The (Drabble). LFEng 821-823.
Neely, Richard. M&D 1269-1272.
Negative Dialectics (Adorno). LTh 14.
Negative Dialektik. See *Negative Dialectics.*
"Negatives" (Sissman). PEng 2618-2619.
Nègres, Les. See *Blacks, The.*
Negri, Ada. PFor 2047.
"Negro Speaks of Rivers, The" (Hughes, L.).
PEng 3393.
Negromante, Il. See *Necromancer, The.*
"Négy-ökrös szekér, A." *See* "Ox Cart, The."
Nehru, Jawaharlal. LFFor 2214, 2216.
Nei (Heiberg, J.). DFor 905.
Neiderman, Andrew. ShF 2743.
Neidhartspiel (Saint Paul of Lavanthal). DFor
2178.
"Neige, La." *See* "Snow, The."
"Neighbor Rosicky" (Cather). ShF 605-607,
1079-1080.
Neighbors (Berger). LFEng 258-259.
"Neighbors" (Carver). ShFSup 77.
"Neighbors" (West). ShFSup 364.
Neither a Candle Nor a Pitchfork (Porter).
M&D 1340.
Nekrasov, Nikolai. LTh 442; PFor 2141.
Nekrassov (Sartre). DFor 1643-1644.
Neljätoista hallitsijaa (Haavikko). PSup 145-
146.
Nelson, Kent. ShF 2744.
Nelson, Rodney. ShF 2745.
Němcová, Božena. LFFor 2065.
**Nemerov, Howard. LFEng 3254-3255, 3292;
PEng 2076-2089; PSup 408.**
Nemesianus. PFor 2106.
Németh, László. DFor 2288.
Nemiroff, Robert. *See* **Hansberry, Lorraine.**
Nemureru bijo. See *House of the Sleeping
Beauties, The.*
"Nemzeti Dal." *See* "National Ode."
Neon Wilderness, The (Algren). ShF 856.
Neostorozhnost. See *Carelessness.*
Nepenthe (Karyotákis). PFor 1960.
Nephelai. See *Clouds, The.*
Nephew, The (Purdy). LFEng 2171-2172.
Nepočin-polje. See *Unrest-Field.*
Nepos, Cornelius. PFor 2094.
"Nerthus" (Heaney). PEng 1270.
Neruda, Jan. PFor 1801-1802.
Neruda, Pablo. DFor 2443; PFor 1069-1080.

Nerval, Gérard de. PFor 1801-1809, 1872-
1873.
Neshome Ekspeditsyes. See *Shosha.*
Nesiga mislat. See *Retreat, The.*
Nesnesitelná lehkost byti. See *Unbearable
Lightness of Being, The.*
Nest, The (Kroetz). DFor 1124-1125.
Nestroy, Johann. DFor 1415-1427, 2372-
2373.
"Net of Moon, the" (Blackburn). PEng 198.
Netherwood (White). DSup 396.
Nettles (Lawrence, D. H.). PEng 1681.
Neuber, Karoline. DFor 2362.
Neuberg Anthology. PFor 1797.
Neue Gedichte. See *New Poems.*
Neue Lieder. See *New Poems.*
Neue Menoza, Der (Lenz). DFor 1168-1169.
Neue Reich, Das. See *Kingdom Come, The.*
Neue Sachlichkeit. DFor 257, 2019, 2020-
2021.
Neuen Leiden des jungen W., Die. See *New
Sufferings of Young W., The.*
"Neuer Frühling." *See* "New Spring."
Neugeboren, Jay. ShF 2746.
Neumann, Stanislav Kostka. PFor 1804.
"Neutral Tones" (Hardy). PEng 1218-1219.
"Never Again" (Foscolo). PFor 494. *See also*
"Sonetti."
Never Come Morning (Algren). LFSup 24-26.
"Never Let Them Kill You, Brother!" (Yosano
Akiko). PFor 1714.
"Nevertheless" (Moore). PEng 2046.
Neveu de Rameau, Le. See *Rameau's Nephew.*
New Account of Tales of the World, A (Liu I-
ching). LFFor 2087.
New Apologists for Poetry, The (Krieger). LTh
825.
New Art of Writing Plays, The (Vega). DFor
2205; PFor 1602-1603.
"New Birth, A" (Hoffman). PEng 1359.
New Criticism, The (Ransom). LTh 1204,
1206.
New Criticism or New Fraud? (Picard). LTh
106.
New Dominion, A. See *Travelers.*
New Don Quixote, The. See *Tartarin of
Tarascon.*
New Drama, A (Tamayo y Baus). DFor 1809-
1811, 2500.
"New Dress, The" (Woolf). ShF 2456.

"New England: A Memory" (Coxe). PEng 628.

"New England Nun, A" (Freeman). ShF 228-229, 1418-1420.

New England Tragedies, The (Longfellow). PEng 1753-1754.

"New Forms of Short Fiction" (Fuller). ShF 77.

New Found Land (MacLeish). PEng 1855.

New Grub Street (Gissing). LFEng 1113-1115.

New Héloïse, The (Rousseau). LFEng 3114-3115; LFFor 1458-1460, 2120.

"New Invisible Man, The" (Carr). ShF 763.

New Left Church, The (Eagleton). LTh 415.

New Life, The (Dante). LTh 340-343; PFor 390, 393-397, 2007; ShF 679.

New Lives for Old (Snow). LFEng 2458.

New Machiavelli, The (Wells). LFEng 2812-2813.

"New Pastoral, The" (Boland). PSup 35.

New Poems (Goethe). PFor 582.

New Poems (Heine). PFor 648, 649-650.

New Poems (Kinsella). PSup 235.

New Poems (Rilke). PFor 1329, 1330-1331.

New Poetic Works (Musset). PFor 1065.

New Poetics, The (Geoffrey of Vinsauf). LTh 1652.

New Science, The (Vico). LTh 1508-1511.

"New-Sense" (Baraka). ShF 923-924

"New Spirit, The" (Ashbery). PEng 59-60, 61.

"New Spring" (Heine). PFor 649-650.

New Sufferings of Young W., The (Plenzdorf). LFFor 2204.

New Tenant, The (Ionesco). DFor 2357.

New Verses (Ady). PFor 4.

New Way of Making Fowre Parts in Counterpoint, A (Campion). PEng 425.

New Way to Pay Old Debts, A (Massinger). DEng 1297-1298, 2291.

"New Ways of Analyzing Narrative Structure, With an Example from Joyce's *Dubliners*" (Chatman). ShF 73.

"New World" (Walcott). PEng 3005.

"New World A-Comin" (Brathwaite). PEng 271.

New Worlds. ShF 780.

"New Year's Eve" (Housman). PEng 1411.

"New Year's Eve Adventure, A" (Hoffmann). ShF 1648.

"New Year's Sacrifice, The" (Lu Hsün). ShFSup 178-179.

New Yorker, The. ShF 314-315.

Newbound, Bernard Slade. *See* **Slade, Bernard.**

Newcastle, Margaret Cavendish, Duchess of. PEng 2090-2097.

Newcomes, The (Thackeray). LFEng 2623-2624.

Newman, John Henry. PEng 2098-2106.

News of the Night (Bird). DEng 214.

"News Report" (Ignatow). PEng 1471.

Newton, David C. *See* **Chance, John Newton.**

Newton Letter, The (Banville). LFSup 48-49.

Nexø, Martin Andersen. LFFor 2348-2349.

Next (McNally). DEng 1231-1232.

"Next Day" (Jarrell). PEng 1484.

Next of Kin (Eberhart). M&D 565-566.

Nezval, Vítězslav. PFor 1805.

Ngugi, James. *See* **Ngugi wa Thiong'o.**

Ngugi wa Thiong'o. DEng 2419; DSup 264-274; LFEng 1973-1985; LFFor 2041, 2044, 2052; LFSup 406; LTh 1060-1065.

Nibelungen, Die (Hebbel). DFor 889-890.

Nibelungenlied, The. PFor 1747, 1762, 1763, 1764-1766, 1899-1900; ShF 137-138.

Niccolini, Giovanni Battista. DFor 1428-1434, 2409.

"Nice Day at School" (Trevor). ShFSup 321-322.

Nich zehn Minuten bis Buffalo. See *Only Ten Minutes to Buffalo*.

Nichijō-Seikatsu no bōken (Ōe). LFFor 1197.

Nicholas Nickleby (Dickens, C.). LFEng 748-749.

Nichols, Leigh. *See* **Koontz, Dean R.**

Nichols, Peter. DSup 275-287.

Nicht der Mörder, der Ermordete ist schuldig. See *Not the Murderer.*

Nicht Fisch nicht Fleisch (Kroetz). DFor 1125-1126.

Nick Adams Stories, The (Hemingway). ShF 1623.

"Nick and the Candlestick" (Plath). PEng 2228.

Nickel Mountain (Gardner, J.). LFEng 1076-1078.

Nicolas, F. R. E. *See* **Freeling, Nicolas.**

Nicomède (Corneille). DFor 435-436.

Nido ajeno, El. See *Another's Nest.*

Niebla. See *Mist.*

Nie-Boska komedia. See *Undivine Comedy, The.*

Niech Sczena Artysci. See *Let the Artists Die.*

Niedecker, Lorine. PSup 294-302.

Niels Ebbesen (Munk). DFor 2480.

Niels Klims underjordisketreise. See *Journey of Niels Klim to the World of the Underground*.

Niels Lyhne (Jacobsen). LFFor 2339.

Niemandsrose, Die (Celan). PFor 313-314.

"Nieto del Cid." *See* "Descendant of El Cid, A."

Nietzsche, Friedrich. DEng 2198; DFor 457; LTh 194, 459, 987, 995, **1066-1071,** 1317-1318, 1328, 1719, 1721.

Nieva, Francisco. DFor 2507.

Nievo, Ippolito. LFFor 2231.

Niezwyciężony i inne opowiadania. See *Invincible, The*.

Nigg, J. E. ShF 2747.

"Nigger, A" (Himes). ShF 1642.

Nigger Heaven (Van Vechten). LFEng 2710.

"Nigger Jeff" (Dreiser). ShF 1308.

Nigger of the "Narcissus," The (Conrad). ShF 814.

Night (O'Brien, E.). LFEng 2022.

Night (Wiesel). LFFor 1916, 1919-1922.

Night and Day (Woolf). LFEng 2945, 2946-2947.

"Night and Morning" (Clarke). PSup 69-70.

Night and Morning (Clarke). PSup 68-69.

Night at an Inn, A (Dunsany). DEng 540-541.

Night Feed (Boland). PSup 34.

"Night Fishing for Blues" (Smith, D.). PEng 2645-2647.

Night Flight (Saint-Exupéry). LFFor 1484.

Night Flight on a Sweet Saturday. See *Killing Ground, The*.

Night in Acadie, A (Chopin). LFEng 524.

"Night in Hell" (Rimbaud). PFor 1340. See also *Season in Hell, A*.

Night in Lisbon, The (Remarque). LFFor 1402-1403.

"Night in the Royal Ontario Museum, A" (Atwood). PEng 65-66.

Night Light (Justice). PEng 1530, 1531.

Night Lodging, A. See *Lower Depths, The*.

'night Mother (Norman). DSup 291-292.

Night Music (Odets). DEng 1402.

Night Must Fall (Williams, E.). DEng 2061-2063.

Night Notes (Booth). PEng 243-244.

Night of Snow (Bracco). DFor 226-227.

Night of the Iguana, The (Williams, T.). DEng 2080-2083; ShF 2434-2435.

Night of the Poor (Prokosch). LFEng 2167.

Night of the Twelfth, The (Gilbert, M.). M&D 735.

Night of Wenceslas, The (Davidson). M&D 456.

Night on Bald Mountain (White). DSup 395.

"Night Owls" (Leskov). ShFSup 161.

Night Rider (Warren). LFEng 2773-2775.

"Night-Sea Journey" (Barth). ShF 929-930.

"Night Song of a Nomadic Shepherd in Asia" (Leopardi). PFor 862. See also *Canti*.

Night Thoughts (Young, E.). PEng 3325-3326, 3327.

"Night Thoughts over a Sick Child" (Levine). PEng 1714.

Night-World (Bloch). M&D 147.

"Nightfall" (Asimov). ShF 878-879.

"Nightingale, The" (Andersen). ShF 864-865.

Nightmare Abbey (Peacock). LFEng 2082-2083.

Nightmare Begins Responsibility (Harper). PSup 164.

"Nightmare by Day" (Untermeyer). PEng 2950.

Nights at the Circus (Carter). LFSup 75.

"Night's for Cryin', The" (Himes). ShF 1641.

"Night of the Curlews" (García Márquez). ShF 1454.

Nightspawn (Banville). LFSup 44-45.

"Nightwalker" (Kinsella). PSup 232-235.

Nightwing (Smith). M&D 1503-1506.

Nihon shoki. See *Chronicles of Japan*.

Niihara, Ryūnosuke. *See* **Akutagawa, Ryūnosuke.**

Nikal Seyn (Coxe). PEng 631-632.

"Nikki-Rosa" (Giovanni). PEng 3400.

"Nile, The" (Hunt). PEng 1464.

Nile, Dorothea. *See* **Avallone, Michael.**

Nils Holgerssons underbara resa genom Sveriga. See *Further Adventures of Nils, The* and *Wonderful Adventures of Nils, The*.

Nims, John Frederick. PEng 2107-2115.

Nin, Anaïs. LFEng 1986-1997; ShF 1947-1952.

Niña en casa y la madre en la máscara, La (Martínez de la Rosa). DFor 1272.

Nine Coaches Waiting (Stewart). M&D 1528-1529.

Nine Days to Mukalla (Prokosch). LFEng 2165.

"Nine Monsters, The" (Vallejo). PFor 1592. See also *Human Poems*.

"Nothing Is Really Hard But to Be Real" (Ciardi). PEng 504.

Nothing Like the Sixteenth Floor (Vilalta). DSup 377.

Nothing Like the Sun (Burgess). LFEng 368-369.

Noticen des Feuerwerkers Christopher Magalan, Die (Meckel). ShFSup 189.

"Notre Dame" (Mandelstam). PFor 937. See also *Stone*.

"Notre Dame de Chartres" (Meredith). PEng 1955-1956.

Notre-Dame de Paris. See *Hunchback of Notre Dame, The*.

Notre-Dame des Fleurs. See *Our Lady of the Flowers*.

Notte di neve. See *Night of Snow.*

Nourritures terrestres, Les. See *Fruits of the Earth*.

Nouveau Discours du récit (Genette). LTh 563.

Nouveaux Essais de critique et d'histoire (Taine). LTh 1391, 1419-1420.

Nouvelle critique ou nouvelle imposture? See *New Criticism or New Fraud?*

Nouvelle Héloïse, La. See *New Héloïse, The*.

Nouvelles méditations poétiques (Lamartine). PFor 833.

Nov. See *Virgin Soil*.

Nova (Delany). LFEng 718.

Nova Express (Burroughs). LFEng 387-388, 390.

Novalis. LFFor 2165, 2166; LTh 437-438, 1697, 1701-1702, 1706, 1709; **PFor 1090-1101,** 1916-1917.

"Novel and the Story--The Long and Short of It, The" (Gold, Herbert). ShF 77.

Novel of Master F. J., The (Gascoigne). ShF 489, 490.

Novelas Ejemplares. See *Exemplary Novels*.

Novelle (Goethe). LFEng 3239-3242; ShFSup 101-102.

Novelle napoletane. See *Neapolitan Short Stores*.

Novellino. ShF 677-678, 680.

Novels and Novelists (Mansfield). ShF 815.

"November" (Pastan). PEng 2173.

"November Cotton Flower" (Toomer). ShF 2340-2341.

November 1918 (Döblin). LFFor 478-479.

"Novice, The" (Lermontov). PFor 869, 870.

"Novice, A" (Rossetti, C.). PEng 2420.

Novikov, Nikolay. LTh 1694.

Novius. DFor 2136.

"Novotny's Pain" (Roth). ShF 2161-2162.

Novum Organum (Bacon). LTh 76-77.

"Now and Then" (Baraka). ShF 924.

"Now, Dear Me!" (de la Mare). PEng 776.

"Now in These Days" (Everson). PEng 988.

Now That April's Here and Other Stories (Callaghan). ShFSup 70-71.

"Now the Sky" (Van Doren). PEng 2958.

Nowhere City, The (Lurie). LFSup 252-253.

Noyes, Stanley. ShF 2749.

"NRACP, The" (Elliott). ShF 1345-1347.

Nü Chuang Yüan (Hsü). DFor 2323-2324.

"Nube que trae un viento, La." See "Cloud That Bears Wind, The."

Nubes, Las (Cernuda). PFor 321-323.

"Nude" (Guillén). PFor 626.

9, El. See *Number 9*.

"+9 de febrero de 1913" (Reyes). PFor 1320.

"Nueve monstruos, Los." See "Nine Monsters, The."

Nuit, La. See *Night*.

"Nuit de l'enfer." See "Night in Hell."

"Nuit de mai, La." See "May Night."

"Nuit du Walpurgis classique." See "Classical Walpurgis Night."

Number 9 (Vilalta). DSup 375-376.

"Number of Ways of Looking at It, A" (Booth). PEng 242.

Numbered, The (Canetti). LFFor 267.

"NUMBERS" (Creeley). PEng 687-688.

Nummisuutarit (Kivi). DFor 1065-1066.

"Nun, The" (Alarcón). ShF 845-846.

Nun, The (Behn). LFEng 221.

Nun, The (Diderot). LFFor 463-464.

Nun in the Closet, A (Gilman). M&D 747.

Nunquam (Durrell). LFEng 847.

"Nun's Priest's Tale, The" (Chaucer). PEng 488; ShF 381, 1112-1113.

Nuorena nukkunut. See *Maid Silja, The*.

"Nuptial Torches, The" (Harrison). PSup 168.

Nursery Crimes (Gill). M&D 742-743.

Nušić, Branislav. DFor 2291.

Nutricia (Poliziano). LTh 1669; PFor 1256. See also *Sylvae*.

Nychtologio (Sinópoulos). PFor 1972.

Nymphidia (Drayton). PEng 885.

"Nymph's Reply to the Shepherd, The" (Raleigh). PEng 1901-1902.

O

O Babylon! (Walcott, D. A.). DEng 2002-2003.

"O Basne i basniakh Krylova" (Zhukovsky). LTh 1612-1613.

O Beulah Land (Settle). LFSup 345-346. *See also* Beulah Quintet, The.

"O Cheese" (Hall). PEng 1206.

"O Daedalus, Fly Away Home" (Hayden). PEng 1248.

"O. Genri i teoriia novelly." *See* "O. Henry and the Theory of the Short Story."

"O happy dames, that may embrace" (Surrey). PEng 2788.

"O. Henry and the Theory of the Short Story" (Eikhenbaum). LTh 443; ShF 75.

"O literaturnoy evolyutsii." *See* "On Literary Evolution."

O locura o santidad. See *Folly or Saintliness.*

O noapte furtunoasa. See *Stormy Night, A.*

Ô Pays, mon beau peuple! (Sembène). LFFor 1538-1540, 2045-2046.

O Pioneers! (Cather). LFEng 478; ShF 1569.

"O poete i sovremennom ego znachenii" (Zhukovsky). LTh 1614.

"O pokolenii, rastrativshem svoikh poetov." *See* "On a Generation That Squandered Its Poets."

"O repertuare dramaticheskikh teatov i merakh po ego ulucheniiu." *See* "On the Repertoire of the Dramatic Theaters and Measures for Its Improvement."

"O satire i satirakh Kantemira" (Zhukovsky). LTh 1613.

O scrisoare pierdută. See *Lost Letter, The.*

"O Shekspire i o drame." *See* "Shakespeare and the Drama."

"O Sol, di cui questo bel sol è raggio" (Bembo). PFor 167.

"O stepeni uchastiia narodnosti v razvitii russkoi literatury" (Dobrolyubov). LTh 388.

"O Vanke Kaine, slavnom vore i moshennike kratkaya povest." LFFor 2306.

"O Yes" (Olsen). ShF 2022.

"O zhurnalnoy kritike." *See* "On Journal Criticism."

"Oaks, The" (Castro). PFor 280. See also *Beside the River Sar.*

Ōan shinshiki. See *Renga shinshiki.*

"O-A-O-A" (Sachs). PFor 1375-1376.

Oasis, The (McCarthy). LFEng 1721-1722.

Oates, Joyce Carol. LFEng 2007-2016; LFSup 406; PEng 2116-2121; PSup 408; ShF 552, 1961-1968; ShFSup 389.

Oath, The (Wiesel). LFFor 1927-1928.

Obaka san. See *Wonderful Fool.*

Obermann (Senancour). LFFor 2123-2124.

Oberon (Weber). DEng 2460.

"Obit" (Lowell, R.). PEng 1796.

"Object of Virtue" (Hale, N.). ShF 1570.

"Objects and Apparitions" (Paz). PEng 184.

"Oblako, ozero, bashnya." *See* "Cloud, Castle, Lake."

Oblako v shtanakh. See *Cloud in Pants, A.*

Oblivion Ha-Ha, The (Tate, J.). PEng 2836.

Oblomov (Goncharov). LFFor 705-707, 2315-2316; LTh 389.

"Oblong Box, The" (Poe). M&D 1333-1334.

Obra gruesa (Parra). PFor 1134.

Obrestad, Tor. LFFor 2363-2364; PFor 2195.

O'Brien, Edna. LFEng 2017-2023; ShF 1969-1976; ShFSup 390.

O'Brien, Edward J. ShF 561.

O'Brien, Fitz-James. ShF 1977-1981.

O'Brien, Flann. LFEng 2024-2032; ShF 666.

Obryv. See *Precipice, The.*

Obscene Bird of Night, The (Donoso). LFFor 498-500.

Obsceno pájaro de la noche, El. See *Obscene Bird of Night, The.*

"Observance" (Berry). PEng 149.

Observations in the Art of English Poesie (Campion). PEng 423-424.

"Observatory Ode, The" (Nims). PEng 2113.

Obstfelder, Sigbjørn. DFor 2473; PFor 2173.

Obyčejný život. See *Ordinary Life, An.*

Obyknovennaya istoriya. See *Common Story, A.*

O'Casey, Sean. DEng 1382-1393, 2376, 2447-2448.

Occasion for Loving (Gordimer). LFEng 1162-1164.

"Ode, Written during the Negociations with Buonaparte, in January 1814" (Southey). PEng 2683.
Odes (Horace). PFor 710, 715-718.
Odes and Eclogues (Dixon). PEng 819.
Odes et ballades (Hugo). PFor 732-733.
Odessa File, The (Forsyth). M&D 648.
Odets, Clifford. DEng 1394-1405.
Odi barbare. See *Barbarian Odes.*
Odin den Ivana Denisovicha. See *One Day in the Life of Ivan Denisovich.*
Odlévání zvonů. See *Casting of Bells, The.*
Odor of Sanctity, An (Yerby). LFEng 2989-2990.
"Odour of Chrysanthemums" (Lawrence, D. H.). ShF 1790-1791.
Odysseia. See *Odyssey, The.*
Odysseia. See *Odyssey: A Modern Sequel, The.*
Odyssey (Homer). LFFor 1999; PEng 2862; PFor 698-702, 706-708, 1750-1751, 1754-1756; ShF 1652, 1653-1654.
Odyssey, The (Kazantzakis). LFFor 918-919.
Odyssey: A Modern Sequel, The (Kazantzakis). PFor 787-790.
Ōe, Kenzaburō. LFFor 1192-1204; ShFSup 231-237.
Oedipus (Seneca). DFor 1691-1692, 2149.
Oedipus (Voltaire). DFor 1967.
Oedipus at Colonus (Sophocles). DFor 2109-2110.
Oedipus Rex. See *Oedipus Tyrannus.*
Oedipus the King. See *Oedipus Tyrannus.*
Oedipus Tyrannus (Sophocles). DEng 2141; DFor 1732-1733, 2105-2108; LTh 41.
Oehlenschläger, Adam Gottlob. DFor 1435-1442, 2468; LFFor 2335; PFor 2163-2164.
Œuvre au noir, L'. See *Abyss, The.*
Of All Mysteries (Ady). PFor 5-7.
"Of an European Literature" (Mazzini). LTh 1017, 1020.
Of Being Numerous (Oppen). PEng 2140.
Of Dramatic Poesy (Dryden). LTh 312, 406, 783.
Of Education (Milton). LTh 1349.
Of Flesh and Bone (Nims). PEng 2112.
"Of God we ask one favor" (Dickinson). PEng 808.
Of Grammatology (Derrida). LTh 357, 359, 1152-1153.

"Of His Majesty's receiving the news of the Duke of Buckingham's death" (Waller). PEng 3012-3013.
Of Human Bondage (Maugham). LFEng 1846-1847.
Of Love and Dust (Gaines). LFEng 1045-1047.
Of Men and Women (Buck). LFEng 338-339.
Of Mice and Men (Steinbeck). LFEng 2523.
"Of Modern Poetry" (Stevens). PEng 2744-2745.
"Of Pilgrimage" (Rilke). PFor 1330. See also *Book of Hours, The.*
"Of Poor B.B." (Brecht). PFor 223-224.
"Of Poverty and Death" (Rilke). PFor 1330. See also *Book of Hours, The.*
"Of the Different Stops and Cadences in Blank Verse" (Watts). PEng 3046-3047.
Of the Farm (Updike). LFEng 2687, 2689.
"Of the lady who can sleep when she pleases" (Waller). PEng 3013-3014.
"Of the last verses in the book" (Waller). PEng 3017.
"Of the Monastic Life" (Rilke). PFor 1330. See also *Book of Hours, The.*
"Of the Muse" (Sarton). PEng 2464.
Of the Progress of the Soule (Donne). PEng 834, 835.
Of Thee I Sing (Kaufman and Ryskind). DEng 1032-1034.
Of Time and the River (Wolfe). LFEng 2934-2936.
Of Women and Their Elegance (Mailer). LFEng 1785.
O'Faoláin, Seán. ShF 177, 253, 666, 669-670, 671-672, 673-674, 1996-2004; ShFSup 390.
Offending the Audience (Handke). DFor 858-859.
"Offering for Mr. Bluehart, An" (Wright, J.). PEng 3160-3161.
"Office Romances" (Trevor). ShFSup 322.
Officers and Gentlemen (Waugh). LFEng 2801-2802.
Oficio de tinieblas, 5 (Cela). LFFor 299-300.
O'Flaherty, Liam. ShF 253, 669-671, 2005-2012; ShFSup 390.
"Often I Am Permitted to Return to a Meadow" (Duncan). PEng 902.
Ogier, François. LTh 310.
Ogiwara Seisensui. PFor 2076.

Ognall, Leopold Horace. *See* **Carmichael, Harry.**

"Ogni bol'shogo goroda." *See* "Big-City Lights."

Ogniem i mieczem. See *With Fire and Sword.*

"Ogon', ty slyshish'." *See* "Fire Is Dying Down, The."

Ogre, The (Tournier). LFFor 1743-1745.

Oh Dad, Poor Dad, Mamma's Hung You in the Closet and I'm Feelin' So Sad (Kopit). DEng 1070-1071.

"Oh, I could laugh to hear the midnight wind" (Lamb). PEng 1634.

"Oh Thy Bright Eyes Must Answer Now" (Brontë). PEng 297-298.

"Oh, Welcome May" (Poliziano). PFor 1254-1255.

"Oh! were my Love" (Allingham). PEng 41-42.

Oh What a Paradise It Seems (Cheever). LFEng 502.

"Oh, Whistle, and I'll Come to You, My Lad" (James, M. R.). ShF 1691-1693.

O'Hara, Frank. PEng 191-192, **2122-2129.**

O'Hara, John. LFEng **2041-2054;** ShF 267, 546-547, **2013-2019.**

Ohmann, Richard. PEng 3452.

Ohrfeige und Sonstiges, Eine. See *Slap in the Face et cetera, A.*

Oidipous epi Kolōnōi. See *Oedipus at Colonus.*

Oidipous Tyrannos. See *Oedipus Tyrannus.*

"Oil of Dog" (Bierce). M&D 127-128.

"Oiseau blanc, L'." *See* "White Bird, The."

Oiseaux. See *Birds.*

"Oiseaux sont en neige" (Cocteau). PFor 371. See also *Vocabulaire.*

Ojciec zadżumionych. See *Father of the Plague-Stricken, The.*

Ojos de los enterrados, Los. See *Eyes of the Interred, The.*

Okhlopkov, Nikolai. DEng 2238-2239.

Oklahoma! (Rodgers and Hammerstein). DEng 1591, 1595, 2471.

Økland, Einar. LFFor 2364; PFor 2195.

Okno bez krat (Slonimski). PFor 1434.

Oktave (Pavlović). PFor 1165.

Oku no hosomichi. See *Narrow Road to the Deep North, The.*

Ōkuma Kotomichi. PFor 2073.

Ōkura Toraaki. LTh 1789.

Okura, Yamanoe no. *See* Yamanoe no Okura.

Okuretekita seinen (Ōe). LFFor 1195-1197.

Olav Audunssøn. See *Master of Hestviken, The.*

Old and the Young, The (Pirandello). LFFor 1302.

"Old Apple Tree, The" (Dunbar). PSup 117-118.

Old Bachelor, The (Congreve). DEng 402-404.

Old Cap. Collier Library. ShF 759.

Old Creole Days (Cable). ShF 225, 534, 616.

"Old Doc Rivers" (Williams, W. C.). ShF 2442-2443.

Old English Apollonius of Tyre, The. LFFor 2014-2015.

Old English Peep Show, The (Dickinson). M&D 511.

"Old Familiar Faces, The" (Lamb). PEng 1635.

"Old Fashioned Cincinnati Blues, The" (Young). PEng 3215.

"Old Fools, The" (Larkin). PEng 1675.

Old Fortunatus (Dekker). PEng 767-768.

"Old Gypsy, The" (Vörösmarty). PFor 1669.

Old Heads and Young Hearts (Boucicault). DEng 268.

Old House in the Country, The (Reese). PEng 2346.

"Old Ironsides" (Holmes). PEng 1371-1372.

"Old King, The" (de la Mare). PEng 775-776.

Old Man (Gorky). DFor 785.

"Old Man and Jim, The" (Riley). PEng 2379-2380.

Old Man and the Sea, The (Hemingway). LFEng 1339, 1347-1348, 3061-3062, 3272-3274.

Old Man Dies, The (Simenon). LFFor 1600.

Old Man Rubbing His Eyes (Bly). PEng 225.

Old Man Savarin and Other Stories. ShF 636.

"Old Man's Journey" (MacLeish). PEng 1859.

"Old Manuscript, An" (Kafka). ShF 1732.

Old Men at the Zoo, The (Wilson, A.). LFEng 2903-2904.

Old Mortality (Porter). LFEng 2104-2105; ShF 13.

Old Mortality (Scott). LFEng 2371-2373.

"Old Neighborhood, The" (Dreiser). ShF 1309-1310.

"Old Night and Sleep" (Dubie). PSup 107.

Old Ones, The (Wesker). DEng 2018-2019.

Old Saint Paul's (Ainsworth). LFEng 31-32.

"Old Swimmin'-Hole, The" (Riley). PEng 2381-2382.

"On Imagination" (Wheatley). PEng 3052-3053, 3058.

On Imitation (Dionysius). LTh 1192.

"On Inhabiting an Orange" (Miles). PSup 276.

"On Journal Criticism" (Pushkin). LTh 1179.

"On Literary Evolution" (Tynyanov). LTh 1480-1481.

"On Looking at a Copy of Alice Meynell's Poems" (Lowell, A.). PEng 1769.

"On Lookout Mountain" (Hayden). PEng 1252.

"On Love" (Shelley). PEng 2544, 2552.

"On Marriage" (Crashaw). PEng 669.

"On Mrs. Arabella Hart, Singing" (Congreve). PEng 557.

On Moral Fiction (Gardner, J.). LFEng 1070-1071; LTh 535.

"On My First Daughter" (Jonson). PEng 1510, 3307.

"On My First Son" (Jonson). PEng 1510, 3307; PSup 76.

"On My Shield" (Archilochus). PFor 89-90.

On Naïve and Sentimental Poetry (Schiller). LTh 670, 1298; PFor 1401, 1404.

On ne badine pas avec l'amour. See No Trifling with Love.

On Neoclassicism (Praz). LTh 1168.

On Oratory (Cicero). LTh 294-295, 1638.

On Photography (Sontag). LTh 1365-1366.

"On Poetry" (George). LTh 573.

On Poetry: A Rapsody (Swift). PEng 2808.

"On Poetry in General" (Hazlitt). LTh 653.

On purge bébé. See Going to Pot.

On Racine (Barthes). LTh 103, 106, 1195.

"On Reading Books" (Brecht). ShF 1005.

"On Reason and Imagination" (Hazlitt). LTh 650.

"On Recollection" (Wheatley). PEng 3059-3060.

On Religion (Schleiermacher). LTh 1702.

On Romances (Giraldi Cinthio). LTh 585.

"On Saturday Afternoon" (Sillitoe). ShF 2227, 2228.

"On Seeing the Elgin Marbles" (Keats). PEng 1549.

On Sepulchers (Foscolo). PFor 495-496.

"On Sitting Down to Read King Lear Once Again" (Keats). PEng 1547.

On Socialist Realism (Sinyavsky) LFFor 1628, 1630; LTh 1352-1354.

"On Some Verses of Vergil" (Montaigne). LTh 1044.

"On Stella's Birth-day 1719" (Swift). PEng 2807.

"On Stories" (Lewis, C. S.). ShF 81.

On the Aesthetic Education of Man (Schiller). LTh 1297.

"On the Affray in King Street" (Wheatley). PEng 3054.

On the Ancient Orators (Dionysius). LTh 1643.

"On the Ancient Sepulchral Bas-Relief" (Leopardi). PFor 863-864. See also Canti.

On the Arrangement of Words (Dionysius). LTh 383-384.

"On the Arrival in England of Lord Byron's Remains" (Lamb). PEng 1636-1637.

"On the Banks of the Kalota" (Ady). PFor 6.

"On the Beach" (Hale, N). ShF 1570.

On the Big Wind (Madden). LFEng 1761, 1768.

"On the Building of Springfield" (Lindsay). PEng 1725.

"On the Coronation of the Most August Monarch K. James II, and Queen Mary" (Prior). PEng 2288.

"On the Death of Dr. Robert Levet" (Johnson). PEng 1506.

"On the Death of Edmund Waller" (Behn). PEng 129-130.

"On the Death of Mr. Snider Murder'd by Richardson" (Wheatley). PEng 3053-3054.

"On the Death of the Late Earl of Rochester" (Behn). PEng 129.

"On the Death of the Rev. Dr. Sewell, 1769" (Wheatley). PEng 3057.

"On the Death of the Rev. Mr. George Whitefield, 1770" (Wheatley). PEng 3056-3057.

On the Education of an Orator. See Institutio oratoria.

"On the Eve" (Simpson). PEng 2606-2607.

On the Eve (Turgenev). LFFor 1775.

"On the Excellent Poems of My Most Worthy Friend, Mr. Thomas Flatman" (Cotton). PEng 585.

"On the Genius and Tendency of the Writing of Thomas Carlyle" (Mazzini). LTh 1019.

"On the Hill Late at Night" (Berry). PEng 153.

"On the Historical Drama" (Mazzini). LTh 1020.

On the History of Religion and Philosophy in Germany (Heine). LTh 662.

"On the Holidays of All Saints' Day" (León). PFor 841.

"On the Industrial Highway" (Hoffman). PEng 1359.

"On the Journals *Zvezda* and *Leningrad*" (Zhdanov). LTh 1607.

"On the Lake" (Goethe). PFor 583.

"On the Living Poets" (Hazlitt). LTh 652.

On the Marriage of Mercury and Philology (Capella). PFor 2111-2112.

"On the Minor Works of Dante" (Mazzini). LTh 1018.

"On the Morning of Christ's Nativity" (Milton). PEng 2006-2007.

On the Motion and Immobility of Douve (Bonnefoy). PSup 44-45.

"On the Move" (Gunn). PEng 1171-1172, 1176.

On the Nature of Things. See *De rerum natura*.

On the Origin of Species (Darwin). PEng 3348.

On the Principles of Human Action (Hazlitt). LTh 798.

"On the Puppet Theatre" (Kleist). LFEng 3247-3248.

"On the Receipt of My Mother's Picture Out of Norfolk" (Cowper). PEng 613-615.

"On the Repertoire of the Dramatic Theaters and Measures for Its Improvement" (Zhdanov). LTh 1603.

On the Road (Kerouac). LFEng 1520-1522, 1524.

"On the Road to San Romano" (Breton). PFor 234.

"On the Short Story" (Canby). ShF 72-73.

On the Sublime (Longinus). LTh 904-909, 1596, 1642, 1679-1680; PEng 3466-3467.

On the Sublime (Schiller). LTh 1298-1299.

"On the Supernatural in Poetry" (Radcliffe). ShF 472.

"On the Teaching of Modern Literature" (Trilling). LTh 1455.

"On the Tram" (Kafka). ShF 1734.

On the Twofold Abundance of Words and Things. See *De Duplici Copia Verborum ac Rerum*.

"On the Universality and Other Attributes of the God of Nature" (Freneau). PEng 1036-1037.

"On the Walpole Road" (Freeman). ShF 370-371.

"On this auspicious, memorable morn" (Byrom). PEng 395-396.

"On Trains" (McPherson). ShF 582-583.

"On Wit and Humour" (Hazlitt). LTh 653.

On World Government (Dante). PFor 390.

On Your Toes (Rodgers and Hart, L.). DEng 903-904.

Once in a Lifetime (Kaufman and Hart, M.). DEng 908-909.

"Once Only" (Seifert). PSup 354.

"Once-Over, The" (Blackburn). PEng 199.

Oncle Charles s'est enfermé (Simenon). LFFor 1598-1599.

Onde estivestes de noite (Lispector). ShFSup 168.

"Ondes." See "Waves."

"Ondine" (Barnard). PSup 28-29.

"1(a" (Cummings). PEng 705.

"One Against Thebes" (Gordon). ShF 1521-1522.

"One Arm" (Williams, T.). ShF 2438-2439.

"One Bone to Another" (Popa). PFor 1270.

One Day in the Life of Ivan Denisovich (Solzhenitsyn). LFFor 1636-1637, 1642-1643, 2327-2328.

"One Evening at Home" (Petőfi). PFor 1218.

One Flew over the Cuckoo's Nest (Kesey). LFEng 1526, 1532-1534.

One Foot in the Grave (Dickinson). M&D 513.

One for My Dame (Webb). M&D 1692-1693.

158-Pound Marriage, The (Irving). LFEng 1420-1421.

150,000,000 (Mayakovsky). PFor 989-990.

One Hundred More Poems from the Japanese (Rexroth, trans.). PFor 1716.

One Hundred Years of Solitude (García Márquez). LFFor 617-619.

"One-Legged Man, The" (Sassoon). PEng 2472.

One Lonely Night (Spillane). M&D 1511.

One Million Dead (Gironella). LFFor 663-665.

One, None and a Hundred-Thousand (Pirandello). LFFor 1305-1306.

One O'Clock! (Lewis). DEng 1137-1139.

One of Life's Slaves (Lie). LFFor 2341.

One of Our Girls (Howard, B.). DEng 971.

One of Ours (Cather). LFEng 480.

"One of These Days" (Garcia Márquez). ShF 702-704.

One Sentence on Tyranny (Illyés). PFor 742, 744.

"One True Friend" (O'Faoláin). ShF 1998-1999.

One Way or Another (Sciascia). LFFor 1522.

"One Word" (Benn). PFor 173.

O'Neill, Egan. See **Linington, Elizabeth.**

O'Neill, Eugene. DEng 1406-1417, 2401.

O'Neill-O'Flaherty series, The (Farrell). LFEng 910-912.

"One's-Self I Sing" (Whitman). PEng 3065.

"Ones Who Walk Away from Omelas, The" (Le Guin). ShFSup 145.

Onetti, Juan Carlos. LFFor 1205-1215, 2295.

Ong, Walter J. LTh 296, 957, **1079-1085.**

Onion Eaters, The (Donleavy). LFEng 786.

Onkel, Onkel. See *Mister, Mister.*

Only a Fiddler (Andersen). LFFor 2336.

Only Children (Lurie). LFSup 251, 253-254.

Only Game in Town, The (Gilroy). DEng 781-782.

"Only Man on Liberty Street, The" (Kelley). ShF 582.

"Only One, The" (Hölderlin). PFor 688.

Only Ten Minutes to Buffalo (Grass). DSup 157.

Ono no Komachi. PFor 2059-2060.

Onofri, Arturo. PFor 2038, 2045-2046.

O'Nolan, Brian. See **O'Brien, Flann.**

Ooblyfsels (Breytenbach). PSup 56.

"Open Boat, The" (Crane, S.). ShF 236, 1217-1219.

Open Couple--Very Open, An (Fo and Rame). DSup 113.

Open Heart. See *Book of Bebb, The.*

Open House (Roethke). PEng 2409.

Open Mind, The (Bernanos). LFFor 150-151.

"Open Parable, The" (Eastman). ShF 75.

"Open the Gates" (Kunitz). PSup 244.

"Open Window, The" (Saki). ShF 2173.

"Open Window, The" (Tranströmer). PFor 1527-1528.

Opening of the Field, The (Duncan). PEng 902.

Openings (Berry). PEng 150-151.

Opéra (Cocteau). PFor 372.

Opera dello sghigazzo, L' (Fo). DSup 114.

"Opéra des girafes, L'" (Prévert). PFor 1279.

Opera omnia (Poliziano). PFor 1255.

"Operation, The" (Sexton). PEng 2523.

Operation Sidewinder (Shepard). DEng 1762.

"Opere minori di Dante." *See* "On the Minor Works of Dante."

Operetta (Gombrowicz). DFor 774-775.

Opitz, Martin. LFFor 2150, 2151; PFor 1908.

Opowieści o pilocie Pirxie. See *Tales of Pirx the Pilot.*

Oppen, George. PEng 2136-2141; PSup 408.

Oppenheim, E. Phillips. M&D 1273-1278.

Oppenheimer, Joel. PEng 2142-2147; PSup 408.

"Öppna fönstret, Det." *See* "Open Window, The."

Optimist's Daughter, The (Welty). LFEng 2827-2828.

Or: La Merveilleuse Histoire du géneral Johann August Suter, L'. See *Sutter's Gold.*

"Or Else" (Middleton, C.). PEng 1991.

"Oracion del 9 de febrero de 1913." *See* "Prayer of the Ninth of February."

Orality and Literacy (Ong). LTh 1084.

Oralloossa (Bird). DEng 216-217.

"Orange, The" (Ponge). PFor 1264.

Oration Delivered Before the Phi Beta Kappa Society, Cambridge, An. See *American Scholar, The.*

Orator, The (Cicero). LTh 294-295.

Orator ad M. Brutum (Cicero). LTh 1638.

Orators, The (Foote). DEng 646-648.

Orazia, La (Aretino). DFor 100-101.

Orbecche (Giraldi Cinthio). DFor 716-717.

Orchard, The (Sa'di). PFor 1379-1381.

Orchard Keeper, The (McCarthy). LFSup 267.

"Orchards, The" (Thomas). ShF 2324.

Orchestra (Davies). PEng 747, 750-753, 754, 3290.

Orczy, Baroness. M&D 1279-1285; ShF 752-753.

Ordeal of Richard Feverel, The (Meredith). LFEng 1865-1867.

"Ordeal of the Bier" (Arany). PFor 82.

Order, The (Hochwälder). DFor 931-932.

"Order of Insects" (Gass). ShF 1480.

Orderly Life, An (Yglesias). LFEng 2997-2999.

Ordet. See *Word, The.*

"Ordinance of Wine" (Neruda). PFor 1076.

See also *Residence on Earth.*

Ordinary Life, An (Čapek). LFFor 278.

Ördög, Az. See *Devil, The.*

Oreach Nata Lalun. See *Guest for the Night, A.*

"Oread" (H. D.). PEng 1257-1261, 1262.

Oresteia (Aeschylus). DFor 20-21, 2101, 2103.

Orestes (Euripides). DFor 2117.

Orestēs (Rítsos). PFor 1970.

Orfalea, Greg. ShF 2752.

Orfeo (Poliziano). DFor 2394; PFor 1249, 1251-1252, 2011.

"Orgy: An Idyll, The" (de la Mare). ShF 1252.

Oriani, Alfredo. LFFor 2238.

Oricellari, Orti. LTh 1459.

Orientales, Les (Hugo). PFor 733.

Origen. LTh 1644.

"Origin of Sadness, The" (Morris). ShFSup 206.

Origin of the Brunists, The (Coover). LFEng 620-621.

Original Child Bomb (Merton). PEng 1976.

Orison (Arrabal). DFor 2261.

Örkény, István. DSup 294-301.

Orlandino (Edgeworth). ShF 1329.

Orlando furioso (Ariosto). LTh 131, 366, 584, 1662; PFor 97-100, 2012-2014; ShF 138.

Orlando Furioso (Greene, R.). DEng 839-840.

Orlando innamorato (Boiardo). PFor 97-98, 2012-2013.

Orléans, Charles d'. *See* **Charles d'Orléans.**

Orley Farm (Trollope). LFEng 2654-2656.

Orlock, Carol. ShF 2753.

Ormond (Edgeworth, M.). LFEng 867-868.

Ornithes. See Birds, The.

Ørnsbro, Jess. PFor 2196.

Oroonoko (Behn). DEng 168-170; LFEng 222, 3019; ShF 502.

Oroonoko (Southerne). DEng 2451.

Orphan, The (Otway). DEng 1440-1441, 1449-1450.

Orphan, The (Rabe). DEng 1549-1550.

Orphan Island (Macaulay). LFSup 261.

"Orpheus" (Snodgrass). PEng 2659.

Orr, Gregory. PEng 2148-2155; PSup 408.

Orrego Luco, Luis. LFFor 2286-2287.

Országh-Hviezdoslav, Pavol. DFor 2285.

Ortadirek. See Wind from the Plain, The.

Ortega y Gasset, José. LFEng 3224-3225; LTh 194.

Orthodoxy (Chesterton). PEng 496.

Orton, Joe. DEng 1418-1427.

O'Ruddy, The (Crane and Barr). LFEng 646.

Örvar-Odds saga. LFFor 2333.

Orwell, George. LFEng 2055-2064; PEng 1699-1700.

Orzeszkowa, Eliza. LFFor 2063.

87 pesama (Pavlović). PFor 1164-1165.

Osanai Kaoru. DFor 2432-2433.

Osborn, Carolyn. ShF 2754.

Osborne, John. DEng 1428-1437, 2385-2386.

"Oskar" (Walser, R.). ShFSup 347.

Osman (Gundulić). PFor 2260-2261.

Osman (Tristan). DFor 1893-1895.

Ossi di seppia. See Bones of the Cuttlefish.

Ossian. LTh 669-671.

Ossian tales (Macpherson). PEng 3329.

"Ostanovka v pustyne." *See* "Halt in the Wilderness, A."

Osterman Weekend, The (Ludlum). M&D 1107.

Östersjöar. See Baltics.

Ostrekoff Jewels, The (Oppenheim). M&D 1275.

"Ostrov Borngolm." *See* "Song of Bornholm, The."

Ostrovityane. See Islanders, The.

Ostrovsky, Alexander. DFor 1443-1452, 2454.

Osudy dobrého vojáka Švejka ve světove války. See *Good Soldier Schweik, The.*

O. T. (Andersen). LFFor 2336.

Otero, Blas de. PFor 1109-1118.

Otfrid von Weissenburg. PFor 1897.

Othello (Shakespeare). DEng 1717-1719, 2281, 2282.

Other, The (Unamuno y Jugo). DFor 1914-1915.

Other Inquisitions (Borges). LTh 192.

Other Karen, The (Johnston). M&D 940.

"Other Kingdom" (Forster). ShF 1388-1389, 1390-1391.

Other Men's Daughters (Stern). LFSup 364-365.

"Other Paris, The" (Gallant). ShF 1438-1439.

Other Paris, The (Gallant). LFEng 1052-1053.

Other Times (Lawler). DEng 1117. See also *Doll Trilogy, The.*

"Other Two, The" (Wharton). ShF 707.

Other Voices, Other Rooms (Capote). LFEng 444, 445-446, 447-448.

"Other Way, The" (Grau). ShF 1531.

Other Worlds (Cyrano). LFFor 396-403.

Otherwise Engaged (Gray). DEng 809-811.

Ōtomo no Tabito. PFor 2057.

Ōtomo no Yakamochi. PFor 2057-2058.

Otoño del patriarca, El. See Autumn of the Patriarch, The.

Otras inquisiciones. See Other Inquisitions.

Otro, El. See Other, The.

Ottar Trallings leftnads-målning (Cederborgh). LFFor 2335.

"Ottawa Valley, The" (Munro). ShFSup 211-212.

"Otto and the Magi" (Connell). ShF 1181.

8 anime in una bomba (Marinetti). LTh 996, 233, 859.

Ottsy i deti. See *Fathers and Sons.*

Otuel. ShF 445.

Otway, Thomas. DEng 1438-1452.

Otzhitoye vremya. See *Case, The.*

Our Ancestors (Calvino). LFFor 237, 238.

Our Betters (Maugham). DEng 1309-1310.

"Our Cousin, Mr. Poe" (Tate). LTh 1428.

"Our English Syllabus" (Lewis). LTh 896.

Our Father's Failing (Horovitz). DEng 962.

Our Flowers & Nice Bones (Middleton, C.). PEng 1988-1989.

Our Gang (Roth). LFEng 2304.

Our Husband Has Gone Mad Again (Rotimi). DEng 1624-1625, 1629.

Our Lady of the Flowers (Genet). LFFor 628-629.

Our Late Night (Shawn). DSup 335.

Our Mrs. McChesney (Ferber and Hobart). DEng 586, 589.

Our Mutual Friend (Dickens, C.). LFEng 754-755.

Our Time Is Gone. See *Fury Chronicle, The.*

Our Town (Wilder). DEng 2046-2049.

Ours (Robertson). DEng 1608-1609.

Oursler, Fulton. *See* **Abbot, Anthony.**

Ousmane Sembène. *See* **Sembène, Ousmane.**

Out at Sea (Mrożek). DFor 1381.

Out of Africa (Dinesen). ShF 1281.

Out of His Head (Aldrich). M&D 12; ShF 750-751.

"Out of Lycophron" (Sedley). PEng 2507.

"Out-of-the-Body Travel" (Plumly). PEng 2237.

Out-of-the-Body Travel (Plumly). PEng 2237-2238.

"Out of the Cradle Endlessly Rocking" (Whitman). PEng 3071.

Out of the Silent Planet (Lewis, C. S.). LFEng 1654-1655.

Outcast, The (Pirandello). LFFor 1301.

"Outcasts of Poker Flat, The" (Harte). ShF 587, 594-595, 1594-1597.

Outcry, The (James, H.). DEng 995.

Outer Dark (McCarthy). LFSup 267-268.

"Outlaw, The" (Heaney). PEng 1269.

Outlyer and Ghazals (Harrison). PEng 1229-1231.

"Outsider, The" (Lovecraft). ShF 1822.

Outsider, The (Sabato). LFFor 1464-1465.

Outsider, The (Wright, R.). LFEng 2981-2983.

Outsider in Amsterdam (van de Wetering). M&D 1629-1631.

Ou-yang Hsiu. PFor 1788.

"Oval Portrait, The" (Poe). ShF 474.

"Ove romita e stanca si sedea" (Bembo). PFor 167-168.

Over ævne, annet stykke. See *Beyond Our Power.*

Over ævne, første stykke. See *Pastor Sang.*

"Over Colorado" (Walcott). PEng 3005.

"Over Sir John's Hill" (Thomas, D.). PEng 2886-2887.

"Over the Carnage Rose Prophetic a Voice" (Whitman). PEng 3072.

"Over the Rivers That Flow" (Camões). PFor 262.

"Over 2000 Illustrations and a Complete Concordance" (Bishop). PEng 185-186.

Overcoat, The (Gogol). LFEng 3267, 3276-3278; ShF 120, 187-188.

Overholser, Stephen D. LFEng 3198.

Overkomplet, En (Drachmann). LFFor 2339.

Overlaid (Davies). DEng 468.

Øverland, Arnulf. PFor 2183.

Overland Monthly. ShF 587.

Overskou, Thomas. DFor 2469.

Overture to Death (Marsh). M&D 1192.

Ovid. LTh 1654; **PFor 1119-1128,** 1282, 1283, 2097; **ShF 2025-2034.**

Ovid's Banquet of Sense (Chapman). PEng 458-460.

Ovonramwen Nogbaisi (Rotimi). DEng 1625, 1626-1627.

"Ovtsebyk." *See* "Musk-ox, The."

Owen, Philip. *See* **Pentecost, Hugh.**

Owen, Wilfred. PEng 2156-2163.

Owens, Rochelle. DEng 1453-1462.

Owl Answers, The (Kennedy). DSup 214-215.

"Owl King, The" (Dickey, J.). PEng 796.

Ox-Bow Incident, The (Clark). LFEng 545-546, 548-550; ShF 607.

"Ox Cart, The" (Petőfi). PFor 1221.

"Oxenhope" (Warner). ShFSup 357-358.

Oxford Blood (Fraser). M&D 658.

Oxyrhynchus (MacLennan). LFEng 1741.

Oyono-Mbia. DFor 2268, 2270-2271.
"Oyster, The" (Ponge). PFor 1263, 1264.
Ozaki, Hōsai. PFor 2076.
Ozhog. See *Burn, The.*

Ozick, Cynthia. ShF 2035-2039; ShFSup 390.
Ozidi (Clark). DSup 57-58.
Ozu Norinaga. *See* **Motoori Norinaga.**
"Ozymandias" (Shelley). PEng 1608.

P

P., W. S. *See* **Henry, O.**
Pa Chin. LFFor 2107.
Pabellón de reposo. See *Rest Home.*
Pachmuss, Temira. LFEng 3297-3298.
Packer, Nancy Huddleston. ShF 2755.
Pact with Satan, A (Holton). M&D 902.
Pacuvius, Marcus. DFor 2146.
Padmasambhava. PFor 2242.
Padrona, La (Betti). DFor 207-208.
"Paean to Place" (Niedecker). PSup 299-300.
"Paese infido" (Calvino). ShF 1044.
Paesi tuoi. See *Harvesters, The.*
Pagan Place, A (O'Brien, E.). LFEng 2021.
Pagan Salute (Radnóti). PFor 1312.
Page, Thomas Nelson. ShF 616.
"Page d'écriture" (Prévert). PFor 1278.
Pagenstreiche (Kotzebue). DFor 1087-1088.
Paige, Richard. *See* **Koontz, Dean R.**
Pai-mao mü. See *White-Haired Girl, The.*
"Pain, Le." *See* "Loaf of Bread, The."
"Pain for a Daughter" (Sexton). PEng 2524-2525.
"Painful Case, A" (Joyce). ShF 1722.
Painted Bird, The (Kosinski). LFEng 1559-1561.
Painted Face, The (Stubbs). M&D 1549-1551.
Painted Lady, The (Sagan). LFFor 1478.
"Painted Skin, The" (P'u). ShFSup 246-248.
"Painter Dreaming in the Scholar's House, The" (Nemerov). PEng 2088.
Painter of His Dishonor, The (Calderón). DFor 308-309.
Painter of Signs, The (Narayan). LFEng 1971.
"Painture" (Lovelace). PEng 1761.
Pair of Drawers, A. See *Bloomers, The.*
"Pair So Unequal" (Salinas). PFor 1388-1389. See also *Sea of San Juan, The.*
Paixão segundo G. H., A (Lispector). LFSup 244.
"Pájaro, El." *See* "Bird, The."
Pal Joey (Rodgers and Hart, L.). DEng 904.
"Palace, The" (Bates). ShF 270; ShFSup 31.
Palace of Eternal Youth, The (Hung). DFor 2326.

Palace of Pleasure, The (Painter). ShF 147, 487.
Palace of the Peacock (Harris). LFSup 144-147. See also *Guiana Quartet, The.*
Palacký, František. PFor 1799-1800.
"Palais de Justice" (Helprin). ShFSup 119.
Palazzeschi, Aldo. LFFor 2240-2241.
Pale Fire (Nabokov). LFEng 1953.
Pale Horse, Pale Rider (Porter). LFEng 2106-2107.
"Pale Pink Roast, The" (Paley). ShF 2042.
Paley, Grace. ShF 551, **2040-2044;** ShFSup 390.
Palimpsestes (Genette). LTh 563.
Palm, Göran. PFor 2192.
Palm-Wine Drinkard, The (Tutuola). LFFor 1785-1787.
Palmàs, Kostìs. PFor 1952-1954.
"Palmatoria de cobre, La." *See* "Copper Ferule, The."
Palmer, Leslie John. *See* **Beeding, Francis.**
Palmer, Stuart. M&D 1286-1292.
Palombe (Camus, J. P.). ShF 498.
Palomino (Jolley). LFSup 178-179.
Pálsson, Sigurthur. PFor 2200-2201.
Paludan, Jacob. LFFor 2354.
Paludan-Müller, Frederik. PFor 2166-2167.
Pamela (Richardson, S.). LFEng 2246, 2248-2250, 3013, 3072-3073, 3112-3114. See also *Shamela.*
"Pamiętnik." *See* "Monument."
Pamiętnik znaleziony w wannie. See *Memoirs Found in a Bathtub.*
Pan (Hamsun). LFFor 771-773, 2346
"Pan and Pitys" (Landor). PEng 1644.
Pan Cogito (Herbert). PFor 657, 659.
Pan Geldhab (Fredro). DSup 137-138.
Pan Jowialski (Fredro). DFor 2277; DSup 140.
Pan Ku. LTh 1773-1774.
Pan Michael (Sienkiewicz). LFFor 1565, 1573, 1574-1575.
Pan Tadeusz (Mickiewicz). PFor 1017, 1022-1024, 2125.
Pan Wołodyjowski. See *Pan Michael.*
Panama (McGuane). LFSup 293-294.

Passing Time (Butor). LFFor 216-217.

"Passion" (Cunningham). PSup 75.

"Passion, The" (Elýtis). PFor 465, 1967. See also *Axion Esti, The.*

Passion Artist, The (Hawkes). LFEng 1310-1312.

Passion Flower, The (Benavente). DFor 179-180, 2502.

Passion of New Eve, The (Carter). LFSup 74.

Passion Play (Nichols). DSup 284.

Passionate North, The (Sansom). ShF 275.

Passionate Shepheard (Breton, N.). PEng 279.

"Passionate Shepherd to His Love, The" (Marlowe). PEng 1901-1902.

Passione (Innaurato). DSup 203-204.

"Passione, La" (Manzoni). PFor 959. See also *Sacred Hymns, The.*

"Passos da cruz." *See* "Stations of the Cross."

Passport to the War (Kunitz). PSup 243.

"Past One at Rooney's" (Henry). ShF 1631.

Pastan, Linda. PEng 2169-2177; PSup 408.

Pasternak, Boris. LFFor 1229-1239, 2327; PFor 1153-1162, 2149-2150; ShF 2057-2063.

Pastime of Pleasure, The (Hawes). PEng 3285.

"Pastime of the Queen of Fairies, The" (Newcastle). PEng 2095.

Pastor fido, Il. See *Faithful Shepherd, The.*

Pastor Sang (Bjørnson). DFor 218-219, 2473.

"Pastoral Care" (Gardner). ShF 1462.

Pastoral Symphony, The (Gide). LFFor 641, 645-646.

Pastorales (Jiménez). PFor 751.

Pastorall Elegie, A (Drummond). PEng 867.

Pata de la raposa, La. See *Fox's Paw, The.*

Pataxanadu and Other Prose (Middleton, C.). PEng 1987, 1990.

Patchen, Kenneth. PEng 2178-2183.

Pater, Walter. LFEng 2065-2076; LTh 1086-1090, 1245, 1400, 1405-1407, 1410-1411, 1731-1732, 1734-1735; ShF 515.

Paterson (Williams, W. C.). PEng 3113-3119, 3366-3367, 3392.

Path, The (Delibes). LFFor 449-450.

Path to the Nest of Spiders, The (Calvino). LFFor 234-236, 2251.

Patience (Gilbert and Sullivan). DEng 764-765.

Patience (Pearl-Poet). PEng 2197, 2200-2202, 3254; ShF 2068, 2069-2070.

"Patience, Hard Thing" (Hopkins). PEng 1402.

"Patience of Job in Detroit, The" (Berrigan). ShF 372-373.

Patmore, Coventry. PEng 2184-2195.

"Patmos" (Hölderlin). PFor 688.

Patraput (Tagore). PFor 1484-1485.

Patrasket (Bergman). DFor 190-191.

"Patriarch, The" (Colette). ShF 1165-1166.

"Patricia, Edith and Arnold" (Thomas). ShF 2322.

Patrick, John. DEng 1463-1471.

Patrick, Q. *See* **Quentin, Patrick.**

Patrick, Robert. DEng 1472-1480.

Patrick Pearse Motel, The (Leonard). DSup 229-230.

Patrie (Sardou). DFor 1634-1637.

Patriot, The (Connell). LFEng 577-578.

"Patriotic Debate, The" (Chartier). PFor 347-348.

Patriotic Gore (Wilson). LTh 1549.

"Patriotism" (Mishima). ShF 1937-1938.

Patriots, The (Kingsley). DEng 1042.

"Patrol, The" (Lem). ShFSup 153.

"Pattern of Perfection, The" (Hale, N.). ShF 1571.

Pattern of Perfection, The (Hale, N.). ShF 1570-1571.

Patterns of Childhood (Wolf). LFFor 1933.

Pattes de mouche, Les. See *Scrap of Paper, A.*

Paul, Jean. See **Jean Paul.**

Paul Among the Jews (Werfel). DFor 1999.

Paul and Mary. See *Paul and Virginia.*

Paul and Virginia (Saint-Pierre). LFFor 2121.

Paul Campenhaye, Specialist in Criminology (Fletcher). M&D 622.

Paul Lange and Tora Parsberg (Bjørnson). DFor 219-220.

Paul Schippel Esq. (Sternheim). DFor 1742-1743.

Paulding, James Kirke. LTh 1743.

Paulinus of Nola. PFor 2109-2110.

"Paul's Case" (Cather). ShF 252, 800-801, 1077-1078.

Paulus unter den Juden. See *Paul Among the Jews.*

"Paura alla Scala." *See* "Scala Scare, The."

Pause Under the Sky (Beck). ShF 935.

Pauvre Christ de Bomba, Le. See *Poor Christ of Bomba, The.*

Pavese, Cesare. LFFor 1240-1250, 2249; PFor 2048, 2049; ShF 2064-2067.

Pavić, Milorad. PFor 2257-2258.

Pavičić, Ante Tresić. PFor 2264.
Pavlović, Miodrag. PFor 1163-1168, 2257;
PSup 408.
"Pavlovic Variations" (Middleton, C.). PEng
1988-1989.
Pavlovski, Radovan. PFor 2273.
Pavlovsky, Eduardo. DFor 2445.
Pavšič, Vladimir. *See* Bor, Matej.
Pawnbroker, The (Wallant). LFEng 2762-2763.
Payack, Paul J. J. ShF 2758.
Payment Deferred (Forester). M&D 641-643.
Payne, John Howard. DEng 1481-1487,
2397.
"Paysages tristes." *See* "Sad Landscapes."
Paysan parvenu, Le. See *Fortunate Peasant,*
The.
"Paysans, Les." *See* "Peasants, The."
Paz, Octavio. PFor 1169-1175, 2228; PSup
408.
Pazos de Ulloa, Los. See *Son of the*
Bondwoman, The.
Pea, Enrico. LFFor 2240.
Peabody, Richard Myers, Jr. ShF 2759.
Peace (Aristophanes). DFor 2126.
"Peace" (Brooke). PEng 306.
"Peace" (Rítsos). PFor 1350.
Peace After War (Gironella). LFFor 665.
"Peace and Plenty" (Kennedy). PEng 1573.
"Peace of Mowsle Barton, The" (Saki). M&D
1456.
Peace of the Augustans, The (Saintsbury). LTh
1266.
"Peace of Utrecht, The" (Munro). ShFSup 209-
211.
Peach Blossom Fan, The (K'ung). DFor 2327.
"Peach Blossom Spring" (T'ao Ch'ien). PFor
1492.
"Peaches, The" (Thomas). ShF 2320-2321.
Peacock, Thomas Love. LFEng 2077-2086;
LTh 1696-1698, 1710.
Peacock's Tail, The (Hoagland). LFSup 154-
155.
Pearl, The (Pearl-Poet). PEng 2197, 2204-
2206, 3253-3254; ShF 2068, 2072-2075,
2078.
Pearl, The (Steinbeck). LFEng 2526-2527.
Pearl-Poet, The. PEng 2196-2209; ShF 2068-
2078.
Pearson's Magazine. ShF 771.
"Peasant Marey, The" (Dostoevski). ShF 205,
1295.

"Peasant Poet" (Clare). PEng 514.
Peasants, The (Reymont). LFFor 1409-1410.
"Peasants, The" (Verhaeren). PFor 1621-1622.
See also *Flamandes, Les.*
Peau de chagrin, La. See *Wild Ass's Skin, The.*
Pechos privilegiados, Los (Ruiz de Alarcón).
DFor 1607.
Pedersen, Knut. *See* **Hamsun, Knut.**
"Pederson Kid, The" (Gass). ShF 1480-1481.
"Pedestrian Accident, A" (Coover). ShF 1193.
Pedigree (Simenon). LFFor 1599-1600.
"Pedlar's Revenge, The" (O'Flaherty). ShF
671.
Peele, George. DEng 1488-1495, 2271.
Peggy-Ann (Rodgers and Hart, L.). DEng 902.
Pegnitz Junction, The (Gallant). LFEng 1055.
Péguy, Charles-Pierre. PFor 1176-1184,
1881-1882.
Peirce, Charles Sanders. LTh 422, 913-914,
1826, 1831.
"Pelican Chorus, The" (Lear). PEng 1700-
1706.
Pell, Derek. ShF 2760.
Pelle the Conqueror (Nexø). LFFor 2348.
Pelléas and Mélisande (Maeterlinck). DFor
1239-1241.
Pellico, Silvio. DFor 2408-2409.
Pellinen, Jyrki. PFor 2199.
Pelopidas (Bird). DEng 214-215.
Peltonen, Vihtori. *See* Linnankoski, Johannes.
Peña, Ramón José Simón Valle. *See* **Valle-**
Inclán, Ramón María del.
Pendzíkis, Nikos. *See* **Pentzíkis, Nikos.**
Penelope (Cunningham). M&D 439.
Penguin Island (France). LFFor 577.
Penhally (Gordon). LFEng 1175-1176.
Pénitencier, Le (Martin du Gard). LFFor 1114.
See also *World of the Thibaults, The.*
"Penitential Psalm, A" (Everson). PEng 990.
Penny for a Song, A (Whiting). DEng 2023-
2025.
"Pensar en ti esta noche." *See* "To Think of
You Tonight."
Pensée sauvage, La. See *Savage Mind, The.*
Pensées (Sainte-Beuve). LTh 1259.
"Penseroso, Il" (Milton). PEng 2007, 3035.
"Pensiero dominante, Il." *See* "Ascendant
Thought, The."
Pentamerone, The (Basile). ShF 682-683.
"Pentecost" (Manzoni). PFor 959-960. See also
Sacred Hymns, The.

Pentecost, Hugh. M&D 1305-1310.
Pentelogia (Quarles). PEng 2298.
Penthesilea (Kleist). DFor 1078.
Pentzíkis, Nikos. PFor 1185-1191.
Penultimate Truth, The (Dick). LFSup 96.
Peony Pavilion (T'ang). DFor 2325.
People Betrayed, A. See *November 1918.*
People from the Sea, The (Johnston). M&D 940.
People in the Summer Night (Sillanpää). LFFor 1580.
People in the Wind. See *Bus Stop.*
People of Hemsö, The. See *Natives of Hemsö, The.*
People of Juvik, The (Duun). LFFor 2351.
People of Seldwyla, The (Keller). LFFor 930.
People of the Cave, The. See *Ahl al-kahf.*
People of the City (Ekwensi). LFFor 2046-2047.
People of the Valley (Waters). LFEng 2784-2785.
People, Yes, The (Sandburg). PEng 2452.
Peopled Landscape, A (Tomlinson). PEng 2908-2909.
Pepita Ximenez (Valera). LFFor 1817, 1819-1820.
Pequeña historia de horror (y de amor desenfrenado). See *Little Tale of Horror (and Unbridled Love), A.*
Per Abad. PFor 2205.
Perceval: Or, The Story of the Grail (Chrétien de Troyes). PFor 1838.
Percy, Walker. LFEng 2087-2100; LFSup 406.
Père de famille, Le. See *Father of the Family, The.*
Père Goriot, Le. See *Father Goriot.*
Perec, Georges. LTh 269.
Pereda, José María de. LFFor 2384.
Peregrine Pickle (Smollett). LFEng 2448-2449.
Perelandra (Lewis, C. S.). LFEng 1654-1655.
Perelman, S. J. LFEng 2842; ShF 2079-2084.
Peresmeshnik (Chulkov). LFFor 2305.
Peretz, Isaac Leib. ShF 2085-2090.
Pérez de Ayala, Ramón. LFFor 1251-1263, 2391.
Pérez Galdós, Benito. DFor 1453-1463, 2501; LFFor 1264-1285, 2382, 2384, 2385, 2386-2387.
"Perfección." *See* "Perfection."

"Perfección de la tarde." *See* "Afternoon Perfection."
Perfect Circle of Sun, A (Pastan). PEng 2173-2174.
"Perfect Day for Bananafish, A" (Salinger). ShF 2176-2177.
Perfect Murder, The (Keating). M&D 949-951.
Perfect Vacuum, A (Lem). LFFor 1012, 1013; ShFSup 150.
Perfect Wagnerite, The (Shaw). LTh 1327-1328.
Perfect Wife, The (León). PFor 842-843.
Perfecta casada, La. See *Perfect Wife, The.*
"Perfection" (Guillén). PFor 625. See also *Cántico.*
Perfectionist, The (Williamson). DEng 2092-2093.
Perfectionists, The (Godwin). LFSup 135, 137.
Perfil del aire (Cernuda). PFor 319-320.
"Performance, The" (Dickey, J.). PEng 795.
"Performers, The" (Hayden). PEng 1248, 1252.
Perfume of the Lady in Black, The (Leroux). M&D 1074-1076.
Pérgola de las flores, La (Aguirre). DFor 33-34.
"Perhaps Because of the Fateful Quiet" (Foscolo). PFor 494. *See also* "Sonetti."
Peri hypsous. See *On the Sublime* (Longinus).
Perì Kharean kai Kalliróēn, Ta. See *Chaereas and Callirhoe.*
Peribáñez (Vega). DFor 1933-1934.
Pericles (Shakespeare). DEng 1711.
Perikeiromenē. See *Girl Who Was Shorn, The.*
"Period" (Herbert). PFor 657. See also *Struna swiatla.*
"Periodical Articles of the American Short Story" (Smith, F.). ShF 89-90.
Periquillo sarniento, El. See *Itching Parrot, The.*
Perjur'd Beauty, The (Behn). ShF 502.
Perkin Warbeck (Ford). DEng 664-666, 2290.
Perkins, Michael. ShF 2761.
Perkins, William. LTh 1740-1741.
Perlemorstrand (Hauge). LFFor 803, 804.
"Permanence, A" (Blackburn). PEng 195.
Permanent Errors (Price). ShF 2123, 2126.
Perrault, Charles. LTh 479, 836, 841, 1684.
Perro del hortelano, El. See *Gardener's Dog, The.*

Pharsalia (Lucan). PFor 894, 896-901.

Pharsamond (Marivaux). LFFor 1099-1100.

Pheander the Mayden Knight (Roberts, H.). ShF 495-496.

Phèdre. See *Phaedra*.

Phelps, Samuel. DEng 2357.

"Phenomenology of Reading" (Poulet). LTh 1149-1150.

Phenomenology of Spirit, The (Hegel). LTh 656, 658.

Pherecrates. DFor 2122.

"Phihellene" (Cavafy). PFor 298.

Philadelphia Comedy, The. See *City Looking Glass, The*.

Philadelphia, Here I Come! (Friel). DEng 674.

Philadelphia Story, The (Barry). DEng 135.

Philaster (Beaumont and Fletcher). DEng 631-632, 2290.

Philby, Kim. LFEng 1217.

Philemon. DFor 2133-2134.

Philip. See *Phillip II*.

Philip Sparrow (Skelton). PEng 2637.

Philipe, Gérard. DFor 2354.

Philips, Judson. *See* **Pentecost, Hugh.**

Philistines, The. See *Smug Citizen*.

Philistion of Nicaea. DFor 2135.

"Phillida and Coridon" (Breton, N.). PEng 278-279.

Phillip II (Alfieri). DFor 47, 2406.

Phillips, Louis. ShF 2766.

Phillips, Robert. ShF 2767.

Phillips, Thomas. *See* **Davies, L. P.**

Phillis (Lodge). PEng 1733.

"Phillis: Or, The Progress of Love" (Swift). PEng 2808.

Phillpotts, Eden. M&D 1325-1330.

Philoctetes (Müller). DSup 259-260.

Philoctetes (Sophocles). DFor 2108-2109.

Philoktet. See *Philoctetes*.

Philoktētēs (Rítsos). PFor 1351, 1970.

Philosophe sans le savior, Le (Sedaine). DFor 2342.

"Philosopher, The" (Anderson). ShF 870-871.

"Philosopher, The" (Brontë). PEng 297.

"Philosopher, The" (Graves). PEng 1129.

Philosopher's Stone, The (Lagerkvist). DFor 1156-1157, 2478.

Philosophes classiques du XIXᵉ siècle en France, Les (Taine). LTh 1419-1421.

Philosophes français du XIXᵉ siècle, Les. See *Philosophes classiques du XIXᵉ siècle en France, Les*.

Philosophiae Naturalis Principia Mathematica. See *Mathematical Principles of Natural Philosophy, The*.

Philosophic Words (Wimsatt). LTh 1556.

Philosophical Enquiry into the Origin of Our Ideas of the Sublime and Beautiful, A (Burke, E.). LTh 238, 1218, 1601, 1700; ShF 470.

"Philosophy of Composition, The" (Poe). LTh 1135-1136; PEng 2248.

Philosophy of the Short Story, The (Matthews). ShF 82.

Philotas (Lessing). DFor 1202-1203.

"Phineas" (Knowles). ShF 1767-1769.

Phlyakes. DFor 2137.

"Phoebe's Garden." See *Quality Street*.

Phoenician Women, The (Euripides). DFor 2116-2117.

Phoenician Women, The (Seneca). DFor 2148.

Phoenissae (Phrynichus). DFor 2090.

Phoenix and the Tortoise, The (Rexroth). PEng 2353.

"Phoenix and the Turtle, The" (Shakespeare). PEng 2529.

Phoenix Nest, The (Breton, N.). PEng 278.

Phormio (Terence). DFor 1827, 2143.

Photograph, A (Shange). DSup 329.

Phrynichus. DFor 2089-2090, 2095, 2122.

Phyllis (Cunningham). M&D 440.

Physical Universe (Simpson). PEng 2609-2610.

P'i-p'a chi. See *Lute, The*.

Piacere, Il. See *Child of Pleasure, The*.

"Piano Kissed by a Fragile Hand, The" (Verlaine). PFor 1630-1631.

"Piano que baise une main frêle, Le." *See* "Piano Kissed by a Fragile Hand, The."

"Piazza Piece" (Ransom). PEng 2330-2331.

Picano, Felice. ShF 2768.

Picard, Raymond. LTh 103, 106.

Picaro. LFEng 3101-3107.

Piccadilly Bushman, The (Lawler). DEng 1115-1116.

"Piccolo Berto, Il" (Saba). PSup 345.

Piccolo mondo antico. See *Little World of the Past, The*.

Piccolo santo, Il. See *Little Saint, The*.

Piccolominis, The (Schiller). DFor 1658. See also *Death of Wallenstein, The*.

Pick Your Victim (McGerr). M&D 1143-1144.

"Porcupine, The" (Kinnell). PEng 1593.
"Pordenone" (Howells). PEng 1422.
Porgy (Heyward and Heyward). DEng 936-937.
Porgy and Bess (Heyward and the Gershwins). DEng 934, 937, 2470.
"Pork Chop Paradise" (Himes). ShF 1641-1642.
Pornografia (Gombrowicz). LFFor 699.
Porphyras (Solomòs). PFor 1457-1458.
"Porphyria's Lover" (Browning, R.). PEng 337-339.
Porphyry. LTh 1645.
Port-Royal (Montherlant). DFor 1355-1356.
Port sepolto, Il. See *Allegria, L'*.
Portable Faulkner, The (Cowley). LTh 316.
"Portable Phonograph, The" (Clark). ShF 1152-1153.
Porte étroite, La. See *Strait Is the Gate.*
Porten (Bergman). DFor 188-189.
Porter, Joyce. M&D 1338-1341.
Porter, Katherine Anne. LFEng 2101-2109; ShF 260-261, 542, **2111-2116.**
Porter, Sydney. *See* **Henry, O.**
Porter, William Sydney. *See* **Henry, O.**
Portes de la forêt, Les. See *Gates of the Forest, The.*
Portico of the Mystery of the Second Virtue, The (Péguy). PFor 1181.
Portnoy's Complaint (Roth). LFEng 2303-2304.
Porto-Riche, Georges de. DFor 2349.
Portrait in Brownstone (Auchincloss). LFEng 107-109.
"Portrait in Georgia" (Toomer). PEng 2917.
Portrait of a Lady, The (James, H.). LFEng 1443-1446, 3162-3163.
Portrait of a Man Unknown (Sarraute). LFFor 1502-1503.
Portrait of an Artist with Twenty-six Horses (Eastlake). LFEng 851-853.
"Portrait of Shunkin, A" (Tanizaki). ShFSup 316-317.
Portrait of the Artist as a Young Dog (Thomas). ShF 2320.
Portrait of the Artist as a Young Man, A (Joyce). LFEng 1500-1502, 3057.
Portraits (Sainte-Beuve). LTh 1259, 1263.
Portraits of the Day (Gautier). LTh 554.
Portuguese Letters (Guilleragues). LFEng 3109-3110.

Posies of George Gascoigne Esquire, The (Gascoigne). LTh 543.
Positions (Derrida). LTh 360.
Positives (Gunn). PEng 1169.
Positivo, Lo (Tamayo y Baus). DFor 1806.
"Posledniaia nepriiatnost." *See* "Final Unpleasantness, A."
"Poslednye literaturnye yavleniya." *See* "Latest Literary Controversies, The."
Possessed, The (Dostoevski). LFFor 513-514, 2317; LTh 396.
"Posson Jone" (Cable). ShF 225.
Post, Melville Davisson. M&D 1342-1348; ShF 754-755.
Post Man, The. *See* **Henry, O.**
"Post Office, The" (O'Flaherty). ShF 2011.
Post Office, The (Tagore). DFor 1796.
"Postcard from the Volcano, A" (Stevens). PEng 2748-2749.
"Postcards from Cape Split" (Van Duyn). PEng 2964-2965.
"Posthumous Collection, A" (Sissman). PEng 2618-2622.
Posthumous Memoirs of Brás Cubas, The (Machado de Assis). LFFor 1038, 1042-1045.
Posthumous Papers of the Pickwick Club, The. See *Pickwick Papers.*
Postille a "Il nome della rosa." See *Postscript to "The Name of the Rose."*
Postman Always Rings Twice, The (Cain). M&D 257-258; ShF 1024.
"Postmodernism" (Jameson). LTh 763.
"Postscript" (Kunitz). PSup 242.
Postscript to "The Name of the Rose" (Eco). LTh 425.
Postures. See *Quartet.*
Pot of Earth, The (MacLeish). DEng 1217; PEng 1852-1853.
Pot of Gold, The (Plautus). DFor 2141.
"Pot Roast" (Strand). PEng 2772-2773.
Potok, Chaim. LFSup 313-321.
Potomak, Le (Cocteau). LFFor 360.
Potop. See *Deluge, The.*
Potterism (Macaulay). LFSup 260-261.
Potting Shed, The (Greene, G.). DEng 829-831.
Potts, Jean. M&D 1349-1354.
Poudre aux yeux, La. See *Throwing Dust in People's Eyes.*
Poulet, Georges. LTh 1033, 1147-1153, 1808.

"Preludio e canzonette" (Saba). PSup 345.

Preludios (González Martínez). PFor 610.

Prem Chand, Munshi. LFFor 2224.

"Premier manifeste du futurisme." *See* "Founding and Manifesto of Futurism, The."

"Première du monde" (Éluard). PFor 459.

Premios, Los. See *Winners, The.*

Preradović, Petar. PFor 2262-2263.

"Presence, The" (Everson). PEng 988.

Presence of the Word, The (Ong). LTh 1082.

"Present State of the Short Story, The" (Pattee). ShF 86.

"Présentation de la Beauce à Notre-Dame de Chartres" (Péguy). PFor 1183. See also *Tapisserie de Notre-Dame, La.*

"Presented to His Highness" (Fanshawe). PEng 999.

Prešeren, France. PFor 2267-2268.

President, The (Asturias). See *Mr. President.*

President, The (Cassill). LFEng 469-470.

"Presso l'urna di P. B. Shelley." *See* "Near the Urn of P. B. Shelley."

Prestupleniye i nakazaniye. See *Crime and Punishment.*

Pretenders, The (Ariosto). DFor 107-108.

Pretty Leslie (Cassill). LFEng 468.

"Pretty Polly Barlow" (Coward). ShF 1208.

Preussengeist (Ernst). DFor 560-561.

Preussischer Ikarus (Biermann). PFor 192.

Prévert, Jacques. PFor **1275-1281,** 1887.

Prévost, Abbé. LFFor **1308-1318,** 2030, 2119.

"Priapus" (H. D.). PEng 1261.

Price, The (Miller). DEng 1348-1349.

Price, Nancy. ShF 2772.

Price, Reynolds. LFEng **2129-2137;** LFSup 406; ShF 368, **2122-2127.**

Pricksongs & Descants (Coover). ShF 1190.

Pričo o vezirovom slonu. See *Vizier's Elephant, The.*

Pride and Prejudice (Austen). LFEng 119-120.

Pride of Heroes, A. See *Old English Peep Show, The.*

Pride of Life, The. DEng 2253.

"Priest and the Pigeons, The" (Anand). ShF 645-646.

Priest in the House, A. See *Conquest of Plassans, The.*

Priestley, J. B. DEng **1531-1544;** LFEng **2138-2147;** LFSup 406; LTh 1264, 1266; M&D **1355-1362.**

Prigozhaia povarikha. See *Comely Cook, The.*

"Prikliucheniia obeziany." *See* "Adventures of a Monkey, The."

Prima Pastorum. See *First Shepherds' Play, The.*

"Primative, The" (Madhubuti). PEng 1893.

"Primavera hitleriana." *See* "Hitler Spring, The."

"Primaveral" (Darío). PFor 422. See also *Azul.*

"Prime Leaf" (Warren). ShF 2405-2406.

Prime of Miss Jean Brodie, The (Spark). LFEng 2476, 2479-2482.

Primele poème (Tzara). PFor 1549.

Primer for Combat (Boyle). LFEng 279.

"Primero sueño" (Cruz). PFor 380.

"Primeval Words, Orphic" (Goethe). PFor 585.

Primitivism and Decadence (Winters). LTh 1566.

Primo Basílio, O. See *Cousin Bazilio.*

"Primo rapporto sulla terra del' Inviato speciale della luna" (Moravia). ShFSup 196.

Primo vere (D'Annunzio). PFor 385.

Prince, F. T. PSup **313-318.**

Prince, Gerald. LTh 1437.

Prince and the Pauper, The (Twain). LFEng 2666.

Prince Caspian (Lewis, C. S.). LFEng 1657-1658.

Prince frivole, Le (Cocteau). PFor 370.

Prince of Abissinia, The. See *Rasselas.*

"Prince of Darkness" (Powers). ShF 2118.

Prince of Homburg, The (Kleist). DFor 1080-1081, 2369.

Prince of Parthia, The (Godfrey). DEng 2395.

"Prince Who Was a Thief, The" (Dreiser). ShF 1308.

Princely Pleasures at Kenelworth Castle, The (Gascoigne). DEng 724-725.

"Prince's Progress, The" (Rossetti, C.). PEng 2419.

Princess, The (Tennyson). PEng 2867-2868.

"Princess and the Pea, The" (Andersen). ShF 864.

Princess Brambilla (Hoffmann). ShF 1648.

Princess Far-Away, The. See *Far Princess, The.*

Princess Ligovskaya (Lermontov). LFFor 1020-1021.

Princess of Cleve, The (Lee). DEng 1121-1122.

Providence (Brookner). LFSup 63-64.

Provincial Lady, A (Turgenev). DFor 1902.

Provincial Tale, A (Zamyatin). LFFor 1977-1979.

Provintsialka. See *Provincial Lady, A.*

Provok'd Husband, The (Vanbrugh and Cibber). DEng 367-368, 1975-1976.

Provok'd Wife, The (Vanbrugh). DEng 1971-1975.

Prozess, Der. See *Trial, The.*

Prudence in Woman (Tirso). DFor 1847.

Prudence Palfrey (Aldrich). LFEng 53-55.

Prudencia en la mujer, La. See *Prudence in Woman.*

Prudentius. PFor 211.

Prudhomme, Sully. PFor 1872, 1874.

Prus, Bolesław. LFFor 2063.

"Prussian Vase, The" (Edgeworth). ShF 1323-1324.

"Przebudzenie." *See* "Awakening."

Przybyszewski, Stanisław. DFor 2278; LFFor 2183.

Przyrost naturalny. See *Birth Rate.*

Psalam 44 (Kiš). LFSup 213-214.

Psalle et sile (Calderón). PFor 249.

Psalm 38 (Wyatt). PEng 3179.

Psalm 55 (Surrey, paraphrase). PEng 2791.

Psalm 75 (Surrey, paraphrase). PEng 2791.

Psalm 88 (Surrey, paraphrase). PEng 2791.

"Psara, To" (Solomòs). PFor 1455-1456.

Pseudo-Callisthenes. LFFor 2014.

Psyché. See *Body's Rapture, The.*

Psycho (Bloch). M&D 145-146.

Psycho II (Bloch). M&D 146.

"Psychoanals, The" (Kraus). PFor 798.

Psychoanalyse du feu, La. See *Psychoanalysis of Fire, The.*

Psychoanalysis of Fire, The (Bachelard). LTh 1149.

P'u Sung-ling. LFFor 209; **ShFSup 238-249.**

Public Burning, The (Coover). LFEng 617, 624-625.

"Public Garden, The" (Lowell, R.). PEng 1792.

Public Image, The (Spark). LFEng 2476.

"Public Pool, A" (Adams). ShFSup 4-5.

Público, El. See *Audience, The.*

Publikumsbeschimpfung. See *Offending the Audience.*

Publilius. DFor 2147.

Publius Cornelius Scipio Aemilianus. *See* Scipio Aemilianus.

Publius Ovidius Naso. *See* **Ovid.**

Publius Vergilius Maro. *See* **Vergil.**

Puccini, Giacomo. DEng 2196-2197.

Puce à l'oreille, La. See *Flea in Her Ear, A.*

Puchmajer, Antonín Jaroslav. PFor 1799.

Puck. ShF 587.

Puebla de las mujeres. See *Women's Town, The.*

"Pugachov" (Esenin). PFor 479.

Puig, Manuel. LFFor 1347-1358; M&D 1370-1374.

Pulci, Luigi. PFor 2012.

"Pull-Push" (Malgonkar). ShF 650.

Puñal del godo, El. See *Dagger of the Goth.*

"Punch, The" (Friedman, B.). ShF 1426-1427.

Punishment Without Revenge. See *Justice Without Revenge.*

Pupil of Nature, The. See *Ingenuous.*

"Pupils of the Eyes That Talked, The" (P'u). ShFSup 244-245.

Puppet Play of Don Cristóbal, The. See *In the Frame of Don Cristóbal.*

"Purchase's Living Wonders" (Bates). ShF 270; ShFSup 31.

Purdy, James. LFEng 2169-2177; LFSup 406; ShF 2134-2140.

"Pure and Impure Poetry" (Warren). LTh 1524; PEng 3430, 3432-3433.

Pure and the Impure, The (Colette). LFFor 369.

"Pure Diamond Man, The" (Laurence). ShF 1778-1779.

Purgatory (Dante). PFor 405-411. See also *Divine Comedy, The.*

Purgatory (Yeats). DEng 2120-2121.

Purgatory of St. Patrick, The (Marie de France). ShF 1891.

Purity. See *Cleanness.*

"Purloined Letter, The" (Poe). M&D 1336; ShF 750, 2108.

"Purple Dress, The" (Henry). ShF 1630.

Purple Dust (O'Casey). DEng 1390.

"Purple Jar, The" (Edgeworth). ShF 1322.

Purple Land, The (Hudson). LFEng 1382-1384.

Purposes of Love. See *Promise of Love.*

Purse of Copper, A (O'Faoláin). ShF 1997.

"Purse Seine, The" (Blackburn). PEng 198.

"Pursuit, A" (Atwood). PEng 66.

Q

Q.E.D. See *Things as They Are.*

Quaderni di Serafino Gubbio, operatore, I. See *Shoot! The Notebooks of Serafino Gubbio, Cinematograph Operator.*

"Quaker Graveyard in Nantucket, The" (Lowell, R.). PEng 1787-1788.

"Qualcosa era successo." *See* "Catastrophe."

Quality of Mercy, A (West). LFSup 370.

"Quality of Sprawl, The" (Murray). PSup 292.

Quality Street (Barrie). DEng 119-121.

Quand le navire. . . . See *Love's Questing.*

"Quand vous serez bien vieille." *See* "When You Are Old."

"Quangle Wangle's Hat, The" (Lear). PEng 1701-1702.

Quare Fellow, The (Behan). DEng 164-165.

Quarles, Francis. PEng 2293-2300.

Quarry, The (Dürrenmatt). M&D 559.

Quartet (Rhys). LFEng 2228.

Quartet in Autumn (Pym). LFEng 2182, 2184-2185.

Quartier Nègre (Simenon). LFFor 1599.

"Quartz Pebble, The" (Popa). PFor 1269-1270. See also *Bark.*

Quasimodo, Salvatore. PFor 1303-1309, 2032, 2043-2044, 2046, 2049.

"14 juillet, Le." *See* "July 14."

Quatre-vingt-treize. See *Ninety-three.*

"Que bien sé yo la fonte." *See* "Although by Night."

"¿Que lle digo?" *See* "What Should I Tell Her?"

Que ma joie demeure. See *Joy of Man's Desiring.*

Que trata de España (Otero). PFor 1116-1117.

Que van quedando en el camino, Los (Aguirre). DFor 35-37.

Queen, Ellery. M&D 1375-1383; ShF 526, 763. *See also* **Hoch, Edward D.**

Queen After Death (Montherlant). DFor 1352-1353.

Queen Is Dead, The. See *Queen on Tour, The.*

Queen Mary (Tennyson). DEng 1915-1917.

Queen of Spades, The (Pushkin). ShF 170; ShFSup 255-256.

Queen on Tour, The (Abell). DFor 6.

Queene of Navarres Tales, The. See *Heptameron, The.*

Queen's Comedy, The (Bridie). DEng 278.

Queen's Husband, The (Sherwood). DEng 1801-1802.

Quem quaeritis. DEng 2150, 2244-2245; DFor 2155-2156.

Queneau, Raymond. LFSup 322-332; LTh 269, 1234; PFor 1890.

Quentin, Patrick. M&D 1384-1388.

Quer pasticciaccio brutto de via Merulana. See *That Awful Mess on Via Merulana.*

Querelle of Brest (Genet). LFFor 631-633.

Qu'est-ce que la littérature? See *What Is Literature?*

Quest for Christa T., The (Wolf). LFFor 1935-1938.

Quest for Karla, The. See *Tinker, Tailor, Soldier, Spy, Honourable Schoolboy, The,* and *Smiley's People.*

Quest of the Absolute, The (Balzac). LFFor 92, 93.

Quest of the Gole, The (Hollander). PEng 1364.

Question of Upbringing, A (Powell). LFEng 2117-2118.

Question Time (Davies). DEng 467-468, 471-472.

Questions de critique (Brunetière). LTh 235.

Questions of Travel (Bishop). PEng 187.

"Quia Multum Amavit" (Swinburne). PEng 2820.

Quiet American, The (Greene, G.). LFEng 1221.

Quiet as a Nun (Fraser). M&D 657-658.

"Quiet Work" (Arnold). PEng 53.

"Quiete dopo la tempesta, La." *See* "Calm After the Storm, The."

Quill, Monica. *See* **McInerny, Ralph.**

"Quilt Pattern, A" (Jarrell). PEng 1483.

Quimera, La (Pardo Bazán). LFFor 1227.

Quinault, Philippe. DFor 1503-1509.

Quinn, Martin. *See* **Smith, Martin Cruz.**

Quinn, Simon. *See* **Smith, Martin Cruz.**

R

Raabe, Wilhelm. LFFor 1373-1386, 2174-2176.

Rabbit Is Rich (Updike). LFEng 2698-2699.

Rabbit Race, The (Walser, M.). DSup 385-386.

Rabbit Redux (Updike). LFEng 2695-2698.

Rabbit, Run (Updike). LFEng 2689, 2692-2695.

Rabe, David. DEng 1545-1554, 2413; DSup 408.

Rabelais, François. LFFor 1387-1394, 2022, 2111-2112.

Rabelais and His World (Bakhtin). LTh 85.

Rabinowitz, Solomon. *See* Aleichem, Sholom.

Racconto d'autunno (Landolfi). ShFSup 129.

Race Rock (Matthiessen). LFEng 1823-1824, 1826.

"Race," Writing, and Difference (Gates). LTh 550.

"Racer's Window, The" (Glück). PSup 135.

Rachlin, Nahid. ShF 2774.

Racin, Kosta. PFor 2272.

Racine, Jean. DEng 2173; DFor 1510-1522; LTh 669, 708-709, 837, 839-840, 880, 1195-1201, 1306, 1393, 1419.

Racine, Louis. PFor 1861.

Racine and Shakespeare (Hugo). LTh 709.

Racine and Shakespeare (Stendhal). LTh 1393-1395, 1696.

"Radagon in Dianem" (Greene). PEng 1149-1150.

Radcliffe, Ann. LFEng 2195-2204, 3122, 3126; M&D 1389-1394; ShF 472, 730.

Radetzky March, The (Roth). LFFor 1452-1453.

RADI OS I-IV (Johnson). PSup 214.

Radiance of the King, The (Laye). LFFor 2035-2036.

Radičević, Branko. PFor 2253-2254.

Radishchev, Aleksandr. LFFor 2308.

Raditzer (Matthiessen). LFEng 1824-1825, 1826.

Radnóti, Miklós. PFor 1310-1316, 1986-1987.

Radović, Burislav. PFor 2258.

Radunitsa (Esenin). PFor 478.

"Radwechsel, Der." *See* "Changing the Wheel."

"Rady." *See* "Counsels."

"Rafaelova 'Madonna'" (Zhukovsky). LTh 1613.

Raffel, Burton. ShF 2775.

Raffles, the Amateur Cracksman. See *Amateur Cracksman, The.*

Raft, The (Clark). DSup 56-57.

Raft of the Medusa, The (Kaiser). DFor 1025-1026.

"Raggedy Man, The" (Riley). PEng 2380-2381.

"Ragman's Daughter, The" (Sillitoe). ShF 2227.

Ragtime (Doctorow). LFEng 770, 777-778.

"Ragtime" (Nin). ShF 1950-1951.

Rai Sanyō. PFor 2073.

Raičković, Stevan. PFor 2258.

Railroad (McPherson and Williams, M.). ShF 1855.

Raimann, Jakob. *See* Raimund, Ferdinand.

Raimund, Ferdinand. DFor 1523-1534, 2372.

"Rain" (Booth). PEng 246-247.

"Rain, The" (Creeley). PEng 679-680.

"Rain" (Maugham). ShF 1903-1904.

"Rain" (Ponge). PFor 1263-1264.

"Rain Down Home" (Foote). LFEng 978.

Rain from Heaven (Behrman). DEng 186, 187.

"Rain on the Cumberlands" (Still). PEng 2764.

Rainbow, The (Lawrence, D. H.). LFEng 1589-1591.

"Rainbow" (Plumly). PEng 2238.

"Rainy Moon, The" (Colette). ShF 1166-1167.

"Rainy Mountain Cemetery" (Momaday). PEng 2021.

Raisin in the Sun, A (Hansberry). DEng 877, 878-880.

"Raison d'Être of Criticism in the Arts, The" (Forster). LTh 498.

Raj Duszny (Biernat of Lublin). PFor 2119.

Raj Mohan's Wife (Chatterjee). LFFor 2216; ShF 642.

Rājā. See *King of the Dark Chamber, The.*

Rake's Progress, The (Auden and Kallman). DEng 56-57.

Rakić, Milan. PFor 2255.

Rakovy korpus. See *Cancer Ward.*
Raktakarabi. See *Red Oleanders.*
Raleigh, Sir Walter. LFEng 1094-1095; **PEng 2301-2309.**
Ralph Roister Doister (Udall). DEng 1960-1963.
"Ram in the Thicket, The" (Morris). ShFSup 202-203.
Ramayana. ShF 137, 642.
"Ramble in St. James's Park, A" (Rochester). PEng 2400-2401.
Rambler, The (Johnson, S.). LTh 771, 773-774, 777, 1685; ShF 1707, 1708-1709.

Rame, Franca. DSup 108-109.
Rameau's Nephew (Diderot). LFFor 464-465, 2120.
Ramos, José Antonio. DFor 2442.
Ramsay, Allan. PEng 3334.
Ramus, Petrus. LTh 1081.
Ranch, Hieronymus Justesen. DFor 2464.
Randall, Dudley. PEng 2310-2318; PSup 409.
Randisi, Robert J. *See* **Carter, Nick.**
Randolph, Georgiana Ann. *See* **Rice, Craig.**
Randolph, Thomas. PEng 2319-2323.
Ranger, Ken. *See* **Creasey, John.**
Ransom (Cleary). M&D 363.
Ransom, John Crowe. LTh 158, 1011, 1148, **1202-1207,** 1424-1425, 1522, 1554, 1753, 1818; **PEng 2324-2333.**
"Ransom of Red Chief, The" (Henry). ShF 1632.
Rao, Raja. LFEng 2205-2215; LFFor 2220; ShF 648.
"Rape" (Rich). ShF 124.
Rape of Lucrece, The (Shakespeare). PEng 2529; ShF 2210.
Rape of the Bucket, The (Tassoni). PFor 2018.
Rape of the Lock, The (Pope). PEng 2255-2257, 3324.
Rape upon Rape (Fielding). DEng 603.
"Rapids, The" (Barnard). PSup 26.
Rapin, René. LTh 277.
Raport z oblężonego miasta (Herbert). PFor 659-660.
"Rappaccini's Daughter" (Hawthorne). ShF 191, 369-370, 475, 801, 1612.
"Rapsodhia skeseon" (Pentzíkis). PFor 1189. See also *Ikones.*
"Rapture, to Laura" (Schiller). PFor 1406-1407.

"Rapunzel" (Grimm). ShF 1558-1559.
"Rapunzel" (Morris). PEng 2054.
Raquel encadenada (Unamuno y Jugo). DFor 1913-1914.
Rasa, Risto. PFor 2200.
"Rashōmon" (Akutagawa). ShFSup 9.
Rask, Rasmus. PFor 1732.
Raspberry Picker, The (Hochwälder). DFor 931-932.
Rasselas (Johnson). LFEng 1468-1473.
"Rasskas o tom, kak zhena ne razreshila muzhu umeret." *See* "Hen-Pecked."
"Rasskaz o samom glavnom." *See* "Story About the Most Important Thing, A."
Rastell, John. DEng 2258-2259.
Rat Man of Paris (West). LFSup 376-377.
Ratablillo de don Cristóbal, El. See *In the Frame of Don Cristóbal.*
Ratner's Star (DeLillo). LFSup 87-88.
Rats (Horovitz). DEng 961-962.
"Rats in the Walls, The" (Lovecraft). ShF 735.
Rat's Mass, A (Kennedy). DSup 215.
Rattigan, Terence. DEng 1555-1565.
Rattray, Simon. *See* **Trevor, Elleston.**
Räuber, Die. See *Robbers, The.*
Ravagers, The (Hamilton). M&D 819-820.
Ravenna (Wilde). PEng 3103-3104.
"Ravens, the Sexton, and the Earthworm, The" (Gay). PEng 1076-1077.
Ravishing of Lol Stein, The (Duras). LFFor 534, 537-538.
Ravisht Soule, and the Blessed Weeper, The (Breton, N.). PEng 280-281.
Raw Flesh (Popa). PFor 1272.
Raw Youth, A (Dostoevski). LFFor 514-515.
Ray, David. ShF 2776.
Ray, Raja Rammohan. LFFor 2214.
Raymond, Marcel. LTh 1151, 1808.
Raymond, René Brabazon. *See* **Chase, James Hadley.**
Rayner, Olive Pratt. *See* **Allen, Grant.**
Rayons et les ombres, Les (Hugo). PFor 734.
Rayuela. See *Hopscotch.*
"Razglednicas" (Radnóti). PFor 1316.
Razgovor na bolshoy doroge. See *Conversation on the Highway. A.*
Razgovor ugodni naroda slovinskoga (Miošić). PFor 2261.
Razgrom. See *Nineteen, The.*
Razón de amor (Salinas). PFor 1387.
"Razor, The" (Nabokov). ShFSup 218.

Razor's Edge, The (Maugham). LFEng 1849-1850.

"Razrushenie estetiki" (Pisarev). LTh 1107.

Răzvan și Vidra (Hașdeu). DFor 2297.

Re cervo, Il. See *King Stag, The.*

Re Torrismondo, Il (Tasso). DFor 1819-1821.

"Re Travicello, Il." *See* "King Travicello."

"Reach, The" (King). ShFSup 125.

Read, Sir Herbert. LTh 1208-1213.

Reade, Hamish, *See* **Gray, Simon.**

"Reader, The" (Lewis). PSup 255.

Reading and Feelings (Bleich). LTh 1764.

"Reading and Writing of Short Stories, The" (Welty). ShF 93, 815-816.

"Reading Nijinsky's Diary" (Young). PEng 3213-3214.

Reading the Spirit (Eberhart). PEng 928.

"Readville Stars, The" (Hale, N.). ShF 1570.

Real Life of Sebastian Knight, The (Nabokov). LFEng 1951.

Real People (Lurie). LFSup 251, 253.

"Real Thing, The" (James, H.). ShF 1680-1682.

Real Thing, The (Stoppard). DEng 1877-1879.

Realidad (Pérez Galdós). DFor 2501.

Realism in Our Time (Lukács). LTh 938.

"Realists, The" (Pisarev). LTh 1107-1108.

"Realisty." *See* "Realists, The."

Realities of Fiction, The (Hale, N.). ShF 1573.

Reality and the Poet in Spanish Poetry (Salinas). PFor 1383, 1389-1390.

"Reality *(dreamed)*, A" (Ekelöf). PFor 450-451.

"Reality in America" (Trilling). LTh 1454.

Realms of Gold, The (Drabble). LFEng 823-825.

Reaney, James. DEng 1566-1578.

"Rear Window." *See* "It Had to Be Murder."

Reardon Poems, The (Blackburn). PEng 200-201.

Reasons for Moving (Strand). PEng 2769.

Reasons of State (Carpentier). LFFor 286-287.

"Reassurances and Revisions" (Biermann). PFor 190.

Rebecca (du Maurier). M&D 553-554.

Rebel Angels, The (Davies). LFEng 671.

Rebels, The (Ngugi). DSup 269-270.

Rèbora, Clemente. PFor 2045.

Recapitulation (Stegner). LFEng 2502-2503.

"Recapture of the Storyable, The" (Munson). ShF 84.

Recensenten og dyret (Heiberg, J.). DFor 902-903.

Recherche de l'absolu, La. See *Quest of the Absolute, The.*

"Recit d'un berger" (Malherbe). PFor 921-922.

"Reckless Abuse" (Biermann). PFor 1820.

Reckless Eyeballing (Reed). LFSup 340-341.

Reckoning, A (Sarton). LFEng 2351-2352.

Recognitions, The (Gaddis). LFEng 1034-1035, 1036-1039.

"Recollection of Bellagio" (Meredith). PEng 1956.

"Recollections" (Dazai). ShFSup 93.

Record of Travels in the West, The. ShF 135.

Records of Ancient Matters. LFFor 2259-2260; LTh 787, 1784; PFor 2053, 2054.

Recruiting Officer, The (Farquhar). DEng 582-583.

Rector of Justin, The (Auchincloss). LFEng 109-111.

Recurso del método, El. See *Reasons of State.*

"Red" (Maugham). ShF 1901-1903.

Red and the Black, The (Stendhal). LFFor 1655-1657.

Red Badge of Courage, The (Crane). LFEng 641-643.

"Red Barbara" (O'Flaherty). ShF 2008.

"Red Coal, The" (Stern). PSup 372-373.

Red Gardenias (Latimer). M&D 1029.

Red Gloves. See *Dirty Hands.*

Red Harvest (Hammett). LFEng 1236-1237; M&D 826.

"Red-Headed League, The" (Doyle). ShF 1301-1302.

"Red Herring, The" (MacBeth). PEng 1836.

Red House Mystery, The (Milne). M&D 1226-1228.

Red Lily, The (France). LFFor 579, 2138.

Red Magic (Ghelderode). DFor 697-698.

Red Men, The (McGinley). M&D 1149-1150.

Red Mill, The (Herbert). DEng 2467.

Red Noses (Barnes). DSup 14.

Red Oleanders (Tagore). DFor 1797.

"Red Pavement" (Nebel). M&D 1266.

"Red Petticoat, The" (O'Flaherty). ShF 2010.

Red Pony, The (Steinbeck). LFEng 2523-2524; ShF 2278-2279.

Red Redmaynes, The (Phillpotts). M&D 1328.

Red Robe, The (Brieux). DFor 252-253.

Red Room, The (Strindberg). LFFor 1689-1690, 2340.

Red Roses for Me (O'Casey). DEng 1390-1391.

"Red Shirt, A" (Atwood). PEng 68.

Red Sun at Morning (Cusack). DEng 2433.

"Red-Tailed Hawk and the Pyre of Youth" (Warren). PEng 3025.

"Red Wind" (Chandler). ShF 1095-1096, 1097-1098.

Redbook. ShF 314-315.

"Redemption" (Gardner). ShF 1463.

"Redemption" (Sassoon). PEng 2474.

Redliche Mann von Hofe, Der (Loën). LFFor 2152.

Redoble de conciencia (Otero). PFor 1115.

Reductorium morale (Ovid). LTh 1654-1655.

Reed, Eliot. *See* **Ambler, Eric.**

Reed, Henry. PEng 2334-2339; PSup 409.

Reed, Ishmael. LFSup 333-341.

Reeds and Mud (Blasco Ibáñez). LFFor 173-175.

Reef, The (Wharton, Edith). LFEng 2856-2857.

"Reena" (Marshall). ShF 582.

Reese, Lizette Woodworth. PEng 2340-2347.

Reeve, Arthur B. M&D 1395-1400; ShF 753-754.

"Reeve's Tale, The" (Chaucer). ShF 1112.

Reflections in a Golden Eye (McCullers). LFEng 1733-1734.

"Reflections on April 4, 1968" (Giovanni). PEng 1100.

Reflections on the Paintings and Sculpture of the Greeks (Winckelmann). LTh 1560.

Reflex (Francis). M&D 653.

Réflexions sur Longin (Boileau). LTh 179, 1684.

"Reformation of Calliope, The" (Henry). ShF 1630.

"Refrigerium" (Tuckerman). PEng 2940.

"Refutation of the Apologie for Actors, A" ("I. G."). LTh 1668.

Regain. See Harvest.

Regard du roi, Le. See Radiance of the King, The.

Regarding Wave (Snyder). PEng 2674.

Regenbogen, Der (Ausländer). PSup 18.

Regenta, La (Clarín). LFFor 346-350.

Regiment of Women (Berger). LFEng 256.

"Register of Mournful Verses, A" (Newcastle). PEng 2096.

Registro de representantes (Rueda). DFor 1596-1597.

Regnard, Jean-François. DFor 1535-1546, 2338.

Régnier, Henri. PFor 1879-1880.

Rehabilitations and Other Essays (Lewis). LTh 895-896.

Rehearsal, The (Villiers). DEng 1982-1985.

Rehearsal at Goatham, The (Gay). DEng 735.

Rehearsal Transpros'd, The (Marvell). PEng 1910.

Reich, Ebbe Kløvedal. LFFor 2367.

Reich Gottes in Bohmen, Das. See Kingdom of God in Bohemia, The.

Reid, Barbara. ShF 2777.

Reid, Randell. ShF 2778.

Reiling, Netty. *See* **Seghers, Anna.**

Reilly, Helen. M&D 1401-1405.

Reilly, William K. *See* **Creasey, John.**

Reina di Scotia (Della Valle). PFor 2018-2019.

Reine morte, La. See Queen After Death.

Reinhardt, Max. DEng 2237.

Reinhart in Love (Berger). LFEng 253.

Reinhart's Women (Berger). LFEng 259-261.

Reino de este mundo, El. See Kingdom of This World, The.

Reis, Ricardo. *See* **Pessoa, Fernando.**

"Reisekamerad, Der." *See* "Traveling Companion, The."

Reizenstein, Elmer Leopold. *See* **Rice, Elmer.**

Rej, Mikolaj. PFor 2119.

Rejected Guest (Aldington). LFEng 45-46.

Rejment, Stanisław Władysław. *See* **Reymont, Władysław.**

Rejoicings (Stern). PSup 369.

Rekviem. See Requiem.

Relapse, The (Vanbrugh). DEng 1967-1971.

"Relating to Robinson" (Kees). PEng 1564.

Relation d'un voyage en Limousin (La Fontaine). LTh 856.

Relic, The (Eça de Queiróz). LFFor 545.

Religieuse, La. See Nun, The.

Religio Laici (Dryden). PEng 876-877, 3298, 3299.

"Religion and Literature" (Eliot). LTh 451.

Religione del mio tempo, La (Pasolini). PFor 1150.

"Religious Articles" (Hall). PEng 1200.

Relíquia, A. See Relic, The.

Reljković, Matija Antun. PFor 2261.

Remains of Elmet (Hughes, L.). PEng 1446.

Remarque, Erich Maria. LFFor 1395-1403, 2191.

"Rembrandt, The" (Wharton). ShF 2428-2429.

Remedia amoris. See *Cure for Love.*

"Remedies, Maladies, Reasons" (Van Duyn). PEng 2965.

Remember (Jones, P.). DEng 1012.

Remember Me (Tremblay). DSup 356.

Remember Reuben (Beti). LFFor 2051.

"Remembering Maria A." (Brecht). PFor 223.

"Remembrance" (Brontë). PEng 296-297.

"Remembrance" (Byron). PEng 405.

Remembrance (Walcott, D. A.). DEng 2003-2004.

"Remembrance from a Dream in 1963" (Różewicz). PFor 1367-1368.

Remembrance of Things Past (Proust). LFFor 1322-1324, 1334-1335, 2140-2141; LTh 1172.

"Remembrances" (Clare). PEng 512.

Remizov, Alexsey. LFFor 2322.

Removalists, The (Williamson). DEng 2093-2094.

Renaissance, The (Pater). LTh 1086-1090.

Renaissance in Italy, The (Symonds). LTh 1406, 1408.

Renan, Ernest. LTh 231, 235, 1417.

"Renascence" (Lawrence, D. H.). PEng 1682.

Renault, Mary. LFEng 2216-2225; LFSup 406.

Renault, Rick. *See* **Pronzini, Bill.**

Rendell, Ruth. M&D 1406-1411.

Rendez-vous de Senlis, Le. See *Dinner with the Family.*

Rendezvous in Black (Woolrich). M&D 1727.

Rendezvous in Tokyo. See *Stopover: Tokyo.*

René (Chateaubriand). LFEng 3142; LFFor 339-341.

Renée (Zola). DFor 2051-2052.

Renée Mauperin (Goncourts). LFFor 713-714.

"Renegade, The" (Camus, A.). ShF 1050.

"Renegade, The" (Jackson). ShF 1670.

"Renewal, The" (Roethke). PEng 2412-2413.

Renga (Paz). PFor 1174.

Renga (Tomlinson). PEng 3370.

Renga shinshiki (Yoshimoto). LTh 1594.

"Renner" (Powers). ShF 2120.

"Renovación" (González Martínez). PFor 611.

Renri hishō (Yoshimoto). LTh 1594.

Repas du lion, Le. See *Lion's Meal, The.*

Repeat Performance (Mrożek). DFor 1384.

Repent in Haste (Marquand). LFEng 1818.

Reply to Gosson's Schoole of Abuse, in Defence of Poetry, A (Lodge). LTh 609, 613.

"Reply to Matthew Arnold of My Fifth Day in Fano, A" (Wright, J.). PEng 3168.

"Report to an Academy, A" (Kafka). ShF 1733.

Repos de septième jour, Le (Claudel). DFor 407.

Representación a la muy bendita pasión y muerte de nuestro precioso Redentor (Encina). DFor 2172.

Representación a la santisima resurrectión de Christo (Encina). DFor 2172.

Representación de la parabola de San Mateo (Horozsco). DFor 2172.

Representación del nacimiento de Nuestro Señor (Manrique). DFor 1255-1256, 2171.

"Repression of War Experience" (Sassoon). PEng 2471-2472.

Reprobate, The (James, H.). DEng 995.

"Reproof" (Smollett). PEng 2651, 2653-2654.

Republic (Plato). LTh 1116, 1118, 1635-1636, 1667; PEng 3462-3463.

Repuesta de la poetisa a la muy ilustre Sor Filotea de la Cruz (Cruz). PFor 375.

Requena, María Asunción. DFor 2443.

Requiem (Akhmatova). PFor 13-14.

Requiem for a Spanish Peasant (Sender). LFFor 1553-1554.

"Requiem for Dvořák, A" (Seifert). PSup 356.

Resa till Italien (Ehrensvärd). LFFor 2335.

"Rescue Party" (Clarke, A.). ShF 1157-1158.

Rescue the Dead (Ignatow). PEng 1474-1475.

"Research on the Technique of the Novel" (Butor). LTh 251.

"Resemblance Between a Violin Case and a Coffin, The" (Williams, T.). ShF 2435-2436.

Residence on Earth (Neruda). PFor 1075-1076, 1077.

Residencia en la tierra. See *Residence on Earth.*

"Residential Streets" (Hall). PEng 1199-1200.

"Resignation" (Schiller). PFor 1407-1408.

Resistance to Theory, The (de Man). LTh 351.

"Resolution and Independence" (Wordsworth). ShF 180.

Résponce aux injures et calomnies de je ne sçay quels predicans et ministres de Genève (Ronsard). PFor 1359.

"Response to a Request" (Walser, R.). ShFSup 348.

"Rest" (Newman). PEng 2104.

Rest Home (Cela). LFFor 292.

Rest in Pieces (McInerny). M&D 1162.

Restif de la Bretonne, Nicholas. LFFor 2121.

Restlessness of Shanti Andia, The (Baroja). LFFor 110.

Resurrection, The (Gardner, J.). LFEng 1071-1072.

Resurrection (Tolstoy). LFFor 1722.

Resurrection of the Word (Shklovsky). LTh 1341.

Resurreição (Machado de Assis). LFFor 1042.

"Resuscitation of a Vampire, The" (Rymer). ShF 732.

"Reszket a bokor, mert." *See* "Bush Trembles, Because, The."

Retablo de las maravillas, El. See *Wonder Show, The.*

Retenue d'amours (Charles d'Orléans). PFor 340.

"Retornos de Chopin a través de unas manos ya idas." *See* "Returns: Chopin by Way of Hands Now Gone."

Retornos de lo vivo lejano (Alberti). PFor 22-23.

"Retornos del amor en una noche de verano." *See* "Returns: A Summer Night's Love."

Retour imprévu, Le. See *Unexpected Return, The.*

Retreat, The (Appelfeld). LFSup 39.

"Return, The" (Berry). PEng 151.

Return, The (de la Mare). LFEng 709-710.

"Return" (Sikelianos). PFor 1957-1958.

Return from the Stars (Lem). LFFor 1010-1011.

"Return of a Private, The" (Garland). ShF 1469-1470.

Return of A. J. Raffles, The (Greene, G.). DEng 833.

Return of Ansel Gibbs, The (Buechner). LFEng 351-352.

"Return of Aphrodite, The" (Sarton). PEng 2461.

"Return of Iphigenia, The" (Rítsos). PFor 1970.

Return of Moriarty, The (Gardner, J.). M&D 696.

Return of Peter Grimm, The (Belasco). DEng 196-197.

"Return of the Goddess" (Graves). PEng 1132.

Return of the King, The. See *Lord of the Rings, The.*

Return of the Native, The (Hardy). LFEng 1268-1270.

Return of the Sphinx (MacLennan). LFEng 1746-1747.

"Return to Hinton" (Tomlinson). PEng 2909.

Return to My Native Land (Césaire). PFor 327-328, 329.

Return to Región. See *Volverás a Región.*

Returning to Earth (Harrison). PEng 1233-1234.

"Returns: A Summer Night's Love" (Alberti). PFor 23.

"Returns: Chopin by Way of Hands Now Gone" (Alberti). PFor 23.

Reuben, Reuben (De Vries). LFEng 740.

"Reuben, Reuben" (Harper). PSup 162.

"Reunion" (Goethe). PFor 588. See also *West-Eastern Divan.*

Reunion in Vienna (Sherwood). DEng 1803-1804.

Reuter, Christian. LFFor 2152.

"Revelation and Evolution" (Gullason). ShF 78.

"Revelation in the Short Story" (Sullivan, W.). ShF 91.

Revenge (Fredro). DFor 2277.

"Revenge, The" (Pardo Bazán). ShF 2049-2050.

Revenge for Love, The (Lewis, W.). LFEng 1687.

Revenge of Bussy d'Ambois, The (Chapman). DEng 359-360, 2288.

"Revenge of Hannah Kemhuff, The" (Walker). ShFSup 337-338.

Revenge of the Lawn (Brautigan). ShFSup 55.

Revenger's Tragedy, The (Tourneur). DEng 1934-1941, 2292.

Reverdy, Pierre. PFor 1888-1889; **PSup 319-327.**

"Reverend Father Gaucher's Elixir, The" (Daudet). ShF 1239-1240.

"Reversion to Type, A" (Norris). ShF 1957.

Reviczky, Gyula. PFor 1983.

"Review of *Twice-Told Tales*" (Poe). ShF 87-88.

Revizor. See *Inspector General, The.*

Revolt of Islam, The (Shelley). LTh 1334, 1336.

"Revolt of 'Mother,' The" (Freeman, M.). ShF 1417-1418.

Revolt of the Angels, The (France). LFFor 579.

Revolt of the Fishermen, The (Seghers). LFFor 1526-1527.

Révolte des anges, La. See *Revolt of the Angels, The.*

Revolution der Lyrik (Holz). LTh 693.

"Revolution in the Revolution in the Revolution" (Snyder). PEng 2674.

"Revolutions, Les" (Lamartine). PFor 834-835. See also *Harmonies poetiques et religieuses.*

"Revolver, The" (Pardo Bazán). ShF 2050-2051.

Rexroth, Kenneth. PEng 2348-2355.

Reyes, Alfonso. PFor 1317-1323.

Reymont, Władysław. LFFor 1404-1411, 2063.

Reynolds, Henry. LTh 1675.

Reynolds, Sir Joshua. LTh 91, 1214-1220.

Reznikoff, Charles. PEng 2356-2362.

"R. F. at Bread Loaf His Hand Against a Tree" (Swenson). PEng 2798.

Rhesus (Euripides?). DFor 2130-2131.

"'Rhetoric' and Poetic Drama" (Eliot). LTh 448.

Rhetoric of Fiction, The (Booth). LTh 184-186, 560; ShF 299.

Rhetoric of Irony, A (Booth). LTh 186.

Rhetoric of Religion, The (Burke, K.). LTh 247.

Rhetoric, Romance, and Technology (Ong). LTh 1082.

Rhetorica ad Herrenium (Cicero). LTh 1653.

Rhinoceros (Ionesco). DFor 1001-1002, 2253-2255, 2357.

Rhinthon of Tarentum. DFor 2137.

Rhodanes et Simonis. See *Babyloniaca.*

Rhode, John. M&D 1412-1419.

Rhodes, Eugene Manlove. ShF 603, 604-605.

Rhodius, Apollonius. *See* **Apollonius Rhodius.**

"Rhodora, The" (Emerson). PEng 959.

R'Hoone, Lord. *See* **Balzac, Honoré de.**

"Rhotruda" (Tuckerman). PEng 2939.

"Rhyme" (Bogan). PEng 235.

Rhymes, The (Bécquer). PFor 154, 155-158.

Rhymes (Petrarch). See *Canzoniere.*

Rhymes of a Red Cross Man (Service). PEng 2514.

Rhys, Jean. LFEng 2226-2233; ShF 244-245, 2779; **ShFSup 258-263.**

Riba, Carles. PFor 1774-1775.

Ribman, Ronald. DSup 309-316.

Ricahembra, La (Tamayo y Baus). DFor 1805-1806.

Rice, Craig. M&D 1420-1426.

Rice, Elmer. DEng 1579-1588.

Riceyman Steps (Bennett). LFEng 246.

Rich, Adrienne. PEng 2363-2371; PSup 409.

"Rich Boy, The" (Fitzgerald). ShF 1372.

Richard, Jean-Pierre. LTh 1151.

"Richard Hunt's 'Arachne'" (Hayden). PEng 1251.

Richard Hurdis (Simms). LFEng 2412-2413.

Richard II (Shakespeare). DEng 1700-1701, 2277.

Richard III (Shakespeare). DEng 1699-1700.

Richards, Francis. *See* **Lockridge, Richard, and Frances Lockridge.**

Richards, I. A. LTh 158, 306, 463, 465, 873, 895, 1204, 1206, **1221-1226,** 1523, 1554-1555, 1753, 1805, 1818, 1822.

Richardson, Dorothy. LFEng 2234-2243, 3056-3057.

Richardson, Samuel. LFEng 2244-2253, 3112-3114; LTh 887; ShF 469.

Richelieu (Bulwer-Lytton). DEng 313, 314-315.

Richelieu, Cardinal de. DFor 430.

Richler, Mordecai. LFEng 2254-2262; ShF 640, **2148-2152.**

Richter, Conrad. LFEng 2263-2273; ShF 600, 602.

Richter, Johann Paul Friedrich. *See* **Jean Paul.**

Richter und sein Henker, Der. See *Judge and His Hangman, The.*

"Rick of Green Wood, The" (Dorn). PEng 841-842.

Rickshaw Boy (Lao Shê). LFFor 2107.

Ricœur, Paul. LTh 850, **1227-1232,** 1763.

"Ricordanze, Le." *See* "Memories."

"Riddle, The" (de la Mare). ShF 257, 1251-1252.

Riddle of Samson, The (Garve). M&D 702-703.

Riddle of the Sands, The (Childers). M&D 342-343.

Riddle of the Third Mile, The (Dexter). M&D 499.

Ride Across Lake Constance, The. (Handke).
DFor 862-863.
"Ride Out" (Foote). LFEng 978.
Rider on the White Horse, The (Storm). LFFor
1683.
Riders in the Chariot (White, P.). LFEng
2870-2872
Riders of the Purple Sage (Grey). LFEng 3193-
3194.
Riders to the Sea (Synge). DEng 1904-1906.
Riding, Laura. LFEng 1193, 1198.
Riding to Lithend, The (Bottomley). DEng 256-
258.
"Ridotto of Bath, The" (Sheridan). PEng 2566.
Riede, David G. PEng 2813.
Riel (Coulter). DEng 2441.
Rifbjerg, Klaus. LFFor 2365-2366; PFor 2196.
Riffaterre, Michael. LTh 768, 889-890; PEng
3450-3451.
Riggs, Lynn. DEng 1589-1598.
"Right Hand, The" (Solzhenitsyn). ShF 2249.
Right Madness on Skye, The (Hugo, R.). PEng
1452-1453.
Right to an Answer, The (Burgess). LFEng
367.
Right You Are (If You Think So) (Pirandello).
DFor 1466-1467; LFFor 1296.
Right You Are, Mr. Moto. See *Stopover: Tokyo.*
Rigley, Dane. *See* **Gardner, Erle Stanley.**
Rihlah ila al-ghad. See *Voyage to Tomorrow.*
Rijmsnoer (Gezelle). PFor 559-560.
Riley, James Whitcomb. PEng 2372-2383.
Riley, Tex. *See* **Creasey, John.**
Rilke, Rainer Maria. LFFor 2189; PFor
1324-1333, 1925-1926.
Rimado de palacio (López de Ayala). PFor
2213-2214.
Rimas. See *Rhymes, The.*
Rimas (Vega). PFor 1604.
Rimbaud, Arthur. PFor 1334-1343, 1877-
1878.
Rime (Bembo). LTh 136; PFor 167.
Rime (Poliziano). PFor 2011.
Rime (Stampa). PFor 1461-1464.
"Rime d'amore" (Stampa). PFor 1461.
Rime e ritmi. See *Lyrics and Rhythms, The.*
Rime of the Ancient Mariner, The (Coleridge, S.
T.). LTh 1525; PEng 536-539; ShF 180.
"Rime of the Swallows" (Bécquer). PFor 158.
See also *Rhymes, The.*
"Rime varie" (Stampa). PFor 1461-1462.

Rimers of Eldritch, The (Wilson). DEng 2099-
2100.
Rinaldo (Tasso). PFor 1498.
"Rinconete and Cortadillo" (Cervantes). ShF
1090-1092.
Rinehart, Mary Roberts. M&D 1427-1433.
Ring and the Book, The (Browning, R.). PEng
344-346.
Ring of the Löwenskölds, The (Lagerlöf).
LFFor 985-986, 2344.
"Ringing the Bells" (Sexton). PEng 2521.
Ringwood, Gwen Pharis. DEng 2440-2441.
Rintala, Paavo. LFFor 2369.
Río, un amor, Un (Cernuda). PFor 320-321.
"Rip Van Winkle" (Irving). ShF 157-159,
1664-1665.
Rise of Silas Lapham, The (Howells). LFEng
1375-1376, 3049, 3086.
"Rise of the Short Story, The" (Harte). ShF
79.
Rishel, Mary Ann. ShF 2780.
"Risurrezione, La" (Manzoni). PFor 958-959.
See also *Sacred Hymns, The.*
"Rite, The" (Randall, D.). PEng 2316-2317.
Rites of Passage (Brathwaite). PEng 268; PFor
212.
Rites of Passage (Golding). LFEng 1136.
"Rites of Passage" (Gunn). PEng 1176.
Rítsos, Yánnis. PFor 1344-1352, 1967-1970.
Ritt über den Bodensee, Der. See *Ride Across
Lake Constance, The.*
"Ritter Gluck" (Hoffmann). ShF 1646.
"Ritual I" (Blackburn). PEng 196-197.
"Ritual IV" (Blackburn). PEng 197.
Ritz, The (McNally). DEng 1232-1233.
Rival Queens, The (Lee). DEng 1119-1121.
Rivals, The (Sheridan). DEng 1774-1776.
Rivas, Duke of. *See* **Saavedra, Ángel de.**
Riven Doggeries (Tate, J.). PEng 2839-2840.
"River, The" (Patmore). PEng 2189.
River Between, The (Ngugi). LFEng 1978-
1980; LFFor 2041, 2044.
"River by Our Village, The" (Tu Fu). PFor 1543.
River of Madness, The (Hakim). DSup 175.
"Riverman, The" (Bishop). PEng 186.
"Rivers, The" (Ungaretti). PFor 1566. See also
Allegria, L'.
Rivers and Forests, The (Duras). DFor 511.
Rivière, Jacques. LFFor 24, 25, 26.
Road, The (Martinson). LFFor 2351.
Road, The (Soyinka). DEng 1851-1854.

Road Block (Waugh). M&D 1685-1686.

"Road from Colonus, The" (Forster). ShF 1391.

Road Leads On, The (Hamsun). LFFor 768.

Road to Mecca, The (Fugard). DEng 705-707.

Road to Rome, The (Sherwood). DEng 1799-1801.

"Road to Shu Is Hard, The" (Li Po). PFor 891-892.

Road to the City, The (Ginzburg). LFSup 129.

Roads of Destiny, The (Henry). ShF 1631.

Roads to Freedom (Sartre). LFFor 1514-1517.

"Roan Stallion" (Jeffers). PEng 1492.

Roaring Girl, The (Middleton and Dekker). DEng 1327-1329.

Rob Roy (Scott). LFEng 2373-2377.

"Roba, La." *See* "Property."

Robbe-Grillet, Alain. LFFor 1412-1422, 2146-2147; LFSup 406; LTh 251, 1233-1238; M&D 1434-1441; ShF 2153-2157.

Robber, The (Čapek). DFor 336-337.

Robber Bridegroom, The (Welty). LFEng 2822-2823; ShF 481.

Robbers, The (Schiller). DFor 1657, 2367-2368.

Robe rouge, La. See *Red Robe, The.*

Robert Browning (Chesterton). ShF 714.

"Robert Kennedy Saved from Drowning" (Barthelme). ShF 99-100; ShFSup 25.

Roberts, Charles G. D. ShF 636.

Roberts, Elizabeth Madox. LFEng 2274-2283.

Roberts, James Hall. M&D 1442-1447.

Roberts, Lawrence. *See* **Fish, Robert L.**

Robertson, Mary Elsie. ShF 2781.

Robertson, Thomas William. DEng 1599-1611, 2364-2365; DFor 2237.

Robeson, Kenneth. *See* **Dent, Lester,** and **Goulart, Ron.**

Robin, Ralph. ShF 2782.

"Robin Redbreast" (Kunitz). PSup 245-246.

Robinson, Edwin Arlington. PEng 2384-2394, 3388.

Robinson, Lennox. DEng 1612-1621.

Robinson, Leonard Wallace. ShF 2784.

Robinson, Nugent. ShF 589.

Robinson Crusoe (Defoe). LFEng 688-690, 3019-3020.

Robinson Crusoë (Pixérécourt). DFor 1479-1480.

"Robles, Los." *See* "Oaks, The."

Robortello, Francesco. LTh 310, 1664.

Robson, Deborah. ShF 2785.

Rocannon's World (Le Guin). LFEng 1632-1633.

Rocher, Jean-Antoine. PFor 1862.

Rochester, John Wilmot, Earl of. PEng 2395-2404.

"Rock-of-the-Mas" (Corkery). ShF 667, 668.

Rock Wagram (Saroyan). LFEng 2337-2338.

Rocket to the Moon (Odets). DEng 1401-1402.

Rocket to the Morgue (Boucher). M&D 171.

"Rocking-Horse Winner, The" (Lawrence, D. H.). ShF 115, 481, 520, 786, 1792-1793.

"Rockpile, The" (Baldwin). ShF 581.

"Rocks, The" (Creeley). PEng 682.

Röda rummet. See *Red Room, The.*

Roderick Random (Smollett). LFEng 2447-2448, 3104.

Roderick, the Last of the Goths (Southey). PEng 2682-2683.

"Rodez" (Davie). PSup 87.

Rodgers, Richard, and Lorenz Hart. DEng 896, 898-899, 900, 901.

Rodríguez Álvarez, Alejandro. *See* **Casona, Alejandro.**

Roethke, Theodore. PEng 2405-2415.

"Roger Malvin's Burial" (Hawthorne). ShF 114.

Rogers, Samuel Shepard. *See* **Shepard, Sam.**

Rogue Cop (McGivern). M&D 1156.

"Rogul'ka." *See* "Buoy, The."

Rohmer, Sax. M&D 1448-1453.

Roi des aulnes, Le. See *Ogre, The.*

Roi sans divertissement, Un (Giono). LFFor 657.

Roi se muert, Le. See *Exit the King.*

Rojas, Fernando de. DFor 2483.

Rojas Zorrilla, Francisco de. DFor 2495.

Roksolanki (Zimorowic). PFor 2121.

Roland, Alan. PEng 3425.

Roland Barthes by Roland Barthes (Barthes). LTh 104.

Role of the Reader, The (Eco). LTh 425.

Rolland, Romain. LFFor 1423-1432, 2141-2142.

Rolls, Anthony. *See* **Vulliamy, C. E.**

"Romagna, The" (Pascoli). PFor 1141.

Romains, Jules. DFor 1547-1556, 2350-2351; LFFor 1433-1445.

Roman bourgeois. See *City Romance.*

Rosa do povo, A (Drummond de Andrade). PSup 99-100.
Rosalynde (Lodge). ShF 492.
"Rosalynds Madrigal" (Lodge). PEng 1732.
Rosamond (Addison). DEng 4-6.
"Rosanna" (Edgeworth). ShF 1326-1327.
"Rosas amo dos jardins do Adónis, As." *See* "Roses of the Gardens of Adonis, The."
"Rose, The" (Creeley). PEng 680.
"Rose, The" (Fanshawe). PEng 999-1000.
Rose Bernd (Hauptmann). DFor 873-874.
Rose caduche (Verga). DFor 1943-1944.
"Rose for Ecclesiastes, A" (Zelazny). ShF 371.
"Rose for Emily, A" (Faulkner). M&D 586-587; ShF 112, 1360-1363.
Rose Garden, The (Sa'di). PFor 1377, 1381-1382.
Rose of Dutcher's Coolly (Garland). LFEng 1087.
Rose of Solitude, The (Everson). PEng 991-992.
Rose of Tibet, The (Davidson). M&D 457.
"Rosebush on the Hillside" (Petőfi). PFor 1225.
"Roselily" (Walker). ShFSup 336-337.
"Rosemary" (Moore). PEng 2047.
Rosencrantz and Guildenstern Are Dead (Stoppard). DEng 1872-1873.
Rosenfeld, Rita L. ShF 2787.
Rosengarten, Theodore. ShF 627.
Rosenstock, Sami. *See* **Tzara, Tristan.**
Rosenthal, Carole. ShF 2788.
"Roses and Revolution" (Randall, D.). PEng 2315-2316.
"Roses of the Gardens of Adonis, The" (Pessoa). PFor 1209-1210.
Roshwald, Mordecai. ShF 2789.
"Rosina Alcona to Julius Branzaida." *See* "Remembrance."
Rosmersholm (Ibsen). DFor 983-985.
Ross (Rattigan). DEng 1562-1563.
Ross, Bernard L. *See* **Follett, Ken.**
Ross, Sinclair. LFEng 2284-2297; ShF 638.
Rossetti, Christina. PEng 2416-2423.
Rossetti, Dante Gabriel. LTh 1398, 1734, 1822; **PEng 2424-2434.**
Rossia i intelligentsia (Blok). PFor 196.
"Rosso Malpelo" (Verga). ShF 2381.
Rostand, Edmond. DFor 1557-1567, 2350.
Rosten, Norman. ShF 2790.
Roth, Joseph. LFFor **1446-1453,** 2191.

Roth, Philip. LFEng 2298-2310, 3324-3325; LFSup 406; ShF **2158-2162.**
Rotimi, Ola. DEng 1622-1630.
Rotrou, Jean de. DFor 1568-1577.
Rotten Skin. ShF 388, 389.
Rouge et le noir, Le. See *Red and the Black, The.*
Rough Field, The (Montague). PEng 2037-2038.
"Rough Justice" (Nebel). M&D 1266.
Rougon-Macquart, Les (Zola). LFFor 1988, 1989-1995.
Round and Round the Garden (Ayckbourn). DEng 65-66. See also *Norman Conquests, The.*
"Round Dozen, The" (Maugham). ShF 1904.
Rousseau, Jean-Baptiste. PFor 1859-1860.
Rousseau, Jean-Jacques. LFEng 3114-3115; LFFor **1454-1460,** 2120-2121; **LTh 1239-1244,** 1381, 1393-1394, 1696, 1709.
Rousset, Jean. LFEng 3118; LTh 1151.
Route antique des hommes pervers, La. See *Job, the Victim of His People.*
Route des Flandres, La. See *Flanders Road, The.*
"Route of Evanescence, A" (Dickinson). PEng 806.
Roux, Paul. *See* Roux, Saint-Pol.
Roux, Saint-Pol. PFor 1880.
Rover, The (Behn). DEng 176-177.
Rovetta, Gerolamo. DFor 2409-2410.
Rowe, Nicholas. DEng 1631-1638, 2344-2345.
Rowley, Thomas. *See* **Chatterton, Thomas.**
Rowse, A. L. PEng 1903-1904.
Rowson, Susanna. LFEng **2311-2320.**
Roxana (Defoe). LFEng 691-694.
Roy, Gabrielle. ShF 639.
Royal Family, The (Kaufman and Ferber). DEng 594.
Royal Hunt of the Sun, The (Shaffer, P.). DEng 1682-1683.
"Royal Jelly" (Dahl). ShF 1224.
"Royal Princess, A" (Rossetti, C.). PEng 2420.
Royal Way, The (Malraux). LFFor 1064-1065.
"Royalist, The" (Fanshawe). PEng 999.
Różewicz, Tadeusz. DFor 1578-1590; PFor 655, 1361-1369; PSup 409.
Rozhdeniye bogov. See *Birth of the Gods, The.*
Rozmowy z Gombrowiczem. See *Kind of Testament, A.*

"Rózsabokor a domboldalon." *See* "Rosebush on the Hillside."

"R-p-o-p-h-e-s-s-a-g-r" (Cummings). PEng 704-705.

Rubaiyat (Hikmet). PSup 179-180.

Rubáiyát (Omar Khayyám). PFor 1103, 1104-1108.

"Rücksichtslose Schimpferei." *See* "Reckless Abuse."

Rude Hiver, Un. See *Hard Winter, A.*

Rudin (Turgenev). LFFor 1773-1774.

Rueda, Lope de. DFor **1591-1600,** 2485.

"Rueda del hambriento, La." *See* "Hungry Man's Wheel, The."

Ruedo ibérico, El (Valle-Inclán). LFFor 1840-1843.

Ruell, Patrick. See **Hill, Reginald.**

Ruffian on the Stair, The (Orton). DEng 1420.

Rufián cobarde, El. See *Registro de representantes.*

Rufián vuido llamado Trampagos, El. See *Trampagos the Pimp Who Lost His Moll.*

Rugel, Miriam. ShF 2791.

Ruibal, José. DFor 2507.

Ruined Map, The (Abe). LFFor 7.

"Ruins of a Great House" (Walcott). PEng 3003-3004.

"Ruins of the *Csárda*" (Petőfi). PFor 1220-1221. See also *Clouds.*

Ruiz, Juan. PFor 2210-2212.

Ruiz de Alarcón, Juan. DFor **1601-1611,** 2493.

"Ruka blishnego." *See* "My Brother's Hand."

Rukeyser, Muriel. PSup **328-335.**

Rule of Metaphor, The (Ricœur). LTh 1763.

Ruling Class, The (Barnes). DSup 11-12.

Rumbold-Gibbs, Henry St. John Clair. *See* **Harvester, Simon.**

Rumi, Jalal al-Din. PSup **336-341.**

"Rumpole and the Golden Thread" (Mortimer). M&D 1249.

"Rumpole and the Heavy Brigade" (Mortimer). M&D 1249.

Run River (Didion). LFEng 759-761.

Run with the Hunted (Bukowski). PEng 359.

"Runagate Runagate" (Hayden). PEng 1253, 3401.

"Runaways, The" (Wescott). ShF 2423.

Runeberg, Johan Ludvig. DFor 2469; PFor 2167.

"Runes" (Nemerov). PEng 2085-2087.

Runius, Johan. PFor 2158.

"Running" (Galvin). PEng 1053-1054.

R.U.R. (Čapek and Čapek). DFor 338-340.

"Rural Meditations." *See* "Poem for a Day."

Rural Sports (Gay). PEng 1076.

"Rus." *See* "In Old Russia."

"Rus' sovetskaia" (Esenin). PFor 477-478.

Rusalka. See *Water Nymph, The.*

Rush for the Spoil, The. See *Kill, The.*

Ruskin, John. LTh 225, 1087, **1245-1249,** 1405-1407, 1731-1732, 1820; PEng 2425; ShF **2163-2169.**

Ruslan and Liudmila (Pushkin). PFor 1293, 1296, 1297-1298.

Ruslan i Lyudmila. See *Ruslan and Liudmila.*

Russell, George William. *See* Æ.

Russell, William. ShF 751.

Russet Mantle (Riggs). DEng 1595-1596.

"Russian at the Rendez-vous, The" (Chernyshevsky). LTh 289.

Russian Life in the Interior. See *Sportsman's Sketches, A.*

"Russkii chelovek na rendez-vous." *See* "Russian at the Rendez-vous, The."

Russo, Albert. ShF 2792.

Russo, Fernando. PFor 2035.

Rusteghi, I. See *Boors, The.*

Rusticus (Poliziano). PFor 1256. See also *Sylvae.*

Rutebeuf. DFor 2164.

Ruth. ShF 352-356.

Ruth (Gaskell). LFEng 1098, 1103-1104.

"Ruth's Blues" (Harper). PSup 162-163.

Ruy Blas (Hugo). DFor 968-969.

Ryan, Tim. *See* **Dent, Lester.**

Rydberg, Viktor. LFFor 2337-2338; PFor 2167.

Ryder, Jonathan. *See* **Ludlum, Robert.**

Ryga, George. DEng **1639-1648.**

Rymer, Thomas. LTh **1250-1255,** 1688.

Ryskind, Morrie. *See* **Kaufman, George S.**

Rytsar nashego vremeni (Karamzin). LFFor 2307.

Ryum, Ulla. LFFor 2366.

S

"S veselym rzhaniem pasutsia tabuny." *See* "Happily Neighing, the Herds Graze."
Sa-skya Pandita. PFor 2247.
S/Z (Barthes). LTh 106, 1765.
Saar, Ferdinand von. LFFor 2187.
Saarikoski, Pentti. PFor 2198-2199.
Saavedra, Ángel de. DFor 1612-1619, 2498.
Saavedra, Miguel de Cervantes. *See* **Cervantes, Miguel de.**
Saba, Umberto. PFor 2042-2043; PSup 342-349.
Sabato, Ernesto. LFFor 1461-1469, 2295-2296.
"Sabato del villaggio, Il." *See* "Saturday Evening in the Village."
"Sabbatha and Solitude" (Williams, T.). ShF 2437.
Sachs, Hans. DFor 1620-1627, 2178-2179.
Sachs, Leonie. *See* **Sachs, Nelly.**
Sachs, Nelly. PFor 1370-1376.
Sackett's Land (L'Amour). LFSup 223.
Sackful of News, The. ShF 497.
Sackler, Howard. DEng 1649-1653.
Sackville, Thomas. PEng 2435-2443.
Sackville, Thomas, and **Thomas Norton.** DEng 1370-1381.
Sacred Hymns, The (Manzoni). PFor 958-960.
"Sacred Mound, The" (Foote). LFEng 979.
"Sacrifice, The" (Herbert). PEng 1302.
"Sad Fate of Mr. Fox, The" (Harris, J.). ShF 1588.
"Sad Hour of Your Peace, The" (Young). PEng 3215-3216.
"Sad Landscapes" (Verlaine). PFor 1628.
Sad Shepherd, The (Jonson). DEng 2286.
Saddest Summer of Samuel S., The (Donleavy). LFEng 785.
Sade, Marquis de. LFFor 2122.
Sa'di. PFor 1377-1382.
Sadler, Mark. *See* **Collins, Michael.**
"Sadness and Happiness" (Pinsky). PEng 2214-2215.
Sadness and Happiness (Pinsky). PEng 2212-2214.
Sado kōshaku fujin. See *Madame de Sade.*

Šafárik, Pavol Jozef. PFor 1799, 1808.
"Safe" (Johnson, J.). ShF 1702-1703, 1705.
"Safe Place, The" (Morris). ShFSup 203-204.
"Safety" (Brooke). PEng 306.
Safety Net, The (Böll). LFFor 188.
Sagan (Bergman). DFor 188.
Sagan, Françoise. LFFor 1470-1479.
Sagan om Fatumeh (Ekelöf). PFor 453.
"Sage in the Sierra, The" (Van Doren). PEng 2957-2958.
Sagesse (Verlaine). PFor 1628, 1631-1632.
"Saget mir ieman, waz ist Minne?" *See* "What Is Loving?"
Saggio metafisico sopra l'entusiasmo nelle belle arti (Paradisi). LTh 1691.
Sahgal, Nayantara. LFFor 2223.
Said, Edward. LTh 506.
"Said King Pompey" (Sitwell). PEng 2629.
Saikaku, Ihara. PFor 2070; ShFSup 264-272.
Saikaku okimiyage (Saikaku). ShFSup 271.
Saikaku shokoku-banashi (Saikaku). ShFSup 270.
Saiko, Georg. LFFor 2206.
"Sail, The" (Lermontov). PFor 871.
"Sailing to Byzantium" (Yeats). PEng 3362.
"Sailor off the Bremen" (Shaw). ShF 2222-2223.
Sailors of Cattaro, The (Wolf). DFor 2020-2021.
Sailor's Song (Hanley). LFEng 1250.
Saint-Aubin, Horace de. *See* **Balzac, Honoré.**
"St. Augustine's Pigeon" (Connell). ShF 1181.
St. Cecilia or The Power of Music (Kleist). ShF 1762.
"St. Columba and the River" (Dreiser). ShF 1311.
"St. Emmanuel the Good, Martyr" (Unamuno). LFEng 3303-3304.
Saint Erkenwald (Pearl-Poet). PEng 2196.
Saint-Exupéry, Antoine de. LFFor 1480-1486, 2143.
Saint-Genet (Sartre). LTh 1274.
Saint Genet: Actor and Martyr (Sartre). DFor 2259.
St. Helena (Sherriff). DEng 1790-1791.

San-kuo chih yen-i. See *Romance of the Three Kingdoms, The.*

San Manuel Bueno, mártir. See *Saint Manuel Bueno, Martyr.*

Sanatorium pod klepsydrą. See *Sanatorium Under the Sign of the Hourglass.*

Sanatorium Under the Sign of the Hourglass (Schulz). ShFSup 279-280.

Sánchez, Florencio. DFor 2442.

Sánchez de Badajoz, Diego. DFor 2171-2173.

Sancho Cargía (Zorrilla y Moral). DFor 2063.

Sanct hansaften-spil. See *Midsummer Night's Play.*

"Sanctity, The" (Williams). PSup 390.

"Sanctuary" (Dreiser). ShF 1308-1309.

Sanctuary (Faulkner). LFEng 923-924; M&D 587-589.

"Sanctuary" (Nemerov). PEng 2079-2080.

Sand and Foam (Gibran). PEng 1085-1086; PFor 568-569.

"Sand from the Urns" (Celan). PFor 311. See also *Mohn und Gedächtnis.*

Sand, George. DFor 1398-1399; LFFor **1487-1499**, 2128.

"Sand Martin" (Clare). PEng 511.

Sand Mountain (Linney). DSup 236-237.

Sand Mountain Matchmaking (Linney). DSup 237. See also *Sand Mountain.*

Sandburg, Carl. PEng **2444-2453.**

Sandel, Cora. LFFor 2352.

Sandemose, Aksel. LFFor 2352, 2353.

Sanders, Daphne. *See* Rice, Craig.

Sanders, Lawrence. M&D 1460-1466.

"Sandman, The" (Hoffmann). LFEng 3246-3247; ShF 714-716, 1648.

"Sandpiper" (Bishop). PEng 182-183.

Sang des autres, Le. See *Blood of Others, The.*

Sanglot de la terre, Le (Laforgue). PFor 824.

"Sanies I" (Beckett). PEng 105-106; PFor 148-149.

Sanity of Art, The (Shaw). LTh 1327, 1329.

Sannazzaro, Jacopo. PFor 2011-2012, 2115.

Sanningsbarriären. See *Truth Barriers.*

Sansom, William. ShF 524, **2182-2186.**

"Sant' Ambrogio." *See* "In Sant' Ambrogio's."

"Santa Escolástica." *See* "Saint Scholastica."

Santa Fe Sunshine (Jones, P.). DEng 1012.

Santa Juana de América (Lizárraga). DFor 2444.

Santiago (Bush). DEng 2438.

Šantić, Aleksa. PFor 2255.

Santillana, Juana de Asbaje y Ramírez de. *See* **Cruz, Sor Juana Inés de la.**

Santob. *See* Sem Tob.

Santos, Bienvenido N. ShF 2793.

"Sapeur, Le" (Follain). PSup 130-131.

Sapho and Phao (Lyly). DEng 1182; PEng 1819.

Sapientia (Hroswitha). DFor 2153.

Sapper. M&D 1467-1471.

Sappho. PFor **1391-1400,** 1759-1761.

Sappho (Daudet). LFFor 424-426.

"Sappho's Last Song" (Leopardi). PFor 860. See also *Canti.*

Sara. ShF 2794.

Sara Videbeck (Almqvist). LFFor 2337.

Sarah (Sackler). DEng 1651.

Sardanapalus (Byron). DEng 329, 340-341.

Sardou, Victorien. DFor 1628-1637, 2346.

Sarmiento, Domingo Faustino. LFFor 2282, 2290, 2294.

Saroyan, William. DEng 1654-1659; LFEng 2330-2342; ShF 264-265, 547, **2187-2192.**

Sarraute, Nathalie. LFFor 1500-1508, 2143, 2146.

Sarton, May. LFEng 2343-2352; LFSup 406; PEng 2454-2465; PSup 409.

Sartor Resartus (Carlyle). LTh 1248.

Sartre, Jean-Paul. DFor 72, **1638-1652,** 2356; LFFor 1123-1124, **1509-1517,** 2143; LTh 104, 808, **1270-1276,** 1806; ShF **2193-2196.**

"Sarugashima." *See* "Island of Monkeys, The."

Sarumino. See *Monkey's Raincoat.*

"Saruzuka." *See* "Mound of the Monkey's Grave, The."

Sarvig, Ole. LFFor 2364-2365; PFor 2188-2189.

Sasame-yuki. See *Makioka Sisters, The.*

Sassoon, Siegfried. PEng **2466-2475.**

Sastre, Alfonso. DFor 2507; DSup 317-325.

"Sat." *See* "Clock, The."

Satan in Goray (Singer, Isaac). LFEng 2433-2434; LFFor 1619-1620.

Satan in Search of a Wife (Lamb). PEng 1637-1638.

Sathianandan, Kamala. ShF 642.

Satin Slipper, The (Claudel). DFor 410-411, 2352.

Satir (Reljković). PFor 2261.

"Satire Against Mankind, A" (Rochester). PEng 2402-2403.

Schernberg, Dietrich. DFor 2169-2170.

Schiller, Friedrich. DEng 2185-2186; DFor 734, **1653-1664**, 2367-2368; LFFor 2160-2161; LTh 118, 437, 531, 596, 599, 663, 670, 790, 985-986, **1295-1300**, 1302, 1305-1306; PFor 682, **1401-1411**, 1914.

Schimmelreiter, Der. See *Rider on the White Horse, The.*

Schindler's Ark. See *Schindler's List.*

Schindler's List (Keneally). LFSup 185.

Schionatulander and Sigune (Wolfram von Eschenbach). PFor 1700-1701.

Schisgal, Murray. DEng **1660-1665;** DSup 408.

Schlacht bei Lobositz, Die (Hacks). DFor 852.

Schlaf, Johannes. LTh 1719-1720.

Schlafwandler, Die. See *Sleepwalkers, The.*

"Schlechte Zeit für Lyrik." *See* "Bad Time for Poetry."

Schlegel, August Wilhelm. DFor 2369; LTh 599, 642, 663, 710, **1301-1307**, 1309, 1360-1361, 1392, 1405, 1697, 1699.

Schlegel, Friedrich. LFEng 3141, 3232-3233; LFFor 2166; LTh 433, 437, 599, **1308-1313**, 1360-1361, 1696-1697, 1699, 1702, 1704, 1708, 1710.

Schleiermacher, Friedrich. LFFor 2164; LTh 377-378, 529-530, 1359, 1702, 1809.

Schloss, Das. See *Castle, The.*

"Schmetterling." *See* "Butterfly."

Schmitten (Braun). DSup 23-24.

Schmitz, Ettore. *See* **Svevo, Italo.**

Schneeman, Peter. ShF 2796.

Schneepart (Celan). PFor 314.

Schneewittchen. See *Snowwhite.*

Schneiderman, Lawrence. ShF 2797.

"Schnellzug." *See* "Fast Train."

Schnitzler, Arthur. DFor **1665-1673**, 2377; LFFor 2188; ShF 2798.

"Scholar-Gipsy, The" (Arnold). PEng 52.

Scholar of the Western Chou Period. *See* **P'u Sung-ling.**

Scholars, The (Wu Ching-tzu). LFFor 1953-1957, 2091, 2102-2103.

Scholem, Gershom. LTh 137-138.

Scholemaster, The (Ascham). LTh 1663.

"Schöne Jugend." *See* "Beautiful Youth."

Schöne Tage. See *Beautiful Days.*

School (Robertson). DEng 1609.

"School for Dark Thoughts" (Simic). PEng 2596.

School for Scandal, The (Sheridan). DEng 1778-1780.

School for Wives, The (Molière). DFor 1333-1334.

"School Novels, The" (Wodehouse). LFEng 2920-2921.

"School of Eloquence, The" (Harrison). PSup 169-171.

"School of Giorgione, The" (Pater). LTh 1088.

School of Rakes, The (Beaumarchais). DFor 147.

Schoole of Abuse, The (Gosson). LTh 612-614, 1345, 1671.

Schoolmaster, The (Lovelace). LFEng 1702.

"Schooner *Flight*, The" (Walcott). PEng 3007.

Schopenhauer, Arthur. LFFor 2171; LTh 636, 987, 1066-1068, **1314-1318**, 1328, 1704.

Schor, Lynda. ShF 2799.

Schorer, Mark. LFEng 3252; ShF **2197-2202.**

"Schreuderspitze, The" (Helprin). ShFSup 117-118.

Schröder, Rudolf Alexander. PFor 1932.

Schroffenstein Family, The (Kleist). DFor 1073-1076.

Schüdderump, Der (Raabe). LFFor 1380, 1382-1383.

Schuler, Ruth Wildes. ShF 2800.

Schultz (Donleavy). LFEng 787.

Schultz, John. ShF 2801.

Schulz, Bruno. LFFor 2064; ShFSup **273-280.**

Schutz, Alfred. LFEng 3223-3224.

Schuyler, James. PEng **2476-2484;** PSup 409.

Schwanger Bauer, Der (Sachs). DFor 1625.

Schwartz, Delmore. PEng **2485-2494;** ShF 548-549, **2203-2208.**

Schwartz, Howard. ShF 2802.

Schwarze Schwan, Der (Walser, M.). DSup 386-387.

Schwarzwälder Dorfgeschichten (Auerbach). ShF 463.

"Schweigen" (Gomringer). PFor 594.

Schwierige, Der. See *Difficult Man, The.*

Sciascia, Leonardo. LFFor **1518-1523**, 2248.

Science and Poetry (Richards). LTh 1753.

"Science of the Night, The" (Kunitz). PSup 244.

Scillaes Metamorphosis (Lodge). PEng 1734-1735.

Scipio Aemilianus. PFor 2087.

"Scissor-Man" (MacBeth). PEng 1836.

Season of the Stranger, The (Becker). LFEng 198-199.

Season of the Strangler (Jones, M.). LFEng 1494-1495.

"Season Opens on Wild Boar in Chianti" (Warren). PEng 3023.

Seasons, The (Thomson). PEng 3326.

Season's Difference, The (Buechner). LFEng 348, 350, 351.

"Seasons of the Soul" (Tate, A.). PEng 2829-2831.

Secchia rapita, La. See *Rape of the Bucket, The.*

"Sechzigjährige dankt, Der" (Zweig). PFor 1726-1727.

"2nd Air Force" (Jarrell). PEng 1480.

Second *Aliya.* LFFor 20.

Second Birth, The (Pasternak). ShF 2062.

Second Coming, The (Percy). LFEng 2098-2099.

"Second Coming, The" (Yeats). PEng 3194-3199.

"Second Eclogue" (Garcilaso). PFor 524-525.

"Second Eclogue" (Radnóti). PFor 1313-1314.

Second Flowering, A (Cowley). LTh 316, 319.

Second Man, The (Behrman). DEng 185, 186.

Second Man and Other Poems, The (Coxe). PEng 627-628.

Second Manifesto of Surrealism (Breton). LTh 214.

Second Mrs. Tanqueray, The (Pinero). DEng 1507-1509.

Second Round, The (Peters). LFFor 2048-2049.

Second Sex, The (Beauvoir). PEng 1615.

Second Shepherds' Play, The (Wakefield Master). DEng 1993-1994.

"Second Song" (Bogan). PEng 235.

Second Sophistic. LFFor 2003, 2004.

Secondary Heaven (Popa). PFor 1270, 1272-1273.

Secondat, Charles-Louis de. *See* Montesquieu.

Secret Adversary, The (Christie). LFEng 540-541.

"Secret Integration, The" (Pynchon). ShF 2146-2147.

Secret Journey, The. See *Fury Chronicle, The.*

Secret Ladder, The (Harris). LFSup 146-148. See also *Guiana Quartet, The.*

Secret Life, The (Granville-Barker). DEng 801-802.

"Secret Life of Walter Mitty, The" (Thurber). ShF 2328.

Secret Masters, The. See *Great Wash, The.*

Secret of Heaven, The (Lagerkvist). DFor 1153-1154.

Secret of High Eldersham, The (Rhode). M&D 1416.

Secret of Luca, The (Silone). LFFor 1589-1590.

"Secret of the Short Story, The" (O'Faoláin). ShF 85.

Secret Rendezvous (Abe). LFFor 8.

"Secret Room, The" (Robbe-Grillet). ShF 2156-2157.

Secret Rose, The (Yeats). ShF 657.

Secret Service (Gillette). DEng 2398-2399.

"Secret Sharer, The" (Conrad). LFEng 3295-3296; ShF 477-478, 795, 1186-1188.

Secret Vengeance for Secret Insult (Calderón). DFor 305-306.

"Secret Woman, The" (Colette). ShF 707-708.

Secrets (Besier). DEng 200-201.

Secrets (Hale, N.). ShF 1571-1572.

Secrets and Surprises (Beattie). ShFSup 38.

Secuestro del general, El. See *Babelandia.*

Secular Masque, The (Dryden). PEng 872.

Secular Scripture, The (Frye). LTh 508, 512.

Secunda Pastorum. See *Second Shepherds' Play, The.*

Sedaine. DFor 2342.

Sédécie. See *Juives, Les.*

Sedley, Sir Charles. PEng 2504-2511.

Seduction of the Minotaur (Nin). LFEng 1966.

Sedulius. PFor 2113-2114.

"See the Moon" (Barthelme). ShFSup 23.

Seeberg, Peter. LFFor 2365.

Seed Beneath the Snow, The (Silone). LFFor 1588.

"Seeds for a Psalm" (Paz). PFor 1173-1174.

Seeds of Tomorrow. See *Virgin Soil Upturned.*

Seele und die Formen, Die. See *Soul and Form.*

"Seer Letter" (Rimbaud). PFor 1336-1337, 1343.

Seersucker Whipsaw, The (Thomas). M&D 1587.

Seesaw Log, The (Gibson). DEng 747, 749.

Seferiades, Giorgos Stylianou. *See* **Seferis, George.**

Seferis, George. PFor 1412-1418, 1947, 1961-1964.

Segelfoss Town (Hamsun). LFFor 773-774.

Seger i mörker (Lagerkvist). DFor 1156.

Seghers, Anna. LFFor **1524-1531,** 2202; ShF 2804.

Segrais. *See* **La Fayette, Madame de.**

Segreto del Bosco Vecchio, Il (Buzzati). LFFor 225-226.

Segreto di Luca, Il. See Secret of Luca, The.

Sei personaggi in cerca d'autore. See Six Characters in Search of an Author.

Seifert, Jaroslav. PFor 1805; PSup 350-358.

Seitsemän veljestä. See Seven Brothers.

Seize the Day (Bellow). LFEng 227-229.

Sejanus His Fall (Jonson). DEng 2286; LTh 1665.

Seken munezan' yō. See Worldly Mental Calculations.

Selbstbezichtigung. See Self-Accusation.

Selby, Hubert, Jr. ShF 2805.

Selected and New Poems (Dubie). PSup 106.

Selected and New Poems (Harrison). PEng 1234-1235.

Selected Essays (Warren). LTh 1524-1525.

Selected Life, A (Kinsella). PSup 236.

Selected Papers in Aesthetics (Ingarden). LTh 726.

Selected Poems (Justice). PEng 1533.

Selected Poems (Moss). PEng 2066.

Selected Poems (Reese). PEng 2346.

Selected Poems (Strand). PEng 2773.

Selected Poems and New (Villa). PEng 2982-2983; PFor 1650-1651.

Selected Poems from the Dīvānī Shamsi Tabrīz. See Divan-e Shams-e Tabriz.

Self-Accusation (Handke). DFor 859.

"Self and the Weather, The" (Whittemore). PEng 3079.

Self Condemned (Lewis, W.). LFEng 1687-1688.

Self-Consuming Artifacts (Fish). LTh 490.

"Self-Hatred of Don L. Lee, The" (Madhubuti). PEng 1892-1893.

"Self-Help" (Beer). PEng 121.

"Self-Portrait, as a Bear" (Hall). PEng 1201.

"Self-Portrait in a Convex Mirror" (Ashbery). PEng 60.

"Self-Reliance" (Emerson). LTh 455, 457-458.

Self-tormentor, The (Terence). DFor 1828, 2143.

"Selige Sehnsucht." *See* "Blessed Longing."

Sellers, Arthur Mann. *See* **Gardner, Erle Stanley.**

"Selling the House" (McPherson). PEng 1879.

Selman juonet (Kivi). DFor 1069.

Seltsame Springinsfeld Der (Grimmelshausen). LFFor 763.

"Seltsame Stadt." *See* "Strange City, A."

Sem Tob. PFor 2213.

Sembène, Ousmane. LFFor **1532-1545,** 2038, 2045-2046, 2052, 2056.

Seme sotto la neve, Il. See Seed Beneath the Snow, The.

"Semeinyi kuporos." *See* "Marriage Bond, The."

"Semejante a la noche." *See* "Like the Night."

"Semillas para un himno." *See* "Seeds for a Psalm."

"Semi-Lunatics of Kilmuir, The" (Hugo, R.). PEng 1449.

Semimaru (Chikamatsu). DFor 397.

Semimaru (Zeami). DFor 2042.

Seminar for Murder (Gill). M&D 741.

"Seminar on 'The Purloined Letter'" (Lacan). LTh 846, 849-850.

Semmelweiss (Sackler). DEng 1652.

Send No More Roses. See Siege of the Villa Lipp, The.

Sender, Ramón José. LFFor **1546-1554.**

Senderos ocultos, Los (González Martínez). PFor 611-612.

Seneca. DEng 2146, 2263; DFor **1685-1694,** 2148-2149; LTh 1045; PFor 2103-2104.

"Senex" (Betjeman). PEng 172.

Senghor, Léopold. LTh 1055-1057; PFor **1419-1429.**

Senilità. See As a Man Grows Older.

"Senility of the Short Story, The" (Cory). ShF 74.

"Senility" (Lavin). ShF 1785.

Senlin (Aiken). PEng 24.

Sennik współczesny. See Dreambook for Our Time, A.

Šenoa, August. LFFor 2076; PFor 2263.

"Señor muy viego con unas alas enormes, Un." *See* "Very Old Man with Enormous Wings."

Señor Presidente, El. See Mr. President

Sense and Sensibility (Austen). LFEng 118-119.

Sense in Sex and Other Stories (Ayyar). ShF 643.

Sense of an Ending, The (Kermode). LTh 810.

"Sense of Humour" (Pritchett). ShF 2131-2132.

Sense of Movement, The (Gunn). PEng 1169, 1170, 1171-1173.

"Sense simbolisme." *See* "Without Symbolism."

Sensenheimer Lieder (Goethe). PFor 1913.

Sensible Wege (Kunze). PFor 806-807.

Sent for You Yesterday (Wideman). LFSup 384-385. See also *Homewood Trilogy, The*.

Sent på jorden (Ekelöf). PFor 448.

Sentence, The. See *Judgment, The.*

"Sententious" (Shalamov). ShFSup 291.

"Sententious Man, The" (Roethke). PEng 2412.

"Sententsiya." *See* "Sententious."

Sentiero dei nidi di ragno, Il. See *Path to the Nest of Spiders, The.*

"Sentimental Colloquium" (Verlaine). PFor 1630.

Sentimental Education, A (Flaubert). LFFor 554-555.

Sentimental Journey, A (Sterne). LFEng 2534, 2540-2542.

"Sentimental Walk" (Verlaine). PFor 1628-1629.

Sentimento del tempo (Ungaretti). PFor 1567-1569.

Sentimento do mundo (Drummond de Andrade). PSup 99-100.

Sentiments de l'Académie française sur "Le Cid," Les (Chapelain). LTh 309-310.

"Sentinel, The" (Clarke, A.). ShF 1158-1159.

"Sephestia's Song to Her Child" (Greene). PEng 1149.

"September" (Coleridge, H.). PEng 530.

September September (Foote). LFEng 979-980.

"Sequence for Francis Parkman, A" (Davie). PSup 87.

"Sequence on the Virgin Mary and Christ, The" (Southwell). PEng 2688-2689.

"Sequence, Sometimes Metaphysical" (Roethke). PEng 2413.

Séquestrés d'Altona, Les. See *Condemned of Altona, The.*

"Ser Cepparello" (Boccaccio). ShFSup 48.

"Sera del dì di festa, La." *See* "Sunday Evening."

Serafimovich, Aleksandr. LFFor 2324.

Serao, Matilde. LFFor 2234.

"Seraph and the Poet, The" (Browning, E. B.). PEng 332-333.

Seraph on the Suwanee (Hurston). LFEng 1393.

"¿Serás, amor?" *See* "Will You Be, Love?"

Serena Blandish (Behrman). DEng 185.

"Serenade" (Sitwell). PEng 2626.

Serenade to the Big Bird (Stiles). ShF 274.

Sergeant Lamb of the Ninth. See *Sergeant Lamb's America.*

Sergeant Lamb's America (Graves, R.). LFEng 1196.

Serjeant Musgrave's Dance (Arden). DEng 46-47.

Serlio, Sebastiano. DEng 2216.

Serment de Kolvillàg, Le. See *Oath, The.*

"Sermon Fourteen" (Taylor). PEng 2847-2849.

"Sermon in a Churchyard" (Macaulay). PEng 1825.

"Sermon on the Warpland" (Brooks, G.). PEng 315.

Sermoni (Manzoni). PFor 957.

Sermons and Soda Water (O'Hara). LFEng 2051-2052.

Serpent and the Rope, The (Rao). LFEng 2210-2212; ShF 648.

"Serpent Knowledge" (Pinsky). PEng 2218-2219.

Serpent of Division, The (Lydgate). PEng 1801.

Serpent's Egg, A (Ribman). DSup 316.

Serpiente de oro, La. See *Golden Serpent, The.*

Service, Robert W. 2512-2518.

Servius. LTh 1650.

"Ses purs ongles très haut dédiant leur onyx." *See* "Her Pure Fingernails on High Offering Their Onyx."

62: Modelo para armar. See *62: A Model Kit.*

Sestra moia zhizn. See *My Sister, Life.*

Set This House on Fire (Styron). LFEng 2592, 2594-2595, 2598-2599.

Seth's Brother's Wife (Frederic). LFEng 1028-1029.

Sette giornate del mondo creato, Le (Tasso). PFor 1497-1498.

"Sette Messaggeri, I." *See* "Seven Messengers."

Settembrini, Luigi. LTh 365.

Setting Free the Bears (Irving). LFEng 1415-1416, 1417-1418.

Setting in the American Short Story of Local Color (Rhode). ShF 88.

Setting Sun, The (Dazai). LFFor 431-433.

"Setting Suns" (Verlaine). PFor 1628.

Setting the World on Fire (Wilson, A.). LFEng 2905-2906.

Settle, Mary Lee. LFSup 342-350.

Settled out of Court. See Body in the Silo, The.

Settlers of the Marsh (Grove). LFEng 1225-1227.

Seugamme (Gryphius). DFor 835.

Seuils (Genette). LTh 563.

"Seurat's Sunday Afternoon Along the Seine" (Schwartz). PEng 2493-2494.

Seven Against Reeves (Aldington). LFEng 45.

Seven Against Thebes (Aeschylus). DFor 2100.

Seven Brothers (Kivi). LFFor 2342.

Seven Conundrums, The (Oppenheim). M&D 1275.

Seven Deadly Sisters, The (McGerr). M&D 1144-1145.

"Seven Destinations of Mayerling" (Cassity). PSup 61.

"Seven Floors" (Buzzati). ShFSup 62.

Seven Gothic Tales (Dinesen). ShF 1281.

Seven Hills Away (Gonzalez). LFEng 1139.

Seven Lamps of Architecture, The (Ruskin). LTh 1248.

Seven Men (Beerbohm). ShF 943.

"Seven Messengers" (Buzzati). ShFSup 61-62.

Seven Rivers West (Hoagland). LFSup 155-156.

Seven Serpents and Seven Moons (Aguilera Malta). LFSup 12-13; LFFor 2295.

"7:VII" (Snyder). PEng 2673.

Seven Sisters, The (Prokosch). LFEng 2165-2166.

"Seven Songs for an Old Voice" (Wagoner). PEng 2990.

Seven Suspects (Innes). M&D 923-924.

Seven Types of Ambiguity (Empson). LTh 461-463, 465.

Seven Who Fled, The (Prokosch). LFEng 2164-2165.

"7 Years from Somewhere" (Levine). PEng 1717.

"17-18 April, 1961" (Oppenheimer). PEng 2144-2145.

"XVII Machines" (Heyen). PEng 1326.

Seventh Cross, The (Seghers). LFFor 1527-1528.

"Seventh House" (Narayan). ShFSup 228.

Seventh Ring, The (George). PFor 549-550.

Seventh Sinner, The (Peters, Elizabeth). M&D 1313.

"Sever." *See* "North, The."

Several Perceptions (Carter). LFSup 73-74.

"Several Voices out of a Cloud" (Bogan). PEng 234.

Sewamono. DFor 2427-2428, 2430.

Sexton, Anne. PEng 2519-2526.

Sexual Perversity in Chicago (Mamet). DEng 1237-1240.

Sexual Politics (Millett). LTh 1768.

Shackles (Césaire). PFor 328-330.

"Shadow, The" (Andersen). ShF 862-863.

Shadow, The (Shvarts). DFor 1698-1699.

Shadow Before, The (Davies). M&D 462-463.

Shadow Behind the Curtain (Johnston). M&D 941.

Shadow Flies, The (Macaulay). LFSup 262.

Shadow-Line, The (Conrad). LFEng 3313-3315.

Shadow of a Gunman, The (O'Casey). DEng 1386, 1388-1389.

"Shadow of Cain, The" (Sitwell). PEng 2630-2631.

Shadow of Night, The (Chapman). PEng 457-458.

Shadow of the Glen, The. See In the Shadow of the Glen.

Shadow of the Mountain (Wilkinson). LFEng 2893-2894.

Shadow Show (Flower). M&D 632-633.

Shadows from the Past (Neely). M&D 1271.

Shadows on the Rock (Cather). LFEng 482-483.

Shadwell, Thomas. DEng 1666-1675, 2297-2298.

Shaffer, Anthony. DEng 1676, 1677.

Shaffer, Peter. DEng 1676-1688, 2389.

Shaftesbury, Third Earl of (Anthony Ashley Cooper). LTh 240, 1319-1324, 1531; PEng 3325.

"Shag" (Booth). PEng 245-247.

Shah, Indries. ShF 177.

Shahnamah (Firdusi). PSup 119-123.

Shakespeare, William. DEng 1689-1724, 2165-2166, 2273-2285; DFor 2228; LTh 90, 301-302, 305, 448, 450, 597, 636, 641-642, 669, 709-710, 774-776, 783, 826, 862, 880, 883, 1144-1145, 1181, 1204, 1253, 1304-1305, 1393, 1398, 1517, 1671-1673, 1688, 1698; **PEng 2527-2537,** 3319-3320; ShF 146-150, **2209-2220.**

Shakespeare and Society (Eagleton). LTh 415.

"Shakespeare and the Drama" (Tolstoy). LTh 1445.

Shih-p'in (Chung Jung). LTh 1775.

Shih-shuo hsin-yü. See *New Account of Tales of the World, A*.

"Shiiku." *See* "Catch, The."

Shikasta (Lessing). LFEng 1647-1648.

Shikibu, Murasaki. *See* **Murasaki Shikibu.**

Shiloh (Foote). LFEng 977-978.

"Shiloh, a Requiem" (Melville). PEng 1948-1949.

Shimamura Hōgetsu. DFor 2432.

Shining, The (King). LFSup 206; M&D 987-988.

Shinjū ten no Amijima. See *Love Suicides at Amijima, The*.

Shintaishisho. PFor 2074.

Shiosai. See *Sound of Waves, The*.

"Ship, The" (Booth). PEng 245.

Ship, The (Ervine). DEng 561, 562, 563.

"Ship of Death, The" (Lawrence, D. H.). PEng 1686.

Ship of Fools (Brant). ShF 141.

Ship of Fools (Porter). LFEng 2101-2102, 2107-2109.

Ship of Heaven, The (Vicente). DFor 1958.

Ship of the Righteous, The (Evreinov). DFor 586.

Shipyard, The (Onetti). LFFor 1212-1213.

"Shirei Ziyyon." *See* "Ode to Zion."

Shires, The (Davie). PSup 89.

Shirley (Brontë, C.). LFEng 302-303.

Shirley, James. DEng **1810-1823**, 2292-2293.

"Shisei." *See* "Tattooer, The."

"Shita de wakareta sakki no hito." *See* "Man I Parted from, Below, The."

Shklovsky, Viktor. LFEng 3226; LFFor 2322; LTh 913-914, 975, **1339-1344**, 1505, 1758, 1803, 1822.

Shock of Recognition, The (Anderson, R.). DEng 39. See also *You Know I Can't Hear You When the Water's Running*.

Shock to the System, A (Brett). M&D 207-208.

Shockley, Ann Allen. ShF 2814.

Shoemakers, The (Witkiewicz). DFor 2011, 2279.

Shoemaker's Holiday, The (Dekker). DEng 485-488; PEng 768-770.

Shoemaker's Prodigious Wife, The (García Lorca). DFor 658-660.

Shōfū. PFor 980.

Sholokhov, Mikhail. LFFor **1555-1562**, 2324-2325.

Shoot! The Notebooks of Serafino Gubbio, Cinematograph Operator (Pirandello). LFFor 1304-1305.

"Shooting-match, The" (Longstreet). ShF 1818.

"Shooting Party, The" (Woolf). ShF 2456.

"Shooting Whales" (Strand). PEng 2773.

"Shoreline" (Barnard). PSup 25.

Short, Luke. LFEng 3196-3197.

"Short Essay on Critics, A" (Fuller). LTh 523.

Short Fiction Criticism (Thurston, Emerson, Hartman, and Wright). ShF 92.

"Short Fiction in Medieval English" (Duncan). ShF 74-75.

"Short Friday" (Singer). ShF 422.

"Short Happy Life of Francis Macomber, The" (Hemingway). ShF 1626-1627.

Short Letter, Long Farewell (Handke). LFFor 785-787.

"Short-Short Story, The" (Torgan). ShF 91.

"Short Song of Congratulation, A" (Johnson). PEng 1506.

"Short Stories" (Prichett). ShF 87.

"Short Stories for the Millions" (Baker, F. O.). ShF 70.

"Short Stories, 1950" (Mirrielees). ShF 83.

Short Stories of the Western World (Current-Garcia and Patrick, eds.). ShF 74.

"Short Story, The" (Bierce). ShF 71.

"Short Story, The" (Farrell). ShF 76.

"Short Story, The" (Gullason). ShF 78.

Short Story, The (Kempton). ShF 80.

"Short Story, The" (Matson). ShF 82.

"Short Story, The" (Maugham). ShF 82.

"Short Story, The" (Millett). ShF 83.

"Short Story, The" (Oates). ShF 84.

Short Story, The (O'Faoláin). ShF 85.

Short Story, The (Pain). ShF 86.

"Short Story, The" (Perry). ShF 87.

"Short Story, The" (Strong). ShF 90.

"Short Story, The" (Suckow). ShF 91.

"Short Story and the Novel, The" (Moravia). ShF 84.

Short Story in America, The (West, R. B.). ShF 94.

"Short Story in Embryo, The" (Steveson, L.). ShF 90.

Short Story in English, The (Canby). ShF 73.

"Short Story in Text and Intact, The" (Bleifuss). ShF 71.

"Short Story in the College Classroom (May). ShF 82.

Short Story Theories (May). ShF 82.
Short Story's Mutations from Petronius to Paul Morand, The (Newman). ShF 84.
Short View of Tragedy, A (Rymer). LTh 1254, 1688.
Shōsetsu shinzui (Tsubouchi). LTh 1005, 1793.
Shosha (Singer, Isaac). LFEng 2439-2441; LFFor 1625-1627.
"Shot, The" (Pushkin). ShFSup 252-253.
Shoten an Goray. See *Satan in Goray.*
"Shoveling Out" (Galvin). PEng 1056.
Show Boat (Kern and Hammerstein). DEng 2469-2470.
"Show me, dear Christ" (Donne). PEng 836.
Showalter, Elaine. LTh 1769, 1807.
"Shower of Gold" (Barthelme). ShFSup 24.
"Shower of Gold" (Welty). ShF 2418-2419.
Shōyō, Tsubouchi. *See* Tsubouchi Shōyō.
Shred of Evidence, A (Sherriff). DEng 1793.
Shrewsbury Fragments. DEng 2246.
Shrimp and the Anemone, The (Hartley). LFEng 1299.
"Shrine, The" (H. D.). PEng 1259.
Shroud for a Nightingale (James). LFSup 165-166; M&D 935.
Shui-hu chuan. See *Water Margin.*
Shu-jên, Chou. *See* Lu Hsün.
Shun-tzŭ chih hsiao pien-wên. LFFor 2088.
"Shunkinshō." *See* "Portrait of Shunkin, A."
Shuttle, The. See *Merry-Go-Round, The.*
Shvarts, Yevgeny. DFor 1695-1702, 2462-2463.
Sí de las niñas, El. See *When a Girl Says Yes.*
Si gira. . . . See *Shoot! The Notebooks of Serafino Gubbio, Cinematograph Operator.*
"¡Si, todo con exceso!" *See* "Yes, Too Much of Everything."
Siamese Twins, The (Gambaro). DFor 2444; DSup 147.
Siameses, Los. See *Siamese Twins, The.*
"Siberia" (McPherson). PEng 1880-1881.
Sibyl, The (Lagerkvist). LFFor 975-976.
"Sic Semper" (Untermeyer). PEng 2948.
"Sic Vita" (King). PEng 1585.
Sicilian Romance, A (Radcliffe). LFEng 2200; M&D 1390-1391.
"Sick Call, A" (Callaghan). ShFSup 71-72.
"Sick Child, The" (Colette). ShF 1166.
Sick Heart River. LFEng 334-335. See also *Mountain Meadow.*

"Sick Rose, The" (Blake). PEng 3416-3417, 3419, 3420-3423, 3424, 3425, 3427-3428.
Siddhartha (Hesse). LFFor 829-830.
Siddons, Sarah. DEng 2524.
"Sides of a Mind, The" (Everson). PEng 987-988.
Sidney, Mary. PEng 2584-2585.
Sidney, Sir Philip. DEng 2164; DFor 2203-2204; LFEng 3014-3015; LTh 609-611, 781-782, 1184, 1186, **1345-1351,** 1442, 1665; PEng 1154-1155, **2569-2581;** ShF 490-491, 492.
Sidney, Sir Robert. PEng 2582-2589.
Sidney Poet Heroical, The (Baraka). DEng 102-103.
Sidonius Apollinaris. PFor 2111.
"Sie tanzt." *See* "She Dances."
Sieben Brüder, Die (Gryphius). DFor 835.
Siebente Ring, Der. See *Seventh Ring, The.*
Siebte Kreuz, Das. See *Seventh Cross, The.*
17 Dikter (Tranströmer). PFor 1529.
"Sieg des Sommers." *See* "Triumph of Summer."
Siege of Ancona, The (Landor). PEng 1644-1645.
"Siege of Berlin, The" (Daudet). ShF 1241.
Siege of Krishnapur, The (Farrell). LFSup 111-112.
Siege of Numantia, The (Cervantes). DFor 362, 364-365.
Siege of Rhodes, The (Davenant). DEng 457-459.
Siege of Szabács, The. PFor 1975.
Siege of the Villa Lipp, The (Ambler). M&D 33.
Siegfried's Death (Hebbel). DFor 890. See also *Nibelungen, Die.*
Sienkiewicz, Henryk. LFFor **1563-1576,** 2063.
Siete lunas y siete serpientes. See *Seven Serpents and Seven Moons.*
"Sieur George" (Cable). ShF 1018-1021.
Sieveking, Alejandro. DFor 2443.
"Sight in Camp in the Daybreak Gray and Dim, A" (Whitman). PEng 3072.
"Sign, The" (Harrison). PEng 1228-1229.
Sign in Sidney Brustein's Window, The (Hansberry). DEng 878, 880-882.
Sign of the Four, The (Doyle). LFEng 809-810.
Signal Driver (White). DSup 396.

Sinclair, May. LFEng 3057.

Sinclair, Upton. LFEng 2416-2427, 3053.

Sinful Stones, The (Dickinson). M&D 511-512.

Sing to Me Through Open Windows (Kopit). DEng 1069-1070.

Singapore Grip, The (Farrell). LFSup 112.

Singer, Isaac Bashevis. LFEng 2428-2442; LFFor 1614-1627; LFSup 407; ShF 422-423, 546, 2240-2245; ShFSup 390.

Singer, Israel Joshua. LFEng 2431, 2432.

Singh, Khushwant. ShF 649-650.

Singing Bone, The (Freeman). ShF 753.

"Singing Bone, The" (Grimm). ShF 1561.

Singoalla (Rydberg). LFFor 2338.

"Singular Event, A" (Machado de Assís). ShF 1850-1852.

Singular Man, A (Donleavy). LFEng 784-785.

Sinisgalli, Leonardo. PFor 2044.

Sinking of the Titanic, The (Enzensberger). PFor 469-471.

Sinners and Shrouds (Latimer). M&D 1031.

Sinngedicht, Das (Keller). ShF 460.

Sins of the Fathers, The (Block). M&D 151.

"Sins of the Third Age" (Gordimer). ShFSup 110.

Sinyavsky, Andrei. LFFor 1628-1635; LTh 1352-1357.

Sio, Kewlian. ShF 654.

Sions Elegies Wept by Jeremie the Prophet (Quarles). PEng 2299.

Sions Sonets Sung by Solomon the King (Quarles). PEng 2299.

Sir Charles Grandison (Richardson, S.). LFEng 2251-2252.

Sir Courtly Nice (Crowne). DEng 437-439.

"Sir Dominick's Bargain" (Le Fanu). ShF 735.

"Sir Emperor" (Walther). PFor 1679.

Sir Fopling Flutter. See *Man of Mode, The.*

Sir Gawain and the Green Knight (Pearl-Poet). PEng 2206-2209, 3257-3259; ShF 2068, 2075-2077, 2078.

Sir John van Olden Barnavelt (Fletcher and Massinger). DEng 636.

Sir Launcelot Greaves (Smollett). LFEng 2449-2450.

Sir Patient Fancy (Behn). DEng 177.

"Sir Patrick Spens." ShF 404.

"Sir Pope" (Walther). PFor 1679.

Sircar, Bidal. DFor 2391.

"Siren' na kamne." *See* "Lilac on the Gravestone."

Sirena varada, La (Casona). DFor 352-355.

Sirens of Titan, The (Vonnegut). LFEng 2725-2726.

Sirin, V. *See* **Nabokov, Vladimir.**

Sirius. *See* **Martyn, Edward.**

Sirof, Harriet. ShF 2819.

"Sirventes on a Sad Occasion" (Oppenheimer). PEng 2154.

Sissman, L. E. PEng 2612-2622.

Sista mänskan (Lagerkvist). DFor 1152-1153.

Siste Athenaren, Den. See *Last Athenian, The.*

Sister, The (Swinburne). DEng 1899.

Sister Carrie (Dreiser). LFEng 831-833, 3051, 3161-3162, 3164.

Sister Mary Ignatius Explains It All for You (Durang). DSup 103.

Sister My Life. See *My Sister, Life.*

Sister Philomène (Goncourts). LFFor 712-713.

"Sisters, The" (Battin). ShF 710.

"Sisters, The" (Joyce). ShF 1719-1720.

"Sisters' Tragedy, The" (Aldrich). PEng 33.

Sitka (L'Amour). LFSup 222.

Sitting Pretty (Young). LFEng 3009-3010.

Sittlichkeit und Kriminalität (Kraus). PFor 793.

Situation Normal (Miller). DEng 1337-1338.

Sitwell, Edith. PEng 2623-2632.

Six and One Remorses for the Sky (Elýtis). PFor 1966-1967.

Six Characters in Search of an Author (Pirandello). DFor 1467-1469; LFFor 1297; LTh 1101.

Six Epistles to Eva Hesse (Davie). PSup 88.

"Six Feet of the Country" (Gordimer). ShFSup 106-107.

"Six Soldiers of Fortune" (Grimm). ShF 1557.

Six Stories Written in the First Person Singular (Maugham). ShF 1904, 1905.

Sixth Heaven, The (Hartley). LFEng 1299-1300.

62: A Model Kit (Cortázar). LFFor 380-382.

Sjæl efter døden, En (Heiberg, J.). DFor 905-907.

Sjálfstætt fólk. See *Independent People.*

Sjöberg, Birger. PFor 2177.

Sjöwall, Maj, and Per Wahlöö. M&D 1495-1501.

Skallagrimsson, Egil. ShF 388-389.

"Skaters, The" (Ashbery). PEng 59, 60.

Skelton, John. PEng 2633-2640, 3286.

Smile in His Lifetime, A (Hansen). M&D 831.
Smiley's People (le Carré). LFEng 1617-1618;
M&D 1044.
Smith, Alexander. LTh 1703, 1706.
Smith, Caesar. *See* **Trevor, Elleston.**
Smith, Cecil Lewis Troughton. *See* **Forester,
C. S.**
Smith, Clark Ashton. ShF 566.
Smith, Cordwainer. ShF 2821.
Smith, Dave. PEng 2641-2648; PSup 409.
Smith, Ernest Bramah. *See* **Bramah, Ernest.**
Smith, June Edith. LFEng 1875-1876.
Smith, Martin Cruz. M&D 1502-1507.
Smith, R. E. ShF 2822.
Smoke (Turgenev). LFFor 1777-1778.
Smoke and Steel (Sandburg). PEng 2451.
Smoking Mountain, The (Boyle). ShF 1002.
Smollett, Tobias. LFEng 2443-2451, 3073;
PEng 2649-2655.
"Smooth Gnarled Crape Myrtle" (Moore).
PEng 2045.
Smrek, Ján. PFor 1810-1811.
Smrt Smail-age Čengijića (Mažuranić). PFor
2262.
Smudging (Wakoski). PEng 2998.
Smug Citizen (Gorky). DFor 781-783.
Smuggler's Bible, A (McElroy). LFSup 283-
284.
"Snail, The" (Giusti). PFor 575-576.
"Snails" (Ponge). PFor 1262.
"Snake" (Lawrence, D. H.). PEng 1684.
"Snake of the Cabin, The" (Simms). ShF 2237-
2238.
Snake Pit, The (Undset). LFFor 1805. See also
Master of Hestviken, The.
Snakes (Young). LFEng 3006-3008.
"Snapshot of Uig in Montana, A" (Hugo, R.).
PEng 1453, 1454.
Snapshots (Robbe-Grillet). ShF 2154.
"Snapshots of a Daughter-in-Law" (Rich).
PEng 2366-2368.
Snarl of the Beast, The (Daly, C.). M&D 446-
447.
Sneaky People (Berger). LFEng 256.
"Sneg." *See* "Snow."
Snezhnaya maska (Blok). PFor 199-200.
Snob, The (Sternheim). DFor 1737-1738.
Snodgrass, Quintus Curtius. *See* **Twain, Mark.**
Snodgrass, Thomas Jefferson. *See* **Twain, Mark.**
Snodgrass, W. D. PEng 1785, 2656-2665;
PSup 409-410.

Snoilsky, Carl. PFor 2167.
Snooks, John. *See* **Twain, Mark.**
Snooty Baronet (Lewis, W.). LFEng 1686.
"Snow" (Annensky). PFor 43.
"Snow" (Beattie). ShFSup 41-42.
"Snow" (Grove). ShF 637.
"Snow, The" (Verhaeren). PFor 1623. See also
Villages illusoires, Les.
Snow, C. P. LFEng 2452-2465, 3058.
"Snow-Bound" (Whittier). PEng 3088-3089.
Snow Country (Kawabata). LFFor 910-911.
Snow Goose, The (Gallico). ShF 1444-1445.
Snow Leopard, The (Matthiessen). LFEng
1825.
"Snow Queen, The" (Andersen). ShF 860-862.
"Snow-Storm, The" (Emerson). PEng 957.
Snow White (Barthelme). LFEng 172-175.
"Snow White" (Grimm). ShF 1560.
"Snowfall in the Afternoon" (Bly). PEng 224.
Snowwhite (Walser, R.). ShFSup 347.
"Snowy Heron" (Ciardi). PEng 503.
Snyder, Gary. PEng 2666-2676, 3380; PSup
410.
"So crewell prison" (Surrey). PEng 2789.
"So Deep We Never Got" (Blackburn). PEng
200.
"So I Said I Am Ezra" (Ammons). PSup 9-10.
So Little Time (Marquand). LFEng 1818.
"So Much Water Close to Home" (Carver).
ShFSup 79.
So the Wind Won't Blow It All Away
(Brautigan). LFEng 294-295.
Soap (Ponge). PFor 1263.
Sobachie serdtse. See *Heart of a Dog, The.*
"Soberba." *See* "Foolish Pride."
"Sobolos os rios que vão." *See* "Over the
Rivers That Flow."
Soboriane. See *Cathedral Folk, The.*
Sobre héroes y tumbas. See *On Heroes and
Tombs.*
Sobre los ángeles. See *Concerning the Angels.*
Society (Robertson). DEng 1607-1608.
"Sociological Approach to Literature, The"
(Witte). PEng 3407.
Socrates. LTh 1634-1635.
Söderberg, Hjalmar. LFFor 2344-2345.
Södergran, Edith. PFor 2180-2181; PSup
359-367.
Sodome et Gomorrhe. See *Cities of the Plain.*
Sodoms Ende. See *Man and His Picture, A.*
Sœur, La (Rotrou). DFor 1574-1575.

Sœur Philomène. See *Sister Philomène.*
Sœurs Vatard, Les (Huysmans). LFFor 861-862.
Sofonisba, La (Trissino). DFor 1882-1885, 2395.
Soft Machine, The (Burroughs). LFEng 387, 389.
"Soil" (Salinas). PFor 1386.
"Soirée perdue, Une." *See* "Wasted Evening, A."
Soirs, Les (Verhaeren). PFor 1622.
Sol, i de dol (Foix). PFor 489.
Solar Lottery (Dick). LFSup 94.
Solaris (Lem). LFFor 1010.
Sólarljóth. See *Lay of the Sun, The.*
"Sold!" (Cheyney). M&D 334-335.
Soldati, Mario. LFFor 2256.
"Soldier, The" (Brooke). PEng 306.
"Soldier, A" (Suckling). PEng 2779.
"Soldier and the Star, The" (Patchen). PEng 2181.
Soldiers (Hochhuth). DFor 918, 921-922.
Soldiers, The (Lenz). DFor 1166-1168.
Soldier's Art, The (Powell). LFEng 2120.
"Soldiers Bathing" (Prince). PSup 316.
"Soldier's Embrace, A" (Gordimer). ShFSup 108-109.
Soldier's Fortune, The (Otway). DEng 1448-1449.
Soledad (Unamuno y Jugo). DFor 1912-1913.
Soledad sonora, La (Jiménez). PFor 751-752.
Soledades (Machado). PFor 913-914.
Soledades. See *Solitudes, The.*
"Soleils chanteurs, Les" (Char). PFor 335.
"Soleils couchants." *See* "Setting Suns."
Solemne Passion of the Soule's Love, A (Breton, N.). PEng 280.
Solger, Karl Wilhelm Ferdinand. LTh 1358-1362, 1702.
Solid Mandala, The (White, P.). LFEng 2872-2873.
"Solid Objects" (Woolf). ShF 2456.
Soliman and Perseda (Kyd). DEng 1095-1096.
"Solitary" (Boland). PSup 39.
"Solitary, The" (Teasdale). PEng 2858.
"Solitary Life, The" (Leopardi). PFor 859. See also *Canti.*
"Solitary Thrush, The" (Leopardi). PFor 861. See also *Canti.*
Solitudes, The (Góngora). PFor 603-604.
Soljan, Antun. PFor 2266.

Sollers, Philippe. LTh 832.
"Solo Song, A" (McPherson). ShF 1857.
Sologub, Fyodor. LFFor 2320.
Solomon (Prior). PEng 2291.
Solomòs, Dionysios. PFor 1450-1458, 1948-1950.
Solon. PFor 1761.
Solovyov, Vladimir. PFor 2144-2145.
Solstad, Dag. LFFor 2364.
"Solstice Poem" (Atwood). PEng 68.
Soluna (Asturias). LFFor 85.
Solzhenitsyn, Aleksandr. LFEng 3154; LFFor 1636-1647, 2327-2328; LTh 938-939; ShF 279-280, 2246-2251; ShFSup 287, 289.
Sombra del padre, La (Martínez Sierras). DFor 1284.
Sombra del paraíso (Aleixandre). PFor 30-31.
"Some Anomalies of the Short Story" (Howells, W. D.). ShF 79.
"Some Clinical Notes" (Shaw, H.). ShF 89.
Some Dames Are Deadly. See *Red Gardenias.*
"Some General Instructions" (Koch). PEng 1628.
"Some Grist for Mervyn's Mill" (Richler). ShF 2151-2152.
"Some Like Them Cold" (Lardner). ShF 1773.
"Some Notes for an Autobiographical Lecture" (Trilling). LTh 1456.
"Some Notes on Recent American Fiction" (Bellow). ShF 949, 951.
"Some of Us Had Been Threatening Our Friend Colby" (Barthelme). ShF 725.
"Some Parishioners" (Moore). ShF 660.
Some Prefer Nettles (Tanizaki). LFFor 1713; ShFSup 315-316.
"Some Recent Fiction" (Young). PEng 3217.
Some Versions of Pastoral (Empson). LTh 461, 463.
Somers, Paul. *See* Garve, Andrew.
Somerset Masque, The (Campion). PEng 427.
Something About a Soldier (Harris). LFEng 1278, 1282-1284.
Something Happened (Heller). LFEng 1334-1335.
"Something Out There" (Gordimer). ShFSup 109-111.
Something Short and Sweet (Bates). ShFSup 31.
Something Terrible, Something Lovely (Sansom). ShF 275.

"Something There" (Beckett). PEng 106; PFor
149.
Something to Be Desired (McGuane). LFSup
295-297.
Sometimes a Great Notion (Kesey). LFEng
1534-1536.
Sommergeschichten (Storm). ShF 463.
"Somnambule Ballad" (García Lorca). PFor
517.
Son Avenger, The (Undset). LFFor 1805. See
also *Master of Hestviken, The.*
"Son du cor, Le." *See* "Sounding of the
Hunting Horn, The."
Son Excellence Eugène Rougon. See *His
Excellency.*
Son of Don Juan, The (Echegaray). DFor 532-
533.
Son of Learning, The (Clarke). DEng 375-376.
Son of Perdition, The (Cozzens). LFEng 631.
Son of the Bondwoman, The (Pardo Bazán).
LFFor 1221-1226.
Son of the Soil, A. *See* **Fletcher, J. S.**
Sonata de otoño. See *Autumn Sonata.*
Sonata tou selēnophōtos, Ē. See *Moonlight
Sonata, The.*
Sonatas. See *Pleasant Memoirs of the Marquis
de Bradomín, The.*
"Sonatina in Green" (Justice). PEng 1533.
Sondheim, Stephen. DEng 2477-2478.
"Soñé con un verso. . ." (González Martínez).
PFor 611.
"Sonet." *See* "Sonnet."
Sonetni venec (Prešeren). PFor 2268.
Sonetos espirituales (Jiménez). PFor 752.
Sonette an Orpheus, Die. See *Sonnets to
Orpheus.*
"Sonetti" (Foscolo). PFor 493-494.
Sonety krymskie. See *Sonnets from the Crimea.*
Sonezaki shinjū. See *Love Suicides at Sonezaki,
The.*
"Song" (Congreve). PEng 554-555.
"Song" (Creeley). PEng 682.
"Song: When Phillis watched her harmless
sheep" (Etherege). PEng 976.
Song (Harper). PSup 163.
"Song: Adieu, farewell earths blisse" (Nashe).
PEng 2073-2074.
"Song: Autumn Hath all the Summer's Fruitfull
Treasure" (Nashe). PEng 2073.
"Song: Fayre Summer droops" (Nashe). PEng
2073.

"Song" (Radnóti). PFor 1314.
"Song: My dear Mistress has a heart, A"
(Rochester). PEng 2399-2400.
"Song" (Schuyler). PEng 2480.
"Song: Not *Celia*, that I juster am" (Sedley).
PEng 2509.
"Song: *Phillis* is my only Joy" (Sedley). PEng
2508.
"Song: *Phillis*, let's shun the common Fate"
(Sedley). PEng 2508.
Song and Idea (Eberhart). PEng 930.
"Song for a Slight Voice" (Bogan). PEng 235.
"Song for Billie" (Hughes, L.). PEng 3402.
"Song for My Comrades" (Biermann). PFor
191.
"Song for St. Cecilia's Day, A" (Dryden).
PEng 878.
"Song in Dialogue, For Two Women"
(Congreve). PEng 555.
"Song in praise of a Ladie, A" (Heywood, J.).
PEng 1335.
Song of a Goat (Clark). DEng 2422; DSup 53-
54.
"Song of a Man Who Has Come Through"
(Lawrence, D. H.). PEng 1683.
"Song of Autumn" (Verlaine). PFor 1629.
Song of Bernadette, The (Werfel). LFFor 1912.
"Song of Bornholm, The" (Karamzin). LFFor
2307.
Song of Death, The (Hakim). DSup 177.
"Song of Grendel, The" (Gardner). ShF 1459-
1460.
Song of Hiawatha, The (Longfellow). PEng
1752.
Song of Hildebrand, The. See *Hildebrandslied.*
Song of Los, The (Blake). PEng 215-216.
"Song of Love" (Carducci). PFor 271.
"Song of Myself" (Whitman). PEng 3066-
3068, 3386.
"Song of Queene Isabel, A" (Deloney). PEng 787.
Song of Roland. LFFor 2110; PFor 1747,
1766-1767, 1830, 1831; ShF 134, 135.
Song of Solomon. ShF 348-349.
Song of Solomon (Morrison). LFEng 1919-
1922.
"Song of the Bell, The" (Schiller). PFor 1402,
1410.
"Song of the Borderguard, The" (Duncan).
PEng 901.
"Song of the Chattahoochee" (Lanier). PEng
1662-1663.

"Song of the Fort Donald Railroad Gang" (Brecht). PFor 222-223.

"Song of the Horseman, The" (García Lorca). PFor 516.

Song of the Lark, The (Cather). LFEng 478-479.

"Song of the Shirt, The" (Hood). PEng 1388.

"Song of the Son" (Toomer). PEng 2917.

Song of the World, The (Giono). LFFor 655-656.

Song 6 (Sidney, R.). PEng 2585-2586.

"Song, To my Inconstant Mistress" (Carew). PEng 433-434.

Song Turning Back into Itself, The (Young). PEng 3215.

"Song Which the Old Man Heard in His Dreams, The" (Castro). PFor 280. See also *Beside the River Sar.*

Songe de Vaux, Le (La Fontaine). PFor 812, 813, 814-815.

Songe en complainte (Charles d'Orléans). PFor 341-343.

Songes and Sonettes. See *Tottel's Miscellany.*

Songs and Lyrics from the Plays (MacDonald, H., ed.). PEng 96-97.

Songs Before Sunrise (Swinburne). PEng 2819-2820.

"Song's Eternity" (Clare). PEng 512.

"Songs for Signare" (Senghor). PFor 1427-1428. See also *Nocturnes.*

Songs of Dream and Death, The (George). LTh 575.

Songs of Experience (Blake). PEng 207, 208-209.

Songs of Innocence (Blake). PEng 207, 208-209.

"Songs of Sorrow" (Awoonor). PFor 112-113.

Songs of the Earth (Johnson). PSup 213-214.

Songs of the Sourdough (Service). PEng 2517.

Songs of Travel (Stevenson). PEng 2756-2757.

Sonim de Geshichte fun a Liebe. See *Enemies.*

"Sonne, The" (Herbert). PEng 1301.

Sonne, Jørgen. PFor 2197.

"Sonnet 49" (Berryman). PEng 161.

"Sonnet" (Brodsky). PFor 238-239.

"Sonnet--To Science" (Poe). PEng 2242-2243.

Sonnet 15 (Shakespeare). PEng 2532.

Sonnet 60 (Shakespeare). PEng 2532.

Sonnet 64 (Shakespeare). PEng 2534.

Sonnet 116 (Shakespeare). PEng 2533, 2536.

Sonnet 124 (Shakespeare). PEng 2535-2536.

Sonnet 126 (Shakespeare). PEng 2536.

Sonnet 144 (Shakespeare). PEng 2535.

Sonnet 21 (Sidney, R.). PEng 2585.

"Sonnet X" (Tuckerman). PEng 2939-2940.

"Sonnet (Remembering Louise Bogan), The" (Hoffman). PEng 1359.

"Sonnet to My Father" (Justice). PEng 1529.

Sonnets (Boker). DEng 219.

Sonnets (Shakespeare). DEng 1689-1690, 2274; PEng 2529-2537.

Sonnets and Stanzas of Petrarch, The. See *Canzionere.*

Sonnets for Helen (Ronsard). PFor 1357.

Sonnets from the Crimea (Mickiewicz). PFor 1019-1020.

Sonnets from the Portuguese (Browning, E. B.). PEng 329-330.

Sonnets pour Hélène. See *Sonnets for Helen.*

Sonnets to Orpheus (Rilke). PFor 1329.

Sonnevi, Göran. PFor 2192-2193.

"Sonny's Blues" (Baldwin, James). ShF 909-910.

"Sono namida." *See* "Tears in Your Eyes."

Sons and Lovers (Lawrence, D. H.). LFEng 1226, 1585-1589.

Sontag, Susan. LTh 1363-1368; ShF 816, 817.

"Sopa" (Reyes). PFor 1322.

Sophie's Choice (Styron). LFEng 2593, 2601-2603.

Sophist (Plato). LTh 1635.

Sophocles. DEng 2141; **DFor 1722-1733,** 2090, 2120, 2103-2110.

Sophonisba (Marston). DEng 1273-1274.

Sophonisbe (Mairet). DFor 1249-1251.

Šopov, Aco. PFor 2273.

"Sopra un basso rilievo antico sepolcrale." *See* "On the Ancient Sepulchral Bas-Relief."

Sopro de vida, Um (Lispector). LFSup 247.

"Sora no kaibatsu Agui." *See* "Aghwee the Sky Monster."

"Sorcerer's Daughter, The" (Bogan). PEng 233.

"Sorceress in the Forest, The" (Eichendorff). PFor 440.

Sorel, Charles. LFFor 2027.

Sorellina, La (Martin du Gard). LFFor 1116. See also *World of the Thibaults, The.*

Sorge, Reinhard Johannes. LTh 1726.

Sorgen un die Macht, Die (Hacks). DFor 852.

"Sorrow Acre" (Dinesen). ShF 481, 1283-1284.

Sorrow Beyond Dreams, A (Handke). LFFor 787-788.

"Sorrow, I Do Not Wish You" (Salinas). PFor 1388.

Sorrows of Frederick, The (Linney). DSup 237-238.

Sorrows of Han, The (Ma). DFor 2315.

Sorrows of Young Werther, The (Goethe). LFEng 3028, 3112, 3115-3117; LFFor 670-673, 2159; ShFSup 99-101.

Sōseki, Natsumi. LFFor 2276-2277.

Sosies, Les (Rotrou). DFor 1573-1574.

Sositheus. DFor 2120.

Sot-Weed Factor, The (Barth). LFEng 162-165.

Sotades of Maronea. DFor 2135.

Sotoba Komachi (Mishima). DFor 1322-1323.

Sottie. DFor 2176.

Soul and Form (Lukács). LTh 935-936.

Soul Enchanted, The (Rolland). LFFor 1430-1431.

"Soul Longs to Return Whence It Came, The" (Eberhart). PEng 930-931.

Soule's Immortal Crowne (Breton, N.). PEng 282.

Soul's Tragedy, A (Browning). DEng 296.

Soulier de satin, Le. See *Satin Slipper, The.*

Sound and the Fury, The (Faulkner). LFEng 918-922.

Sound of the Mountain, The (Kawabata). LFFor 912-913.

Sound of Waves, The (Mishima). LFFor 1158-1159.

"Sounding of the Hunting Horn, The" (Verlaine). PFor 1632.

"Soundings" (Pastan). PEng 2172, 2174.

"Sounds of Eger" (Petőfi). PFor 1218.

Soupault, Philippe. LTh 214.

"Source, The" (Porter). ShF 2114.

"Source" (Walker). ShFSup 341-342.

Source of Light, The (Price). LFEng 2135-2136.

Sous le soleil de Satan. See *Star of Satan, The.*

"Sousa" (Dorn). PEng 841.

"South Africa" (Gordimer). ShF 78.

South Star (Fletcher, J. G.). PEng 1028.

Southern, Terry. LFEng 2466-2472.

Southern Cross, The (Wright, C.). PEng 3153-3154.

Southern Exposure (Akalaitis). DSup 3-4.

Southern Mail (Saint-Exupéry). LFFor 1483-1484.

Southern Review. ShF 627-628.

Southey, Robert. LTh 258, 299, 1697; PEng 2677-2685.

Southpaw, The (Harris). LFEng 1281-1282.

Southwell, Robert. PEng 2686-2692.

Souvenirs romantiques (Gautier). LTh 553-554.

Sova, Antonín. PFor 1803.

"Sovremennaya russkaya literatura." See "Contemporary Russian Literature."

Sowdone of Babylon, The. ShF 446.

Soyinka, Wole. DEng 1845-1857, 2422; DSup 408; LFFor 2037, 2054-2055; LFSup 351-359; LTh 1063, 1369-1377.

"Space" (Kennedy). PEng 1573-1574.

Space (Michener). LFSup 303-304.

"Space Spiders, The" (Hall). PEng 1204.

Spach, John Thom. ShF 2823.

"Spacious Firmament on High, The" (Addison). PEng 12.

Spacks, Patricia Meyer. LTh 1769.

Spain, John. See Adams, Cleve F.

Spain, Take This Cup from Me (Vallejo). PFor 1593-1595. See also *Human Poems.*

"Spaniard Speaks of His Homeland, A" (Cernuda). PFor 321-322. See also *Nubes, Las.*

Spaniards in Peru, The (Kotzebue). DFor 1088.

Spanier, Muriel. ShF 2824.

Spanish Bawd, Represented in Celestina, The. See *Celestina, La.*

"Spanish Lady's Love, The" (Deloney). PEng 789.

Spanish Tragedy, The (Kyd). DEng 1088-1094, 1096; ShF 729.

Sparagus Garden, The (Brome). DEng 286-287.

Spark, Muriel. LFEng 2473-2487; LFSup 407; ShF 2252-2258; ShFSup 390.

"Sparrows" (Abbas). ShF 649.

Späth, Gerold. LFFor 2201, 2210-2211.

Spatz, Ronald. ShF 2825.

Spaziergang, Der. See *Walk and Other Stories, The.*

"Speak a Welcome" (Walther). PFor 1675.

Speak, Parrot (Skelton). PEng 2638.

Speaking Likenesses (Rossetti, C.). PEng 2416.

Special Occasions (Slade). DEng 1842-1843.

"Sprache." *See* "Language."
"Sprache als Hort der Freiheit, Die" (Böll). ShF 972.
Sprachgitter. See *Speech-Grille.*
Sprat, Thomas. PEng 3496.
Spreading the News (Gregory). DEng 852, 853.
"Spring, The" (Barnard). PSup 27.
"Spring" (Hopkins). PEng 1400.
Spring and Asura (Miyazawa). PSup 283-284.
"Spring in Fialta" (Nabokov). ShFSup 221-222.
Spring of the Thief (Logan). PEng 1741.
"Spring on Troublesome Creek" (Still). PEng 2764.
Spring Snow (Mishima). LFFor 1159.
"Spring Sowing" (O'Flaherty). ShF 2009.
Springer, Mary Doyle. LFEng 3253-3254.
Springhouse, The (Dubie). PSup 106-107.
"Springing of the Blade, The" (Everson). PEng 989-990.
Spring's Awakening (Wedekind). DFor 1975-1976.
Sputniki. See *Train, The.*
Spy in the House of Love, A (Nin). LFEng 1995.
Spy in the Vodka. See *Cold War Swap, The.*
Spy Who Came in from the Cold, The (Le Carré). LFEng 1612-1614.
Square, The (Duras). DFor 510.
Square in the Eye (Gelber). DEng 743-744.
Square Root of Wonderful, The (McCullers). DEng 1198-1200.
"Squares" (Hollander). PEng 1364.
"Squire's Daughter, The" (Pushkin). ShFSup 255.
"Sredni Vashtar" (Saki). M&D 1455; ShF 2173.
S.S. San Pedro (Cozzens). LFEng 631-632.
Ssu-k'ung T'u. LTh 1776.
Stab in the Dark, A (Block). M&D 151-152.
Stadler, Ernst. PFor 1928-1929.
Staël, Madame de. LFFor 2124; LTh 863, 1243, 1302, 1306, **1378-1384**, 1392, 1696, 1699, 1704, 1706; PFor 1864-1865.
Staff, Leopold. PFor 2128.
Stafford, Jean. ShF **2259-2263.**
Stafford, William. PEng **2719-2723**; PSup 410.
Stage Door (Kaufman and Ferber). DEng 593-594.

Stage for Poetry, A (Bottomley). DEng 255-256.
Stagge, Jonathan. *See* **Quentin, Patrick.**
Stagnelius, Erik Johan. LFFor 2335; PFor 2165.
Stained Glass (Buckley). M&D 234-235.
Stallerhof. See *Farmyard.*
"Stalnaia cikada." *See* "Steel Cicada, The."
Stalnaya ptitsa. See *Steel Bird, The.*
Stampa, Gaspara. PFor **1459-1465.**
Stand, The (King). LFSup 206.
Standiford, Les. ShF 2830.
Standish, Lorraine. ShF 2831.
Stanfill, Dorothy. ShF 2832.
Stanislavsky, Konstantin. DEng 2233-2234, 2522, 2526-2527, 2532; DFor 2237, 2455.
Stanley, Thomas. PEng **2724-2730.**
Stanton, Charles M. *See* **Gardner, Erle Stanley.**
Stanton, Vance. *See* **Avallone, Michael.**
"Stantsia Zima." *See* "Zima Junction."
"Stantsionnyi smotritel." *See* "Station Master, The."
"Stanzas from the Grande Chartreuse" (Arnold). PEng 53.
"Stanzas in Meditation" (Stein). PEng 2740.
"Stanzas in Terza Rima" (Hofmannsthal). PFor 674, 675.
Stanze (Poliziano). PFor 1252-1253, 2011.
Stanze cominciate di Giuliano de' Medici. See *Stanze.*
"Star, The" (Clarke, A.). ShF 371-372, 1159-1160.
"Star-Apple Kingdom, The" (Walcott). PEng 3007.
"Star in the Valley, The" (Murfree). ShF 227.
Star Light, Star Bright (Ellin). M&D 577.
Star of Satan, The (Bernanos). LFFor 148-149.
Star of the Covenant, The (George). LTh 575-576.
Star of the Unborn (Werfel). LFFor 1908, 1912-1913.
Stara kobieta wysiaduje. See *Old Woman Broods, The.*
Starik. See *Old Man.*
Stark, Richard. *See* **Westlake, Donald E.**
Starke Stamm, Der (Fleisser). DFor 624-625.
"Starlight Night, The" (Hopkins). PEng 1400.
Starobinski, Jean. LTh 1151-1152.
Starrett, Vincent. M&D **1514-1520.**
Starry Ticket, A. See *Ticket to the Stars, A.*

"Stivale, Lo." *See* "Boot, The."

Stockanes, Anthony E. ShF 2841.

Stockton, Frank R. M&D 1533-1539; ShF 2279-2290.

Stockwell, Nancy. ShF 2842.

Stone (Mandelstam). PFor 936-937, 941.

Stone, Zachary. *See* **Follett, Ken.**

Stone Angel, The (Laurence). LFEng 1571-1573.

Stone Guest, The (Pushkin). DFor 1499-1500. See also *Little Tragedies*.

Stone Maiden, The (Johnston). M&D 941.

Stones of Venice, The (Ruskin). LTh 1248-1249.

"Stony Limits" (MacDiarmid). PSup 263-264.

Stony Limits and Other Poems (MacDiarmid). PSup 263-264.

Stop It, Whoever You Are (Livings). DEng 1155.

Stopfkuchen. See *Tubby Schaumann*.

Stopover: Tokyo (Marquand). M&D 1187.

Stoppard, Tom. DEng 1866-1879, 2204, 2389; DSup 408.

"Stopping a Kaleidoscope" (Eberhart). PEng 934.

"Stopping by Woods on a Snowy Evening" (Frost). PEng 3388.

Stops of Various Quills (Howells). PEng 1424-1425.

Storey, David. DEng 1880-1891.

Storia della letteratura. See *History of Italian Literature*.

Storia di una capinera (Verga). LFFor 1860.

"Storie of Wyllyam Canygne, The" (Chatterton). PEng 470, 473.

"Stories" (Heine). PFor 651.

"Stories" (Jarrell). ShF 80.

Stories and Texts for Nothing (Beckett). ShF 939.

Stories from Indian Christian Life (Sathianandan). ShF 642.

Stories of Liam O'Flaherty, The (O'Flaherty). ShF 2006.

Stories of Red Hanrahan (Yeats). ShF 657, 2472.

Stories of Three Burglars, The (Stockton). M&D 1536-1537.

"Storm, The" (Chopin). ShF 1135.

Storm, The (Drinkwater). DEng 509.

Storm, The (Ostrovsky). DFor 1450-1451, 2454.

Storm, Elliott. *See* **Halliday, Brett.**

Storm, Theodor. LFFor 1675-1684, 2172-2173; PFor 1921, 1922.

Storm and Echo (Prokosch). LFEng 2167.

Storm and Other Poems, The (Montale). PFor 1051-1052.

Storm in Shanghai. See *Man's Fate*.

Storm over Chandigarh (Sahgal). LFFor 2223.

Stormy Night, A (Caragiale). DFor 346-347, 2298.

"Story, The" (Pasternak). ShF 2061-2062.

"Story About the Most Important Thing, A" (Zamyatin). ShFSup 372.

Story and Discourse (Chatman). ShF 120-121.

Story of a Bad Boy, The (Aldrich). LFEng 51-53.

"Story of a Contraoctave, The" (Pasternak). ShF 2059.

Story of a Novel, The (Wolfe). LFEng 2932.

"Story of an Hour, The" (Chopin). ShF 707, 1133.

Story of Belphagor the Arch Demon, The (Machiavelli). ShF 1681.

Story of Gísli the Outlaw, The. See *Gísli saga*.

Story of Gösta Berling, The. See *Gösta Berling's Saga*.

Story of Him, The (Vilalta). DSup 377-378.

"Story of Justin Martyr, The" (Trench). PEng 2943.

Story of Marie Powell, Wife to Mr. Milton, The (Graves, R.). LFEng 1197-1198.

"Story of Maupassant, A" (O'Connor, Frank). ShF 1993.

"Story of Our Lives, The" (Strand). PEng 2771.

Story of Our Lives, The (Strand). PEng 2771-2772.

"Story of Phoebus and Daphne, applied, The" (Waller). PEng 3014, 3015.

Story of Rimini, The (Hunt). PEng 1463-1464.

"Story of Serapion, The" (Hoffmann). ShF 1646.

Story of Sigurd the Volsung and the Fall of the Nibelungs, The (Morris). PEng 2060.

"Story of Stories, A" (Dreiser). ShF 1308.

Story of the Stone, The. See *Dream of the Red Chamber*.

Story of Thebes, The (Lydgate). PEng 1804.

Story Teller's Story, A (Anderson, S.). ShF 815.

Strittmatter, Eva. PFor 1817, 1824.
Strong Are Lonely, The (Hochwälder). DFor 928-929.
Strong Wind (Asturias). LFFor 87.
Strongbox, The (Sternheim). DFor 1740-1742.
Stronger, The (Giacosa). DFor 708-710.
Stronger Climate, A (Jhabvala). ShF 650-651.
Stronghold (Ellin). M&D 576.
Strophe. See *Turning Point.*
"Strophi." *See* "Turn."
"Struck by a Boomerang" (Stockton). M&D 1535.
"Structural Analysis in Linguistics and in Anthropology" (Lévi-Strauss). LTh 888.
"Structural Analysis of Literature, The" (Todorov). ShF 92.
"Structural Analysis of Narrative" (Fodorov). ShF 92.
Structural Anthropology (Lévi-Strauss). LTh 1762.
"Structural Study of Myth, The" (Lévi-Strauss). LTh 888.
"Structuralism and Literary Criticism" (Genette). LTh 559.
Structuralism in Literature (Scholes). ShF 89.
Structure of Complex Words, The (Empson). LTh 463-465.
"Structure of Gogl's 'The Overcoat,' The" (Eichenbaum). ShF 75.
"Structure of Rime, The" (Duncan). PEng 903.
Structure of Scientific Revolutions, The (Kuhn). LTh 765.
"Structure of the Modern Short Story, The" (Bader). ShF 70.
"Structure, Sign and Play in the Discourse of the Human Sciences" (Derrida). LTh 354, 1765.
Strudlhofstiege, Die (Doderer). LFFor 484.
Struna swiatla (Herbert). PFor 657.
Stseny iz rytsarskikh vryemen (Pushkin). DFor 1501.
Stuart, Ian. *See* MacLean, Alistair.
Stuart, Jesse. LFEng 2567-2578; LFSup 407; ShF 262, 2291-2296; ShFSup 390.
Stuart, Sidney. *See* Avallone, Michael.
Stub, Ambrosius. PFor 2160.
"Stub-Book, The" (Alarcón). ShF 847.
Stub sećanja (Pavlović). PFor 1165.
Stubbs, Jean. M&D 1548-1552.
Studenbuch, Das. See *Book of Hours, The.*
Studenti, I. See *Pretenders, The.*

Studia z estetyki. See *Selected Papers in Aesthetics.*
Studies in Classic American Literature (Lawrence, D H.). LTh 867-868; ShF 814.
Studies in the History of the Renaissance (Pater). LTh 1734.
"Studies in the Literature of Sherlock Holmes" (Knox). M&D 998.
Studies in the Narrative Technique of the First-Person Novel (Romberg). ShF 120.
Studium przedmiotu (Herbert). PFor 657, 659.
Studs Lonigan: A Trilogy (Farrell). LFEng 909-910.
Study in Scarlet, A (Doyle). LFEng 810.
"Study of Poetry, The" (Arnold). LTh 48; PEng 3482, 3483-3484.
Study of Prose Fiction, A (Perry). ShF 182.
Study of the Short Story, A (Canby and Dashiell). ShF 73.
Study of Thomas Hardy (Lawrence). LTh 867.
Stuff of Sleep and Dreams (Edel). LTh 428-429.
"Stumble Between Two Stars" (Vallejo). PFor 1593. See also *Human Poems.*
Stundeslose, Den. See *Fussy Man, The.*
Stupid Lady, The. See *Lady Nit-Wit, The.*
Štúr, Ludovít. PFor 1808-1809.
Sturgeon, Theodore. LFEng 2579-2588; LFSup 407; ShF 2297-2303; ShFSup 390.
See also Queen, Ellery.
Sturhahn, Lawrence. ShF 2845.
Sturlunga saga (Narfason). LFFor 2332.
Sturluson, Snorri. ShF 389-390.
Sturm, M. *See* Millar, Margaret.
"Stuttgart Trilogy" (Raabe). LFFor 1380-1381.
"Style" (Durrell). PEng 918-919.
"Style" (Moore). PEng 2047.
Styles of Radical Will (Sontag). LTh 1365.
Styron, William. LFEng 2589-2603, 3154-3155.
Su Pao-pi. DFor 2304.
"Su persona." *See* "Her Person."
Su T'ung-p'o. PFor 1788-1789.
Su único hijo. See *His Only Son.*
Subhasitaratnanidhi (Sa-skya Pandita). PFor 2247.
Subida del Monte Carmelo, La. See *Ascent of Mount Carmel, The.*
Subject Was Roses, The (Gilroy). DEng 776-779.
Subjective Criticism (Bleich). LTh 688, 1764.

Sublette, Walter. ShF 2846.
"Sublime Adventure, The" (Guillén). PFor 627. See also *Homenaje*.
Subterraneans, The (Kerouac). LFEng 1522-1523, 1524.
"Suburban Mad Song" (Corso). PEng 578.
"Success" (Empson). PEng 972.
"Such hap as I am happed in" (Wyatt). PEng 3177.
Such Is My Beloved (Callaghan). LFEng 432-435.
Suchbild (Meckel). ShFSup 190.
Suckling, Sir John. PEng 2775-2783.
Suckow, Ruth. ShF 177, 541-542.
Sud idyot. See *Trial Begins, The.*
Sudermann, Hermann. DFor 1757-1770; LTh 1722.
Sudraka. DFor 2386-2387.
Suds in Your Eye (Kirkland). DEng 1052.
Sue, Eugène. M&D 1553-1559.
Suekichi, Aono. LTh 1006.
"Suelo." *See* "Soil."
Sueño de la razón, El. See *Sleep of Reason, The.*
Suetonius. LTh 964.
"Suffolk" (Davie). PSup 89.
Suffrage of Elvira, The (Naipaul). LFEng 1959.
Sugimori Nobumori. See **Chikamatsu Monzaemon.**
Suhrawardy, Shahid. PFor 2001.
Sui principi di belle lettere (Parini). LTh 1691.
"Suicide Eaters, The" (Smith, D.). PEng 2644.
Suicide's Wife, The (Madden). LFEng 1761-1762, 1766.
"Suicidio al parco" (Buzzati). ShFSup 64.
Suitable Match, A (Fontane). LFFor 561-562, 2177.
Sukenick, Ronald. ShF 817.
Sukhovo-Kobylin, Alexander. DFor 1771-1778.
Sula (Morrison). LFEng 1917-1918.
Sulayman al-hakim. See *Wisdom of Solomon, The.*
Sulkin, Sidney. ShF 2847.
Sullen Lovers, The (Shadwell). DEng 1669-1670, 2297-2298.
Sullivan, Sir Arthur. *See* **Gilbert, W. S.**
"Sullivan's Trousers" (O'Faoláin). ShF 2001.
Sult. See *Hunger.*
Sultan, Stanley. ShF 2848.

Sultan al-ha'ir, al-. See *Sultan's Dilemma, The.*
Sultaness, The. See *Bajazet.*
Sultan's Dilemma, The (Hakim). DSup 175.
Sumarokov, Aleksandr Petrovich. DFor 1779-1788, 2451; LTh 1693.
"Sumerki svobody." *See* "Twilight of Freedom, The."
Summer (Wharton, Edith). LFEng 2855-2856.
Summer Anniversaries, The (Justice). PEng 1529
Summer Bird-Cage, A (Drabble). LFEng 817.
"Summer Cannibals" (Ballard). ShF 915.
Summer Evening (Shawn). DSup 335-336. See also *Three Short Plays.*
Summer Folk (Gorky). DFor 784-785.
"Summer Gone, A" (Moss). PEng 2065, 2066.
"Summer Home" (Heaney). PEng 1270-1271.
Summer Knowledge (Schwartz). PEng 2492-2493.
"Summer My Grandmother Was Supposed to Die, The" (Richler). ShF 2149-2151.
"Summer Night" (Bowen). ShF 984-985.
Summer 1914. See *World of the Thibaults, The.*
"Summer of the Beautiful White Horse, The" (Saroyan). ShF 2190.
Summer of the Seventeenth Doll, The (Lawler). DEng 1109, 1110-1115, 2434-2435. See also *Doll Trilogy, The.*
"Summer People, The" (Merrill). PEng 1906-1961.
"Summer Pilgrim, A" (Tuohy). ShF 2348.
Summer's Last Will and Testament (Nashe). DEng 1364-1369; PEng 2073.
"'Summertime and the Living. . .'" (Hayden). PEng 1253.
Summing Up, The (Maugham). DEng 1308.
Summoned by Bells (Betjeman). PEng 169.
Summoning of Stones, A (Hecht). PEng 1275.
"Summons, The" (Vörösmarty). PFor 1668.
Sump'n Like Wings (Riggs). DEng 1594.
"Sun" (Moore). PEng 2047-2048.
Sun Also Rises, The (Hemingway). LFEng 1338, 1340-1343.
Sun Chemist, The (Davidson). M&D 457.
Sun, He Dies, The (Highwater). LFEng 1364-1366.
Sun Rock Man (Corman). PEng 569-570.
Suna no onna. See *Woman in the Dunes, The.*
"Sunčane pesme" (Dučić). PFor 429-430.
Sunday (Simenon). LFFor 1600.
"Sunday" (Tzara). PFor 1549.

"Sunday Afternoon Hanging" (Stuart). ShF
2294-2295.
"Sunday Evening" (Leopardi). PFor 858-859.
See also *Canti*.
"Sunday Morning" (Stevens). PEng 2747-2748.
Sunday of Life, The (Queneau). LFSup 329-
330.
"Sunday Painter, The" (Cassill). ShF 1070,
1072.
Sunday Sunlight (Pérez de Ayala). LFFor
1258.
Sundial, The (Jackson). LFEng 1428-1430.
Sundman, Per Olof. LFFor 2360-2361.
"Sunflower Kid, The" (Gill). ShF 1487.
"Sunflower Sutra" (Ginsberg). PEng 1092.
"Sunlight" (Gunn). PEng 1176-1177.
Sunlight Dialogues, The (Gardner, J.). LFEng
1074-1076.
Sun's Darling, The (Ford and Dekker). DEng
652-653.
"Super Flumina Babylonis" (Swinburne). PEng
2820.
"Supermarket in California, A" (Ginsberg).
PEng 1092.
Superstition (Barker). DEng 105, 112-113.
Supervielle, Jules. PFor 1888.
"Supplement to Bougainville's Voyage"
(Diderot). ShF 1279.
Suppliants, The (Aeschylus). DFor 2090, 2100-
2101.
Suppliants, The (Euripides). DFor 2114.
Supposes (Gascoigne). DEng 726, 2257, 2264.
"Supremacy of the Hunza, The" (Greenberg).
ShF 1536-1538.
"Sur la Route de San Romano." *See* "On the
Road to San Romano."
Sur le Fil (Arrabal). DFor 129-130.
Sur Racine. See *On Racine*.
"Sur une morte." *See* "On a Dead Woman."
Suréna (Corneille). DFor 436.
Surface of the Earth, The (Price). LFEng 2134-
2135.
Surfacing (Atwood). LFEng 96-98.
Surgeon of His Honor, The (Calderón). DFor
302-303.
**Surrey, Henry Howard, Earl of. PEng 2784-
2792.**
"Survey of Short Story Textbooks, A" (Beeke).
ShF 71.
"Survey of the Short Story Criticism in
America, A" (May). ShF 82-83.

Surviving and Other Essays (Bettleheim). ShF
290.
"Survivor in Salvador, A" (Tuohy). ShF 2347.
Survivors of the Chancellor (Verne). LFFor
1874-1875.
"Susanna at the Beach" (Gold). ShF 1503.
"Sussex" (Davie). PSup 90.
Sutras (Pānini). PFor 1731.
Sutter's Gold (Cendrars). LFFor 318-320.
Suttree (McCarthy). LFSup 268-269.
Suze sina razmetnoga (Gundulić). PFor 2260.
Svadba Krechinskogo. See *Krechinsky's
Wedding*.
Svåra studen, Den. See *Difficult Hour, I-III,
The*.
Světlá, Karolina. LFFor 2065-2066.
Svetli i tamni praznici (Pavlović). PFor 1166-
1167.
Svevo, Italo. LFFor 1697-1707, 2242.
Svoi lyudi--sochtemsya. See *It's a Family Affair*.
"Swaddling Clothes" (Mishima). ShF 1936-
1937.
Swami and Friends (Narayan). LFEng 1968.
Swamp Angel (Wilson, E.). LFEng 2914-2916.
"Swan, The" (Baudelaire). PFor 136-138.
Swan, The (Molnár). DFor 1347.
Swan, Gladys. ShF 2849.
Swann, Brian. ShF 2850.
Swann's Way (Proust). LFFor 1324-1327. See
also *Remembrance of Things Past*.
"Swans on an Autumn River" (Warner).
ShFSup 355-356.
"Swastika Poems, The" (Heyen). PEng 1323-
1324.
Swedenhielms, The (Bergman). DFor 189-190,
2478.
Sweeney Todd (Prest). ShF 732.
Sweet Cheat Gone, The (Proust). LFFor 1339-
1342. See also *Remembrance of Things Past*.
Sweet Lavender (Pinero). DEng 1503-1505.
"Sweet Lullabie, A" (Breton, N.). PEng 279.
"Sweet Shop Around the Corner, The"
(Graves). PEng 1132-1133.
Sweet Table at the Richelieu (Ribman). DSup
315-316.
Sweets of Pimlico, The (Wilson). LFSup 387-
388, 391.
"Sweets to the Sweet" (Bloch). ShF 565-566.
Swenson, May. PEng 2793-2799; PSup 410.
Świadkowie albo nasza mała stabilizacja. See
Witnesses, The.

T

T Zero (Calvino). LFFor 244-245.
Ta'am li-kull fam, al-. See *Food for the Millions.*
"Tabacaria." *See* "Tobacco-Shop."
Tabermann, Tommy. PFor 2199-2200.
Tabito, Ōtomo no. *See* Ōtomo no Tabito.
Table for Critics, A (Lowell, J. R.). PEng 1779-1780.
Table Manners (Ayckbourn). DEng 63-64. See also *Norman Conquests, The.*
"Table of Balin, The" (Malory). ShF 1866-1867.
"Tables of the Law, The" (Yeats). ShF 2473.
Tabte land, Det (Jensen). LFFor 882. See also *Long Journey, The.*
Tacey Cromwell (Richter). LFEng 2268-2270.
Tacitus, Cornelius. LTh 1193.
Tade kuu mushi. See *Some Prefer Nettles.*
"Tag, Der." *See* "Day, The."
"Tag der Gesichter, Der" (Bernhard). PFor 181. See also *Auf der Erde und in der Hölle.*
"Tagebuchblatt 1980." *See* "Diary Page 1980."
Tagger, Theodor. *See* **Bruckner, Ferdinand.**
Tagore, Rabindranath. DFor 1789-1799; LFFor 2215; PFor 1477-1485, 1998-1999.
Tai-ching T'ang shin-hua (Wang Shih-chen). LTh 1780.
Taine, Hippolyte-Adolphe. LTh 231, 235, 260, 753, 1122-1123, 1258, 1391, **1416-1423.**
Takamura Kōtarō. PFor 2077.
Takarai Kikaku. PFor 2071.
Take a Girl Like You (Amis). LFEng 63-64, 65-67.
"Take It and Like It" (Nebel). M&D 1266.
Takemoto Gidayū. DFor 2426.
"Taking a Poem to Pieces" (Sinclair, J.). PEng 3455.
"Taking Notice" (Hacker). PEng 1192-1193.
Taking of Miss Janie, The (Bullins). DEng 306-307.
Taking the Side of Things (Ponge). PFor 1260, 1261.
"Taking the Wen Away" (Dazai). ShFSup 95.

Takitarō, Shimamura. *See* **Hōgetsu, Shimamura.**
Taková láska (Kohout). DSup 221-222.
Tala (Mistral). PFor 1040, 1042-1043.
Talanta, La (Aretino). DFor 99-100.
Tale for Midnight, A (Prokosch). LFEng 2167.
Tale of a Tub, A (Swift). LFEng 2606-2608; LTh 1690.
Tale of Gamelyn, The. PEng 3251.
Tale of Genji, The (Murasaki). LFFor 1174-1175, 1177-1182, 2259, 2260-2265, 2275; LTh 1049, 1051, 1786-1787.
Tale of Hemetes the Hermit, The (Gascoigne). LTh 542.
"Tale of King Arthur, The" (Malory). ShF 1866.
Tale of Mystery, The (Pixérécourt). DFor 1477-1478.
Tale of Orpheus (Henryson). PEng 1288, 1291-1292.
Tale of the Heike, The. See *Heike monogatari.*
"Tale of the Hunchback, The." ShF 412-413.
"Tale of the Ragged Mountains, A" (Poe). ShF 2107.
"Tale of the Seven Beggars, The" (Nahman). ShF 1944-1946.
"Tale of the Squint-eyed Left-handed Gunsmith from Tula and the Steel Flea, The." *See* "Lefty."
Tale of Two Cities, A (Dickens, C.). LFEng 3153.
Talented Mr. Ripley, The (Highsmith). M&D 869.
Tales (Baraka). ShF 923.
Tales and Short Stories in Verse (La Fontaine). PFor 815-816.
"Tales from a Family Album" (Justice). PEng 1530.
Tales from the Calendar (Brecht). ShF 1006.
Tales from the Vienna Woods (Horvath). DFor 958-960.
Tales in Verse (Crabbe). PEng 643-644.
Tales of Belkin, The (Pushkin). ShFSup 251.
Tales of Hoffmann, The (Hoffmann). ShF 714.
Tales of Jacob, The (Mann). LFFor 1082.

Taylor, H. Baldwin. *See* **Waugh, Hillary.**
Taylor, Peter. ShF 550-551, **2304-2311;** ShFSup 390.
Taylor, Phoebe Atwood. M&D **1567-1572.**
Taylor, Robert, Jr. ShF 2853.
"Te nudrice alle muse." *See* "You Nurturer of the Muses."
Tea and Sympathy (Anderson, R.). DEng 34-35, 36.
Teach Me How to Cry (Joudrey). DEng 2440.
"Teacher, The" (Anderson). ShF 871-872.
"Teacher of Wisdom, The" (Wilde). PEng 3108-3109.
Teahouse of the August Moon, The (Patrick, J.). DEng 1468-1470.
Teares, on the Death of Moeliades (Drummond). PEng 862-863, 864.
"Tears" (Reese). PEng 2341, 2344-2345.
Tears and Smiles (Barker). DEng 105, 108-110.
"Tears at the Grave of Sr Albertus Morton *(who was buried at* Southampton) *wept by Sir H.* Wotton" (Wotton). PEng 3142.
"Tears in Your Eyes" (Yosano Akiko). PFor 1717-1718.
"Tears of Scotland, The" (Smollett). PEng 2652.
Tears of the Blind Lions, The (Merton). PEng 1975-1976.
Teasdale, Sara. PEng 2855-2858.
Teatr vechnoy voyny. See Unmasked Ball, The.
Teatralny roman. See Black Snow.
Teatro comico all'osteria del Pellegrino, Il (Gozzi). DFor 793-794.
"Teatro como espectáculo, El" (Feijóo). LTh 476.
Teatro crítico universal (Feijóo). LTh 475-476.
Teatro de ensueno (Martínez Sierras). DFor 1283.
Technē rhetorikē. See On the Ancient Orators.
"Technical Manifesto of Futurist Literature" (Marinetti). LTh 994.
"Teck, The" (Hölderlin). PFor 683.
Tecumseh (Mair). DEng 2439.
Teeth 'n' Smiles (Hare). DSup 184-185.
Tegnér, Esaias. PFor 2166.
Teilhet, Darwin L. M&D 1573-1578.
Teitoku, Matsunaga. *See* Matsunaga Teitoku.
Teleclides. DFor 2122.
"Telefon." *See* "Telephone, The."

Télémaque travesti, Le (Marivaux). LFFor 1100-1101.
"Telephone, The" (Zoshchenko). ShFSup 380.
"Telephone Call, A" (Parker). ShF 2053, 2054.
"Telephone Number of the Muse, The" (Justice). PEng 1533.
Teleutaios peirasmos, Ho. See *Last Temptation of Christ, The.*
"Tell Me a Riddle" (Olsen). ShF 2022-2024.
"Tell Me Yes or No" (Munro). ShFSup 212-213.
"Tell the Women We're Going" (Carver). ShFSup 79.
Téllez, Gabriel. *See* **Tirso de Molina.**
"Telling a Short Story" (Wharton). ShF 94.
"Telling Stories" (Moffett). ShF 83.
"Tell-Tale Heart, The" (Poe). LFEng 3129; ShF 194-195, 790-792, 2107.
Tem, Steve Rasnic. ShF 2854.
Tembladera (Ramos). DFor 2442.
"Temnoe tsarstvo." *See* "Kingdom of Darkness, The."
Témoins, Les. See *Witnesses, The.*
Tempest, The (Césaire). DSup 43.
Tempest, The (Shakespeare). DEng 1712-1713, 2284; PEng 1946, 1949-1950; ShF 149, 2218-2219.
Tempête, d'après "La Tempête" de Shakespeare, Une. See *Tempest, The.*
Temple, The (Herbert). PEng 1296-1297, 1299-1300, 1302, 1303-1304.
Temple, Mary (Minny). LFEng 1438.
Temple, Sir William. LTh 1689-1690.
Temple Beau, The (Fielding). DEng 602.
Temple of the Golden Pavilion, The (Mishima). LFFor 1157-1158.
Temporary Kings (Powell). LFEng 2121.
Temps retrouvé, Le. See *Time Regained.*
Temps sauvage, Le (Hébert). LFFor 806.
Temptation of Eileen Hughes, The (Moore, B.). LFEng 1893.
Temptation of Saint Anthony, The (Flaubert). LFFor 555-556.
Tempter, The (Jones, H. A.). DEng 1004.
Ten. See *Shadow, The.*
Ten North Frederick (O'Hara). LFEng 2048-2051.
Tenants of Moonbloom, The (Wallant). LFEng 2764-2765.

Tender Buttons (Stein). PEng 2738; ShFSup 305-307.

Tender Hands (Hakim). DSup 176.

Tender Husband, The (Steele). DEng 1860-1862.

Tender Is the Night (Fitzgerald, F. S.). LFEng 964-966; ShF 1373.

"Tendril in the Mesh" (Everson). PEng 992.

Tenebrae (Hill, G.). PEng 1353-1354.

Ténébreuse Affaire, Une. See *Historical Mystery, An.*

Tenement of Clay (West). LFSup 370-372.

Tennessee (Linney). DSup 238. See also *Laughing Stock.*

"Tennessee's Partner" (Harte). ShF 210-211.

Tennyson, Alfred, Lord. DEng 1912-1921; PEng 1207-1208, 1209, **2859-2870**, 3345-3346, 3497.

Tenor, The (Wedekind). DFor 1978-1979.

"Tension in Poetry" (Tate). LTh 1427.

Tentativa del hombre infinito (Neruda). PFor 1073-1075.

"Tenth Clew, The" (Hammett). M&D 826.

Tents of Wickedness, The (De Vries). LFEng 739.

"Tenzone" (Ciardi). PEng 504.

"Teoría prosaica" (Reyes). PFor 1321.

"Teoriia 'formalnogo metoda.'" *See* "Theory of the 'Formal Method,' The."

Teppich des Lebens und die Lieder von Traum und Tod, mit einem Vorspiel, Der. See *Tapestry of Life, The.*

Terence. DEng 2147-2148, 2263; DFor **1823-1829**, 2142-2144, 2153.

Teresa (Unamuno). PFor 1555.

Teresa and Other Stories (O'Faoláin). ShF 1997.

"Terminal Beach, The" (Ballard). ShF 914.

Ternura (Mistral). PFor 1043.

"Terra dei morti, La." *See* "Land of the Dead, The."

Terra nostra (Fuentes). LFFor 594-595.

Terra promessa, La (Ungaretti). PFor 1570-1571.

Terras do sem fim. See *Violent Land, The.*

Terre des hommes. See *Wind, Sand and Stars.*

Terrible Twos, The (Reed). LFSup 340.

Territorial Rights (Spark). LFEng 2476.

"Terror" (Tanizaki). ShFSup 315.

Terror Tales. ShF 741.

Terry, Megan. DEng 2486-2487; **DSup 340-346.**

Terternikov, Fyodor. *See* Sologub, Fyodor.

Tertz, Abram. *See* **Sinyavsky, Andrei.**

"Terzinen." *See* "Stanzas in Terza Rima."

Tess of the D'Urbervilles (Hardy). LFEng 1271-1274.

"Test, The" (Lem). ShFSup 153.

Testament (Jean de Meung). PFor 614.

Testament (Lydgate). PEng 1805.

Testament, The (Wiesel). LFFor 1928-1929.

Testament d'un poète juif assassiné. See *Testament, The.*

Testament of Beauty, The (Bridges). PEng 288-289.

Testament of Cresseid (Henryson). PEng 1287, 1288, 1290-1291, 3278-3279.

Testarium. See *Prophets, The.*

Testi, Fulvio. PFor 2018.

Testimony (Reznikoff). PEng 2361-2362.

Testing Tree, The (Kunitz). PSup 244-245, 247.

Testor, A. See *Guardsman, The.*

Testori, Giovanni. LFFor 2256.

Tête d'Or (Claudel). DFor 404-405.

"Tetemre hívas." *See* "Ordeal of the Bier."

Tetmajer, Kazimierz Przerwa. PFor 2127.

Tetradio gymnasmaton. See *Book of Exercises.*

Teufels General, Des. See *Devil's General, The.*

Teutonic Knights, The. See *Knights of the Cross, The.*

Texas (Michener). LFSup 304-305.

Texas Trilogy, A (Jones, P.). DEng 1009-1010, 1011.

Tey, Josephine. M&D **1579-1583.**

Thackeray, William Makepeace. LFEng **2613-2627**, 3078; PEng **2871-2877**; ShF **2312-2318.**

Thaïs (France). LFFor 575-576; ShF 1404.

Thalaba the Destroyer (Southey). PEng 2681-2682.

"Thalia" (Aldrich). PEng 33.

Thalia Rediviva (Vaughan). PEng 2974-2975.

"Thanatopsis" (Bryant). PEng 350-352.

"Thank You Ma'am" (Hughes). ShF 1658.

"Thanksgiving" (Glück). PSup 134.

"Thanksgiving, The" (Herbert). PEng 1303.

"Thar's More in the Man Than Thar Is in the Land" (Lanier). PEng 1660-1661.

That Awful Mess on Via Merulana (Gadda). LFFor 608-610.

"That Evening Sun" (Faulkner). ShF 623.

That Hideous Strength (Lewis, C. S.). LFEng 1655-1656.

"That in Aleppo Once . . ." (Nabakov). ShF 114.

"That Nature Is a Heraclitean Fire and the Comfort of the Resurrection" (Hopkins). PEng 1402-1403.

"That Straightlaced Christian Thing Between Her Legs" (Simic). PEng 2592-2593.

That Summer--That Fall (Gilroy). DEng 779-781.

"That the pear delights me" (Hoffman). PEng 1358.

That Voice (Pinget). LFFor 1292.

"Theater" (Toomer). ShF 2342.

Theater and Its Double, The (Artaud). DFor 2256.

Theater as a Moral Institution, The (Schiller). LTh 1296.

Théâtre de Clara Gazul, Le. See *Plays of Clara Gazul, The.*

Théâtre de Neptune dans la Nouvelle France, Le. See *Theatre of Neptune, The.*

Théâtre et son double, Le. See *Theater and Its Double, The.*

Theatre of Gods Judgements, The (Beard). ShF 499.

Theatre of Neptune, The (Lescarbot). DEng 2437.

Theatre of the Absurd, The (Esslin). DFor 2255-2256.

Theatre of the Soul, The (Evreinov). DFor 584-585.

Thebaid. See *Thebais.*

Thebais (Statius). PFor 1471-1475; ShF 150.

Theban Mysteries, The (Cross). M&D 428.

Their Eyes Were Watching God (Hurston). LFEng 1393, 1395-1397.

"Them" (Galvin). PEng 1055.

Them (Oates). LFEng 2012-2013.

"Thematics" (Tomashevsky). ShF 92-93.

Then Came Violence (Ball). M&D 70.

"Then the Ermine" (Moore). PEng 2047.

Theōn dialogoi. See *Dialogues of the Gods.*

Theocritus. PFor 1503-1510.

Theognidea (Theognis). PFor 1511-1515.

Theognis. PFor 1511-1516, 1761-1762.

Theogony (Hesiod). PFor 662, 663, 664-666, 1757-1758.

Theophilus. DFor 2169.

Theophilus North (Wilder). LFEng 2887-2888.

Theophrastus. LTh 384; ShF 155.

Théorie des Romans, Die. See *Theory of the Novel, The.*

Theory of Criticism (Krieger). LTh 828.

Theory of Flight (Rukeyser). PSup 330.

Theory of Literature (Wellek and Warren, A.). LTh 1426, 1535-1536, 1758.

"Theory of the 'Formal Method,' The" (Eikhenbaum). LTh 443.

Theory of the Novel, The (Lukács). LTh 936; ShF 174-175.

"Theory of the Short Story, A" (Lawrence, J. C.). ShF 81.

"There Are Chaste Charms" (Mandelstam). PFor 937. See also *Stone.*

There Is No Natural Religion (Blake). LTh 1700.

There Shall Be No Night (Sherwood). DEng 1808-1809.

"There Was a Jesus" (Ady). PFor 7.

"There was One I met upon the road" (Crane, S.). PEng 662.

Thérèse (Mauriac). LFFor 1127-1129.

Thérèse Desqueyroux. See *Thérèse.*

Thérèse Raquin (Zola). DFor 2050; LFFor 1989.

Theriault, Yves. ShF 639-640.

Theroux, Paul. LFEng **2628-2634;** LFSup 407.

These Are the Ravens (Everson). PEng 985-986.

"These Images Remain" (Sarton). PEng 2461.

"These Trees Stand. . ." (Snodgrass). PEng 2659.

These Twain (Bennett). LFEng 245-246.

Thésée. See *Theseus.*

Theseus (Gide). LFFor 639, 649.

Thesmophoriazusae (Aristophanes). DFor 2127.

"They" (Kipling). ShF 510- 1749, 1751-1753.

"They" (Sassoon). PEng 2472.

"They are all gone into the world of light" (Vaughan). PEng 3314-3315.

They Are Dying Out (Handke). DFor 863.

"They Clapped" (Giovanni). PEng 1102.

"They Feed, They Lion" (Levine). PEng 1716.

"They flee from me, that sometime did me seek" (Wyatt). PEng 3175-3176.

They Found Him Dead (Heyer). M&D 862-863.

They Hanged My Saintly Billy (Graves, R.). LFEng 1195-1196.

They Knew What They Wanted (Howard, S.). DEng 975-976.

"They Say That Plants Do Not Speak" (Castro). PFor 280. See also *Beside the River Sar.*

They Were Defeated. See *Shadow Flies, The.*

They Wouldn't Be Chessmen (Mason). M&D 1198.

Thibaudet, Albert. LTh 1421.

Thibault, Jacques-Anatole-François. *See* **France, Anatole.**

Thibaults, The. See *World of the Thibaults, The.*

Thief, The (Leonov). M&D 1060-1061.

"Thief, The" (Tanizaki). ShFSup 315.

Thierry of Chartres. LTh 20.

"Thieves, The" (Grau). ShF 1531.

Thieves in the Night (Koestler). LFEng 1553.

"Thin Edge of Happiness, The" (Guimarães Rosa). ShF 1564-1566.

Thin Man, The (Hammett). LFEng 1235-1236, 1240-1241; M&D 827.

Thin Red Line, The (Jones, J.). LFEng 1480-1481, 1482-1483.

Thing at Their Heads, The (Phillpotts). M&D 1327.

"Thing in the Cellar, The" (Keller). ShF 565.

Things as They Are (Godwin). See *Caleb Williams.*

Things as They Are (Horgan). LFSup 161-162.

Things as They Are (Stein). PEng 2737.

Things Fall Apart (Achebe). LFEng 6-8; LFFor 2039-2040, 2042-2044.

Things Hidden Since the Foundation of the World (Girard). LTh 592.

"Things in Their Season" (Greenberg). ShF 1539.

Think Black! (Madhubuti). PEng 1892.

"Thinking of the Lost World" (Jarrell). PEng 1485.

Third and Fourthe Booke of Ayres, The (Campion). PEng 427-428.

Third and Oak (Norman). DSup 290-291.

"Third Avenue in Sunlight" (Hecht). PEng 1281.

Third Book About Achim, The (Johnson). LFFor 890-891.

"Third Circle, The (Norris). ShF 1955-1957.

Third Deadly Sin, The (Sanders). M&D 1464.

Third Life of Grange Copeland, The (Walker). LFEng 2749, 2750-2753.

Third Policeman, The (O'Brien, F.). LFEng 2028-2029.

Third Satire (Oldham, trans.). PEng 2134.

Third Violet, The (Crane). LFEng 643-644.

"Thirteen for Centaurus" (Ballard). ShF 913-914.

"13,000 People" (Lawrence, D. H.). PEng 1685.

"Thirteen Ways of Looking at a Blackbird" (Stevens). PEng 3509-3510, 3511-3512.

Thirty-nine Steps, The (Buchan). LFEng 332; M&D 225.

31 Letters and 13 Dreams (Hugo, R.). PEng 1454-1458.

Thirty Poems (Merton). PEng 1974.

XXXVI Lyrics and XII Sonnets (Aldrich). PEng 31.

XXXIII Kleengedichtjes (Gezelle). PFor 557-558.

This Body Is Made of Camphor and Gopherwood (Bly). PEng 225-226.

This Business of Living (Pavese). LFFor 1243.

This Gun for Hire. See *Gun for Sale, A.*

This in Which (Oppen). PEng 2139.

This Is New York (Sherwood). DEng 1803.

"This Is No Yarn" (Diderot). ShF 1278.

This Is Our Chance (Henshaw). DEng 927-928.

"This Last Pain" (Empson). PEng 970.

"This Lime-Tree Bower My Prison" (Coleridge, S. T.). PEng 535.

"This Morning, This Evening, So Soon" (Baldwin). ShF 581.

This Music Crept by Me upon the Waters (MacLeish). DEng 1220.

"This Past Must Address Its Present" (Soyinka). LTh 1376.

"This Poem" (Plumly). PEng 2234.

This Rough Magic (Stewart). M&D 1530-1531.

This Scheming World. See *Worldly Mental Calculations.*

This Side Jordan (Laurence). LFEng 1571.

This Side of Paradise (Fitzgerald, F. S.). LFEng 958-959, 960.

This Sunday (Donoso). LFFor 495-497.

This Time of Morning (Sahgal). LFFor 2223.

This Time Tomorrow (Ngugi). DEng 2419; DSup 269-270.

"This Tokyo" (Snyder). PEng 2673.

"This World" (Creeley). PEng 690.

Tomb for Boris Davidovich, A (Kiš). LFSup 215-216.

"Tomb of Stéphane Mallarmé, The" (Simic). PEng 2594.

Tomb of the Kings, The (Hébert). LFFor 806, 810, 815.

"Tombeaux" (Cocteau). PFor 371. See also *Vocabulaire*.

Tomlinson, Charles. PEng 2905-2911; PSup 410.

Tomodachi. See *Friends.*

"Tomorrow--Fairly Cloudy" (Perelman). ShF 2081-2082.

"Tomorrow Morning" (Cowley, M.). PEng 606.

"Tomorrow-Tamer, The" (Laurence). ShF 1776-1778.

"Tomorrow's Song" (Snyder). PEng 2675.

"Tone in the Short Story" (Howe). ShF 79.

"Tonging at St. James Harbor" (Heyen). PEng 1323.

"Tonight at Seven-Thirty" (Auden). PEng 78.

Tonio Kröger (Mann). LFFor 1079, 2186; ShF 1876-1877.

Tono-Bungay (Wells). LFEng 2810-2811.

Tonson, Jacob. See **Bennett, Arnold.**

"Tontine Curse, The" (de la Torre). M&D 479-480.

"Tony's Story" (Silko). ShF 570-571.

"Too Late to Marry, Too Soon to Die" (Gill). ShF 1487.

Too Many Husbands. See *Home and Beauty.*

Toomer, Jean. PEng 2912-2920; ShF 251-252, 554-555, **2339-2344.**

"Tooth, The" (Jackson). ShF 1670.

Tooth of Crime, The (Shepard). DEng 1761.

Topelius, Zacharias. LFFor 2342.

"Topoghrafia" (Pentzíkis). PFor 1189.

Topology of a Phantom City (Robbe-Grillet). LFFor 1419-1421.

Tor-ha-pela'ot. See *Age of Wonders, The.*

Tor und der Tod, Der. See *Death and the Fool.*

Torelli, Achille. DFor 2409.

Tornimparte, Alessandra. See **Ginzburg, Natalia.**

Törnrosens bok (Almqvist). LFFor 2337.

"Török Bálint" (Arany). PFor 80.

Torquato Tasso (Goethe). DFor 740-741, 2366.

Torquemada cycle (Pérez Galdós). LFFor 2387.

"Torrent, The" (Hébert). LFFor 811.

Torres Naharro, Bartolomé de. DEng 2162; **DFor 1866-1876,** 2484-2485.

Torrie, Malcolm. See **Mitchell, Gladys.**

Torse 3 (Middleton, C.). PEng 1987.

Tortilla Flat (Kirkland). DEng 1051.

Tory Lover, The (Jewett). LFEng 1461-1463.

Tosa Diary (Tsurayuki). LTh 1470.

Tosa Nikki. See *Tosa Diary.*

"Toska." See "Depression."

Tot, kto poluchayet poshchechiny. See *He Who Gets Slapped.*

"Total Stranger" (Cozzens). ShF 1211-1212.

Tóték. See *Tóts, The.*

Toten bleiben jung, Die. See *Dead Stay Young, The.*

Tóth, Árpád. PFor 1985.

Tóts, The (Örkény). DSup 299.

Tottel's Miscellany (Surrey). PEng 3286-3288.

Totten, Caroline B. ShF 2859.

Tou Ô yüan. See *Injustice Done to Tou Ngo, The.*

Touch (Gunn). PEng 1169-1171.

Touch Not the Cat (Stewart). M&D 1531.

Touch of Silk, The (Roland). DEng 2433.

Touissant l'Ouverture (James, C. L. R.). DEng 2452.

"Toupee Artist, The" (Leskov). ShFSup 161.

Tour de Force (Brand). M&D 195.

Tour de Nesle, La (Dumas, *père*). DFor 489-490.

Tour du monde en quatre-vingts jours, Le. See *Around the World in Eighty Days.*

Tour du Pin, Patrice de la. PFor 1890.

"Tournament, The" (Chatterton). PEng 471.

Tournament (Foote). LFEng 973-974.

Tourneur, Cyril. DEng 1933-1944, 2292; LTh 450.

Tournier, Michel. LFFor 1738-1748; LFSup 407.

Tous contre tous (Adamov). DFor 16-17.

Tous les hommes sont mortels. See *All Men Are Mortal.*

"Tout le long du jour" (Senghor). PFor 1424. See also *Chants d'ombre.*

"Toute l'âme résumée. . . ." See "All the Soul Indrawn. . . ."

"Towards an Open Universe" (Duncan). PEng 905.

Towards the Last Spike (Pratt). PEng 2286.

Tower, The (Hofmannsthal). DFor 941-942.

"Trois Messes basses, La." *See* "Three Low Masses, The."
Trois Mousquetaires, Les. See *Three Musketeers, The.*
Trois Prétendants. . .un mari. See *Three Suitors One Husband Until Further Notice.*
Trojan Horse, The (MacLeish). DEng 1219-1220.
"Trojan Horse" (Queen). ShF 763.
Trojan Women, The (Euripides). DFor 2115.
Trojan Women, The (Seneca). DFor 2148.
Trollope, Anthony. LFEng 2648-2659, 3034, 3078-3079.
"Tropic Death" (Walrond). ShF 578.
Tropic Moon (Simenon). LFFor 1599.
Tropic of Cancer (Miller). LFEng 1873-1874, 1878-1879.
Tropic of Capricorn (Miller). LFEng 1879-1881.
"Tropics in New York, The" (McKay). PEng 1843-1844.
Tropisms (Sarraute). LFFor 2143.
Troteras y danzaderas (Pérez de Ayala). LFFor 1257.
Trotsky, Leon. LTh 1058.
Trotsky in Exile (Weiss). DFor 1990.
"Trouble, The" (Powers). ShF 2120.
Trouble at Turkey Hill, The (Knight). M&D 991-992.
"Trouble Man, The" (Rhodes). ShF 603-604.
Trouble on Triton. See *Triton.*
Troubled Sleep (Sartre). LFFor 1515-1516. See also *Roads to Freedom.*
Troubles (Farrell). LFSup 110.
Troublesome Raigne of John King of England, The. DEng 2265-2266, 2276.
Trout Fishing in America (Brautigan). LFEng 294; ShFSup 53-54.
"Trout Fishing on the Bevel" (Brautigan). ShFSup 54.
Troy Book (Lydgate). PEng 1804.
Troy Romances (Dictys). LFFor 2014.
True Confessions of an Albino Terrorist, The (Breytenbach). PSup 50.
True History, A (Lucian). LTh 932.
"True Maid, A" (Prior). PEng 2290.
"True Relation of the Apparition of One Mrs. Veal, A" (Defoe). ShF 729-730.
"True Story, A" (Twain). ShF 2362.
True Story of Ah Q, The (Lu Hsün). LFFor 2107; ShFSup 177-178.

True West (Shepard). DEng 1766-1767.
Trumbull, John. LTh 1742.
Trumpets and Raspberries. See *About Face.*
Truth, The (Fitch). DEng 621-622, 2399.
Truth About Them, The (Yglesias). LFEng 2999.
"Truth and Consequences" (Gill). ShF 1486-1487.
Truth and Life of Myth, The (Duncan). PEng 901.
Truth and Method (Gadamer). LTh 527-528, 530-531.
Truth Barriers (Tranströmer). PFor 1529.
"Truth or Consequences" (Adams). ShFSup 4.
Truth Suspected, The (Ruiz de Alarcón. DFor 1604-1605.
"Truth the Dead Know, The" (Sexton). PEng 2523.
"Truth's Complaint over England" (Lodge). PEng 1733.
"Trying to Tell You Something" (Warren). PEng 3027-3028.
Trzy zimy (Miłosz). PFor 1032.
"Tsai chiu-lou shang." *See* "Upstairs in a Wineshop."
"Ts'ai-sang tzu." *See* "Tune: Song of Picking Mulberry."
Ts'ai Yen. PFor 1783.
Tsai Yen-an wen-i tso-t'an-hui shang-te chiang-hua. See *Talks at the Yenan Literary Conference.*
Ts'ang-lang shih-hua (Yen Yü). LTh 1777.
Tsang Mou-hsün. DFor 2324.
Ts'ao Chan. *See* Ts'ao Hsüeh-ch'in.
Ts'ao Hsüeh-ch'in. LFFor 1749-1768, 2091, 2099-2102.
Ts'ao P'i. LTh 901, **1465-1469,** 1774.
Ts'ao Yü. DFor 2336.
Tsar golod. See *King Hunger.*
Tsê-ch'êng. *See* Kao Ming.
Tsubouchi Shōyō. DFor 2432; LTh 1005, 1793-1794.
"Tsui hua-yin." *See* "Tune: Tipsy in the Flowers' Shade."
Tsuki ni hoeru. See *Howling at the Moon.*
Tsukuba mondō (Yoshimoto). LTh 1593.
Tsukubashū (Yoshimoto). LTh 1593.
Tsurayuki, Ki no. LTh **1470-1475,** 1785-1786; PFor 2058-2059.
Tsuruya Nanboku. DFor 2429.
Tsushima, Shūji. *See* **Dazai, Osamu.**

Tzara, Tristan. DEng 2203; DFor 2238; LTh 214; PFor **1545-1553,** 1885.

Tzili (Appelfeld). LFSup 38-39.
Tzu yeh. See *Midnight.*

U

"Ubasute." *See* "Putting Granny Out to Die."

Über Anmut und Würde. See *On Grace and Dignity.*

Über das Erhabene. See *On the Sublime* (Schiller).

"Über das Marionettentheater." *See* "About the Marionette Theater."

"Über das Studium der griechischen Poesie" (Schlegel, F.). LTh 1697.

"Über das Wesen des Dramas" (Grillparzer). LTh 636.

"Über den gegenwärtigen Zustand der dramatischen Kunst in Deutschland" (Grillparzer). LTh 635.

"Über Dichtung." *See* "On Poetry."

Über die neuere deutsche Literatur (Herder). LTh 670-671.

Über die Religion. See *On Religion.*

Über naïve und sentimentalische Dichtung. See *On Naïve and Sentimental Poetry.*

"Über Shakespeare" (Herder). LTh 669.

"Über Vergänglichkeit" (Hofmannsthal). PFor 674-675.

Überlebensgross Herr Kott (Walser, M.). DSup 386.

Ubik (Dick). LFSup 97.

Ubohý vrah. See *Poor Murderer.*

Ubu Cuckolded (Jarry). DFor 1013-1014.

Ubu roi (Jarry). DEng 2203; DFor 1010-1013.

Udall, Nicholas. DEng 1955-1964.

Uden fædreland, De. See *Denied a Country.*

"Uder." *See* "Blow, The."

Ughniyah al-mawt. See *Song of Death, The.*

"Ugly Little Boy, The" (Asimov). ShF 876.

Uhland, Ludwig. LTh 438.

Új versek. See *New Verses.*

Ujević, Tin. PFor 2265.

"Ulalume" (Poe). PEng 2244-2246.

"Ultima Calaverada, La." *See* "Last Escapade, The."

"Ultima giornata, L." *See* "Last Day The."

"Última ilusión de Don Juan, La". *See* "Don Juan's Last Illusion."

"Ultima Ratio Regum" (Spender). PEng 2698.

Ultima Thule (Longfellow). PEng 1751.

Ultime lettere di Jacopo Ortis, Le. See *Last Letters of Jacopo Ortis.*

"Ultimo canto di Saffo." *See* "Sappho's Last Song."

Ulysses (Joyce). LFEng 1502-1505, 3057, 3105-3106; LTh 1574; ShF 11, 14.

"Ulysses" (Saba). PSup 346, 348.

"Ulysses" (Tennyson). PEng 2863-2867.

"Ulysses and Circe" (Lowell, R.). PEng 1799.

Ulysses in Traction (Innaurato). DSup 203.

"Umanitari." *See* "Humanitarians, The."

Umarła Klasa. See *Dead Class, The.*

Umbstaetter, Herman Daniel. ShF 589.

Umi to dokuyaku. See *Sea and the Poison, The.*

Umorismo, L'. See *Humor.*

Un de Baumugnes. See *Lovers Are Never Losers.*

Un di Velt hot geshvign. See *Night.*

Un millón de muertos. See *One Million Dead.*

Una cosa è una cosa. See *Command and I Will Obey You.*

"Una-ha vez tiven un cravo." *See* "I Used to Have a Nail."

Una, nessuno e centomila. See *One, None and a Hundred-Thousand.*

Unaddressed Letters (Plekhanov). LTh 1123-1124.

Unamuno y Jugo, Miguel de. DFor 1909-1916, 2503; LFEng 3303-3305; LFFor 1789-1797, 2390-2391; LTh 1483-1488; PFor 911, 1554-1560.

Unbearable Lightness of Being, The (Kundera). LFFor 956-957.

Unclassed, The (Gissing). LFEng 1112-1113.

"Uncle" (Narayan). ShFSup 228.

Uncle Abner, Master of Mysteries (Post). M&D 1345.

"Uncle Ben's Choice" (Achebe). ShF 821-822.

"Uncle Ernest" (Sillitoe). ShF 2227-2228.

"Uncle Grant" (Price). ShF 2123-2124.

Uncle Silas (Le Fanu). LFEng 1626-1627; M&D 1050-1051; ShF 1796.

Uncle Tom's Cabin (Stowe). LFEng 2558-2559; ShF 530.

Uncle Tom's Children (Wright). ShF 579.

V

V. (Pynchon). LFEng 2188-2190.
V As in Victim (Treat). M&D 1598-1599.
V lyudyakh. See *In the World.*
"V Peterburge my soidemsia snova." *See* "In Petersburg We Shall Meet Again."
Vade-mecum (Norwid). PFor 2126.
Vadim (Lermontov). LFFor 1020, 2313.
Vagabonds (Hamsun). LFFor 775-776.
Vägen till Klockrike. See *Road, The.*
Vägvisare till underjorden. See *Guide to the Underworld.*
Vajanský, Svetozár Hurban. LFFor 2068; PFor 1809.
Vajda, János. PFor 1983.
Valaská škola (Gavlovič). PFor 1807.
Valčik no roz oučenou. See *Farewell Party, The.*
Valdez, Luis Miguel. DSup 366-372.
"Vale of teares, A" (Southwell). PEng 2689.
"Vale of Tears" (Leskov). ShFSup 161.
"Valediction: Forbidding Mourning, A" (Donne). PEng 831-832.
Valentine (Sand). LFFor 1490-1491.
Valentine, Jo. *See* **Armstrong, Charlotte.**
"Valentines to the Wide World" (Van Duyn). PEng 2962.
Valentinian (Fletcher). DEng 635.
Valera, Juan. LFFor 1813-1829, 2384.
"Valeria" (Monroe). PEng 2027.
Valeria and Other Poems (Monroe). PEng 2027.
Valerius Catullus, Gaius. *See* **Catullus.**
Valéry, Paul. LTh 213, 555-556, 858, 979, **1489-1494;** PFor **1572-1583,** 1881, 1883.
"Valiant Woman, The" (Powers). ShF 2119-2120.
Validity in Interpretation (Hirsch). LTh 809.
Valin, Jonathan. M&D 1622-1627.
Valle Peña, Ramón José Simón. *See* **Valle-Inclán, Ramón María del.**
Vallejo, César. PFor **1584-1595,** 2228.
"Valley, The" (Lamartine). PFor 833. See also *Poetical Meditations, The.*
Valley of Bones, The (Powell). LFEng 2120.

Valley of the Many-colored Grasses (Johnson). PSup 211.
Valley of the Moon, The (London). LFEng 1698.
Valle-Inclán, Ramón María del; DFor 1917-1927, 2503-2504; LFFor **1830-1843,** 2389.
Vallfart och vandringsår (Heidenstam). LFFor 817, 820.
"Vallon, Le." *See* "Valley, The."
Valperga (Shelley, M.). LFEng 2389-2390.
Valse aux adieux, La. See *Farewell Party, The.*
Valse des toréadors, La. See *Waltz of the Toreadors.*
"Value Is an Activity" (Empson). PEng 969.
Vampire, The (Planché). DEng 1524-1525.
"Vampyre, The" (Polidori). ShF 476.
Vanbrugh, Sir John. DEng 1965-1977.
Vance, Arthur. ShF 589.
Vance, John Holbrook. *See* **Queen, Ellery.**
Vance, Ronald. ShF 2863.
Vančura, Vladislav. LFFor 2066.
Vandaleur's Folly (Arden and D'Arcy). DEng 48.
Van de Wetering, Janwillem. M&D 1628-1633.
Van Dine, S. S. M&D **1634-1640;** ShF 756. *See also* Wright, Willard Huntington.
Van Doren, Mark. PEng 2954-2959.
Vandover and the Brute (Norris). LFEng 2002, 2004.
Van Duyn, Mona. PEng 2960-2967.
Van Dyke, Henry. ShF 2864.
"Van Gogh" (Snodgrass). PEng 2663.
Van Gulik, Robert H. M&D 1641-1647.
"Vanishing Point" (Pastan). PEng 2172.
Van Itallie, Jean-Claude. DEng 2483, 2485-2486.
"Vanitas Vanitatum" (Thackeray). PEng 2876.
Vanity Fair (Thackeray). LFEng 2618-2620, 3078.
Vanity of Human Wishes, The (Johnson). PEng 1504-1505.
Vanity Row (Burnett). M&D 245, 247.
"Vanna's Twins" (Rossetti, C.). PEng 2416.
Van Vechten, Carl. LFEng 2705-2711.

Vergne, Marie-Madeleine Pioche de la. *See* La Fayette, Madame de.

Vergonzoso en palacio, El (Tirso). DFor 1845.

Verhaeren, Émile. PFor 1619-1624, 1879.

Véritable Saint-Genest, La (Rotrou). DFor 1575-1576.

Verkehrte Welt, Die (Tieck). DFor 1836-1839.

"Verklighet *(drömd)*, En." *See* "Reality *(dreamed)*, A."

Verlaine, Paul. PFor 1625-1633, 1876, 1877.

Verliebtes Gespente und die gelible Dornrose. See *Beloved Hedgerose, The.*

Verlorene Ehre der Katharina Blum, Die. See *Lost Honor of Katharina Blum, The.*

"Verlorenes Ich." *See* "Lost Self."

"Vermont: Indian Summer" (Booth). PEng 242.

"Vermont Tale, A" (Helprin). ShFSup 118-119.

Verne, Jules. LFFor 1866-1878.

Vernisáž. See *Private View.*

Verre d'eau, La. See *Glass of Water, The.*

Vérrokonok. See *Blood Relations.*

"Vers dorés." *See* "Golden Verses."

Verschwender, Der. See *Spendthrift, The.*

Verschwörung des Fiesko zu Genua, Die. See *Fiesco.*

Verschwundene Mond, Der (Hochwälder). DFor 933.

Verses (Rossetti, C.). PEng 2417.

Verses About the Beautiful Lady. See *Stikhi o prekrasnoy dame.*

"Verses on Sir Joshua Reynold's Painted Window" (Warton). PEng 3039.

Verses on the Death of Dr. Swift (Swift). LFEng 2606; PEng 2809.

"Verses to the Memory of Garrick" (Sheridan). PEng 2565.

"Verses wrote in a Lady's Ivory Table-Book" (Swift). PEng 2804-2805.

Versi et regole della nuova poesia toscana (Tolomei). LTh 1663.

Versi sciolti (Paradisi). LTh 1691.

Versos de salón (Parra). PFor 1133.

Versos del capitán, Los. See *Captain's Verses, The.*

Versprechen, Das. See *Pledge, The.*

Verstörung. See *Gargoyles.*

Versty I (Tsvetayeva). PFor 1534, 1536.

Versuch einer kritischen Dichtkunst vor die Deutschen (Gottsched). LTh 617.

Versuch über Schiller (Mann). LTh 986.

"Versuch über uns." *See* "Attempt About Us."

Verte y no verte. See *To See You and Not to See You.*

Verteidigung der Wölfe (Enzensberger). PFor 469.

"Vertical Ladder, The" (Sansom). ShF 2184.

Vertical Man (Kinsella). PSup 236.

Veruntreute Himmel, Der. See *Embezzled Heaven.*

"Verwandlung, Die." *See* "Metamorphosis."

Verwirrungen des Zöglings Törless, Die. See *Young Törless.*

Very Heaven (Aldington). LFEng 44-45.

"Very Old Man with Enormous Wings, The" (García Márquez). ShF 1456-1457.

Very Rich Hours of Count von Stauffenberg, The (West). LFSup 375-376.

Vesaas, Tarjei. LFFor 2352-2353; PFor 2189-2190.

Veselovsky, Alexander. LTh 1341, 1501-1506.

"Vesna v Fialte." *See* "Spring in Fialta."

Vestris, Madame. DEng 2357.

Vesyolaya Smert. See *Merry Death, A.*

Vetere, Richard. ShF 2865.

Vetezović, Pavao Ritter. PFor 2261.

Via crucis do corpo, A (Lispector). ShFSup 168.

Via del male, La (Deledda). LFFor 439.

Viaduct Murder, The (Knox). M&D 999-1000.

Viaducts of Seine-et-Oise, The (Duras). DFor 511.

"Viagem a Petrópolis." *See* "Journey to Petrópolis."

Viaje de invierno, Un (Benet). LFFor 140-142.

Vialis, Gaston. *See* **Simenon, Georges.**

Viallis, Gaston. *See* **Simenon, Georges.**

Vic Makropulos. See *Macropulos Secret, The.*

"Vicar, The" (Praed). PEng 2278-2279.

Vicar of Tours, The (Balzac). LFFor 95-96.

Vicente, Gil. DFor 1950-1960, 2172-2173, 2484.

Vicerè, I. See *Viceroys, The.*

Viceroys, The (De Roberto). LFFor 2223.

Vico, Giambattista. LTh 31, 329, 1507-1512.

Vicomte de Bragelonne, The (Dumas, *père*). LFFor 526.

Victim, The (Bellow). LFEng 226-227.

"Victim No. 5" (Keeler). M&D 955.

Victim of the Aurora, A (Keneally). LFSup 188-189.

"Victor Hugo romancier" (Butor). LTh 253.

Victorian Village, A (Reese). PEng 2342.

Victories of Love, The (Patmore). PEng 2192.

Victory (Conrad). LFEng 597-600.

Vida breve, La. See *Brief Life, A.*

Vida de Don Quixote y Sancho. See *Life of Don Quixote and Sancho, The.*

Vida de Lazarillo de Tormes y de sus fortunas y adversidades, La. See *Lazarillo de Tormes.*

Vida de Santa Maria Egipciaca. PFor 2207.

Vida es sueño, La. See *Life Is a Dream.*

Vida y dulzura (Martínez Sierras). DFor 1283-1284.

Vida y obra de Medrano (Alonso). LTh 27.

Vidaković, Milovan. LFFor 2075.

Vidal, Gore. LFEng 2712-2721, 3154; LFSup 408. *See also* **Box, Edgar.**

Vidocq, François-Eugène. M&D 1648-1653; ShF 749.

Vidrić, Vladimir. PFor 2264.

Vie de Marianne, La. See *Life of Marianne, The.*

Vie de Rancé (Chateaubriand). LFFor 2124.

Vie de Shakespeare (Guizot). DEng 2188.

Vie est ailleurs, La. See *Life Is Elsewhere.*

Vie Passionée of Rodney Buckthorne, La (Cassill). LFEng 468.

Viebig, Clara. LFFor 2183.

Viejo celoso, El. See *Jealous Old Husband, The.*

Viejo y la niña, El (Moratín). DFor 1361-1362.

"Vielleicht" (Gomringer). PFor 594-595.

Vienna: Lusthaus (Clarke). DSup 65-66.

Vienna (Spender). PEng 2697-2698.

Viento fuerte. See *Strong Wind.*

Vierte Gebot, Das. See *Fourth Commandment, The.*

Vierundzwanzigste Februar, Der. See *Twenty-fourth of February, The.*

Vierzig Tage des Musa Dagh, Die. See *Forty Days of Musa Dagh, The.*

Viet Rock (Terry). DSup 343.

Vietnam Discourse (Weiss). DFor 1989-1990.

Vietnam Project, The. See *Dusklands.*

Vietnamization of New Jersey, The (Durang). DSup 102.

"View, A" (Van Duyn). PEng 2965-2966.

"View from an Attic Window, The" (Nemerov). PEng 2081-2082.

View from the Bridge, A (Miller). DEng 1343-1345.

"View of Birds" (George). PFor 547-548. See also *Algabal.*

"Vigil Strange I Kept on the Field One Night" (Whitman). PEng 3072.

Vigny, Alfred de. DFor 2344; LTh 1029-1030, 1702; **PFor 1634-1643,** 1868-1869.

Vikrama and Urvaśī (Kālidāsa). DFor 1031-1033.

Vikramorvaśiya. See *Vikrama and Urvaśī.*

Vilalta, Maruxa. DSup 373-379.

Vilar, Jean. DFor 2354.

Vilhjálmsson, Thor. LFFor 2371.

Villa, Die (Dorst). DSup 96.

Villa, José Garcia. PEng 2976-2984; **PFor 1644-1652;** PSup 410.

Village, The (Crabbe). PEng 634, 637-640.

Village Romeo and Juliet, A (Keller). LFFor 930-931. See also *People of Seldwyla, The.*

"Villager, The" (Jackson). ShF 1669-1670.

Villages illusoires, Les (Verhaeren). PFor 1623.

Villano en su rincón, El. See *King and the Farmer, The.*

Ville, La. See *City, The.*

Ville de la chance, La. See *Town Beyond the Wall, The.*

Villette (Brontë, C.). LFEng 303-304.

Villette, Reverend John. ShF 748.

Villiers, George. DEng 1978-1985.

"Villon" (Bunting). PEng 370.

Villon, François. PFor 1653-1661, 1845-1846.

"Villon's Epitaph" (Villon). PFor 1660.

Vinaver, Stanislav. PFor 2256.

Vine, Barbara. *See* **Rendell, Ruth.**

Vingt Ans après. See *Twenty Years After.*

Vingt Mille Lieues sous les mers. See *Twenty Thousand Leagues Under the Sea.*

Vino e pane. See *Bread and Wine.*

Vintage Murder (Marsh). M&D 1193.

"Vintage Thunderbird, A" (Beattie). ShFSup 38.

Violence and the Sacred (Girard). LTh 591.

Violence et le Sacré, La. See *Violence and the Sacred.*

Violent Bear It Away, The (O'Connor, Flannery). LFEng 2038-2039.

Violent Land, The (Amado). LFFor 52-53.
Violet Clay (Godwin). LFSup 138-139.
Violio, G. *See* **Simenon, Georges.**
Violis, G. *See* **Simenon, Georges.**
"Viotti Stradivarius, The" (de la Torre). M&D 480-481.
Viper Jazz (Tate, J.). PEng 2839.
Vipers' Tangle (Mauriac). LFFor 1124, 1129-1131.
Virgiliana continentia. See *Content of Virgil.*
Virgin Martyr, The (Massinger and Dekker). DEng 1295-1296.
Virgin Soil (Turgenev). LFFor 1778-1779.
Virgin Soil Upturned (Sholokhov). LFFor 1556, 1559, 1561-1562.
Virginia (Alfieri). DFor 44-45.
Virginia (Glasgow). LFEng 1121-1122.
"Virginia" (Macaulay). PEng 1827.
Virginia (Montiano y Luyando). LTh 1692.
Virginia (Tamayo y Baus). DFor 1807-1808.
"Virginia Britannia" (Moore). PEng 2045.
Virginian, The (Wister). LFEng 3192-3193; ShF 593-594.
Virginians, The (Thackeray). LFEng 2624-2626.
Virginius (Knowles). DEng 1056-1057, 1061.
"Virility" (Dzick). ShF 2038-2039.
"Virtue" (Maugham). ShF 1904.
Virtuous Orphan, The. See *Life of Marianne, The.*
Visconte dimezzato, Il. See *Cloven Viscount, The.*
Viscount of Blarney, The (Clarke). DEng 377-378.
Vises sten, De. See *Philosopher's Stone, The.*
Vishnyovy sad. See *Cherry Orchard, The.*
"Vision and Form" (Harris, W.). ShF 78-79.
"Vision Between Waking and Sleeping in the Mountains" (Wright, J.). PEng 3158-3159.
Vision of Delight, The (Jonson). LTh 1677.
Vision of Judgment, The (Byron). LTh 258.
"Vision of Mizrah, The" (Addison). ShF 826-827.
"Vision of Repentance, A" (Lamb). PEng 1635.
"Vision of Spring in Winter, A" (Swinburne). PEng 2821.
Vision of the Last Judgment, A (Blake). LTh 1700.

Vision of William, Concerning Piers the Plowman, The (Langland). PEng 1646-1655, 3256-3257.
Visionary, The (Lie). LFFor 2341.
Visions of the Daughters of Albion (Blake). PEng 216-217.
Visit, The (Dürrenmatt). DFor 521-524, 2262-2263, 2381.
"Visit, The" (Jackson). ShF 1670-1671.
"Visit to Grandpa's, A" (Thomas). ShF 2320.
"Visita de Dios, La." *See* "God's Visit."
Visitatio sepulchri. DFor 2156-2157.
"Visitation, A" (Snodgrass). PEng 2663-2664.
"Visiting the Temple of Gathered Fragrance" (Wang Wei). PFor 1687-1689.
"Visitor, The" (Thomas). ShF 2325.
"Visitor from Egypt, A" (Long). ShF 565.
Vita, Una. See *Life, A.*
Vita Christi por coplas (Mendoza). DFor 2171.
Vita d'un uomo: Tutto le poesie (Ungaretti). PFor 1570.
Vita dei campi. See *Under the Shadow of Etna.*
"Vita fugge, La" (Stampa). PFor 1463.
Vita nuova, La. See *New Life, The.*
"Vita solitaria, La." *See* "Solitary Life, The."
"Vital Matter of Environment, The" (Kopit). DEng 1065.
Vital Parts (Berger). LFEng 255-256.
Vitéz, Mihály Csokonai. *See* Csokonai Vitéz, Mihály.
Vitrac, Roger. DFor 2239.
Vittorini, Elio. LFFor **1879-1889**, 2244-2245.
Viuda de Padilla, La (Martínez de la Rosa). DFor 1271-1272.
Viva mi dueño. See *Ruedo ibérico, El.*
Vivas, Eliseo. LTh 824.
Vivat! Vivat Regina! (Bolt). DEng 236-238.
Vivisector, The (White, P.). LFEng 2860, 2873-2874.
Vizier's Elephant, The (Andrić). LFFor 65-66.
Vladimir Mayakovsky (Mayakovsky). DFor 1292-1294; PFor 986.
Vlast tmy. See *Power of Darkness, The.*
"Vlastní životopis." *See* "Autobiography."
Vo ves' golos. See *At the Top of My Voice.*
Vocabulaire (Cocteau). PFor 371.
"Voce, La." *See* "Voice, The."
Voci della sera, Le. See *Voices in the Evening.*
Vodicka, Felix. LTh 1476.
Vodnik, Valentin. PFor 2267.
Vogan, Sara. ShF 2866.

Vögel über dem Tau (Kunze). PFor 805.

"Vogelschau." *See* "View of Birds."

"Voice, The" (Nin). LFEng 1992.

"Voice, The" (Pascoli). PFor 1142.

Voice from the Chorus, A (Sinyavsky). LTh 1356.

"Voices" (Hardy). PEng 1221.

"Voices" (Pastan). PEng 2172.

Voices in the City (Desai). LFEng 728-729.

Voices in the Evening (Ginzburg). LFSup 130.

Voices in the Night (Johnston). M&D 941.

Voices in Time (MacLennan). LFEng 1747-1748.

Voices of the Night (Longfellow). PEng 1748-1749.

Voie royale, La. See *Royal Way, The.*

"Voitel'nitsa." *See* "Amazon, The."

Voiture embourbée, La (Marivaux). LFFor 1100.

Voix et le phénomène, La. See "Speech and Phenomena."

Vojnović, Ivo. DFor 2293.

Vol de nuit. See *Night Flight.*

Volcano (Endō). LFSup 103.

Vold, Jan Erik. PFor 2195.

Volkslieder (Herder). PFor 1798.

Volpone (Jonson). DEng 1019-1021, 2285; ShF 1714-1715.

Volshebny fonar (Tsvetayeva). PFor 1536.

Völsunga saga. LFFor 2332; ShF 138, 394.

Volsunga Saga (Morris). PEng 2059-2060.

"Volt egy Jézus." *See* "There Was a Jesus."

Voltaire. DEng 2180-2181, 2343-2344; **DFor 1961-1971**, 2340-2341; **LFFor 1890-1904**, 2118; LTh 90-91, 862, 1242, **1513-1520**, 1687-1688; **M&D 1654-1658**; PFor 1860-1861; **ShFSup 326-333.**

Volume II (Villa). PEng 2981-2982; PFor 1649-1650.

Voluntad, La (Azorín). LFFor 2389.

Volunteers (Friel). DEng 676-677.

Völuspá: The Song of the Sybil. PFor 2153.

Volverás a Región (Benet). LFFor 135-138.

"Vom armen B.B." *See* "Of Poor B.B."

Von Dalin, Olaf. LFFor 2334.

Von dem Einfluss und Gebrauche der Einbildungs-Krafft (Bodmer). LTh 176.

Von deutscher Art und Kunst (Herder). LTh 669.

Von Linné, Carl. *See* Linnaeus.

Von morgens bis mitternachts. See *From Morn to Midnight.*

Von Schwelle zu Schwelle (Celan). PFor 312-313.

Vonnegut, Kurt, Jr. LFEng **2722-2732;** LFSup 408; ShF **2391-2398.**

"Voprosy izucheniya literatury yazyka" (Tynyanov and Jakobson). LTh 1477.

Voprosy literatury i estetiki. See *Dialogic Imagination, The.*

Vor. See *Thief, The.*

"Vor dem Gesetz". *See* "Before the Law."

Vor dem Sturm (Fontane). LFFor 566-567.

Vor Sonnenaufgang. See *Before Dawn.*

Vorlesungen über Ästhetik (Solger). LTh 1360, 1362.

Vorlesungen über dramatische Kunst und Literatur. See *Course of Lectures on Dramatic Art and Literature, A.*

Vörösmarty, Mihály. DFor 2286-2287; **PFor 1662-1670**, 1980.

"Vorrede aus dem Jahre 1881" (Storm). LFFor 1679.

Vortex, The (Coward). DEng 426-427.

Voskreseniye. See *Resurrection.*

Voskreshenie slova. See *Resurrection of the Word.*

Voskresshiye bogi. See *Romance of Leonardo da Vinci, The.*

Voss (White, P.). LFEng 2869-2870.

Voss, Johann Heinrich. LTh 663.

"Vowels" (Rimbaud). PFor 1338.

Vox Clamantis (Gower). PEng 1113, 1114, 1115, 1118-1120.

"Voyage, Le." *See* "Trip, The."

Voyage au bout de la nuit. See *Journey to the End of the Night.*

Voyage de M. Perrichon, Le. See *Journey of Mr. Perrichon, The.*

Voyage en Orient. See *Journey to the Orient.*

Voyage of St. Brendan. ShF 432-433.

Voyage of the Dawn Treader, The (Lewis, C. S.). LFEng 1658.

Voyage Out, The (Woolf). LFEng 2945-2946.

Voyage Round My Father, A (Mortimer). DEng 1356-1358.

Voyage to Tomorrow (Hakim). DSup 177-178.

Voyageur sans bagage, Le. See *Traveller Without Luggage.*

"Voyelles." *See* "Vowels."

Voyeur, Le. See *Voyeur, The.*

W

W Szwajcarii. See *In Switzerland.*

"Waage der Baleks, Die." *See* "Balek Scales, The."

Wackenroder, Wilhelm Heinrich. LTh 437, 1699, 1706.

Waclaw (Słowacki). PFor 1443.

Wade, Henry. M&D 1665-1670.

"Wading at Wellfleet" (Bishop). PEng 188.

Wagatomo Hittora. See *My Friend Hitler.*

Wager, The (Giacosa). DFor 702-704.

Wager, The (Medoff). DSup 242-243.

Wages of Zen, The (Melville, J.). M&D 1214.

Wagner, Richard. DEng 2197; DFor 2374-2375; LTh 987, 1068-1069, 1328-1329.

Wagner the Were-Wolf (Reynolds). ShF 732.

Wagon (Ważyk). PFor 1695.

Wagoner, David. PEng 2985-2993; PSup 410.

Wahlöö, Per, and Maj Sjöwall. M&D 1495-1501.

Wahlöö, Peter. *See* **Wahlöö, Per.**

Wahlverwandtschaften, Die. See *Elective Affinities.*

Wahre Muftoni, Der (Meckel). ShFSup 190

Wahrheit und Methode. See *Truth and Method.*

Wain, John. LFEng 2733-2745; LFSup 408; ShF 2399-2402.

"Wait by the Door Awhile, Death, There Are Others" (Dorn). PEng 842.

"Wait Not Till Slaves Pronounce the Word" (Thoreau). PEng 2901.

Waiting for Godot (Beckett). DEng 150-152, 2384; DFor 158-160, 2245-2246, 2359; LFFor 122.

Waiting for Lefty (Odets). DEng 1397-1398.

Waiting for My Life (Pastan). PEng 2173-2174.

Waiting for Sheila (Braine). LFEng 284, 287, 288.

"Waiting for the Barbarians" (Cavafy). PFor 297-298.

Waiting for the Barbarians (Coetzee). LFSup 80-81.

Waiting for the End (Fiedler). LTh 487.

Waiting Room, The (Harris). LFSup 148-149.

Wake in Ybor City, A (Yglesias). LFEng 2995-2997.

Wake of Jimmy Foster, The (Henley). DSup 196-197.

Wake Up, Stupid (Harris). LFEng 1284-1285.

"Wakefield" (Hawthorne). ShF 112.

Wakefield Master. DEng 1986-1996, 2250.

Waking, The (Roethke). PEng 2411-2412.

"Waking Early Sunday Morning" (Lowell, R.). PEng 1794.

Wakoski, Diane. PEng 2994-3000; PSup 410.

Walahfrid Strabo. PFor 2113.

Walcott, Derek, A. DEng 1997-2005, 2453-2454; PEng 3001-3007; PSup 411.

Walcott, Roderick. DEng 2453.

"Walcourt" (Verlaine). PFor 1631.

"Wald, Der" (Walser, R.). ShFSup 347.

Walden (Thoreau). PEng 2897.

"Walesi bardok, A." *See* "Welsh Bards, The."

Walk and Other Stories, The (Walser, R.). ShFSup 348-349.

Walk in the Night, A (La Guma). LFFor 2050.

Walk on the Wild Side, A (Algren). LFSup 28-29.

Walke, John. ShF 2867.

Walker, Alice. LFEng 2746-2757; LFSup 408; ShFSup 334-343.

Walker, Harry. *See* **Waugh, Hillary.**

Walker, Max. *See* **Avallone, Michael.**

Walker, London. DEng 118-119.

Walking Drum, The (L'Amour). LFSup 225.

"Walking Lessons" (Price). ShF 2125-2126.

Walking Stick, The (Graham). M&D 777.

"Walking Swiftly" (Bly). PEng 226.

"Walking to Sleep" (Wilbur). PEng 3098-3099.

Wall, The (Hersey). LFEng 1356-1357.

"Wall, The" (Montale). PFor 1048-1049. See also *Bones of the Cuttlefish.*

"Wall, The" (Sartre). LFFor 1516; ShF 2193, 2194-2195.

Wall of Masks, The (Koontz). M&D 1006.

Wallace, The (Blind Harry). PEng 3278.

Wallace, Edgar. M&D 1671-1677.

Wallant, Edward Lewis. LFEng 2758-2766.

Wallensteins Lager. See *Camp of Wallenstein, The.*

Warton, Joseph, and Thomas Warton. LTh 1528-1533.

Warton, Thomas. PEng 3030-3040.

"Warum gabst du uns die tiefen Blicke?" *See* "Why Did You Give Us the Deep Glances?"

"Was I never yet of your love grieved" (Wyatt). PEng 3174.

"Was it some sweet device of Faery" (Lamb). PEng 1634.

"Washing My Face" (Orr). PEng 2150.

Washington Square (James, H.). LFEng 1441.

Wasps, The (Aristophanes). DFor 2125-2126.

Wästberg, Per. LFFor 2360.

Waste (Granville-Barker). DEng 800.

Waste Land, The (Eliot). PEng 943-946, 3356, 3363, 3364, 3389.

Waste of Timelessness and Other Early Stories (Nin). ShF 1949.

"Wasted Evening, A" (Musset). PFor 1066-1067.

"Watakushi." *See* "Thief, The."

Watch on the Rhine (Hellman). DEng 923-924.

Watch That Ends the Night, The (MacLennan). LFEng 1746.

Watch the North Wind Rise (Graves, R.). LFEng 1202.

Watchboy, What of the Night? (Cassity). PSup 62.

"Watcher by the Dead, A" (Bierce). M&D 126.

Watchers (Koontz). M&D 1007.

"Water" (Creeley). PEng 682.

"Water Hen, The" (O'Flaherty). ShF 2006-2007.

Water Hen, The (Witkiewicz). DFor 2009-2011, 2279.

Water Margin (Shih Nai-an). LFFor 2091, 2094-2095.

"Water Message" (Barth). ShF 928.

Water-Method Man, The (Irving). LFEng 1418-1420.

Water Nymph, The (Pushkin). DFor 1500-1501.

"Water Picture" (Swenson). PEng 2796.

"Water Poems" (McPherson). PEng 1880-1882.

Water Street (Merrill). PEng 1962.

"Water Them Geraniums" (Lawson). ShFSup 140.

Watercress Girl and Other Stories, The (Bates). ShFSup 32.

Waterfall, The (Drabble). LFEng 820-821.

Waterloo Bridge (Sherwood). DEng 1802-1803.

Waters, Frank. LFEng 2781-2792; LFSup 408.

Waters of Babylon, The (Arden). DEng 45-46.

Waters of Kronos, The (Richter). LFEng 2272.

Watmough, David. ShF 2869.

Watson, Lawrence. ShF 2870.

Watson, Robert. ShF 2871.

Watt (Beckett). LFEng 209-210; LFFor 126.

Watts, Isaac. PEng 3041-3049, 3331.

Watts, Theodore. PEng 2817.

Watźlaw. See *Vatzlav.*

Waugh, Evelyn. LFEng 2793-2804.

Waugh, Hillary. M&D 1683-1688.

Waverley (Scott). LFEng 2366-2371, 3031, 3133, 3150.

Waverley novels, The (Scott). LFEng 2364-2365, 2366-2383.

"Waves" (Apollinaire). PFor 54-55.

Waves, The (Woolf). LFEng 2954-2955.

Waxwork (Lovesey). M&D 1096-1097.

"Way Back, The" (Grau). ShF 1533-1534.

"Way Back, The" (Robbe-Grillet). ShF 2155.

"Way Men Live Is a Lie, The" (Patchen). PEng 2182.

Way of a World, The (Tomlinson). PEng 2909.

Way of All Flesh, The (Butler). LFEng 392, 393, 397-399; ShF 108.

Way of the World, The (Congreve). DEng 409-412.

Way Some People Live, The (Cheever). ShF 553.

"Way Through the Woods, The" (Kipling). PEng 1607-1608.

Way to Rainy Mountain, The (Momaday). PEng 2020-2021.

"Wayfarer Comes Home, The" (Awoonor). PFor 115.

Wayfarers. See *Vagabonds.*

Wayne, Anderson. *See* Halliday, Brett.

Wayside Lute, A (Reese). PEng 2344.

Wayside Motor Inn, The (Gurney). DSup 167.

Wayward Lover, The (Goethe). DFor 735.

Ważyk, Adam. PFor 1691-1695.

We (Zamyatin). LFFor 1979-1980, 2323.

"--We Also Walk Dogs" (Heinlein). ShF 1616-1617.

We Always Treat Women Too Well (Queneau). LFSup 326-327.

Welt als Wille und Vorstellung, Die. See *World as Will and Idea, The.*

Welt von Gestern, Die. See *World of Yesterday, The.*

Welty, Eudora. LFEng 2817-2829; ShF 262-263, 547-548, 815-816, **2413-2420**; ShFSup 391.

Wên fu. See *Essay on Literature.*

Wên-hsin tiao-lung. See *Literary Mind and the Carving of Dragons, The.*

Wên I-to. LTh 1782; PFor 1794.

"Wenn nicht dein Brunnen, Melusine." *See* "Melusine, If Your Well Had Not."

Wentworth, Patricia. M&D 1694-1699.

Weöres, Sándor. PFor 1986.

We're Friends Again (O'Hara). LFEng 2052.

"Werewolf, The" (Housman). LFEng 3204.

"Werewolf Raspberries" (Brautigan). ShFSup 57.

Werewolf Trace, The (Gardner, J.). M&D 696-697.

Werfel, Franz. DFor 1992-2001; **LFFor 1905-1914,** 2196; PFor 1929.

Wergeland, Henrik. DFor 2470; LFFor 2338; PFor 2168.

Werner (Byron). DEng 330, 337-339.

Werner, Zacharias. DFor 2370.

Werther, der Jude (Jacobowsky). LFFor 2182.

"Werwolf, Der." *See* "Banshee, The."

Wescott, Glenway. LFEng 2830-2839; ShF **2421-2425.**

Wesele. See *Wedding, The.*

Wesker, Arnold. DEng 2012-2019, 2387.

Wessel, Johan Herman. DFor 2467.

Wessex Poems (Hardy). PEng 1218-1219.

West, Edward. *See* **Household, Geoffrey.**

West, Jessamyn. ShFSup 360-365.

West, Martin. *See* **Christie, Agatha.**

West, Nathanael. LFEng 2840-2847.

West, Owen. *See* **Koontz, Dean R.**

West, Paul. LFSup 369-377; ShF 2879.

West-Eastern Divan (Goethe). PFor 584, 588.

West Indian, The (Cumberland). DEng 447-448, 2330.

West of Suez (Osborne). DEng 1435-1436.

West-östlicher Divan. See *West-Eastern Divan.*

"West-Running Brook" (Frost). PEng 1047.

West Side Story (Laurents and Bernstein). DEng 2474.

"Westering" (Heaney). PEng 1271.

Westlake, Donald E. M&D 1700-1706.

Westmacott, Mary. *See* **Christie, Agatha.**

"W. H. Auden and Mantan Moreland" (Young). PEng 3218.

"Whale's Tale, The" (Berrigan). ShF 374-375.

"Wharf Rats" (Walrond). ShF 578.

Wharton, Edith. LFEng 2848-2858, 3054; ShF 539, 707, **2426-2432.**

Wharton, Edward (Teddy) Robbins. LFEng 2851.

"What Are Years?" (Moore). PEng 2045-2046.

What Did I Do Tomorrow? (Davies). M&D 462.

"What Do the Trees Say?" (Heyen). PEng 1327-1328.

What Do You Want, Peire Vidal? (Owens). DEng 1460.

What D'ye Call It, The (Gay). DEng 731-732.

"What Happened to the Short Story?" (Brickell). ShF 72.

"What I Believe" (Forster). LTh 500.

"What I Found in the Sea" (Stockton). M&D 1536.

What If You Died Tomorrow (Williamson). DEng 2092.

What I'm Going to Do, I Think (Woiwode). LFSup 394-395.

"What Is a Classic?" (Eliot). LTh 449.

"What Is a Story?" (Saroyan). ShF 88.

"What Is an Initiation Story?" (Marcus). ShF 81.

What Is Art? (Tolstoy). LTh 790, 1445.

What Is Literature? (Sartre). LTh 104, 1272; PSup 52.

"What Is Loving?" (Walther). PFor 1675.

"What Is Oblomovism?" (Dobrolyubov). LTh 390.

What Is Pure French? (Gourmont). LTh 624.

"What Is the Connection Between Men and Women" (Oates). ShF 1963.

What Is the Short Story? (Current-Garcia and Patrick, eds.). ShF 74.

What Is to Be Done? (Chernyshevsky). LTh 285-286, 396.

"What Jorkens Has to Put Up With" (Dunsany). ShF 1317-1318.

"What Makes a Short Story Short?" (Friedman, N.). ShF 76.

"What Metre Is" (MacBeth). PEng 1834.

"What of the Night?" (Kunitz). PSup 248.

What Price Glory? (Anderson, M., and Stallings). DEng 27, 2400.

Whole Art of the Stage, The (d'Aubignac). LTh 309-310.

"Whole Loaf, A" (Agnon). ShF 834-835.

Who'll Save the Plowboy? (Gilroy). DEng 774-776.

"Whorf, Chomsky, and the Student of Literature" (Steiner). LTh 1389.

Whoroscope (Beckett). PEng 100-104; PFor 143-147.

Who's Afraid of Virginia Woolf? (Albee). DEng 15-17, 2409.

Who's Who (Hall and Waterhouse). DEng 872, 873.

Whose Body? (Sayers). LFEng 2358-2359.

"Whoso list to hunt" (Wyatt). PEng 3174-3175.

Why Are We in Vietnam? (Mailer). LFEng 1781-1783.

Why Are We So Blest? (Armah). LFEng 88-90; LFFor 2052-2053.

"Why Can't They Tell You Why?" (Purdy). ShF 2137.

Why Come Ye Not to Court (Skelton). PEng 2639.

"Why Did You Give Us the Deep Glances?" (Goethe). PFor 583.

"Why Do We Read Fiction?" (Warren). LTh 1523.

"Why Do You Write About Russia?" (Simpson). PEng 2609.

"Why Don't You Dance?" (Carver). ShFSup 78.

"Why I Like Country Music" (McPherson). ShF 1857-1858.

"Why I Live at the P.O." (Welty). ShF 2415-2416.

"Why ist damnation" (Nashe). PEng 2073.

"Why so pale and wan, fond Lover?" (Suckling). PEng 2780.

Why the Lord Came to Sand Mountain (Linney). DSup 236-237. See also *Sand Mountain.*

Wibberley, Leonard Patrick O'Connor. *See* **Holton, Leonard.**

Wicked Cooks, The (Grass). DSup 158.

Wickford Point (Marquand). LFEng 1817.

Wickram, Jörg. LFFor 2150.

Wide Sargasso Sea (Rhys). LFEng 2228-2232.

Wideman, John Edgar. LFSup 378-385.

Widening Gyre, The (Parker). M&D 1302.

Wider den missverstandenen Realismus. See *Realism in Our Time.*

Widmungen (Kunze). PFor 806, 807.

Widow Lerouge, The (Gaboriau). M&D 682.

"Widow of Ephesus, The" (Petronius). ShF 2093-2094.

Widower's Son, The (Sillitoe). LFEng 2402.

Widow's Blind Date, The (Horovitz). DEng 962-963.

Wie die Alten den Tod gebildet. See *How the Ancients Represented Death.*

"Wiederfinden." *See* "Reunion."

Wieland (Brown, C. B.). LFEng 315-320; ShF 528, 737.

Wieland, Christoph Martin. LFFor 2157-2158; LTh 438.

Wielkość urojona. See *Imaginary Magnitude.*

Wier, Allen. ShF 2883.

"Wiese im Park." *See* "Lawn in the Park."

Wiesel, Elie. LFFor 1915-1929; LFSup 408; ShF 423.

Wife and His Youth and Other Stories of the Color Line, The (Chesnutt). ShFSup 87-88.

Wife Next Door, The (Cassill). LFEng 468.

Wife of Bath, The (Gay). DEng 731.

"Wife of Bath's Prologue and Tale, The" (Chaucer). PEng 3264-3265; ShF 1113-1114.

"Wife of His Youth, The" (Chesnutt). ShFSup 87-88.

Wife of His Youth, The (Chesnutt). LFEng 513.

"Wife of Nashville, A" (Taylor). ShF 2307-2309.

"Wife-wooing" (Updike). ShF 2373-2374.

Wilbur, Richard. PEng 3091-3100; PSup 411.

Wild Ass's Skin, The (Balzac). LFFor 94-95.

Wild Boys, The (Burroughs). LFEng 390.

"Wild Dog Rose, The" (Montague). PEng 2037.

Wild-Goose Chase, The (Fletcher, J.). PEng 1018-1019.

"Wild Honey Suckle, The" (Freneau). PEng 1036.

Wild Hunter in the Bush of Ghosts, The (Tutuola). LFFor 1783, 1784.

Wild Irish Boy, The (Maturin). LFEng 1839.

Wilde, Oscar. DEng 2030-2041; LTh 1089, 1400, 1736; PEng 3101-3109; ShF 518.

Wildenwey, Herman. PFor 2176.

Wilder, Thornton. DEng 2042-2055; LFEng 2880-2888.

"Wilderness, The" (Coxe). PEng 628-629.

Wilderness (Warren). LFEng 2778.

Winds of April, The (Gonzalez). LFEng 1142.
Winds of Morning (Davis). LFEng 678-679.
Winds of War, The (Wouk). LFEng 2971-2972.
Windsor Forest (Pope). PEng 2255.
Windsor Magazine, The. ShF 771.
Windy McPherson's Son (Anderson). LFEng 73, 75.
"Wine" (Gay). PEng 1071-1072.
Wine of Astonishment, The (Lovelace). LFEng 1703-1704.
Wine of the Puritans, The (Brooks, V.). LTh 226.
"Wine Song" (Petőfi). PFor 1228.
Winesburg, Ohio (Anderson). LFEng 76-78, 79; ShF 247-248, 723, 869-870, 871, 872.
Wings (Kopit). DEng 1073-1075.
Winners, The (Cortázar). LFFor 377-379.
"Winter: 1978" (Beattie). ShFSup 39-40.
"Winter" (Cotton). PEng 586.
"Winter Come, A" (Moss). PEng 2065-2066.
"Winter Diary, A" (Van Doren). PEng 2957.
"Winter Dreams" (Fitzgerald). ShF 1371-1372.
"Winter Evening" (Barnard). PSup 26-27.
"Winter in the Air" (Warner). ShFSup 353-354.
Winter in the Hills, A (Wain). LFEng 2738, 2741-2742.
"Winter Landscapes" (Davie). PSup 87.
"Winter Night" (Boyle). ShF 1001-1002.
"Winter Noon" (Saba). PSup 347.
Winter of Artifice (Nin). LFEng 1992.
"Winter Orchard, The" (Johnson, J.). ShF 1701-1702.
Winter Palace, The (Haavikko). PSup 144.
"Winter Runner, The" (Galvin). PEng 1054.
"Winter Sleepers" (Atwood). PEng 65.
Winter Song. See Fury Chronicle, The.
Wintering Out (Heaney). PEng 1264, 1266, 1269-1271.
Winters, Yvor. LTh 158, 1206, **1565-1570;** **PSup 253, 255-256, 393-400.**
"Winter's Day, A" (Leskov). ShFSup 161.
Winter's Tale, The (Shakespeare). DEng 1712; ShF 2217-2218.
Winter's Tales (Dinesen). ShF 1281.
Winterset (Anderson, M.). DEng 2403.
Winterton, Paul. *See* **Garve, Andrew.**
Winther, Christian. PFor 2166.
"Wiper, The" (MacNeice). PEng 1875-1876.
Wir werden schon noch handeln (Walser, M.). DSup 388.

Wire Harp, The (Biermann). PFor 190.
"Wireless" (Kipling). ShF 1751.
Wisdom Amok (Innaurato). DSup 201.
Wisdom of Solomon, The (Hakim). DSup 175.
Wisdom of Solomon, Paraphrased, The (Middleton, T.). PEng 1994-1995.
Wisdom of the Sands, The (Saint-Exupéry). LFFor 1485.
Wise Blood (O'Connor, Flannery). LFEng 2036-2038.
Wise Child (Gray). DEng 806.
Wise Virgin (Wilson). LFSup 389-390.
Wise Woman of Hogsdon, The (Heywood, T.). DEng 953-955.
"Wiser Than a God" (Chopin). ShF 1132.
Wister, Owen. LFEng 3192-3193; ShF 595, 596, 597, 609.
Wit and Mirth (D'Urfey). PEng 910.
Wit and Science (Redford). DEng 2259.
Wit at Several Weapons (Fletcher). DEng 634.
Wit Works Woe. See Mischief of Being Clever, The.
Witch of Edmonton, The (Ford, Dekker, and Rowley). DEng 651-652.
"Witch Trial at Mount Holly, A" (Franklin). ShF 1412-1413.
Witch Wood (Buchan). LFEng 330.
Witches' Brew, The (Pratt). PEng 2285-2286.
"Witching" (Boland). PSup 39-40.
Witching Times (De Forest). LFEng 699-700, 702.
Witch's House, The (Armstrong). M&D 37-38.
With Eyes at the Back of Our Heads (Levertov). PEng 1706.
With Fire and Sword (Sienkiewicz). LFFor 1565, 1572-1574.
"With Garments Flowing" (Clare). PEng 512-513.
With Ignorance (Williams). PSup 390.
"With rue my heart is laden" (Housman). PEng 1412.
With Shuddering Fall (Oates). LFEng 2010-2011.
With Strings (Sondhi). DEng 2418.
"Withered Arm, The" (Hardy). ShF 1580-1581.
Within a Budding Grove (Proust). LFFor 1327-1330. *See also Remembrance of Things Past.*
"Within the House" (Claudel). PFor 358, 361-362. *See also Five Great Odes.*
"Without Love" (Pasternak). ShF 2059.

"Wünschelrute." *See* "Divining Rod."

Wunschloses Unglück. See *Sorrow Beyond Dreams, A.*

Wuthering Heights (Brontë, E.). LFEng 306-307, 308, 309-311, 3145-3146.

Wyatt, Sir Thomas. PEng 3170-3180, 3287.

"Wyatt resteth here, that quick could never rest" (Surrey). PEng 2788.

Wycherley, William. DEng 2104-2114.

Wylder's Hand (Le Fanu). LFEng 1625-1626; M&D 1050; ShF 1796.

"Wyrta," 3489.

Wyspiański, Stanisław. DFor 2026-2035, 2278-2279; PFor 2127-2128.

Wyszedł z domu. See *Gone Out.*

X

X. See **Simenon, Georges.**
X, Mr. See **Hoch, Edward D.**
X = O (Drinkwater). DEng 509-510.
Xala (Sembène). LFFor 1542, 1543-1544.

Xenophanes of Colophon. LTh 1634.
Xenophon of Athens. LFFor 2000.
Xenophon of Ephesus. LFFor 2003-2004.

Y

Y nos dijeron que éramos inmortales (Dragún). DFor 2443-2444.
Ya tali' al-shajarah. See *Tree Climber, The.*
"Yabu no naka." *See* "In a Grove."
Yakamochi, Ōtomo no. *See* Ōtomo no Yakamochi.
Yama no oto. See *Sound of the Mountain, The.*
Yamanoe no Okura. PFor 2057.
Yang Shên. DFor 2324.
Yang Wan-li. LTh 1776-1777.
Yankee Ranger. See *Tory Lover, The.*
"Yao." *See* "Medicine."
Yard of Sun, A (Fry). DEng 688-689.
Yasunari Kawabata. *See* **Kawabata, Yasunari.**
"Yawahada no." *See* "You Have Yet to Touch."
Yayá Garcia. See *Iaia Garcia.*
Ye Bare and Ye Cubb. See *Bare and Ye Cubb, Ye.*
Year Before Last (Boyle). LFEng 275-276.
Year 1905, The (Pasternak). PFor 1159-1160.
Year of the Dragon, The (Chin). DSup 48-51.
Year of the Soul, The (George). LTh 575; PFor 548-549.
Years, The (Woolf). LFEng 2955-2957.
"Years Behind, The" (Awoonor). PFor 114.
"Years Go By, The" (Niedecker). PSup 296, 299.
Yeats, William Butler. DEng 2115-2122, 2199, 2375, 2376, 2379, 2445, 2446; LTh 979, 1412-1413, **1585-1590,** 1737; PEng **3181-3209,** 3349, 3361-3362; PSup 411; ShF 292, **2468-2474.**
Yegor Bulychov and Others (Gorky). DFor 786.
Yellen, Samuel. ShF 2895.
Yellow Back Radio Broke-Down (Reed). LFSup 338.
"Yellow Dog, The" (Guest). PEng 1165.
Yellow Room, The (Hall). PEng 1202-1204.
Yemassee, The (Simms). LFEng 2413.
Yen Hsieh. LTh 1778.
Yen Yü. LTh 1777.
"Yentl the Yeshiva Boy" (Singer). ShF 2243-2244.

Yeomen of the Guard, The (Gilbert and Sullivan). DEng 766-767.
Yerby, Frank. LFEng 2985-2992; LFSup 408; **ShF 2475-2480.**
Yerkes, C. T. LFEng 835.
Yerma (García Lorca). DFor 663-664, 2505.
"Yes" (Harvey). ShF 129.
"Yes, Too Much of Everything" (Salinas). PFor 1387-1388.
Yesenin, Sergei. *See* Esenin, Sergei.
"Yesterday and To-morrow" (Dunbar). PSup 115.
"Yet Do I Marvel" (Cullen). PEng 694-696.
"Yeux d'Elsa, Les." *See* "Elsa's Eyes."
Yevtushenko, Yevgeny. PFor 1704-1712, 2150.
"Yew-Trees" (Wordsworth). PEng 3458-3459.
Yglesias, José. LFEng 2993-3003.
Yin, Leslie Charles Bowyer. *See* **Charteris, Leslie.**
"Yin and Yang" (Rexroth). PEng 2351.
"Ynn Auntient Dayes" (Chatterton). PEng 471.
Yö ja päivä (Kivi). DFor 1068-1069.
Yogi and the Commissar and Other Essays, The (Koestler). LFEng 1549.
Yogi of Cockroach Court, The (Waters). LFEng 2787-2788.
York, Jeremy. *See* **Creasey, John.**
Yorke, Henry Vincent. *See* **Green, Henry.**
Yosano Akiko. PFor 1713-1719, 2075.
Yoshimoto, Nijō. LTh 1591-1595, 1787-1788.
Yoshioka Minoru. PFor 2078.
Yosimochi, Ki no. LTh 1785.
You and I (Monroe). PEng 2028.
"You Are Happy" (Atwood). PEng 67.
You Are Happy (Atwood). PEng 67-68.
"You Are Not I" (Bowles). ShF 992.
"You Are Odysseus" (Pastan). PEng 2175.
"You Are What You Own" (Adams). ShFSup 5.
"You Blue" (Gomringer). PFor 595.
"You Can Always Tell Newark" (O'Hara). ShF 2017-2018.
You Can't Go Home Again (Wolfe). LFEng 2936, 2937-2938.

Z

Zabawa. See Party, The.

"Zabitye liudi" (Dobrolyubov). LTh 389.

Zacharias, Lee. ShF 2896.

Zadig (Voltaire). LFFor 1895-1898; M&D 1655-1657.

Zagoskin, Mikhail. LFFor 2310-2311.

"Zähle die Mandeln." See "Count the Almonds."

Zahradní salvnost. See Garden Party, The.

Zaïde. See Zayde.

Zaïre (Voltaire). DFor 1967-1968.

Zalacaín el aventurero (Baroja). LFFor 109-110.

Zalán futása (Vörösmarty). PFor 1665-1666.

Zamyatin, Yevgeny. LFFor 1973-1981, 2323.

Zangirimono. DFor 2432.

Zangwill, Israel. M&D 1730-1734; ShF 516.

Zanzotto, Andrea. PFor 2050.

Zapatera prodigiosa, La. See Shoemaker's Prodigious Wife, The.

Zapatero y el rey, El (Zorrilla y Moral). DFor 2062-2063.

Zapiski iz myortvogo doma. See House of the Dead, The.

Zapiski iz podpolya. See Notes from the Underground.

Zauberberg, Der. See Magic Mountain, The.

"Zauberin im Walde, Die." See "Sorceress in the Forest, The."

Zavist. See Envy.

Zavrian, Suzanne Ostro. ShF 2897.

Zayde (La Fayette). LFFor 959-961.

Zazie in the Metro (Queneau). LFSup 330-332.

Zdarzenia (Ważyk). PFor 1695.

Ze wspomnień Ijona Tichego: Kongres futurologiczny. See Futurological Congress, The.

Ze zivota hmyzu. See Insect Play, The.

Zeami Motokiyo. DFor 2036-2043, 2422-2423; LTh 1788-1789.

Zebra-Striped Hearse, The (Macdonald). LFSup 275.

Žebrácká opera (Havel). DFor 881.

Zee & Co. (O'Brien, E.). LFEng 2021-2022.

"Zeitgedichte" (George). See "Time Poems."

"Zeitgedichte" (Heine). See "Poems of the Times."

Zeko (Andrić). LFFor 67-69.

Zelazny, Roger. ShF 2898.

Zelman, Anita. ShF 2899.

Zement. See Cement.

Zemganno Brothers, The (Goncourt, E.). LFFor 717.

Zemsta. See Revenge and Vengeance, The.

Zeno, Apostolo. DFor 2402.

Zensur, Die (Wedekind). DFor 1981-1982.

"Zero" (Salinas). PFor 1389.

Zeromski, Stefan. LFFor 2063.

Zerrissene, Der. See Man Full of Nothing, A.

Žert. See Joke, The.

Zesen, Philipp von. LFFor 2151.

Zhdanov, Andrey. LTh 1125, 1505, 1603-1608.

Zhelezny potok. See Iron Flood, The.

Zhirmunsky, V. M. LTh 1504.

Zhizn cheloveko. See Life of Man, The.

Zhizn Matveya Kozhemyakina. See Life of Matvei Kozhemyakin, The.

Zhukovsky, Vasily. LTh 118-119, 1609-1614; PFor 2135-2136.

Ziemia obiecana. See Promised Land, The.

Zig-Zag Walk, The (Logan). PEng 1741.

"Zima Junction" (Yevtushenko). PFor 1708-1709.

Zimmerschlacht, Die (Walser, M.). DSup 387-388.

Zimpel, Lloyd. ShF 2900.

Zinberg, Leonard S. See Lacy, Ed.

Zindel, Paul. DEng 2123-2131.

Zinnes, Harriet. ShF 2901.

"Zip!" (Davie). PSup 85.

Živo meso. See Raw Flesh.

Život a dílo skladatele Foltýna. See Cheat, The.

Zivot de jinde. See Life Is Elsewhere.

Zmaj, Jovan Jovanović. PFor 2254.

Żmija (Słowacki). PFor 1441.

Zola, Émile. DEng 2195; DFor 2044-2057; LFEng 3170, 3174-3175; LFFor 1982-1995, 2134; LTh 233, 690, 1420, 1497, 1615-

24.95